New Frontiers in Asia-Pacific International Arbitration and Dispute Resolution

International Arbitration Law Library

VOLUME 59

Editors

Professor Julian D.M. Lew QC has been involved with international arbitration for more than forty years as counsel, as arbitrator and as an academic. He is the founder and has been the Head of the School of International Arbitration, Centre for Commercial Law Studies, Queen Mary University of London since its creation in 1985. He is now an independent international arbitrator at 20 Essex Street, London.

Stavros Brekoulakis is Professor at Queen Mary University of London and an associate member of 3 Verulam Buildings (Gray's Inn). He is a leading academic in international arbitration and has led, or been involved in, several projects with ICCA, ICC Commission and ILA. He also acts as an independent arbitrator and has been appointed as chairman, sole arbitrator, co-arbitrator and emergency arbitrator under the rules of all the major arbitration rules.

Introduction

Since its first volume published in 1993, this authoritative practitioner-oriented series has published in-depth and analytical works on niche aspects of international arbitration, authored by specialists in the field.

Objective

This authoritative and established series covering in-depth analyses of niche areas appeals to both practitioners and academics. The series includes specific monographs and PhD dissertations of high quality, which are practical and cover issues not fully explored in general texts.

Frequency

A volume is published whenever an interesting topic presents itself.

The titles published in this series are listed at the end of this volume.

New Frontiers in Asia-Pacific International Arbitration and Dispute Resolution

Edited by

Luke Nottage
Shahla Ali
Bruno Jetin
Nobumichi Teramura

Wolters Kluwer

Published by:
Kluwer Law International B.V.
PO Box 316
2400 AH Alphen aan den Rijn
The Netherlands
E-mail: international-sales@wolterskluwer.com
Website: lrus.wolterskluwer.com

Sold and distributed by:
Wolters Kluwer Legal & Regulatory U.S.
7201 McKinney Circle
Frederick, MD 21704
United States of America
Email: customer.service@wolterskluwer.com

e-Book: ISBN 978-94-035-2863-2
web-PDF: ISBN 978-94-035-2871-7

Editors

Dr Luke Nottage is Professor of Comparative and Transnational Business Law at the University of Sydney Law School, founding Co-Director of the Australian Network for Japanese Law (ANJeL) and Special Counsel at Williams Trade Law. He specialises in comparative and transnational business law (especially arbitration and product safety law), with a particular interest in Japan and the Asia-Pacific. Luke has or had executive roles in the Australia-Japan Society (NSW), the Law Council of Australia's International Law Section, the Australian Centre for International Commercial Arbitration, and the Asia-Pacific Forum for International Arbitration. Luke is also a Rules Committee Member of the Australian Centre for International Arbitration (ACICA) and listed on the Panel of Arbitrators for the AIAC (formerly KLRCA), BAC, JCAA, KCAB, NZIAC, SCIA and TAI. Luke serves on Working Group 6 (examining arbitrator neutrality) for the Academic Forum on ISDS. He qualified as a lawyer in New Zealand in 1994 and in New South Wales in 2001 and has consulted for law firms and organisations worldwide (including ASEAN, the EC, OECD, UNCTAD and the Japanese government). His seventeen other books include *International Arbitration in Australia* (Federation Press, 2010, eds) and *International Investment Treaties and Arbitration Across Asia* (Brill, 2018, eds). He is or has been Visiting Professor teaching and researching at universities throughout Asia, Oceania, Europe and North America.

Dr Shahla Ali is Professor and Associate Dean (International) and Director of the LLM in Arbitration and Dispute Resolution at the Faculty of Law of the University of Hong Kong. Her research and practice centre on questions of governance, development and the resolution of cross-border disputes in the Asia-Pacific region. Shahla is the author of *Court Mediation Reform* (Edward Elgar, 2018), *Governing Disasters: Engaging Local Populations in Humanitarian Relief* (Cambridge University Press, 2016), *Consumer Financial Dispute Resolution in a Comparative Context* (Cambridge University Press, 2013), and *Resolving Disputes in the Asia Pacific Region* (Routledge, 2010), and she writes for law journals in the area of comparative ADR. She has consulted with USAID, IFC/World Bank and the United Nations on issues pertaining to access to justice, peace process negotiation training and land use conflict resolution. She serves as a bilingual arbitrator (English/Chinese) with CIETAC, HKIAC (ADNDRC) and SIAC and has served on the IBA Drafting Committee for Investor-State Mediation Rules, the DOJ Mediation Regulatory Committee, the UN Mediation Roster and the FDRC Appointments Committee. Prior to HKU, she worked as an international trade attorney with Baker & McKenzie in its San Francisco office. She received her JD and PhD in Jurisprudence and Social Policy from the University of California, Berkeleyand BA from Stanford University.

Dr Bruno Jetin is Associate Professor and Director of the Institute of Asian Studies, University of Brunei Darussalam (UBD). His current work focuses on the ASEAN Economic Community, the One Belt One Road initiative, Chinese investments in South-East Asia, and the impact of income distribution on growth in Asia. He is also an expert in the automobile industry. Before joining UBD, he was a researcher at the Institute for Research on Contemporary Southeast Asia (IRASEC, CNRS-MAEE, Bangkok) and Associate Professor at the University of Paris 13 Sorbonne Paris Cité in France, where he obtained his PhD in Economics and was Deputy Director of the Research Center in Economics. He was also involved in promoting taxes on financial transactions as alternative sources for financing development as well as innovative regulation of global finance. Bruno's recent publications include *ASEAN Economic Community: A Model for Asia-Wide Integration?* (Palgrave McMillan 2016, edited with Mia Mikic); *Global Automobile Demand* (Palgrave McMillan 2015, two edited volumes); International Investment Policy for Small States: The Case of Brunei, in *International Investment Treaties and Arbitration Across Asia* (Julien Chaisse and Luke Nottage eds., Brill 2018, with Julien Chaisse); One Belt-One Road Initiative and ASEAN Connectivity, in *China's Global Rebalancing and the New Silk Road* (B.R. Deepak ed., Springer 2018).

Dr Nobumichi Teramura is Assistant Professor of the Institute of Asian Studies, University of Brunei Darussalam (UBD), Associate at the Centre for Asian and Pacific Law at the University of Sydney (CAPLUS), and Legal Consultant at Bun & Associates (Cambodia). He is the author of *Ex Aequo et Bono as a Response to the Over-Judicialisation of International Commercial Arbitration* (Wolters Kluwer, 2020), based on his doctoral thesis from the University of New South Wales in Australia, which received a PhD Excellence Award when completed in 2018. Nobu also published recently in the *Asian International Arbitration Journal* (2019) and *ASA Bulletin* (2020) and has co-authored a chapter comparing Australia in Larry di Matteo et al (eds.), *The Cambridge Handbook of Judicial Control of Arbitral Awards* (Cambridge University Press, 2020). Specialising in commercial law, his current research interests include legal integration in Asia and legal development for South-East Asian nations severely affected by colonisation and the Cold War, including Cambodia, Vietnam, Laos and Myanmar. He has teaching and research experience in Asia-Pacific jurisdictions including the Philippines, Australia, Japan, Taiwan, Hong Kong, Indonesia, Cambodia and Brunei.

Contributors

Vivienne Bath is Professor of Chinese and International Business Law at Sydney Law School in Australia and Director of the Centre for Asian and Pacific Law at the University of Sydney (CAPLUS). Her teaching and research interests are in international business and economic law, private international law and Chinese law. She has first-class honours in Chinese and in law from the Australian National University, and an LLM from Harvard Law School. She has also studied in China and Germany and has extensive professional experience in Sydney, New York and Hong Kong, specialising in international commercial law, with a focus on foreign investment and commercial transactions in China and the Asian region. Representative publications include: Vivienne Bath & Gabriël Moëns, *Law of International Business in Australasia* (2nd ed., Federation Press 2019); *Overlapping Jurisdiction and the Resolution of Disputes Before Chinese and Foreign Courts*, 17 Yearbook of International Private Law 111-150 (2015-2016) and The South and Alternative Models of Trade and Investment Regulation – Chinese Outbound Investment and Approaches to International Investment Agreements, in *Recalibrating International Investment Law: Global South Initiatives* (Fabio Morosini & Michelle Ratton Sanchez Badin eds., Cambridge University Press, 2018).

James Claxton is Professor of Law at Rikkyo University, Tokyo and Adjunct Faculty for the White & Case International Arbitration LLM at University of Miami Law School in Florida, as well as an independent arbitrator and mediator. He teaches and researches in the fields of international investment law, business and human rights, and international dispute settlement. Previously, he was Legal Counsel at the International Centre for Settlement of Investment Disputes (ICSID) in Washington and attorney in the international arbitration practices of law firms in Paris. James regularly advises dispute resolution institutions in Asia and is a member of various working groups devoted to improving international dispute resolution systems.

The Hon Clyde Croft AM SC is Professor of Law at Monash University in Melbourne, Australia, as well as a commercial arbitrator and mediator. Until retiring in 2019 he was the judge in charge of the Arbitration List, the Taxation List, and a General Commercial

List in the Commercial Court of the Supreme Court of Victoria. Prior to his Court appointment in 2009, he practised extensively in property and commercial law and was an arbitrator and mediator in property, construction and general commercial disputes, domestically and internationally. Dr Croft was appointed Senior Counsel in 2000 and holds the degrees of BEc, LLB and LLM from Monash University and PhD from the University of Cambridge. He has chaired the Expert Advisory Committee of the UNCITRAL National Co-ordination Committee of Australia (UNCCA) to support UNCITRAL Working Group II (Disputes) since May 2018. He represented the Asia Pacific Regional Arbitration Group (APRAG) at UNCITRAL from 2005 to 2010, revising the UNCITRAL Model Law and Arbitration Rules, and later co-authored *A Guide to the UNCITRAL Arbitration Rules* (Cambridge University Press, 2013). Dr Croft is Life Fellow of the Australian Centre for International Commercial Arbitration (ACICA) and of the Resolution Institute (incorporating the Institute of Arbitrators and Mediators Australia), Fellow of the Arbitrators' and Mediators' Institute of New Zealand (AMINZ), the Chartered Institute of Arbitrators, the Australian Academy of Law and UNCCA.

Weixia Gu is Associate Professor at the University of Hong Kong Faculty of Law and Co-Chair of the American Society of International Law Asia-Pacific Interest Group. Her research focuses on international arbitration, dispute resolution, private international law and cross-border legal issues. She is the author, editor, and co-editor of three books, including *The Developing World of Arbitration in the Asia Pacific* (Hart, 2018) and *Arbitration in China: Regulation of Arbitration Agreements and Practical Issues* (Sweet & Maxwell, 2012). She is the author of more than fifty journal articles, and her recent works appear in leading international and comparative law journals, such as the *American Journal of Comparative Law*, *Vanderbilt Journal of Transnational Law*, *Cornell International Law Journal*, among others. Her scholarship has been cited by the US Federal Court 11th Circuit, Texas Supreme Court, Hong Kong High Court, Singapore Law Gazette, and China Council for the Promotion of International Trade. Dr Gu is an elected member of the International Academy of Comparative Law and sits on the governing councils of Hong Kong Institute of Arbitrators and China Society of Private International Law. She also serves as a panel-listed arbitrator in a number of leading arbitration institutions in China and Asia. Before joining the Faculty, she was selected as an Honorary Young Fellow to the New York University Law School, in association with her Fulbright Award from the US Department of State.

Dr Jiaxiang Hu is Professor at the KoGuan Law School at the Shanghai Jiao Tong University in China. His research areas include public international law, international economic law and WTO law. He holds BA and MA from Hangzhou University, MPhil in Law from Zhejiang University, and PhD from the University of Edinburgh in Scotland. In the past three decades, Professor Hu has published more than ten books and one hundred articles in both Chinese and English. He has been awarded various honours by the Ministry of Education of China and Shanghai Municipality for his excellence in teaching and is currently leading several national research programmes.

Dr Jie (Jeanne) Huang is Associate Professor at the University of Sydney Law School. She was previously Senior Lecturer at the University of New South Wales, and Associate Professor/Associate Dean at Shanghai University of International Business and Economics School of Law in China. She obtained her Doctor of Juridical Science (SJD) from Duke University School of Law in 2010. She was Foreign Research Fellow at the Max Planck Institute for Comparative and International Private Law in Hamburg, and also had research experience at The Hague Academy of International Law, and the Paris-based Academy of International Arbitration Law. Jeanne teaches and researches in the fields of private international law, e-commerce regulation, international investment law and dispute resolution (international litigation and arbitration). She has published four books including *Interregional Recognition and Enforcement of Civil and Commercial Judgments: Lessons for China from US and EU Laws* (Hart, 2014) and her articles have appeared in many peer-reviewed law journals, with extensive competitive funding, including from the China National Social Science Fund. In 2015, she won the First Prize of Excellent Scholarship awarded by the China Society of Private International Law and the Nomination Award of the Dong Biwu Prize for Youth Research in Law. Jeanne serves as an arbitrator at the Hong Kong International Arbitration Center, Shanghai International Economic and Trade Arbitration Commission (Shanghai International Arbitration Center), Nanjing Arbitration Commission and Xi'an Arbitration Commission. She also serves as an expert witness on issues of private international law and Chinese law in courts in Australia and the US.

Dr Michael Hwang SC is a Singapore-based international arbitrator. He was the Deputy Chief Justice of the Dubai International Financial Centre (DIFC) Courts upon its establishment in 2005, and subsequently was appointed as Chief Justice in 2010, retiring at the end of 2018. Throughout that period, he has continued practising as an international arbitrator in commercial and treaty arbitrations. He has written two volumes of essays on international arbitration and international dispute resolution, respectively, and was awarded an honorary LLD from the University of Sydney.

Albert Monichino QC is a Melbourne-based barrister and arbitrator, with over twenty-five years of experience in resolving commercial disputes domestically and internationally. He was appointed Senior Counsel in 2010 and is a former Vice President (Convenor) and Co-Chair of the Arbitration and ADR Section for the Commercial Bar Association of the Victorian Bar (COMMBAR). Albert is a Chartered Arbitrator and Past President of the Chartered Institute of Arbitrators Australian Branch (CIArb, 2014-2017), and is a Fellow of CIArb, ACICA, the Resolution Institute and the Singapore Institute of Arbitrators. He writes extensively on international commercial arbitration in Australia and the Asia-Pacific, including an annual Australian survey for the *Australian Dispute Resolution Journal*.

Anselmo Reyes SC practises as an arbitrator. He was Professor of Legal Practice at Hong Kong University from October 2012 to September 2018. Before that, he was a judge of the Hong Kong High Court from September 2003 to September 2012, when he was in charge of the Construction and Arbitration List (2004-2008) and the Commercial and Admiralty Lists (2008-2012). He was Representative of the Hague Conference on

Private International Law's Regional Office Asia Pacific from April 2013 to July 2017. He became an International Judge of the Singapore International Commercial Court in January 2015.

Dr Jaivir Singh is Professor at the Centre for the Study of Law and Governance, Jawaharlal Nehru University, having previously taught at the University of Delhi in India. Trained as an economist at the Delhi School of Economics, University of Delhi, his research work aims at an interdisciplinary exploration of the interaction between the law and the economy. He has published on diverse topics including the Indian constitution, regulation, labour law, competition law, corporate law and international investment treaties.

Dr S.I. Strong is Associate Professor at the University of Sydney Law School, specialising in international dispute resolution and comparative law, particularly international commercial arbitration and large-scale (class and collective) suits. Prior to joining the University of Sydney, she taught at the Universities of Cambridge and Oxford as well as Georgetown Law Center and the University of Missouri. Dr Strong is an experienced practitioner, having acted as Counsel at Baker & McKenzie after working as a dual-qualified lawyer (US attorney and English solicitor) in the New York and London offices of Weil, Gotshal & Manges. She has published over 130 award-winning books, chapters and articles in Europe, Asia and the Americas, including *Legal Reasoning Across Commercial Disputes: Comparing Judicial and Arbitral Analyses* (anticipated 2021), *Arbitration of Trust Disputes: Issues in National and International Law* (2016), and *Class, Mass, and Collective Arbitration in National and International Law* (2013) from Oxford University Press as well as *International Commercial Arbitration: A Guide for U.S. Judges* (2012) from the Federal Judicial Center. Dr Strong's scholarly work has been translated into Spanish, French, Russian and Chinese and has been cited as authority by numerous state and federal courts and international tribunals. She sits as an arbitrator and mediator on a variety of international commercial and trust-related matters.

Ana Ubilava is Research Assistant and PhD candidate at the University of Sydney Law School, where she is in the final stages of completing a thesis on investor-state mediation. She has published on international dispute resolution in several periodicals including the *Journal of World Investment and Trade*. Ana is also Executive Coordinator of the Australian Network for Japanese Law (ANJeL).

The Hon Marilyn Warren AC QC is Vice-Chancellor's Professorial Fellow at Monash University, where she is a member of its Global Leaders Summit, and teaches postgraduate commercial law and international arbitration. She was a long-serving Chief Justice of the Supreme Court of Victoria (2003-2017), and earlier on that Court (1998-2003) included service as the Judge in Charge of the Commercial List and the Corporations List (now combined as the Commercial Court). Professor Warren was a foundation Council member of the Asian Business Law Institute in Singapore. She now also sits as a domestic and international commercial arbitrator and is a member of the

Dawson Chambers Senior Arbitrator Group at the Victorian Bar (where she became Queen's Counsel in 1997).

Dr A. Vijayalakshmi Venugopal is Senior Lecturer at Taylor's University Law School in Malaysia. Her teaching and postgraduate supervisory experience includes WTO law, international dispute resolution, international sale of goods and intellectual property law. She was a visiting lecturer at the University of Rotterdam Business School in the Netherlands. She holds Master's in Law and Educational Psychology and has presented conference papers in these fields. She is the author of three books, and articles in peer-reviewed law journals.

Dr Brett Williams is an Australian Legal Practitioner, is the principal of Williams Trade Law and an Honorary Senior Lecturer at the University of Sydney Law School. His legal practice specialises in the law of the World Trade Organization and of bilateral and regional trade agreements, including representation in WTO dispute settlement, accession issues, and also trade issues under Australian law. He has taught WTO law at Sydney Law School since 2001 and is Research Affiliate of both the Sydney Centre International Law and the Centre for Asian and Pacific Law at the University of Sydney. His publications include the co-edited book *China and the World Trade System* (Cambridge University Press, 2003), building on his PhD research, and articles on WTO negotiations on agricultural trade, China's WTO accession, trade in services and innovations in dispute settlement mechanisms in trade agreements. Brett also serves on the Editorial Board of the *Australian International Law Journal*. He has held various professional positions, including on the Executive of the International Law Section of the Law Council of Australia (2012-2016) and as inaugural co-chair of the International Economic Law Interest Group of the Australia New Zealand Society of International Law (2010-2012).

Summary of Contents

Table of Contents

Foreword

This is a book which looks forward to possible future outcomes in the development of cross-border dispute resolution in the Asia-Pacific region, focusing on major economies in East and South Asia, as well as neighbouring countries such as Australia which are closely linked economically and geographically. The principal questions posed are: (a) whether international commercial arbitration can improve its attractiveness through law reform and case law development, overcoming criticisms about cost and delay; (b) whether growing concerns about ISDS issues in current investment treaties will lead to Asian states to become rule-makers in international investment law, rather than continue as rule-takers; and (c) whether innovations in existing or new fields can assist the Asia-Pacific region in developing international dispute settlement mechanisms further. It is therefore an exciting book that challenges existing procedures and frameworks for cross-border dispute resolution both in commercial and in treaty arbitration, rather than being another book which is simply descriptive of the existing mechanisms (valuable as such books might be).

There are clearly catalysts for change within the existing framework of dispute resolution in Asia, and several could be real game-changers, like China's Belt and Road Initiative (examined in detail in Chapter 7) and the Singapore Convention on Mediation (Chapter 14). The team of writers specially assembled for this project have impressive credentials, led by the prolific and perceptive Professor Luke Nottage, and supported by several authors whom I have the privilege of knowing personally, and whose work I can wholeheartedly recommend as being worth reading, for both their knowledge and their experience, but particularly for their insight.

The various authors are not simply writing about existing practices and procedures in the region, but are examining the situation on the ground with a critical eye, and making informed observations about where changes are needed and educated guesses about the chances of reforms being successful, and the consequences if they are not. It has been written in the time of COVID-19 and accordingly points out the special challenges to the field of international dispute resolution in this unprecedented situation. Those include whether lawyers can adapt to new technological solutions to overcome the difficulties of conducting virtual hearings, and whether players in the field of dispute resolution can continue to afford the time and cost of long drawn-out forensic procedures to resolve the inevitable disputes that have been caused by the pandemic, or whether there will be added impetus to use mediation in place of confrontation. There are also protectionist issues affecting the future of maintaining the rule of law in settling cross-border commercial disputes. Local judges might be influenced by the fact that certain apparent breaches of contract have been caused by events beyond the control of their local businesses, and the law may become stretched or even disregarded for what may be perceived to be a fairer commercial solution when performance of a contractual obligation has been rendered impossible in the light of conditions brought on by the pandemic. Such situations could lead possibly to foreign judgments and/or foreign arbitration awards not being recognised or enforced, relying on an overly liberal interpretation of the doctrine of public policy to justify such non-enforcement.

There are also challenges arising from internal social and political challenges in certain Asian jurisdictions such as Malaysia and Hong Kong, where rule of law issues may affect investor confidence in those territories. This mistrust of the application of the rule of law will likely also lead to an international lack of confidence in the reliability of the dispute resolution system of the countries concerned, and Hong Kong in particular may find it difficult to maintain the hitherto proud record of independence and efficiency of its courts and arbitral tribunals. And there are legacy challenges which were there in several Asian countries before COVID-19 and remain as challenges to be overcome, without which their attractiveness as international investment and commercial centres will surely decrease if the legacy problems are not resolved.

The best introduction to this book is actually to start from the succinct final chapter (Chapter 15) jointly authored by Professors Anselmo Reyes, Shahla Ali and Nobumichi Teramura. This gives an excellent summary of the aims and contents of the fourteen preceding chapters and will highlight to readers which chapters might be of particular interest and therefore help determine in which order to read which chapters, although all fourteen are worth reading.

I therefore congratulate Professors Nottage, Ali, Jetin and Teramura and their team of authors on producing a timely and lively study. It will certainly stimulate ideas and discussion among its readers and perhaps also contribute to some positive changes in the jurisdictions which are the subject of this critical study.

Dr Michael Hwang SC
Singapore, 31 July 2020

List of Abbreviations

AANZFTA	ASEAN Australia-New Zealand FTA
ACIA	ASEAN Comprehensive Investment Agreement
ACICA	Australian Centre for International Commercial Arbitration
ADR	Alternative Dispute Resolution
AFTINET	Australian Fair Trade and Investment Network
AG	Australia Group
A-HKFTA	Australia-Hong Kong Free Trade Agreement
AHKIA	Australia-Hong Kong Investment Agreement
AIAC	Asian International Arbitration Centre
AIIB	Asian Infrastructure Investment Bank
APEC	Asia-Pacific Economic Cooperation
ASEAN	Association of Southeast Asian Nations
BAC	Beijing Arbitration Commission
BIT	Bilateral Investment Treaty
BRI	Belt and Road Initiative
CAJAC	China-Africa Joint Arbitration Centre
CCJA	Cour Commune de Justice et d'Arbitrage
CEDR	Centre for Effective Dispute Resolution
CEPA	Closer Economic Partnership Agreement
CFA	Court of Final Appeal
CFI	Court of First Instance
CICC	China International Commercial Court
CIDS	Geneva Center for International Dispute Settlement
CIETAC	China International Economic and Trade Arbitration Commission

CISTEC	Center for Information on Security Trade Control
CITES	Convention on International Trade in Endangered Species of Wild Fauna and Flora
CJEU	Court of Justice of the European Union
CLC	International Convention on Civil Liability for Oil Pollution Damage
CMAC	China Maritime Arbitration Commission
CMG	China Merchants Group
CPTPP	Comprehensive and Progressive Agreement for Trans-Pacific Partnership
DSB	Dispute Settlement Body
DSD	Dispute System Design
DSU	Dispute Settlement Understanding
ETCO	Export Trade Control Order
EU	European Union
FDI	Foreign Direct Investment
FEO	Foreign Exchange Order
FET	Fair and Equitable Treatment
FOC	Flag of Convenience
FTA	Free Trade Agreement
GATT	General Agreement on Tariffs and Trade
GDPR	General Data Protection Regulation
GFC	Global Financial Crisis
GVC	Global Value Chains
HKAO	Hong Kong Arbitration Ordinance
HKIAC	Hong Kong International Arbitration Commission
HKMAAL	Hong Kong Mediation Accreditation Associated Limited
IAA	International Arbitration Act
IA-CEPA	Indonesia-Australia Comprehensive Economic Partnership Agreement
IACT	International Arbitration Centre in Tokyo
IBA	International Bar Association
ICA	International Commercial Arbitration
ICC	International Chamber of Commerce
ICCA	International Council for Commercial Arbitration
ICJ	International Court of Justice
ICP	Internal Control Procedure
ICSID	International Centre for Settlement of Investment Disputes

IHR	International Health Regulations 2005
IIA	International Investment Agreement
ILA	International Law Association
IMO	International Maritime Organization
IOPP	International Oil Pollution Prevention
ISA	Investor-State Arbitration
ISDS	Investor-State Dispute Settlement
JAA	Japan Association of Arbitrators
JCAA	Japan Commercial Arbitration Association
JIDRC-Osaka	Japan International Dispute Resolution Centre-Osaka
JIMC-Kyoto	Japan International Mediation Centre-Kyoto
JSCOT	Joint Standing Committee on Treaties
KCAB	Korean Commercial Arbitration Board
KLRCA	Kuala Lumpur Regional Centre for Arbitration
LCIA	London Court of International Arbitration
LDP	Liberal Democratic Party
MARPOL 73/78	The International Convention for the Prevention of Pollution from Ships 1973 as Modified by the Protocol of 1978
MEA	Multilateral Environmental Agreement
METI	Ministry of Economy, Trade and Industry (Japan)
MFN	Most-Favoured Nation
MNE	Multinational Enterprise
MSTCR	Missile Technology Control Regime
NAFTA	North American Free Trade Agreement
NDB	New Development Bank
NDRC	National Development and Reform Commission (People's Republic of China)
NGO	Non-governmental Organisation
NSG	Nuclear Suppliers Group
NT	National Treatment
NYC	New York Convention on the Recognition and Enforcement of Foreign Arbitral Awards
OBOR	One Belt One Road
OECD	Organisation for Economic Co-operation and Development
OHADA	Organization for the Harmonization of African Business Law
Paris-MoU	Paris Memorandum of Understanding
PCA	Permanent Court of Arbitration
PRC	People's Republic of China

PTPA	Peru Trade Promotion Agreement
RCEP	Regional Comprehensive Economic Partnership
ROK	Republic of Korea
SCC	Stockholm Chamber of Commerce
SCIA	Shenzhen Court of International Arbitration
SIMC	Singapore International Mediation Centre
SPC	Supreme People's Court
TFAAB	Trade for All Advisory Board
TOMAC	Tokyo Maritime Arbitration Commission
TPP	Trans-Pacific Partnership
UN	United Nations
UNCITRAL	United Nations Commission on International Trade Law
UNCLOS	United Nations Convention on the Law of the Sea
UNCTAD	United Nations Conference on Trade and Development
UNTS	United Nations Treaty
USD	United States Dollar
VCLT	Vienna Convention on the Law of Treaties
WA	Wassenaar Arrangement
WHO	World Health Organization
WMD	Weapons of Mass Destruction
WTO	World Trade Organization

List of Figures

List of Tables

Acknowledgements

We co-editors are very grateful for all other fourteen authors to this fifteen-chapter book, for completing their manuscripts so efficiently despite the extra challenge of the global COVID-19 pandemic. That unexpectedly created a further 'new frontier' for Asia-Pacific international arbitration and dispute resolution, and also impacted on the original two overarching themes for this book. One of those was how different jurisdictions can develop as attractive seats for international commercial arbitration despite concerns about its delays and costs, amidst established and emerging venues as well as new competition from international commercial courts and mediation. The second theme was whether and how Asia-Pacific states could be becoming 'rule-makers' rather than 'rule-takers' when engaging in international investment treaty making and dispute settlement with foreign investors.

Many of us were fortunately able to meet in person over 2019 to discuss these themes and present some earlier versions of this book's chapters or related papers, in conferences hosted in July at the University of Hong Kong (HKU) and in November at the University of Sydney. We are grateful for other presentations and feedback, and funding provided by both universities' central administrations to facilitate those public events as well as for research assistance (University of Sydney/HKU Strategic Partnership Award). Nottage also acknowledges further research funding from the Sydney Law School's Legal Scholarship Support Fund, and Ali acknowledges the Government of Hong Kong's University Grants Committee for its kind support through its GRF Grant (HKU 17604318) and a 2019 University of Hong Kong Knowledge Exchange Award. For editorial and other assistance, we also thank student interns for 2019 (Grace Huang) and 2020 (Troy Lee and Novea Chan), from the Centre for Asian and Pacific Law at the University of Sydney.

We are also grateful for several journals (some as copyright holders) for permission to publish significantly updated and/or expanded versions of several chapters in this book, as indicated in their respective opening footnotes.

Luke Nottage
Shahla Ali
Bruno Jetin
Nobumichi Teramura
(31 July 2020)

CHAPTER 1

New Frontiers in Asia-Pacific Trade, Investment and International Business Dispute Resolution

Luke Nottage & Bruno Jetin

Asia-Pacific trade and investment flows have burgeoned over recent decades, albeit impacted by China-US trade tensions and especially the COVID-19 pandemic (§1.02). International investment agreements (IIAs) have proliferated to liberalise and protect investments (§1.03), mostly adding the option of investor-state dispute settlement (ISDS). Asia-related ISDS cases have also started to grow, albeit somewhat belatedly (§1.04), complementing a more long-standing upward trend in international commercial arbitration (ICA) cases involving Asian parties filed in the region as well as the traditional Western centres (§1.05). The eastward shift in international dispute resolution has already involved initiatives not only to improve the support for ICA and ISDS arbitrations but also to develop alternatives, such as international commercial courts and mediation. Core arguments from ensuing chapters (§1.06) cover the main existing venues for international dispute resolution in Asia (China, Hong Kong and Singapore) but also some emerging contenders (Japan, Malaysia, India and Australia). Overall (§1.07), can ICA venues improve their attractiveness through law reforms, case law development and other measures, despite growing concerns about costs and delays? Will some emerging concerns about ISDS prompt Asia-Pacific states to become more active 'rule-makers' in international investment law? How might these issues be affected by the COVID-19 pandemic?

§1.01 INTRODUCTION

Asia-related trade and investment flows have burgeoned over recent decades, although impacted by the US-China trade tensions from 2018 and especially the coronavirus disease of 2019 (COVID-19) pandemic declared from early 2020, as elaborated in §1.02 below. §1.03 outlines the parallel proliferation of stand-alone bilateral investment treaties (BITs), especially from the 1990s, and then free trade agreements (FTAs). These comprehensive FTAs go beyond commitments under the multilateral World Trade Organization (WTO) regime by including investment chapters aimed at both protecting and liberalising foreign investment. Both types of IIAs typically allow foreign investors to bring ISDS arbitrations directly against host states for violating substantive treaty commitments, like non-discrimination or adequate compensation for expropriation.

Accordingly, but somewhat belatedly compared to other parts of the world, Asia-related ISDS cases have also started to grow, as explained in §1.04 and the Appendix to this chapter. This complements a more long-standing upward trend in ICA cases involving Asian parties. The growth in ICA filings has occurred not only in the 'core' Western seats and arbitral institutions (France, Switzerland, England and US) but now also through those that have emerged in the Eastern 'periphery'.[1] Section 1.05 outlines this eastward shift for international dispute resolution services, tracking Asia's emergence as a global economic powerhouse. The shift may be dampened in the short term by restrictions on international travel and other logistical impediments because of the COVID-19 pandemic. Yet its disruptions to cross-border contracts and investments combined with pressures on profitability are likely to generate more disputes, and innovations in how to resolve them.[2] The eastward shift in international dispute resolution has already involved initiatives not only to improve support for ICA and ISDS arbitrations but also to develop alternatives, such as international commercial courts and mediation in and for the region. These new types of procedures, as well as innovations within ICA and ISDS, combine with geographical expansion to generate significant 'new frontiers' for Asia-Pacific cross-border business dispute resolution.

Section 1.06 provides further background and summarises core arguments from ensuing chapters. It outlines key developments not only in the existing key jurisdictions in Asia for international dispute resolution (China, Hong Kong and Singapore) but also in some emerging contenders (especially Japan, Malaysia, India, and Australia – itself on the periphery of Asia but, like neighbouring New Zealand, closely entwined economically and in other ways with the region). As reiterated in the concluding §1.07, one key theme throughout the book is whether existing and new venues for ICA can improve their attractiveness through law reforms, case law development and other

---

1. Luke Nottage, *The Vicissitudes of Transnational Commercial Arbitration and the Lex Mercatoria: A View from the Periphery*, 16 Arb. Int'l 53 (2000); Luke Nottage, *In/formalization and Glocalization of International Commercial Arbitration and Investment Treaty Arbitration in Asia*, in *Formalisation and Flexibilisation of Dispute Resolution* 211 (Joachim Zekoll, et al., eds., Martinus Nijhoff / Brill 2014).
2. *See generally*, e.g., Gary Benton, *How Will the Coronavirus Impact International Arbitration?*, Kluwer Arbitration Blog (13 Mar. 2020), http://arbitrationblog.kluwerarbitration.com/2020/03/13/how-will-the-coronavirus-impact-international-arbitration/; Constantin-Adi Gavrila, *Reflections in the Age of Coronavirus (COVID-19)*, Kluwer Mediation Blog (14 Mar. 2020), http://mediationblog.kluwerarbitration.com/2020/03/14/reflections-in-the-age-of-coronavirus-covid-19/; Luke Nottage, *Will the COVID-19 Be a Long-Term Game Changer for International Arbitration?*, Kluwer Arbitration Blog (16 Jul. 2020), http://arbitrationblog.kluwerarbitration.com/2020/07/16/will-the-covid-19-pandemic-be-a-long-term-game-changer-for-international-arbitration/; and Teramura, Ali and Reyes, Chapter 15 in this volume.

measures,[3] despite growing concerns about costs and delays in arbitration. A second is whether evolving controversy about ISDS-backed investment treaty commitments will prompt Asian states to become ever more 'rule-makers' in international investment law rather than mostly 'rule takers'.[4] Both questions may well be impacted by changes in legal instruments, practices and attitudes related to the spread of COVID-19 from 2020, making that pandemic a further 'new frontier' for Asia-Pacific international dispute resolution.

§1.02 TRANSFORMATIONS IN TRADE AND INVESTMENT FLOWS IN AND AROUND ASIA

Asia-Pacific economies have increased their share of global trade over the last few decades, and this has underpinned a wave of international investment in the region. The reason is the development of global value chains (GVCs), which are generated by the fragmentation of the production of goods and services into discrete segments.[5] These are localised in the best-suited countries in terms of costs, natural resources, logistics and technology. Around 50% of global trade is related to GVCs,[6] and multinational enterprises (MNEs) are the core actors within GVCs. MNEs coordinate large flows of intermediate products within their networks of affiliates, contractual partners (in non-equity modes of international production) and arm's-length suppliers.[7]

GVC trade operates mostly in three regions called 'Factory Asia', 'Factory Europe' and 'Factory North America'.[8] On average, the higher the degree of the economic integration of a region, the higher the intra-regional GVC participation. Thanks to the European Union (EU), 'Factory Europe' had the highest share of intra-regional GVC participation in 2000, followed by 'Factory North America' and 'Factory Asia'. Ten years after the Global Financial Crisis (GFC) and economic slowdown over 2008-2009, 'Factory Asia's' share of intra-regional participation exceeded that of 'Factory North America',[9] which reveals the progress of economic integration of Asia supported by

3. Anselmo Reyes & Weixia Gu eds., *The Developing World of Arbitration: A Comparative Study of Arbitration Reform in the Asia Pacific* (Hart Publishing 2018).
4. Julien Chaisse & Luke Nottage, *International Investment Treaties and Arbitration: Across Asia: A Bird's Eye View*, in *International Investment Treaties and Arbitration Across Asia* 1 (Julien Chaisse & Luke Nottage eds., Brill | Nijhoff 2018).
5. Richard Baldwin, *The Great Convergence: Information Technology and the New Globalization* (Harvard University Press 2016).
6. World Bank, *World Development Report 2020: Trading for Development in the Age of Global Value Chains* 19 (World Bank Group 2020). The GVC participation measure is computed as the share of GVC exports in total international exports. GVC exports include transactions in which a country's exports embody value added that it previously imported from abroad (backward GVC participation), as well as transactions in which a country's exports are embodied in the importing country's exports to third countries (forward GVC participation).
7. UNCTAD, *Global Value Chains and Development: Investment and Value Added Trade in the Global Economy* (United Nations 2013).
8. Richard Baldwin & Javier Lopez Gonzalez, *Supply Chain Trade: A Portrait of Global Patterns and Several Testable Hypotheses*, 38 World Econ. 1682 (2015).
9. UNCTAD, *World Investment Report 2019: Special Economic Zones* (United Nations 2019).

regional and bilateral treaties (elaborated in §1.03 below).[10] The intra-regional share of GVC activity has increased more regionally than globally in the Asia-Pacific region. This contrasts with Europe and North America, where the share of extra-regional GVC trade has increased, in particular, due to their growing links with Asia.[11] The automobile industry is a good example: this value chain has become more regional and integrated more of Asia's sub-regions.[12] China traditionally played the key role of final assembler of many of the regional supply chains of 'Factory Asia'.[13] However, the local content of Chinese exports has increased recently as China has been rebalancing its economy,[14] upgrading its technological capacities and investing more in the region.

GVC trade and foreign investment are 'inextricably intertwined through the international production networks of firms'.[15] Recent and earlier studies have demonstrated that GVC trade and Foreign Direct Investment (FDI) have grown in parallel.[16] An econometric study shows that 'the higher the GVC participation, the higher the bilateral FDI inward stocks'.[17] The rise of GVC participation by 'Factory Asia', plus the stronger links of other regions with Asia, explains the continued increase of FDI inflows into the region. By 2018, they amounted to 36% of the world total, as shown in §1.02 Figure 1.1 (and this chapter's Appendix).

10. Gianluca Orefice & Nadia Rocha, *Deep Integration and Production Networks: An Empirical Analysis*, 37 World Econ. 106 (2014).
11. World Bank, *supra* n. 6, at 23-5 reaches the same conclusion.
12. Bruno Jetin, *Production Networks of the Asian Automobile Industry: Regional or Global?*, 18 Int'l J. Automotive Tech. & Mgt. 302 (2018).
13. Prema-chandra Athukorala, *Southeast Asian Countries in Global Production Networks*, in *ASEAN Economic Community: A Model for Asia-Wide Regional Integration?* 79 (Mia Mikic & Bruno Jetin eds., Palgrave Macmillan 2016).
14. Bruno Jetin & Luis Reyes, *Wage-led Demand as a Rebalancing Strategy for Economic Growth in China*, 43 J. Post Keynesian Econ. 341 (2020).
15. UNCTAD, *supra* n. 7, at 3.
16. World Bank, *supra* n. 6, at 33; UNCTAD, *supra* n. 7, at 137-9.
17. Enrique Martínez-Galán & Maria Paula Fontoura, *Global Value Chains and Inward Foreign Direct Investment in the 2000s*, 42 World Econ. 175 (2019).

Figure 1.1 Inflows of FDI in Asia, 1990-2018

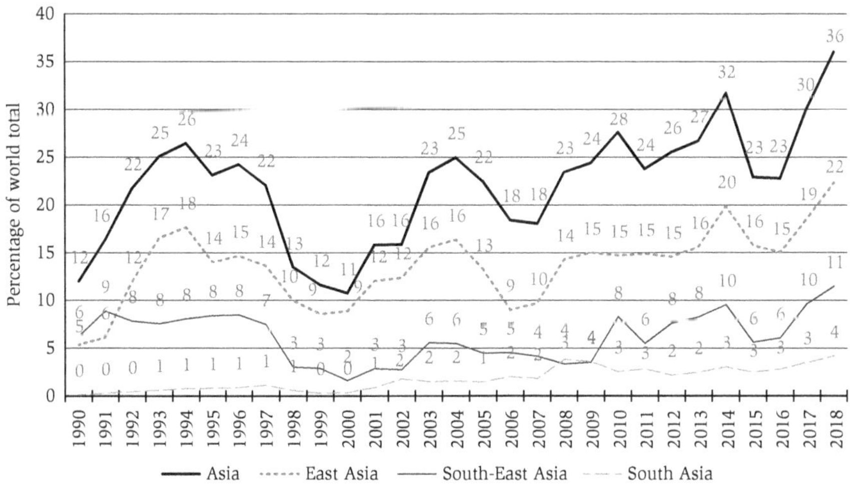

Source: Authors' calculations based on data from UNCTAD.

Although East Asia contributed to most of the rise, Southeast Asia and more modestly South Asia have also increased their share of global FDI. This is in sharp contrast with Europe and North America, whose share of FDI inflows declined in 2018 to respectively 21.4% and 22.5% – down from 50% and 28% in 2000.[18] Asia has also become the main global outbound investor. In 2018, FDI outflows from Asia amounted to 49% of the world total, exceeding the EU (38.5%) and the USA (27% in 2017).

These FDI flows give only an approximate view of the importance of MNE investment from a home country in the economy of a host country. This is due to 'conduit FDI', which 'arises when an MNE investing from home country A in host country B establishes an intermediate step through a third country C'.[19] One of the main motivations for conduit FDI is tax avoidance, but another consideration is increasingly an investment treaty between the intermediate and the host countries. In Asia, Singapore and Hong Kong are important hosts for conduit FDI whose final destination is other countries in the Asia Pacific. The existence of conduit FDI 'augments and blurs the scope of international treaties, producing a de facto multilateralising effect'.[20] Accordingly, a significant share of ultimate beneficiaries of the 'mega-regional' trade and investment agreements (like those outlined below in §1.03 and in several subsequent chapters) may be outside the regions involved. Table 1.1 (including some authors' calculations) gives a view of FDI shares by the ultimate investor in the accumulated stock of selected Asia-Pacific economies.

18. *Source*: Authors' estimations with UNCTAD data.
19. Bruno Casella, *Looking Through Conduit FDI in Search of Ultimate Investors: A Probabilistic Approach*, 26 Transnatl. Corporations 109, 111 (2019).
20. *Ibid.*, 139.

Table 1.1 UNCTAD FDI Estimates by Ultimate Investor, Share in Inward FDI Stock, 2017, Selected Countries

Investor	*Australia*	*Bangladesh*	*Cambodia*	*China*	*Hong Kong*	*India*	*Indonesia*	*Japan*	*South Korea*	*Malaysia*	*Mongolia*	*Myanmar*	*Nepal*	*Pakistan*	*Philippines*	*Singapore*	*Sri Lanka*	*Thailand*
Australia	0.1	6.2	1.5	1.1	0.6	0.7	1.8	1.3	0.5	1.7	2.2	0.6	3.6	0.7	2.6	2.1	1.4	1.4
Bangladesh	-	-	0.1	-	-	-	-	-	-	-	-	0.0	2.6	0.0	-	0.0	0.1	0.0
Canada	4.6	1.5	2.8	1.6	2.4	1.0	2.0	1.5	1.8	0.6	26.2	0.3	0.1	0.7	0.9	2.0	2.6	1.1
China	5.5	3.3	24.9	7.8	25.6	0.8	3.5	1.7	3.5	5.1	26.7	34.1	10.7	7.6	2.0	5.1	12.0	3.7
EU	9.9	7.7	4.6	14.5	16.8	16.3	14.9	30.3	20.0	12.8	8.9	4.3	4.6	12.3	19.3	13.8	14.7	10.7
Hong Kong	1.3	2.3	4.9	18.3	1.0	0.7	1.6	1.8	1.4	3.7	2.3	1.2	1.2	1.0	3.3	1.9	3.0	2.9
India	0.2	3.8	0.4	0.2	0.2	1.6	0.4	0.2	0.4	0.2	0.1	1.7	19.6	0.2	0.4	2.3	11.5	0.6
Indonesia	0.0	0.5	0.1	0.1	0.1	0.1	0.1	0.2	0.1	0.1	0.1	0.2	0.0	0.0	0.5	1.6	0.1	0.2
Japan	11.4	2.9	8.7	8.2	4.5	11.8	10.7	1.0	23.2	13.8	4.3	5.4	1.0	5.7	25.2	8.1	3.9	37.5
South Korea	0.7	5.8	6.4	2.9	0.4	2.5	1.9	2.0	0.1	2.4	2.5	4.1	2.1	0.5	2.1	1.0	0.8	1.8
Malaysia	1.7	4.9	5.3	0.4	0.3	0.7	6.1	0.5	1.0	0.3	0.3	1.6	0.4	2.0	1.3	4.4	10.2	1.8
Singapore	2.3	4.7	4.5	3.8	2.9	8.7	16.6	6.5	5.0	14.1	6.4	20.0	2.9	0.7	5.9	0.5	6.1	10.3
Sri Lanka	-	1.9	1.8	-	-	0.0	-	-	-	-	-	-	0.1	-	-	0.0	-	0.0
Switzerland	1.6	0.9	0.5	2.3	3.4	5.4	2.6	4.3	3.3	5.8	1.3	0.6	0.4	14.3	7.2	4.1	5.9	2.5
Taiwan	0.1	1.9	6.2	1.5	0.9	0.1	0.2	2.8	0.4	1.0	0.2	0.7	0.0	0.0	1.9	1.5	0.2	1.6
Thailand	0.3	2.1	5.4	0.8	2.0	0.5	1.7	0.2	0.1	0.4	0.3	8.7	0.1	0.1	0.9	0.9	0.4	0.2
U K	8.6	9.7	4.0	3.7	6.0	13.7	9.0	7.4	7.3	4.3	3.3	6.5	2.0	24.3	3.5	6.2	6.4	4.2
U S	25.3	26.8	6.0	9.7	12.8	24.3	16.6	30.3	20.6	10.7	7.6	3.7	2.9	10.1	15.5	25.5	8.0	11.7
Viet Nam	-	-	4.6	-	-	-	0.0	-	-	-	0.1	0.9	-	-	0.0	0.0	-	-
Confidential/ Unspecified	*24.1*	*4.1*	*5.5*	*18.0*	*14.1*	*5.0*	*6.6*	*5.6*	*5.9*	*20.4*	*4.0*	*3.9*	*40.2*	*6.3*	*4.3*	*10.4*	*3.7*	*4.1*
Total bilateral	100.0	100.0	100.0	100.0	100.0	100.0	100.0	100.0	100.0	100.0	100.0	100.0	100.0	100.0	100.0	100.0	100.0	100.0

Source: Annex table 22, World Investment Report 2019, UNCTAD. Details in Casella, 2019, pages 109-146. *For the EU estimate, authors' calculations by summation of EU country members' shares.*
Note: Estimates cover 108 recipient countries, corresponding to 93% of the value of global inward FDI stock.

The USA and the EU remain large investors and still eclipse China in many key Asia-Pacific countries (Australia, India, Indonesia, Malaysia, Pakistan, Philippines, Singapore and Thailand). China is the largest investor in only three neighbouring countries (Cambodia, Mongolia and Myanmar). Japan remains the largest investor in Korea, the Philippines and Thailand, and is the second-largest in Malaysia. Singapore is an important investor in Indonesia, India, Malaysia and Myanmar and Thailand, while Hong Kong is an important investor only in China. This wide range of investors means that the investment agreements signed in the region need to appeal to a large variety of interests.

Two recent shocks will likely have long-term consequences for the region, including perhaps for the central role that China has come to play in Asian GVCs: the trade tensions between the USA and China that escalated over 2019, and the COVID-19 pandemic since 2020. United Nations Conference on Trade and Development's (UNCTAD's) *World Investment Report 2020* notes that:[21]

> *The COVID-19 crisis will cause a dramatic fall in FDI.* Global FDI flows are forecast to decrease by up to 40 per cent in 2020, from their 2019 value of $1.54 trillion. This would bring FDI below $1 trillion for the first time since 2005. FDI is projected to decrease by a further 5 to 10 per cent in 2021 and to initiate a recovery in 2022. A rebound in 2022, with FDI reverting to the pre-pandemic underlying trend, is possible, but only at the upper bound of expectations. ...
>
> Developing economies are expected to see the biggest fall in FDI because they rely more on investment in [GVC]-intensive and extractive industries, which have been severely hit, and because they are not able to put in place the same economic support measures as developed economies. ...
>
> Flows to *developing Asia* will be severely affected due to their vulnerability to supply chain disruptions, the weight of GVC-intensive FDI in the region and global pressures to diversify production locations. FDI is projected to fall by 30 to 45 per cent. In 2019, FDI flows to the region declined by 5 per cent, to $474 billion, despite gains in South-East Asia, China and India.

The US-China trade tensions and then the pandemic have caused many MNEs, especially in high technology, to consider the risks of over-reliance on China for manufacturing. Trade tensions, which escalated from 2018, had led several MNEs to close some plants in China and relocate to Vietnam and other Southeast Asian countries.[22] The continuous rise of real wages in China was an additional motive for those seeking primarily to minimise costs. The pandemic from 2020 accelerated the trend.[23] The severity of the supply chain disruptions is intense: an estimated 20% of

21. UNCTAD, *World Investment Report 2020: International Production Beyond the Pandemic* (June 2020) x-xi (original emphasis), available via https://unctad.org/en/Pages/DIAE/World Investment Report/World_Investment_Report.aspx.
22. Rei Nakafuji & Ken Moriyasu, *Multinationals Reroute Supply Chains from China – for Good?: Komatsu, Daikin and Asics Shift Operations Elsewhere,* Nikkei Asian Review (15 Feb. 2020), https://asia.nikkei.com/Spotlight/Coronavirus/Multinationals-reroute-supply-chains-from-China-for-good.
23. For example, Google and Microsoft are shifting their production of mobile phone, smart speakers and laptops to Vietnam and Thailand. *See* Cheng Ting-Fang & Lauly Li, *Google, Microsoft Shift Production from China Faster Due to Virus: 'Made in Vietnam' Pixel Phones and Surface Laptops*

global trade in manufacturing of intermediate products originates in China, and the COVID-19 outbreak could result in a USD 50 billion decrease in exports across GVCs in 2020.[24] Accordingly, some products (and related investment)[25] could be relocated to Japan, Europe and North America. This is the case for many products that are considered critical for national security. For the Trump Administration, even before the pandemic during the China-US trade tensions, these have included several products entering the defence industry supply chain, such as steel, aluminium, and possibly even cars were considered eligible for 'national security-based tariffs'. Finished pharmaceuticals, drug ingredients and medical supplies might also be added to the list of products which, according to the Trump administration, should be produced in the USA.[26] The COVID-19 pandemic is a further game changer that is likely to transform globalisation or even lead to some de-globalisation. The big difference compared to even two decades ago is that GVCs, including across Asia, have become overlaid with another complex network: substantive commitments and dispute resolution enforcement mechanisms under bilateral and regional investment treaties.

§1.03 PROLIFERATION OF IIAs IN ASIA

Asian states remain very diverse in political or legal systems and economic development and overall have tended to be less open to formalising international cooperation through treaty-based commitments. However, IIAs are somewhat of an exception,[27] and more generally regarding economic cooperation (say compared to security matters), there is a greater tendency to commit to 'hard law' (specific commitments linked to enforcement mechanisms) and/or formalised cooperation (regular meetings, etc.).[28] One example comes from the Association of Southeast Asian Nations (ASEAN). It has committed increasingly to trade and investment liberalisation within that subregion and with other Asia-Pacific economies through 'ASEAN + ' FTAs, and formalised its arrangements in other ways, e.g., through the 2008 ASEAN Charter, although in some important 'behind the borders' areas (such as consumer law) policymakers are still

---

Expected in 2020, Nikkei Asian Review (26 Feb. 2020), https://asia.nikkei.com/Spotlight/Coronavirus/Google-Microsoft-shift-production-from-China-faster-due-to-virus.

24. According to estimates of UNCTAD. *See* UNCTAD, *Global Trade Impact of the Coronavirus (COVID-19) Epidemic, Trade and Development Report Update* (4 Mar. 2020), https://unctad.org/en/PublicationsLibrary/ditcinf2020d1.pdf.
25. For instance, the fact that China produces 50% of the world's face mask supply explain their global shortage. *See* Izabella Kaminska, *The under Appreciated Importance of Non-woven Markets,* Financial Times (21 Feb. 2020), https://ftalphaville.ft.com/2020/02/21/1582279827000/The-under-appreciated-importance-of-non-woven-markets/. Diversification of supply may be accelerated by government responses. *See*, for example, *Japan to Pay Firms to Leave China,* Bloomberg (9 Apr. 2020), https://www.scmp.com/news/asia/east-asia/article/3079126/japan-pay-firms-leave-china-relocate-production-elsewhere-part.
26. James Politi, *US Trade Adviser Seeks to Replace Chinese Drug Supplies: Navarro Says Coronavirus Is 'Wake-Up Call' to Create American Pharmaceutical Supply Chain,* Financial Times (12 Feb. 2020), https://www.ft.com/content/73751cca-4d1a-11ea-95a0-43d18ec715f5.
27. Simon Chesterman, *Asia's Ambivalence about International Law and Institutions: Past, Present and Futures,* 27 Eur. J. Int'l L. 945 (2016).
28. Saadia M. Pekkanen, *Asian Designs: Governance in the Contemporary World Order* (Cornell University Press 2016).

largely engaging in voluntary harmonisation and capacity-building in the older-style 'ASEAN Way'.[29] Another example comes from the Asia-Pacific Economic Forum (APEC). From 1994, APEC issued non-binding and general principles to assist Member States voluntarily improving their foreign investment regimes, but more recently, it has been providing detailed manuals and other capacity-building relating to negotiating and drafting IIAs as well as dealing with treaty-based disputes with investors.[30]

Most Asian states significantly expanded signings of BITs especially over the 1990s and into the 2000s,[31] as socialist and other economies started to deregulate and engage in more regional and global trade, underpinned by the WTO system and trends outlined in §1.02 above. The BITs even from this era mostly still focused on protection for foreign investments once made, for example, by requiring the host state to provide to counterparty investors the same 'national treatment' (NT) as for its local investors or 'most-favoured-nation' (MFN) treatment as for foreign investors from third states. In contrast to such 'post-establishment' NT and MFN, these BITs did not tend to offer much liberalisation of market access through 'pre-establishment' NT or MFN and even then qualified such commitments through extensive negative lists where discrimination was still permitted in favour of local investors. More liberalisation commitments have emerged in recent BITs, but especially through investment chapters contained in FTAs. The latter started to be concluded from the early twenty-first century, first bilaterally and then regionally (e.g., through ASEAN+ FTAs), as it became clear that the WTO (or the Organization for International Cooperation and Development: OECD) would find it difficult to promote a multilateral investment treaty protecting and liberalising investment.[32]

In stand-alone BITs and especially FTA investment chapters, it also became more common to include broadly applicable ISDS provisions, whereby the host state consented in advance to an arbitration claim being brought directly by an aggrieved foreign investor. Earlier treaties sometimes provided only for inter-state arbitration, a procedure that is still given in recent treaties as an extra option (and for resolving trade rather than investment disputes, as also under the WTO system). Yet, this option was hardly ever taken by foreign investors, despite the costs involved in pursuing ISDS arbitration instead because they would need to mobilise their home state (at its cost

29. Luke Nottage, et al., *ASEAN Consumer Law Harmonisation and Cooperation: Achievements and Challenges* Chs. 1 & 2 (Cambridge University Press 2019), partially available also via https://papers.ssrn.com/sol3/papers.cfm?abstract_id=3398046. *See also generally* Anna Tevina, *Regional Economic Integration and Dispute Settlement in East Asia: The Evolving Legal Framework* (Hart Publishing 2018).
30. Vivienne Bath & Luke Nottage, *International Investment Agreements in Asia, in Handbook of International Investment Law and Policy* (Julien Chaisse, et al., eds., Springer 2020). A longer version is available at https://papers.ssrn.com/sol3/papers.cfm?abstract_id=3544458, adding a part on Australia and New Zealand plus an Appendix (initially drafted by Nottage) adapted for this present chapter.
31. Sandra Friedrich & Claudia Salomon, *Investment Arbitration in East Asia and the Pacific*, 16 J. World Inv. & Trade (2015). *See also* their Appendix available at https://ssrn.com/abstract=2591186.
32. On the stalling of the OECD treaty in the late 1990s, *see* Joachim Karl, *The Negotiations on the OECD Multilateral Agreement on Investment*, in *International Investment Law* 283 (Marc Bungenberg, et al., eds., Hart Publishing 2015).

and despite potential diplomatic embarrassment) to commence the inter-state arbitration against the host state. However, perhaps reflecting some traditional ambivalence about IIAs and/or international arbitration, several Asian states (including important economies, such as India, Thailand and Vietnam) did not go as far ratification of the 1965 Washington Convention establishing the International Centre for Settlement of Investment Disputes (ICSID). This framework, ICSID Convention, facilitates enforcement of ISDS commitments made separately by a host state through IIAs or in an ICSID arbitration clause in ad hoc investment contracts. Notably, the Convention requires the host state to enforce an award given in favour of a foreign investor from another state that has acceded to the ICSID Convention, after running through an arbitral process administered under the ICSID Arbitration Rules, as if the award is a final judgment of the host state's courts.

If the ICSID option is unavailable because the host state has not consented in advance to ICSID Arbitration Rules or because it has not ratified the ICSID Convention, the foreign investor typically can only invoke the host state's advance consent to ad hoc proceedings under United National Commission on International Trade Law (UNCITRAL) Arbitration Rules – or occasionally other agreed rules. Awards are then typically enforced under the 1958 New York Convention on the Recognition and Enforcement of Foreign Arbitral Awards (NYC). A key difference compared to the enforcement of an ICSID Convention Arbitration Rules award is that courts in an NYC Member State where the award creditor is pursuing assets of the losing party can refuse enforcement as contrary to that state's 'public policy' (NYC Convention Art V(2)). Although that public policy exception is supposed to be interpreted in an internationalist spirit,[33] it is likely to be a major hurdle where the arbitral award from ISDS is sought to be enforced through the courts of the host state. This is presumably why, for example, the German award creditor (Walter Bau) from a 2009 UNCITRAL Arbitration Rules award did not attempt to enforce it through the courts in Thailand, but instead through the US and then successfully Germany – although that took around a decade, as the Thai Government vigorously contested NYC enforcement through Germany courts.[34] Given such problems, it is unsurprising that investors choose the option of ICSID Convention arbitration (528 out of 983 treaty-based ISDS cases known since 1987), if available, rather than ad hoc UNCITRAL Rules arbitration (308 cases).[35]

33. *See generally* UNCITRAL, *UNCITRAL Secretariat Guide on the Convention on the Recognition and Enforcement of Foreign Arbitral Awards (New York, 1958)* 225 (United Nations Publishing and Library Section 2016), also available at http://newyorkconvention1958.org/index.php?lvl=cmspage&pageid=10&menu=626&opac_view=-1.

34. Luke Nottage & Sakda Thanitcul, *International Investment Arbitration in Thailand: Limiting Contract-Based Claims While Maintaining Treaty-Based ISDS*, 18 J. World Inv. & Trade 767 (2017), with a more detailed chronology at https://ssrn.com/abstract=2770889.

35. Data from https://investmentpolicy.unctad.org/investment-dispute-settlement/advanced-search (as of 26 Feb. 2020). There were also sixty-one arbitration cases administered by the ICSID Additional Facility Rules, which can be offered in the IIA if either the host state or the foreign investor's home state has ratified the Convention. But this does not benefit from the ICSID Convention arbitration applicable if both states have ratified, and Additional Facility awards must be enforced instead through the NYC for example.

On the one hand, the selective ratification of the ICSID Convention, combined with some unusual wording in Thailand's IIAs plus consistency in drafting IIAs by some other ASEAN states relative to economic scale (e.g., by Malaysia and Indonesia),[36] suggests that at least some Asian states have tried to be rule-makers rather than just accepting the early templates proposed by European and then US treaty negotiators.[37] The picture is now further complicated first because several Asian states have recently been subjected to ISDS claims, notably Indonesia but also especially India (in a case brought by White Industries under an old BIT with Australia). Both states have therefore terminated old BITs, perceived as having wider commitments favouring foreign investors, and in India's case have sought to conclude new treaties based on a publically debated and then disclosed 2016 Model BIT that retains but with significantly *reduced* commitments to foreign investors.[38] A second complication, by contrast, is that several Asian states (notably Singapore and China / Hong Kong, but also in some years Thailand) have recently become significant exporters of FDI, rather than just destinations for FDI, especially since the 1990s. This shift generates a greater incentive to (re)negotiate instead *more expansive* ISDS-backed commitments, not only for their bilateral IIAs but also in the growing number of 'mega-regional' FTAs containing investment treaties.

Adding to the 2009 ASEAN Comprehensive Investment Agreement (ACIA, protecting and partly liberalising investment within Southeast Asian states) and the five ASEAN+ IIAs, including the 2009 ASEAN Australia-New Zealand FTA (AANZFTA),[39] the ten ASEAN states plus Australia, New Zealand, Japan, Korea and China (but not India) concluded in late 2019 the Regional Comprehensive Partnership (RCEP) FTA. [[When available for signature it will be possible to check what extra liberalisation and other commitments are made. It has already been disclosed that the fifteen states did not agree to add the ISDS option in RCEP, but that issue will be revisited within two years of the FTA coming into force, and the COVID-19 pandemic created uncertainty about whether Japan (and others) would be able to sign RCEP in 2020 as originally planned.[40] Anyway, Table 1.2 below shows that ISDS-backed commitments are already available (at least for core substantive protections, if not extensive

36. Nottage & Thanitcul, *supra* n. 34; Luke Nottage, et al., *International Investment Treaties and Arbitration Across Asia: A Bird's Eye View*, in *International Investment Treaties and Arbitration Across Asia* 1 (Luke Nottage & Julien Chaisse eds., Brill | Nijhoff 2018), especially Figure 1.5 on treaty drafting consistency by ASEAN Member States.
37. Compare the studies by Lauge Poullsen, reviewed in Luke Nottage, *Rebalancing Investment Treaties and Investor-State Arbitration: Two Approaches*, 17 J. World Inv. & Trade 1015 (2016).
38. Antony Crockett, *The Termination of Indonesia's BITs: Changing the Bathwater, but Keeping the Baby?*, in *International Investment Treaties and Arbitration Across Asia* 159 (Luke Nottage & Julien Chaisse eds., Brill | Nijhoff 2018); Prabhash Ranjan & Pushkar Anand, *Investor State Dispute Settlement in the 2016 Indian Model Bilateral Investment Treaty: Does It Go Too Far?*, in *International Investment Treaties and Arbitration Across Asia* 579 (Luke Nottage & Julien Chaisse eds., Brill | Nijhoff 2018).
39. Bath & Nottage, *supra* n. 30.
40. *See* https://dfat.gov.au/trade/agreements/negotiations/rcep/Pages/regional-comprehensive-economic-partnership.aspx and Julien Chaisse, *The Regional Comprehensive Economic Partnership's Investment Chapter: One Step Forward, Two Steps Back*, Columbia FDI Perspectives (10 Feb. 2020), http://ccsi.columbia.edu/files/2018/10/No-271-Chaisse-FINAL.pdf; and *Pandemic*

liberalisation commitments) among almost all fifteen RCEP states (and even partly India):[41]

Table 1.2 Separate ISDS-Backed Investment Treaty Commitments Among RCEP Parties (and India)

	ASEAN	*Australia*	*NZ*	*Korea*	*Japan*	*China*	*(India)*
ASEAN	Y (among AMS under ACIA)	Y		Y	N (with Philippines ISDS-backed BITs or FTAs with all other AMS	Y (for most commitm-ents)	(N – ISDS in 2014 Investment Agreement but not yet in force)
Australia	Y	n/a	N	Y	Y (CPTPP)	Y (but BIT & FTA both limited)	(N – BIT terminated in 2017 but sunset clause for existing investments)
NZ	Y	N	n/a	Y	Y (CPTPP)	Y	(N)
Korea	Y	Y	Y	n/a	Y (BIT and trilateral IIA)	Y (trilateral Investment Agreement & FTA)	(Y – CEPA)[42]
Japan	N (with Philippines: all others via BIT or FTA)	Y (CPTPP)	Y (CPTPP)	Y (BIT & trilateral IIA)	n/a	Y (trilateral IIA)	(Y – FTA)
China	Y (for most commitm-ents)	Y (but limited[43])	Y	Y (FTA & trilateral IAA & FTA)	Y (trilateral IIA)	n/a	(Y – BIT 2006)
(India)	(N – Agreem-ent not yet in force)	(N – BIT terminated in 2017 but sunset clause)	(N)	Y (CEPA)	(Y – FTA)	Y (BIT 2006)	(n/a)

May Force Japan to Give Up on RCEP in 2020, Japan Times (19 Apr. 2020), https://www.japantimes.co.jp/news/2020/04/19/business/coronavirus-pandemic-japan-give-up-rcep-trade-2020/#.XrSYuJolGUZ.

41. Treaties analysed from https://investmentpolicy.unctad.org/international-investment-agreements.
42. The India-Korea BIT also had an ISDS clause, but the BIT was denounced by India in 2017. However, the ISDS-backed bilateral FTA (Closer Economic Partnership Agreement) was signed in 2009 and came into force from 2010.
43. But *cf.*, a more expansive (re-)interpretation proposed recently by Tania Voon & Elizabeth Sheargold, *Australia, China, and the Co-Existence of Successive International Investment Agreements, in the China-Australia Free Trade Agreement: A 21st-Century Model* 215 (Colin Picker, et al., eds., Hart Publishing 2017).

On the other hand, suggesting that Asian states are also still partly rule takers, the ASEAN + FTAs and indeed most Asia-Pacific FTAs, as well as many recent stand-alone BITs, do largely follow contemporary US-style IIA drafting.[44] That template was based originally on the 1993 North American FTA (NAFTA, renegotiated recently by the Trump Administration[45]), with provisions somewhat revised in later US FTAs and a Model BIT in light of experiences with NAFTA ISDS cases, seeking to rebalance host state and foreign investor interests. It is epitomised by the Trans-Pacific Partnership (TPP) signed in 2016 by twelve Asia-Pacific states,[46] including by the Obama Administration although the Trump Administration withdrew US signature in 2017. These US-style provisions are very largely retained in the Comprehensive Partnership for TPP, signed by the original signatories (other than the US) and in force since 2019 among six Asia-Pacific states.[47]

Asian states have, therefore, been contributing to investment treaty-making significantly but in complex ways at the regional level.[48] Diverse states are also now participating in diverse ways to multilateral reform discussions. They are engaged by the UNCTAD, which has gone from being a keen proponent of 1990s-style (and arguably quite pro-investor) IIAs for developing countries, to an advocate for reform or rebalancing in newer treaties.[49] Some Asian states have also provided written submissions and made active oral interventions in the UNCITRAL deliberations underway since 2018 on reforming the ISDS system generally.[50] Yet their interests somewhat diverge,[51] arguably reflecting interests as outbound versus inbound investor states but also their experiences with ISDS cases, as indicated in some of this book's later chapters.

---

44. Wolfgang Alschner & Dmitriy Skougarevskiy, *The New Gold Standard? Empirically Situating the TPP in The Investment Treaty Universe*, 17 J. World Inv. & Trade 339 (2016).
45. Orlando F. Cabrera, *The US-Mexico-Canada Agreement: The New Gold Standard to Enforce Investment Treaty Protection?*, Columbia FDI Perspectives (13 Jan. 2020), http://ccsi.columbia.edu/files/2018/10/No-269-Cabrera-C.-FINAL.pdf. *See also* Niyati Ahuja, *USMCA: An Analysis of the Proposed ISDS Mechanism*, Kluwer Arbitration Blog (26 Nov. 2019), http://arbitrationblog.kluwerarbitration.com/2019/11/26/usmca-an-analysis-of-the-proposed-isds-mechanism/.
46. Luke Nottage, *The TPP Investment Chapter and Investor-State Arbitration in Asia and Oceania: Assessing Prospects for Ratification*, 17 Melb. J. Int'l L. 313 (2016). *See also generally* Julien Chaisse, Henry Gao & Chang-fa Lo, (eds.), *Paradigm Shift in International Economic Law Rule-Making: TPP as a Model for Trade Agreements?* (Springer 2017).
47. https://dfat.gov.au/trade/agreements/in-force/cptpp/Pages/comprehensive-and-progressive-agreement-for-trans-pacific-partnership.aspx.
48. Luke Nottage & Ana Ubilava, *Asia's Changing International Investment Regime: Sustainability, Regionalization and Arbitration – Review Essay* 44 U. W. Australia L. Rev. 195 (2018).
49. *See generally* Nicholas Perrone, *UNCTAD's World Investment Reports 1991–2015: 25 Years of Narratives Justifying and Balancing Foreign Investor Rights*, 19 J. World Inv. & Trade 7 (2018).
50. https://uncitral.un.org/sites/uncitral.un.org/files/report_1004-add1_for_submission_rev_002.pdf.
51. *See generally* the blog postings co-authored by a semi-official delegate from Australia, Professor Anthea Roberts: https://www.ejiltalk.org/author/aroberts/.

§1.04 BELATED EXPANSION OF ASIA-RELATED ISDS ARBITRATIONS

The growth in FDI and IIAs, including ISDS-backed commitments, has led to more investment disputes around Asia, but somewhat later and in lower proportions as compared to other parts of the world. Initially, some attributed this to a general 'cultural' aversion in Asia to formal dispute resolution processes generating binding outcomes by impartial adjudicators. Yet this rubbed up against the growth in ICA cases in Asia, and the belated increase in ISDS arbitrations involving Asian parties. Arguably, a better explanation for greater use of ISDS lies in diminishing 'institutional barriers' to initiating or defending claims, including greater availability of experienced counsel and arbitrators in the region and learning from the experience of initial cases.[52]

Like treaty-based ISDS cases generally, most of these arbitrations are conducted under ICSID rather than UNCITRAL Rules. A few treaties with Malaysia as party add the option for investors to use instead of the rules of the Kuala Lumpur Regional Centre for Arbitration (recently renamed the Asian International Arbitration Centre or AIAC, as mentioned in Chapter 9 of this volume). There is no known case using them, despite the institution's efforts to promote itself as a suitable venue for ISDS (as well as ICA) cases.[53] But it is also very rare for investors to choose the option of non-ICSID or non-UNCITRAL Rules, even when offered in treaties.[54] Nonetheless, arbitration rules tailored to ISDS proceedings have been developed or promoted by various regional arbitration centres, notably the Singapore International Arbitration Centre, but also in Hong Kong and China (as discussed in Chapters 6-8 of this volume). The development and incorporation of such rules as an option in treaties was proposed for Australia and Japan a decade ago but to no avail.[55] A key difference for such rules is enhanced transparency, rather than the usual default rule of confidentiality generally valued by commercial parties to ICA because of the greater public interest in ISDS cases where an investor claims against a host state.[56]

Most ISDS claims nowadays are based on treaty-based consent to arbitration, and such treaties (or arbitral rulings) generally provide significant transparency around key aspects of proceedings and especially the outcomes.[57] However, sometimes the

52. Luke Nottage & J Romesh Weeramantry, *Investment Arbitration in Asia: Five Perspectives on Law and Practice*, 28 Arb. Int'l 19 (2012).
53. AIAC, *First Ever AALCO Annual Arbitration Forum Held to Discuss Business, Economy, and ADR Mechanisms to Safeguard Investments in Asia and Africa*, AIAC News (21 Jul. 2018), https://www.aiac.world/news/263/First-Ever-AALCO-Annual-Arbitration-Forum-Held-to-Discuss-Business,-Economy,-and-ADR-Mechanisms-to-Safeguard-Investments-in-Asia-and-Africa.
54. According to UNCTAD's ISDS Navigator website, as of 26 Feb. 2020, *supra* n. 35, there had been seventeen arbitrations through the otherwise very active International Chamber of Commerce (ICC), and forty-eight by the Stockholm Chamber of Commerce.
55. Luke Nottage & Kate Miles, *'Back to the Future' for Investor-State Arbitrations: Revising Rules in Australia and Japan for Public Interests*, 26 J. Int'l Arb. 25 (2009).
56. Chief Justice James Allsop, *Commercial and Investor-State Arbitration: The Importance of Recognising Their Differences*, ICCA Congress 2018, Sydney, Opening Keynote Address, at https://www.fedcourt.gov.au/digital-law-library/judges-speeches/chief-justice-allsop/allsop-cj-20180416.
57. Luke Nottage & Ana Ubilava, *Costs, Outcomes and Transparency in ISDS Arbitrations: Evidence for an Investment Treaty Parliamentary Inquiry*, 21 Int'l Arb. L. Rev. 111 (2018).

advance consent is provided through an arbitration clause in an investment contract negotiated individually between the foreign investor and a host state. If this consent is to ICSID arbitration, some transparency is available through its website.[58] But if to non-ICSID arbitration, the proceedings and even awards are generally confidential under the applicable Rules and/or arbitration law at the chosen seat (devised primarily with ICA in mind). This means a paucity of data on such cases unless there are challenges relating to the proceedings or arbitral award enforcement that end up in the courts of the seat and/or where assets of the award-debtor are located, and such courts provide public access to proceedings or awards.

Apart from growing public concerns about transparency around ISDS arbitrations, there are issues around delays and especially costs in arbitration. Arguably, these problems are exacerbated by confidentiality, and hence a lack of accurate information about service provider quality. Another contributing factor may be the spread of large law firms into Asia, including 'billable hours' models of delivery (and internal promotion) for their lawyers.[59] As with ICA but even more so for ISDS arbitration, given its greater public interests, more discussions and initiatives are underway promoting alternatives or complements to arbitration for international dispute resolution. One example is a unique mediation step before ISDS arbitration that can be compelled by the host state, found in the Australia-Indonesia FTA signed in 2019 (analysed in Chapter 5).[60] Another is the 2019 UN Convention on International Settlement Agreements Resulting from Mediation (Singapore Convention on Mediation) aimed at facilitating enforcement of settlement agreements, in force from 12 September 2020 (described in Chapter 14).[61] A third 'new frontier' is the establishment of international commercial courts in Singapore and more recently in China (Chapter 8), and proposed for Australia (Chapter 2).

---

58. Available via https://icsid.worldbank.org/en/Pages/cases/AdvancedSearch.aspx.
59. Nottage *supra* n. 1.
60. *See also* James Claxton, Luke Nottage & Ana Ubilava, *Pioneering Mandatory Investor-State Conciliation Before Arbitration in Asia-Pacific Treaties: IA-CEPA and HK-UAE BIT*, Kluwer Arbitration Blog (5 Sep. 2020), http://arbitrationblog.kluwerarbitration.com/2020/09/05/pioneering-mandatory-investor-state-conciliation-before-arbitration-in-asia-pacific-treaties-ia-cepa-and-hk-uae-bit/, discussing the mandatory investor-state mediation step added to the Hong Kong-United Arab Emirates BIT (also signed in 2019); and a comparison by Ana Ubilava, *Mandatory Investor-State Conciliation in New International Investment Treaties: Innovation and Interpretation*, Kluwer Mediation Blog (5 Sep. 2020), http://mediationblog.kluwerarbitration.com/2020/09/05/mandatory-investor-state-conciliation-in-new-international-investment-treaties-innovation-and-interpretation/.
61. *See* UNCITRAL, *United Nations Convention on International Settlement Agreements Resulting from Mediation (New York, 2018) (the 'Singapore Convention on Mediation')*, Texts and Status: International Commercial Mediation (20 Dec. 2018), https://uncitral.un.org/en/texts/mediation/conventions/international_settlement_agreements. *See also Mediation in International Commercial and Investment Disputes* (Catharine Titi & Katia Fach Gómez eds., Oxford University Press 2019).

§1.05 EMERGENCE OF REGIONAL CENTRES AND NEW INITIATIVES FOR INTERNATIONAL DISPUTE RESOLUTION

This expansion in Asia-related ICA cases, and more recently ISDS cases, has underpinned the growth and new initiatives for regional centres providing international dispute resolution services. For example, the China International Economic and Trade Arbitration Commission (CIETAC) has developed the highest annual caseload of international cases filed in the world, although this also counts ICA cases between foreign-owned subsidiaries and local firms. The attraction is partly due to comparatively poor-quality (although improving) court procedures, which foreign investors and traders try to avoid by consenting instead to arbitration, combined with some strong negotiating power from Chinese parties seeking to secure China as the seat. Some foreign parties may not push for a foreign seat of arbitration out of concern for extra problems enforcing foreign awards even under the NYC, although the Chinese courts' record for enforcement has been improving. Chinese arbitration law also still does not allow ad hoc arbitrations, which further boosts the caseloads of CIETAC and other arbitral centres like the Beijing International Arbitration Centre. But they have also been innovating recently through publishing rules tailored for ISDS cases. Further momentum comes from the Chinese Government establishing an International Commercial Court. These initiatives also aim to attract cases arising from China's westward investments and other projects along the Belt and Road, as also elaborated in Chapters 6-8 of this volume

Hong Kong also has a high caseload and very strong reputation, including from early on for its courts applying the UNCITRAL Model Law on ICA (as template legislation) in an internationalist and pro-arbitration spirit.[62] Parties to contracts and their legal advisors have agreed on Hong Kong as a more neutral seat for arbitration between mainland Chinese and foreign parties. Hong Kong practitioners and policymakers have been trying to promote new initiatives, such as third-party funding for arbitration and mediation services,[63] while the government continues to negotiate comprehensive IIAs (including recently with ASEAN and Australia, each providing for ISDS), as elaborated in Chapters 5 and 8. However, political tensions since 2019 and

62. *See* Dean Lewis, *The Interpretation and Uniformity of the UNCITRAL Model Law on International Commercial Arbitration: Focusing on Australia, Hong Kong and Singapore* (Wolters Kluwer 2016), comparing mainly with Singapore and Australia, reviewed at https://japaneselaw.sydney.edu.au/2017/04/book-review-dean-lewis-the-interpretation-and-uniformity-of-the-uncitral-model-law-on-international-commercial-arbitration/.

63. Singapore has also been recently competing in this space: *see* Gary Benton, *The Whispered Conversation: Hong Kong v. Singapore*, Kluwer Arbitration Blog (2 Jan. 2019), http://arbitrationblog.kluwerarbitration.com/2019/01/02/whispered-conversation-hong-kong-v-singapore/. Curiously, Australia has not been actively promoting itself for ICA by emphasising a laissez-faire regime for third-party funding created much earlier through the High Court's decision in *Campbells Cash and Carry Pty Ltd v. Fostif Pty Limited* [2006] HCA 41. After the COVID-19 pandemic, some limits on third-party funding have been legislated but primarily only impacting on grouped 'retail' claimants (rather than corporate claimants in ICA cases): *New Rules for Litigation Funders After Jump in Class Actions*, Sydney Morning Herald (22 May 2020), https://www.smh.com.au/politics/federal/new-rules-for-litigation-funders-after-jump-in-class-actions-20200521-p54vak.html.

the coronavirus from early 2020 have created challenges for Hong Kong. Those may enhance the relative attraction of Singapore, which had already emerged as a similarly attractive venue for ICA, ISDS, mediation and international litigation.[64]

As for smaller players in the region, Malaysia and Korea have been making sustained efforts particularly to attract ICA cases. This has prompted new initiatives by Australia once more (like Hong Kong, an earlier adopter of the Model Law style of arbitration law) and more recently Japan, as elaborated in Chapters 3, 6 and 10 of this volume. Even India has undergone legislative, case law and institutional developments in recent years that aim to promote more efficient arbitration in India. Arguably, these initiatives are prompted by losing in 2011 an ISDS claim brought by White Industries from Australia claiming violation of a treaty commitment to provide 'effective means' of enforcing ICA awards (elaborated in Chapter 12).[65] However, previous studies and other chapters in this volume show how important it is for ICA venues to have and amend legislation carefully, develop consistent and widely disseminated case law, and expand arbitration 'infrastructure' and publicity generally. These countries also compete against the well-established reputations of the three more popular regional venues, not to mention the ongoing attraction (and marketing efforts into Asia) of 'core' arbitral institutions in the West. One strategy may be to focus on niche markets. These can include arbitration of particular types of disputes (e.g., intellectual property in Japan, or resources in Australia) or particular regions (e.g., along the Belt and Road) or new types of dispute resolution processes (such as stand-alone mediation or hybrid Arb-Med).

§1.06 KEY DEVELOPMENTS IN KEY JURISDICTIONS: CHAPTER SUMMARIES AND FURTHER CONTEXT

[A] Australia (and New Zealand)

Australia and neighbouring New Zealand lie on the periphery of the Asian region, incorporate growing Asian and Eurasian populations, and have many close trade and investment links, especially with each other but also across Asia. Their geographical location and other factors have so far prevented them from attracting many ICA cases. But they have internationally minded and respected courts, and various current and past judges, in particular, are exploring the potential for Australia to develop an international commercial court (inspired by Singapore and others) to offer enhanced international business dispute resolution services in the region. Australia and more recently New Zealand have also experienced intense political and media debate discussion over ISDS in IIAs, which risks giving arbitration more generally a bad

64. Chan Leng Sun, *Making Arbitration Work in Singapore*, *in The Developing World of Arbitration: A Comparative Study of Arbitration Reform in the Asia Pacific* 143 (Anselmo Reyes & Weixia Gu eds., Hart Publishing 2018).
65. Harisankar K. Sathyapalan, *Indian Judiciary and International Arbitration: A BIT of a Control?*, 33 Arb. Int'l 503 (2017).

name,[66] and such concerns around ISDS are also impacting on counterparties with which they have been negotiating IIAs.

In Chapter 2, as former senior judges from Victoria now practising as commercial arbitrators, Marilyn Warren and Clyde Croft, argue that the time has come for Australia to join others in establishing a new 'International Commercial Court' as another international dispute resolution option, especially for the Asia-Pacific region. They outline the existing international legislative architecture (the 1958 NYC for international arbitration, inspiring the 2005 Hague Choice of Court Convention), and the models provided by London's venerable Commercial Court and since 2015 the Singapore International Commercial Court (including the latter's composition, jurisdiction, procedure and confidentiality provisions, appeals, and cross-border enforceability of its judgments – facilitated by Singapore ratifying the 2005 Hague Convention). Warren and Croft use these topics to frame their proposal for an Australian International Commercial Court, including the possibility of allowing its litigants to exclude the application of the Australian Consumer Law (which otherwise may also apply to many business-to-business disputes).[67] They conclude that the COVID-19 pandemic has bolstered the case for such a new court, by minimising the obstacle of Australia's physical distance as litigation has had to move rapidly online, and because the pandemic's economic dislocation will undoubtedly lead to more cross-border disputes.[68]

In Chapter 3, Albert Monichino and Nobumichi Teramura discuss largely positive recent trends in ICA case law and other developments in Australia. They discuss interesting judgments recently applying the Model Law based International Arbitration Act (IAA) regarding (still comparatively few) ICA proceedings seated in Australia, as well as those seated abroad (including enforcement of awards from Singapore, China and New York).[69] They conclude by recommending a suite of further useful reforms to the IAA, based on this case law and developments abroad, including allowing commercial parties to opt-out of the Australian Consumer Law.[70] These initiatives

66. *See also* e.g., Luke Nottage, *International Arbitration and Society at Large,* in *Cambridge Compendium on International Arbitration* (Andrea Bjorklund et al. eds. Cambridge University Press, forthcoming), with a draft manuscript available at https://ssrn.com/abstract=3116528; and generally, George Bermann, *International Arbitration: Out of the Shadows*, 21 Asian Disp. Rev. 48 (2019).

67. For an earlier more pessimistic assessment of the need for a separate court, *see* the speech by the President of the New South Wales Court of Appeal quite soon after his appointment: Justice Andrew Bell, *An Australian International Commercial Court – Not a Bad Idea or What a Bad Idea?*, 2019 ABA Biennial International Conference, Singapore, http://www.supremecourt.justice.nsw.gov.au/Documents/Publications/Speeches/2019%20Speeches/Bell_20190712.pdf.

68. *See also*, on the economics and psychology behind likely increases in disputes and various ways to promote their resolution especially out of court, Joerg Risse & Antje Baumann, *Thinking Ahead: Dispute Resolution After the Corona Crisis*, 18(4) German Arb. J. (SchiedsVZ) 165 (2020).

69. *See also* Russell Thirgood & Erika Williams, *Arbitrating Down Under: Highlights and Lessons Learned from 2018 to 2019*, 15(2) Asian Int'l Arb. J. 133 (2019).

70. Monichino and Teramura focus on the statutory prohibitions regarding misleading and unconscionable conduct, which are indeed broadly worded and thus of major concern for commercial parties. But allowing ICA parties to opt-out of mandatory 'consumer' guarantees and broader unfair terms regulation is also important, and may be even more justifiable on public policy grounds given that these provisions have fewer repercussions (or third-party effects) on market

could combine with ICA's widespread adoption of e-proceedings, since the COVID-19 pandemic, to put Australia more prominently on the map for ICA filings.[71] The authors of this introductory chapter consider it plausible that not updating legislation concerning major issues, after significant stakeholder consultation as in Hong Kong and Singapore,[72] might have further diminished Australia's relative attractiveness as a regional seat – or at least may do so into the future.

The need for legislative reform can become clearer by comparing statutes, especially in other Model Law states. An example is a review by seat courts of tribunals' positive (not just negative) jurisdictional rulings, as from 2012 in Singapore (and earlier English law), as proposed by Teramura and Monichino. In addition, statutory reforms can focus on issues raised directly or indirectly by one or more court judgments. For example, Monichino and Teramura highlight how a first-instance judgment in 2016 by the Federal Court of Australia declined to follow case law in Hong Kong that has progressively applied the principle that indemnity costs should be awarded by courts against those challenging the arbitration, and indeed moves in that direction by some other judges in Australia.[73] Nonetheless, extending the traditional approach with due recognition that arbitration is supposed to be a cost- and time-effective process, Beach J did manage to award indemnity costs for two of three grounds of challenge that were held not to have sufficiently reasonable prospects of success. However, we find it curious that one such ground was a challenge to an

generally. Under Australian Consumer Law s. 3, 'consumer' guarantees (e.g., for fitness of purpose under s. 55) apply even to business-to-business supplies goods or services under AUD 40,000 (with the *Treasury Laws Amendment (Acquisition as Consumer – Financial Thresholds) Regulations 2020* raising this threshold to AUD 100,000 from 1 Jul. 2021), as well as in principle to supplies above the threshold if the goods or services are ordinarily for personal use (even if subjectively purchased for business purposes), unless for re-supply or using up in an industrial process. The Full Federal Court has furthermore interpreted s. 67 as requiring consumer guarantees to be applied to imports even if the objective governing law is foreign: *see* paras 96-115 of *Valve Corporation v. Australian Competition and Consumer Commission* [2017] FCAFC 224. If an Australian-seated arbitrator applied a chosen foreign law in such a scenario, rather than the Australian Consumer Law, the award, therefore, could well be challenged in Australian courts as contrary to public policy. Similar problems could arise regarding allegedly unfair terms, voided since 2016 in 'small business contracts' under s. 23. For early discussion of such problems (evident already with the Law's predecessor statute), *see* Luke Nottage & Richard Garnett, *The Top 20 Things to Change In or Around Australia's International Arbitration Act, in International Arbitration in Australia* 149, 153-5 (*ibid.*, eds., Federation Press 2010), with a manuscript version at https://ssrn.com/abstract=1378722. *See also* Nobumichi Teramura, Luke Nottage & James Morrison, *Judicial Control of Arbitral Awards in Australia, in The Cambridge Handbook of Judicial Control of Arbitral Awards* 173, 183-7 (Larry di Matteo et al., eds., Cambridge University Press, 2020); and, focusing on transactions involving individual consumers for non-business purposes, Richard Garnett, *Arbitration of Cross-Border Consumer Transactions in Australia: A Way Forward?*, 39 Sydney L. Rev. 569 (2017).

71. For an early (2016) initiative by the Australian Centre for International Commercial Arbitration to promote 'e-arbitrations', but which attracted little attention, *see* ACICA draft Procedural Order for the Use of Online Dispute Resolution Technologies, available via https://acica.org.au/acica-practice-procedures-toolkit/.
72. For a possible further legislative innovation being suggested recently for Singapore, *see also* Weiyi Tan, *Allowing the Exclusion of Set-aside Proceedings: An Innovative Means of Enhancing Singapore's Position as an Arbitration Hub*, 15(2) Asian Int'l Arb. J. 87 (2019).
73. *Sino Dragon Trading Ltd v. Noble Resources International Pte Ltd (No 2)* [2016] FCA 1169, available at http://www.austlii.edu.au/cgi-bin/viewdoc/au/cases/cth/FCA/2016/1169.html.

arbitrator for apparent bias, which seems a stronger ground as this chairperson had been appointed by a co-arbitrator (with the other), despite them having worked together – albeit only for a few years ending six years prior to the appointment. By contrast, in a decision that provides helpful guidance given the shift to virtual hearings during the COVID-19 pandemic in 2020, Beach J did not award indemnity costs for the unsuccessful challenge based on the award-debtor encountering difficulties in witness examinations using videoconferencing technology (as well as problems with interpreters), even though this challenge seems weak as the witnesses were their own and there had been prior agreement on videoconferencing. The time and costs associated with such challenges might have been avoided if Australia moved to an indemnity costs principle, as in Hong Kong and suggested now by the authors (and earlier by others[74]).

Other issues could be usefully addressed by legislators even if there is less or less conflicting case law within Australia, or indeed if what seems to be the position might be debatable on policy grounds. For example, the earlier decision by Beach J in the same case indicated that the perspective for judging whether there was a 'real danger of bias' of arbitrators, as required by section 18A of the Act as amended in 2010 (elaborating on the Model Law) in light of English law, was that of the court itself 'as opposed to merely that of a reasonable lay person'.[75] As laypeople may be more sceptical than judges about apparent bias or conflicts of interest, this might somewhat narrow the scope for challenges, consistently with specifying a 'real danger of bias'. As mentioned above, Beach J ended up finding that there was insufficient apparent bias, which might have been connected to adopting the perspective of the court itself. However, Beach J added that the same result would apply in this particular situation even if the perspective was instead that of a 'fair-minded lay observer'.[76] In a judgment rendered the next year, Beach J instead adopted the latter view, before finding apparent bias by the arbitrator. He was brought around to the view that the correct perspective even for the English 'real danger' test is that of a 'reasonable bystander'. Beach J was bolstered in this shift partly by that the fact that IAA 's18A is silent on perspective', and partly because 'the difference in perspective may not make much practical difference'.[77]

Yet these limited Australian judgments indicate that the law remains uncertain, especially as Beach J's evolving thinking was only expressed at first-instance in one of the many courts within Australia with jurisdiction over ICA cases. Such uncertainty generates delays and costs not only in the two cases before Beach J but also potentially for other challenges to arbitrators that have not ended up in court, as well as for future cases. It is also disappointing that the Australian legislator still has not addressed this perspective issue, which raises interesting policy questions about whether and how to

74. *See* e.g., Diana Hu & Luke Nottage, *The International Arbitration Act Matters in Australia: Where to Litigate and Why (Not)*, 35(1) The Arbitrator & Mediator 91 (2016), manuscript at https://ssrn.com/abstract=2862256.
75. *Sino Dragon Trading Ltd v. Noble Resources International Pte Ltd* [2016] FCA 1131, at [197], available at http://www.austlii.edu.au/cgi-bin/viewdoc/au/cases/cth/FCA/2016/1131.html.
76. *Ibid.*, at [198].
77. *Hui v. Esposito Holdings Pty Ltd* [2017] FCA 648, at [241], available at http://www.austlii.edu.au/cgi-bin/viewdoc/au/cases/cth/FCA/2017/648.html.

limit challenges to arbitrators, despite attention being drawn to it by commentators from around 2010.[78] The reflex of those working within the common law tradition may be to hope that courts will develop applicable principles gradually and optimally, but this is complicated because of multiple courts as well as still few Australia-seated ICA cases. In addition, this attitude may seem curious for legal advisors from its regional neighbours, more influenced by the civil law tradition and therefore putting less weight on case law and precedent.

In Chapter 4, focusing on Australia and Japan in the Asian context, Luke Nottage examines transparency (increasing around treaty-based ISDS) and confidentiality (still largely seen as preferred by parties to ICA, and thus reflected in laws and especially arbitration rules). Australia has seen more legislative action in this field, although quite confusingly through three IAA amendments since 2010, whereas Japan has gradually increased confidentiality in ICA by revising arbitral institution rules. Nottage argues that growing transparency around ISDS arbitration (especially perhaps in Australia's treaties) is welcome given the greater public interests involved in such cases, but transparency should not be simply transposed into commercial dispute resolution through ICA, as the fields are overlapping but distinct. Confidentiality in ICA has the disadvantage of exacerbating information asymmetry, making it harder for clients and advisors to assess whether particular arbitrators and lawyers provide value for money. Yet confidentiality allows arbitrators, in particular, to be more robust in proceedings and drafting rulings, thus countering the rise in ICA delays and especially costs. More transparency around ISDS, as well as initiatives like 'Arbitrator Intelligence' and experiments in reforming arbitral rules, can help reduce information asymmetry for users anyway[79] while retaining various advantages of confidentiality, particularly in ICA.

In Chapter 5, Ana Ubilava and Luke Nottage provide an update on Australia's recent treaty-making related to international investment and ISDS. Including insights from participation in parliamentary inquiries into ratifying recent treaties, they mostly compare aspects of the Comprehensive and Progressive Agreement for Trans-Pacific Partnership (CPTPP) (also ratified by New Zealand) with Australia's treaties signed in 2019 with Indonesia (IA-CEPA) and Hong Kong (AHKIA), along with the UN Mauritius Transparency Convention that seeks to retrofit more transparency around ISDS provisions contained in pre-2014 investment treaties. As well as transparency, delays and costs are persistent contemporary concerns nowadays, so the analysis focuses mainly on those features.

78. Sam Luttrell, *Australia Adopts the 'Real Danger' Test for Arbitrator Bias*, 26(4) Arb. Int'l 625 (2010). As further indication of the topicality of questions around tests for arbitrator neutrality in Australia, see a recent article by the former President of the New South Wales Court of Appeal: Margaret Beazley, 'Apparent Bias and Conflicts of Interest in the Arbitral Process' (August 2020) *Bar News* 57-61, with a version also available at https://www.disputescentre.com.au/adr-address-supreme-court-of-nsw-2019/.

79. *See* Catherine Rogers, *The Market for Arbitrators and the Market for Lemons*, Kluwer Arbitration Blog (10 Jun. 2020) http://arbitrationblog.kluwerarbitration.com/2020/06/10/the-market-for-arbitrators-and-the-market-for-lemons/.

By way of further background, it is worth looking more closely already at investment treaty-making by Australia and New Zealand for several reasons. First, they have mainly concluded treaties with Asian counterparties, thus already or potentially influencing those counterparties' approaches to negotiating investment treaties with other states. Second, Australia and New Zealand may provide some other ideas for intra-Asian economic integration because they have long-standing shared interests and widespread cooperation in legal and economic affairs, and a comprehensive arrangement for closer economic relations bilaterally. These cover cross-border trade and investment, mutual recognition, free movement of people and agreements for the enforcement of court judgments and regulatory cooperation.[80]

Neither Australia nor New Zealand has been a particularly enthusiastic proponent of BITs, although Australia has signed twenty-four (of which six have since been terminated, four because of subsequent FTAs). The most recent is a BIT with Uruguay designed to replace the 2001 BIT, which is not yet in effect, and the AHKIA was signed in 2019 and came into force on 17 January 2020.[81] Both contain language derived from the CPTPP, but do not contain an NT provision, either for the pre-establishment phase (which means liberalising market access for foreign investors, unless a negative list schedules exclusions) or even for the post-establishment phase. Since 2003, Australian policymakers have been much more focused on negotiating comprehensive FTAs, including regional FTAs, such as the AANZFTA, the CPTPP and the RCEP.[82] Australia has signed twenty-two FTAs (including the Closer Economic Relations agreement and its 2011 investment protocol with New Zealand, and the 2019 IA-CEPA), although a few are not in effect, and the RCEP has not yet been finalised for signature. These, in fact, reflect more accurately Australia's close economic integration with the Asian region and the USA. New Zealand only ever signed four BITs, with China and Hong Kong (in force) and Chile and Argentina (not in force), but it has entered into sixteen FTAs (including the Closer Economic Relations bilateral trade agreement and its later investment protocol with Australia) plus the RCEP.[83] These are, like Australia's, focused on the Asian region. Collectively, therefore, the two nations could exercise a 'middle power' role in regional investment treaty-making.[84]

Like many of its Asian counterparties, Australia and New Zealand have followed a NAFTA style in their negotiations of investment chapters in FTAs. Although New Zealand does not have an FTA with the US, they are both parties to the CPTPP, with its detailed and comprehensive investment chapter and ISDS provision. They are both

80. Vivienne Bath & Gabriël Moens, *Law of International Business in Australasia* (The Federation Press 2nd ed. 2019); Luke Nottage, *Asia-Pacific Regional Architecture and Consumer Product Safety Regulation Beyond Free Trade Agreements*, in *Trade Agreements at the Crossroads* 114-38 (Susy Frankel & Meredith Kolsky-Lewis eds., Routledge 2014).
81. Agreement between Australia and the Oriental Republic of Uruguay on the Promotion and Protection of Investments, signed on 5 Apr. 2019.
82. UNCTAD, https://investmentpolicy.unctad.org/international-investment-agreements/countries/11/australia.
83. UNCTAD, https://investmentpolicy.unctad.org/international-investment-agreements/countries/150/new-zealand.
84. Amokura Kawharu & Luke Nottage, *Models for Investment Treaties in the Asian Region: An Underview*, 34 Ariz. J. Int'l & Comp. L. 461 (2016).

also quite accommodating when dealing with their more cautious neighbours, particularly in relation to market access commitments, since trade liberalisation and market access for goods and services is a fundamental aspect of FTAs for both countries. However, both are quite cautious in relation to market access for foreign investment. In the CPTPP, for example, although they both agreed to pre-establishment NT and MFN provision, this was subject to a negative list setting out measures and sectors in which investment may be restricted. They were also careful to maintain exceptions for legitimate public welfare objectives (CPTPP investment chapter fn 11) and to ensure that the ISDS provision did not apply to pre-admission screening decisions made by either country (Annex 9-H).

Australia has only had a few ISDS claims made against it,[85] but experienced a similar shock to India (mentioned above) when in 2011 it too was subjected to a significant ISDS claim. This was initiated formally by Philip Morris Asia under the succinct 1993 Hong Kong-Australia BIT,[86] over Australia's pioneering tobacco plain packaging legislation. The claim under UNCITRAL Rules was dismissed on jurisdictional grounds in December 2015. An eminent tribunal found an abuse of rights by Philip Morris (under background customary international law) which reorganised its corporate structure to ensure that the Hong Kong subsidiary of the (originally US) tobacco company held the affected trademarks in Australia when there was a reasonable prospect of a dispute arising though the Australian legislation.[87] The case nonetheless attracted much discussion in Australian media and politics, which retains a comparatively open market but also some historical ambivalence towards foreign investment (and perhaps the US generally).[88]

Australia's policy towards to ISDS has reflected both changes in government and a growing public debate. In 2010, the government's Productivity Commission recommended that Australia no longer agree to ISDS in future treaties, a policy shift that was adopted by the centre-left Gillard Government from 2011 until it lost the general election of 2013. The new government reverted to Australia's past policy of including ISDS provisions in treaties on a case-by-case assessment. ISDS was omitted from the 2004 Australia-US FTA, the 2012 bilateral FTA with Malaysia (but anyway applicable under AANZFTA) and the FTA with Japan in 2014 (but anyway applicable under the

85. For details of claims filed or threatened, curiously under the Australia-US FTA that had omitted advance consent to ISDS, *see ibid.*, and https://investmentpolicy.unctad.org/investment-dispute-settlement/cases/816/.
86. Agreement between the Government of Hong Kong and the Government of Australia for the Promotion and Protection of Investments [1993] ATS 30, signed 15 Sep. 1993, effective 15 Oct. 1993; terminated 17 Jan. 2020 on the coming into effect of the Investment Agreement between the Government of Australia and the Government of the Hong Kong Special Administrative Region of the People's Republic of China [2020] ATS 5, signed 26 Mar. 2019, effective 17 Jan. 2020.
87. *Philip Morris Asia Limited v. The Commonwealth of Australia*, UNCITRAL, PCA Case No. 2012-12, Award on Jurisdiction and Admissibility (17 Dec. 2015) noted in Jarrod Hepburn & Luke Nottage, *Case Note: Philip Morris Asia v. Australia*, 18 J. World Inv. & Trade 307 (2017).
88. Luke Nottage, *The Evolution of Foreign Investment Regulation, Treaties and Investor-State Arbitration in Australia*, 21 N.Z.B.L.Q. 266 (2015). *See also* Vivienne Bath, *Australia and the Asia Pacific, in Reconceptualizing International Investment Law from The Global South* 95 (Fabio Morosini & Michelle Ratton Sanchez Badin eds., Cambridge University Press 2017).

CPTPP).[89] The PACER-Plus FTA with New Zealand and small Pacific Island states (2017) also omits ISDS,[90] seemingly because such micro-states would lack the capacity to defend arbitration claims and rely much more anyway on trade than foreign investment. Similarly, Australia and New Zealand do not consider it necessary to provide for ISDS as between themselves, so it was omitted from the Australia-New Zealand Investment Protocol[91] and by side letter from the AANZFTA[92] as well as the CPTPP.[93]

All other FTAs signed by Australia have added the ISDS option for foreign investors, including the bilateral FTA signed with Indonesia signed in 2019. Australia has also begun procedures to ratify the 2014 Mauritius Convention, which retrofits transparency provisions to past treaties (where the counterparty ratifies the Convention as well).[94] Enhanced transparency in ISDS has, in any event, become a feature of Australia's treaty practice (although less evident in the Indonesia treaty, for example, compared to the Hong Kong treaty recently).[95]

In contrast to the limited number of cases against Australia, Australia's outbound investors (notably in the resources area) have now become active in utilising Australia's treaties bringing treaty-based claims against host states, including Indonesia, Pakistan and Thailand.[96] Most of these outbound ISDS claims are commenced under Australia's older BITs, signed mostly over 1988-2005. Those treaties were not based on any (at least publically disclosed) Model BIT. However, they largely followed then European and US treaty drafting, and offered quite wide protections for investors, without the various express qualifications found in the FTAs signed since 2003 with Singapore (on an updated US FTA approach).[97] Australian outbound investors' treaty

89. Luke Nottage, *Investment Treaty Arbitration Policy in Australia, New Zealand and Korea*, 25 J. Arb. Stud. 185 (2015).
90. Deborah Gleeson & Ronald Labonté, *Trade Agreements and Public Health: A Primer for Health Policy Makers, Researchers and Advocates* 30 (Palgrave Pivot 2020).
91. [2013] ATS 10, signed 16 Feb. 2011, effective 1 Mar. 2013.
92. An exchange of letters between Australia's Minister for Trade and New Zealand's Minister of Trade on the application of AANZFTA between Australia and New Zealand, 27 Feb. 2009, https://dfat.gov.au/trade/agreements/in-force/aanzfta/official-documents/Pages/official-documents.aspx. Accessed 14 Feb. 2020.
93. Agreement between Australia and New Zealand regarding Investor State Dispute Settlement, Trade Remedies and Transport Services, 8 Mar. 2018, https://dfat.gov.au/trade/agreements/in-force/cptpp/official-documents/Documents/sl15-australia-new-zealand-isds.pdf. Accessed 14 Feb. 2020.
94. United Nations Convention on Transparency in Treaty-based Investor-State Arbitration, [2019] ATNIF 13.
95. *See* Luke Nottage, *New Frontiers in International Arbitration for The Asia-Pacific Region (7): Australia's Parliamentary Inquiries into ISDS in HK, Indonesia and UN/Mauritius Treaties*, Japanese Law and the Asia-Pacific (1 Sep. 2019), https://japaneselaw.sydney.edu.au/2019/09/new-frontiers-in-international-arbitration-for-the-asia-pacific-region-7-australias-parliamentary-inquiries-into-isds-in-hk-indonesia-and-un-mauritius-treaties/; elaborated in Ubilava and Nottage, Chapter 5 in this volume.
96. *See* https://investmentpolicy.unctad.org/investment-dispute-settlement/country/11/australia. The 2019 claim against Georgia invoking the Energy Charter Treaty is curious because Australia has signed but not yet ratified that treaty.
97. *See generally* Andrew D. Mitchell, *Australia and New Zealand, in Research Handbook on Foreign Direct Investment* 390 (Markus Krajewski & Rhea Tamara Hoffmann eds., Edward Elgar Publishing 2019). Australia resumed signing BITs in 2019 through one with Uruguay, closely

claims have occurred despite one ICSID tribunal finding that Australia's 1992 BIT with Indonesia (and indeed with several other states, including with Pakistan) lacked sufficient advance consent to ISDS.[98] However, several of these cases also involve investment contract claims containing ad hoc consent to ICSID arbitration (e.g., unsuccessfully recently against Timor Leste, and a claim against Papua New Guinea registered in 1996 and discontinued in 2001).[99]

The overlapping nature of investment treaties in Asia may also offer investors a choice of treaties when seeking to institute a claim. Australia has terminated and replaced a number of its BITs, particularly in conjunction with the ratification of FTAs with investment chapters. However, its 1988 BIT with China coexists with Chinese-Australia Free Trade Agreement (ChAFTA),[100] although it may be reviewed as part of the overall work program provided under the FTA's investment chapter (Article 9.9).

New Zealand has followed developments in nearby Australia, although it has never been subjected to an inbound treaty-based ISDS claim.[101] Public debate escalated after the US and others joined the negotiations from 2010 for the TPP (signed in Auckland in 2016), and Korea obtained ISDS provisions in its bilateral FTA (signed in 2015). The New Zealand First Party submitted the 'Fighting Foreign Corporate Control Bill', which would have prevented the government from including ISDS provisions in future treaties, but this Bill was defeated in 2015. The Party joined, however, the Labour Government's coalition government from late 2017, which announced that New Zealand would seek not to agree to ISDS. New Zealand nonetheless ratified the CPTPP in 2018 (little changed from the TPP signed by the previous centre-right government). It excluded ISDS bilaterally through side letters with some Member States (Brunei Darussalam, Malaysia, Viet Nam and Peru),[102] but for the first of those three ISDS-backed protections remain available anyway under AANZFTA.

tracking (CP)TPP drafting and thus including extensive qualifications and some transparency provisions. Curiously, however, it did not contain an express exclusion for ISDS claims related to tobacco measures despite Uruguay having also successfully defended a claim over tobacco legislation against Philip Morris under a BIT with Switzerland. *See* generally Jarrod Hepburn, *After Respective Battles with Philip Morris, Australia and Uruguay Unveil New Bilateral Investment Treaty*, IA Reporter (15 Apr. 2019), https://www.iareporter.com/; and compare the express exclusion in Australia's IIA signed with Hong Kong in 2019, as elaborate by Ubilava and Nottage, Chapter 5 in this volume.

98. For a critical analysis of that argument, *see* Luke Nottage, *Do Many of Australia's Bilateral Treaties Really Not Provide Full Advance Consent to Investor-State Arbitration? Analysis and Regional Implications*, 12 TDM 1 (2015), also available at, http://ssrn.com/abstract=2424987.
99. Searchable via https://icsid.worldbank.org/en/Pages/cases/AdvancedSearch.aspx.
100. *See* Voon & Sheargold, *supra* n. 43.
101. For an early claim by Mobil Oil that provided advance consent by investment contract, which settled, *see* Amokura Kawharu & Luke Nottage, *Renouncing Investor-State Dispute Settlement in Australia, Then New Zealand: Déjà Vu*, 18/03 Sydney Law School Research Paper 1 (2018).
102. Available via https://www.mfat.govt.nz/en/trade/free-trade-agreements/free-trade-agreements-in-force/cptpp/comprehensive-and-progressive-agreement-for-trans-pacific-partnership-text-and-resources/.

The New Zealand Government has created a Trade For All Advisory Board (TFAAB) for public consultations over New Zealand's international trade and investment policy. Its November 2019 Report[103] reviewed the pros and cons of ISDS for a developed country and legal system. In particular, it considered the implications for New Zealand's indigenous population. The TFAAB Report did not recommend changing the coalition government's policy shift against ISDS when negotiating new treaties, announced already two years earlier, but recommended caution, particularly if the alternative to agreeing to ISDS is to lose the broader benefits of the overall treaty.[104] TFAAB also recommended that New Zealand should become more prominent in regional and global public debates over international investment law:

> TFAAB supports the reform of investment arbitration systems. The Government should:
>
> a swiftly complete and implement the [Waitangi Tribunal Report] Wai 2522 recommendation for an ISDS Protocol [for consultation if disputes could affect New Zealand's indigenous people];
> b take a more active approach to international processes to reform arbitration arrangements and consider alternatives to ad hoc arbitration, particularly in the UNCITRAL Working Group and [UNCTAD];
> c seek membership of UNCITRAL at the next available opportunity;
> d review current arrangements in trade agreements with its partners as new arrangements become available.[105]

On the multilateral front, Australia is engaged in the UNCITRAL Working Group III discussions, although it does not appear to have made any written submissions. It was also one of the primary advocates of a WTO discussion on Investment Facilitation, which has been slowly moving forward multilaterally. New Zealand is involved in the WTO discussions,[106] but is not a member of UNCITRAL and is not involved in the UNCITRAL Working Group III meetings (although the TFAAB notes that membership is not required for New Zealand to participate). This may change if New Zealand decides to play a more significant role at a multilateral level. Until 2020, and even now given the larger size of its economy, Australia is better placed to play a 'rule-maker' role in international investment law. Arguably, however, it could improve that potential through even closer coordination with New Zealand in treaty-making, especially given the extra challenges for negotiating and implementing trade and investment treaties following the COVID-19 pandemic. The pandemic has also raised concerns, from those

103. Available via the top page of https://www.tradeforalladvisoryboard.org.nz/. *See especially* 53-6 (paras 133-153).
104. *Ibid.*, [149]-[150].
105. *Ibid.*, [8].
106. New Zealand Foreign Affairs & Trade, WTO plurilateral discussions on investment facilitation for development, https://www.mfat.govt.nz/en/trade/our-work-with-the-wto/wto-plurilateral-discussions-on-investment-facilitation-for-development/.

in Australia long critical about any form of ISDS, about claims being brought by investors impacted by public health countermeasures.[107]

[B] Japan (and Korea)

Japan initially concluded a similar number of BITs to Australia, which is comparatively low given Japan's much larger outbound flows and overall stock of FDI (as illustrated in the Appendix), and the wording of these BITs was quite flexible. Japan also then began to conclude FTAs (mostly all with investment chapters) from the early twenty-first century, after a new WTO negotiation round and OECD initiatives for a multilateral IIA foundered while income from Japan's investments abroad became increasingly significant. Drafting also became more consistent as these FTAs were mostly drafted in contemporary US style.[108] A difference from Australia is that Japan has recently kept signing more stand-alone BITs, under pressure from business associations, as Japanese firms find themselves with less treaty protection compared to outbound investors from Korea or China (both with much larger IIA networks).[109] Japan has also pushed in UNCITRAL deliberations to keep ISDS while reforming particular aspects at different rates.[110] It also declined to sign an investment protection treaty alongside its FTA with the EU, presumably because the latter insisted on its 'investment court' alternative preferred since 2015 (and subsequently achieved in the EU's agreements with Vietnam, Singapore and Mexico).[111]

However, Japan has shown pragmatism and patience in other IIA negotiations, including recently. For example, Japan agreed to omit ISDS in its bilateral FTA with Australia signed in 2014, arguably because of domestic politics in Australia. Presumably, Japan hoped to obtain ISDS anyway through regional treaty negotiations, and it, in fact, did obtain ISDS through the CPTPP (in force for disputes arising from 2019, including for pre-existing investments) although reportedly not also via RCEP (for now). Earlier, Japan had also agreed to omit ISDS in its 2006 FTA with the Philippines, seemingly at the latter's request and presumably because it hoped to obtain ISDS anyway through an FTA with ASEAN. In fact, the ASEAN-Japan FTA ended up omitting ISDS. However, other than with the Philippines (where Japan has relatively little

107. Patricia Ranald, *Corporations Prepare to Sue Over Action to Save Lives as Pandemic Reveals Trade Flaws*, The Conversation (23 April 2020), https://theconversation.com/corporations-prepare-to-sue-over-action-to-save-lives-as-pandemic-reveals-trade-flaws-136604. Compare generally, e.g., UNCTAD, *The Changing IIA Landscape: New Treaties and Recent Policy Developments*, IIA Issues Note No. 1, 5 (July 2020), https://investmentpolicy.unctad.org/publications/1230/the-changing-iia-landscape-new-treaties-and-recent-policy-developments.
108. Shotaro Hamamoto & Luke Nottage, *Japan*, in *Commentaries on Selected Model Investment Treaties* 347 (Chester Brown ed., Oxford University Press 2013), with a partial version also at https://ssrn.com/abstract=1724999.
109. Tomoko Ishikawa, *A Japanese Perspective on International Investment Agreements: Recent Developments*, in *International Investment Treaties and Arbitration Across Asia* 513–543 (Luke Nottage & Julien Chaisse eds., Brill | Nijhoff 2018).
110. *See* https://undocs.org/en/A/CN.9/WG.III/WP.163; http://undocs.org/en/A/CN.9/WG.III/WP.182; http://undocs.org/en/A/CN.9/WG.III/WP.163.
111. *See* https://ec.europa.eu/trade/policy/countries-and-regions/negotiations-and-agreements/.

investment) there are ISDS-backed commitments (even sometimes ICSID Rules options) between Japan and all the other nine ASEAN Member States through BITs and/or bilateral FTAs, as shown in Table 1.3 below:

Table 1.3 ISDS-Backed Commitments in IIAs Between Japan and ASEAN Member States

	FTA Investment Chapter	*BIT*	*ICSID Arbitration (as an Option for ISDS)*
Indonesia	Yes (in force from July 2008)	No	Yes: Article 69 EPA
Malaysia	Yes (July 2006)	No	Yes: Article 85 EPA
Philippines	Yes (December 2008)	No	No ISDS: Article 107 EPA only requires negotiations towards an ISDS mechanism, otherwise only if by mutual consent of disputing parties)
Singapore	Yes (originally in force November 2002; amended September 2007)	No	Yes: Article 82 EPA
Thailand	Yes (in force from November 2007)	No	No (because Thailand not a party to ICSID) but Yes under UNCITRAL Rules: Article 106 EPA
Brunei	Yes (July 2008)	No	Yes: Article 67 EPA
Laos	No	Yes (in force August 2008)	No (because Laos not a party to ICSID) but Yes under UNCITRAL Rules: Article 17 BIT
Myanmar	No	Yes (in force August 2014)	No (because Myanmar not a party to ICSID) but Yes under UNCITRAL Rules: Article 18 BIT
Cambodia	No	Yes (in force July 2008)	Yes: Article 17 BIT
Viet Nam	Yes (October 2007)	Yes (in force 2004)	No (because Viet Nam not a party to ICSID) but Yes under UNCITRAL Rules: Article 14 BIT

In addition, although Japan traditionally has attracted few ICA cases, policymakers since 2017 have tried to bring the nation out of the shadow of other regional centres (including recently Korea). In Chapter 10, James Claxton, Nottage and Teramura show how the Japanese government, supported by various stakeholders, has recently been attempting to develop Japan as another hub for international business dispute resolution services. Tracking this development is important for both theoretical and practical reasons. How it unfolds should reveal which of various theories for explaining law-related behaviour in Japan (and perhaps other Asian jurisdictions) have more traction nowadays, especially the debate over whether general or legal 'culture' is more important than practical institutional barriers. Assessing Japan's new initiatives is also important for legal practitioners and others interested in the practical question of where to arbitrate or mediate cross-border business disputes. This chapter, therefore, reports on current attempts to promote existing and new international arbitration centres in Japan,[112] as well as the recent establishment of the Japan International Mediation Centre – Kyoto, in the context of intensifying competition from other Asian venues for dispute resolution services. The new Centre's prospects are arguably enhanced by the COVID-19 pandemic, given its extensive impact on international business and related disputes. Mediation's advantages over arbitration of these disputes, including more scope for preserving business relations, fewer costs and delays, and lesser challenges from trying to run formal online hearings or managing travel restrictions.

New frontiers for international dispute resolution processes have also been highlighted for Japan given some emerging disputes between Japan and Korea since 2019. In Chapter 11, Claxton, Nottage and Brett Williams first describe the trade tensions between Korea and Japan that escalated from mid-2019. They first assess Korea's prospects in a formal claim now brought before the WTO, noting difficulties under substantive law (especially Japan's likely arguments based on national security), but especially procedure (given the general breakdown in the WTO's usual two-tier inter-state dispute resolution process). The chapter then outlines the possibility of Japan bringing claims under a 1965 Treaty that purported to settle claims resulting from Japan's colonisation of Korea, or under bilateral or trilateral investment treaties, regarding Korean courts recently ordering Japanese companies to pay compensation to colonisation-era Korean labourers. Yet such claims also face procedural and/or substantive law difficulties. The chapter further elaborates the possibility of affected Japanese companies instead or in parallel bringing ISDS claims against Korea, similarly alleging denial of justice in Korean court proceedings, under the two investment treaties. The chapter concludes that these extra complications bolster the attraction of a formal mediation to bring both countries and the affected companies together in order to achieve an overall negotiated settlement. An approach involving formal mediation may also provide inspiration for other states in the region, and indeed globally. Many are also increasingly face complex issues intertwining economics with national security issues and potentially involving multiple treaty regimes.

112. *See also* Huw Watkins, *Product Differentiation and the JCAA's 2019 Sets of Arbitration Rules*, 21(3) Asian Dispute Rev. 114 (2019).

[C] Hong Kong, China and BRI

China has emerged not just as a major destination for inbound FDI but also more recently for outbound FDI, prompting a shift to more expansive substantive commitments in IIAs and wider ISDS protections.[113] Because much inbound and outbound FDI is with Hong Kong, it is also important to examine the latter jurisdiction's recent initiatives regarding ISDS and IIAs. Both are also important, as mentioned, for existing and future ICA and other forms of international dispute resolution services, especially as the Belt and Road Initiative (BRI) projects extend westwards from China.[114]

In Chapter 6, Shahla Ali examines the impact of both the BRI and the UNCITRAL Model Law on ICA on international commercial and investor-state arbitration practice in Hong Kong. Given the significance of Hong Kong as a gateway to BRI project financing and logistics, understanding current dispute resolution policy is critical for gaining insights into China's approach to the resolution of BRI disputes. Measures taken to modernise the practice of arbitration, include training programmes and legislative reforms, including with regard to third-party funding, which are examined with a view to gaining insights into challenges and future developments. However, the COVID-19 pandemic combined with revived political disturbances in Hong Kong in 2020[115] have cast somewhat of a shadow over its future as a leading neutral forum for international dispute resolution, opening up additional space for other contenders as outlined in this volume.

In Chapter 7, in the context of a rising volume of cross-border transactions generated by the BRI, Weixia Gu argues that a robust legal framework for dispute resolution is required to forge investor confidence and enable BRI's integral goal of economic integration.[116] In light of the substantial levels of harmonisation among arbitration laws, arbitration is argued to constitute a primary vehicle of international commercial dispute resolution in an economically integrated Asia under the BRI. Against this backdrop, this chapter argues that the BRI provides a unique opportunity to contemplate the possibility of regional harmonisation, as within the Asian economies along the BRI, of the public policy exception to arbitral award enforcement. Such an arbitration initiative in Asia, in which China is anticipated to take a proactive role, holds considerable potential to project renewed momentum on China as an engine of

113. *See generally* Julien Chaisse ed., *China's International Investment Strategy: Bilateral, Regional, and Global Law and Policy* (Oxford University Press 2019).

114. For earlier analogues to the Belt and Road, promoted through the Asian Development Bank under strong influence from Japan, *see also* Nikolay Murashkin, *Not-So-New Silk Roads: Japan's Foreign Policies on Asian Connectivity Infrastructure Under the Radar*, 72 Australian J. Int'l Aff. 455 (2018).

115. For a pessimistic assessment generally, *see* Jeppe Mulich, *The End of Hong Kong Autonomy*, East Asia Forum (31 May 2020), https://www.eastasiaforum.org/2020/05/31/the-end-of-hong-kong-autonomy/.

116. It should be added that the COVID-19 pandemic may exacerbate some diplomatic tensions, as well as economic stresses, resulting in additional or more difficult disputes along the Belt and Road. *See generally*, e.g., Raffaello Pantucci, *Rising Nationalism Tests China's Uneasy Partnerships in Central Asia*, East Asia Forum (29 May 2020), https://www.eastasiaforum.org/2020/05/29/rising-nationalism-tests-chinas-uneasy-partnerships-in-central-asia/#more-259021.

not only economic power but also 'soft power' transformation in pioneering international legal norms.

In Chapter 8, Vivienne Bath outlines the latest developments in the People's Republic of China as it promotes itself as a regional hub not only for inbound investment (with 2019 legislation regulating foreign investment) but also for international dispute resolution. China is actively reviewing ISDS through UNCITRAL Working Group III and participating in WTO dispute settlement developments. The Supreme People's Court has been working on setting up new institutions (notably the China International Commercial Court) and improving mechanisms for the review and enforcement of arbitral awards and encourage mediation, both domestically and internationally.[117] Much of this activity has been encouraged by the BRI and an associated increase in related cross-border disputes. It also reflects the desire to encourage and expand the international use of Chinese law and to build up China as a centre for international dispute resolution. However, the Chinese Communist Party is tightening its ideological and administrative control over the courts and judicial system, potentially creating tensions.

[D] India and Malaysia

Malaysia and India are other Asian jurisdictions that have adopted both the NYC and then the UNCITRAL Model Law. In addition, Malaysia's case has a long-standing arbitration centre (recently renamed the AIAC).[118] However, delays throughout India's court system and decades of complex case law interpreting these international instruments, plus a preference for ad hoc arbitration including by former senior judges, have encouraged parties to India-related transactions to arbitrate elsewhere (notably recently in Singapore). India has also gone through significant changes in its approach to ISDS and investment treaties over the last decade, arguably prompting potentially significant reforms to the law and practice for ICA within India as well.

In Chapter 12, Jaivir Singh provides a perspective on investment treaty practice from India, which (somewhat like Australia) lies at the periphery of what is traditionally associated with the Asia-Pacific region. While seemingly on the frontier of this collection of states, India has signed investment and trade treaties with many of them. It has also recently become involved in disputes under them, and so has started to terminate many BITs. India now seeks to renegotiate fresh treaties using a template provided by a new model treaty that is oriented towards privileging state rights. The chapter looks at the narrative led to this point, including emergent nationalism (even before the COVID-19 pandemic), which also helps explain why India did not agree to

117. *See also* Vicky Priskich, *The Recognition and Enforcement of New York Convention Awards in the People's Republic of China: Recent Reform of the Prior Reporting System and Trends in Recognition and Enforcement*, 21(2), Asian Dispute Rev. 70 (2019).

118. Lam Ko Luen, *Arbitration Reform in Malaysia: Adopting the Model Law, in The Developing World of Arbitration* 123 (Anselmo Reyes & Weixia Gu eds., Hart Publishing 2018); Hiro Naraindas Aragaki, *Arbitration Reform in India: Challenges and Opportunities, in The Developing World of Arbitration: A Comparative Study of Arbitration Reform in the Asia Pacific* 221 (Anselmo Reyes & Gu Weixia eds., Hart Publishing 2018).

join RCEP in late 2019. Singh sketches key ISDS claims brought against India, the most against any Asian state, including that the case decided in 2011 in favour of White Industries under a BIT with Australia (but terminated by India in 2017).[119] He then summarises original econometric evidence of the positive impact of India's investment treaties (cumulatively, until 2015) on the country's inbound foreign investment.[120] The analysis highlights the risks for India of its newfound caution towards ISDS-backed investment treaties, including the curious elision of trade and investment law in a new BIT with Brazil. Singh does note how the ISDS claims have recently prompted Indian legislators and judges to start improving the legal regime for arbitration generally within India. For example, the Supreme Court has started to limit public policy challenges to enforcing arbitral awards (discussed generally by Gu, in Chapter 7). Yet a recent judgment nonetheless refused enforcement and highlighted the pervasive delays that have afflicted arbitration-related proceedings in India.[121]

In Chapter 9, A Vijayalakshmi Venugopal reviews Malaysia's involvement in international business dispute resolution. This includes actual involvement in cases in the WTO and through ISDS, and as a venue for international dispute resolution especially through the recently rebranded AIAC.[122] This chapter also extends to Malaysia's potential involvement in dispute resolution of international business disputes, especially through rather disparate provisions in its FTAs. The chapter, therefore, highlights how Malaysia has been involved in international dispute resolution and the continuing significance of this for Malaysia. Its analysis should be seen against the backdrop of significant domestic political changes in recent years.[123]

119. Jarrod Hepburn, *India Round-Up: An Update on Seven Investment Treaty Cases Against the State*, Investment Arbitration Reporter (11 Jun. 2020).
120. Compare more generally Shiro Armstrong & Luke Nottage, *The Impact of Investment Treaties and ISDS Provisions on Foreign Direct Investment: A Baseline Econometric Analysis*, 16/74 Sydney Law School Research Paper 1 (2016) on SSRN, https://papers.ssrn.com/sol3/papers.cfm?abstract_id=2824090.
121. *Compare* Sathyapalan, *supra* n. 65, with R. Harikrishnan, *NAFED v. Alimenta S.A.: Has the Indian Supreme Court Opened a Pandora's Box on Enforcement of Foreign Awards?*, Kluwer Arbitration Blog (11 Jul. 2020, http://arbitrationblog.kluwerarbitration.com/2020/07/11/nafed-v-alimenta-s-a-has-the-indian-supreme-court-opened-a-pandoras-box-on-enforcement-of-foreign-awards.
122. *See also* comparing the burgeoning field of statutory adjudication of construction disputes, John Cock, *Statutory Construction Adjudication: An International Overview*, 21 Asian Disp. Rev. 98 (2019); more generally Tatiana Polevshchikova, Niveta Venkatraman & Chelsea Pollard, *Panorama of Arbitration in Malaysia: Developments in Review*, Kluwer Arbitration Blog (2 Jul. 2020), http://arbitrationblog.kluwerarbitration.com/2020/07/02/panorama-of-arbitration-in-malaysia-developments-in-review/?doing_wp_cron=1594082006.16206693649 29199218750; and a settlement reported recently of a BIT dispute notified by a Malaysian investor against South Korea: Damien Charlotin, *South Korea Round-up*, Investment Arbitration Reporter (24 Jul. 2020).
123. For ongoing upheavals in 2020 following a remarkable general election ousting the long-ruling party, in the context of the 1MDB corruption scandal, *see* Ahmad Fauzi Abdul Hamid, *The Return of Old-Style Malay-Centric Politics?* East Asia Forum (25 Apr. 2020), https://www.eastasiaforum.org/2020/04/25/the-return-of-old-style-malay-centric-politics/#more-249463.

[E] Other Regional Developments

The rest of this book then turns to some wider developments on the 'frontiers' of Asia-Pacific international dispute resolution but focusing more on new fields rather than particular jurisdictions. In Chapter 13, Jeanne Huang and Jiaxiang Hu examine whether provisions in FTAs can be adapted to more effectively encourage states to comply with other international instruments that have weaker dispute resolution provisions, to promote better protection of the environment and public health – including pandemics, such as COVID-19. This question has not been well researched, although the International Convention for the Prevention of Pollution from Ships and its Protocols has been incorporated by references into FTAs since the 2006 US-Peru FTA and most recently in the CPTPP. This chapter explores the CPTPP's achievements and deficiencies to enhance marine environment protection from four aspects: flags of convenience, the vague role of coastal states, affecting trade or investment, and dispute resolution. It adds proposals to address the deficiencies and draws on this analysis to consider how FTAs could also enhance enforcement of international instruments to promote public health. It concludes by assessing the broader potential for using FTA dispute resolution processes to assist in ensuring compliance with inter-linked treaties, especially for the Asia-Pacific region.

In Chapter 14, Strong seeks to provide insights into the 'black box' of early treaty-making processes by undertaking a case study of the development of the 2019 Singapore Convention on Mediation.[124] The discussion focuses on several issues that have seldom been discussed in the legal literature, including the way in which a proposal for an international treaty makes its way to the relevant decision-makers and how those decision-makers determine which of the various alternatives to pursue. In so doing, the article focuses particularly on the role that dispute system design (DSD) and empirical research played in the early development of the 2019 Convention. The analysis also considers how interested individuals can assist the treaty-proposing process, particularly if they are not Non-Governmental Organisation (NGO) members. The chapter concludes with implications for international business dispute resolution policy development and treaty-making, including for the Asia-Pacific region.

As a related 'new frontier', an innovative recent hybrid avenue for engagement in international treaty-making can be found in the context of the deliberations underway since late 2017 in UNCITRAL's Working Group III, considering multilaterally whether and how to reform ISDS. The Academic Forum on ISDS (ACFI) operates, on the basis of transparent governance arrangements, mainly to provide 'concept papers' elucidating key issues and evidence for national delegations to UNCITRAL. ACFI now comprises around a hundred professors expert in ISDS and international investment law, and often also international commercial dispute resolution, including some East Asia, Oceania and the wider Pacific Rim.[125] A few ACFI members are even full or partial

124. *See also* Eunice Chua, *Enforcement of International Mediated Settlement Agreements in Asia: A Path Towards Convergence*, 15(1) Asian Int'l Arb. J. 1 (2019).

125. *See* https://www.jus.uio.no/pluricourts/english/projects/leginvest/academic-forum/academic-forum-isds-members.html. For example, from Australia there are two members from the

members of national delegations engaged in UNCITRAL's formal deliberations. ACFI is a recognised Observer at those deliberations, and if new questions arise, has followed up with new research and papers. ACFI also organises side events when the UNCITRAL Working Group meets (usually twice a year).[126]

§1.07 CONCLUSIONS

As elaborated in the brief concluding Chapter 15 by Reyes, Ali and Teramura, the Asian region is a path-breaking frontier for 'rulemaking' initiatives in international commercial and investment treaty arbitration,[127] as well as other forms of cross-border business dispute resolution, especially given the disruptions caused by the COVID-19 pandemic. They suggest that the significant regional rule-makers are China (especially through BRI leadership) and Malaysia (through institutional innovation, such as rules for Islamic law-related arbitrations), followed by Hong Kong (and Singapore), with Australia, India and Japan also now starting to experiment. They end with recommendations for how these states and the wider Asia-Pacific region can work through and learn from the COVID-19 pandemic. They include more proactive engagement with new and emerging technologies, coming up with new procedures (rather than mainly adopting those developed outside the region, like an emergency arbitrator or expedited procedures), and expanded communication and consultation channels (including regional stakeholders). These constitute promising ways forward to further expand Asia-Pacific frontiers for international business resolution.

University of Sydney, one from the Australian National University (with a role on the Australian delegation to UNCITRAL), one from the European University Institute (but from and still with an affiliation with the University of Melbourne). There are also members from universities in China/Taiwan/Hong Kong (five professors), the National University of Singapore (although one of the two is non-Singaporean), Seoul National University and Yonsei University, Kyoto University (a full member of Japan's delegation to UNCITRAL), Auckland University, as well as for example a professor from the Philippines now at the University of Notre Dame in the United States. There are also many members from universities in the Americas.

126. *See* https://www.cids.ch/academic-forum.

127. *See also* generally Carlos Esplugues ed., *Foreign Investment and Investment Arbitration in Asia* (Intersentia 2019).

APPENDIX: INVESTMENT, TREATIES AND ISDS CLAIMS IN THE ASIAN REGION

A. Investment, Treaties and ISDS Claims in ASEAN (Ranked by GDP)

Country (& **GDP**, USD in 2018)[128]	**Inbound FDI stock** (USD in 2018)[129]	**Outbound FDI stock** (USD in 2018)[130]	**Inbound FDI flow** (USD in 2018)[131]	**Outbound FDI flow** (USD in 2018)[132]	**BITs** signed (years) [or in force][133]	**FTAs with investment chapters /IIAs** signed (years) [or in force or concluded][134]	**Inbound treaty ISDS claims** (years) [won by investor][135]	**Outbound treaty ISDS claims** [won by investor][136]	**Inbound ICSID contract claims**[137]	**Outbound ICSID contract claims**[138]
Indonesia ($1 trillion)	$226b	$72b	$22b	$8b	72 (1968-2018) [26]	14 (1987-2019) [9]	7 (2004-2016) [nil]	nil	3 (1981-2007)	2 (1981 & 2007)
Thailand ($505 billion)	$222.7b	$121.4b	$10.5b	$17.7b	42 (1961-2015) [36]	24 (1980-2017) [21]	2 (2005-2017) [1]	nil	nil	nil
Singapore ($364 billion)	$1.5t	$1t	$77b	$37b	51 (1972-2-19) [39]	36 (1980-2019) [31]	nil	5 (2000-2019) [0]	nil	1 (2004)

128. Data via https //data.worldbank.org/country (accessed at the indicated webpages as of 12 Dec. 2019, except for FTAs data accessed 3 Feb. 2020).
129. https://unctadstat.unctad.org/wds/ReportFolders/reportFolders.aspx?sCS_ChosenLang=en.
130. *Ibid.*
131. *Ibid.*
132. *Ibid.*
133. https://investmentpolicy.unctad.org/.
134. *Ibid.*
135. *Ibid.*
136. *Ibid.*
137. https://icsid.worldbank.org/en/Pages/cases/AdvancedSearch.aspx.
138. *Ibid.*

Country (& **GDP**, USD in 2018)[128]	**Inbound FDI stock** (USD in 2018)[129]	**Outbound FDI stock** (USD in 2018)[130]	**Inbound FDI flow** (USD in 2018)[131]	**Outbound FDI flow** (USD in 2018)[132]	**BITs** signed (years) [or in force][133]	**FTAs with investment chapters /IIAs** signed (years) [or in force or concluded][134]	**Inbound treaty ISDS claims** (years) [won by investor][135]	**Outbound treaty ISDS claims** [won by investor][136]	**Inbound ICSID contract claims**[137]	**Outbound ICSID contract claims**[138]
Malaysia ($354 billion)	$152.5b	$119b	$8b	$5.2b	71 (1960-2012) [54]	26 (1980-2018) [22]	3 (1994-2005) [0]	4 (2001-2018) [1]	nil	nil
Philippines ($330 billion)	$83b	$52b	$6.5b	$0.6b	38 (1976-2009) [32]	17 (1980-2017) [14]	5 (2002-2016) [1]	nil	nil	nil
Viet Nam ($245 billion)	$145b	$10.6b	$15.5b	$0.6b	66 (1990-2014) [48]	25 (1980-2019) [18]	8 (2004-2018) [1]	nil	nil	nil
Myanmar ($71 billion)	$31b	nil	$3.5b	Nil	11 (1998-2019) [8]	16 (1980-2017) [13]	1 (2010) [0]	nil	nil	nil
Cambodia ($25 billion)	$23.7b	$1b	$3.1b	$0.124b	27 (1994-2018) [14]	16 (1980-2017) [14]	nil	nil	1 (2010)	nil
Laos ($18 billion)	$8.7b	$0.15b	$1.3b	$0	26 (1989-2013) [20]	17 (1980-2017) [14]	4 (2012-2017) [0]	nil	nil	nil
Brunei ($14 billion)	$6.7b	nil	$0.5b	Nil	8 (1998-2009) [6]	8 (1998-2009) [6]	nil	nil	nil	nil

B. Investment, Treaties and ISDS Claims in Key States in Non-ASEAN Asia Plus Oceania (Ranked Geographically then by GDP)

Country (& USD GDP in 2018)	**Inbound FDI stock (USD in 2018)**[139]	**Outbound FDI stock (USD in 2018)**[140]	**Inbound FDI flow (USD in 2018)**[141]	**Outbound FDI flow (USD in 2018)**[142]	**BITs signed [or in force]**[143]	**FTAs/IIAs signed [or in force or concluded]**[144]	**Inbound treaty ISDS claims [won by investor]**[145]	**Outbound treaty ISDS claims**[146]	**Inbound ICSID contract claims**[147]	**Outbound ICSID contract claims**[148]
China ($13.6 trillion)	$1.6t (excl. HK&Macao)	$2t (excl. HK&Macao)	$139b (excl. HK&Macao)	$129b (excl. HK&Macao)	145 (1982-2015) [109]	22 (1985-2017) [19]	3 (2011-2017) [0]	6 (2007-2017) [3]	nil	2 (2010 & 2016) [2]
Japan ($5 trillion)	$213b	$1.7t	$10b	$143b	33 (1977-2018) [29]	20 (1994-2018) [19]	nil	4 (2015-2018)	nil	Nil
Korea ($1.7 trillion)	$231b	$387.6b	$14.5b	$39b	105 (1964-2019) [90]	21 (1996-2018) [17]	3 (2012-2018) [1]	6 (2014-2018) [1]	1 (1984)	Nil
India ($2.7 trillion)	$386b	$166.6b	$42b	$11b	84 (1994-2018) [14]	13 (1993-2014) [13]	24 (2003-2017) [1]	7 (2000-2018) [1]	nil	Nil

139. https://unctadstat.unctad.org/wds/ReportFolders/reportFolders.aspx?sCS_ChosenLang=en.
140. *Ibid.*
141. *Ibid.*
142. *Ibid.*
143. https://investmentpolicy.unctad.org/.
144. *Ibid.*
145. *Ibid.*
146. *Ibid.*
147. https://icsid.worldbank.org/en/Pages/cases/AdvancedSearch.aspx.
148. *Ibid.*

Country (& USD GDP in 2018)	Inbound FDI stock (USD in 2018)[139]	Outbound FDI stock (USD in 2018)[140]	Inbound FDI flow (USD in 2018)[141]	Outbound FDI flow (USD in 2018)[142]	BITs signed [or in force][143]	FTAs/IIAs signed [or in force or concluded][144]	Inbound treaty ISDS claims [won by investor][145]	Outbound treaty ISDS claims[146]	Inbound ICSID contract claims[147]	Outbound ICSID contract claims[148]
Pakistan ($312.5 billion)	$42b	$1.9b	$2.35b	$0.008b	53 (1959-2014) [32]	7 (1981-2007) [6]	10 (2001-2013)	nil	nil	Nil
Bangladesh ($274 billion)	$17b	$0.31b	$3.6b	$0.023b	31 (1980-2014) [24]	4 (1981-2009) [3]	1 (2005) [1]	nil	6 (1992-2018)	Nil
Sri Lanka ($89 billion)	$12.7b	$1.4b	$1.6b	$0.068b	29 (1963-2011) [24]	6 (1994-2018) [5]	5 (1987-2018) [2]	nil	nil	Nil
Australia ($1.4 trillion)	$683b	$491b	$60b	$3.6b	24 (1988-2019) [18]	22 (1976-2019) [17]	2 (2011-2017)	7 (2010-2019) [3]	nil	5 (1996-2015)
New Zealand ($205 billion)	$75b	$17b	$1.4b	$0.4b	4 (1988-1999) [2]	16 (1980-2018)	nil	nil	1 (1987)	Nil
Papua New Guinea ($23 billion)	$4.56b	$0.5b	$335m	$-0.34b	6 (1980-2011) [5]	3 (1976-2000) [3]	nil	nil	2 (1996 & 2017)	Nil

CHAPTER 2

An International Commercial Court for Australia: An Idea Worth Taking to Market*

Marilyn Warren & Clyde Croft

The time has come for Australia to join others in establishing a new 'international commercial court' as another international dispute resolution option, especially for the Asia-Pacific region. This chapter outlines the existing international legislative architecture (the 1958 NYC (New York Convention) for international arbitration, inspiring the 2005 Hague Choice of Court Convention), and the models provided by London's venerable Commercial Court and since 2015 the Singapore International Commercial Court (SICC) (including the latter's composition, jurisdiction, procedure and confidentiality provisions, appeals, and cross-border enforceability of its judgments – facilitated by Singapore ratifying the 2005 Hague Convention). It uses these topics to frame the proposal for an Australian international commercial court (AICC), including the possibility of allowing its litigants to exclude the application of the Australian Consumer Law (which otherwise may apply also to many business-to-business disputes). It concludes that the COVID-19 pandemic has bolstered the case for such a new court, by minimising the obstacle of Australia's physical distance as litigation has had to move rapidly online, and because the pandemic's economic dislocation will undoubtedly lead to more cross-border disputes.

* The authors acknowledge the research assistance of Michaela Glass of the Faculty of Law, Monash University. The opinions expressed are the authors' own.

§2.01 INTRODUCTION

It is commonly thought that we are now living in a unique period of internationalisation or globalisation.[1] Never before has there been such accessibility to communications and (until the coronavirus disease of 2019 (COVID-19) pandemic) to international air travel, but this is, in itself, deceptive. In many respects we are, at least from a legal perspective, only now moving again to a period of internationalism. Internationalism declined during the twentieth century for a variety of reasons, the exploration of which time does not permit. Nevertheless, an important factor seems to have been the rise of the nation state at the expense of former world empires or other transnational organisations. Global trading empires, such as the British Empire, provided coherent and coordinated legal systems throughout the world, together with some consistent legislative models, enforceability of judgments and court process available between different parts of the Empire and, of course, appeals to one court, the Privy Council.[2]

The development of coherent systems of transnational law continued into the twentieth century in this context. There were, for example, a variety of proposals for the federation of the British Empire and, in that context, it was proposed that there be established a court akin to the United States (US) Supreme Court to resolve constitutional and other matters or, perhaps more broadly, a similarly reconstituted House of Lords.[3] This transnational or international thinking had its origins in the eighteenth century, but it seems that as the commercial dominance and power of England rose throughout the nineteenth century, the readiness of the common law to accept settled rules of international law declined. So, in the latter part of the eighteenth century, 'if English law was silent, it was the opinion of both Lord Mansfield and Blackstone that a settled rule of international law must be considered to be part of English law, and enforced as such'.[4] By the latter part of the nineteenth century, however, a threshold question had been interposed - namely 'whether the particular rule of international law has been received into, and so become a source of, English law'.[5]

As the power and significance of the nation state grew, we moved into our legal silos - with apologies to more twenty-first-century terminology - and away from the free flow of commerce and the law merchant with its transnational mercantile courts, which were so active in the middle ages. Consequently, it became necessary to explore new ways of providing support for world trade - with transnational legislation and transnational dispute resolution.[6] This process led to the development of one of the

1. Cf., earlier great internationalisation or globalisation events brought about as a result of technology, such as the invention of the electrical telegraph: *see* Tom Standage, *The Victorian Internet: The Remarkable Story of the Telegraph and the Nineteenth Century's On-Line Pioneers* (Walker Publishing Company 1998).
2. *See* Frank Safford & George Wheeler, *Privy Council Practice* (Sweet & Maxwell 1901).
3. *See*, e.g., Seymour Ching-Yuan Cheng, *Schemes for the Federation of the British Empire* 72, 112 (Columbia University Press 1931).
4. William S. Holdsworth, *The Relation of English Law to International Law*, in *Essays in Law and History* 260, 261 (A.L. Goodhart & H.C. Hanbury eds., Clarendon Press 1946).
5. *Ibid.*, 267.
6. In the present context, this includes the Convention on the Recognition and Enforcement of Foreign Arbitral Awards (10 Jun. 1958) ('NYC'), the UNCITRAL Model Law on International

most important pieces of international 'legislation', namely, the 1958 *Convention on the Recognition and Enforcement of Foreign Arbitral Awards* - generally known in this context as the New York Convention (NYC).

The ready enforcement of arbitral awards internationally had, by the 1950s, become critical as the then rapid rise of nation states, particularly given the post-Second World War independence movements, posed significant problems for the enforcement of court judgments internationally - problems that were not solved by international conventions or domestic legislation.[7] Neither could produce the universality of enforceability of determinative decisions, by way of court judgments, as was achieved by the NYC with respect to arbitral awards. Additionally, the enforceability of a court judgment obviously follows determination of the matter by a national court. As one party's national court in an international dispute is not generally going to be neutral from the point of view of the other party, it is unlikely to be an attractive venue - no matter how good the quality of the particular national court. There are, however, some exceptions, such as the English Commercial Court, the reasons for which are explored further in this chapter.

Consequently, to date, international arbitration, with neutral arbitrators selected by the parties or an impartial international arbitral institution and seated in a neutral forum, has proved much more attractive than litigation in the courts.[8] These issues would only have become more pressing but for the conclusion and success of the NYC, as globalisation and privatisation produced a plethora of parties to international transactions and consequent disputes and litigation.[9]

Without in any way denigrating or detracting from the process and success of international commercial arbitration, a variety of factors - to which we will turn shortly - indicate a desire by international commercial parties to have the option of access to, what may generally be described as, an international commercial court or courts. Moreover, the developing architecture of international 'legislation' marks this as a propitious time for the development of international commercial courts. As will be discussed, this is also an ideal time for Australia to establish an international commercial court.

Commercial Arbitration 1985 (amended on 7 Jul. 2006) ('Model Law'), and in terms of more substantive law, United Nations Convention on Contracts for the International Sale of Goods (11 Apr. 1980) ('CISG'). The CISG is applied in Victoria by the Sale of Goods (Vienna Convention) Act 1987 (Vic).

7. *See*, e.g., the Convention on the Recognition and Enforcement of Foreign Judgments in Civil and Commercial Matters (1 Feb. 1971) ('Hague Convention'); and, in terms of domestic legislation, *see*, e.g., Foreign Judgments Act 1991 (Cth).
8. References to the 'seat' of an arbitration are to 'Juridical Seat', which has consequences in terms of the *lex arbitri* and court 'supervision'. *See* Article 20 of the Model Law.
9. *See* Robert Briner, *Philosophy and Objectives of the Convention*, Conference Paper for New York Convention Day on 10 Jun. 1998, published in *Enforcing Arbitration Awards under the New York Convention - Experience and Prospects* 9, 10 (United Nations 1999).

§2.02 EXISTING INTERNATIONAL LEGISLATIVE ARCHITECTURE

Before considering existing international commercial court models, it is helpful to provide two brief examples of transnational legislation which form an important part of the international legislative architecture to which reference has been made. As will become apparent, the success of the NYC in particular serves to emphasise the need for simple 'single-tiered' structures which do not involve anything in the nature of double exequatur or 'localisation'. Moreover, the Hague *Convention on Choice of Court Agreements* ('the Choice of Court Convention'),[10] which came into force in 2015, has the potential to revolutionise international dispute resolution on a scale equivalent to the NYC.

[A] The New York Convention

The NYC has been described as 'the single most important pillar on which the edifice of international arbitration rests'[11] and also as a Convention which 'perhaps could lay claim to be the most effective instance of international legislation in the entire history of commercial law'.[12] The outstanding success of the NYC is demonstrated very clearly by the fact that the network of convention countries has grown to 160 during the sixty-one years since its birth.[13] The application of the NYC and its provisions for the enforcement of foreign arbitration agreements and the recognition and enforcement of foreign arbitral awards is regulated in Australia by Part II of the *International Arbitration Act* 1974 (Cth).[14]

The NYC greatly simplified and expedited the recognition and enforcement process established by the Geneva Convention because it eliminated the double exequatur problem that had existed since 1927.[15] More particularly, this difficulty, which arose under the Geneva Convention, arose because, in relation to recognition and enforcement, it was necessary, in effect, to demonstrate that an arbitral award which was sought to be enforced outside the country of its origin had become final in the country where it was made. This was known as the problem of double exequatur - because it meant that international arbitral awards, far from being rendered as something in the nature of international instruments, were fundamentally dependent

10. Convention on Choice of Court Agreements (30 Jun. 2005) ('Convention on Choice of Court Agreements').
11. J. Gillis Wetter, *The Present Status of the International Court of Arbitration of the ICC: An Appraisal*, 1 Am. Rev. Int'l Arb. 91 (1990).
12. Lord Michael Mustill, *Arbitration: History and Background* 6(2) J. Int'l Arb. 43 (2019). *See also* Stephen Schwebel, *A Celebration of the United Nations New York Convention on the Recognition and Enforcement of Foreign Arbitral Awards*, 12 Arb. Int'l 823 (1996); Alan Redfern & Martin Hunter, *Law and Practice of International Commercial Arbitration* 441 (Sweet & Maxwell 4th ed. 2004).
13. Information as to the extent of the application of the NYC is available from the UNCITRAL website, at www.uncitral.un.org.
14. *See further* Monichino & Teramura, Chapter 3 in this volume.
15. Convention on the Execution of Foreign Arbitral Awards (26 Sep. 1927) ('Geneva Convention'), which followed on from the Protocol on Arbitration Clauses (24 Sep. 1923).

upon the arbitration laws in the country of their origin, regardless of any international consensus or views in the country in which enforcement may have been sought. The need to 'delocalise' these measures increased as a result of the expansion of international trade after the conclusion of the Second World War. The NYC, in eliminating this double exequatur problem, thereby significantly 'delocalised' and institutionalised international arbitral awards. They became 'international currency' to be considered and assessed in the courts of a country or countries of enforcement, rather than the instruments the validity and effectiveness of which was always to be determined in a critical respect by the laws and courts of the country of their origin, namely the seat of the arbitration.

The process of 'enlightenment' or the 'Eureka moment' that occurred in the development of the NYC in this critical respect is described in a paper given by Pieter Sanders presented at 'New York Convention Day', which was held at the United Nations Headquarters on 10 June 1998 to celebrate the fortieth anniversary of the NYC. It should be noted that Pieter Sanders was described as 'the principal architect of the New York Convention' when delegates at the Eleventh International Bar Association (IBA) International Arbitration Day, held on 1 February 2008 at New York to commemorate the fiftieth anniversary of the Convention, viewed the premiere screening of 'Pieter Sanders at 95 – Reflections on the New York Convention'. In any event, Pieter Sanders recalled, in 1998:[16]

> My review of the Convention's history will deal in particular with what, during the Conference, was called the 'Dutch proposal'. It was conceived during the first weekend of the Conference. I spent that week-end at the house of my father-in-law in a suburb of New York. I can still see myself sitting in the garden with my small portable type-writer on my knees. It was there, sitting in the sun, that the 'Dutch proposal' was conceived. Upon return to New York on Monday, 26 May, this draft was presented to the Conference.
>
> At the meeting of Tuesday, 27 May, this proposal was welcomed by many of the delegates. The meeting decided that the Dutch proposal would be the basis for further discussions. I will not go into details of these discussions and the amendments made. I will only mention that the Conference, initially, preferred not to deal in the Convention with the arbitration agreement, as the Dutch proposal did. Preference was first given to a separate Protocol, as we knew from the Geneva Protocol on Arbitration Clauses (Geneva, 1923) (the 1923 Geneva Protocol). Nevertheless, at a very late stage of the Conference, a provision on the arbitration agreement was inserted in the Convention, the present article II.
>
> Was the Dutch proposal really, as Professor Matteucci called it, 'a very bold innovation'? At the time, I regarded that as rather a logical follow-up of the Geneva Convention on the Execution of Foreign Arbitral Awards (Geneva, 1927) (the 1927 Geneva Convention), taking into account the experience gained since then in the increased use of arbitration for solution of international business disputes.
>
> The main elements of the 'Dutch proposal' were, first of all, the elimination of the double exequatur, one in the country where the award was made and another one

16. Pieter Sanders, *The Making of the Convention*, Conference Paper for New York Convention Day (10 Jun. 1998), published in *Enforcing Arbitration Awards under the New York Convention – Experience and Prospects* 3, 3-4 (United Nations 1999).

> in the country of enforcement of the award. Under the 1927 Geneva Convention we always requested both. It is logical to require an exequatur only in the country where enforcement of the award is sought and not also in the country where the award was made, but no enforcement is sought. Another element of the proposal was to restrict the grounds for refusal of recognition and enforcement as much as possible and to switch the burden of proof of the existence of one or more of these grounds to the party against whom the enforcement was sought. This again stands to reason.
>
> However, nothing is perfect in this world. After 40 years of practice with the Convention its text could certainly be improved. For example, one could consider the introduction of uniform rules for the procedure of enforcement. In this respect, the Convention only contains the requirement that the award and arbitration agreement shall be supplied to the court (article IV) and that no more onerous conditions or higher fees should be imposed than when enforcement of a domestic award is sought (article III).

The Convention provides for two possible reservations: the first that the Convention applies only on the basis of reciprocity and the second that it will apply only to disputes which are considered to be commercial under the national law of the state relying upon this reservation.[17] A significant proportion of states have relied upon the reciprocity reservation, which has the effect of limiting the application of the NYC to arbitral awards within the jurisdiction of another convention state only, and not arbitral awards regardless of whether they are made within the jurisdiction of a convention state.[18]

[B] The Hague Choice of Court Convention

A recent addition to the international legislative architecture directed towards international commercial dispute resolution is the Hague Choice of Court Convention. The Convention of 30 June 2005, which came into force on 1 October 2015, aims at ensuring the effectiveness of choice of court agreements – also known as 'forum selection clauses' or 'jurisdiction clauses' – between parties to international commercial transactions.

Parties to international commercial transactions often seek to agree in advance on how disputes arising out of the transaction between them will be resolved. Well-advised parties realise that this is desirable, if not essential, in order to manage the risk associated with disputes that may arise in the future. For reasons already discussed, parties have tended to refer disputes which may arise to arbitration, thereby seeking to take advantage of the international enforcement mechanisms of the NYC. In some cases, parties will agree to litigate before a designated court but, as already discussed, this is less likely where the potential court is a national court of one of the parties.

17. *See* the NYC Article I(3).
18. Approximately 30% of 'Convention' states have applied the 'reciprocity' reservation and also approximately 30% the 'commercial' reservation. Australia has not applied either reservation.

Moreover, choice of court agreements have not always been respected under divergent national rules, particularly when cases are brought before a court other than one designated by the parties. This is a position sought to be rectified by the Choice of Court Convention, with a view to promoting greater legal certainty for cross-border business and creating a climate more favourable to international trade and investment. The Convention contains 'three basic rules' to give effect to choice of court agreements:[19]

(1) the chosen court must in principle hear the case (Article 5);
(2) any court not chosen must in principle decline to hear the case (Article 6); and
(3) any judgment rendered by the chosen court must be recognised and enforced in other Contracting States, except where a ground for refusal applies (Articles 8 and 9).

The Convention applies in international cases to exclusive choice of court agreements 'concluded in civil or commercial matters' (Article 1). The Convention does not apply to exclusive choice of court agreements to consumer and employment contracts and to a number of other specified matters, including wills and succession, insolvency, composition and analogous matters and the carriage of passengers and goods (Article 2). These exclusions generally reflect the existence of more specific international instruments and national, regional or international rules which provide for exclusive jurisdiction for some of these matters.

The Convention applies to 'exclusive choice of court agreements' (Article 1). Article 3 provides that for the purposes of the Convention an 'exclusive choice of court agreement' means an agreement concluded by two or more parties that meets the requirements specified in paragraph (c) of Article 3 and designates, for the purpose of deciding disputes which may have arisen or may arise in connection with a particular legal relationship, the courts of one Contracting State or one or more specific courts of one Contracting State to the exclusion of the jurisdiction of any other courts. The formalities for such an agreement, as specified in Article 3(c), are that the agreement must be concluded or documented in writing or by any other means of communication which renders information accessible so as to be useable for subsequent reference. In other words, the Convention well accommodates the digital age. Additionally, a Contracting State may declare that it will recognise and enforce judgments given by courts designated in a non-exclusive choice of court agreement (Article 22).

Also of particular importance are Articles 6 and 9. Article 6 makes provision for the obligations of a court which has not been chosen by the parties in their agreement:

19. Hague Conference on Private International Law, *The Hague Convention of 30 June 2005 on Choice of Court Agreements – Outline of the Convention*, Conference Paper for Workshop on Effective Enforcement of Business Contracts and Efficient Resolution of Business Disputes Through the Hague Choice of Court Agreements Convention 1 (1 Sep. 2015).

Article 6

Obligations of a court not chosen

A court of a Contracting State other than that of the chosen court shall suspend or dismiss proceedings to which an exclusive choice of court agreement applies unless–

a) the agreement is null and void under the law of the State of the chosen court;
b) a party lacked the capacity to conclude the agreement under the law of the State of the court seised;
c) giving effect to the agreement would lead to a manifest injustice or would be manifestly contrary to the public policy of the State of the court seised;
d) for exceptional reasons beyond the control of the parties, the agreement cannot reasonably be performed; or
e) the chosen court has decided not to hear the case.

Article 9 of the Convention makes provision for the refusal of recognition or enforcement, but in very limited terms, terms which are reminiscent of the limited grounds for refusal of enforcement of foreign arbitral awards under the NYC. It will be seen that one of the grounds for refusal of the recognition is manifest incompatibility with 'public policy' of the state in which enforcement is sought. The 'public policy' exception has been a vexed issue with respect to enforcement under the NYC.[20] It would be expected that a similarly restrictive interpretation of the expression 'public policy' under Article 9 of the Choice of Court Convention would be adopted. The provisions of Article 9 are as follows:

Article 9

Refusal of recognition or enforcement

Recognition or enforcement may be refused if–

a) the agreement was null and void under the law of the State of the chosen court, unless the chosen court has determined that the agreement is valid;
b) a party lacked the capacity to conclude the agreement under the law of the requested State;
c) the document which instituted the proceedings or an equivalent document, including the essential elements of the claim,
    i. was not notified to the defendant in sufficient time and in such a way as to enable him to arrange for his defence, unless the defendant entered an appearance and presented his case without contesting notification in the court of origin, provided that the law of the State of origin permitted notification to be contested; or
    ii. was notified to the defendant in the requested State in a manner that is incompatible with fundamental principles of the requested State concerning service of documents;
d) the judgment was obtained by fraud in connection with a matter of procedure;

20. *See Indian Farmers Fertiliser Cooperative Ltd., v. Gutnick* [2015] VSC 724 and, on appeal, *Gutnick v. Indian Farmers Fertiliser Cooperative Ltd.* (2016) 49 V.R. 732; as well as Monichino & Teramura, Chapter 3 in this volume. Proposing regional harmonisation for the public policy exception, *see also* Gu, Chapter 7 in this volume.

e) recognition or enforcement would be manifestly incompatible with the public policy of the requested State, including situations where the specific proceedings leading to the judgment were incompatible with fundamental principles of procedural fairness of that State;
f) the judgment is inconsistent with a judgment given in the requested State in a dispute between the same parties; or
g) the judgment is inconsistent with an earlier judgment given in another State between the same parties on the same cause of action, provided that the earlier judgment fulfils the conditions necessary for its recognition in the requested State.

Finally, it is also important to observe that the provisions of Article 3(b) provide that a choice of court agreement which designates the courts of one Contracting State or one or more specific courts of one Contracting State are deemed to be exclusive unless the parties have expressly provided otherwise.

To date, thirty-two states, including the European Union Member States, the US, Singapore and China, have signed the Convention. Australia is yet to become a signatory. However, the Convention was tabled in the Federal Parliament along with a detailed National Interest Analysis in June 2016.[21] The National Interest Analysis states:[22]

> Accession to the Convention is in Australia's national interest. Implementing the Convention will provide greater clarity and certainty for Australian businesses in the resolution of disputes arising from international transactions. Furthermore, accession to the Convention by Australia will facilitate party autonomy in civil and commercial contracts, making the process of determining jurisdiction more transparent and predictable.

The National Interest Analysis goes on to set out the proposed implementation of the Convention in Australia and states:[23]

> [21] It is proposed that the Convention will be implemented domestically through a new International Civil Law Act. This Act will also implement the *Hague Principles on Choice of Law in International Commercial Contracts* approved by the Hague Conference on Private International Law on 19 March 2015 ('Principles'). The Principles consist of 12 articles designed to clarify the operation of contracts with cross-border elements in international commercial law. They establish the basic rule that international commercial contracts are to be governed by the law chosen by the parties, subject to certain limitations. The Principles are a guide to best practice with respect to the recognition of party autonomy in choice of law in international commercial contracts. They are neither binding in international law, nor a model law, but are designed to be incorporated into State law in the manner most appropriate to each State, so as to develop and harmonise State laws.
> [22] The Convention and the Principles are well suited to implementation via a single Act, which will provide clear, consistent and accessible Australian

21. *National Interest Analysis on Australia's Accession to the Convention on Choice of Court Agreements*, A.T.N.I.A. 7 (2016).
22. *Ibid.*, [6].
23. *Ibid.*, 7 [21]-[24].

> private international law rules and principles to litigants in Australia and abroad.
>
> [23] For international proceedings, the treatment of exclusive choice of court agreements is currently governed by the common law, and the Trans-Tasman Proceedings Act for Trans-Tasman litigation. Exclusive choice of court agreements are generally regarded as enforceable in Australia, subject to certain limitations relating to the validity of the agreement and public policy considerations.
>
> [24] The proposed International Civil Law Act will codify the common law relating to choice of court agreements, clarify areas of uncertainty, and broaden the range of situations in which choice of court agreements will be given effect by Australian courts, consistent with Convention obligations. It will also set out the circumstances in which the recognition and enforcement of foreign judgments can occur in Australia. In accordance with the provisions of the Convention, the new Act will limit the possible grounds for refusing to give effect to an exclusive choice of court agreement.

It is, of course, early days for the development of the Choice of Court Convention, and it remains to be seen whether it will replicate the success of the NYC in providing a global web of enforceability for the judgments of courts of Contracting States the same way as the NYC has achieved for arbitral awards. There are, however, reasons for thinking that commercial parties will see the need for such global coverage and that states, including Australia, will respond accordingly. Of particular note in the present context, the Choice of Court Convention also has the potential to help further facilitate the effectiveness and attractiveness of international commercial courts, as well as helping drive the establishment of such courts.

§2.03 INTERNATIONAL COMMERCIAL COURTS

There are presently at least five well-established examples of courts which have been described as 'international commercial courts'. They are the relatively newly established SICC,[24] the London Commercial Court,[25] the Qatar International Court (QIC),[26] the courts of the Dubai International Financial Centre (DIFC)[27] and the Abu Dhabi Global Market (ADGM).[28] The London Commercial Court has a long lineage which is readily traceable to the work of Lord Mansfield who, as Chief Justice of the Court of Kings Bench, drew on the expertise of special commercial juries for the purpose of

24. *See* SICC, *Singapore International Commercial Court*, www.sicc.gov.sg (accessed 28 Apr. 2020).
25. *See Courts and Tribunals Judiciary*, www.judiciary.gov.uk/you-and-the-judiciary/going-to-court/high-court/queens-bench-division/courts-of-the-queens-bench-division/commercial-court/ (accessed 28 Apr. 2020).
26. *See Qatar International Court and Dispute Resolution Centre*, www.qicdrc.com.qa (accessed 28 Apr. 2020). The QIC was formerly known as the Civil and Commercial Court of the Qatar Financial Centre.
27. *See* DIFC Courts, *Dubai International Financial Centre Courts*, http://difccourts.ae/ (accessed 28 Apr. 2020).
28. *See* ADGM, *Abu Dhabi Global Market*, http://adgm.com/doing-business/adgm-courts/about-us/ (accessed 28 Apr. 2020).

informing the court in deciding commercial cases.[29] When one looks at these courts, it is readily seen that, beyond the common feature that they hear disputes involving international parties, they provide examples of the variety of international commercial court models.

In the last two years, several further courts have also been founded and styled as 'international commercial courts'. Evidently they reflect major shifts in world order, such as Brexit and China's Belt and Road initiative. In the mould of the more established forebears, there is now the Netherlands Commercial Court (NCC),[30] the International Commercial Chamber of the Paris Court of Appeal (CICAP),[31] the Chamber for International Commercial Disputes of the Landgericht Frankfurt am Main,[32] the Chinese International Commercial Courts (CICCs) in the cities of Shenzhen and Xi'an,[33] and the Astana International Financial Court (AIFC) in Kazakhstan.[34]

These courts are municipal courts in that they are established under the legislation of the states in which they are situated, with jurisdiction to hear international cases. They commonly deal with international commercial matters, sometimes including matters where more than one party is foreign to the state within which the court is based. It is therefore imperative that these courts are attuned to the needs and realities of international commerce and in the course of their work set standards for resolving international disputes. Before considering these existing international commercial court models further, though, it is necessary to say something about the developing need for an alternative to international commercial arbitration.

[A] An Alternative to International Commercial Arbitration

Despite the undeniable success of international commercial arbitration – success which is attributable in no small part to the widespread adoption and implementation of the NYC and the Model Law – there is a growing recognition of a need for an alternative to arbitration for international disputing parties. In the Opening Lecture for the DIFC Courts Lecture Series 2015, Singapore's Chief Justice Sundaresh Menon attributed the

29. John Thomas, *Commercial Justice in the Global Village: The Role of Commercial Courts* [41]–[43], Speech for DIFC Academy of Law Lecture in Dubai (1 Feb. 2016).
30. *See* NCC, *Netherlands Commercial Court*, https://www.rechtspraak.nl/English/NCC/Pages/default.aspx (accessed 28 Apr. 2020).
31. Guillaume Croisant, *The Belgian Government Unveils Its Plan for the Brussels International Business Court (BIBC)*, Kluwer Arbitration Blog (25 Jun. 2018), http://arbitrationblog.kluwerarbitration.com/2018/06/25/the-belgian-government-unveils-its-plan-for-the-brussels-international-business-court-bibc/ (accessed 28 Apr. 2020); Xandra Kramer, *The International Business Courts Saga Continued: NCC First Judgment – BIBC Proposal Unplugged*, Conflict of Laws.net (27 Mar. 2019), http://conflictoflaws.net/2019/the-international-business-courts-saga-continued-ncc-first-judgment-bibc-proposal-unplugged/ (accessed 28 Apr. 2020).
32. *See Chamber for International Commercial Disputes*, https://ordentliche-gerichtsbarkeit.hessen.de/ordentliche-gerichte/lgb-frankfurt-am-main/lg-frankfurt-am-main/chamber-international (accessed 28 Apr. 2020).
33. *See* CICC, *China International Commercial Court*, http://cicc.court.gov.cn/html/1/219/index.html (accessed 28 Apr. 2020); and Bath, Chapter 8 in this volume.
34. *See* AIFC, *Astana International Financial Centre*, http://aifc-court.kz/ (accessed 28 Apr. 2020).

preference of some commercial parties for litigation over arbitration to a variety of push and pull factors. As Menon CJ put it:[35]

> 12. The main pull factors are that certain cases are better suited for a process that is relatively open and transparent, equipped with appellate mechanisms, the options of consolidation and joinder, and the assurance of a court judgment.
> 13. The main push factors relate to the actual or perceived problems with arbitration. There are some well-rehearsed (if not universally accepted) issues relating to the lack of regulation in the arbitration industry. Among other things, there is said to be a lack of ethical consensus to guide the increasingly amorphous and diverse body of practitioners, resulting in various ethical issues; a lack of visibility and public accountability in decision making; increasing judicialisation and laboriousness in process resulting in delay accompanied by rising costs; some unpredictability in the enforcement of arbitral awards due to the ad hoc nature of courts' oversight of the enforcement process; and some lack of consistency in arbitral decisions due to the lack of corrective appellate mechanisms or an open body of jurisprudence.

The Chief Justice went on to address what, in our view, forms the crux of the need for an alternative to arbitration, observing that:[36]

> 14. ... arbitration, by its very nature, cannot provide a complete solution to propel the vessel of global commerce forward. Arbitration was conceived as an ad hoc, consensual, convenient and confidential method of resolving disputes. It was not designed to provide an authoritative and legitimate superstructure to facilitate global commerce. It cannot, on its own, adequately address such things as the harmonisation of substantive commercial laws, practices and ethics.
> 15. This is where I believe that international commercial courts have a potentially important role to play. Such courts can be instrumental in facilitating the harmonisation of commercial laws and practices. They also represent an avenue for the advancement of the rule of law as a normative ideal in global commerce. This is because there will be greater external scrutiny of their decisions and processes, with increased pressure to justify decisions against international norms.

Similar sentiments have been expressed by the former Chief Justice of the High Court of Australia, Robert French, who has questioned the capacity for arbitration to contribute to the 'development and international convergence of commercial law'.[37] Recognition of the inherently different conceptual bases of arbitration and litigation also helps demonstrate why the establishment of international commercial courts does not pose an existential threat to the practice of international commercial arbitration. This is because international commercial courts are not a replacement for arbitration, but rather they add to the range of options available to parties involved in international commerce. Indeed, Menon CJ gives the example of the London Commercial Court,

35. Sundaresh Menon, *International Commercial Courts: Towards a Transnational System of Dispute Resolution* [12]–[13], Opening Lecture for DIFC Courts Lecture Series 2015 in Dubai (2015) (citations omitted).
36. *Ibid.*, [14]–[15].
37. Robert French, *Transnational Dispute Resolution* [14]–[15], Speech for Supreme and Federal Court Judges' Conference in Brisbane (25 Jan. 2016).

which has operated 'alongside a vibrant arbitration market' for many years.[38] Space does not permit a more comprehensive consideration of the differences between arbitration and litigation, but it is clear that commercial parties will welcome the greater choice.[39]

[B] The London Commercial Court: Building on a History of Innovation

The London Commercial Court is a division of the Queen's Bench and has a long history dating back to its establishment in 1895. Although the court is, in essence, a municipal court and not a court newly and specially established to deal with international disputes – unlike the SICC and the DIFC courts for example – it does attract an enormous amount of international commercial litigation, including in circumstances where neither the parties nor the subject matter of the disputes has any real or significant connection with the United Kingdom (UK). As indicated previously, international dispute resolution in municipal courts, particularly the courts of the country of nationality of one of the international transactional parties, is generally thought to be unattractive, both for the reasons of lack of a 'neutral' forum and difficulties in the enforceability of judgments. Nevertheless, the London Commercial Court, based, as it is, in one of the world's preeminent financial centres, has attracted this international position through its long history of excellence in its work in the hands of judges of impeccable ability and impartiality.

Consequently, the position of the London Commercial Court might be regarded in this context as unique. So, apart from the clear message with respect to the establishment of any international commercial court – that is, the requirement of judges of impeccability and impartiality – the more immediate issues which need to be addressed in Australia are better illustrated by looking to other international commercial court models. Nevertheless, the English experience does highlight the importance of, and the capacity for, international commercial courts to keep abreast with innovation in the world of commerce. This was particularly well illustrated by former Lord Chief Justice Thomas in his lecture to the DIFC Academy of Law in Dubai in February 2016:[40]

> 41. ... [A] court must understand the markets and the commercial world. The London Commercial Court has developed and adapted its links with the financial and business community. The aim of those links is to ensure that the judiciary remained abreast of changes in the market. London has a historic advantage. In the 18th Century Lord Mansfield, the creator of the basis of modern English commercial and insurance law, often used special juries drawn from experts in the field: being, for instance, commercial merchants, insurance brokers, traders and so on. Their expertise would be practical expertise. In Lewis v Rucker from 1794, for instance, Lord Mansfield drew on the expertise of

38. Menon, *supra* n. 35, [10].
39. For a comprehensive discussion of the differences between international commercial arbitration and litigation in an international commercial court, *see especially ibid.*, [37]–[56].
40. *See* Thomas, *supra* n. 29, at [41]–[44].

a special jury to enable him to fashion principles of insurance law. As he explained it, the jury:[41]

> understood the question very well, and knew more about the subject of it than anybody else present; and formed their judgment from their own notions and experience, without much assistance from anything that passed.

42. That experience helped form the principles which he then went on to articulate in his judgments. In these, and other ways, Lord Mansfield ensured that the courts, and their search for principle, were not divorced from practice and thus the law was moulded to underpin the rapid growth of the UK as a trading state. It was also his common practice to invite his 'jurymen' to dinner, in order to discuss mercantile principles and customs so that he was as up to date as possible. I am afraid to say that even if it were still thought appropriate for judges to invite jurors to dinner, the idea that a modern Chief Justice would be able to invest the same amount of time as Lord Mansfield did in this way is one that bears little scrutiny.
43. The courts in London may no longer have special juries or leisurely dinners, but the London Commercial Court and the Financial List must keep properly abreast with rapidly changing market developments. This is now done through the provision of market seminars by an independent body originally established by the Bank of England, the Financial Markets Law Committee.[42] It ensures that senior members of the judiciary, and particularly the judges of the Commercial Court and the Financial List, are provided with regular and well-informed updates on changing market practices and the development of new financial products. In addition, to ensure that the Financial List remains relevant to court users and that change is demand-motivated, but judge led, a Financial List Users Committee has been established. Akin to the Commercial Court Users Committee, it is intended to have a broad membership drawn from representatives of legal and market associations, as well as Financial List judges.
44. The creation of the Financial List User Committee is a demonstration of a commitment to court users in the widest sense. In an interconnected world it has long seemed to me that London needed to develop a similar forum for debate at the international level. The London Commercial Court and the Financial List are international in their focus. 80% of work before the London Commercial Court has, at least, one party who is based outside the jurisdiction. Singapore and the DIFC Courts of Dubai, amongst others, are equally outward looking. Business and markets require us to be so. In truth all our Commercial Courts are international dispute resolution centres underneath their individual differences.

The message then is clear – successful international commercial courts must be inherently outward looking, and adapt their processes to the changing needs and expectations of the international market. In furtherance of this goal, Chief Justice Menon and former Lord Chief Justice Thomas have separately indicated their support for the creation of a network or forum of commercial courts which would encourage collaboration between courts and aid the development of best dispute resolution

41. (1761) 2 Burrow 1167.
42. *See Financial Markets Law Committee*, http://www.fmlc.org/ (accessed 28 Apr. 2020);

practice.[43] As former Lord Chief Justice Thomas put it – expressing sentiments with which we wholeheartedly agree:[44]

> In our interconnected world, our global village, the judges of the Commercial Courts have a ... role in ensuring our global prosperity continues to be underpinned by an effective legal framework and by law which develops in harmony with the rapidly changing markets and commerce brought about by the digital revolution. The Commercial Courts of the world are not unconnected islands, but have a common duty working together to innovate and to lead.

[C] Other International Models

Returning to Menon CJ's illuminating paper delivered at the DIFC Courts Lecture Series 2015, Singapore's Chief Justice observed that the SICC and the DIFC courts share some fundamental similarities, many of which have already been mentioned. The Chief Justice then turned to focus on the different underlying motivations and ideologies of the two courts:[45]

> 19. The DIFCC was created to support the economic activities within the Dubai International Financial Centre (DIFC), a purpose-built financial centre strategically located between the East and West.[46] It seeks to provide a 'platform for business and financial institutions to reach into and out of the emerging markets of the region'. It is conceived of as an independent zone specially created for the specific purpose of supporting a financial market for multinational companies.[47] The idea is that a capital market could be created in order to provide global businesses with a familiar environment governed by financial regulations and legal rules that are substantially similar to those found in leading common law jurisdictions.[48] To this end, the DIFCC is a common law court that applies either the law governing the contract in question, or the DIFC's common law system, which is 'based substantially on English law in codified form but with civil law influence'.
>
> 20. When the DIFCC was launched about a decade ago, it focused on dealing with matters that arose within the DIFC. The 'internationalisation' of the DIFCC came about in 2011, when its jurisdiction was expanded to include consent jurisdiction. This allowed the DIFCC to hear disputes that were not connected to its physical jurisdiction. With this expansion of its jurisdiction, the DIFCC

43. Menon, *supra* n. 35, at [67(d)]; Thomas, *supra* n. 29, at [47]–[51].
44. Thomas, *supra* n. 29, at [47].
45. Menon, *supra* n. 35, at [19]–[21] (citations omitted).
46. *See* DIFC Courts, *FAQ Dubai International Finance Centre Courts*, https://www.difccourts.ae/faq/ (accessed 28 Apr. 2020), which states 'The Dubai International Financial Centre is an onshore financial centre in the UAE. The DIFC's strategic location, between the markets of the east and west, provides a secure and efficient platform for business and financial institutions to reach into and out of the emerging markets of the region. The Centre offers independent regulation, supportive infrastructure and a tax-efficient regime, as well as a common law system.'
47. Denise Huiwen Wong, *The Rise of the International Commercial Court: What Is It and Will It Work?*, 33 C.J.Q. 205, 208 (2014).
48. *Ibid.*, 209.

plays an even more important role in making the DIFC a legal hub for the Middle East and North Africa.

21. This is to be contrasted with the SICC, which is located in South-East Asia, and therefore will likely serve a different demographic. From its inception, the SICC was envisaged as a forum dedicated to handling only international commercial disputes.[49] As such, unlike the DIFCC, the SICC's jurisdiction does not have a significant domestic component, if at all.

Moreover, the drivers for the establishment of the SICC and the DIFC courts were different. As Chief Justice Menon emphasised, the massive growth of transnational trade in Asia and the need for a centre to resolve transnational disputes was the genesis of the SICC.[50] The driver for establishing the DIFC courts was, however, somewhat different:[51]

25. For instance, the DIFCC was effectively established from a blank slate, with all the attendant pioneering benefits. While some of the laws in the DIFC involve fusion between the civil law and the common law, the DIFCC was primarily designed as a common law court operating within a purpose-built English-language common law jurisdiction. The opening page of the DIFCC website proclaims that '[t]he DIFC Courts are an *independent common law judiciary* based in the Dubai International Financial Centre (DIFC) with jurisdiction governing civil and commercial disputes'. In similar vein, Chief Justice Michael Hwang has described the DIFC as 'a common law island in a civil law ocean'. The DIFC's common law system was specifically intended to be 'independent from, but complementary to, the UAE's Arabic-language civil law system, thus offering a choice that strengthens both processes while ensuring public access to world-class justice'. While a French-heritage Arabic language civil law system is available in the Dubai national courts, parties opting for English common law processes go to the DIFCC instead. Consonant with these objectives, the DIFCC's international judges are experienced common law legal professionals from Australia, Malaysia, Singapore and the UK.[52]

The models for the ADGM Courts in Abu Dhabi, and the QIC in Qatar, are more like that of the DIFC courts. The ADGM Courts commenced operation in 2016 and, like the DIFC courts in Dubai and the AFIC Courts in Kazakhstan, the ADGM Courts service a specially created economic zone within the United Arab Emirates. The ADGM Courts are modelled on the English judicial system and administer legislation based on English, Scots and Australian statutes. The *Application of English Law Regulations* 2015[53] also makes the English common law directly applicable in the ADGM – an approach which the ADGM Courts' website proclaims as unique in the Middle East.[54]

49. *Ibid.*, 211.
50. Menon, *supra* n. 35, at [22]–[23].
51. *Ibid.*, [25] (citations omitted and emphasis in original).
52. As of 5 Feb. 2015, the international judges are: Chief Justice Michael Hwang, SC (Singapore), Deputy Chief Justice Sir John Murray Chadwick (UK), Justice Sir David Steel (UK), Justice Roger Giles (Australia), Justice Tun Zaki Azmi (Malaysia) and Justice Sir Anthony David Colman (UK).
53. *See ADGM Legal Framework*, https://en.adgm.thomsonreuters.com/rulebook/application-english-law-regulations-2015-0 (accessed at 28 Apr. 2020).
54. *See Frequently Asked Questions – What Are ADGM Courts?*, http://adgm.com/doing-business/adgm-courts/frequently-asked-questions/ (accessed at 28 Apr. 2020).

Pursuant to the *ADGM Courts, Civil Evidence, Judgments, Enforcement and Judicial Appointments Regulations* 2015, the Court of First Instance has jurisdiction to hear commercial matters which are connected with the ADGM,[55] as well as 'jurisdiction as is conferred on it by any request, in writing, by the parties to have the Court of First Instance determine the claim or dispute'.[56]

§2.04 SICC: A CASE STUDY

Returning to the (East) Asian region, the SICC has been established as a curial forum which accommodates parties foreign to its sovereign jurisdiction, where neither the parties nor the subject matter of the dispute have or has any connection with Singapore. Moreover, the SICC will not decline to assume jurisdiction solely on the ground that the dispute is connected to a jurisdiction other than Singapore.[57] As a result, the SICC provides a useful case study with respect to issues to be considered in establishing an AICC.

[A] Composition of the Court

The SICC is a division of the Singapore High Court and thus part of the Supreme Court of Singapore. The panel of SICC judges is constituted by the existing Supreme Court Judges, as well as international judges appointed for a fixed period and assigned to cases on an ad hoc basis. These Associate International Judges have been appointed from a variety of countries, both within and beyond the region, and are preeminent and experienced commercial judges. As the SICC is part of the Supreme Court of Singapore, provision is made for appeals from the SICC to the Court of Appeal of Singapore, with the appellate Bench drawn from the SICC panel of judges – which, for this purpose, also includes the Associate International Judges. The composition of the SICC generally reflects the position for Singapore High Court proceedings in that proceedings may be disposed of by a single judge, who may be a Singapore Supreme Court Judge or an Associate International Judge. The Chief Justice may, on the application of a party, designate three judges to hear a case. In this respect, regard would be had to the nature of the dispute, its subject matter and, no doubt, the nationality of parties in designating a particular judge or judges to hear the case.

---

55. *See* Civil Evidence, Judgments, Enforcement and Judicial Appointments Regulations 2015 (Abu Dhabi Global Market Courts) s. 16(2)(a)-(d); Law No. 4 of 2013 Concerning the Abu Dhabi Global Market, Article 13(6). For legislation affecting the Abu Dhabi Global Market, *see ADGM Rulebook*, https://en.adgm.thomsonreuters.com/ (accessed at 28 Apr. 2020).
56. Civil Evidence, Judgments, Enforcement and Judicial Appointments Regulations 2015 (Abu Dhabi Global Market Courts), s. 16(2)(e).
57. SICC, *Singapore International Commercial Court User Guides*, Note 1 [5] (31 Jan. 2019), https://www.sicc.gov.sg/docs/default-source/legislation-rules-pd/sicc-user-guides 31jan19.pdf (accessed 28 Apr. 2020).

[B] Governing Legislation

Provision has been made for the SICC in amendments to the Singapore *Supreme Court of Judicature Act*, particularly in section 18D and 18F, which provide for the jurisdiction of the court, certification as to the nature of the intended action and the effect of the parties' jurisdiction agreement.[58]

There are other provisions added to this legislation providing for the composition of the SICC, its powers, the transfer of cases from the SICC to the High Court of Singapore and, significantly, provisions with respect to the rules of evidence, determination of foreign law on submissions rather than as a factual matter to be proved, and for representation by foreign lawyers. These provisions are contained in section 18K, 18L and 18M.[59] They are also supported by court rules,[60] and perhaps more significantly from the perspective of an intending international party, by comprehensive and

58. Singapore, cap. 322, 2014 rev. ed. ('*Supreme Court of Judicature Act*'). These provisions state:

Jurisdiction of Singapore International Commercial Court

18D. –The Singapore International Commercial Court shall have jurisdiction to hear and try any action that satisfies all of the following conditions:
(a) the action is international and commercial in nature;
(b) the action is one that the High Court may hear and try in its original civil jurisdiction;
(c) the action satisfies such other conditions as the Rules of Court may prescribe.
(2) Without limiting subsection (1), the Singapore International Commercial Court (being a division of the High Court) has jurisdiction to hear any proceedings relating to international commercial arbitration that the High Court may hear and that satisfy such conditions as the Rules of Court may prescribe.

Effect of jurisdiction agreement

18F. -

(1) Subject to subsection (2), the parties to an agreement to submit to the jurisdiction of the Singapore International Commercial Court shall be considered to have agreed–
 (a) to submit to the exclusive jurisdiction of the Singapore International Commercial Court;
 (b) to carry out any judgment or order of the Singapore International Commercial Court without undue delay; and
 (c) to waive any recourse to any court or tribunal outside Singapore against any judgment or order of the Singapore International Commercial Court, and against the enforcement of such judgment or order, insofar as such recourse can be validly waived.
(2) Subsection (1)(*a*), (*b*) and (*c*) applies only if there is no express provision to the contrary in the agreement.

59. These provisions state:

Rules of evidence in certain cases

18K.

(1) The Singapore International Commercial Court–
 (a) shall not be bound to apply any rule of evidence under Singapore law in such cases and to such extent as the Rules of Court may provide; and
 (b) may, in those cases, apply other rules of evidence (whether such rules are found under any foreign law or otherwise) in accordance with the Rules of Court.
(2) In subsection (1), 'rule of evidence' includes any rule of law relating to privilege, or to the taking of evidence.

helpful *Singapore International Commercial Court User Guides*[61] and a very detailed and comprehensive *Singapore International Commercial Court Practice Direction.*[62]

[C] Approach to Procedure

The approach to procedure generally is encapsulated in the *Report of the Singapore International Commercial Court Committee* in the opening of the discussion on procedure in the then proposed SICC:[63]

> The SICC Rules and practice directions will govern proceedings before the SICC. It is envisaged that these provisions would follow international best practices for commercial dispute resolution. In particular, reference will be taken from the procedure of institutions such as the English Commercial Court. The provisions adopted must be sensitive to the unique needs of commercial users and the commercial Bar. In addition, a model similar to the English Commercial Court Guide which, through consultation with the Users' Committee, may be considered to allow for a flexible and efficient mode of amending the SICC Rules.

In terms of case management generally, interlocutory proceedings are heard by judges in a docket system. The SICC places emphasis on case management, including encouragement of Alternative Dispute Resolution (ADR), and the use of technology, such as electronic filing and the like.[64]

It is worthwhile reflecting on the way in which the SICC has developed in a very short period. Chief Justice Menon described the administrative and operational issues with the establishment of the SICC in the following terms:

Determination of foreign law on submissions

18L.

(1) The Singapore International Commercial Court may, in such cases as the Rules of Court may prescribe, order that any question of foreign law be determined on the basis of submissions instead of proof.

(2) In determining any question of foreign law on the basis of submissions, the Singapore International Commercial Court may have regard to such matters as the Rules of Court may prescribe.

Representation by foreign lawyers

18M. A party to a case in the Singapore International Commercial Court, or to an appeal from that Court, may in accordance with the Rules of Court be represented by a foreign lawyer who is registered in accordance with Part IVB of the Legal Profession Act (Cap. 161).

60. Supreme Court of Judicature Act, *supra* n. 58, at s. 80.
61. SICC, *supra* n. 57.
62. SICC, *Singapore International Commercial Court Practice Directions* (22 Jul. 2019), https://www.supremecourt.gov.sg/docs/default-source/default-document-library/sicc-practice-directions---amended-version-(15-july-2019).pdf (accessed 28 Apr. 2020).
63. Singapore International Commercial Court Committee, *Report of the Singapore International Commercial Court Committee* [29] (November 2013), https://www.sicc.gov.sg/docs/default-source/modules-document/news-and-article/-report-of-the-singapore-international-commercial-court-committee-_90a41701-a5fc-4a2e-82db-cc33db8b6603-1.pdf (accessed 28 Apr. 2020) (citations omitted).
64. SICC, *supra* n. 62, at [75]–[86], [42]–[60].

> [it was necessary] to consider a number of administrative and operational issues with the establishment of the SICC. This included such matters as the possible need for a special website; promotional and marketing work to raise awareness; IT and infrastructure needs and the manpower needs of this new division of the court. Underlying all of that was the need for funds. We submitted a bid to the Reinvestment Fund (a government innovation fund) and our bid was successful, as a result of which we were given funds over and above our baseline budget for the specific purpose of financing the SICC.

[D] Confidentiality

As a general rule, SICC proceedings take place in open court. The *Report of the Singapore International Commercial Court Committee* observed that:[65]

> Transparency is attractive to some parties and is important for the branding of the SICC. The Committee agreed that confidentiality militates against the development of a body of jurisprudence which will be necessary to enable prospective users of SICC dispute resolution to model their future commercial relations.

The Committee continued, observing that the position may be different where the dispute is one which has no connection with Singapore:[66]

> Nevertheless, it is intended that special rules apply for cases which have no substantial connection to Singapore. What constitutes the absence of substantial connection will be further refined in consultation with stakeholders, but will include cases where parties confirm that either (i) Singapore law is not the governing law; or (ii) the choice of Singapore law is the sole connection to Singapore, and agree that it is desirable to maintain confidentiality, the hearing will be conducted in camera, with other appropriate measures, such as the redaction of judgments. Confidentiality will immediately attach on filing unless the position is shown to be misstated later. On the other hand, if one party wishes to have confidentiality but the other does not, the SICC Rules will allow the party requesting for confidentiality to apply to the court, which will consider all the circumstances of the case, including the private interest of the contesting parties and any public interest considerations. In such cases, confidentiality will be extended until the court has disposed of the application.

Parties may apply for hearings in camera and the sealing of court files,[67] which would result in a position similar to that available in international arbitral proceedings.[68]

65. Singapore International Commercial Court Committee, *supra* n. 63, at [32].
66. *Ibid.*, [33].
67. Supreme Court of Judicature Act, *supra* n. 58, s. 80, ord. 110 r. 30. Provision for a pre-action procedure that included the power for a certificate of confidentiality to be granted was removed from the Singapore Court Rules by amendment in 2018: Supreme Court of Judicature (Amendment) Act (Singapore, 2018 rev. ed.), s. 3.
68. *See*, e.g., International Arbitration Act 1974 (Cth) ss 23C–23G; Arbitration Act 1996 (NZ) ss 14-14I.
    See, e.g., *Australian Centre for International Commercial Arbitration Rules* (2016) r. 22; AMINZ Arbitration Rules (2009) r. 102; Arbitration Rules of the Singapore International

[E] Rules of Evidence, Determining Foreign Law, and Joinder

As will be seen from the provisions of section 18K and 18L of the Singapore *Supreme Court of Judicature Act*, considerable flexibility is accorded to the SICC with respect to the application of the rules of evidence and also in relation to the determination of foreign law.[69] The considerable flexibility provided to the SICC by these provisions mirrors the flexibility enjoyed by arbitral tribunals but with the court having many other advantages flowing from its position and from its sovereign rather than consensual source of power and authority. One particular advantage in this respect is the power to join additional parties under Order 110 of the Singapore Court Rules.[70] The intent of those powers is summarised in the *SICC User Guides*:[71]

> 7. Once an action is in the Court (i.e. the Court has and has assumed jurisdiction), a person may be joined as a party, including as an additional plaintiff, defendant or as a third or subsequent party, to the action. This is provided that:
>   (a) the requirements in the Rules of Court for joining the person are met (the relevant provisions include Orders 15 and 16);
>   (b) the claims by or against the person:
>   (i) do not include a claim for any relief in the form of, or connected with, a prerogative order (including a mandatory order, a prohibiting order, a quashing order or an order for review of detention); and
>   (ii) are appropriate to be heard in the Court.
> 8. Unlike the claims between the plaintiffs and the defendants named in the originating process when it was first filed, there is no requirement that the claims by or against a person sought to be joined to the action must be of an international and commercial nature. However, the Court, in exercising its discretion on whether to join that person, would have to decide whether the claims by or against that person are appropriate to be heard in the Court. In exercising that discretion, the Court would have regard to its international and commercial nature: see Order 110, Rule 9(3).
> 9. There is also no requirement that a person sought to be joined to the action must have submitted to the Court's jurisdiction under a written jurisdiction agreement. There is one exception. A State or the sovereign of a State may not be made a party to an action in the Court (whether by joinder or otherwise) unless the State or the sovereign has submitted to the jurisdiction of the Court under a written jurisdiction agreement: see Order 110, r 9(2).
> 10. Where the person sought to be joined has not agreed in writing to submit to the jurisdiction of the Court, the Court may examine the connecting factors to Singapore in deciding whether to exercise its compulsory jurisdiction and join that person to the action. There is therefore no equivalent of Order 110, Rule 8(2) for joinder cases.
> 11. However, this does not mean that the Court is bound to consider and give weight to arguments based on connecting factors made by persons sought to

---

Arbitration Centre (5th ed. 2013) r. 35. *See also* Supreme Court of Singapore, *Singapore International Commercial Court Practice Directions* (1 Jan. 2015, as amended by Amendment No. 1 of 2016) [97]; and generally Nottage, Chapter 4 in this volume.

69. *See* SICC, *supra* n. 57, at Note 4.
70. Supreme Court of Judicature Act, *supra* n. 58, at s. 80.
71. SICC, *supra* n. 57, at Note 1, [7]–[11].

> be joined. Where the person sought to be joined has submitted to the Court's jurisdiction under a written jurisdiction agreement, for example, the Court may decide to disregard such arguments in deciding whether to join that person. This would be in the discretion of the Court.

These are very extensive powers and avoid the problems encountered in arbitral proceedings in attempting to 'join' other parties to the proceedings. Given the consensual basis of arbitral proceedings, absent cooperation and agreement of the parties to the arbitration agreement and parties to be joined, there are limits to the extent that arbitration legislation and rules can assist to, in effect, achieve joinder.[72] Powers of joinder such as this also complement and are complemented by the extensive powers of the SICC with respect to Mareva injunctions and associated remedies.[73]

In relation to foreign law, section 18L of the Singapore *Supreme Court of Judicature Act* represents a significant departure from the usual position at common law, which is that foreign law is a matter to be proved as a question of fact. However, the recommendation of the SICC Committee was that greater flexibility should be allowed in this respect and the same practice adopted with respect to questions of foreign law as is adopted by international arbitral tribunals. Thus, the Committee reported:[74]

> *Questions of Foreign Law.* In line with the international character of the SICC, foreign law need not be pleaded and proved as a fact in proceedings before the SICC, as the Judges can take judicial notice of foreign law with the assistance of oral and written legal submissions, supported by relevant authorities. The SICC would then apply foreign law[75] to determine the issues in dispute. This would facilitate buy-in from foreign counsel to bring their disputes to the SICC and, at the same time, aligns SICC procedure with the practice in international arbitration. Notwithstanding the position on the applicable conflict of laws rules, consideration should be given to the extent to which Singapore's public policy would be applicable in each case, and if so, the relevant implications it might have on the resolution of SICC disputes.[76]

Furthermore, the provisions of section 18M with respect to representation by foreign lawyers are clearly significant and important. Apart from reflecting the flexibility enjoyed in this respect in most jurisdictions in the arbitration field, it is important in the present context in two particular respects. First, if foreign law is to be established by submission rather than proof as a fact, considerable advantage may flow from involvement of foreign practitioners from relevant foreign jurisdictions. Second, to

72. *See* Clyde Croft, Christopher Kee & Jeff Waincymer, *A Guide to the UNCITRAL Arbitration Rules* 185-92 (Cambridge University Press, 2013) (in relation to Article 17(5) of the *UNCITRAL Arbitration Rules*).
73. SICC, *supra* n. 57, at Note 5.
74. Singapore International Commercial Court Committee, *supra* n. 63, at 17-18, at [34].
75. This can extend to civil law, and the relevant rules can allow for the appointment of judges from civil law jurisdictions.
76. An example raised in the SICC Committee meeting would be the consideration of the SICC's position towards disputes based on gaming contracts, or otherwise claims which are pre-supposed upon contracts which ordinarily be considered illegal in many jurisdictions.

close off representation against foreign lawyers engaged by parties would put an international court at considerable disadvantage as compared to international arbitral proceedings. Provision is also made for foreign representation in the Singapore Court Rules, and Practice Directions, as summarised in the SICC User Guides.[77] For present purposes, it is sufficient to note that the main category of cases in which foreign lawyers may represent parties in the SICC is offshore cases – that is, cases which have no substantial connection to Singapore.

[F] Appeals

Decisions of the SICC are appealable, in the same way as other Singapore High Court decisions, to the Singapore Court of Appeal. The difference with respect to SICC appeals is that the Court of Appeal may be composed of Associate International Judges from the SICC panel and, or alternatively, comprised of judges from the Singapore Court of Appeal – or a mixture of both.[78] Significantly, the right of appeal is subject to any prior agreement between the parties to limit or vary the scope of an appeal. Apart from wholesale exclusion of the right to appeal, parties may agree to a limited scope of appeal or review on specific grounds modelled after the international arbitration regime, such as breaches of natural justice or defects in the validity and scope of the agreement to submit matters to the SICC.[79]

[G] Enforceability of Judgments

In relation to enforceability, the approach of the SICC is to rely upon existing mechanisms for the enforcement of Singapore judgments, which may be complemented by the provision of model SICC dispute resolution clauses. Additionally, the SICC Committee suggested that the Singapore government may wish to consider negotiating multilateral judgment enforcement agreements, especially within the Association of Southeast Asian Nations (ASEAN) community, bilateral government agreements and the possibility of court to court arrangements. Moreover, it was suggested that an aspect of multilateral government agreements would be for Singapore to consider signing the Choice of Court Convention.

The Committee recommendations with respect to the international enforceability of SICC judgments generally and court to court arrangements are applicable to any jurisdiction and are, consequently, of particular interest and importance in the present context. The Committee's commentary and recommendations in this respect are as follows:[80]

77. SICC, *supra* n. 57, at Note 3. *See also* SICC, *supra* n. 62, at [26]–[28].
78. SICC, *supra* n. 62, [23]–[25] (noting that in varying circumstances the Court of Appeal may be constituted by two, three or five judges).
79. *Ibid.*, [139].
80. Singapore International Commercial Court Committee, *supra* n. 63, at 20 [42]–[43], 21-2 [48]–[51] (emphasis in original).

42. As with the judgments of the Supreme Court of Singapore, judgments of the SICC may be enforced in other jurisdictions through reciprocal enforcement provisions, such as the Reciprocal Enforcement of Commonwealth Judgments Act[81] and the Reciprocal Enforcement of Foreign Judgments Act,[82] is a key factor to be emphasised in marketing and promotion.
43. The existing position may be complemented by the provision of model SICC dispute resolution clauses. A party who has submitted or who has agreed to submit to the SICC's jurisdiction may be deemed to have waived its right to defend against an action based on a SICC judgment in all jurisdictions. This may be expressly agreed upon or incorporated by reference to the SICC Rules in the SICC model dispute resolution clauses. The written consent of parties should be required so as to create issue estoppels which will bind parties to the decision of the referred jurisdiction.

...

48. *Court to Court Arrangements.* A unique method to market the internationality of SICC judgments would be to have a tie up with a friendly foreign international court, to refer appropriate proceedings to each other's jurisdiction. For example, Order 101 of the Rules of Court reflects the procedure of the Memorandum for Understanding signed between Singapore and New South Wales. The order prescribes that if, in any proceeding before the Singapore High Court or Court of Appeal, a question of foreign law relating to the New South Wales jurisdiction arises, our courts have the power to, on its own motion or upon a party's application, order that an action be commenced in New South Wales for that question of foreign law to be determined.
49. The SICC could have similar arrangements with a friendly and prominent jurisdiction, for example, the English Commercial Court, such that:
    (a) Where parties have commenced proceedings in the SICC, and a party to the dispute brings an independent but related set of proceedings in the English Commercial Court to determine a question of English law, the English Commercial Court could refuse the continuation of the proceedings and refer the matter back to the SICC. This would be an express recognition of the SICC's competence to deal with questions involving foreign law, in view of the SICC Panel's international make up.
    (b) If a party to an agreement to resolve commercial disputes in the SICC commences proceedings in the English Commercial Court, the latter would refer parties to bring their dispute to the SICC as a matter of course. A low threshold is needed: so long as there is the *prima facie* existence of a written SICC dispute resolution agreement, the referral will be made, any dispute on whether the commercial dispute falls within the agreement, or the validity of the agreement, would essentially be a dispute over the SICC's jurisdiction, which can and should be decided by the SICC itself.

---

81. In addition to the UK, the RECJA covers several major jurisdictions in the region: Australia (New South Wales, Queensland, Victoria, etc.), New Zealand, Malaysia, Brunei and India (except the state of Jammu and Kashmir).
82. In particular, the domestic legislation of India recognises Singapore as a 'reciprocating territory' and provides a regime which facilitates the enforcement of a judgment given by a Singapore court. *See* The Code of Civil Procedure (Singapore) ss 13, 37 & 44A. To maximise the enforceability of a Singapore judgment in India, sufficient regard may have to be accorded to the public policy of India where applicable, and the laws of India would have to be applied where it is expressed to be the governing law of a contract: Rishi Agrawala, *Executability and Enforceability of Foreign Judgments and Decrees in India: Judicial Trends,* Mondaq (23 Oct. 2000), https://www.mondaq.com/india/Employment-and-HR/9190/Executability-Enforceability-Of-Foreign-Judgments-And-Decrees-In-India-Judicial-Trends-Part-4 (accessed 28 Apr. 2020); and generally Singh, Chapter 12 in this volume.

This obviates the existing position in the English common law, which permits the party to continue with the proceedings in the English Commercial Court notwithstanding an *exclusive* SICC dispute resolution clause if it can show strong cause to do so.

50. Singapore would likely need to offer to reciprocate on both (a) and (b).
51. A Memorandum of Guidance with jurisdictions which do not have any reciprocal enforcement treaty with Singapore may also enhance the international enforceability of SICC judgments. The Memorandum would set out the understanding of the court procedures required for the enforcement of each jurisdiction's judgment in the other court, and would promote a positive perception of SICC judgments. A written example would be the Memorandum of Guidance signed between the English Commercial Court and the DIFCC in January 2013.

Finally, it should not be forgotten that judgments for a definite sum of money can also be enforced at common law in a variety of circumstances.[83]

§2.05 AN AUSTRALIAN INTERNATIONAL COMMERCIAL COURT

As has been discussed, the manner in which other international commercial courts have been established and developed provides useful guidance and issues for consideration in the establishment of an AICC. This does not mean, however, that in establishing an AICC, we should slavishly follow any particular model. Moreover, the Australian legal landscape is, unsurprisingly, different from that in which the international commercial courts that have been considered have been established and developed. An obvious difference in Australia is its federal system of government and courts. On one level, it might be thought that this is an inhibition to national action. Yet thoughtful consideration of possible models indicates, rather, that the federation has the strength of bringing together diverse thought and experience and the legal and economic environments and experience from throughout a diverse continent. Moreover, the establishment of an international commercial court provides the opportunity for the nation as a whole to present an integrated commercial court to the region and to the world. Any legislation would necessarily require clarification and resolution of Australian constitutional aspects that do not arise in England and Singapore.

[A] Sovereign Base and Composition of the Court

Clearly, the 'AICC' would require a sovereign base if it is to be established as a court, rather than something in the nature of an arbitral tribunal. This sovereign base is readily provided by an Australian court which, with enabling legislation, would be empowered to establish a panel of national and international judges along the same lines as the model adopted in Singapore by the SICC.

With the cooperation of these courts, together with the various governments, there would appear to be no inhibition in appointing to the judicial panel the finest

83. Supreme Court of Victoria, *Practice Note SC Gen 15: Enforcement of Foreign Judgments* (30 Jan. 2017).

sitting and retired commercial judges from the various Australian Courts across the nation. The benefit to Australia, both domestically and internationally, in being able to bring this commercial judicial expertise together needs no further explanation. It should, however, be emphasised that though the AICC would have an analogous international focus to that of the other international commercial courts considered above, there is no reason why the AICC could not also have a national domestic jurisdiction enabling commercial parties from anywhere in Australia to litigate in a forum populated by the best commercial judicial minds in the country.

The panel of judges appointed for the purposes of the AICC would not, of course, be limited to Australian sitting or retired judges or judges within this region. Similarly to the approach taken to populating the panel of international judges adopted by the SICC, the AICC panel would consist of leading commercial judges from jurisdictions across the world, including, for example, Singapore, Hong Kong, New Zealand, the UK, and other jurisdictions where it might be expected or it is found that disputes arise, or in which disputing parties conduct their business. Additionally, consideration should be given to the appointment of international judges from beyond the common law world.

As has been observed, the environment in which the DIFC courts exist has been described as something in the nature of a civil law sea in which the DIFC courts are a common law 'island'. As is clear from experience with international arbitral tribunals, it is often the case and helpful where parties come from common law and civil law jurisdictions to include within the arbitral tribunal panel of three, arbitrators from both the common law and civil law tradition. This mix of judicial backgrounds may also be very beneficial if, as is contemplated, the AICC is empowered to determine foreign law on the basis of submissions without the need for formal proof as a factual matter.

[B] Appeals

As is clear from the Singapore model, attention also needs to be given to the appellate arrangements, particularly the constitution of the Court of Appeal from judgments at first instance in the AICC. As with the SICC, it is desirable that flexible appellate arrangements be provided for and, particularly, that the Court of Appeal Bench, whether it be composed of two, three or five judges, is able to be selected from the AICC panel of Australian and international judges.

It goes without saying that the appellate procedures from an international commercial court must be flexible and expeditious. In this respect, legislation empowering the Court of Appeal to dispose of matters on the papers and for the filtering of appeals through a leave to appeal mechanism is highly desirable. Experience with expedited appeals and leave to appeal requirements has proved very successful in expediting civil appeals. In light of this experience, there could be no objection to these type of appeal 'constraints' with respect to Australian commercial litigation conducted in the AICC and, internationally, such 'constraints' would likely be very attractive as they more closely replicate the international arbitral regime where, under the Model

Law and the NYC, appeals and challenges to international arbitral awards are severely constrained, with merits appeals simply not permitted.

There will be important policies and aspects of the legislative framework to be developed by state and federal governments taking account of the Australian constitutional structure.

[C] Scope of Jurisdiction, Procedure, and the Enforceability of Judgments

In terms of substantive jurisdiction, there seems every reason to adopt the approach of the SICC and to accommodate and encourage disputes which are 'disconnected' from Australia – an approach which is, similarly, adopted by the other courts discussed above. Moving from substance to procedure, it is clear from the nature of an international commercial court and the experience in Singapore and London, particularly, that procedures must be flexible, be provided for clearly in readily accessible court rules, practice notes and user guides, and be supported by administrative structures and court technology which will accommodate the hearing of disputes from across the globe. With respect to technology, clearly basic things like electronic filing, videoconferencing and, as technology develops, e-dispute resolution fora are essential, in order to ensure that the court keeps pace with developments in international commerce.[84] The 2020 COVID-19 pandemic further highlights both this necessity and the potential for Australia, as elaborated in section §2.06 below.

In relation to enforceability of judgments of the AICC, the same issues arise as with respect to the SICC, at least internationally. Singapore, as a member of the Commonwealth of Nations, is in much the same position as Australia and the Australian States and Territories in relation to international enforcement of judgments, and so the Singapore experience and position adopted in this respect is readily applicable to the AICC. A matter which does, however, require particular attention from an Australian perspective is the question of accession to the Choice of Court Convention. As momentum develops internationally in this respect, national accessions to this Convention will become more and more important if countries are to be connected to the international commercial litigation network.

[D] The Australian Consumer Law

One common argument against an AICC is that international parties would be deterred from electing such a court because they do not wish to be subject to the Australian Consumer Law. Specifically, its regulation of unconscionable conduct has been considered by some commercial litigators to be subjective and unpredictable, working

84. *See*, e.g., Thomas, *supra* n. 29, at [37]–[39].

against the ideal of a neutral dispute resolution forum.[85] Whenever one of the disputing parties has a substantive nexus with Australia, it is most likely the unconscionability provisions apply. The legislation establishing the AICC could allow the parties the option of agreeing to the application of, for example, English law (as readily occurs in contracts). Given the substantial similarities between Australian and English law, the application of such law by Australian sitting and retired judges should be seamless.

There is a longstanding history of English law governing international trade, which would give the AICC the advantage of a familiar element to make it more palatable to the global market. This also promotes international consistency by complementing the London Commercial Court's strict application of English law and the DIFC Court and ADGM Courts' systems, both based on English law. Alternatively, parties might elect New York law, which is frequently used in international commercial transactions. This approach enables parties to experience the benefits of the AICC. There will be legislative policies to be refined in the finalisation of the AICC framework.

§2.06 IMPACT OF COVID-19

The recent global pandemic caused by the COVID-19 outbreak provides pressing incentive to advance the establishment of the AICC. First, because it will lead to a substantial amount of work for such a court. Second, because it minimises the obstacle of Australia's physical distance from the rest of the world.

The virus is likely to generate extensive and significant transborder litigation, not just arbitration or mediation.[86] Many companies previously involved in international commercial agreements will find themselves insolvent as a result of collapsed supply chains, loss of consumer demand and disruptions to shipping and distribution. Their business partners may sue to recover losses. We can also expect to see manufacturers sued over missed deadlines and extensive litigation over force majeure clauses, with parties seeking to be freed from their contractual obligations on the basis the virus is an 'act of God'.

Another area which may lend itself to transnational litigation is insurance contracts. Typically, businesses have been insured for physical disruptions, such as factories burning down, but may not have contemplated forced closures to stop the spread of a virus. Lastly, the rapid global shift towards digital and remote working and learning functionalities has sparked a swift uptake of AI, software and technology. These contracts typically cross sovereign borders and raise concerns around privacy and international data transfer and storage. All of these developments would be suitable cases for the AICC to hear and provide a substantial amount of work for the court in its early years.

---

85. *See*, from the current President of the New South Wales Court of Appeal, Andrew S. Bell, *An Australian International Commercial Court – Not a Bad Idea or What a Bad Idea?* 94 Austl. L.J. 24, 38 (2020).
86. *See further generally* Nottage & Jetin, Chapter 1 and other chapters discussing the impact of COVID-19 on international dispute resolution, in this volume.

Another element of the coronavirus pandemic which supports the development of the AICC is that it has forced the commercial world to shift to digital, remote working models. Previously, Australia's distance from the rest of the world deterred international parties from choosing it as a dispute resolution hub. This is especially the case for parties located in Europe and America. However, from early 2020 due to the pandemic, most major corporations were operating almost entirely via distance, with most staff working from home. This experience of relying on online databases, cloud hosting services and teleconferencing has proven to commercial parties the effectiveness of these resources. This should make them more receptive to e-dispute resolution fora, electronic filing and the use of videoconferencing during dispute resolution.

Furthermore, Australian Courts are gaining valuable experience with these technologies. At present, in the Commercial Court, the Common Law Division and also the Court of Appeal of the Supreme Court of Victoria matters are being conducted via Zoom and other web platforms. Increased willingness to utilise these technologies, particularly in light of the experience gained from doing so in the pandemic shutdown, means parties would not necessarily need to travel to Australia to use the AICC. This saves parties time and money and can be expected to encourage uptake of the court.

§2.07 CONCLUSION

When the significant trade and investment agreements concluded or being negotiated by Australia are considered with respect to Asia (especially China / Hong Kong, Japan, Korea, India and ASEAN[87]) and the Pacific, the opportunities offered by an Australian international court are almost boundless. Indeed, there is a symmetry in the establishment of an Australian court which would complement the trade agreements.

The proposal for an international commercial court for Australia cannot be left to the courts themselves or the legal profession to develop and agitate. The experiences of Singapore, Dubai, Abu Dhabi, and indeed London, demonstrate that it is vital for there to be government interest and support for such a proposal.

It is also important to be reminded that a proposal for an Australian court occurs within an international context. We have already cited the international trade agreements. Recently, an important legal institute was established in the Asian region in which Australia is an active participant. The Asian Business Law Institute (ABLI) was launched on 21 February 2016 in conjunction with the International Conference on *Doing Business Across Asia – Legal Convergence in an Asian Century*. The purpose or 'mission' of ABLI is to:[88]

> Undertake and facilitate research into transnational business law possibility for the region, publish in the area of Asian business laws, provide guidance in the field of Asian legal development and to promote the convergence of Asian business laws. The specific 'mission' statement of ABLI states that it is to:

87. *See further*, the chapters respectively by Ali, Claxton/Nottage/Teramura, Claxton/Nottage/Williams, Singh, and Venugopal, in this volume.
88. ABLI, *About Us: Asian Business Law Institute*, http://abli.asia/ABOUT-US/Introduction (accessed 28 Apr. 2020).

- Evaluate and stimulate the development of Asian law, legal policy, and practice and in particular make proposals for the further convergence of business law among Asian countries and regions;
- Study Asian approaches regarding business laws and practice in drafting legal instruments, restatement law or model rules;
- Conduct and facilitate Pan-Asian research, in particular to draft, evaluate or improve principles and rules which are common to Asian legal systems; and
- Provide a forum, for discussion and cooperation, between the business community and the legal fraternity including, inter alia judges, lawyers, academics and other legal professionals, who take an active interest in business law development.

ABLI has a board of governors. The Australian representatives on the board are former Chief Justice French and the Honourable Kevin Lindgren (formerly on the Federal Court of Australia).

In his keynote address to launch ABLI, the Singaporean Chief Justice Sundaresh Menon said:

> Business today is conducted in an environment that is dramatically different from what we have, until recently, been accustomed to. Once upon a time, the market place referred to riotous fairs and bazaars in which merchants gathered to barter and trade. Today, we think of the market place as a metaphysical global interface for the exchange of goods and services, unbounded by both in its reach and its potential.

Indeed, there is considerable international interest in sharing information or, in the words of former Chief Justice French, engaging in 'convergence'. For example, in 2016 the Supreme Court of Victoria received an invitation for the Commercial Court to join an international forum or college of commercial courts across the world. In his invitation, former Lord Chief Justice Thomas wrote:

> Such a forum might allow the commercial court judiciary worldwide to share experiences and hold discussions on subjects of mutual interest. It could promote the possibility of common practices. It could even consider developing common or at least converging rules and procedures.

Needless to say, the court accepted the invitation, as did the Supreme Court of New South Wales, the Federal Court of Australia and the High Court of New Zealand. The Standing International Forum of Commercial Courts was thus founded and today extends in its membership to courts more than thirty-five jurisdictions across the Asia-Pacific region, Europe, Africa, the Gulf States and the Americas. Annual meetings commenced in 2017, at which all Australian Courts involved have been represented. The Standing Committee recently achieved one of its founding objectives: a Multilateral Memorandum on Enforcement of Commercial Judgments for Money.[89] The Memorandum sets out an understanding of the procedures for the enforcement of a

89. Standing International Forum of Commercial Courts, *Multilateral Memorandum on Enforcement of Commercial Judgments for Money* (June 2019), https://www.judiciary.uk/wp-content/uploads/2019/06/Multilateral-Memorandum-on-Enforcement.pdf (accessed 28 Apr. 2020).

judgment by the courts of one jurisdiction obtained in the courts of another jurisdiction, with each section contributed by the judiciary of the jurisdiction concerned.

A stronger contribution can be made to the rule of law by courts working together than if they are working separately. The early twenty-first century is being defined by something of a return to internationalisation and globalisation, although the form and forms that will take remain to be seen. It is for us to shape those forms in the capacity we can and to make contributions towards global stability, harmonisation and due recognition of the law in the context of commercial enterprise. These common purposes, as well as quality of justice and the manner of its administration provided at commercial courts and arbitral tribunals, international and domestic, should be promoted and indeed marketed.

CHAPTER 3

New Frontiers for International Commercial Arbitration in Australia: Beyond the 'Lucky Country'

Albert Monichino & Nobumichi Teramura[*]

Australia is not a lucky country in the context of international commercial arbitration (ICA) due to its geographical isolation. However, the problem of remoteness has luckily been ameliorated since the COVID-19 pandemic, thanks to the dramatic spread of videoconferencing technologies in arbitrations and even in some court proceedings. 'Luck' can no longer excuse Australia for running behind other regional competitors. Analysing recent cases in Australian judiciary, this chapter puts forward seven proposals for legislative reform that may be useful for Australia to attract more ICA cases on its shores: establishing an indemnity costs principle for failed challenges in ICA matters, notably regarding arbitral awards; enabling Australian courts to issue subpoenas to support foreign arbitrations; clarifying choice of law rules on the existence and scope of arbitration agreements; limiting or excluding the application of Australian Consumer Law (ACL) to cross-border business-to-business transactions; defining 'Australian Law'; provisions to catch up with recent arbitration innovations; clarifying arbitrability of trust disputes; and centralising judicial power for ICA appeals. Implementing those proposals will pave the way for Australia to become an attractive arbitration hub in the Asia-Pacific region.

§3.01 INTRODUCTION

In the mid-twentieth century, Donald Horne famously described Australia as a 'lucky' country to express the irony that the country was able to accumulate power and wealth

* The authors are grateful to Professor Luke Nottage for valuable comments and input that significantly improved earlier versions of the manuscript. Responsibility for any remaining errors is solely our own.

without relying on its own efforts, thanks to natural resources and distance from problems elsewhere in the world.[1] Unfortunately, however, Australia is not so lucky in the context of ICA. It has been struggling to attract arbitration cases to its shores despite substantial perseverance by leading Australian arbitrators, arbitration practitioners, judges, academics and various organisations.[2] The tyranny of distance has impeded its efforts to become an attractive arbitration hub, in contrast with regional competitors in the Asia-Pacific region.[3] Horne's book was a wake-up call to an unimaginative nation, mired in mediocrity. The message of the book still resonates today. Wisdom and discernment are needed to survive, let alone prosper, in this age of pandemic and uncertainty. A 'she'll be right' optimism will not suffice. Rather, objectivity and creativity are required for Australia to create its own luck in the field of international arbitration.[4]

Since around 2010, Australia has renewed its efforts to attract more ICA filings, while ICA has grown exponentially in the Asia-Pacific region. First, Australia has established a harmonised legal framework for both domestic arbitration and ICA in line with international standards.[5] The International Arbitration Act 1974 (Cth) (IAA) – a federal statute regulating ICA – gives the force of law to the UNCITRAL Model Law on ICA (UNCITRAL Model Law),[6] including most of its 2006 revisions.[7] The IAA also implements the 1958 New York Convention on the Recognition and Enforcement of Foreign Arbitral Awards (NYC).[8] Second, the Australian judiciary has become more consistently internationalist and pro-arbitration.[9] Leading (current and former) judges have been actively promoting Australian developments in ICA both domestically and worldwide through various mediums.[10] Third, Australia has succeeded in producing a critical mass of prominent arbitrators and arbitration practitioners. In fact, a relatively

1. Donald Horne, *The Lucky Country* (Penguin Books 2008 (First Published in 1964 from Angus & Robertson)).
2. Nobumichi Teramura, et al., *Judicial Control of Arbitral Awards in Australia*, in *The Cambridge Handbook of Judicial Control of Arbitral Awards* 173 (Larry A. DiMatteo, et al. eds., Cambridge University Press 2020); Luke Nottage, *International Commercial and Investor-State Arbitration: Australia and Japan in Regional and Global Contexts* (Elgar, forthcoming, early 2021).
3. Luke Nottage & Nobumichi Teramura, *Australia's (In)Capacity in International Commercial Arbitration*, Kluwer Arbitration Blog (20 Sep. 2018), http://arbitrationblog.kluwerarbitration.com/2018/09/20/australias-incapacity-international-commercialarbitration/.
4. Steve Harris, *A Failure to Create Our Own Luck Results in New Tyranny*, The Australian (1 Nov. 2019), https://www.theaustralian.com.au/inquirer/a-failure-to-create-our-own-luck-results-in-new-tyranny/news-story/e64d2527ddf2c947ec75137c8313c80b.
5. Albert Monichino & Luke Nottage, *Australia Country Update*, 20 Asian Disp. Rev. 131 (2018).
6. *See* s. 16 of the IAA.
7. Other than allowing interim relief to be sought on an ex parte basis.
8. Monichino & Nottage, *supra* n. 5, 132.
9. The Federal Court of Australia and the superior courts of the six States and two Territories exercise concurrent jurisdiction in ICA matters, while the superior courts of the six States and two Territories exercise jurisdiction in respect of domestic arbitration regulated by a suite of uniform Acts based on the Model Law.
10. *See* e.g., Chief Justice James Allsop, *The Role of Law in International Commercial Arbitration*, Chartered Institute of Arbitrators Inaugural Annual Lecture (15 Oct. 2018), https://www.fedcourt.gov.au/digital-law-library/judges-speeches/chief-justice-allsop/allsop-cj-20181015; James Allsop, *Commercial and Investor-State Arbitration: The Importance of Recognising their Difference*, ICCA Congress Speech (16 Apr. 2018), www.fedcourt.gov.au/__data/assets/pdf_file/0003/49413/16_April_2018.pdf ;James Allsop & Clyde Croft, *The Role of Courts in Australia's*

large number of Australian arbitrators are appointed every year to handle arbitration cases administered, for example, by the International Chamber of Commerce (ICC), a premier arbitration institution in the world.[11] Fourth, the government has become more active in promoting Australia as an arbitration hub.[12] For instance, in the last few years, it has supported several large ICA-related international events, including the International Council for Commercial Arbitration (ICCA) Congress 2018[13] and the Biennial Conference of the International Law Association 2018.[14] Fifth, Australia has a sophisticated arbitration institution – the Australian Centre for International Commercial Arbitration (ACICA) – which offers credible and competitive dispute resolution services and facilities in the country's major cities. Under ACICA sits the Australian Maritime and Transport Arbitration Commission (AMTAC) and the Perth Centre for Energy and Resources Arbitration (PCERA). In addition, a grid of hearing centres has been established across the country: the Australian Disputes Centre (ADC) in Sydney, the Melbourne Commercial Arbitration and Mediation Centre (MCAMC) in Melbourne, and the David Malcolm Justice Centre in Perth.

Notwithstanding these concerted efforts by the Australian government, judiciary and legal profession, there has been no discernible increase in the number of Australia-seated ICA cases.[15] ACICA struggles to compete with its counterparts in Hong Kong and Singapore.[16] Only a handful of ICA cases administered by other institutions

---

Arbitration Regime, Commercial CPD Seminar Series (11 Nov. 2015), https://www.fedcourt.gov.au/digital-law-library/judges-speeches/chief-justice-allsop/allsop-cj-20151111.

11. For example, ICC statistics demonstrate that thirty-nine Australian arbitrators were confirmed or appointed for ICC arbitrations in 2017, which means that Australian arbitrators comprise 2.6% of total ICC appointments despite the fact that the population of the country is around 25 million and so much smaller than that of other major arbitration players – the United Kingdom, France, the United States of America and Germany. It should also be noted that those major players are also geographically much closer to the ICC headquarters in Paris. *See* Julien Fouret & Samaa Haridi, *2017 ICC Dispute Resolution Statistics*, ICC Disp. Res. Bull. 51 (2018).
12. *See* e.g., Nottage & Teramura, *supra* n. 3.
13. https://www.arbitration-icca.org/conferences-and-congresses/ICCA_2018_Congress_Sydney.html.
14. https://www.ila-hq.org/index.php/component/easyblog/2016-ila-conference-77th-johannesburg-south-africa?Itemid=347.
15. Admittedly, a number of arbitrations seated in Australia are ad hoc and thus 'fly under the radar', although some surface in related court proceedings (as mentioned below). However, this is also true of other jurisdictions regionally, with leading venues additionally recording much higher numbers of institutionally administered ICA cases.
16. Although ACICA does not publicise statistics on its arbitration case filings, unusually among regional competitors, ACICA reportedly averaged eight filings per annum between the 2010 amendments and May 2015 (compared to 1-3 ICA filings annually over the 1990s): *see* Luke Nottage & James Morrison, *Accessing and Assessing Australia's International Arbitration Act*, 34 J. Int'l Arb. 1 (2017). Compare generally Anselmo Reyes & Weixia Gu, *Conclusion: An Asia Pacific Model of Arbitration Reform*, in *The Developing World of Arbitration: A Comparative Study of Arbitration Reform in the Asia Pacific* 279-300 (Anselmo Reyes & Weixia Gu eds., Hart Publishing 2018); Anselmo Reyes & Weixia Gu, *Introduction: Towards a Model of Arbitration Reform in the Asia Pacific*, in *The Developing World of Arbitration: A Comparative Study of Arbitration Reform in the Asia Pacific* 1-16 (Anselmo Reyes & Weixia Gu eds., Hart Publishing 2018).

are seated in Australia each year.[17] The country, therefore, still has a long way to go to become a popular arbitration hub for ICA cases.

Why then is Australia failing to attract more ICA cases? One common explanation is geographical bad luck. That is, Australia is an isolated country distant from parts of the world where arbitrating parties come from or where most arbitration cases take place,[18] such as Hong Kong, Singapore, Tokyo, Shanghai, Paris, Geneva, New York and London. The persistent paucity of ICA cases seated in Australia might simply be attributed to what Geoffrey Blainey dubbed the 'tyranny of distance'.[19] Yet, this perennial disadvantage does not necessarily pose an insurmountable challenge for Australia to become a prominent arbitration centre. For example, Australia could and should develop its capacity to facilitate e-arbitrations (i.e., arbitrations utilising virtual hearings).[20] In fact, the necessity or at least potential of e-arbitrations has attracted renewed attention among the global arbitration community from early 2020, after the spread of coronavirus (COVID-19) from China around the region and then further afield.[21] Australia has already undertaken efforts in this regard,[22] although it is early days. It could also market itself a seat for resources-based arbitrations.[23]

There are other causes that inhibit the growth of Australia's ICA caseload. This chapter aims at identifying some of these causes by analysing recent developments in Australia's arbitration law and practice. Specifically, §3.02 will examine a selection of recent ICA court cases related to IAA, especially since 2016. Based on this, §3.03 will put forward several options for further developing Australian arbitration law in the context of ICA (bearing in mind that a country's legal infrastructure is an important factor in determining its attractiveness as a seat for arbitration).[24] Section 3.04 will conclude that some legal adventurism is necessary for Australia to become a viable arbitration hub.

---

17. For example, only three ICC cases were seated in Australia in 2018. *See* ICC, *2018 ICC Dispute Resolution Statistics*, ICC Disp. Res. Bull. 12 (2019).
18. Clyde Croft, *Recent Developments in Arbitration: At Home and Abroad*, Speech, Arbitration Special Interest Group, Resolution Institute, Melbourne (16 Oct. 2017), https://www.supremecourt.vic.gov.au/sites/default/files/assets/2017/10/ec/f671a35d4/Recentdevelopmentsinarbitrationathomeandabroad.pdf. *See also* Nobumichi Teramura, et al., *International Commercial Arbitration in Australia: Judicial Control over Arbitral Awards*, Sydney Law School Research Paper No. 19/24; U. of Adelaide Law Research Paper No. 2019-72 (10 Apr. 2019), https://ssrn.com/abstract=3379494.
19. Blainey Geoffrey, *The Tyranny of Distance: How Distance Shaped Australia's History* (Macmillan 1966).
20. Nottage and Teramura *supra* n. 3.
21. John A. Trenor & Hyun-Soo Lim, *Revisiting Force Majeure and Dispute Resolution Clauses in Light of the Recent Outbreak of the Coronavirus*, WilmerHale (27 Feb. 2020), https://www.wilmerhale.com/-/media/ad0a9c50aa1d4e2ea3bd63cf109f54e2.pdf?la=en&hash=5E9FE1BA9CDACD97351B8685D83848809D66ED6D.
22. ACICA is active in developing online arbitration platforms and holding webinars. *See* e.g., https://acica.org.au/use-online-dispute-resolution-technologies/; https://acica.org.au/acica-webinars (respectively).
23. Perth Centre for Energy and Resources Arbitration, https://pcera.org/.
24. Queen Mary University of London & White & Case, *2018 International Arbitration Survey: The Evolution of International Arbitration* (2018).

§3.02 IAA-RELATED DEVELOPMENTS IN AUSTRALIAN COURTS SINCE 2016

Over the past ten years, there has been a shift in the attitude of Australian courts towards greater judicial support and less judicial intervention in the arbitration process.[25] As noted by two prominent Australian judges, 'Australian courts are moving to a significantly more positive, pro-arbitration, position',[26] adapting a more consistently internationalist approach to the Model Law and NYC.[27] A snapshot of the number of published arbitration judgments provides some instruction concerning ICA cases related to Australia.

Table 3.1 Domestic and International Commercial Arbitration Judgments in Australia (2010-2018)

Type of Matter	*2010/ 2011*[28]	*2011/ 2012*[29]	*2012/ 2013*[30]	*2013/ 2014*[31]	*2014/ 2015*[32]	*2015/ 2016*[33]	*2016/ 2017*[34]	*2017/ 2018*[35]
International	14	10	6	10	17	17	11	18
Domestic - new CAA	3	5	9	6	17	10	13	15
Domestic - old CAA	18	21	11	12	6	2	2	3
Total:	35	36	26	28	40	29	26	36

25. *See* e.g., Leon Trakman, *The Reform of Commercial Arbitration in Australia: Recent and Prospective Developments*, in *The Developing World of Arbitration: A Comparative Study of Arbitration Reform in the Asia Pacific* 251-78 (Anselmo Reyes & Weixia Gu eds., Hart Publishing 2018).
26. James Allsop & Clyde Croft, *Judicial Support of Arbitration*, A Paper Presented at the APRAG Tenth Anniversary Conference, Melbourne (28 Mar. 2014), http://www.austlii.edu.au/au/journals/FedJSchol/2014/5.html.
27. *See* Dean Lewis, *The Interpretation and Uniformity of the UNCITRAL Model Law on International Commercial Arbitration: Focusing on Australia, Hong Kong and Singapore* (Wolters Kluwer 2016).
28. *See* Albert Monichino, *International Arbitration in Australia: 2010/2011 in Review*, 22 Australasian Disp. Res. J. 215 (2011).
29. *See* Albert Monichino & Alex Fawke, *International Arbitration in Australia: 2011/2012 in Review*, 23 Australasian Disp. Res. J. 234 (2012).
30. *See* Albert Monichino & Alex Fawke, *International Arbitration in Australia: 2012/2013 in Review*, 24 Australasian Disp. Res. J. 208 (2013).
31. *See* Albert Monichino & Alex Fawke, *International Arbitration in Australia: 2013/2014 in Review*, 25 Australasian Disp. Res. J. 187 (2014).
32. *See* Albert Monichino & Alex Fawke, *International Arbitration in Australia: 2014/2015 in Review*, 26 Australasian Disp. Res. J. 192 (2015).
33. *See* Albert Monichino & Alex Fawke, *International Arbitration in Australia: 2015/2016 in Review*, 27 Australasian Disp. Res. J. 211 (2016).
34. *See* Albert Monichino & Alex Fawke, *International Arbitration in Australia: 2016/2017 in Review*, 25 Australasian Disp. Res. J. 215 (2018).
35. *See* Albert Monichino & Alex Fawke, *International Arbitration in Australia: 2017/2018 in Review*, 29 Australasian Disp. Res. J. 215 (2019).

The table indicates some step-up in annual judgments since the 2010 amendments to the IAA, but this is quite small and erratic. Domestic arbitration judgments under the old Commercial Arbitration Acts (CAAs) (based on the 1979 English Arbitration Act) have diminished as judgments have grown under the new CAAs enacted gradually around the country since 2010. The latter enactments for domestic arbitrations are based on the UNCITRAL Model Law, as is the IAA for ICA cases, although they add some additional features (like the possibility of opting-in to appeals to courts for serious errors of law by arbitral tribunals).

During this time, the High Court of Australia has decided three arbitration-related cases. First, in *Westport Insurance Corporation v. Gordian Runoff Limited,*[36] the court had occasion to consider the required standard of reasons under the old Uniform Act. Secondly, in *TCL v. Castel,*[37] the High Court rejected a challenge to the constitutional validity of Articles 35 and 36 of Model Law (as given the force of law by section 16 of the IAA) on the basis that those Articles impermissibly purport to confer the judicial power of the Commonwealth on arbitral tribunals, as opposed to a court specified in Chapter III of the Constitution. Thirdly, and most recently, in *Rinehart v. Hancock Prospecting Pty Ltd.*,[38] the High Court considered the proper approach to the interpretation of arbitration agreements, as well as the ability of third parties (i.e., non-signatories to the arbitration agreement) to 'claim through or under' a party to an arbitration agreement, and thus take advantage of an arbitration agreement.[39] Taken together, the recent Australian jurisprudence illustrates a new enlightened judicial approach to arbitration in Australia. It might be compared to the old judicial approach to arbitration, which has been described extra-curially by a current member of the High Court as 'two steps forward, one step back'.[40]

To identify the necessity of further reforms based on updated information and new developments, nationally and internationally, the remainder of this section reviews a selection of recent judgments referring to the IAA in relation to ICAs seated in and outside Australia after 2016. This section focuses on cases with Asia-Pacific connections and identifies some pressure points that the subsequent section will build on in proposing further useful legislative reforms for Australia.

[A] *Sino Dragon Trading Ltd. v. Noble Resources International Pte Ltd.*

Sino Dragon (Hong Kong), as a purchaser, and Noble Resources (Singapore), as a seller, entered into a contract for the sale of 170,000 dry metric tons of iron ore. The contract contained an arbitration clause requiring the parties to resolve their differences by arbitration in Australia under UNCITRAL Arbitration Rules. The ad hoc

36. [2011] HCA 37.
37. *TCL Air Conditioner (Zhongshan) Co. Ltd. v. The Judges of the Federal Court of Australia* [2013] HCA 5.
38. [2019] HCA 13.
39. Vicky Priskich, *Binding Non-Signatories to Arbitration Agreements: Who Are Persons 'Claiming Through or under' a Party?*, 35 Arb. Int'l 375 (2019).
40. Patrick A. Keane, *The Prospects for International Arbitration in Australia: Meeting the Challenge of Regional Forum Competition or Our House, Our Rules*, 79 Arb. 195 (2013).

arbitration was held at the ADC in Sydney, and the three-member tribunal decided in favour of Noble Resources after Sino Dragon's failed attempt to challenge the arbitrators (on the grounds of perceived bias) in the Federal Court of Australia.[41]

Sino Dragon later applied to set aside the final award, invoking Article 34 of the Model Law (given effect to by section 16 of the IAA).[42] The grounds for Sino Dragon's challenge were threefold: (1) the tribunal's excess of jurisdiction by hearing matters not contemplated by the arbitration agreement (Article 34(2)(a)(iii)); (2) lack of procedural fairness and the tribunal's violation of other procedural rights by conducting witness examination with ill-equipped videoconferencing and interpreting facilities (Articles 34(2)(a)(ii), 34(2)(a)(iv) and 34(2)(b)(ii)); and (3) the appointment of arbitrators was not in accordance with the agreement of the parties and violated procedural public policy (Articles 34(2)(a)(iv) and 34(2)(b)(ii)).[43] None of these challenges to the award was accepted by the Federal Court.[44]

Noble Resources sought indemnity costs in respect of the failed application to challenge (and remove) the arbitrators and, separately, to set aside the final award. In respect of the first application for indemnity costs, Edelman J doubted the legitimacy of a default indemnity costs rule in arbitration-related court proceedings.[45] In respect of the second application for indemnity costs, Beach J went further and gave detailed reasons why there should not be a default indemnity costs rule – in particular:[46]

(1) The Model Law is silent on the question of costs.
(2) The Model Law leaves it to the law of the forum to determine how costs are to be decided.
(3) An award of costs is a question of public policy of the forum and is not an international issue.
(4) England and Hong Kong have adopted different approaches to the question of indemnity costs. This is explicable by the fact that each country is applying its own public policy.
(5) Whether Australia requires a default indemnity costs rule depends on Australia's public policy.
(6) While 102 jurisdictions in 72 States have adopted the Model Law, there is no uniform approach to costs in these jurisdictions. Adopting a default indemnity costs rule is not necessary for the purposes of adopting a uniform approach to the interpretation of the Model Law.
(7) It is not necessary, nor is it justified, for Australian law to embrace a new costs rule in arbitration-related court proceedings which carries a reverse onus, for the following reasons:

41. *Sino Dragon Trading Ltd v. Noble Resources International Pte Ltd* [2015] FCA 1028.
42. *Sino Dragon Trading Ltd v. Noble Resources International Pte Ltd* [2016] FCA 1131.
43. [2016] FCA 1131, at [6]. On the question of which perspective should be used to assess arbitrator neutrality, not clarified when the IAA adopted the 'real danger of bias' threshold in 2010, *see* Nottage & Jetin, Chapter 1 in this volume.
44. [2016] FCA 1131, at [7].
45. *Sino Dragon Trading Ltd v. Noble Resources International Pte Ltd* [2015] FCA 1046.
46. *Sino Dragon Trading Ltd v. Noble Resources International Pte Ltd (No 2)* [2016] FCA 1169.

(a) there is no legislative intention manifest on the face of the IAA to recognise any special category for an award of indemnity costs. In particular, there is nothing in section 27 of the IAA which supports the existence of a default indemnity costs rule in arbitration-related court proceedings;
(b) there is no special reason why Article 34 challenges should attract a special rule on costs as compared with other arbitration applications;
(c) the contention that challenges to arbitral awards are inconsistent with the contractual nature of arbitration breaks down at several levels: (i) Article 34 (setting aside) challenge does not involve a breach of the arbitration agreement. Rather, the parties should be taken to have objectively intended that either of them could pursue an Article 34 challenge that had reasonable prospects of success; (ii) a similar position applies to an Article 36 (resisting enforcement) challenge; and (iii) nor does a stay application warrant a special rule. It is no different than a breach of the covenant to sue. An award of costs should not be a proxy for damages. If damages are sought to be recovered, they should be recovered in a separate application;[47]
(d) sections 2D and 39(2) of the IAA do not justify any special cost rule with a reverse onus. However, they may require a different application of existing principles is applied to arbitration-related court proceedings (as discussed below);
(e) different considerations may apply as to whether the application involves a stay application, setting aside application, resisting of enforcement application, or some other arbitration-related challenge (e.g., removal of an arbitrator for bias). Creation of a special costs rule for only some of the contexts in which the court may be called on to award costs in arbitration-related matter lacks conceptual coherence; and
(f) it has not been demonstrated that the existing principles as to costs cannot accommodate special considerations relating to arbitration.

In short, Beach J advocated a nuanced approach to the award of costs of arbitration-related court proceedings; that is, applying the existing cost principles but in the context of the IAA which emphasises the finality of arbitration awards. In such situations, it should be easier for the successful party to establish that an unsuccessful court application should not have been brought (or resisted) and that, therefore, indemnity costs are appropriate. However, there should not be a default rule that the losing party should pay costs of the court proceedings and have an onus cast upon it to demonstrate that it should not pay costs.

47. Following Edelman J in *Sino Dragon*, but contrast Martin CJ in *KNM Process Systems* [2014] WASC 437.

In contrast, Allsop CJ is a strong supporter of a default indemnity costs rule in arbitration-related court matters. In *Ye v. Zeng (No 5)*,[48] he left the door open as to whether the Federal Court of Australia should adopt a default indemnity costs rule in arbitration-related court proceedings, as is the case in Hong Kong. His Honour remarked (at [23]):

> It is both unnecessary, and, sitting at first instance, inappropriate, to decide the obiter question whether the Hong Kong approach should be preferred and adopted in Australia. There can be seen to be powerful considerations to that effect. ... The parties have had their dispute resolved under contract by the tribunal of their choice. The NYC and the [IAA] have limited and constrained bases for resistance to paying an award sum that is the contractually provided outcome of a dispute. It is not merely a debt, it is the resolution of a dispute by a chosen contractual mechanism. Courts should be astute to distinguish between conduct that reflects no more than an attempt to delay or impede payment and the reasonable invocation of the proper protections built into the NYC and the [IAA].

Therefore, the Australian judiciary is still divided as to the necessity of a default indemnity costs rule in arbitration-related court matters in Australia. This point will be further explored in §3.03[A] below.

[B] *Re Samsung C&T Corporation*[49]

Samsung C&T Corporation (Samsung) requested the court's permission under section 23 of the IAA to issue subpoenas to produce documents in aid of a Singapore-seated ICA.[50] Samsung made two applications for document production. Gilmour J granted leave to issue subpoenas on the first application, but refused to grant leave to issue further subpoenas on the second application and, further, concluded that his earlier decision on the first application was 'clearly wrong'.[51]

IAA section 23 allows a party to apply to the Federal Court of Australia (and also a State Supreme Court) for leave to issue a subpoena in aid of an ICA, to require a person to attend a witness examination before the arbitral tribunal[52] and/or to produce to the arbitral tribunal the documents specified in the subpoena.[53] The court must not grant leave to issue a subpoena to a person who is not a party to the arbitration unless it considers it reasonable to do so.[54] Two issues arose in the *Samsung* case. First, whether the court had jurisdiction to issue a subpoena in aid of a foreign-seated arbitration. Second, and, if so, whether the court was satisfied that issuing the subpoenas was reasonable in the circumstances.[55]

48. [2016] FCA 850. This case post-dated Edelman J's decision but pre-dated Beach J's decision in *Sino Dragon*.
49. [2017] FCA 1169. The following case summary is based on Monichino & Fawke, *supra* n. 35.
50. [2017] FCA 1169, at [1].
51. [2017] FCA 1169, at [2].
52. IAA s. 23(3)(a).
53. IAA s. 23(3)(b).
54. IAA s. 23(5).
55. [2017] FCA 1169, at [11].

Adopting a narrow interpretation of section 23, the court held that it had no jurisdiction to grant leave to issue a subpoena in aid of a foreign-seated arbitration. In Gilmour J's view, section 23 was concerned with domestic arbitral proceedings undertaken in a State or Territory of Australia.[56] This conclusion was justified by the proper interpretation of section 23 in conjunction with section 22A. According to section 22A, a 'court' having the power to issue subpoenas is: in relation to arbitral proceedings that are, or are to be, conducted in a State, the Supreme Court of that State; in relation to arbitral proceedings that are, or are to be, conducted in a Territory, the Supreme Court of the Territory or, if there is no such court, the Supreme Court of the State or Territory that has jurisdiction in relation to that Territory; and, in any case, the Federal Court of Australia. Accordingly, Gilmour J emphasised that a State and Territory referred in section 22A meant a State or Territory of Australia.[57]

Second, in his Honour's view, the Model Law did not confer authority on Australian courts to issue subpoenas to support foreign arbitral proceedings. Gilmour J invoked Article 27 of the Model Law: 'The arbitral tribunal or a party with the approval of the arbitral tribunal may request from *a competent court of this State* assistance in taking evidence.'[58] Also, referring to the Explanatory Memorandum relating to the amendment of the IAA in 2010, Gilmour J pointed out that the Model Law was not intended generally to govern any arbitrations conducted outside a country adopting it.[59]

This judgment is persuasive in that the express wording of IAA sections 22A and 23 does not support the issuing of subpoenas in aid of foreign-seated arbitrations. By contrast, for instance, Model Law Article 17J provides that a court has the authority to issue an interim measure in relation to arbitration proceedings, 'irrespective of whether their place[60] is in [Australia]'; IAA section 23 does not contain such wording.[61] This judgment usefully highlights a shortcoming of the IAA which should be addressed by statutory reform so that Australia may demonstrate a pro-arbitration stance and improve its prospects for attracting more ICA. This point will be further discussed in §3.03[B] below.

[C] *Trina Solar (US) Inc. v. Jasmin Solar Pty Ltd.*[62]

Trina Solar (US) Inc (Trina), a US company, and Jasmin Solar Pty Ltd (Jasmin), an Australian company,[63] negotiated for the supply by Trina to Jasmin of solar panels. For

56. [2017] FCA 1169, at [14].
57. [2017] FCA 1169, at [13]ff.
58. [2017] FCA 1169, at [35] (emphasis added).
59. [2017] FCA 1169, at [47].
60. Properly interpreted, meaning the seat.
61. Monichino & Fawke, *supra* n. 35. Contrast *UDP Holdings Pty Ltd v. Esposito Holdings Pty Ltd* [2018] VSC 316 where Croft J granted an application made under s. 23 of the IAA for the issue of subpoenas for the cross-examination of two persons not party to the arbitration proceedings seated in Victoria.
62. [2017] FCAFC 6. *See also* Albert Monichino & Alex Fawke, *International Arbitration in Australia: 2016/2017 in Review*, 28 Australasian Disp. Res. J. 215, 215-18 (2018).
63. [2017] FCAFC 6, at [11].

tax reasons, the supply agreement named JRC Services LLC (JRC), a US company related to Jasmin, as the purchaser under the agreement.[64] The supply agreement provided for arbitration in New York under New York law.[65] The solar panels supplied by Trina were delivered late, were of the wrong model and did not comply with Australian regulations. JRC and Jasmin refused to pay the invoices issued by Trina.[66] Trina commenced an arbitration in New York against the two companies seeking compensation.[67] Jasmin challenged the jurisdiction of the arbitral tribunal, claiming that it was not bound by the arbitration agreement contained in the supply agreement.[68] The tribunal issued a preliminary ruling that it had jurisdiction to determine the claim brought against Jasmin, notwithstanding it was a non-signatory to the arbitration agreement contained in the supply agreement. The ruling was confirmed by a New York court following an application by Jasmin to challenge the ruling. Jasmin did not take any further part in the arbitration.[69]

Subsequently, Jasmin commenced legal proceedings against Trina before the Federal Court of Australia, seeking compensation for misleading or deceptive conduct in contravention of the ACL.[70] Jasmin sought leave to serve the originating process on Trina in the US.[71] Trina opposed the application contending that it was futile to grant leave to serve it out of the jurisdiction because it would then make an application under section 7 of the IAA to stay the proceeding on the grounds that the parties had agreed to arbitrate disputes of the kind that Jasmin sought to agitate before the court. In response, Jasmin contended that there was no arbitration agreement in existence between it and Trina. The question therefore arose, what system of law should be applied in determining whether there was an arbitration agreement in existence between the parties before the court – the law of the forum (i.e., Australian law) or the law of the putative arbitration agreement (i.e., New York law)?

Edelman J at first instance considered that the relevant system of law was the law of the forum. According to his Honour, it did not make sense to apply the law of the putative arbitration agreement in circumstances where the very existence of the arbitration agreement was in question. Applying the law of the forum, Edelman J found that Jasmin was not a party to the alleged arbitration agreement and proceeded to exercise his discretion to grant leave to Jasmin to serve Trina with court proceedings out of the jurisdiction.[72] Trina appealed.

The Full Federal Court dismissed the appeal. While all three judges of the court shared the view that the trial judge's exercise of discretion to grant leave to serve out of the jurisdiction did not miscarry, they disagreed on the proper law to determine the existence of any arbitration agreement between Trina and Jasmin.[73] The majority

64. [2017] FCAFC 6, at [12].
65. [2017] FCAFC 6, at [14]-[15].
66. [2017] FCAFC 6, at [11], [16].
67. [2017] FCAFC 6, at [16].
68. [2017] FCAFC 6, at [17].
69. [2017] FCAFC 6, at [17].
70. [2017] FCAFC 6, at [112].
71. [2017] FCAFC 6, at [113].
72. *Jasmin Solar Pty Ltd v. Trina Solar Australia Pty Ltd* [2015] FCA 1453.
73. [2017] FCAFC 6, at [4]ff, [97]ff.

(Beach and Dowsett JJ) took the position that different laws may apply to determine the existence and validity of an arbitration agreement. Invoking common law choice of law rules in Australia,[74] Beach J stated that questions relating to contract formation, including whether a party was a proper party to the arbitration agreement, were to be tested in accordance with the *lex fori*, while questions relating to the validity of the contract were to be examined in light of the putative proper law of the contract.[75] As for the consistency of choice of law rules in sections 7 and 8(5)(b) of the IAA, Beach J observed:

> The fact that s 8(5)(b)[76] provides for a choice of law different to the law of the forum in relation to whether an 'arbitration agreement' exists to which a party is bound, does not entail that the same choice of law needs to be made for s 7(2)[77] ... s 7(2) contains no provision requiring the creation of a legal fiction purportedly justified by some perceived consistency with s 8(5)(b). Notably, Trina ... has not cited any compelling international authority that supports its position.[78]

Dowsett J generally concurred with Beach J.[79]

In contrast, Greenwood J (in dissent) emphasised 'the structured integrated coherence' of the Model Law, NYC and IAA, which required that 'the question of whether a party to a stay application under section 7 of the IAA is a party to an arbitration agreement should be determined by the same choice of law rules selected in IAA section 8(5)(b) of the IAA (reflecting NYC Article V(1)(a)) – namely, the proper law of the putative arbitration agreement, or failing any indication thereon, the law of the seat'.[80]

Accordingly, Australian law is still divided as to the appropriate approach to be taken to selecting the law applicable to determine whether there is an arbitration agreement in existence between two named parties. How to deal with this issue is discussed below in §3.03[C].

§3.03 FUTURE IAA REFORMS TO ENHANCE AUSTRALIA AS A REGIONAL ICA HUB

The IAA was amended significantly in 2010 following the publication of a discussion paper by the Attorney General's Office and submissions made by various

74. For this purpose, Beach J cited *Oceanic Sun Line Special Shipping Co Inc v. Fay* [1988] HCA 32.
75. [2017] FCAFC 6, at [128]. Here, Beach J stated: 'I consider there to be a distinction between two types of scenarios: (a) the choice of law to determine whether there is a consensus ad idem between the parties; and (b) the choice of law to apply where one is dealing with the validity and interpretation of the contract, mode of performance and consequences of breach.'
76. In the context of enforcement of arbitral awards.
77. In the context of stay of proceedings in the face of an arbitration agreement.
78. [2017] FCAFC 6, at [182].
79. [2017] FCAFC 6, at [1].
80. Monichino & Fawke, *supra* n. 35, 217. *See also* [2017] FCAFC 6, at [82]ff.

stakeholders.[81] Since then, several further minor amendments have been made to the IAA, usually in omnibus Bills and therefore 'flying under the radar',[82] most notably by:

- amending the confidentiality provisions such that an ICA seated in Australia is confidential unless the parties expressly opt-out;
- removal of any reciprocity requirement regarding Australia's adoption of the NYC;
- clarification that the persons bound by a foreign award are the parties to the award, rather than the parties to the arbitration agreement;[83] and
- modernisation of the language on arbitrators' power to award costs by removing the archaic reference to 'taxation' of costs.

There are further substantive amendments that could be made to improve the arbitration law in Australia. International dispute resolution is a fast-moving area of practice, and Australia cannot afford to stand still, especially as it is still coming from behind compared to popular ICA seats in the region. Some desired amendments are discussed below.

[A] Indemnity Costs for Failed Challenges to Arbitral Awards

One reform option for Australia is to introduce a default cost rule in respect of arbitration-related court proceedings, such that award debtors who unsuccessfully apply to set aside (or unsuccessfully resist enforcement of) an award, or parties who unsuccessfully apply for a stay of court proceedings in the face of an arbitration agreement, should (absent good cause) be required to pay costs of the court proceedings on an indemnity basis.[84] As mentioned in §3.02[A] above, the Australian judiciary is still divided on this issue. The history of the division is not so short, as introduced below.

In *Altain Khuder LLC v. IMC Mining Inc & Anor (No 2)*[85] *('Altain Khuder')* Croft J awarded indemnity costs against an award debtor who successfully sought to resist enforcement of a foreign award. His Honour's decision enforcing the foreign award was reversed on appeal.[86] While it was not necessary for the Victorian Court of Appeal to do so, it disagreed with Croft J on the indemnity cost issue. Emphasising Croft J's

81. *See* generally Luke Nottage & Richard Garnett eds., *International Arbitration in Australia* (Federation Press 2010).
82. Monichino & Nottage, *supra* n. 5, 133.
83. This addresses the difficulty which led to the Victorian Court of Appeal refusing to enforce a foreign award in *IMC Aviation Solutions Pty Ltd v. Altain Khuder LLC* (2011) 38 VR 303; [2011] VSCA 248.
84. Albert Monichino, *When High Risk Strategies are 'Worth a Go'*, The ACICA Rev. 23, 23-6 (June 2013).
85. [2011] VSC 12.
86. *IMC Aviation Solutions Pty Ltd. v. Altain Khuder LLC* [2011] VSCA 248.

reliance on arbitration jurisprudence in Hong Kong,[87] the court of Appeal found that his Honour acted on a wrong principle in embracing the approach taken in Hong Kong.

However, in his public speech during Sydney Arbitration Week in 2014,[88] Allsop CJ argued that public policy considerations arise in the award of costs, that both the United Kingdom and Hong Kong jurisprudence recognises this, and that the approach of the Victorian Court of Appeal in *Altain Khuder* operates on the (mistaken) assumption that enforcement proceedings are substantially the same as other proceedings brought between Australian courts. His Honour stated:

> Commencing litigation to resist enforcement (if without foundation) may be viewed first and foremost as an abandonment of that contractual bargain. It may be said that there is a public policy interest in discouraging parties from abandoning promises by way of contract. Distinguishing it from other kinds of proceedings, the very act of commencing (unsuccessful) litigation to resist enforcement is itself an attempt to subvert a dispute resolution agreed upon by the parties, a repudiation of a contractual undertaking that causes further unnecessary damage to the innocent party.[89]

Since then, the decisions of Edelman and Beach JJ in *Sino Dragon* have rejected any default indemnity costs rule in relation to arbitration-related court proceedings. This is an important debate that is not closed. Both Singapore[90] and Hong Kong[91] have default indemnity costs rules that have been developed by the courts. Given the division of judicial opinion on the question, it is highly unlikely that Australia will follow suit with its Asia-Pacific neighbours in the absence of legislative amendment.[92] Whether there should be a default indemnity costs rule is a question of Australian public policy, which ultimately is a question for the Australian legislature. Such a rule would sit comfortably with the objects of the IAA. The authors, as well as other commentators, support the introduction of such a rule by statute.[93]

87. *See*, e.g., *A v. R* [2009] HKCFI 342. The Hong Kong Court of Appeal confirmed this approach in *Gao Haiyan v. Keeneye Holdings Ltd (No 2)* [2012] HKCA 43, and also in *Pacific China Holdings Ltd (in liq) v. Grand Pacific Holdings Ltd CACV* [2012] HKCA 200.
88. James Allsop, *The Enforcement of International Arbitration Awards and Public Policy*, Speech Delivered at AMTAC and Holding Redlich Seminar, 30-40 (10 Nov. 2014); Malcolm Holmes, *Open Policy in the New York Convention and the Model Law*, Speech Delivered at AMTAC and Holding Redlich Seminar, 14-23 (10 Nov. 2014).
89. Allsop, *supra* n. 88, 38-9 [74].
90. *Tjong Very Sumito v. Antig Investments Pte Ltd* [2009] 4 SLR(R) 732; *Quarella SpA v. Scelta Marble Australia Pty Ltd* [2012] SGHC 166.
91. *Gao Haiyan v. Keeneye Holdings* [2012] 1 HKC 491.
92. In *John Holland Pty Ltd v. Kellogg Brown & Root Pty Ltd* [No 2] [2015] NSWSC 564 (15 May 2015) [38], Hammerschlag J noted that, in the context of an arbitration under the *Commercial Arbitration Act 2010* (NSW), one of the reasons for not following the Hong Kong approach is the fact that 'the Legislature could have, but did not, create or recognise any such categories for an award of indemnity costs in the Act.'
93. Diana Hu & Luke Nottage, *The International Arbitration Act Matters: Where to Litigate and Why (Not)*, The Arbitrator & Mediator 91 (December 2016) (suggesting that legislating an indemnity costs principle is the best way forward, since case law already varied across Australia, in order to streamline arbitration-related court challenges); Teramura, et al., *supra* n. 2; Nottage & Jetin, Chapter 1 in this volume.

[B] Subpoenas for Supporting Foreign Arbitration

Another desirable reform for the IAA concerns the question of whether Australian courts should be able to issue subpoenas to assist the taking of evidence in foreign arbitral proceedings.[94] Australian courts currently have the power to grant interim measures in aid of foreign-seated arbitrations. It is a short step to also give them the power to issue subpoenas to produce documents and to give evidence in aid of foreign-seated arbitrations. As mentioned above in §3.02[B], neither the IAA nor the Model Law delegate clearly to the Australian courts such authority. Born suggests that such territorial limitation imposed under Article 27 of the Model Law is 'ill-considered; it contrasts with the treatment of court-ordered provisional measures [under revised Model Law Article 17] and unduly restricts judicial support for the international arbitral process',[95] although that is the result of a legislative compromise during the negotiation of drafting Article 27.[96] Accordingly, the Federal Court's refusal to issue subpoenas in *Re Samsung C&T Corporation*[97] is not something that attracts global criticism. It is rather along the lines of the international arbitration trend in which State courts in the most of major arbitration hubs have never issued such subpoenas, except some in the US.[98]

Absent any legislative amendment, under Australian law, the only plausible means for the parties participating in arbitrations abroad to obtain evidence located in Australia is, as Gilmour J rightly pointed out, to rely on the Hague Evidence Convention.[99] However, the cross-border evidence-taking scheme offered by the Convention may slow the arbitral proceedings[100] and has been criticised even in the context of international litigation for its lack of expediency and other reasons.[101] Moreover, there

94. *See* WA Arbitration Initiative, *2019 Arbitration Report*, https://static1.squarespace.com/static/59427471d2b857e78324f18f/t/5cc91aa6ee6eb061011dafb8/1556683450381/WA+Arbitration+Report+2019.pdf.
95. Gary Born, *International Commercial Arbitration* 2397 (Wolters Kluwer 2nd ed. 2014).
96. Howard M. Holtzmann & Joseph E. Neuhaus, *A Guide to the UNCITRAL Model Law on International Commercial Arbitration: Legislative History and Commentary* 737-8 (Wolters Kluwer 1989).
97. [2017] FCA 1169.
98. *See* generally Robert Bradshaw, *How to Obtain Evidence from Third Parties: A Comparative View*, 36 J. Int'l Arb. 629 (2019).
99. Convention of 18 March 1970 on the Taking of Evidence Abroad in Civil or Commercial Matters; [2017] FCA 1169, at [50]ff.
100. Article 1 of the Hague Evidence Convention provides: 'In civil or commercial matters a judicial authority of a Contracting State may, in accordance with the provisions of the law of that State, request the competent authority of another Contracting State, by means of a Letter of Request, to obtain evidence, or to perform some other judicial act.' Accordingly, the parties are required to go through at least two extra judicial examinations: a judicial authority of a Contracting State and that of another contracting State. *See also* Article 12. Besides, the person then may refuse to give evidence. *See* Article 11.
101. *See* e.g., Gary Born, *The Hague Evidence Convention Revisited: Reflections on Its Role in U.S. Civil Procedure*, 57 Law & Contemp. Probs. 77, 98 (1994); Brian Friederich, *Reinforcing the Hague Convention on Taking Evidence Abroad after Blocking Statutes, Data Privacy Directives, and Aerospatiale*, 12 San Diego Int'l L.J. 263 (2010); Marissa L.P. Caylor, *Modernizing the Hague Evidence Convention: A Proposed Solution to Cross-Border Discovery Conflicts during Civil and Commercial Litigation*, 28 B.U. Int'l L.J. 341 (2010).

may be many situations where parties and/or tribunals cannot rely on the Convention since only around one-third of countries in the world have ratified it, and many in the Asia-Pacific region have not.[102] Accordingly, the preferred approach is to amend section 23(3) of the IAA to provide to the effect that an Australian court may issue a subpoena requiring a person in Australia to attend for examination before or produce documents to, an arbitral tribunal conducting arbitral proceedings in Australia,[103] irrespective of whether the arbitration is seated in Australia or not.[104]

[C] Choice of Law Rules on the Existence and Scope of Arbitration Agreements

In *Trina Solar*, Edelman J, at first instance, noted that identifying the governing law to determine whether a named party (such as Jasmin) was a party to an agreement (such as the Supply Agreement) was '[o]ne of the more notoriously intractable problems of the modern conflict of laws'.[105] His Honour then observed that there are three possible choices: '(1) the *lex fori*; (2) the law which the parties purport to choose (i.e., the law which would apply if the parties had contracted); or (3) the law which would be the proper law in the absence of express choice'.[106]

Edelman J went on to note that by reason of the Rome Convention, the position adopted in England to the question in issue is the law of the putative agreement.[107] He also noted that the Australian Law Reform Commission recommended the same solution, thus applying the same system of law to both questions of contract formation and questions of contract validity.[108] His Honour further noted that Professor Briggs argued forcefully that the *lex fori* must be applied for the question of whether the parties have reached an agreement[109] (with whom Edelman J agreed), but that there 'may be understandable pragmatic reasons why a legislature would instead ... apply the proper law of a contract to determine whether the parties had entered into that contract'.[110]

102. As of March 2019, the number of contracting parties to the Convention is 62: https://www.hcch.net/en/instruments/conventions/status-table/?cid = 82.
103. An arbitral tribunal may hold hearings in a place other than the seat of the arbitration.
104. Albert Monichino, *The Future of International Arbitration in Australia*, 5 V.U.L.J.J. 60, 70 (2015).
105. [2015] FCA 1453 at [74] (citing Adrian Briggs, *The Formation of International Contracts*, L.M.C.L.Q. 192 (1990)).
106. [2015] FCA 1453 at [75] (citing Lawrence Collins, et al. eds., *Dicey, Morris & Collins on the Conflict of Laws*, 1814 [32-066] §2 (Sweet & Maxwell 15th ed. 2012)).
107. [2015] FCA 1453 at [83]. From 1991 the EEC Convention on the Law Applicable to Contractual Obligations (the Rome Convention) came into operation, and from 17 Dec. 2009, the Rome I Regulation replaced the Rome Convention). Both the Rome Convention and the Rome 1 Regulation adopt the same rule, provided a defendant falls within the Rome I Regulation.
108. [2015] FCA 1453, at [84] (citing ALRC Report No. 58 titled 'Choice of Law' (March 1992), at [8.59], available at http://www.austlii.edu.au/au/other/lawreform/ALRC/1992/58.html).
109. 'The question of whether a person has manifested consent to be bound cannot be governed by matters contained within the very contract about which the person disputes having manifested agreement': Edelman J at [86].
110. At [86].

Professor Briggs was not concerned with 'the structured integrated coherence' of the Model Law and the NYC that was under discussion in *Trina Solar*. Born notes that there have been a wide range of divergent views expressed on the choice of law rules on the existence and scope of arbitration agreements, and resulting uncertainty, suggesting that in order to produce a consistent and effective legal regime for the recognition and enforcement of international arbitration agreements, and to avoid the possibility of inconsistent results, the same choice of law rules should apply under both NYC Articles II and V at the different stages of the arbitration process.[111]

The views of Greenwood J in *Trina Solar* are preferable. The same choice of the rule of law rule should apply to both questions of the existence of an arbitration agreement as well as the validity and scope of an arbitration agreement.[112] Thus, the authors suggest that the IAA should be amended to make clear that a national court entertaining an application under section 7 of the IAA (giving effect to NYC Article II) to stay a proceeding should apply the choice of law rule expressed in NYC Article V (i.e., the law expressed in the agreement to be applicable to it or when no law is so expressed to be applicable, under the law of the seat)[113] to questions of the existence, validity and scope of the alleged arbitration agreement. This too might be usefully clarified by an IAA amendment.

[D] Limiting or Excluding the Application of ACL to Cross-Border Business-to-Business Transactions

International commercial parties seek relative certainty and predictability for the resolution of the disputes. They wish to avoid nasty surprises. The ACL contains provisions dealing notably with misleading or deceptive conduct, and unconscionability, both of which involve subjective judicial evaluation, and raise a degree of uncertainty which is anathema to many commercial parties.[114] Even when international commercial parties choose a different governing law to Australian law to regulate the determination of the merits of their dispute by arbitration, the spectre of ACL application still arises. That is, there is some uncertainty as to whether the ACL provisions referred to above are mandatory laws of the forum in an arbitration seated in Australia, conversely whether parties may contract out of the ACL.[115] The extent to which the ACL is a mandatory law operating to override a foreign exclusive jurisdiction

111. Albert Monichino, *Enforcement of Arbitration Agreements Against Non-Signatories: Which Law (the Chicken and the Egg)?*, The ACICA Rev. 43, 45 (December 2017); Born, *supra* n. 95, 493-7.
112. There is no question that the law of the putative arbitration agreement applies to determine questions of validity and scope of the arbitration agreement.
113. Reflected in s. 8(5)(b) of the IAA.
114. Andrew Bell, *An Australian International Commercial Court – Not a Bad Idea or What a Bad Idea?*, Paper Presented at 2019 ABA Biennial International Conference, at [71] (12 Jul. 2019), http://www.supremecourt.justice.nsw.gov.au/Documents/Publications/Speeches/2019%20Speeches/Bell_20190712.pdf.
115. Analogously, in the recent decision of the Full Court of the Federal Court in *Valve Corporation v. ACCC* (2017) 351 ALR 584, at [108-13], the court held that the consumer guarantee provisions of the ACL applied even where the proper law of the contract was not the law of Australia.

clause has been described as unsettled.[116] In those circumstances, international parties whose dispute has no connection with Australia may be reticent to choose Australia as the seat of their arbitration, alternatively to choose Australian law as the governing law to regulate the determination of the merits of the dispute (irrespective of the seat of arbitration).[117] For example, more than ten years ago, one commentator referred to the predecessor of the ACL as 'Australia's international arbitration headache'.[118]

Consideration might thus be given to making it clear by a legislative amendment that in international arbitrations seated in Australia involving a foreign party, alternatively where the parties have chosen Australian law as the governing law in their arbitration, the parties are free to exclude the ACL provisions relating to misleading or deceptive conduct as well as statutory unconscionability.[119]

[E] Defining 'Australian Law'

Somewhat relatedly, Allsop CJ of the Federal Court, speaking extra-curially, has noted that the inability of the national parties to adopt 'Australian law' as their governing (or applicable) law to determine the merits of the dispute may be a possible disincentive to choose an Australian city as a seat for international arbitration.[120] This is because Australia is a federation and the law in the various States (and Territories) differs unless they enact identical legislation, and/or the High Court issues a binding precedent. However, Australia's primary competitors in the Asia-Pacific region (in particular, Hong Kong and Singapore) operate in unitary jurisdictions. The question arises as to whether the IAA may be usefully amended to provide a definition as to what constitutes 'Australian law' for the purposes of selecting a governing law in an international arbitration seated in Australia. Does Australian law comprise Federal legislation, the legislation of the State or Territory where the arbitration is seated and the common law (i.e., judge-made law) of Australia? It is undesirable for there to be any doubt about this.

116. Martin Davies, et al., *Nygh's Conflict of Laws in Australia* 160 (LexisNexis 9th ed. 2014). *See also* Reid Mortensen, et al., *Private International Law in Australia* 464 (LexisNexis Butterworths 4th ed. 2019).
117. Roger Gyles, *Report on Enhancing International Arbitration Opportunities*, Inquiry, Australian Bar Association, at [118] (9 Jul. 2019).
118. Max Bonnell, *The Trade Practices Act: Australia's International Arbitration Headache*, 10 Int'l Arb. L. Rev. 170 (2007), cited in Nottage & Morrison, *supra* n. 16, 980.
119. Except perhaps where one of the parties is a consumer. That is, parties should only be free to exclude the ACL in business-to-business transactions.
120. Stephanie Garber, *Lack of 'Australian Law' a Barrier to Arbitration*, Lawyers Weekly (4 Jun. 2015), http://www.lawyersweekly.com.au/wig-chamber/news/16613-lack-of-australian-law-a-barrier-to-arbitration. *See also* Doug Jones, *Arbitration in Australia – Rising to the Challenge*, Clayton Utz IALecture 15-17 (20 Nov. 2019), https://www.claytonutz.com/ArticleDocuments/501/Clayton-Utz-University-of-Sydney-Annual-Lecture-Doug-Jones.pdf.aspx?Embed = Y.

[F] Catching Up with Recent Innovations

The current version of the IAA does not reflect relatively recent innovations concerning negative jurisdictional rulings, emergency arbitration and Arb-Med.[121] First, Model Law Article 16 only allows review by the seat court of a tribunal's positive jurisdictional ruling (i.e., upholding jurisdiction). By 2015, Singapore had revised its *International Arbitration Act* to provide for court review of negative jurisdictional rulings (i.e., rulings by the arbitral tribunal declining jurisdiction).[122] Australia should follow suit. Second, though many Asia-Pacific arbitral institutions (including ACICA) have introduced rules for emergency interim relief prior to the constitution of the arbitral tribunal, the IAA is silent about the enforceability of emergency arbitral awards, unlike arbitration statutes in Singapore and Hong Kong.[123] The existing uncertainty in the IAA should be removed. Third, again in contrast with arbitration statutes in Hong Kong and Singapore,[124] and even Australia's CAAs enacted since 2010 for domestic arbitrations, the IAA does not expressly recognise an Arb-Med procedure – whereby the tribunal may assume the role of a mediator or conciliator to facilitate settlement of the dispute referred to arbitration and then revert to acting as an arbitrator if the mediation/conciliation is unsuccessful. The absence of statutory recognition of an Arb-Med process might hamper enforcement of an international arbitral award made in Australia following a failed Arb-Med procedure. The IAA should be updated to reflect those three relatively recent developments, again as suggested for many years by various commentators.[125]

[G] Clarifying Arbitrability of Trust Disputes

Disputes regarding the existence of a trust, as well as breaches of trust,[126] have been found to be arbitrable.[127] However, difficulties arise where beneficiaries may not have agreed to be bound by the terms of the trust deed and indeed may not be born, or may lack legal capacity at the time the trust deed (containing an arbitration agreement) is established.[128] In several jurisdictions, legislation has been passed to remedy this

121. For details, *see* Monichino, *supra* n. 104, 70.
122. International Arbitration Act (Singapore) s. 10(3)(b).
123. International Arbitration Act (Singapore) s. 2(1); Cap. 609 Arbitration Ordinance (Hong Kong) s. 22B.
124. International Arbitration Act (Singapore) s. 17.
125. *See*, e.g., Luke Nottage & Richard Garnett, *The Top 20 Things to Change In or Around Australia's International Arbitration Act*, *in International Arbitration in Australia* 149-90, 179-84 (Luke Nottage & Richard Garnett eds., Federation Press 2010); Luke Nottage, *International Commercial Arbitration in Australia: What's New and What's Next?*, 35 J. Int'l Arb. 465 (2013); Monichino, *supra* n. 104.
126. *Rinehart v. Hancock Prospecting Pty Ltd* [2019] HCA 13, at [73].
127. *Fitzpatrick v. Emerald Grain Pty Ltd* [2017] WASC 206 ('*Fitzpatrick*'); *Rinehart v. Welker* [2012] NSWCA 95.
128. S.I. Strong, *Arbitration of Trust Disputes: Two Bodies of Law Collide*, 45 Vand. J. Transnat'l L. 1157, 1184 (2012).

problem – most recently, in New Zealand.[129] The UK Trust Law Committee has also recommended that the *Arbitration Act 1996* (UK) be amended to allow the arbitration of internal trust disputes.[130] Commonly, such legislation ensures that representatives are appointed to protect the interests of beneficiaries who are unascertained or lack capacity and, if necessary, agree to be bound by an arbitration agreement on the beneficiaries' behalf.[131]

Different mechanisms have been embraced to appoint such representatives. For example, the New Zealand *Trusts Act* requires that if a trust has beneficiaries who are unascertained or lack legal capacity, then the court must appoint representatives for those beneficiaries if the trust is subject to an alternative dispute resolution process.[132] On the other hand, the UK Trust Law Committee has proposed providing arbitrators in such matters with authority to appoint and remove representatives, make appropriate representation orders and provide that persons represented under such orders be bound by the award.[133] This proposal has not yet been implemented, and the UK awaits legislation regulating arbitration of internal trust disputes. Alternatively (or in addition), legislation regarding internal trust arbitration may simply deem that the beneficiaries' have consented, thereby putting it beyond doubt that arbitration agreements in trust deeds are enforceable.[134]

Without legislative reinforcement, a degree of uncertainty remains as to the arbitrability of trust disputes in many cases. Arbitration of internal trust disputes is desirable and gaining support internationally.[135] Given the importance of trusts in commerce, this area deserves legislative attention.

[H] Centralisation of Judicial Power

A controversial and delicate proposal is an IAA amendment to establish the Federal Court as the single intermediate appellate court to hear ICA matters.[136] The proposal, initially developed in 2012, aims to promote a uniform approach to ICA in Australian

129. Trusts Act 2019 (NZ) ss 142-148; Arbitration Act 1996 (NZ) s. 10A. However, the changes will not come into force until 30 Jan. 2021.
130. Trust Law Committee, *Arbitration of Trust Disputes*, 18 Trusts & Trustees 296 (2012).
131. Trusts Act 2019 (NZ) ss 142-148; Guernsey Trusts Law (2007) s. 63; *See also*, Washington Probate and Trust Law ss 11.96A.120, 11.96A.270 and 11.96A.310 (2013) which uses 'virtual representation' where a party represents persons or classes of persons with similar economic interests without making the represented persons parties.
132. Trusts Act 2019 (NZ) s. 144.
133. Trust Law Committee, *supra* n. 130, 306; This approach has been adopted in the Bahamas, *see* Trustee Act 1998 (Bahamas) s. 91B.
134. Arbitration Act (1996), Cap. 387 (Malta) Article 15A; Florida Probate Code s. 731.401 (2007); Trustee Act 1998 (Bahamas) s. 91A.
135. S.I. Strong, *Arbitration of Internal Trust Disputes: The Next Frontier for International Commercial Arbitration?*, 20 ICCA Congress Series (Evolution and Adaptation: The Future of International Arbitration) 971 (2020).
136. Albert Monichino, *International Arbitration in Australia: the Need to Centralise Judicial Power*, 86 The Australian L. J. 118 (2012); Monichino, *supra* n. 104, 72-3. *See also* Nottage, *supra* n. 125.

jurisprudence.[137] It involves removing the appellate jurisdiction from the State and Territory superior courts such that the State/Territory and Federal Courts retain concurrent first-instance jurisdiction, but that all appeals in ICA-related matters would be heard by the Federal Court as the single intermediate appellate court.[138] The proposal has been favourably received by not only the past Chief Justice of the Federal Court but also the past Commonwealth Solicitor-General.[139] The proposal is far more modest than the exclusive jurisdiction proposal, floating the idea that the Federal Court might deal with all IAA-related cases, including at first instance, which was raised for discussion by the Federal Attorney General's Department in its 2009 Discussion Paper.[140] Roger Gyles AO QC, in a 2019 report commissioned by the Australian Bar Association to identify opportunities in ICA by Australian barristers, noted recently that the fragmentation in judicial power under the IAA was unsatisfactory.[141] He recommended that Australia re-visit the exclusive jurisdiction proposal.

In 2015, Bathurst CJ of the Supreme Court of New South Wales argued against the idea of centralising jurisdiction under the IAA for three principal reasons.[142] First, there is a single common law of Australia, so any differences between intermediate appellate courts are ultimately resolved by the High Court of Australia and, further, arguing that nothing suggests that there is any significant divergence in the approach taken between State and Territory jurisdictions regarding the IAA.[143] Second, the State/Territory courts arguably have special expertise in IAA-related matters, while the Federal Court does not.[144] Third, a divide between the Federal Court hearing matters under the IAA and the State/Territory courts hearing matters in relation to domestic arbitration may result in divergent jurisprudence under the respective international arbitration and domestic arbitration regimes.[145]

Each of Bathurst CJ's arguments may be rebutted. First, the single common law of Australia does not necessarily help the country to compete against other jurisdictions in attracting ICA cases. Most pro-ICA jurisdictions in the Asia-Pacific such as Singapore have a unitary court system, unlike Australia that has nine superior courts exercising appellate jurisdiction under the IAA. Notwithstanding this unwieldy structure, it is conceded that Australian superior courts have so far avoided any substantial conflicts in the interpretation of the IAA.[146] Yet differences have emerged in arbitration matters

137. Monichino, *supra* n. 136. The author also argued for establishment of a specialist arbitration list to promote uniformity.
138. As presently occurs in intellectual property matters. *See* e.g., Patents Act 1990 (Cth) s. 154.
139. *See*, respectively, Keane, *supra* n. 40; Justin Gleeson, *Commentary on Paper by Professor Luke Nottage*, in *International Commercial Law and Arbitration* 343-8, 347 (Nye Perram ed., Ross Parsons Centre of Commercial, Corporate and Taxation Law 2014).
140. For contemporaneous discussion of this proposal, and others in the Discussion Paper as well as other topics for potential reform, *see* Nottage & Garnett, *supra* n. 125, 174-5.
141. Gyles, *supra* n. 117, at [118].
142. Thomas F. Bathurst, *Judicial Support for Arbitration – A Reprise*, 162 Austrl. Constr. L. Newsltr. 6 (2015).
143. *Ibid.*, 13.
144. *Ibid.*
145. *Ibid.*
146. Cf., the conflict between the Victorian and New South Wales Courts of Appeal as to the interpretation of s. 29 of the Old Uniform Acts concerning the adequacy of arbitral reasons in

between intermediate appellate courts regarding the standard of arbitral reasons under the old uniform domestic arbitration Acts[147] and the proper approach to the interpretation of arbitration agreements.[148] In a public speech, Allsop CJ observed:

> The central concepts that affect the success of arbitration procedures, and the degree to which courts will assist or impede arbitration are open to a significant degree of interpretation. Depending upon the court's intellectual predisposition or predilection, *widely different approaches are possible to the same problem* at hand.[149]

Certainly, the High Court may ultimately resolve any conflicts between intermediate courts of appeal, but this takes time, expense and the preparedness of the losing party to appeal the case to the High Court. Meanwhile, conflicts between intermediate appellate courts in ICA matters does not engender confidence in Australia as a seat for arbitration.

Bathurst CJ's second concern is that vesting jurisdiction under the IAA solely in the Federal Court would cause the loss of the arbitration expertise of the State and Territory Supreme Courts. This problem can be resolved by conferring a number of State Supreme Court Judges a dual commission in both Supreme Court and Federal Court, to enable the Judges to deal with important arbitration matters at any court. Separately, since 2015 when Bathurst CJ presented his remarks, the Federal Court has had further extensive experience in ICA matters (as the table above attests to).

Bathurst CJ's third concern is about the creation of 'an unfortunate divide' that is likely to be brought about by a division whereby the Federal Court hears ICA matters, while the State and Territory Supreme Courts hear domestic arbitration matters.[150] However, section 2A of the revised uniform CAA promotes the harmonisation of jurisprudence in respect of international and domestic arbitration by requiring State and Territory courts to interpret provisions of the domestic arbitration Acts conformably with the manner in which the equivalent provisions in the IAA are interpreted.

Accordingly, it is still worth considering investing in the idea of concentrating judicial power (or at least appellate judicial power) under the IAA in a single court. As a former ACICA President put it recently: 'Australia needs a single institution operating nationally, and comprised of the very best commercial judicial talent from across the country'.[151]

a domestic arbitration award. This conflict was resolved by the High Court in *Westport Insurance Corporation v. Gordian Runoff Limited* (2011) 244 CLR 239.

147. Resolved by the High Court in *Westport* (*supra*).
148. Resolved by the High Court in *Rinehart* (*supra*).
149. James Allsop, *International Arbitration and the Courts – the Australian Approach*, The Australian ADR Rep. 18, 20 (2012) (emphasis added).
150. Bathurst, *supra* n. 142, at 13.
151. Jones, *supra* n. 120.

§3.04 CONCLUSION

Over the past ten years, Australia has devoted significant efforts to promoting international arbitration in Australia. It is yet to see the rewards for its efforts. While much has been done, much remains to be done to establish Australia as a viable Asia-Pacific hub for ICA, in what is an increasingly competitive environment. Hope should not be lost. It is to be remembered that Singapore has established itself as arguably the leading arbitral hub in the Asia-Pacific in only the past ten years or so.

Two major challenges face Australia: the perennial problem of the tyranny of distance, and the fragmentation of its legal system caused by the Federation. The relevance of geographical isolation is fading.[152] As demonstrated by the impact of COVID-19, developments in technology are doing away with the need for face-to-face meetings. There is arguably no need for international arbitrations to be conducted in person. Conducting substantive as well as procedural hearings may be conducted remotely with less need to travel to Australia for arbitrations,[153] or even occasional arbitration-related court proceedings (with Australian courts proving very well-equipped for remote hearings).[154] It is a 'no-brainer' that Australia should develop its capacity in conducting remote hearings. Moreover, the problems caused by fragmentation of Australia's legal system could be addressed by a simple amendment to the IAA – either giving exclusive jurisdiction under the IAA to the Federal Court, alternatively (and more modestly) making the Federal Court the single intermediate appellate court in respect of matters under the IAA.[155] Most importantly, Australia needs to be innovative (like Singapore) if it is to make its mark in this space. It cannot afford to simply play 'catch up' with its competitors.

152. *Ibid.*, 13.
153. As a result of COVID-19, a plethora of webinars and guidelines has emerged on conducting remote hearings, including several by ACICA, as listed by Teramura, Ali & Reyes, Chapter 15, in this volume.
154. *See* generally [Warren & Croft, Chapter 2 in this volume.
155. Instead of there being nine intermediate appellate superior courts exercising appellate jurisdiction under the IAA, as presently is the case.

CHAPTER 4

Confidentiality and Transparency in International Arbitration: Asia-Pacific Tensions and Expectations*

Luke Nottage

Confidentiality is considered a significant advantage for international commercial arbitration (ICA) over cross-border litigation, as seen in rules of most arbitral institutions. Automatic (opt-out) confidentiality is also now found in many national laws, including statutory add-ons to the UNCITRAL Model Law and/or through case law for example in New Zealand, then Hong Kong, Singapore, Malaysia, and eventually Australia. Yet there remain variations in the timing of these developments as well as the scope and procedures associated with exceptions. There is also no confidentiality provided in Japan's later Model Law adoption, although parties mostly choose the Japan Commercial Arbitration Association (JCAA) so opt-in to its Rules, which have gradually extended confidentiality obligations.

Another complication is growing public concern over arbitration procedures through investor-state dispute settlement (ISDS), particularly in Australia since an ultimately unsuccessful treaty claim by Philip Morris. Statutory amendments in 2018 reverse automatic confidentiality for Australia-seated ISDS arbitrations applying the 2014 UNCITRAL Rules on Transparency. Concerns over ISDS may even impede Australia enacting provisions for the confidentiality of arbitration-related court proceedings. These provisions could not be revised recently in New Zealand against the backdrop of its new government's anti-ISDS stance.

* Originally published in 16(1) Asian International Arbitration Journal 1-23 (2020), earlier presented at a seminar of ARBIT (Italian Forum for Arbitration and ADR) at the Italian Arbitration Association, Rome, 30 Sep. 2019. I thank discussants and other attendees for that opportunity, especially Andrew Paton as main organiser, and Dr Nobumichi Teramura and Ashley Taylor Kelaita (CAPLUS intern) for excellent editorial and research assistance for this chapter. I am also grateful for Kevin Lindgren QC for helpful feedback. I remain solely responsible for any misconceptions or errors.

This chapter elaborates such expectations and tensions regarding the double-edged sword of confidentiality in international arbitration, focusing on Australia and Japan in a regional context.

§4.01 INTRODUCTION: CONFIDENTIALITY VERSUS TRANSPARENCY IN ASIA-PACIFIC INTERNATIONAL ARBITRATION

Practitioners and users of ICA still see confidentiality as a significant advantage compared to cross-border litigation. For example, 36% of respondents to last year's Queen Mary University of London arbitration survey, with White & Case, listed 'privacy and confidentiality' within the 'three most valuable characteristics of international arbitration' (compared to 64% listing award enforceability and 60% listing the avoidance of specific legal systems and national courts). Focusing just on confidentiality in ICA, 40% saw it as quite important (including 57% of in-house counsel respondents), 33% as quite important, and 14% as somewhat important. Similarly, around three quarters (74%) thought confidentiality should be available on an opt-out (automatic) basis for ICA.[1] The perceived advantage of confidentiality may also have been stronger among users of international arbitration in Asia, compared to the West, according to earlier surveys respectively by Shahla Ali and Christian Buhring-Uhle.[2]

However, such surveys also confirm that neutrality of forum and award enforceability are ICA's most prized features. This is despite the 2005 Hague Choice of Courts Convention and the 2019 Singapore Mediation Convention.[3] There is also significant variation among national laws and arbitral rules. The 1976 Rules of the United Nations Commission on International Trade Law (UNCITRAL), designed originally for ad hoc

1. *See* Queen Mary University of London, White & Case, *2018 International Arbitration Survey: The Evolution of International Arbitration*, 7, 28-30, https://www.whitecase.com/publications/insight/2018-international-arbitration-survey-evolution-international-arbitration (accessed 28 Aug. 2019).
2. Luke Nottage, *Addressing International Arbitration's Ambivalence: Hard Lessons from Australia*, in *Discourse and Practice in International Commercial Arbitration* 15 (Vijay Bhatia, Christopher Candlin & Maurizio Gotti eds., Ashgate 2012), referring to Shahla Ali, *Resolving Disputes in the Asia-Pacific Region: International Arbitration and Mediation in East Asia and the West* (Routledge 2012).
3. The former so far has few ratifying states (although they include the EU, UK and Singapore): Hague Conference on Private International Law, *Status Table: Convention of 30 June 2005 on Choice of Court Agreements*, https://www.hcch.net/en/instruments/conventions/status-table/?cid=98 (accessed 28 Aug. 2019). The latter is not yet in force, but attracted forty-six signatories at the diplomatic conference on 7 Aug. 2019 (including notably China, India, Malaysia, Korea and Singapore, as well as the US): United Nations Treaty Collection, *United Nations Convention of International Settlement Agreements Resulting from Mediation*, https://treaties.un.org/pages/ViewDetails.aspx?src=TREATY&mtdsg_no=XXII-4&chapter=22&clang=_en (accessed 28 Aug. 2019). The Singapore Convention does not deal with confidentiality or privacy in court proceedings to enforce cross-border settlement agreements, but Article 10 of the 2018 Model Law on International Commercial Mediation (like Article 9 of the 2002 Model Law on International Commercial Conciliation) states: 'Unless otherwise agreed by the parties, all information relating to the mediation proceedings shall be kept confidential, except where disclosure is required under the law or for the purposes of implementation or enforcement of a settlement agreement.' Both treaties and related texts are available via UNCITRAL, *International Commercial Mediation*, https://uncitral.un.org/en/texts/mediation (accessed 28 Aug. 2019).

arbitrations, merely required hearings to be held *in camera* (privacy for the parties) and for awards to be made public only if parties agreed (limited confidentiality), and the 2010 revisions left those rules unchanged.[4] The 1985 UNCITRAL Model Law on ICA, which generally followed the wording of the UNCITRAL Rules to create a template for national arbitration laws, did not even include such provisions. This remained true in the Model Law as amended in 2006. Most UNCITRAL delegates saw confidentiality as an interesting but not high-priority topic, despite some delegates arguing that parties were increasingly concerned about the lack of provisions on confidentiality.[5]

Even the Arbitration Rules of the International Chamber of Commerce (ICC) have persisted in not imposing confidentiality obligations on the parties, although the ICC Court and Secretariat are bound under internal rules.[6] The Stockholm Chamber of Commerce 2017 Arbitration Rules require confidentiality by SCC, along with the arbitral tribunal and any tribunal secretary appointed, but not on the part of the parties themselves.[7] Yet almost all other Rules of arbitration, including those from institutions proliferating across the Asian region, impose quite wide-ranging confidentiality obligations.

It could be that the SCC, ICC and UNCITRAL Rules (influencing, in turn, the Model Law drafting) do not specify much confidentiality because it applies anyway under the law of the seat directly chosen by the parties (or otherwise sometimes ordered by the tribunal). However, most SCC arbitrations have their seat in Sweden, where arbitration law does not provide for a general duty of confidentiality. Nor is this provided under the law applicable to many ICC arbitrations, such as those seated in France (except for domestic arbitrations, by statutory amendments in 2011[8]), Switzerland and the USA.[9] In 2018, these three jurisdictions attracted respectively 137, 78 and 75 ICC cases. However, ICC arbitrations were also seated in 72 cases in the UK, 27 in Singapore and 10 in Hong Kong, where confidentiality applies by default.

4. UNCITRAL Rules and other texts related to arbitration are available via https://uncitral.un.org/en/texts/arbitration/contractualtexts/arbitration (accessed 28 Aug. 2019).
5. Referring to UNCITRAL deliberations in 1999 over amending the Model Law, *see* Michael Hwang, Katie Chung, Si Cheng Lim & Hui Min Wong, *Defining the Indefinable: Practical Problems of Confidentiality in Arbitration*, in *International Arbitration: Issues, Perspectives and Practice: Liber Amicorum Neil Kaplan* (HIKAC ed., Kluwer Law International 2019). This updates Michael Hwang's Second Kaplan Lecture, 17 Nov. 2008, with extensive comparative analysis across many issues around confidentiality in international arbitration.
6. *See* ICC Arbitration Rules (2017), Appendix I (Statute of the International Court of Arbitration), Article 6 and Appendix II (Internal Rules). There also does not appear to be public information on how often parties and the tribunal nonetheless subsequently agree to confidentiality (e.g., through Terms of Reference), when not anyway provided under the arbitration law of the seat.
7. Article 3 of Arbitration Rules of the Arbitration Institute of The Stockholm Chamber of Commerce (2017), https://sccinstitute.com/our-services/rules/ (accessed 28 Aug. 2019).
8. Marlon Meza Salas, *Confidentiality in International Commercial Arbitration: Truth or Fiction?*, Kluwer Arbitration Blog (23 Sep. 2018), http://arbitrationblog.kluwerarbitration.com/2018/09/23/confidentiality-in-international-commercial-arbitration-truth-or-fiction/ (accessed 18 Oct. 2019). Note that a significant minority of ICC arbitrations have been domestic, not international, so may attract confidentiality under the 2011 amendments when seated in France.
9. *See 2018 ICC Dispute Resolution Statistics*, ICC Disp. Res. Bull. 12 (2019).

In addition, parties to ICC arbitrations remain free to agree (opt-in) to confidentiality obligations even after filing for arbitration. This apparently occurs quite frequently, which is quite remarkable given that typically it is difficult for claimant and respondent to agree on anything much of significance once the dispute gets formally underway. The ICC Arbitration Rules (current Article 22(3)) further allow the tribunal to order measures to protect 'trade secrets and confidential information' if one party so requests. This also apparently occurs sometimes, although in far fewer additional cases dealt with annually in recent years.[10]

Another possible reason why the ICC, SCC and UNCITRAL Rules still stand out as not providing expressly for a general confidentiality obligation is that they were and still are used in ISDS arbitrations, where the involvement of a host state and other features generate more public interest in transparency. Although the ICC and SCC do not now administer many investment treaty arbitrations,[11] they still have many cases that involve state entities.[12] However, the latter do include commercially-oriented state-owned entities (SOEs) and cases based on one-off investment contracts, which would generally raise fewer public interests.

Whatever the historical and current rationales for not including expansive confidentiality obligations in the UNCITRAL Rules and especially the Model Law, jurisdictions adopting the Model Law (notably across the Asia-Pacific region[13]) have usually often added in legislative provisions providing automatically for confidentiality (as in New Zealand, Hong Kong, Australia and Malaysia). Policymakers and stakeholders seem to view this additional provision as helpful in moving the jurisdiction towards the next stage in developing an attractive seat for ICA filings. Alternatively, they have achieved a similar default position through case law development (as in Singapore, following earlier English law). However, a closer analysis uncovers differences in the timing and scope of such automatic confidentiality connected to arbitration proceedings, including the listing and possible interpretations of exceptions to confidentiality. There is even more variability concerning the question of whether confidentiality should be maintained for arbitration-related court proceedings. This probably reflects the extra public interest in 'open justice' involved when matters exceptionally end up in court.

10. According to former ICC Secretary General Andrea Carlevaris at the 30 Sep. 2019 Rome seminar (mentioned in the opening footnote), parties agreed to add confidentiality in 120 cases in 2016 (with the tribunal ordering measures in another 16 cases); 197 (plus eleven orders) in 2017; and 199 (plus twenty-four orders) in 2018.
11. Out of 942 known ISDS arbitrations based on investment treaties, SCC and ICC Rules have been applied in 46 and 17 cases respectively, with 295 UNCITRAL Rules and 508 ICSID Rules arbitrations (calculated as of 22 Aug. 2019: UNCTAD, *Investment Policy Hub, Investment Dispute Settlement Navigator* (22 Aug. 2019), https://investmentpolicy.unctad.org/investment-dispute-settlement (accessed 28 Aug. 2019).
12. *See* further ICC Commission, *State, State Entities and ICC Arbitration*, https://iccwbo.org/publication/arbitration-involving-states-state-entities-icc-rules-arbitration-report-icc-commission-arbitration-adr/(accessed 28 Aug. 2019).
13. *See* generally Anselmo Reyes & Weixia Gu, *Introduction: Towards a Model of Arbitration Reform in the Asia Pacific*, in *The Developing World of Arbitration: A Comparative Study of Arbitration Reform in the Asia Pacific* 1 (Anselmo Reyes & Weixia Gu eds., Hart Publishing 2018), also available at https://www.ssrn.com/abstract=3183550 (accessed 28 Aug. 2019).

Thus, for example, Australia had case law in 1995 maintaining that only privacy but not confidentiality applied automatically to arbitrations, 2010 legislative amendments added statutory exceptions on the parties if they opted in to confidentiality for international arbitration proceedings, but 2015 amendments made confidentiality automatic unless parties opted out.[14] New Zealand's 1996 enactment of the Model Law provided automatic confidentiality. However, after an arbitration involving the national broadcaster ended up in court in 2000 followed by a Law Commission Report, legislative amendments in 2007 specified exceptions that applied to arbitration-related court proceedings as well the prior arbitration.[15] Malaysia followed the original New Zealand law by providing for confidentiality around arbitrations when enacting Model Law based legislation in 2005, with 2018 amendments providing that related court proceedings should not generally be in open court.[16]

As for jurisdictions in the Asian region that attract many more ICA cases, Hong Kong also has adopted the Model Law (in 1989, like Australia) but first added legislation (in 1997) allowing a party to apply to have arbitration-related court proceedings to be held in closed court and to restrict reporting of such proceedings.[17] In 2011, the legislation made such proceedings closed unless a party applied or the court decided they should be held openly, and also extended case law to create automatic confidentiality around arbitral proceedings and awards.[18] Singapore still

14. *See Esso Australia Resources Ltd v. Plowman* (1995) 183 CLR 10 and the International Arbitration Act 1974 (Cth) as amended, with Australian case law and legislation available via www.austlii .edu.au (accessed 28 Aug. 2019). India is the latest Model Law jurisdiction to add express confidentiality provisions around arbitration, with one exception – regarding disclosure of the award for enforcement: *see* Subhiksh Vasudev, *The 2019 Amendment to the Indian Arbitration Act: A Classic Case of One Step Forward Two Steps Backward?*, Kluwer Arbitration Blog (25 Aug. 2019), http://arbitrationblog.kluwerarbitration.com/2019/08/25/the-2019-amendment-to-the-indian-arbitration-act-a-classic-case-of-one-step-forward-two-steps-backward/ (accessed 31 Mar. 2020). This amendment is despite some criticism that the Bill (now enacted) did not adequately address other possible exceptions to confidentiality or indeed, from a comparative perspective, whether confidentiality should apply automatically: *see* Pranav Rai, *Proposed 2018 Amendments to Indian Arbitration Law: A Historic Moment or Legislative Blunder?*, Kluwer Arbitration Blog (24 Nov. 2018), http://arbitrationblog.kluwerarbitration.com/2018/11/24/proposed-2018-amendments-to-indian-arbitration-law-a-historic-moment-or-legislative-blunder-2/ (accessed 31 Mar. 2020).
15. *See TVNZ v. Langley* [2000] N.Z.L.R. 250 and ss 14-14I of the *Arbitration Act 1996* (New Zealand) at http://www.legislation.govt.nz/act/public/1996/0099/18.0/DLM403277.html (accessed 28 Aug. 2019).
16. *See* s. 41B of the Arbitration Act (Malaysia). For an overview of the 2018 amendments, *see* Asian International Arbitration Centre, *The Arbitration (Amendment) (No. 2) Act 2018 Comes Into Force: The New Era of Arbitration in Malaysia*, https://www.aiac.world/news/254/The-Arbitration-(Amendment)-(No.-2)-Act-2018-Comes-Into-Force--%E2%80%93-The-New-Era-of-Arbitration-in-Malaysia (accessed 28 Aug. 2019). *See also* Venugopal's Chapter 9 in this volume.
17. *See* ss 2D and 2E of the 1997 Arbitration Ordinance (Hong Kong) at www.wipo.int (accessed 28 Aug. 2019). On the latest developments in Hong Kong, *see also* Ali's Chapter 6 in this volume.
18. *See* respectively ss 16-18 of the 2011 Arbitration Ordinance (Hong Kong). These provisions are carried over into the current Arbitration Ordinance (Hong Kong), https://www.elegislation.gov .hk/hk/cap609, attracting interest recently e.g., regarding the exception for disclosures anyway required by Hong Kong listed companies under its securities regulation: Joanna Du, *Hong Kong: A Listed Company's Duty of Confidentiality in Arbitration and Its Duty of Disclosure to the Public*, Kluwer Arbitration Blog (12 Jan. 2019), http://arbitrationblog.kluwerarbitration.com/2019/01

relies on case law to establish such a default rule for confidentiality regarding arbitration proceedings themselves. In addition, however, its 2002 International Arbitration Act (IAA) (sections 22-23) followed the 1997 Hong Kong legislation in allowing a party to apply for arbitration-related court proceedings to be otherwise than in open court and for restrictions on reporting such cases.[19]

Nonetheless, this tendency towards more confidentiality around arbitration in the Asian region is somewhat offset by Japan declining to deal with the issue when it replaced old German-law-inspired legislation with a Model Law based Arbitration Act in 2003.[20] In other jurisdictions, legislative and potentially case law developments may also now be influenced by the evolution of ISDS arbitration. For example, in its 2019 amendments, New Zealand did not enact provisions proposed in 2017 to restore more confidentiality to arbitration-related court proceedings. This non-reform could have been influenced by general public sentiment[21] leading the new Labour Government to declare in late 2017 that it would not accept ISDS provisions at all in future trade and investment treaties.[22]

Growing public concern about ISDS arbitration may also make it harder for Australia ever to amend its legislation to implement even partial confidentiality regarding arbitration-related court proceedings. This would be despite longstanding calls for such legislation (as in Hong Kong, Singapore and New Zealand),[23] and even though most ICA involves far fewer public interests that ISDS arbitration. The visibility around ISDS is certainly reflected in 2018 amendments to Australia's IAA excluding from automatic confidentiality arbitrations where the 2013 UNCITRAL Rules on Transparency in Treaty-based Arbitration apply to Australia-seated cases.[24] Provisions promoting transparency being added to investment treaties, sometimes with related amendments to national legislation on ICA, reflects and in turn impacts on the potential of such jurisdiction to play more of an active role in developing international investment law especially in the region.

The rest of this analysis, therefore, takes a closer look at such tensions between *confidentiality* (especially in and for ICA) and *transparency* (especially in and for ISDS). Against the context of wider developments in the Asian region outlined above

---

/12/hong-kong-a-listed-companys-duty-of-confidentiality-in-arbitration-and-its-duty-of-disclosure-to-the-public/ (accessed 28 Aug. 2019).

19. Hwang et al., *supra* n. 5.
20. Arbitration Law (Law No. 138 of 2003) (Japan) at http://japan.kantei.go.jp/policy/sihou/arbitrationlaw.pdf (accessed 28 Aug. 2019).
21. Jack Wass, *Arbitration Law Reform in New Zealand: A Lesson in Competing Values*, Kluwer Arbitration Blog (21 May 2019) http://arbitrationblog.kluwerarbitration.com/2019/05/21/arbitration-law-reform-in-new-zealand-a-lesson-in-competing-values/ (accessed 28 Aug. 2019).
22. *See generally* Amokura Kawharu & Luke Nottage, *Renouncing Investor-State Dispute Settlement in Australia, Then New Zealand: Déjà Vu*, 18/03 Sydney Law School Research Paper (2018), https://ssrn.com/abstract=3116526 (accessed 28 Aug. 2019).
23. *See*, e.g., Luke Nottage & Richard Garnett, *The Top Twenty Things to Change In or Around Australia's International Arbitration* Act, in *International Arbitration in Australia* 149, 187 (Luke Nottage & Richard Garnett eds., Federation Press 2010). Also available at https://ssrn.com/abstract=1378722 (accessed 28 Aug. 2019).
24. UNCITRAL, *UNCITRAL Rules on Transparency in Treaty-Based Investor-State Arbitration*, https://uncitral.un.org/en/texts/arbitration/contractualtexts/transparency (accessed 28 Aug. 2019).

and in the conclusions, particular emphasis will be placed on Australia and Japan.[25] Both countries lie geographically on the periphery of the Asian region, where international arbitration has been burgeoning especially over the last fifteen years. Yet both have struggled to attract significantly more arbitration cases, despite quite extensive efforts (especially by Australia);[26] most cases still go to Hong Kong, Singapore and (albeit especially where local parties are involved) China.[27] This is despite increasingly strict *confidentiality* obligations being introduced through the rules of the major arbitration institutions, and/or legislation, in Japan and especially Australia over recent years. Although aiming to meet the usual expectations of businesspeople and their legal advisors in international commercial dispute resolution, such changes may be 'too little, too late' to attract significantly more ICA filings.

By contrast, moreover, *transparency* obligations have been added increasingly around the ISDS option included in almost all investment treaties concluded respectively by Australia and Japan. This tendency may reflect growing concerns (especially in Australia[28]) about the public interests implicated by ISDS cases, although empirically there is already significant transparency at least around treaty-based ISDS awards or outcomes.[29] As mentioned above, Australia has gone the next step of revising its legislation in 2018 to automatically exempt some investment treaty arbitrations from the confidentiality obligations otherwise imposed by default on parties and others in Australia-seated international arbitration proceedings since 2015. Japan does not need to because its legislation does not apply confidentiality to arbitrations by default.

---

25. For an earlier suggestive analysis of Australia, *see* Esme Shirlow, *Recent Developments in Australia's Approach to Confidentiality and Transparency in International Arbitration*, Kluwer Arbitration Blog (19 Dec. 2015), http://arbitrationblog.kluwerarbitration.com/2015/12/19/recent-developments-in-australias-approach-to-confidentiality-and-transparency-in-international-arbitration/ (accessed 28 Aug. 2019). For a nuanced analysis of confidentiality versus transparency principles in the Italian context, including a distinction between ICA from ISDS, *see also* Bernadetta Coppa, *Confidentiality in the Arbitration Rules of the Milan Chamber* 137 (Alberto Malatesta & Rinaldo Sali eds., Juris 2013).
26. For the latest effort, through an Australian Bar Association inquiry, *see* Roger Gyles, *Report on Opportunities for Australian Barristers in International Arbitration* (2019), https://austbar.asn.au/singapore-2019/papers (accessed 18 Oct. 2019).
27. For recent developments in China, *see especially* Bath's Chapter 8 in this volume. For a report on the first of two symposiums on Asia-Pacific international arbitration generally, co-hosted by the University of Sydney and the University of Hong Kong, *see* Nobumichi Teramura, *New Frontiers in International Arbitration for the Asia-Pacific Region*, Japanese Law and the Asia-Pacific Blog (31 Jul. 2019), https://japaneselaw.sydney.edu.au/2019/07/new-frontiers-in-international-arbitration-for-the-asia-pacific-region-4-guest-blog-report-on-15-july-symposium-with-at-hku/ (accessed 28 Aug. 2019).
28. Luke Nottage, *Investor-State Arbitration Policy and Practice in Australia*, in *Second Thoughts: Investor-State Arbitration between Developed Democracies* 377 (Armand de Mestral ed., Centre for International Governance Innovation 2017), https://ssrn.com/abstract=2802450 (accessed 28 Aug. 2019).
29. Luke Nottage & Ana Ubilava, *Costs, Outcomes and Transparency in ISDS Arbitrations: Evidence for an Investment Treaty Parliamentary Inquiry*, 21 Int. Arb. L. Rev. 111 (2018). Also available at https://ssrn.com/abstract=3227401 (accessed 28 Aug. 2019). *See also* Malcolm Langford, Daniel Behn & Laura Letourneau-Tremblay, *Empirical Perspectives on Investment Arbitration: What Do We Know? Does It Matter?*, ISDS Academic Forum Working Group 7 Paper (15 Mar. 2019), https://www.cids.ch/academic-forum-concept-papers (accessed 28 Aug. 2019).

Lessons from the tensions between these two trajectories in each country may be particularly interesting for other jurisdictions. They include those adopting the Model Law but also countries with other arbitration law traditions, including in Asia and Europe, which are seeking to attract international arbitration filings away from the most popular jurisdictions amidst evolving expectations in business and wider communities. As concluded below, how those tensions play out may also influence the European Union's (EU's) ongoing negotiations for investment protection treaties with respectively Australia and Japan, as well as other regional and even global developments.

§4.02 AUSTRALIA: AMBITIOUS BUT AMBIVALENT?

[A] ICA

Australia's highest court famously decided in 1995 that there was no implied duty of confidentiality in arbitration, but only an implied duty of privacy.[30] Although that *Esso* case involved a domestic arbitration and the government, a similar reasoning was widely thought to extend to international arbitration involving purely commercial parties and transactions. Because that was considered out of kilter with most expectations among businesspeople and the international arbitration community, when the first Arbitration Rules for the Australian Centre for International Commercial Arbitration (ACICA) were published in 2005 based otherwise generally on the UNCITRAL Rules, confidentiality obligations were added that were relatively strict.[31] These were retained in subsequent Rules, with the 2016 version extending confidentiality to party-called witnesses:[32]

> 22.2 The parties, the Arbitral Tribunal and ACICA shall treat as confidential and shall not disclose to a third party without prior written consent from the parties all matters relating to the arbitration (including the existence of the arbitration), the award, materials created for the purpose of the arbitration and documents produced by another party in the proceedings and not in the public domain except: (a) for the purpose of making an application to any competent court; (b) for the purpose of making an application to the courts of any state to enforce the award; (c) pursuant to the order of a court of competent jurisdiction; (d) if required by the law of any State which is binding on the party making the disclosure; or (e) if required to do so by any regulatory body.

30. James Morrison & Luke Nottage, *Country Report on Australia for: International Commercial Arbitration – An Asia-Pacific Perspective*, 14/95 Sydney Law School Research Paper (2014), https://ssrn.com/abstract=2514124 (accessed 28 Aug. 2019).
31. Simon Greenberg, Luke Nottage & J. Romesh Weeramantry, *The 2005 Rules of the Australian Centre for International Commercial Arbitration – Revisited*, in *International Arbitration in Australia* 79 (Luke Nottage & Richard Garnett eds., Federation Press 2010). Also available at https://ssrn.com/abstract=1479348 (accessed 28 Aug. 2019).
32. ACICA Arbitration Rules, Article 22.2 (2016), outlined in Malcolm Holmes, Luke Nottage & Robert Tang, *The 2016 Rules of the Australian Centre for International Commercial Arbitration: Towards Further 'Cultural Reform'*, 12(2) A.I.A.J. 211 (2016) (emphasis added). Also available at https://ssrn.com/abstract=2786839 (accessed 28 Aug. 2019).

22.3 Any party planning to make disclosure under Article 22.2 must within a reasonable time prior to the intended disclosure notify the Arbitral Tribunal, ACICA and the other parties (if during the arbitration) or ACICA and the other parties (if the disclosure takes place after the conclusion of the arbitration) and furnish details of the disclosure and an explanation of the reason for it.

22.4 *To the extent that a witness is given access to evidence or other information obtained in the arbitration, the party calling such witness is responsible for the maintenance by the witness of the same degree of confidentiality as that required of the party.*

In public consultations from 2008, drafting committee members,[33] ACICA itself and others also pressed the government to add confidentiality provisions to the IAA. Section 16 of Australia's international arbitration legislation had given the force of law to the UNCITRAL Model Law as early as 1989, but like the Model Law, the initial enactment did not mention confidentiality. As mentioned above, 2010 amendments added confidentiality obligations only on the parties,[34] subject to statutory exceptions (section 23C-23G), but provided the parties expressly opted in. This default position was criticised as being little different from that established already by the *Esso* case, and therefore as still being incongruent with usual expectations among ICA users and legal advisors.[35] Another critique was the IAA's inconsistency with new legislation also introduced from 2010 (based around the Model Law) that automatically applied confidentiality for domestic arbitration. The IAA was, therefore, further amended in 2015 to similarly apply confidentiality on an opt-out basis, for international arbitrations seated in Australia.[36]

However, it remains unclear whether this will be enough to establish Australia as an arbitration-friendly jurisdiction, and attract significantly more ICA cases to its shores. The situation may be similar to developments in Australian case law, especially over the last decade. Judgments have generally become more pro-arbitration and

33. Nottage & Garnett, *supra* n. 23.
34. The IAA does not impose direct obligations on arbitrators, any chosen arbitral institution, or other third parties. An unresolved scenario that could, therefore, arise as follows. Assume that a party to an Australia-seated arbitration is under an agreed obligation of confidentiality to a third party in relation to the contractual relationship between them. Assume further that the other party to the arbitration seeks the arbitrator's permission under IAA s. 23(2) to apply to a court for the issue of a subpoena requiring the third party to produce documents evidencing that contractual relationship to the arbitral tribunal. Finally, assume that those documents are relevant and material to the issues before the tribunal. Without further guidance from the IAA, the tribunal (and then the Australian court) will have to consider the competing interests of all parties in exercising its discretion whether to grant permission and later to permit inspection, and, to the extent possible, devise a regime that will protect those interests.
35. At a seminar presented on 15 Aug. 2019 at 12 Wentworth Selborne Chambers in Sydney, Michael Hwang SC and former NSW Supreme Court Justice Robert McDougall further suggested that *Esso's* reasoning might still be relevant, especially when assessing whether the an Australian court should allow disclosure after weighing the 'public interest' under s. 23G(1) of the International Arbitration Act 1974 (Cth).
36. Luke Nottage, *Australia's International Arbitration Act Amendments: Rejuvenation by a Thousand Cuts?*, Kluwer Arbitration Blog (13 May 2017), http://arbitrationblog.kluwerarbitration.com/2017/05/13/australias-international-arbitration-act-amendments-rejuvenation-thousand-cuts/ (accessed 28 Aug. 2019).

internationalist, especially over the last decade.[37] Yet this does not seem to have generated many more ICA filings, at least so far.[38]

There is also the irony that when Australia hosted the International Council for Commercial Arbitration (ICCA) Congress in Sydney last year,[39] the 2015 legislative amendment switching to opt-out confidentiality was criticised by a leading practitioner (Constantine Partasides QC) as going against a broader shift towards transparency in a global society. Against that backdrop, he argued that confidentiality only on an opt-in basis, may be the way forward. Another unresolved issue in Australia is whether and how to limit confidentiality and privacy around IAA-related court proceedings (such as challenges to arbitrators or awards), as in Hong Kong or Singapore compared to (more transparent) New Zealand.[40]

[B] Australia's Investment Treaties and Arbitration

In addition, the IAA was further amended in late 2018 to exempt international investment arbitrations in Australia from the opt-out confidentiality provision if subject to the 2014 UNCITRAL Rules on Transparency in Treaty-based Investor-State Arbitration.[41] None of Australia's treaties (even recently concluded, such as with Korea) specifically adopts those Rules, although they do incorporate directly into the treaty

37. *See*, e.g., *Casaceli v. Natuzzi S.p.A.* (2012) 292 A.L.R. 143. The Federal Court of Australia stayed its proceedings in favour of Milan-seated arbitration, accepting expert witness evidence that the tribunal might apply as mandatory rules the 'Australian Consumer Law' prohibitions against misleading conduct in trade, which apply to B2B as well as B2C transactions. (However, if the arbitrators did not there remains the possibility of the resultant award not being enforced in Australia on public policy grounds.) *See also* Nobumichi Teramura, Luke Nottage & James Morrison, *International Commercial Arbitration in Australia: Judicial Control over Arbitral Awards*, 19/24 Sydney Law School Research Paper (2019), https://ssrn.com/abstract=3379494 (accessed 28 Aug. 2019).
38. Diana Hu & Luke Nottage, *The International Arbitration Act Matters: Where to Litigate and Why (Not)*, 35 The Arbitrator & Mediator 91 (2016). Also available at https://ssrn.com/abstract=2862256 (accessed 4 Sep. 2019). A more recent study also finds, for example, that almost all international arbitration work among practitioners in Western Australia (with significant energy resources and related disputes) relates to hearings and cases seated overseas: *WA Arbitration Report* (2019), https://www.francisburt.com.au/waarbitrationinitiative (accessed 6 Sep. 2019).
39. *See* Partasides' presentation video-recorded: ICC, *Arbitrations Involving Public Bodies and Public Interests: Salient Issues (Continued)*, https://www.arbitration-icca.org/conferences-and-congresses/ICCA_SYDNEY_2018-video-coverage/ICCA_SYDNEY_2018-Panel_8.html (accessed 18 Oct. 2019). For an overview of the ICCA Congress and its side initiatives in Sydney, *see* Luke Nottage & Nobumichi Teramura, *Australia's (In)Capacity in International Commercial Arbitration*, Kluwer Arbitration Blog (20 Sep. 2018), http://arbitrationblog.kluwerarbitration.com/2018/09/20/australias-incapacity-international-commercial-arbitration/ (accessed 4 Sep. 2019).
40. *See*, e.g., Luke Nottage, *International Commercial Arbitration in Australia: What's New and What's Next?*, in *International Commercial Law and Arbitration* 287 (Nye Perram ed., Ross Parsons Centre of Commercial, Corporate and Taxation Law 2014). Also available at https://ssrn.com/abstract=2393232 (accessed 4 Sep. 2019). At present the question remains governed by general Court Rule and Practice Notes across State, Territorial and Federal Courts.
41. Adam Firth, Luke Carbon, Prajesh Shrestha & Maggie Kearney, *Staying on the 'Cutting Edge' – Proposed Amendments to the International Arbitration Act 1974 (Cth)*, Ashurst (24 Sep. 2018), https://www.ashurst.com/en/news-and-insights/legal-updates/international-arbitration-update-staying-on-the-cutting-edge-180924/ (accessed 4 Sep. 2019).

text somewhat similar transparency provisions around ISDS. However, Australia in 2017 signed the 2014 United Nation (UN) Convention on Transparency on Transparency in Treaty-based Investor-State Arbitration.[42] This Mauritius Convention later entered into force for a few other states, and from 17 March 2021 for Australia,[43] thus giving the 2018 IAA amendment more traction because the Convention extends or retrofits the UNCITRAL Transparency Rules to investment treaties concluded before 1 April 2014.

This 2018 amendment arguably had two aims. First, it could help address growing concerns and debate about ISDS generally among the public in Australia, especially since it was subjected to its first treaty-based claim from 2011. The claim over Australia's tobacco plain packaging legislation brought by Philip Morris Asia under an old investment treaty with Hong Kong was dismissed on jurisdictional grounds in 2015. However, the tribunal (applying 2010 UNCITRAL Arbitration Rules) ordered the application of a confidentiality regime.[44] That was criticised by some, including those concerned about the costs spent by the Australian government to defend the case.[45] Second, the minister introducing the 2018 amendment argued that it 'broadens the scope of arbitration work which can be conducted in Australia under the IAA'.[46]

However, both arguments only apply if the parties conduct their investment treaty arbitrations seated in Australia.[47] That is unlikely where the Australian government or investors are involved; the arbitration will almost invariably instead take place overseas. (In the Philip Morris case, for example, it persuaded the tribunal to order Singapore as the seat; Australia had argued for London, somewhat curiously.[48]) The expected benefits from the 2018 IAA amendment, notably to increase the scope and work for investment arbitrations in Australia, will only really arise if governments and investors from other countries choose Australia as a neutral third-country seat. That

42. Department of Foreign Affairs and Trade, *Australia Signs the Mauritius Convention on Transparency* (19 Jul. 2017) https://dfat.gov.au/news/news/Pages/australia-signs-the-mauritius-convention-on-transparency.aspx (accessed 4 Sep. 2019).
43. UNCITRAL, *Status: United Nations Convention on Transparency in Treaty-based Investor-State Arbitration (New York, 2014)*, https://uncitral.un.org/en/texts/arbitration/conventions/transparency/status (accessed 4 Sep. 2019). (Italy signed but also hasn't yet ratified; Japan has not signed).
44. *Philip Morris Asia Limited (Hong Kong) v. The Commonwealth of Australia (Procedural Order No 12)* PCA Case No. 2012-12 (14 Nov. 2014).
45. Cf. e.g., Gareth Hutchens & Christopher Knaus, *Revealed: $39m Cost of Defending Australia's Tobacco Plain Packaging Laws*, The Guardian (2 Jul. 2018), https://www.theguardian.com/business/2018/jul/02/revealed-39m-cost-of-defending-australias-tobacco-plain-packaging-laws (accessed 4 Sep. 2019).
46. Cited in Nottage, *supra* n. 36.
47. Both the 2014 UNCITRAL Transparency Rules and the 2017 Mauritius Convention provisions only cover treaty-based ISDS arbitrations, not those where the consent to arbitration and investment protections are in one-off contracts between investors and host states.
48. A negative jurisdictional ruling (as eventually made by the tribunal) could have been appealed to courts at the seat in England, thus prolonging the dispute, but not at the time in Singapore: *see* Jarrod Hepburn & Luke Nottage, *Case Note: Phillip Morris Asia v. Australia*, 18 J. World Inv. & Trade 307 (2017). Also available at https://ssrn.com/abstract=2842065 (accessed 4 Sep. 2019).

seems unlikely, given the difficulties of attracting even (typically smaller) ICA cases to Australia.

Still, Australia's 2018 IAA amendment may promote transparency generally around ISDS if similar legislation is enacted in other countries. Australia has the opportunity to elaborate these points in the ongoing UNCITRAL deliberations on ISDS reform, where transparency has been a significant issue,[49] as well as through Australia's evolving treaty practice (outlined in the conclusions below).

§4.03 JAPAN: MODEST AND MEASURED?

[A] ICA

Japan also adopted the UNCITRAL Model Law on ICA, but only in 2003 as part of a broader package of justice system reforms.[50] Like Australia in 1989, Japan did not add any confidentiality provisions. Unlike Australia, however, Japan has not subsequently added provisions – indeed, it has not amended its Arbitration Act 2003 at all. It remains unclear whether there are current plans to do so, despite a push since 2017 mainly from the governing Liberal Democratic Party to belatedly promote Japan as a new regional hub for international dispute resolution services (following also initiatives in Korea and Malaysia).[51]

Again, however, arbitration institutions have stepped into the breach. Notably, the JCAA administers most of the (still comparatively few) ICA cases seated in Japan,[52] and its Arbitration Rules have long included a confidentiality provision. The Rules

49. *See* summaries, e.g., by Anthea Roberts & Taylor St. John, *UNCITRAL and ISDS Reform: China's Proposal*, Ejil:Talk (5 Aug. 2019), https://www.ejiltalk.org/author/aroberts/ (accessed 4 Sep. 2019).

50. Tatsuya Nakamura & Luke Nottage, *Arbitration in Japan*, in *International Commercial Arbitration in Asia* 223 (Tom Ginsburg & Shahla Ali eds., Juris 2013). Also available at https://ssrn.com/abstract=2070447 (accessed 4 Sep. 2019).

51. James M. Claxton, Luke Nottage & Nobumichi Teramura, *Developing Japan as a Regional Hub for International Dispute Resolution: Dream Come True or Daydream?*, 47 J. J. L 109 (2019). Also available at https://ssrn.com/abstract=3299097 (accessed 4 Sep. 2019) and updated as Chapter 10 in this volume.

52. The Tokyo Maritime Arbitration Commission (TOMAC) within the Japan Shipping Exchange, deals with fewer and narrower (maritime law) cases, for example eight arbitrations resolved (and twelve filings accepted) in the 2018 financial year: *see* http://www.jseinc.org/about/pdf/2019/hokoku_2018.pdf (accessed 18 Oct. 2019, in Japanese). The TOMAC Rules also stipulate that the arbitrators (Ordinary Arbitration Rules Article 18(3)) and 'the parties, their agents or attorneys or any other persons concerned shall not reveal to third parties the contents of the arbitration, the names of the parties or anything else related' to the case (Article 21(3)). *See* http://www.jseinc.org/en/tomac/arbitration/ordinary_rules.html (accessed 18 Oct. 2019). For further statistics on JCAA and other arbitrations in Japan, *see* Nobumichi Teramura & Luke Nottage, *Arbitration Reform in Japan: Reluctant Legislature and Institutional Challenges*, in *The Developing World of Arbitration: A Comparative Study of Arbitration Reform in the Asia Pacific* 83-108 (Anselmo Reyes & Weixia Gu eds., Hart Publishing 2018). Also available at https://ssrn.com/abstract=3252270 (accessed 18 Oct. 2019).

amended in 2004, the year after enactment of the Arbitration Act based on the Model Law, included Article 38(2). This was restated in the 2008 Rules as Article 40(2):[53]

> The arbitrators, the officers and staff of the Association, the parties and their representatives or assistants shall not disclose facts related to arbitration cases or facts learned through arbitration cases except where disclosure is required by law or required in court proceedings.

Indeed, subsequent JCAA Rules have imposed somewhat stricter confidentiality obligations. Article 38(2) in 2014 extended them to others involved in the arbitration, presumably including witnesses (emphasis added):[54]

> The arbitrators, the JCAA (including its directors, officers, employees, and other staff), the Parties, their counsel and assistants, *and other persons involved in the arbitral proceedings* shall not disclose facts related to or learned through the arbitral proceedings except where disclosure is required by law or in court proceedings, or based on any other justifiable grounds.

Article 42(2) of the main 2019 Rules further elaborate somewhat (emphasis added):[55]

> The arbitrators, the JCAA (including its directors, officers, employees, and other staff), the Parties, their counsel and assistants, and other persons involved in the arbitral proceedings shall not disclose facts related to or learned through the arbitral proceedings *and shall not express any views as to such facts*, except where disclosure is required by law or in court proceedings, or based on any other justifiable grounds.

This progression has been little noticed or discussed among commentators. The silence contrasts with Australia, where enhancement of confidentiality obligations in ACICA Rules since 2005 and especially through the IAA since 2015 has been publicised as signalling a more pro-arbitration stance. It could be that Japan is being typically more modest in self-promotion, or that it has less scope to do so anyway because the legislation still does not provide automatically for confidentiality. But it could also be wise not to amend the Arbitration Act 2003, and instead maintain confidentiality in the main institutional Rules, given recent suggestions by Partasides and a few others that confidentiality is perhaps best available only on an opt-in basis even in ICA. However, most of the international arbitration cases in Japan seem to involve purely commercial arbitrations, namely contracts between private companies that raise no or minimal

53. *See The Japan Commercial Arbitration Association (JCAA) Commercial Arbitration Rules (2008)*, http://www.jcaa.or.jp/e/arbitration/docs/e_shouji.pdf (accessed 4 Sep. 2019); and Gerald P. McAlinn & Luke Nottage, *Changing the (JCAA) Rules: Improving International Commercial Arbitration in Japan*, 18 J.J.L. 23, 33 (2004). Also available at https://ssrn.com/abstract=837085 (accessed 4 Sep. 2019).
54. *See* JCAA Commercial Arbitration Rules (2015), http://www.jcaa.or.jp/e/arbitration/Arbitration_Rules_2015e.pdf (accessed 4 Sep. 2019); and JCAA Commercial Arbitration Rules (2014), http://www.jcaa.or.jp/e/arbitration/docs/Arbitration_Rules_2014e.pdf (accessed 4 Sep. 2019).
55. *See* JCAA Commercial Arbitration Rules *(2019)*, http://www.jcaa.or.jp/e/arbitration/docs/Commercial_Arbitoration_Rules.pdf (accessed 4 Sep. 2019).

private interests. By contrast, Partasides and others may be influenced by the fact that many ICC and other cases now involve some state entity as a disputing party. Those do tend to raise more public interests and therefore support arguments in favour of greater transparency in arbitration.

[B] Japan's Investment Treaties and ISDS

For many decades, Japan did not actively conclude many bilateral investment treaties (BITs), compared to say Korea, and was quite flexible when drafting them. The pattern is similar to Australia, but the latter had much less outbound investment than Japan and therefore less incentive to pursue a BIT program. Since Japan began to conclude investment treaties as part of broader Free Trade Agreements (FTAs), beginning with Singapore in 2001, Japan has become more consistent with drafting.[56] Japan is mostly now inspired by contemporary US-style treaties, as with many countries in the Asia-Pacific region, evidenced in the new mega-regional Comprehensive and Progressive Agreement for Transpacific Partnership (CPTPP).[57] Japan is also playing catch up by accelerating its program of concluding stand-alone BITs, especially in developing markets or politically unstable destination countries in Africa and the Middle East.[58] By contrast, Australia and other developed Asia-Pacific countries are concluding relatively fewer BITs and concentrating more on FTA negotiations. In UNCITRAL reform deliberations, Japan has been one of the states more supportive of the current ISDS system.

However, a noticeable trend in recent Japanese investment treaties, similarly to those concluded by Australia, has been already to enhance transparency provisions around the ISDS procedure.[59] It will be interesting to see if Japan moves soon to sign and ratify the 2017 Mauritius Convention. If it does, the Arbitration Act will not need an amendment similar to Australia's in 2018 because it does not provide for confidentiality on an opt-out basis. Indeed, this aspect could be used by the Japanese government and arbitration community to promote Japan (rather than Australia at present) as an appropriate neutral venue for ISDS arbitrations. But many other factors are likely to be more important for parties thinking about choosing an appropriate venue. In the Philip Morris Asia case, for example, it was argued that London was

---

56. Shotaro Hamamoto & Luke Nottage, *Foreign Investment in and out of Japan: Economic Backdrop, Domestic Law, and International Treaty-Based Investor-State Dispute Resolution*, 8 TDM (2011). Also available at https://ssrn.com/abstract=1724999 (accessed 4 Sep. 2019).
57. Amokura Kawharu & Luke Nottage, *Models for Investment Treaties in the Asian Region: An Underview*, 34 Ariz. J. Int'l & Comp. L. 462 (2017). Also available at https://ssrn.com/abstract=2845088 (accessed 4 Sep. 2019).
58. As noted recently, 'the Abe Administration since 2012 has signed 16 stand-alone BITs (all with ISDS)': James Claxton, Luke Nottage & Brett G. Williams, *Resolving Disputes Amidst Japan-Korea Trade and Investment Tensions: Part II*, Kluwer Arbitration Blog (12 Aug. 2019), *http:*//arbitrationblog.kluwerarbitration.com/2019/08/12/resolving-disputes-amidst-japan-korea-trade-and-investment-tensions-part-ii/(accessed 4 Sep. 2019).
59. *See* Tomoko Ishikawa, *A Japanese Perspective on International Investment Agreements: Recent Developments*, in *International Investment Treaties and Arbitration Across Asia* 513 (Julien Chaisse & Luke Nottage eds., Brill 2018).

better than Singapore because (at that time) the UK courts had had more experience in investment treaty cases. Japanese courts still have no such experience or even much experience in ICA cases.[60] Indeed, the government has never been subjected to a treaty-based ISDS claim.

§4.04 CONCLUSIONS AND BROADER IMPLICATIONS

We can discern a gradual strengthening of confidentiality obligations around ICA, in Japan and especially Australia, yet a loosening in both countries around ISDS.[61] The latter tendency towards transparency probably results mostly from wider public concerns over ISDS. Those could even have led to Australia reverting to eschewing ISDS altogether in future treaties (as in 2011-2013 under a Labor-Greens government) if the government had lost the general election held in May 2019.[62] The Labor Opposition had further declared that it would also seek to renegotiate Australia's old treaties.[63] However, the Coalition Government unexpectedly won the election,[64] and so resumed parliamentary inquiries into ratification of treaties it had signed with Indonesia and Hong Kong that both contain ISDS provisions.[65] The ISDS-related transparency provisions are far less extensive in the former than the latter treaty.[66] However, in light of Australia's other treaty practice,[67] this probably reflects the counterparty's preferences. The Labor Opposition committee members focused on other aspects of these

60. Teramura & Nottage, *supra* n. 52.
61. Shirlow, *supra* n. 25.
62. Kawharu & Nottage, *supra* n. 22.
63. Esme Shirlow, *2018 in Review: Australia and New Zealand*, Kluwer Arbitration Blog (21 Jan. 2019), http://arbitrationblog.kluwerarbitration.com/2019/01/21/2018-in-review-australia-and-new-zealand/ (accessed 4 Sep. 2019).
64. Luke Nottage, *Settling Investor-state Disputes: Asia Pacific Style*, East Asia Forum (25 May 2019), https://www.eastasiaforum.org/2019/05/25/settling-investor-state-disputes-asia-pacific-style/ (accessed 4 Sep. 2019).
65. The transcript of my evidence for the Joint Standing Committee on Treaties inquiry hearings in Sydney on 26 Aug. 2019 is available via https://www.aph.gov.au/Parliamentary_Business/Committees/Joint/Treaties/Indonesia-AustraliaCEPA/Public_Hearings and https://www.aph.gov.au/Parliamentary_Business/Committees/Joint/Treaties/A-HKFTA/Public_Hearings (accessed 4 Sep. 2019).
66. Compare especially Indonesia-Australia Comprehensive Economic Partnership Agreement, Article 14.31.1 (only public disclosure of tribunal 'awards and decisions') against Australia-Hong Kong Free Trade Agreement, Article 30.1 and 30.2 (much other information too and public hearings). *See also generally* Luke Nottage, *New Frontiers in International Arbitration for the Asia-Pacific Region (7): Australia's Parliamentary Inquiries into ISDS in HK, Indonesia and UN/Mauritius Treaties* and *JSCOT Submission on Australia-Indonesia CEPA (FTA) & Australia-Hong Kong Revised Investment Agreement: Compared*, University of Sydney Japanese Law and the Asia Pacific Blog (1 Sep. 2019), https://japaneselaw.sydney.edu.au/2019/09/new-frontiers-in-international-arbitration-for-the-asia-pacific-region-7-australias-parliamentary-inquiries-into-isds-in-hk-indonesia-and-un-mauritius-treaties/ (accessed 4 Sep. 2019). A similar transparency regime will apply if the investor chooses UNCITRAL Arbitration Rules (incorporating the 2014 UNCITRAL Transparency Rules); but the treaty with Indonesia also allows the investor to choose ICSID (Convention or Additional Facility) Arbitration instead.
67. *See*, e.g., Andrew Mitchell, *Australia and New Zealand*, in *Research Handbook on Foreign Direct Investment* 390 (Markus Krajewski & Rhea Tamara Hoffmann eds., Elgar 2019).

treaties, voicing objections to ISDS and other investment-related provisions, but eventually (unlike the Greens) favoured ratification by Australia.

Neither new treaty for Australia regulates the disclosure of settlement agreements, yet Australia's recent treaty with Indonesia lets the host state force the investor into conciliation before being able to commence arbitration (Articles 14.2 and 14.26.2(b)). Such potentially mandatory conciliation is very unusual for investment treaties and seems likely to have been proposed by Indonesia given its more extensive experience in fielding claims from foreign investors.[68] Curiously, only the treaty with Indonesia (Article 14.32) requires the investor to disclose any third-party funder, even though Hong Kong has recently legislated such as disclosure requirement for arbitrations seated there (or elsewhere where arbitration-related services are provided in Hong Kong).[69] Third-party funding remains essentially unregulated in Australia since a judgment of its High Court in 2006,[70] although this has not been actively marketed to make Australia a more attractive seat for international arbitrations compared to Hong Kong, or Singapore which also recently legislated to allow third-party funding on specified conditions.

In addition, after Australia's general election was completed in 2019, a parliamentary inquiry to ratify the Mauritius Convention was commenced.[71] We can again see some more broad-based political agreement to ratify the Mauritius Convention as a major step towards enhancing transparency around ISDS, extending its transparency provisions to pre-2014 treaties already in force at least between states that ratify this new framework Convention. So far the Convention has attracted few ratifications, but this could be because there is little incentive to do so unless counterparties do too.[72] Ratification now by Australia and hopefully other states, especially perhaps by developed states that are better prepared than some developing states to expose their government's alleged (in)action to wider public scrutiny, would also be in line with other international trends towards greater transparency in ISDS.

A recent example of that tendency comes from the well-advanced process to revise the Rules of the International Centre for Investment Disputes (ICSID). Working Paper 1 had proposed that parties would be deemed to have consented to publication of full ICSID awards unless objecting within sixty days. This idea was reversed in

68. *See* generally Ana Ubilava, *Amicable Settlements in Investor-State Disputes: Empirical Analysis of Patterns and Perceived Problems*, 19/17 Sydney Law School Research Paper (2019), https://ssrn.com/abstract=3352181 (accessed 4 Sep. 2019); and Chapter 5 by Ubilava and Nottage in this volume.
69. Peter Hirst & Mun Yeow, *Comparing Hong Kong Code of Practice for Third Party Funding Arbitration with the Code of Conduct in England & Wales*, Kluwer Arbitration Blog (4 Feb. 2019), http://arbitrationblog.kluwerarbitration.com/2019/02/04/comparing-hong-kong-code-of-practice-for-third-party-funding-arbitration-with-the-code-of-conduct-in-england-wales/ (accessed 4 Sep. 2019).
70. *Campbells Cash and Carry Pty Ltd v. Fostif Pty Ltd* (2006) 229 C.L.R. 386.
71. Joint Standing Committee on Treaties, *ISDS UN Convention*, https://www.aph.gov.au/Parliamentary_Business/Committees/Joint/Treaties/ISDSUNConvention (accessed 4 Sep. 2019).
72. *See* United Nations Treaty Collection, https://treaties.un.org/Pages/ViewDetails.aspx?src=TREATY&mtdsg_no=XXII-3&chapter=22&clang=_en (five ratifications, when accessed 18 Oct. 2019).

Working Paper 2 but reinstated in the current Working Paper 3, which also proposes to publish tribunal orders and decisions as the ICSID Convention requiring party consent only applies to awards. ICSID anyway proposes to publish excerpts from the award, not just of 'legal reasoning' as under current Rules. However, Working Paper 3 does retreat from having open hearings; that will be up to the tribunal to determine.[73] More broadly, ever-greater transparency in investment treaty arbitration may be tempered by the requirement of national data privacy laws, as illustrated by two recent cases involving respectively EU and Korean laws.[74]

The overall tendency towards promoting transparency in investment treaty arbitration could ramp up pressure to revisit Australian legislation and even ACICA Rules[75] favouring confidentiality in other international arbitrations. However, the Chief Justice of the Federal Court of Australia rightly reminded ICCA delegates in Sydney in 2018 that there remain significant differences between ISDS and ICA.[76] This tension is less pronounced in Japan, as its Arbitration Act does not provide automatically for confidentiality anyway. Nonetheless, JCAA (and other) Rules do impose confidentiality obligations, and as with ACICA or other arbitral institutions, some cases may involve public interests. Accordingly, the possible tension with transparency principles should also be considered in Japan too.

For each country, moreover, such tensions may influence the negotiation and drafting of transparency provisions in treaties still being negotiated respectively with the EU. Even with the newly re-elected Coalition government, Australia may be amenable in ongoing negotiations[77] to the permanent investment court alternative to traditional ISDS now insisted on by the EU in its recent investment protection treaties (e.g., with Singapore, Vietnam and Canada), which also aims to make investment

73. ICSID, *Proposals for Amendment of the ICSID Rules – Working Paper #3*, available at https://icsid.worldbank.org/en/amendments (accessed 4 Sep. 2019). *See also* Jarrod Hepburn, *ICSID Releases a Third Version of Working Paper on Proposed Changes to Arbitration Rules, Addressing Transparency, Security for Costs, Third-Party Funding, Timelines and Other Issues*, IA Reporter (19 Aug. 2019), www.iareporter.com /articles/icsid-releases-a-third-version-of-working-paper-on-proposed-changes-to-arbitration-rules-addressing-transparency-security-for-costs-third-party-funding-and-timelines/ (accessed 4 Sep. 2019).

74. Emily Hay, *The Invisible Arm of GDPR in International Treaty Arbitration*, Kluwer Arbitration Blog (29 Aug. 2019), http://arbitrationblog.kluwerarbitration.com/2019/08/29/the-invisible-arm-of-gdpr-in-international-treaty-arbitration-cant-we-make-it-go-away/ (accessed 4 Sep. 2019), discussing *Tennant Energy v. Canada*; Jarrod Hepburn, *UNCITRAL Tribunal Permits Korea to Request Redactions of Personal Information from Filings under Domestic Data Privacy Law*, IA Reporter (1 Sep. 2019), https://www.iareporter.com/articles/uncitral-tribunal-permits-korea-to-request-redactions-of-personal-information-from-filings-under-domestic-data-privacy-law/ (accessed 4 Sep. 2019), discussing *Elliott Associates v. Korea*.

75. *See also* Luke Nottage & Kate Miles, *'Back to the Future' for Investor-State Arbitrations: Revising Rules in Australia and Japan to Meet Public Interests*, in *International Arbitration in Australia* 222 (Luke Nottage & Richard Garnett eds., Federation Press 2010). Also available at https://ssrn.com/abstract=1151167 (accessed 4 Sep. 2019).

76. *See* James Allsop, *Commercial and Investor-State Arbitration: The Importance of Recognising Their Differences* (ICCA Congress 2018, Keynote Address), http://www.fedcourt.gov.au/digital-law-library/judges-speeches/chief-justice-allsop/allsop-cj-20180416 (accessed 4 Sep. 2019).

77. *See* Department of Foreign Affairs and Trade, *Australia-European Union Free Trade Agreement*, https://dfat.gov.au/trade/agreements/negotiations/aeufta/Pages/default.aspx (accessed 4 Sep. 2019).

dispute resolution more transparent. But the court option may seem less pro-investor and therefore more unattractive for Japan, which has much larger foreign direct investment in Europe than vice versa, as the EU and Japan continue to negotiate an investment protection treaty.[78] Some hybrid process, such as traditional ISDS arbitration with appeals to a permanent court comprising members appointed only by treaty partner states, may be another compromise way forward.[79] Interestingly, this hybrid alternative has attracted some support by China in a proposal on ISDS reform to UNCITRAL dated 19 July 2019.[80] Nonetheless, as rather cautious and reactive players in international investment law-making, Australia and especially Japan may well end up waiting for whatever consensus emerges from the protracted and ongoing debates in UNCITRAL.

One problem with such a wait-and-see approach is that opportunities may have been lost for a hybrid dispute resolution mechanism providing a compromise to conclude negotiations since 2012 for the Regional Comprehensive Economic Partnership (ASEAN + 6 FTA, including Singapore and nine other Southeast Asian nations, Australia, New Zealand, Japan, China, Korea and India). Indeed, India did not join that mega-regional FTA as concluded in late 2019, and the FTA reportedly left ISDS to be further considered within two years of the treaty eventually coming into force.[81] Momentum for concluding other Asia-Pacific investment treaties with appropriate dispute settlement procedures may also be hampered. Public concerns over transparency or other issues around ISDS arbitration may even spread to undermine the generally positive image of ICA that has been painstakingly built up around the region.[82]

In particular, reducing confidentiality associated with parties choosing arbitration to resolve purely commercial cross-border disputes, risks further exacerbating longstanding and arguably increasing concerns about over-formalisation (including

78. *See* Andre Sapir, Sonali Chowdhry & Alessio Terzi, *The EU-Japan Economic Partnership Agreement*, Report for the European Parliament's Committee on International Trade, 18-19 (28 Sep. 2018). The Japan-EU FTA (in force from 1 Feb. 2019) only provided for market access commitments, not investment protections and a dispute settlement mechanism, which proved controversial.
79. As proposed by Prof. Gabrielle Kaufmann-Kohler et al: Geneva Center for International Dispute Settlement (CIDS), *ISDS Reform Project*, https://www.cids.ch/conferences-research/projects/isds-project (accessed 4 Sep. 2019).
80. Summarised by Roberts & St. John, *supra* n. 49. Korea's submission of 31 Jul. 2019 (A/CN.9/WG.III/WP.179) is decidedly cooler over any possible 'standing mechanism' (seemingly encompassing the two-tier EU-style court or the permanent appellate review body hybrid). The government's stance may reflect the concerns voiced earlier by an eminent Seoul National University Professor: Jaemin Lee, *Mending the Wound or Pulling It Apart? New Proposals for International Investment Courts and Fragmentation of International Investment Law*, 39 Nw. J. Int'l L. & Bus. 1 (2018).
81. Nottage, *supra* n. 64; with an analysis of an earlier leaked RCEP investment chapter draft in Kawharu & Nottage, *supra* n. 57; and *see* generally Singh's Chapter 12 in this volume.
82. For media analysis of reporting and impressions about different types of arbitration in Australia and elsewhere, *see* Luke Nottage, *International Arbitration and Society at Large*, in *Cambridge Compendium on International Arbitration* (Andrea Bjorklund, Franco Ferrari & Stefan Kroell eds., Cambridge University Press 2021 forthcoming). Also available at https://www.ssrn.com/abstract=3116528 (accessed 4 Sep. 2019).

delays and especially costs) in ICA, even in the Asian region.[83] Confidentiality should be seen as a double-edged sword. It can allow arbitrators to be more robust with procedures and succinct in writing up their decisions. Yet it can also exacerbate information asymmetry common in services markets by making it hard for clients to ascertain whether arbitrators and counsel really provide good value for money.[84] Hopefully, such information asymmetry will decline as information about arbitrators and (perhaps less so) counsel becomes more widely available anyway, through publically available ISDS cases but also initiatives from 'Arbitrator Intelligence'[85] and the ICC.[86] Such initiatives may reduce pressure to take away confidentiality from commercial arbitrations under the slogan of ever-greater transparency.

If confidentiality is to be reduced in ICA, care needs to be taken when using the blunt instrument of legislation. A better approach is probably for arbitral institutions to experiment by amending their rules and best practices. In doing so, they should bear in mind careful research into how various institutions have regulated various aspects of confidentiality, ranging from the existence of the arbitration, confidentiality regarding documents used, obligations on arbitrators, witnesses and others as well as the parties, and confidentiality regarding the award.[87] Arbitral institutions and other stakeholders should also consider a perhaps growing view that confidentiality even in ICA should be less sacrosanct especially regarding final awards, to enhance predictability and legitimacy around arbitration, let alone when arbitration-related disputes end up in court due to the further public interests involved: the principle of open justice.[88]

83. For such concerns, *see* e.g., the Queen Mary University of London and White & Case 2018 Survey, *supra* n. 1, at 7-8.
84. Including also further empirical evidence of burgeoning costs and delays, *see* Luke Nottage, *In/Formalisation and Glocalisation of International Commercial Arbitration and Investment Treaty Arbitration in Asia*, in *Formalisation and Flexibilisation of Dispute Resolution* 211 (Joachim Zekoll, Moritz Baelz & Iwo Amelung eds., Martinus Nijhoff/Brill 2014). Also available at https://ssrn.com/abstract=2987674 (accessed 4 Sep. 2019).
85. *See* Arbitrator Intelligence, https://arbitratorintelligence.com/ (accessed 4 Sep. 2019); and e.g., Catherine A. Rogers, *Arbitrator Intelligence: From Intuition to Data in Arbitrator Appointments*, 11(2) N.Y. Disp. Res. Law. 41 (Spring 2018). Also available at https://ssrn.com/abstract=3113800 (accessed 4 Sep. 2019).
86. *See* ICC, *ICC Court Announces New Policies to Foster Transparency and Ensure Greater Efficiency* (5 Jan. 2016), https://iccwbo.org/media-wall/news-speeches/icc-court-announces-new-policies-to-foster-transparency-and-ensure-greater-efficiency/ (accessed 4 Sep. 2019).
87. Hwang et al., *supra* n. 5 (especially the helpful summary table of different arbitral rules).
88. For example, after careful comparative study and discussion (Coppa, *supra* n. 25), the Arbitration Rules of the Milan Chamber of Commerce were revised in 2010 to widen confidentiality obligations on 'the parties, the Arbitral Tribunal and the expert witnesses' (Article 8(1)), but to change the default position to allow the institution to publish anonymised awards 'for purposes of research' unless any party objects (rather than requiring all parties to opt-in and consent).

CHAPTER 5

Novel and Noteworthy Aspects of Australia's Recent Investment Agreements and ISDS Policy: The CPTPP, Hong Kong, Indonesia and Mauritius Transparency Treaties

Ana Ubilava & Luke Nottage

If Tolstoy had been an international arbitration lawyer, he might have said that 'efficient proceedings are all alike; every inefficient proceeding is inefficient in its own way'.[1]

This chapter updates on recent investment treaty practice by Australia, which attracted regional and global attention when a centre-left government over 2011-2013 declared Australia would no longer agree to investor-state dispute settlement (ISDS) provisions when negotiating further treaties. The chapter compares substantive commitments and ISDS provisions in Australia's treaties signed with Indonesia and Hong Kong in 2019 (Indonesia-Australia Comprehensive Economic Partnership Agreement (IA-CEPA) and Australia-Hong Kong Investment Agreement (AHKIA)) compared especially with the mega-regional Comprehensive and Progressive Agreement for a Trans-Pacific Partnership (CPTPP) signed in 2018. The new bilateral treaties remain quite heavily influenced by US-style drafting, epitomised by the CPTPP. The chapter then elaborates on the costs and delays associated with investor-state arbitration (ISA). It examines empirical studies, then relevant provisions of the three new treaties, including an innovative investor-state mediation provision in IA-CEPA probably proposed by Indonesia. The chapter also considers transparency of proceedings and outcomes. It again examines mainly not only CPTPP, IA-CEPA and AHKIA but also a parliamentary enquiry into Australia ratifying the Mauritius Convention. This seeks to retrofit extensive transparency

1. Anthony Sinclair & Sarah Macrory, *ICSID Arbitration: How Long Does It Take?*, 4 GAR 1 (2009).

provisions on pre-2014 treaties between Australia and other states that might also accede to that framework Convention. More bipartisanship may be emerging in domestic politics regarding international investment treaty-marking, so Australia is now better placed to play a more active role, especially in the Asia-Pacific region.

§5.01 INTRODUCTION

The expansion of foreign direct investment (FDI) and international investment agreements (IIAs), including provisions on ISA, has resulted in the proliferation of ISA cases on both ad hoc and institutional platforms such as the International Centre for the Settlement of Investment Disputes (ICSID). Whereas arbitration was previously often seen as a better impartial alternative to costly and time-consuming domestic court systems, today it faces some similar drawbacks.[2] Concerns are further being voiced over provisions more generally on ISDS contained in IIAs that provide advance consent of the host state to ISA claims brought directly by foreign investors.[3] As shown in evidence provided in 2018 to an Australian parliamentary enquiry into ratifying the CPTPP,[4] critiques often revolve around three major issues: the amounts at stake (awarded amounts and costs of the arbitration or lawyers), delays in ISDS cases, and transparency.[5]

Some developing states have been especially critical about ISA, becoming reluctant to include ISDS provisions in their respective IIAs.[6] However, opposition also began to emerge in some civil societies and political spheres in developed states such as Australia.[7] IIAs, and especially ISDS provisions, became a political hot potato from around 2011 when Philip Morris brought the first-ever ISDS claim against Australia under an early (1993) bilateral investment treaty (BIT) with Hong Kong. A Labour-Greens Government declared that it would no longer agree to ISDS provisions in future

2. *See generally*, e.g., Thomas J. Stipanowich, *Arbitration: The 'New Litigation'*, 2010 U. Ill. L. Rev. 1 (2010).
3. Stephan W. Schill, *Reforming Investor–State Dispute Settlement: A (Comparative and International) Constitutional Law Framework*, 20 J. Int'l Econ. L. 649 (2017).
4. Luke Nottage & Ana Ubilava, *Costs, Outcomes and Transparency in ISDS Arbitrations: Evidence for an Investment Treaty Parliamentary Inquiry*, 21 Int'l Arb. L. Rev. 111 (2018).
5. *See*, e.g., Jeswald W. Salacuse, *Is There a Better Way? Alternative Methods of Treaty-Based, Investor-State Dispute Resolution*, 31 Fordham Int'l L. J. 138, 147 (2007); Susan D. Franck, *Rationalising Costs in Investment Treaty Arbitration*, 88 Wash. U. L. Rev. 769 (2011); Leon Trakman, *The ICSID Under Siege*, 45 Cornell Int'l L.J. 603, 617 (2012).
6. *See*, e.g., Prabhash Ranjan & Pushkar Anand, *Investor State Dispute Settlement in the 2016 Indian Model Bilateral Investment Treaty: Does It Go Too Far?*, in *International Investment Treaties and Arbitration Across Asia* 579 (Luke Nottage & Julien Chaisse eds., Brill | Nijhoff 2018); Rodrigo Polanco Lazo, *Is There A Life for Latin American Countries after Denouncing the ICSID Convention?*, 11 TDM (2014), https://www.transnational-dispute-management.com/article.asp?key=2037; Vivienne Bath & Luke Nottage, *International Investment Agreements in Asia*, in *Handbook of International Investment Law and Policy* (Julien Chaisse, et al. eds., Springer 2020). A longer version is also available at SSRN: https://ssrn.com/abstract=3544458.
7. Luke Nottage, *Investor-State Arbitration Policy and Practice in Australia*, 6 CIGI Investor-State Arbitration Series Paper 1 (2016), available at https://www.cigionline.org/publications/investor-state-arbitration-policy-and-practice-australia, updated in Luke Nottage, *International Commercial and Investor-State Arbitration: Australia and Japan in Regional and Global Contexts* (Elgar, forthcoming, early 2021).

treaties, but when a centre-right Coalition Government regained power from 2013 it reverted to concluding treaties containing ISDS clauses on a case-by-case assessment. Australia therefore agreed to ISDS in Free Trade Agreements (FTAs) with Korea and China, but not the bilateral FTA with Japan.[8] ISDS-backed provisions do apply between Australia and Japan since the CPTPP came into force between them (and five other Asia-Pacific nations so far) from January 2019. Yet the Australian parliament engaged in robust debate about ratifying the CPTPP, with Labour Opposition (and especially Greens) parliamentarians continuing to voice concerns over ISDS provisions.[9] This is despite the CPTPP no longer including the USA as a signatory, unlike the earlier Trans-Pacific Partnership (TPP) (containing largely similar investment chapter provisions),[10] and despite the Philip Morris claim against Australia's tobacco plain packaging legislation having been rejected on jurisdictional grounds in 2015.[11]

Further, parliamentary debate arose after Australia and Indonesia on 4 March 2019 signed a new Comprehensive Economic Partnership Agreement (IA-CEPA). Australia ratified this FTA on 18 December 2019,[12] which entered into force on 5 July 2020 (sixty days after it was also ratified by Indonesia). IA-CEPA is not the only treaty that regulates investment relations between Australia and Indonesia and that carries consent to ISDS. IA-CEPA will coexist with the ASEAN-Australia-New Zealand FTA, which already has an ISDS provision (but quite limited investment liberalisation commitments).[13]

The 1992 BIT between Australia and Indonesia was also originally envisaged as remaining in force. That too incorporates ISDS provisions, although an ICSID tribunal quite controversially found that it (like several similarly worded early Australian BITs) did not contain sufficiently clear advance consent to ISA.[14] However, the majority report from the Australian Parliament's Joint Standing Committee on Treaties (JSCOT) enquiry into IA-CEPA, written by parliamentarians not only from the Coalition Government (which signed the FTA) and the Labour Opposition, agreed with submissions arguing that Australia should seek mutual termination of the old BIT when the

8. Luke Nottage, *Investor-State Arbitration: Not in the Australia-Japan Free Trade Agreement, and Not Ever for Australia?*, 38 J.J.L. 37 (2014). Also available at SSRN: https://ssrn.com/abstract=2602130.
9. Submissions to JSCOT on CPTPP enquiry, https://www.aph.gov.au/Parliamentary_Business/Committees/Joint/Treaties/TPP-11/Submissions.
10. Amokura Kawharu & Luke Nottage, *Renouncing Investor-State Dispute Settlement in Australia, Then New Zealand: Déjà Vu*, 18/03 Sydney Law School Research Paper 1 (2018), https://ssrn.com/abstract=3116526.
11. Jarrod Hepburn & Luke Nottage, *A Procedural Win for Public Health Measures*, 18 J. World Inv. & Trade 307 (2017).
12. https://dfat.gov.au/trade/agreements/not-yet-in-force/iacepa/pages/indonesia-australia-comprehensive-economic-partnership-agreement.aspx.
13. *See generally* Vivienne Bath & Luke Nottage, *The ASEAN Comprehensive Investment Agreement and 'ASEAN Plus' – The Australia-New Zealand Free Trade Area (AANZFTA) and the PRC–ASEAN Investment Agreement*, in *International Investment Law* 283 (Marc Bungenberg, et al. eds., Hart Publishing 2015). Also available at SSRN: https://ssrn.com/abstract=2331714.
14. Luke Nottage, *Do Many of Australia's Bilateral Treaties Really Not Provide Full Advance Consent to Investor-State Arbitration? Analysis and Regional Implications*, 12 TDM 1 (2015). Also available at SSRN: https://ssrn.com/abstract=2424987.

new FTA came into force.[15] This is consistent with Australia's past practice,[16] and contributes to 'upgrading' treaty relations from simple (and arguably more pro-investor) BITs to more elaborated (and arguably better balanced, or at least clearer) IIAs. This approach has been recommended by the United Nations Conference on Trade and Development (UNCTAD) and others as one avenue for rebalancing international investment treaty law.[17] It should also be mentioned that Australia and Indonesia will become bound by investment chapter commitments contained in the Regional Comprehensive Economic Partnership (RCEP), which was agreed in principle on 4 November 2019.[18] Yet that FTA, negotiated originally since December 2012 by the 'ASEAN + 6' states, and at least until 2015 envisaging ISDS,[19] has not yet come into force and reportedly excludes ISDS provisions (and indeed India) for now.[20]

In addition, on 26 March 2019, Australia and Hong Kong signed the Australia-Hong Kong Free Trade Agreement (A-HKFTA) and Investment Agreement (AHKIA), which entered into force on 17 January 2020.[21] AHKIA has replaced the 1993 Australia-Hong Kong BIT. AHKIA includes ISDS provisions, like IA-CEPA, although both IIAs have set restrictions on types of claims that can be resolved through such ISDS clauses.

Section 5.02 of this chapter first provides an overview on some of the similarities and differences in substantive commitments and ISDS provisions of IA-CEPA and AHKIA compared especially with CPTPP. It also makes some passing references to the Australia-Peru FTA (in force from 11 February 2020),[22] the amendments to the early

15. *See JSCOT Report*, via https://www.aph.gov.au/Parliamentary_Business/Committees/Joint/Treaties/Indonesia-AustraliaCEPA, and Submissions via https://www.aph.gov.au/Parliamentary_Business/Committees/Joint/Treaties/Indonesia-AustraliaCEPA/Submissions, especially submissions by Professor Andrew D. Mitchell and Professor Tania Voon (no. 2) and Dr Luke Nottage (no. 24). Both governments subsequently entered into an Exchange of Letters to terminate the old BIT (along with its fifteen-year survival clause contained in Article XV), tabled in Australia's Parliament on 14 May 2020 to be also considered by JSCOT: https://www.dfat.gov.au/trade/agreements/in-force/iacepa/Pages/ia-cepa-news. The BIT was accordingly terminated on 6 August 2020: https://www.dfat.gov.au/trade-and-investment/discussion-paper-review-australias-bilateral-investment-treaties.
16. For example, Australia-Vietnam BIT (1991) was terminated on 14 Jan. 2019, subject to transitional arrangements, upon entry into force of the CPTPP as between Australia and Vietnam. *See* https://dfat.gov.au/trade/agreements/in-force/cptpp/official-documents/Documents/australia-vietnam-termination-of-investment-promotion-and-protection-agreement.PDF.
17. UNCTAD, *Phase 2 of IIA Reform: Modernizing the Existing Stock of Old-Generation Treaties* (June 2017), issue 2, https://unctad.org/en/PublicationsLibrary/diaepcb2017d3_en.pdf.
18. https://dfat.gov.au/trade/agreements/negotiations/rcep/Pages/regional-comprehensive-economic-partnership.aspx.
19. Amokura Kawharu & Luke Nottage, *Models for Investment Treaties in the Asian Region: An Underview*, 34 Ariz. J. Int'l & Comp. L. 461 (2016). Also available at SSRN: https://ssrn.com/abstract=2845088.
20. Julien Chaisse, *The Regional Comprehensive Economic Partnership's Investment Chapter: One Step Forward, Two Steps Back*, Columbia FDI Perspectives (10 Feb. 2020), http://ccsi.columbia.edu/files/2018/10/No-271-Chaisse-FINAL.pdf.
21. https://dfat.gov.au/trade/agreements/in-force/a-hkfta/Pages/default.aspx.
22. https://dfat.gov.au/trade/agreements/in-force/pafta/Pages/peru-australia-fta.aspx.

Singapore-Australia FTA (with latest amendments in force from 1 December 2017),[23] and the revised Australia-Uruguay BIT (signed on 5 April 2019 but not yet ratified or in force).[24] The new provisions in these treaties are heavily influenced by US-style drafting, epitomised by the CPTPP, like Australia's FTAs concluded since 2003 and others around the Asia-Pacific region.[25]

Section 5.03 of this chapter elaborates on the costs and delays associated with ISA. The discussion first builds on the reports of several previous empirical studies. It then examines relevant provisions of CPTPP, IA-CEPA and AHKIA to determine how their provisions deal with concerns particularly about delays and (relatedly) costs.

Section 5.04 of the chapter examines a third common concern about ISDS: transparency of proceedings and outcomes. It again focuses mainly on CPTPP, IA-CEPA and AHKIA. But it examines also the parliamentary enquiry into Australia ratifying the Mauritius ('UN ISDS') Convention. This seeks to retrofit extensive transparency provisions on pre-2014 treaties between Australia and other states that might also accede to that framework Convention, as another way of reforming international investment treaty law.[26]

We conclude from these new developments that more bipartisanship may be emerging in domestic politics regarding international investment treaty-marking, so Australia is now better placed to play a more active role in guiding the future path of international investment treaty-making especially in the Asia-Pacific region. However, we note considerable path-dependence in its treaty practice (relying mainly on contemporary US-style drafting, rather than recent EU-style innovations – such as an investment court in lieu of ISA provisions[27]). There also seems to be considerable flexibility or reactiveness to presumed initiatives originating from counterparties to the recent bilateral treaty negotiations. Australia has also not been particularly proactive in deliberations into multilateral ISDS reform through United Nations Commission on International Trade Law (UNCITRAL) since late 2017,[28] perhaps because of underlying domestic political tensions that still exist around this topic.

§5.02 ISDS IN AHKIA AND IA-CEPA

Both IA-CEPA and AHKIA are generally well drafted, attempting to balance host state and foreign investor interests in the contemporary US style for IIAs. However, these

23. Subsequent amendments entered into force on 24 Feb. 2006, 13 Feb. 2007, 11 Oct. 2007, 2 Sep. 2011 and 1 Dec. 2017: *see* https://dfat.gov.au/trade/agreements/in-force/safta/Pages/singapore-australia-fta.aspx.
24. https://dfat.gov.au/trade/investment/Pages/australias-bilateral-investment-treaties.aspx.
25. Wolfgang Alschner & Dmitriy Skougarevskiy, *The New Gold Standard? Empirically Situating the TPP in The Investment Treaty Universe*, 17 J. World Inv. & Trade 339 (2016).
26. UNCTAD, *supra* n. 17; *World Investment Report 2017: Investment and the Digital Economy. New York and Geneva: United Nations*; the United Nations Convention on Transparency in Treaty-Based Investor-State Arbitration, United Nations General Assembly, Resolution 69/116 (10 Dec. 2014), UN Doc No A/Res/69/116 (18 Dec. 2014).
27. Cf., e.g., Kawharu & Nottage, *supra* n. 19.
28. Working Group III: Investor-State Dispute Settlement Reform, https://uncitral.un.org/en/working_groups/3/investor-state.

two recent IIAs signed by Australia are not identical. This is probably due to the rather different counterparties in question. Hong Kong is a more developed economy that has generated an inbound claim against Australia (by Philip Morris Asia), whereas Indonesia is a developing economy that has been subjected to a claim by Australian investors.

Under IA-CEPA, the definitions of fair and equitable treatment (FET) and of full protection and security fall expressly under the scope of customary international law. In particular Article 14.7.2(c) stipulates:

> [T]he concepts of 'fair and equitable treatment' and 'full protection and security' do not require treatment in addition to or beyond that which is required under the customary international law minimum standard of treatment, and do not create additional substantive rights.[29]

The definition of FET further 'requires each Party to not deny justice in any legal or administrative proceedings'.[30] The wording of the clause suggests that the definition of FET is somewhat limited, to denial of justice, and does not go beyond that. This conclusion can be drawn especially when comparing FET under IA-CEPA with FET under CPTPP and AHKIA. Article 9.6.2(a) of CPTPP and Article 8.2(a) of AHKIA state that FET 'includes' a denial of justice obligation. This formulation is clearly inclusive of other possible features of FET and hence is not limited to denial of justice. Notwithstanding such discrepancies in the wordings of the treaties, the definition of FET under IA-CEPA is not expressly limited, and so should not be read as exclusive and protecting against denial of justice only.[31]

By contrast, an EU-Vietnam Investment Protection Agreement (approved in 2020 but not yet in force) provides for a more detailed FET clause. Under Article 2.5(2), the obligation of FET is breached:

> where a measure or series of measures constitutes: (a) a denial of justice in criminal, civil or administrative proceedings; (b) a fundamental breach of due process in judicial and administrative proceedings; (c) manifest arbitrariness; (d) targeted discrimination on manifestly wrongful grounds, such as gender, race or religious belief; (e) abusive treatment such as coercion, abuse of power or similar bad faith conduct; or (f) a breach of any further elements of the fair and equitable treatment obligation adopted by the Parties in accordance with paragraph 3.[32]

Conversely, the 2016 India Model BIT does not include an overarching FET clause, unlike its predecessor 2003 Model BIT. Instead Article 3.1. of the 2016 India Model BIT simply states:

29. Emphasis added.
30. Article 14.7.2.a. of IA-CEPA.
31. For further analysis of IA-CEPA, *see* Jarrod Hepburn, *Analysis: Australia and Indonesia Sign New FTA, Including Investment Provisions on Security for Costs, Third-Party Funding, Dual Citizens, and Public Health Claims*, IA Reporter (5 Mar. 2019), https://www.iareporter.com/articles/analysis-australia-and-indonesia-sign-new-fta-including-investment-provisions-on-security-for-costs-third-party-funding-dual-citizens-and-public-health-claims/.
32. European Commission on EU-Vietnam trade and investment agreements, http://trade.ec.europa.eu/doclib/press/index.cfm?id=1437.

> No Party shall subject investments made by investors of the other Party to measures which constitute a violation of customary international law through:
>
> (i) denial of justice in any judicial or administrative proceedings; or
> (ii) fundamental breach of due process; or
> (iii) targeted discrimination on manifestly unjustified grounds, such as gender, race or religious belief; or
> (iv) manifestly abusive treatment, such as coercion, duress and harassment.[33]

The scope of protection is arguably limited to these five categories as there is no general reference to FET or the minimum standard of treatment.[34]

Under IA-CEPA, states are required to treat each other's investors and investments no less favourably than they treat investors and investments of other, non-contracting states. However, this most-favoured-nation (MFN) obligation expressly does not extend to the dispute resolution procedures such as ISDS.[35] An investor is not allowed to bring claims alleging the breach of MFN clause because another IIA contains a more favourable ISDS provision.[36] This exclusion of ISDS from MFN in IA-CEPA is similar to that provided under the CPTPP,[37] and consistent with Australia's FTA drafting practice.[38]

Under IA-CEPA, ISDS claims can only be made for the commitments stipulated under the Investment Chapter, but IA-CEPA adds restrictions regarding some claims against the host state. The host state can raise defences for claims against its implemented measures: (a) to protect and promote public health; and (b) in other key areas of social services, welfare, education, arts (including indigenous rights). Decisions of Foreign Investment Review Board of Australia cannot be challenged either.[39] However, unlike AHKIA which has a detailed product-specific carve-out preventing ISDS claims about tobacco product measures, no such direct reference can be found in IA-CEPA.[40] Instead, an Australian foreign affairs representative giving evidence to the JSCOT parliamentary enquiry stated that tobacco control measures would anyway fall under the general exceptions provisions, even without special reference:

---

33. 2016 India Model BIT, https://dea.gov.in/sites/default/files/ModelTextIndia_BIT_0.pdf.
34. Prabhash Ranjan & Pushkar Anand, *The 2016 Model Indian Bilateral Investment Treaty: A Critical Deconstruction*, 38 Nw. J. Int'l L. & Bus. 1 (2017).
35. Article 14.5.3 of IA-CEPA.
36. Article 14.21.1(a) of IA-CEPA.
37. Article 9.5.3 of CPTPP.
38. Tania Voon & Elizabeth Sheargold, *Australia, China, and the Co-Existence of Successive International Investment Agreements*, in *The China-Australia Free Trade Agreement: A 21st-Century Model* 215 (Colin Picker Picker, et al. eds., Hart Publishing 2017); Andrew D. Mitchell, *Australia and New Zealand, in Research Handbook on Foreign Direct Investment* 390 (Markus Krajewski & Rhea Tamara Hoffmann eds., Edward Elgar Publishing 2019).
39. Summary of IA-CEPA by the Department of Foreign Affairs and Trade of Australian Government, 'Outcomes: Investment', https://dfat.gov.au/trade/agreements/not-yet-in-force/iacepa/outcomes-documents/Pages/outcomes-investment.aspx.
40. Brenda Horrigan, et al., *Australian Joint Standing Committee on Treaties Approves New Investment Treaties between Australia, Hong Kong and Indonesia,* Herbert Smith Freehills (15 Nov. 2019), https://hsfnotes.com/arbitration/2019/11/15/australian-joint-standing-committee-on-treaties-approves-new-investment-treaties-between-australia-hong-kong-and-indonesia/#_ftnref5.

> With Indonesia, we had discussions, both internally and we consulted closely with the Attorney-General's Department Office of International Law, on which approach to take. It was felt that the broader carve out for public health protected us not only in the case of, say, the tobacco situation but also more broadly for public health, and, as a consequence, we felt that that broader exception was preferable.[41]

The difference is that under such a general exception, an ISDS arbitration can be commenced by the investor objecting to tobacco control measures and the tribunal would have jurisdiction. The tribunal would then have to interpret and apply specific facts to the public health exception as invoked by the host state. By contrast, an express prohibition on measures, as in AHKIA, means that a tribunal will only have to determine whether the host state's action constitutes a tobacco control measure: if so, the tribunal should reject the claim for lack of jurisdiction. A tobacco company might be able instead to mobilise its home state, however, to bring an interstate arbitration over such a measure.

It is possible that Australian government negotiators requested an express carve-out for tobacco measures in IA-CEPA. After all, Australia had taken that option provided in the CPTPP as well as including the express carve-out in its recently revised FTA with Singapore.[42] Curiously, it is not found in Australia's recently revised BIT with Uruguay, even though the latter had successfully defended an ISDS claim on the merits against Philip Morris over other tobacco packaging legislation.[43] Noting this omission, but nonetheless recommending Australia's ratification of the revised Uruguay BIT, JSCOT remarked:[44]

> 3.18 DFAT [Australia's Department of Foreign Affairs and Trade] suggested that other safeguards in the agreement, such as the explicit reference to the right to regulate in the preamble and a WTO-style general exception, are sufficient to address concerns relating to public health. The Committee sought clarification that the measures designed to protect public health would extend to government regulation of the use, and consumption of tobacco. DFAT assured the Committee that the measures would extend to tobacco regulation and vaping.

Even if Australia had requested an express tobacco carve-out for IA-CEPA, Indonesia may have rejected the proposal as Indonesia is a tobacco-exporting nation that had joined in a World Trade Organization (WTO) claim against Australia over its tobacco plain packaging legislation.[45]

---

41. Ms Nadia Krivetz, Director, Free Trade Agreement Services Branch, Regional Trade Agreements Division, DFAT, Committee Hansard, Canberra, 9 Sep. 2019, at 19, quoted in *JSCOT Report 186 IA-CEPA and A-HKFTA*, para. 4.56, at 54, https://apo.org.au/sites/default/files/resource-files/2019/10/apo-nid262606-1391501.pdf.
42. Article 29.5 of CPTPP, Chapter 8, Article 22 of Singapore-Australia FTA.
43. *Philip Morris Brands Sàrl, Philip Morris Products S.A. and Abal Hermanos S.A. v. Oriental Republic of Uruguay*, ICSID Case No. ARB/10/7.
44. *Report 188*, https://www.aph.gov.au/Parliamentary_Business/Committees/Joint/Treaties/InvestmentsUruguay/Report_188/section?id=committees%2Freportjnt%2F024358%2F27983 (footnotes omitted).
45. https://www.wto.org/english/tratop_e/dispu_e/cases_e/ds467_e.htm; Tania Voon, *Third Strike: The WTO Panel Reports Upholding Australia's Tobacco Plain Packaging Scheme*, 20 J.

It is also quite intriguing that IA-CEPA (as well as AHKIA) does not include as a compromise a 'public welfare notice' procedure, as added in the Australia-China FTA signed in 2015 (and not found in any other Australian or Chinese IIAs).[46] Under Article 9.11.4, an investor cannot challenge measures of a state that are 'non-discriminatory and for the legitimate public welfare objectives of public health, safety, the environment, public morals or public order' and such measures 'shall not be the subject of a claim'.[47] If an investor still challenges such a measure, the unusual provision of the Australia-China FTA allows the host state to issue a 'public welfare notice' stipulating that the challenged measure belongs to the carve-out of Article 9.11.4. Once the 'public welfare notice' is issued, the arbitral proceedings are suspended and consultation begins between the states.[48] Commentators have observed that this can also promote early settlement of disputes.[49]

The ISDS clause in IA-CEPA is a multi-tiered dispute resolution clause with an element that is almost unique to over three thousand IIAs worldwide (found otherwise only in the new Hong Kong-United Arab Emirates BIT, also signed in 2019).[50] Apart from a standard initial consultation during the cooling-off period and the final arbitration phase, IA-CEPA also provides an additional conciliation (mediation) step. The peculiarity of this step is that mediation may be initiated by any disputing party, but it then becomes mandatory for the claimant investor (not for the respondent state):

> If the dispute cannot be resolved within 180 days from the date of receipt by the disputing Party of the written request for consultations, the disputing Party may initiate a conciliation process, which shall be mandatory for the disputing investor ... .[51]

A disputing party may submit a claim to its local tribunals, to ICSID arbitration (under either ICSID Arbitration Rules or Additional Facility Arbitration Rules), or to ad hoc arbitration under UNCITRAL Arbitration Rules. The investor may only proceed to

World Inv. & Trade 146 (2019); Tom Miles, *Australia Wins Landmark WTO Ruling on Plain Tobacco Packaging*, Reuters (29 Jun. 2018), https://www.reuters.com/article/us-wto-tobacco-ruling/australia-wins-landmark-wto-ruling-on-plain-tobacco-packaging-idUSKBN1JO2BF.

46. Anthea Roberts & Richard Braddock, *Protecting Public Welfare Regulation Through Joint Treaty Party Control: A ChAFTA Innovation*, Columbia FDI Perspectives, Perspectives on Topical Foreign Direct Investment Issues (20 Jun. 2016), http://ccsi.columbia.edu/files/2013/10/No-176-Roberts-and-Braddock-FINAL.pdf.
47. Article 9.11.4 of the China-Australia FTA.
48. Article 9.11.5-9.11.6 of the China-Australia FTA.
49. Luke Nottage, *Investment Treaty Arbitration Policy in Australia, New Zealand and Korea*, 25 J. Arb. Studies 185 (2015). Also available at SSRN: https://ssrn.com/abstract=2643926.
50. *See further* James Claxton, Luke Nottage & Ana Ubilava, *Pioneering Mandatory Investor-State Conciliation Before Arbitration in Asia-Pacific Treaties: IA-CEPA and HK-UAE BIT*, Kluwer Arbitration Blog (5 Sep. 2020), http://arbitrationblog.kluwerarbitration.com/2020/09/05/pioneering-mandatory-investor-state-conciliation-before-arbitration-in-asia-pacific-treaties-ia-cepa-and-hk-uae-bit/; and Ana Ubilava, *Mandatory Investor-State Conciliation in New International Investment Treaties: Innovation and Interpretation*, Kluwer Mediation Blog (5 Sep. 2020), http://mediationblog.kluwerarbitration.com/2020/09/05/mandatory-investor-state-conciliation-in-new-international-investment-treaties-innovation-and-interpretation/. The innovative mandatory mediation step before arbitration is not mentioned in an otherwise excellent summary of IA-CEPA's key features by Hepburn, *supra* n. 31.
51. Article 14.24 of IA-CEPA.

ISA in two scenarios. One scenario is when mediation had not been requested by either of the disputing parties. The investor can then submit a claim to ISA after the cooling-off period if consultations are unsuccessful in resolving the dispute. The second scenario is when one of the parties has initiated mediation after an unsuccessful consultations phase. Then the investor may proceed with ISA only if both consultations and mediation (conciliation) are unsuccessful.

It seems likely that this unique provision for (one-sided compulsory) mediation was requested by negotiators for Indonesia rather than for Australia. Indonesia has been subjected to many more inbound claims than Australia,[52] and in UNCITRAL reform deliberations, has recorded its interest in investor-state mediation.[53] In addition, the unusual mediation provision is not found in AHKIA, signed by Australia in the same year.

AHKIA also adopts a narrower definition of investor compared to its predecessor (1993) Australia-Hong Kong BIT. Article 1 of AHKIA stipulates that a claimant must be an investor of a party, either 'a natural person' or 'an enterprise'. For Australia, a natural person is a citizen or a permanent resident of Australia, whereas for Hong Kong a natural person is a permanent resident of Hong Kong:

> [E]nterprise of a Party means:
>
> a. an enterprise constituted or organised under the laws of a Party; or
> b. a branch of an enterprise of a Party located in the Area of a Party, which has substantial business activities in the Area of that Party ... ;[54]

The way the definition of the 'enterprise of a Party' is formulated suggests that the parties have taken cautionary measures to avoid abuse of process from investors, although the meaning of 'substantial business' is left ultimately to the interpretation of a tribunal.[55] This definition is more limited compared to the one provided under IA-CEPA. Article 14.1 of IA-CEPA simply states that an 'enterprise of a Party means an enterprise constituted or organised in accordance with the laws of a Party and carrying out business activities there'. AHKIA definition of investor therefore seems a cautionary step, perhaps sought by negotiators from Australia, not to have its recent past experience with Philip Morris repeated in the future for other types of claims.[56]

The MFN clause in AHKIA also expressly excludes ISDS. This is different from the previous MFN clause that was incorporated in the former Australia-Hong Kong BIT,

52. Antony Crockett, *The Termination of Indonesia's BITs: Changing the Bathwater, but Keeping the Baby?*, in *International Investment Treaties and Arbitration Across Asia* 159 (Luke Nottage & Julien Chaisse eds., Brill | Nijhoff 2018).
53. *Submission from the Government of Indonesia to UNCITRAL, WGIII, Possible Reform of Investor-State Dispute Settlement (ISDS)*, A/CN.9/WG.III/WP.156, 3-4 (2018).
54. Article 1 of the AHKIA (definition of enterprise of a Party).
55. Myfanwy Wood, et al., *Australia-Hong Kong Free Trade Agreement & Investment Agreement*, Ashurst International Arbitration Update (4 Jul. 2019), https://www.ashurst.com/en/news-and-insights/legal-updates/australia-hong-kong-free-trade-agreement-and-investment-agreement-(2019)/.
56. Philip Morris Asia acquired Philip Morris (Australia) Limited with the intention to challenge Australia's Tobacco Plain Packaging Act 2011 through the Australia-Hong Kong BIT (1993): *see* Hepburn and Nottage *supra* n. 11.

and similar to that of IA-CEPA and CPTPP. An investor therefore may not challenge the host state based on the allegation that other IIAs contain a more favourable ISDS provision than AHKIA. The exclusion of ISDS from MFN should be read in conjunction with the general exceptions and tobacco carve-outs. It is to ensure that investors under AHKIA will not bypass the restrictions stipulated in this treaty by claiming breach of MFN obligation through another IIA which does not impose similar restrictions on investment claims.

AHKIA includes an ISDS provision allowing the investor of one state to bring claims against the host state. However, the right to bring investment claims under AHKIA also has restrictions. AHKIA prohibits an investor from bringing claims against the host state notably regarding measures 'comprising or related to the Pharmaceutical Benefits Scheme, Medicare Benefits Scheme, Therapeutic Goods'.[57] Again, following usual Australian FTA practice, the decisions of the Foreign Investment Board on foreign investment proposals cannot be challenged by an investor through an investment claim.

As mentioned above, another restriction applies to both states: a detailed, product-specific carve-out which states that an investor cannot bring claims against the tobacco control measures of the host state. The tobacco control measures include products made or derived from tobacco, cigarettes and imitation smoking products (e-cigarettes).[58] Such comprehensive and detailed restriction is understandable considering the recent history between Australia and Hong Kong regarding the Philip Morris case. However, considering the discussion of IA-CEPA above, it can be argued that Article 18 of AHKIA would anyway extend to tobacco control measures as both treaties have identical provisions for general exceptions.[59]

The ISDS provision under AHKIA is a more typical dispute resolution clause found in the majority of Australia's existing (in both older and new generation) IIAs. When the dispute arises, parties are encouraged to attempt resolving their dispute amicably through consultations. This also may include third-party procedures such as mediation (conciliation). Unlike IA-CEPA, however, investor-state mediation in AHKIA is offered as a choice – a voluntary step during the existing six-month cooling-off period. If the dispute is not resolved through consultations or mediation/conciliation, once the cooling-off period is up the claimant can proceed with ISA under UNCITRAL Arbitration Rules.

It is worth noting that double-hatting by arbitrators is not expressly prohibited in either treaty, unlike under the CPTPP pursuant to a Code of Conduct for ISDS.[60] Arbitrators concurrently serving as counsel is a practice that has otherwise persisted

57. Footnote 13 to *Section C: Settlement of Disputes between an Investor and the Host Party of the AHKIA* (2019), https://investmentpolicy.unctad.org/international-investment-agreements/treaty-files/5830/download.
58. Footnote 14 to *Section C: Settlement of Disputes between an Investor and the Host Party of the AHKIA* (2019), https://investmentpolicy.unctad.org/international-investment-agreements/treaty-files/5830/download.
59. Article 18 of the AHKIA and Article 17.2.(3) of IA-CEPA.
60. Available via https://dfat.gov.au/trade/agreements/in-force/cptpp/official-documents/Pages/official-documents.aspx.

despite growing concern, including at the multilateral level.[61] Adding an express prohibition was urged during JSCOT enquiries into Australia ratifying the CPTPP.[62] Because that is not found in any other Australian IIAs, even after the CPTPP was signed, the express prohibition in the latter's Code of Conduct may have been promoted more by the other signatories to the CPTPP. In addition, even compared to the CPTPP, neither IA-CEPA nor AHKIA contains any mention of (even potential, separately agreed) appellate review mechanisms for ISDS arbitrators. This too suggests a rather conservative stance by the Australian negotiators and/or their counterparties.

§5.03 COSTS AND DELAYS IN ISDS AS ADDRESSED BY CPTPP, IA-CEPA AND AHKIA

International arbitration initially was expected to be a cheaper and faster dispute resolution mechanism compared to court adjudications. However, over the past ten to twenty years, this perception has changed quite drastically.[63] International investment disputes, in particular, generally take many years to resolve through arbitration.[64] Figure 5.1 shows that treaty-based investment arbitration takes approximately 4 years on average under ICSID and UNCITRAL Arbitration Rules (with a median of around 4.5 years).[65] The duration is considerably shorter, 2 years, for ISA cases conducted under non-ICSID and non-UNCITRAL arbitration rules. Those (relatively very few) cases are under Rules of the Stockholm Chamber of Commerce (SCC), the London Court of International Arbitration (LCIA), and the International Chamber of Commerce (ICC).[66]

61. Jeffrey Dunoff, et al., *Working Group 6: Lack of Independence and Impartiality of Arbitrators*, Academic Forum on ISDS (March 2019), https://www.cids.ch/images/Documents/Academic-Forum/6_Independence_-_WG6.pdf.
62. Nottage & Ubilava, *supra* n. 4.
63. Joerg Risse, *Ten Drastic Proposals for Saving Time and Costs in Arbitral Proceedings*, 29 Arb. Int'l 453 (2013); Luke Nottage, *A Weather Map for International Arbitration: Mainly Sunny, Some Cloud, Possible Thunderstorms*, in *The Evolution of International Arbitration* 59 (Stavros Brekoulakis, et al. eds., Wolters Kluwer 2016). Also available at SSRN: https://ssrn.com/abstract=2630401.
64. Thomas J. Stipanowich & Ryan Lamare, *Living with ADR: Evolving Perceptions and Use of Mediation, Arbitration, and Conflict Management in Fortune 1000 Corporations*, 19 Harv. Negot. L. Rev. 1 (2013).
65. These findings are based on the data set compiled by Ana Ubilava for her PhD thesis, consisting of 541 known investor-state arbitration cases that were concluded by December 2017. Sources for the data set include: UNCTAD database, ICSID database, ITAlaw.com, IA Reporter and other government press releases and public sources. These findings are also in line with the recently published statistics by ICSID that reported that it takes approximately three to four years to resolve an ISA case under ICSID. *See* ICSID Secretariat, *Proposals for Amendment of the ICSID Rules – Working Paper Vol. 3* 977-9 (2018), https://icsid.worldbank.org/en/Documents/Amendments_Vol_Three.pdf.
66. Based on 329 ISA cases under ICSID and ICSID AF Arbitration Rules, 103 ISA cases under UNCITRAL Arbitration Rules and 27 ISA cases under other rules (SCC, LCIA, ICC, Moscow Chamber of Commerce and Industry (MCCI), the Cairo International Centre for International Commercial Arbitration (CRCICA) and ad hoc arbitration rules).

Figure 5.1 Averages and Medians of Lengths of ISA Proceedings (In Months)

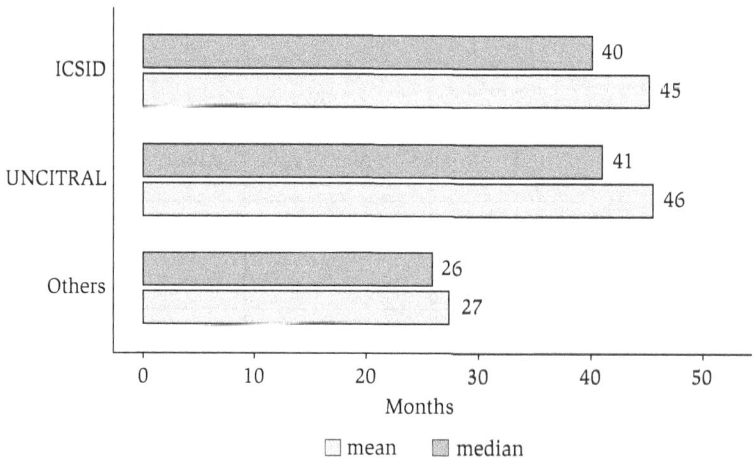

The length of the ISDS has a negative impact on the overall costs of ISA. Arbitration costs can be broken down in two categories: party costs (fees especially for legal counsel, and other expenses of the parties such as for witnesses) and tribunal costs (arbitrator remuneration and administrative/secretariat fees for the tribunal).[67] The findings of some of the recent empirical studies that examine ISA costs of both ICSID and ad hoc (UNCITRAL) arbitrations align with very minor discrepancies (Table 5.1).

67. Susan D. Franck, *Arbitration Costs: Myths and Realities in Investment Treaty Arbitration* 135 (Oxford University Press 2019).

Table 5.1 Average Arbitration Costs from Recent Empirical Studies[68]

Empirical Study	*Study Period*	*Arbitral Rules*	*Sample*	*Average Claimant Costs*	*Sample*	*Average Respondent Costs*	*Sample*	*Average Tribunal Costs*
Behn and Daza (2019)[69]	1987-2019	ICSID & UNCITRAL	169	6,067,184	177	5,223,974	193	947,622
Franck (2019)[70]	1987-2012	ICSID & UNCITRAL	161	5,000,000	161	4,100,000	160	800,000
Hodgson and Campbell (2017)[71]	2013-2017	ICSID & UNCITRAL	96	7,414,000	96	5,188,000	89	1,118,000
Commission and Moloo (2018)[72]	2011-2017	ICSID	90	6,043,915	88	5,217,247	68	922,087
	2010-2017	UNCITRAL	36	6,077,585	41	4,596,807	48	960,641

ISA is not costly per se, but it is the legal services required for conducting the arbitration process that make arbitration costs to skyrocket. When analysed together, the findings of these studies suggest that party costs make up around 90% of the total arbitration costs. While the tribunal costs on average are up to USD 1 million, which is split between the claimant and the respondent, the average party cost for the claimant is USD 6 million and USD 5 million for the respondent. The median party costs are significantly lower than the averages, as those are skewed by occasional large and expensive cases: USD 2.9 million is the median for claimant costs, and USD 3.6 million for respondent costs.[73] Legal costs do not have a cap and are unlikely to be regulated either by separate arbitration rules or through IIAs.[74] It is up to law firm's discretion to set a price for its billable hours and up to an individual party to decide what price it is

68. The table is compiled from a similar table but with addition from the Malcolm Langford, Daniel Behn & Laura Létourneau-Tremblay, *Empirical Perspectives on Investment Arbitration: What Do We Know? Does It Matter?*, ISDS Academic Forum Working Group 7 Paper, Table 1.3 Legal Costs (USD) and Table 1.4: Tribunal Fees (USD).
69. Daniel Behn & Ana Maria Daza, *The Defense Burden in Investment Arbitration*, PluriCourts Working Paper (2019).
70. Franck, *supra* n. 67.
71. Matthew Hodgson & Alastair Campbell, *Damages and Costs in Investment Treaty Arbitration Revisited*, Global Arbitration Review (14 Dec. 2017), https://www.allenovery.com/global/-/media/sharepoint/news/news/news/sitecollectiondocuments/14-12-17_damages_and_costs_in_investment_treaty_arbitration_revisited_.pdf?la=en-gb&hash=D720EA099E8A7D2912FDA054E06350F5.
72. Jeffery Commission & Rahim Moloo, *Procedural Issues in International Investment Arbitration* (Oxford University Press 2018).
73. Jeffery P. Commission, *How Much Does an ICSID Arbitration Cost? A Snapshot of the Last Five Years*, Kluwer Arbitration Blog (29 Feb. 2016), http://arbitrationblog.kluwerarbitration.com/2016/02/29/how-much-does-an-icsid-arbitration-cost-a-snapshot-of-the-last-five-years/.
74. Unusually, for (mainly domestic) arbitrations in Australia, the Resolution Institute Arbitration Rules 2016 Article 40(1)(e) and Schedule 1 imposed a cap on legal costs based on the amount in disputes. However, this cap has vanished in the 2020 Rules, so likely incurred some pushback from legal practitioners. For both Rules, *see* https://www.resolution.institute/resources/rules-for-dispute-resolution-processes/current-arbitration-rules.

willing to pay for certain legal services. Some commentators have argued that the billable hours practices in law firms, including growing law firms even in Asia, have contributed to delays and therefore costs in international arbitration.[75]

Nonetheless, the duration of ISA proceedings is what makes party costs high – the longer the ISA proceedings take the higher are the fees charged by lawyers, unless clients can negotiate a flat-rate fee. While it is unlikely for any international arbitration rules or IIAs to regulate party costs by intervening in the hourly rates of legal services of individual law firms, the timeline for an investment dispute can still be limited by the IIAs. This can be done by setting strict time limits for each of the steps of an ISDS process. Shortening the timelines may help control costs, although it remains possible that legal counsel just crams the same amount of billable hours into the compressed time frames.

Varying time limits are in fact included in the ISDS provisions of IA-CEPA, AHKIA and the CPTPP. According to IA-CEPA, an ISA claim cannot be submitted if, in total, more than three years and six months have passed from the day the claimant knew or must have known about the alleged breach.[76] The ISDS provision further sets time limits for each individual dispute resolution step before submitting a claim to ISA. The disputants are initially given 180 days to try and resolve their dispute amicably through consultations.[77] After this, an investor can submit a claim to ISA: (a) if consultations were unsuccessful; (b) once 180 days have passed since the respondent received the request for consultations from the claimant; and (c) if the notice of intent to submit the claim to ISA was given to the respondent at least 90 days before the investor actually registers its claim to ISA.[78]

If one of the parties has initiated mediation after an unsuccessful consultations phase, an investor may proceed with ISA only: (a) if consultations were unsuccessful; (b) mediation (conciliation) was also unsuccessful; (c) once 120 days have elapsed since the mediation was initiated; and (d) if the claimant has provided the written notice of intent to submit an arbitration claim 60 days before the dispute is registered for ISA.[79]

Mediation potentially increases the otherwise 270-day process by up to 120 additional days. Some commentators suggest that the inclusion of mandatory mediation is 'not particularly innovative' and that it represents a prolonged cooling-off period.[80] This opinion, however, is not completely accurate. Article 14.22: Consultations represents an ordinary cooling-off period where the parties need to attempt and

75. Luke Nottage, *In/formalization and Glocalization of International Commercial Arbitration and Investment Treaty Arbitration in Asia*, in *Formalisation and Flexibilisation of Dispute Resolution* 211-49 (Joachim Zekoll, et al. eds., Martinus Nijhoff / Brill 2014). Also available at SSRN: https://ssrn.com/abstract=2987674.
76. Article 14.26.1 of IA-CEPA.
77. Article 14.22 and 14.23(a) of IA-CEPA.
78. Article 14.26.2(a) of IA-CEPA.
79. Article 14.26.2.b. of IA-CEPA.
80. Esmé Shirlow, *The Indonesia-Australia Comprehensive Economic Partnership Agreement: Repeated Debates, New Issues and Open Questions*, Kluwer Arbitration Blog (24 Apr. 2019),

resolve their disputes amicably during set time limits. This step is a usual component of the great majority (if not all) of the ISDS provisions of known IIAs. However, having a compulsory investor-state mediation as a precondition to arbitration (in any form) is extremely rare, among more than three thousand known IIAs.[81] Even more unusual is a provision as in IA-CEPA by which investor-state mediation can be made mandatory for one party (the claimant investor) but remains voluntary for the other (the respondent state, which does not need to trigger the mediation step).

Under AHKIA, the overall time frame for submitting an investment claim is three years and six months, as in IA-CEPA.[82] It also sets individual time limits for each ISDS step. The parties to the dispute are given a six-month cooling-off period during which time they are encouraged to resolve their dispute amicably, through consultations or other voluntary third-party assisted mechanisms (mediation/conciliation). An investor may submit a claim to ISA: (a) if consultations were unsuccessful; (b) once six months have passed since the respondent received the request for consultations from the claimant; and (b) if the investor has issued a notice of intent to submit the claim to ISA to the respondent at least ninety days before submitting the claim to ISA. Accordingly, it would take a maximum of approximately nine months before the dispute reaches the ISA stage.

AHKIA also sets time limits for the arbitration procedure. For example, there is a 75-day time limit for appointing arbitrators. If the tribunal is not constituted during this time, the Secretary General of the Permanent Court of Arbitration (PCA) shall appoint the arbitrators upon party request.[83] There are time frames for objections and decision on jurisdiction as well. The respondent has 45 days after the constitution of the tribunal to object to the jurisdiction of the tribunal. The tribunal should issue its decision or an award on jurisdiction within 150 days from the day the objection was made by the respondent.[84] This time limit extends by 45 days in case a hearing on the objection of jurisdiction was requested by a party. The time frame for the decision/award on

---

http://arbitrationblog.kluwerarbitration.com/2019/04/24/the-indonesia-australia-comprehensive-economic-partnership-agreement-repeated-debates-new-issues-and-open-questions/; The unilaterally mandatory mediation provisions of IA-CEPA and also the Hong-Kong-United Arab Emirates BIT are discussed in James Claxton, Luke Nottage and Ana Ubilava, *Pioneering Mandatory Investor-State Conciliation Before Arbitration in Asia-Pacific Treaties: IA-CEPA and HK-UAE BIT*, Kluwer Arbitration Blog (5 Sept. 2020), http://arbitrationblog.kluwerarbitration.com/2020/09/05/pioneering-mandatory-investor-state-conciliation-before-arbitration-in-asia-pacific-treaties-ia-cepa-and-hk-uae-bit/.

81. *See generally* UNCTAD, *Investment Dispute Settlement Navigator*, https://investmentpolicy.unctad.org/investment-dispute-settlement; Catherine Kessedjian et al., *Mediation in Future Investor-State Dispute Settlement*, Academic Forum on ISDS Concept Paper 2020/16 (5 Mar. 2020), https://www.jus.uio.no/pluricourts/english/projects/leginvest/academic-forum/papers/2020/isds-af-mediation-paper-16-march-2020.pdf; Ana Ubilava, *Amicable Settlements in Investor-State Disputes: Empirical Analysis of Patterns and Perceived Problems*, 21(4) J. World Inv. & Trade 528 (2020), also available at SSRN: https://ssrn.com/abstract=3352181.
82. Article 27.1 of AHKIA; Ana Ubilava, *Mandatory Investor-State Conciliation in New International Investment Treaties: Innovation and Interpretation*, Kluwer Mediation Blog (5 Sept. 2020), http://mediationblog.kluwerarbitration.com/2020/09/05/mandatory-investor-state-conciliation-in-new-international-investment-treaties-innovation-and-interpretation/ (comparing drafting differences of AHKIA and IA-CEPA as well as timelines for the mediation step).
83. Article 28.3 of AHKIA.
84. Article 29.5 of AHKIA.

jurisdiction may further be extended (with or without the hearing) by 30 days only in exceptional circumstances, which is referred to as an 'extraordinary cause'.[85] Therefore, the maximum time for deliberations on matters of jurisdiction from the constitution of the tribunal to the conclusion of deliberations is 270 days (up to nine months). This timeline is similar to that defined under Article 9.23.5 of CPTPP although the latter gives 30 days if the party requests a hearing, instead of 45 days as in AHKIA.

AHKIA also adds the option for a disputing party (most likely the host state) to have the tribunal provide to the disputing parties plus the non-disputing party (the home state) its draft or 'proposed decision or award on liability'. Any disputing party can then provide comments for up to sixty days, which the tribunal 'shall consider' before issuing its decision or award within another forty-five days. This step therefore extends the ISDS process by up to 3.5 months, increasing delays and costs. However, it might efficiently promote settlement, including through the informal involvement of the host state, although settlement is often more difficult at a late stage after disputing parties have expended much time and expense already.[86] At least this step may reduce errors in decisions or awards on liability (although it is curiously unavailable say for awards on other matters like costs), and thereby enhance prospects for award enforcement or the legitimacy of the ISDS process more generally. The practice derives from WTO dispute settlement and is also found in the 2015 Korea-Australia FTA.[87] Interestingly, this step is not added to IA-CEPA for draft ISDS awards, despite the treaty encouraging early settlement through the host state being able to compel mediation before arbitration commences.

On a normative level, cost allocation in awards is usually left to the discretion of the arbitrators. However, recent practice has shown favouritism towards the English Rule, whereby the loser pays the expenses of the winner.[88] In fact, some commentators now suggest limiting arbitrator discretion. They argue in favour of setting the English Rule as the default cost allocation practice at least for certain types of ISA outcomes under ICSID.[89] This would be similar to Article 42(1) of the 2010 UNCITRAL Arbitration Rules:

> [t]he costs of the arbitration shall in principle be borne by the unsuccessful party or parties. However, the arbitral tribunal may apportion each of such costs between the parties if it determines that apportionment is reasonable, taking into account the circumstances of the case.

---

85. Article 29.5 of AHKIA.
86. On the settlement potential from greater transparency in ISDS, including the involvement of the home state from earlier stages, *see also generally* Micah Burch, et al., *Appropriate Treaty-Based Dispute Resolution for Asia-Pacific Commerce in the 21st Century*, 35 UNSW L. J. 1013 (2012). Also available at SSRN: https://ssrn.com/abstract=2065636.
87. Nottage, *supra* n. 49.
88. Malcolm Langford, et al., *Empirical Perspectives on Investment Arbitration: What Do We Know? Does It Matter?*, ISDS Academic Forum Working Group 7 Paper (15 Mar. 2019), https://www.cids.ch/images/Documents/Academic-Forum/7_Empirical_perspectives_-_WG7.pdf.
89. Sergio Puig, *Contextualizing Cost-Shifting: A Multimethod Approach*, 58 Va. J. Int'l L. 261, 268 (2019), arguing in favour of English Rule for claims that are 'manifestly without legal merit'.

Accordingly, the general expectation would be that the losing party pays the legal costs of the winning party and any divergence from this cost allocation practice would have to be justified by the tribunal. This would tend to make ISA more costly only for one party.

Article 14.34(3) of IA-CEPA sets the English Rule as a default for unsuccessful claimant to pay all costs and attorney's fees of the respondent state if the investor brings a claim under the Most-Favoured-Nation clause, about public health measures, about an investment that was made illegally or through corruption in the first place, or for claims that are found to be frivolous or without merit. It stipulates:

> If the tribunal determines that a claim is brought in contravention of Article 14.21 the tribunal shall make an award requiring the disputing investor to pay all costs and attorney's fees incurred by the disputing Party to respond to the claim, unless the tribunal considers that there are exceptional circumstances that warrant the disputing parties to bear costs in other specified proportions.[90]

Like IA-CEPA, AHKIA also assigns the loser pays principle to its cost allocation. According to Article 29.4, respondent can object to the claim if it alleges that the submitted claim 'is not a claim for which an award in favour of the claimant may be made' and is 'manifestly without legal merit'. If the tribunal finds the respondent's objection to be valid, it may 'award to the prevailing disputing party reasonable costs and attorney's fees incurred in submitting or opposing the objection'.[91]

§5.04 TRANSPARENCY THROUGH CPTPP, IA-CEPA, AHKIA AND THE MAURITIUS CONVENTION

IA-CEPA requires awards and decisions to be made publicly available. However, disputing parties can still maintain confidentiality of certain information that they would not want to make public by simply informing the tribunal that the information they intend to use is confidential.[92]

AHKIA generally provides more comprehensive provisions on transparency requirements compared to IA-CEPA, as discussed further below. However, while IA-CEPA has provisions (Article 14.32) requiring a party to disclose details on a third-party funder, such requirement is absent from AHKIA (despite Hong Kong having recently introduced into its domestic law a disclosure regime for such funding arrangements[93]). Under Article 30 of AHKIA the respondent state is required to make publicly available the following documents: the notice of intent, the notice of arbitration, pleadings, memorials and briefs, minutes/transcripts of hearings, and orders,

90. Article 14.34(3) of the Australia-Indonesia CEPA (FTA).
91. Article 29.6 Australia – Hong Kong Investment Agreement.
92. Articles 14.31.(1), 14.31.(2), 14.31.(3) of IA-CEPA.
93. *See*, e.g., Peter Hirst & Mun Yeow, *Comparing Hong Kong Code of Practice for Third Party Funding Arbitration with the Code of Conduct in England & Wales*, Kluwer Arbitration Blog (4 Feb. 2019), http://arbitrationblog.kluwerarbitration.com/2019/02/04/comparing-hong-kong-code-of-practice-for-third-party-funding-arbitration-with-the-code-of-conduct-in-england-wales/; and Ali, Chapter 6 in this volume.

awards and decisions of the tribunal. However, these requirements are again subject to the provisions that ensure that the state's sensitive information can be protected and remain confidential. It is up to each state to decide what information they will consider as confidential. The confidentiality protections apply to the sensitive information of both the state and the investor. Under Article 30.4(a), 'neither the disputing parties nor the tribunal shall disclose to the non-disputing Party or to the public any protected information if the disputing party that provided the information clearly designates it…'.

Australia has generally secured similar transparency obligations in most of its recent FTAs, including the CPTPP.[94] Its negotiators likely therefore pressed for comparable transparency in IA-CEPA, in which case the toned-down provisions that were agreed would reflect a greater preference for confidentiality from the Indonesian side. Australian negotiators also probably pressed quite strongly for transparency in AHKIA regime, and obtained this compared to IA-CEPA, not only because Hong Kong is a more developed economy but also because of the strong public interest in Australia around the Philip Morris Asia claim brought under the previous BIT with Hong Kong. The latter, like many early BITs, lacked express transparency provisions and therefore resulted in the tribunal having to issue a Procedural Order establishing individualised rules around confidentiality and disclosures.[95] Redactions to the costs award, made under the confidentiality regime, caused delays in publication and the lack of transparency around Australia's first inbound ISA claim generally attracted significant critical commentary in Australia.[96]

Ensuring transparency of ISDS proceedings and outcomes is often seen nowadays as an advantage for developed states. By contrast, governments of developing states (where in fact ISDS-backed treaties have the most impact for encouraging more FDI flows[97]) may be more reluctant to have their (in)actions exposed to public scrutiny. However, a recent empirical study on settlements in ISDS found that the outcomes of ISA cases with larger claimed amounts against developing states in fact increased the probability of outcomes being disclosed, compared to outcomes in claims against developed states.[98]

94. CPTPP Articles 28.13 and 28.18; Peru-Australia FTA Articles 27.12 27.16 of Peru-Australia FTA (2020). However, the (even updated) Singapore-Australia FTA by default sets the arbitration proceedings and related steps confidential. Article 7(11) only requires for the final reports to be made public. Article 7.2 stipulates: 'The deliberations of an arbitral tribunal and the documents submitted to it shall be kept confidential. Nothing in this Article shall preclude a Party from disclosing statements of its own positions or its submissions to the public; provided that a Party shall treat as confidential information submitted by the other Party to the arbitral tribunal which that Party has designated as confidential.' *See* https://www.dfat.gov.au/sites/default/files/SAFTA-chapter-16.pdf.

95. Available via https://pca-cpa.org/en/cases/5/.

96. Hepburn and Nottage, *supra* n. 11 (with further references); Gareth Hutchens & Christopher Knaus, *Revealed: $39m Cost of Defending Australia's Tobacco Plain Packaging Laws*, the Guardian (1 Jul. 2018), https://www.theguardian.com/business/2018/jul/02/revealed-39m-cost-of-defending-australias-tobacco-plain-packaging-laws.

97. Shiro Armstrong & Luke Nottage, *The Impact of Investment Treaties and ISDS Provisions on Foreign Direct Investment: A Baseline Econometric Analysis*, 16/74 Sydney Law School Research Paper 1 (2016), available at SSRN: https://ssrn.com/abstract=2824090.

98. Ubilava, *supra* n. 80.

This study also examined the transparency versus confidentiality of ISA outcomes generally. Instead of only classifying outcomes into two binary categories – public or confidential – the study differentiates three grades of transparency (Figure 5.2):

(a) Confidential – an ISA case where everything was kept confidential (merits, decision/award/settlement agreements, settled/awarded amounts);
(b) Partly Confidential – an ISA case which is confidential but the settlement or awarded amounts are made public; and
(c) Public – an ISA case in which the outcomes are made fully public (merits, decisions/awards/settlement agreements and settled/awarded amounts).

Figure 5.2 Transparency and Outcomes in ISA[99]

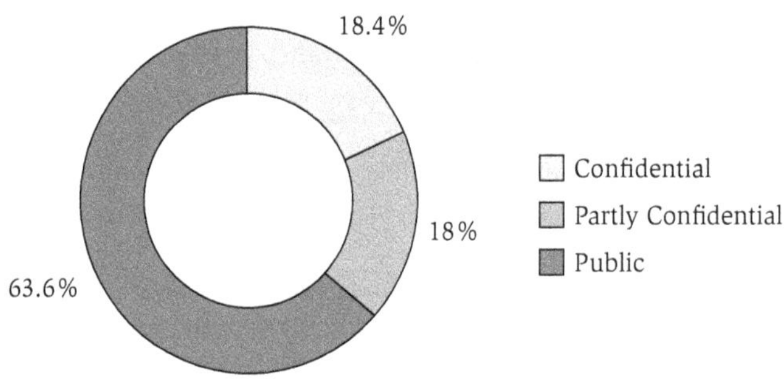

The data suggest that out of examined 495 treaty-based ISA cases 315 involved fully public outcomes, 89 cases although not fully public had final awarded or settled amounts disclosed, and 91 cases were kept completely confidential. The analysis shows that even older treaties can result in significant public disclosures, albeit so far, especially around ISA outcomes (rather than proceedings, such as hearings).[100]

Nonetheless, given the greater public interests in ISA compared to international commercial arbitration,[101] as ISDS claims have increased including against developed states, there have been growing calls to enhance transparency around both outcomes and proceedings in ISDS. After extensive deliberations following the 2010 revisions to the UNCITRAL Arbitration Rules (used for both ISA and international commercial arbitration), UNCITRAL developed the 2014 Rules on Transparency in Treaty-Based

99. Authors' own calculations based on the database by Ubilava, *supra* n. 65.
100. *See recently*, e.g., Lisa Bohmer, *Majority of Kaufmann-Kohler Chaired Tribunal Opts to Make Arbitration Documents Public Despite Silence of Cyprus-Serbia BIT on Transparency; Dissenter Warns of An Excess of Powers*, IA Reporter (5 Feb. 2020), https://www.iareporter.com/articles/majority-of-kaufmann-kohler-chaired-tribunal-opts-to-make-arbitration-documents-public-despite-silence-of-cyprus-serbia-bit-on-transparency-dissenter-warns-of-an-excess-of-powers/.
101. Luke Nottage, *Confidentiality versus Transparency in International Arbitration: Asia-Pacific Tensions and Expectations*, 19/52 Sydney Law School Research Paper 1 (2019). Also available at SSRN: https://ssrn.com/abstract=3444692 (with a revised version in this volume).

Investor-State Arbitration.[102] However, the latter only applies to disputes arising out of treaties concluded on or after 1 April 2014, when ISA is commenced under the UNCITRAL Arbitration Rules (unless the disputing parties otherwise agree). UNCITRAL therefore also developed the 2014 United Nations Convention on Transparency in Treaty-Based Investor-State Arbitration (known as the 'Mauritius Convention on Transparency').[103] Acceding states retrofit the 2014 UNCITRAL Transparency Rules to all ISA cases (whether or not under UNCITRAL Arbitration Rules) in their IIAs concluded even *before* 1 April 2014, if the counterpart state to the IIA has also acceded or the counterpart (or its investor as disputing party) agrees to apply the Transparency Rules.

On 18 July 2017 Australia became the twenty-first signatory to the Mauritius Convention, which came into force from 18 October 2017. On 17 September 2020 Australia became the sixth state to ratify Mauritius Convention, which will enter into force for Australia on 17 September 2021.[104] The Convention was tabled in Parliament on 31 July 2019 (so almost two years after signature), along with the revised Australia-Uruguay BIT (which had been signed on 5 April 2019, and already contains extensive transparency provisions). Following a brief public hearing on 16 September 2019 and review of only five submissions, far fewer than for other parliamentary enquiries into IIA ratifications since the Philip Morris Asia claim was initiated against Australia in 2011, JSCOT's Report 188 (December 2019) recommended that Australia ratifies both treaties. All substantive submissions, including from the Law Council of Australia, had urged ratification of the Mauritius Convention. Nottage's Submission even declared it a 'no-brainer'.[105] It observed how transparency appeals widely not only to (especially developed) host states nowadays but also by many investors bringing claims (by potentially changing host state political dynamics to generate appropriate settlements[106]), as well as ISDS arbitrators and lawyers (keen to showcase their expertise).

The JSCOT Report 188 specifically noted the point made in Nottage's Submission that 'the investment chapter of the new bilateral free trade agreement between Australia and Indonesia (IA-CEPA) has "narrower transparency provisions" than the Convention'.[107] There is little problem if under IA-CEPA an investor chooses UNCITRAL Arbitration Rules, as those already incorporate the 2014 UNCITRAL Transparency Rules, and there are few (if any) derogations in IA-CEPA (Article 14.31). For example, even the latter's exemption from disclosure provided for a host state judging its 'essential security' interests is replicated in the 2014 UNCITRAL Transparency Rules

---

102. https://uncitral.un.org/en/texts/arbitration/contractualtexts/transparency.
103. https://uncitral.un.org/en/texts/arbitration/conventions/transparency.
104. https://www.dfat.gov.au/trade/investment/australias-engagement-isds-reform.
105. Available via https://www.aph.gov.au/Parliamentary_Business/Committees/Joint/Treaties/ISDSUNConvention/Submissions and https://japaneselaw.sydney.edu.au/2019/09/new-frontiers-in-international-arbitration-for-the-asia-pacific-region-7-australias-parliamentary-inquiries-into-isds-in-hk-indonesia-and-un-mauritius-treaties/.
106. *See* further, e.g., Burch, et al., *supra* n. 86.
107. Report 188, para. 4.33 (footnotes omitted), https://www.aph.gov.au/Parliamentary_Business/Committees/Joint/Treaties/ISDSUNConvention/Report_188/section?id=committees%2freportjnt%2f024358%2f27984.

(Article 7.5). A possible but minor derogation in IA-CEPA is that a non-disputing party (home state) has thirty days to request a copy of the Notice of Arbitration at its own cost, whereas Article 3.1 of the Transparency Rules sets no time limits or cost allocation.

Instead, less transparency results under IA-CEPA if the investor chooses rather the treaty's option of ICSID (Convention or Additional Facility) Arbitration Rules. Although ICSID is presently reviewing its Rules, those are partially constrained by the Convention provisions themselves, and how much the new Rules will provide for transparency remains to be seen. For now they provide less than the UNCITRAL Transparency Rules. The ICSID Arbitration Rules allow, for example, publication only of excerpts of legal reasoning from awards, and not for public hearings. IA-CEPA only expands transparency somewhat, by requiring disclosure of full 'awards and decisions', but still not also 'orders' as in the UNCITRAL Transparency Rules or expressly in AHKIA (which also specifically allows amicus curiae submissions).

Further, even if Indonesia also decides to ratify the Mauritius Convention, that will not retrofit the enhanced (UNCITRAL Transparency Rules) provisions to IA-CEPA for both UNCITRAL and non-UNCITRAL (including ICSID) Rules arbitration, as IA-CEPA is a treaty concluded after 1 April 2014. Accordingly, to add such extra transparency, Australia and Indonesia would have to bilaterally agree to revise IA-CEPA. This inefficiency, compared to the multilateral retrofit achieved for treaties concluded before that date through the Mauritius Convention, will also apply for Australia regarding other IIAs concluded after 1 April 2014 that do not achieve transparency to the extent set out in the UNCITRAL Transparency Rules.

Even for pre-2014 treaties, the JSCOT Report also noted that although the Australian Fair Trade and Investment Network (AFTINET) civil society group supported ratification of the Mauritius Convention on Transparency, AFTINET was concerned this would have little impact given that few counterparties have acceded so far.[108] The JSCOT Report responded that DFAT representatives stated that:[109]

> they do not 'necessarily agree' that the Convention has limited practical applications, because of a number of factors, including that:
>
> - investors from a range of countries outside of those five that have ratified, could agree to greater transparency for a variety of reasons; and
> - based on multilateral discussions over the last couple of years, there 'really is a mood to make some reform in relation to ISDS' and that transparency is an issue that continues to be at the centre of reform activities.
>
> More broadly, DFAT indicated that Australia's ratification of the Convention would encourage other countries to take similar action.

The JSCOT Report further noted the argument made in Nottage's submission, similar to that provided in a National Impact Assessment by officials concerning the

108. Current Member States are Cameroon, Canada, Gambia, Mauritius and Switzerland: *see* https://uncitral.un.org/en/texts/arbitration/conventions/transparency/status. Australia only has ISDS-backed commitments in IIAs with Canada, through the CPTPP, which has extensive transparency provisions.
109. JSCOT Report 188, *supra* n. 107, paras 4.35-6 (footnotes omitted).

Mauritius Convention, concerning the role ratification will play in modernising Australia's older-style BITs:[110]

> Australia's ratification of ... [the Convention] will generate a similar expansion of transparency 'retrofitted' to Australia's many other earlier investment treaties, as long as the counterparty states also ratify this framework convention. This is especially important for Australia's early standalone BITs [bilateral investment treaties], as they usually don't add transparency provisions to the treaty text ... This lack of transparency provisions in BITs is different from Australia's more recent (US-style) FTA investment chapters. But such FTA transparency provisions vary too, so ... Convention ratification will be useful even for those FTAs by making transparency obligations more uniform and pervasive.

The JSCOT Report nonetheless noted that:[111]

> Variation in the transparency provisions of more recent FTAs was also raised in AFTINET's submission, which claimed that there 'has been inconsistent application of the Rules on Transparency in Australian trade and investment agreements that have been concluded since the adoption of the Rules'.
>
> In its submission to the inquiry, AFTINET recommended that the Australian Government should ratify the Convention so that investment agreements which include ISDS provisions will be, 'at a minimum', subject to the Rules on Transparency and that the Australian Government should:
>
>> ... address inconsistencies in the application of the Rules on Transparency in existing agreements to ensure they conform to the UNCITRAL rules.

Despite supporting ratification of the Mauritius Convention, the Submission by AFTINET (echoed by that of ActionAid, another civil society group) reiterated its consistent first preference in enquiries into ratification of other IIAs such as the CPTPP and the new treaties with Indonesia and Hong Kong. This is that Australia should not agree to ISDS provisions in new treaties at all anyway, and should seek to remove them from Australia's past IIAs. A similar view was expressed in the JSCOT Report's 'Additional Comments by the Australian Greens' Senator on the Committee:[112] opposition to ISDS provisions, but (if adopted) agreement on ratifying the Mauritius Convention, while seeking similar transparency provisions being extended to Australia's pre-existing treaties even if counterparties have not yet acceded to the Convention.

By contrast, and differently from views expressed in pre-2019 IIA ratification enquiries objecting to ISDS generally,[113] the 'Additional Comments' from the Labour

110. *Ibid.*, para. 4.37 (footnotes omitted).
111. *Ibid.*, paras 4.38-4.39 (footnotes omitted). *See* further Table 1 in AFTINET's Submission to JSCOT Inquiry, identifying some differences in transparency provisions across Australia's IIAs since 2014, at page 6 available via https://www.aph.gov.au/Parliamentary_Business/Committees/Joint/Treaties/ISDSUNConvention/Submissions.
112. Additional Comments by the Australian Greens (16 Sep. 2019),https://www.aph.gov.au/Parliamentary_Business/Committees/Joint/Treaties/ISDSUNConvention/Report_188/section?id=committees%2freportjnt%2f024358%2f72450.
113. *See*, e.g., Kawharu & Nottage, *supra* n. 10.

Opposition members targeted more specific concerns around ISDS, while also agreeing to ratification of the Mauritius and Uruguay treaties:[114]

> The Investments Uruguay Agreement and the ISDS UN Convention make important reforms to the ISDS process to ensure greater public and investor confidence in Australia's trading and international business arrangements.
>
> Despite this, the Labor members of the committee are concerned the lack of consultation may have limited the scope of reforms. In particular, a number of external stakeholders such as trade unions have raised concerns regarding the following ISDS features:
>
> - The capacity for temporary judges to be engaged as counsel in other ISDS proceedings, otherwise referred to as 'double-hatting'
> - The lack of precedence to guide decision making by judges, inconsistent with the rule of law and Australia's judicial principles. The potential for inconsistency in decision making threatens public and investor confidence in the ISDS process and international business arrangements as a result
> - The inability to appeal a decision, also inconsistent with the rule of law and Australia's judicial principles.
>
> The Labor members of the Committee believe that Report 188 should include recommendations which, in consultation with relevant external stakeholders, address the aforementioned concerns.

These Additional Comments from Labour parliamentarians suggest some backtracking from an overarching anti-ISDS policy stance (as maintained instead by the Australian Greens Party). This may create an opportunity for more bipartisanship, with the Coalition Government, in further reviewing and developing Australia's investment treaty programme.

§5.05 CONCLUSIONS

Several general points can be derived from this short review of Australia's recent engagement in international investment treaty lawmaking. First, the drafting of Australia's treaties continues to reflect a largely US-style approach (epitomised by the TPP and then the CPTPP). That approach has been promoted by the US developing a Model BIT in light of its own experiences and some domestic politics around IIAs and ISA. Yet the Australian government has not heeded calls by commentators and earlier parliamentary committees to engage in public consultations to develop its own model provisions.[115] This may have the pragmatic advantage of allowing Australian government negotiators more flexibility in responding to concerns or interests of counterpart states. Such flexibility emerges as the second feature of recent developments, when comparing in particular the provisions eventually agreed in IA-CEPA and AHKIA. However, consultations over model provisions (perhaps beginning around provisions in the revised Australia-Uruguay BIT) could help restore more legitimacy in the public

---

114. *Additional Comments – JSCOT Report 188: Investments Uruguay*, ISDS UN Convention (16 Sep. 2019), https://www.aph.gov.au/Parliamentary_Business/Committees/Joint/Treaties/ISDSUNConvention/Report_188/section?id=committees%2freportjnt%2f024358%2f72451.

115. Cf., generally Nottage, *supra* n. 49.

eye and greater bipartisanship around ISDS-backed commitments in Australia's treaty practice. Anyway, and third, a more nuanced approach to ISDS from Labor Opposition parliamentarians may indicate some emergent bipartisanship and therefore allow Australia to play a more active role in ongoing UNCITRAL deliberations over ISDS reform. This may also result from another recent innovation: the Coalition Government's announcement of a review of Australia's remaining BITs, with DFAT seeking public Submissions by end-September 2020. The associated Discussion Paper called in particular for views on the benefits and concerns related to those BITs, what clauses might be focused on if they were renegotiated (like those with Hong Kong and Uruguay) or folded into wider FTAs (as with Indonesia recently), and what model or approach might be developed more generally for Australia's IIAs.[116]

116. *See* generally https://www.dfat.gov.au/trade-and-investment/discussion-paper-review-australias-bilateral-investment-treaties, and the Submission by Nottage (dated 14 September 2020) available at https://erga-omnes.sydney.edu.au/2020/09/submission-to-dfat-consultation-on-review-of-australias-bilateral-investment-treaties/.

CHAPTER 6

New Frontiers in Hong Kong's Resolution of 'One Belt One Road' International Commercial and Investor-State Disputes

Shahla Ali[*]

Given the rapid increase in Chinese outward foreign direct investment (FDI) since the start of the 'One Belt One Road' Initiative (OBOR), international commercial and investor-state disputes involving Chinese and Hong Kong investors will likely multiply. Given the significance of Hong Kong as a fulcrum for OBOR project financing and logistics, understanding Hong Kong's approach to the resolution of OBOR disputes will offer a window into the region's new frontiers in commercial and investor-state dispute resolution.

§6.01 INTRODUCTION: HONG KONG AND THE BELT AND ROAD INITIATIVE

The Belt and Road Initiative (BRI), also known as the OBOR or the Silk Road Economic Belt and the Twenty-first Century Maritime Silk Road, is an ambitious economic and strategic agenda of the People's Republic of China (PRC). It aims to 'strengthen infrastructure, trade, and investment links between China and between China and some sixty-five other countries that account collectively for over 30 per cent of global GDP, 62 per cent of the world's population, and 75 per cent of known energy reserves'.[1]

* The author thanks the HKU/USydney Strategic Partnership Fund and the Government of Hong Kong's University Grants Committee for its kind support through its GRF Grant (HKU 17604318). Thanks also to Dr Nobumichi Teramura for his assistance in research, drafting and editing. For further elaboration, *see* Shahla Ali, *ICA and ISDS Developments in Hong Kong in the Context of China's Belt and Road Initiative*, C.J.Q (2020).

1. The World Bank, *Belt and Road Initiative*, Brief (29 Mar. 2018), https://www.worldbank.org/en/topic/regional-integration/brief/belt-and-road-initiative.

As in the case of the establishment of regional initiatives, such as the Asian Infrastructure Investment Bank (AIIB) and the New Development Bank (NDB), the BRI is theorised by Djankov to unite China's economic priorities abroad.[2] The BRI seeks the development of external conditions conducive to further expansion of the Chinese economy, including (but not limited to) regional infrastructure development, reduction of trade costs, securing of energy supplies, growth of regional economies and greater international usage of the *renminbi*.[3] Through the BRI initiative, China adopts (in contrast to early days of state-led economic growth) an outward-looking approach to national and regional development.

To realise this initiative, in March 2015, an action plan entitled 'Vision and Action on Jointly Building the Belt and Road' was issued jointly by the National Development and Reform Commission, Ministry of Foreign Affairs, and Ministry of Commerce of the PRC, with State Council authorisation. An objective of the initiative is to establish six major economic cooperation corridors complemented by the sea route corridors across Eurasia and beyond.[4] The 'economic cooperation' extends to the five key areas: policy coordination; facilities connectivity; unimpeded trade; financial integration; and people-to-people linkages.

Funding for the BRI has been offered by the Chinese Government through ensuring that its banks provide a significant outlay of funds for Chinese enterprises operating in the countries participating in the BRI.[5] Further funding is provided by AIIB[6] and NDB (BRICS Bank).[7] Accordingly, Chinese investors have been encouraged to venture into new businesses in countries along the BRI, resulting in increased investment in the region alongside added operational risks.[8] Chinese outward FDI has risen sharply since the launch of the BRI initiative.[9]

2. Simeon Djankov, *Chapter 1: The Rationale Behind China's Belt and Road Initiative*, in *China's Belt and Road Initiative – Motives, Scope and Challenge* 6, 7 (Simeon Djankov & Sean Miner eds., Peterson Institute for International Economics 2016).
3. *Ibid. See also* generally Gu, Chapter 7 in this volume.
4. The action plan is available at http://english.cri.cn/12394/2015/03/29/2941s872030.htm. Those corridors are: New Eurasian Land Bridge Corridor; China-Mongolia-Russia Corridor; China-Central Asia-West Asia Corridor; China-Indochina Peninsula Corridor; China-Pakistan Economic Corridor; and Bangladesh-China-India-Myanmar Economic Corridor.
5. Those policy banks include: China Development Bank; Export-Import Bank of China; the Industrial and Commercial Bank of China Limited; the China Construction Bank Corporation; and the Bank of China. *See* Dini Sejko, *Financing the Belt and Road Initiative: MDBs, SWFs, SOEs and the Long Wait for Private Investors* (November 2017), https://www.rmit.edu.au/content/dam/rmit/documents/college-of-business/industry/apec/apec-currents-dini-sejko-financing-belt-and-road-initiative.pdf.
6. The AIIB was established by the fifty-seven founding members on 29 Jun. 2015. *See* AIIB, *Members and Prospective Members of the Bank*, available at: https://www.aiib.org/en/aboutaiib/governance/members-of-bank/index.html.
7. The NDB was established on 15 Jul. 2014. *See* https://www.ndb.int/about-us/essence/history/.
8. The risks include 'political instability, lack of security, lack of regulation, lack of infrastructure, absence of a fair and impartial legal system, absence of a corporate governance system, and local prejudices that can give rise to a climate of hostility': Sarah Grimmer & Christina Charemi, *Dispute Resolution Along the Belt and Road*, in *The Asia-Pacific Arbitration Review 2018* 1-5, 1 (Global Arbitration Review ed., Law Business Research 2017).
9. Lili Kang, et al., *Harmony in Diversity: Can the One Belt One Road Initiative Promote China's Outward Foreign Direct Investment?*, 10 Sustainability, MDPI, Open Access J. 1 (2018).

This trend may lead to an increase in the number of Chinese and Hong Kong investors involved in legal disputes in BRI countries, including both private and investor-state disputes. A typical scenario would involve a dispute between a Chinese or Hong Kong investor with a local company in a BRI country as a result of a business transaction. In such cases, it is likely that parties would prefer to solve such disputes via International Commercial Arbitration (ICA) given the general importance placed on the neutrality of dispute resolution forum. Another typical scenario would involve harm to a Chinese or Hong Kong investor operating in a BRI country due to policy changes in the country.[10] The investor would then resort to investor-state dispute settlement (ISDS). Other disputes may arise involving third parties against investors seeking recourse for grievances in relation to BRI projects and transactions. For instance, in February 2019, the High Court of Hong Kong accepted the filing of the city's first BRI-related litigation brought by the United Arab Emirates' DP World (a port operator) against the China Merchants Group (CMG) (a state-owned enterprise) in respect of an alleged inducement of breach of contract between DP World and the Djibouti Government granting DP World exclusive rights to operate Djibouti's ports.[11]

Beyond Hong Kong-Mainland China investment disputes, Hong Kong offers an attractive venue for the arbitration of cases between countries along or outside of the Belt and Road. Its user-friendly pro-arbitration environment, including a strong rule of law tradition, speed and minimal court intervention, as well as respect for parties' autonomy, make it a popular choice for regions beyond Hong Kong and Mainland China.[12] Confidentiality provisions under Hong Kong's arbitration law and the jurisdiction's high rate of international arbitral enforcement (capable of being enforced on a near-global basis in jurisdictions party to the New York Convention (NYC)) further increase investor confidence in selecting Hong Kong as the seat of arbitration.[13]

Hong Kong further functions as an effective 'link' between China and foreign jurisdictions.[14] In 2017, it was reported that 55% of arbitrations administered by the Hong Kong International Arbitration Commission (HKIAC) involved a Mainland Chinese party, with a third of total arbitrations involving parties from Mainland China

10. Grimmer & Charemi, *supra* n. 8.
11. Lo Kingling, *Legal Bump in the Belt and Road? A Mideast Port Giant, a Chinese Rival and a Hong Kong Lawsuit over a Djibouti Deal*, South China Morning Post (17 Feb. 2019), https://www.scmp.com/news/china/diplomacy/article/2186411/lawsuit-against-chinese-port-builder-djibouti-highlights-risks (accessed 23 Feb. 2020).
12. Shahla Ali, *Balancing Procedural and Substantive Arbitration Reforms: Advancing International Arbitration Practice in Hong Kong*, in *The Developing World of Arbitration: A Comparative Study of Arbitration Reform in the Asia Pacific* 39 (Anselmo Reyes & Weixia Gu eds., Hart Publishing 2018).
13. Paul Starr, James McKenzie & Suraj Sajnani, *Case Study: Belt and Road Disputes – Choosing Hong Kong as the Seat of Arbitration*, Asia Intelligence (18 Nov. 2016), https://www.kwm.com/en/hk/knowledge/insights/belt-and-road-disputes-choosing-hong-kong-as-the-seat-of-arbitration-20161118 (accessed 21 Oct. 2020). On confidentiality versus transparency, *see* further Nottage, Chapter 4 in this volume.
14. Sarah Grimmer, *Distinction and Connection: Hong Kong and Mainland China, a View from the HKIAC*, in *A Global Arbitration Review Special Report: The Asia-Pacific Arbitration Review 2020* 13-18 (Global Arbitration Review ed., Law Business Research 2019).

and a BRI jurisdiction respectively.[15] It was reported in the same year that over the last five years, the HKIAC had handled almost USD 800 million of disputed claims in 500 cases involving parties from BRI jurisdictions.[16]

As Hong Kong is a leading international dispute resolution hub and a major participant in the BRI given its international repute as a centre for financial and investment services, it is useful to explore how the initiative will influence the dispute resolution industry in the region. This is particularly so in light of its place in the Greater Bay Area (covering Guangdong, Hong Kong and Macao as an integrated 'cluster'), a key financial, transportation and technological hub with enhanced infrastructural connectivity and trade cooperation.[17] In the context of the Greater Bay Area, Hong Kong has been recognised as a 'service centre' for handling commercial and investment disputes arising out of BRI projects.[18]

§6.02 HONG KONG AS A LEADING INTERNATIONAL DISPUTE RESOLUTION HUB

[A] Legislative and Regulatory Framework

The Hong Kong Arbitration Ordinance (HKAO) which came into force on 1 June 2011[19] is currently the law governing arbitrations in Hong Kong. It remains largely based on the UNCITRAL Model Law on International Commercial Arbitration (Model Law), which Hong Kong was one of the earliest jurisdictions in Asia to adopt (in 1989),[20] as well as the Model Law's amendments made in the 2006 version (except for the recognition and enforcement of interim relief from arbitrators). The current HKAO adopted a total of thirty-four articles of the Model Law following a similar pattern: the provisions begin by stating in the first subsection 'Article [X] of the UNCITRAL Model Law, the text of which is set out below, has effect' followed by a verbatim reproduction of the Model Law provision.[21] Amendments or modifications, if any, are contained in ensuing subsections.[22]

The HKAO provides 112 sections in Schedule 1 comprising a unified regime for international and domestic arbitrations. This cohesive model contrasts with Hong

15. HKIAC, *Why HKIAC for Belt and Road Disputes*, https://www.hkiac.org/Belt-and-Road/why-hkiac-belt-and-road-disputes (accessed 30 Mar. 2020).
16. Meghan Tobin, *Hong Kong or Singapore: Who to Trust on China's Belt and Road Disputes?*, South China Morning Post (23 Mar. 2019), https://www.scmp.com/week-asia/economics/article/3002923/hong-kong-or-singapore-who-trust-chinas-belt-and-road-disputes (accessed 23 Feb. 2020).
17. *See* generally *Outline Development Plan for the Guangdong-Hong Kong-Macao Greater Bay Area (Courtesy Translation)*.
18. *Ibid.*, 49.
19. Cap. 609.
20. *See* Law Reform Commission of Hong Kong, *Implementation* (28 Feb. 2020), https://www.hkreform.gov.hk/en/implementation/index.htm.
21. *See* ss 9-12, 19-21, 23-28, 34-42, 47-54 and 64-69, HKAO.
22. *See* e.g., ss 10, 19-20, 23-24 and 26, HKAO.

Kong's prior arbitration law,[23] where the Model Law (1985 version) was applicable to international arbitration and the English Arbitration Act 1950 applied to domestic arbitrations.[24] The HKAO provides for exceptions to this unified regime in Schedule 2, taking seven provisions from the old regime regulating domestic arbitrations.[25] Parties can 'opt-in' to these provisions in whole or part and thereby exclude the respective provisions of Schedule 1.[26] Moreover, unless the parties agree to the contrary,[27] Schedule 2 applies in its entirety to a domestic arbitration agreement entered into before or within a period of six years after the commencement of the HKAO.[28] Schedule 2 likewise applies automatically in construction sub-contracting cases.[29]

Moreover, the HKAO complements and modifies Model Law provisions as follows. First, while the Model Law provides for three arbitrators in case the parties cannot decide on the number of arbitrators,[30] the HKAO leaves the determination of this number to HKIAC,[31] to offer more flexible solutions than a fixed rule providing for three arbitrators.[32] Second, section 46(3)(b) of the HKAO provides that the parties need a 'reasonable opportunity' to present their case, in contrast with a 'full opportunity' in Article 18(3)(b) of the Model Law. The reason for adopting a lower standard in the HKAO was that the drafters were wary of the potential of abusive challenges to arbitral awards based on a 'full' opportunity to present its case, although some scholars have questioned the difference between these two standards in practice.[33] Third, the HKAO in some instances will engage in gap-filling on issues for which the Model Law is silent, as part of a broad-based approach to promote Hong Kong as a seat for arbitration.[34] For example, the HKAO places greater emphasis on confidentiality than the Model Law, as seen in section 16 of the HKAO, which provides that proceedings out of or in connection with a given arbitration are to be heard in closed court proceedings unless one of several limited exceptions apply. Likewise, sections 17 and 18 of the HKAO restrict the reporting of court proceeding and the disclosure of information related to such proceedings.[35] Fourth, the HKAO provides for the option of med-arb in sections 32

23. Old HKAO (Cap. 341).
24. Christopher To & Damon So, *Butterworths Hong Kong Arbitration Law Handbook* 1-2 (LexisNexis Butterworths 2012).
25. David Sandborg, *Arbitration in Hong Kong, in International Commercial Arbitration in Asia* 133, 152-3 (Shahla Ali & Tom Ginsburg eds., Juris 3rd ed. 2013).
26. Section 99, HKAO.
27. Section 102, HKAO.
28. Section 100, HKAO.
29. Section 101, HKAO.
30. Article 10 para. 2, Model Law.
31. Section 23(3), HKAO.
32. John Choong & Romesh J. Weeramantry, *The Hong Kong Arbitration Ordinance: Commentary and Annotations* paras 23.08-23.09 (Sweet & Maxwell/Thomson Reuters 2nd ed. 2015).
33. *See*, for a detailed discussion, John Choong & Michael J. Moser, *Hong Kong SAR*, in *Asia Arbitration Handbook* 189-275, para. 4.172 (John Choong & Michael J. Moser eds., Oxford University Press 2011); Choong & Weeramantry, *supra* n. 32, at para. 46.16; for the Model Law provisions, Howard M. Holtzmann, et al., *A Guide to the 2006 Amendments to the UNCITRAL Model Law on International Commercial Arbitration: Legislative History and Commentary* 549-52 (Wolters Kluwer 2015).
34. Lee Tin Yan, *Introductory Note to the New Arbitration Ordinance of the Hong Kong Special Administrative Region*, 51 I.L.M. 133 (2012).
35. Gary Born, *International Commercial Arbitration* 88-99 (Wolters Kluwer 2nd ed. 2014).

and 33. While some have raised concerns over arbitrator independence given the dual role of acting as both a mediator and arbitrator,[36] the HKAO tackles this issue by stating that an arbitrator may also act as a mediator without affecting his or her independence if all parties give their consent in writing.[37] The HKAO enables parties to avail themselves of med-arb without any concerns as to the validity of an award, although uptake in practice has been less extensive than in Mainland China.[38]

Moreover, Hong Kong, as a part of the PRC,[39] is a signatory to the NYC.[40] Since Mainland China has declared reciprocity as well as a commercial reservation according to Article I(3) of the NYC, these reservations also apply to Hong Kong.[41] However, in Mainland China, arbitration awards from Hong Kong are not considered 'foreign' in the sense of Article I(1) of the NYC. Likewise, Mainland China awards are not considered foreign awards in Hong Kong. As a consequence, a number of awards from Hong Kong have been unable to be enforced in Mainland China and vice versa.[42] In order to circumvent this undesirable result and to provide for an easy enforcement mechanism similar to the NYC,[43] Hong Kong and Mainland China concluded the 'Arrangement Concerning Mutual Recognition and Enforcement of Arbitral Awards Between the Mainland and the Hong Kong Special Administrative Region'. By the same token, in order to ensure the enforceability of Macao awards in Hong Kong and vice versa, Hong Kong and Macao concluded the 'Arrangement Concerning Reciprocal Recognition and Enforcement of Arbitral Awards Between the Hong Kong Special Administrative Region and the Macao Special Administrative Region'.

There are other legal instruments governing ICA-related matters in Hong Kong. Particularly relevant for ad hoc arbitrations is the Host Country Agreement that Mainland China and the Permanent Court of Arbitration (PCA) concluded on 4 January 2015. This agreement enables Hong Kong to serve as a venue for ad hoc arbitrations under the regime of the PCA.[44] Moreover, Hong Kong, being a common law jurisdiction, places great importance on case law, and judgments from the UK, often provide guidance for Hong Kong courts.[45]

As for investment disputes, Mainland China, and thereby Hong Kong, is a signatory to the Convention on the Settlement of Investment Disputes between States and Nationals of Other States (the ICSID Convention). However, the fact does not guarantee that both Beijing and Hong Kong are inclined to let the ICSID to handle all BRI – related disputes as investors from Hong Kong may pursue routes other than ICSID

36. Wei Sun & Melanie Willems, *Arbitration in China* paras 21.1 & 21.5 (Wolters Kluwer 2015).
37. Section 33(1), HKAO.
38. Philip Nunn, *The Med–arb Q&A: The Hong Kong Take on This PRC Phenomenon,* Norton Rose Fulbright Publications (May 2016), https://www.nortonrosefulbright.com/en-hk/knowledge/publications/ec00be49/the-medarb-qa.
39. Since Hong Kong and Macao are part of the PRC, the author will use the term 'Mainland China' to refer to the PRC excluding Macao and Hong Kong.
40. Convention on the Recognition and Enforcement of Foreign Arbitral Awards (New York, 1958).
41. *See* remark at www.uncitral.org/uncitral/en/uncitral_texts/arbitration/NYConvention_status.html.
42. Sun & Willems, *supra* n. 36.
43. Tao Jingzhou, *Arbitration Law and Practice in China* para. 615 (Wolters Kluwer 3rd ed. 2012).
44. *See* www.doj.gov.hk/lawdoc/bilateral/aeio_7e.pdf.
45. Choong & Moser, *supra* n. 33.

to sue Chinese authorities in BRI-related disputes.[46] This point will be further discussed in §6.03[A] below.

[B] Institutional Framework

Several arbitration institutions have offices in Hong Kong, including the International Court of Arbitration of the International Chamber of Commerce (ICC) (in November 2008), the China International Economic and Trade Arbitration Commission (CIETAC) (in September 2012), the China Maritime Arbitration Commission (CMAC) Hong Kong Arbitration Centre (in November 2014), and the Hong Kong International Arbitration Centre (HKIAC) (in September 1985). Among them, the HKIAC is one of the most established centres in the region.[47] Indicators of the HKIAC's status as Hong Kong's foremost arbitration institution are its caseload and functions. In 2019, HKIAC accepted a total of 308 arbitration disputes[48] while the ICC handled almost 842 disputes worldwide in 2018, only about 17% of them were seated in Asia (which includes other popular seats like Singapore).[49] Moreover, CIETAC Hong Kong has not yet published any case statistics.[50]

HKIAC continues to make concerted efforts towards maintaining its leading position amongst global arbitral institutions by upholding its competence and independence. Its governing body is the HKIAC Council, which is comprised of twenty-eight leading figures within the international arbitration community. These highly experienced and skilful arbitrators contribute to the competence of the centre as a whole.[51] HKIAC also maintains a panel of senior arbitrators and a list of younger arbitration practitioners.[52] The arbitrators and practitioners from the panel and the list must adhere to the duties imposed on them by the parties and the law as well as to ethical duties. Otherwise, HKIAC can, on its own or upon a complaint by the parties,

46. However, if the Hong Kong investor is a dual citizen of, say, Hong Kong and Australia, the investor might be able to acquire protection as 'investors' under the ICSID regime; the investor may sue Chinese authorities to the ICSID. *See* Clovis Trevino, *Treaty Claims by Dual Nationals: A New Frontier?*, Kluwer Arbitration Blog (8 Oct. 2015), http://arbitrationblog.kluwerarbitration.com/2015/10/08/treaty-claims-by-dual-nationals-a-new-frontier/; Jarrod Hepburn, *After Australia Fends Off Philip Morris Claim under Hong Kong BIT, Australia and HK Agree to Overhaul of Treaty Terms*, IA Reporter (26 Mar. 2019), https://www.iareporter.com/articles/after-australia-fends-off-philip-morris-claim-under-hong-kong-bit-the-two-countries-release-a-new-treaty-including-tobacco-exception/; Jarrod Hepburn, *After Respective Battles with Philip Morris, Australia and Uruguay Unveil New Bilateral Investment Treaty*, IA Reporter (15 Apr. 2019), https://www.iareporter.com/articles/after-respective-battles-with-philip-morris-australia-and-uruguay-unveil-new-bilateral-investment-treaty/.
47. Department of Justice, *Arbitration – The International Arbitration Centre for the Asia Pacific*, available at www.doj.gov.hk/eng/public/arbitration.html.
48. https://www.hkiac.org/about-us/statistics.
49. ICC, *2018 ICC Dispute Resolution Statistics*, ICC Dispute Resolution Bulletin 12 (2019).
50. *See* for a general overview of CIETAC statistics until 2019, available at http://www.cietac.org/index.php?m = Page&a = index&id = 40&l = en.
51. Chiann Bao, *Hong Kong International Arbitration Centre and Its Rules, in Arbitration in Hong Kong – A Practical Guide*, paras 7.001-7.003 (Geoffrey Ma & Denis Brock eds., Sweet & Maxwell 3rd ed. 2014).
52. *Ibid.*, para. 7.015.

remove the arbitrator from the panel or list.[53] As for HKIAC's independence, while it has received significant financial support from the Hong Kong Government, it nevertheless is independent and free from any external influence.[54]

Moreover, Hong Kong, in general, follows an arbitrator system that is liberal and quality- conscious. The HKAO enables anyone to act as an arbitrator without imposing particular nationality or legal training requirements and also permits anyone to act as counsel in an arbitration even though he/she may not be qualified as a Hong Kong lawyer.[55] An arbitrator must disclose any circumstances likely to give rise to justifiable doubts as to his or her impartiality or independence.[56] If there exist such circumstances or if the arbitrator does not possess the qualifications agreed to by the parties, the arbitrator can be challenged.[57] Moreover, there are several organisations that provide training for arbitrators. The University of Hong Kong, Chinese University of Hong Kong, and the City University of Hong Kong offer LLM programmes in dispute resolution. The Hong Kong Institute of Arbitrators and the Chartered Institute of Arbitrators (East Asia Branch) were all established to enhance the skills of Hong Kong arbitrators.[58]

[C] Judicial Framework

Hong Kong courts are generally viewed as having a pro-arbitration attitude[59] because of minimalist intervention on the part of the courts during the arbitration process.[60] Likewise, the courts generally recognise and enforce arbitral awards,[61] provided that the awards are subject to some degree of scrutiny during the recognition and enforcement process. This can be explained in the context of the four different categories of awards recognised under the HKAO.

The first category comprises awards made in a country that is a signatory to the NYC[62] (convention awards).[63] The grounds for refusal of enforcement of these awards adhere to grounds set out under the Convention,[64] while the enforcement procedure is efficient[65] as the formal requirements for obtaining the enforcement are very limited.[66]

53. www.hkiac.org/en/arbitration/arbitrators.
54. Bao, *supra* n. 51, at para. 7.001.
55. *See* s. 24(1), HKAO.
56. Section 25(1), HKAO.
57. Section 25(2), HKAO.
58. Sandborg, *supra* n. 25.
59. Timothy Hill & Mark Lin, *Role of the Court, in Arbitration in Hong Kong: A Practical Guide*, paras 18.001-18.005 (Geoffrey Ma & Denis Brock eds., Sweet & Maxwell 3rd ed. 2014).
60. Kun Fan, *The New Arbitration Ordinance in Hong Kong*, 29 J. Int'l Arb. 720 (2012).
61. Peter S. Caldwell, *Hong Kong, in Practitioner's Handbook on International Arbitration and Mediation* 689 (Richard Chernick, et al. eds., Juris 3rd ed. 2012).
62. However, this excludes Mainland China; *see* Christopher To & Damon So, *Butterworths Hong Kong Arbitration Law Handbook*, para. 92.01 (LexisNexis Butterworths 2012).
63. Sections 87-91, HKAO.
64. *See* s. 89, HKAO and Article V, NYC.
65. *See* s. 87(1), HKAO; Denis Brock & Laura Feldman, *Recognition and Enforcement of the Arbitral Award, in Arbitration in Hong Kong – A Practical Guide*, para. 19.027 (Geoffrey Ma & Denis Brock eds., Sweet & Maxwell 3rd ed. 2014).

The second and third categories consist of awards made in Mainland China (Mainland awards)[67] and awards made in Macau (Macau awards).[68] In principle, the enforcement of these awards works in the same way as convention awards, because the grounds for refusal, recognition procedures and formal requirements are identical.[69] Yet, due to the enforcement arrangements with Mainland China and Macao, a request for enforcement has to comply with additional procedural steps contained in these arrangements.[70]

The fourth category includes all remaining awards, including awards made in non-NYC countries as well as in Hong Kong (non-convention and Hong Kong awards).[71] The first problem in connection with these awards is that the aforementioned pro-enforcement attitude only extends towards convention, Mainland China and Macau awards,[72] but not necessarily towards non-convention awards.[73] Furthermore, the HKAO provides that a Hong Kong court can refuse recognition of non-convention award 'for any other reason the court considers just to do so'.[74] This provision vests the court with wide discretion to refuse the enforcement of an award.[75] In the event of such non-enforcement, a party may also bring an action at common law to enforce an arbitral award by way of a writ followed by an application for summary judgment.[76] By contrast, the grounds for refusing enforcement of convention, Mainland and Macau awards are limited, and the court has little discretion to refuse enforcement.[77]

The Hong Kong judiciary's pro-enforcement attitude is further confirmed by the high enforceability rate of arbitral awards. According to the enforcement statistics published by the HKIAC, there were thirty-four arbitral award enforcement applications filed in Hong Kong courts in 2017, none of which were refused.[78] It is possible that as a common law jurisdiction, its laws have been in a position to 'evolve more quickly than statute based law in order to adapt to current practices.'[79] It is also possible that being a small jurisdiction means that Hong Kong courts are able to 'assign arbitration cases to specialist judges, who are able to deal with cases efficiently'.[80]

66. *See* s. 88, HKAO.
67. Sections 92-98, HKAO.
68. Section 98A-98D, HKAO.
69. *See* ss 87-91, 92-98 and 98A-98D, HKAO.
70. Brock & Feldman, *supra* n. 65, at paras 19.045-19.049 & 19.063.
71. Sections 82-86, HKAO.
72. Brock & Feldman, *supra* n. 65, at paras 19.028, 19.042 19.063.
73. *Ibid.*, para. 19.037.
74. Section 86(2)(c), HKAO.
75. Choong & Weeramantry, *supra* n. 32.
76. *See Xiamen Xingjingdi Group Ltd v. Eton Properties Ltd* [2008] 4 H.K.L.R.D. 972, paras 47 and 63, affirmed on appeal: [2009] 4 HKLRD. 353; *Re Petrochina International (Hong Kong) Corp Ltd* [2011] 4 HKLRD 604.
77. Choong & Weeramantry, *supra* n. 32, at para. 4.393.
78. HKIAC, *HKIAC – Enforcement of Awards in Hong Kong: 2017*, available at https://www.hkiac.org/about-us/statistics/enforcement-awards.
79. *See* the Law Society of the England and Wales, *England and Wales: The Jurisdiction of Choice*, available at: www.eversheds.com/documents/LawSocietyEnglandAndWalesJurisdictionOfChoice.pdf.
80. *Ibid.*

§6.03 RECENT REFORM OF HONG KONG'S ICA AND ISDS REGIME

[A] Legislative and Regulatory Reform

On 28 June 2017, the Investment Agreement of the Mainland and Hong Kong Closer Economic Partnership Arrangement (Investment Agreement) came into force.[81] The Mainland and Hong Kong Closer Economic Partnership Agreement (CEPA) is a free trade agreement signed on 29 June 2003. The Investment Agreement aims to 'to enhance CEPA in line with a modern and comprehensive free trade agreement, providing for promotion and protection of increasing investments between the two places as well as fostering economic and technical cooperation and exploring new areas of cooperation'.[82]

Of significance to the BRI, is Article 19 of the Investment Agreement, which establishes a dispute settlement mechanism between a Hong Kong investor and the Mainland authority. While not adopting compulsory mediation, for example, the provision recommends that Hong Kong investors solve disputes over losses or damages resulting from a breach by Mainland authorities or institutions through: (i) amicable consultation between the disputing parties; (ii) the complaint handling organisations for foreign investors in the Mainland in accordance with the relevant requirements of the Mainland; (iii) the Committee on Investment under Article 17 of the Investment Agreement; (iv) administrative review in accordance with the laws of the Mainland; (v) a mediation institution of the Mainland; and/or (vi) recourse to the judicial proceedings under the laws of the Mainland. To summarise, Article 19 requires Hong Kong investors to solve their dispute with Mainland authorities/institutions in accordance with the law of the Mainland and, depending on the situation, under the supervision of dispute resolution institutions in the Mainland.

[B] Institutional Reform: BRI Specific Initiatives

As several arbitration centres coexist in Hong Kong, each is continually exploring ways to distinguish itself in attracting a greater share of the arbitration market in light of BRI developments.[83] For example, on 1 October 2017, the CIETAC Investment Arbitration Rules came into force, to regulate both investment treaty arbitration and investor-state arbitration as contractually agreed dispute resolution mechanism. CIETAC seemed to establish the rules to offer dispute resolution service that is effective for the implementation of the BRI.[84]

81. *See* https://investmentpolicyhub.unctad.org/IIA/mostRecent/treaty/3780.
82. *See* https://www.tid.gov.hk/english/cepa/legaltext/cepa1415_note.html.
83. Aisha Nadar, *Construction Arbitration in the Context of China's Belt and Road Projects*, Global Arbitration Review (31 Oct. 2019), https://globalarbitrationreview.com/chapter/1175762/construction-arbitration-in-the-context-of-china%E2%80%99s-belt-and-road-projects#footnote-012.
84. http://www.cietac.org.cn/index.php?m=Article&a=show&id=14473&l=en. For a critical view on the effectiveness of the CIETAC Investment Arbitration Rules, *see* Horia Ciurtin, *The Structural Implications of Belt-and-Road Arbitration: China's Legal Gamble across Eurasia,*

HKIAC is keen to put itself forward as the premier forum for the resolution of BRI-related disputes. On April 2018, the institution announced its new 'Belt and Road Programme' including a Belt and Road Advisory Committee, which consists of experts from the finance, infrastructure, insurance, construction and maritime sectors, and an online dispute resolution platform, which was dedicated to solving BRI disputes.[85] The HKIAC also provided a 'Belt and Road Knowledge Database' that accumulates information relevant to the BRI such as reports, articles and expert analysis. While some commentators criticise the broad categorisation adopted in the database as cumbersome,[86] the database is still useful as a first contact point for accessing the information on BRI and its influence on the legal sector of Hong Kong. Moreover, in January 2018, the ICC established a 'Belt and Road Commission' whose aim is to promote ICC's service as a means to solve disputes arising from BRI-related projects. For now, the HKIAC seems to be in the lead thanks to strong support and backup from the Hong Kong Government,[87] as shown in the active promotion by Teresa Cheng – the Minister of Justice of Hong Kong and renowned arbitrator – of the HKIAC's online platform for BRI-related disputes.[88]

Most arbitration institutions in Hong Kong have been striving to take full advantage of the BRI because:

> [t]he BRI provides unprecedented opportunities for the dispute resolution landscape in Hong Kong, with Hong Kong being ideally placed to become the preferred venue for arbitration between the PRC entities involved in BRI opportunities and parties hailing from the 72 countries participating in the BRI. The proximity to China ... has the potential to help, with the BRI offering Hong Kong a historic opportunity to leverage its status as a modern financial hub combining efficient infrastructure, well-regulated markets and Western-styled legal institutions with a deep understanding of Chinese culture and business practices.[89]

The special status of Hong Kong has been confirmed by the authority of both Mainland China and Hong Kong. Mr Zhang Dejiang – a member of the Standing Committee of the National People's Congress – in his keynote speech at the Belt and Road Summit, expressed the central government's opinion that Hong Kong is 'a key link' for the BRI.[90] Ms Carrie Lam – the Chief Executive of Hong Kong Special

---

Kluwer Arbitration Blog (19 Mar. 2018), http://arbitrationblog.kluwerarbitration.com/2018/03/19/structural-implications-belt-road-arbitration-chinas-legal-gamble-across-eurasia/.

85. http://www.hkiac.org/news/hkiac-announces-belt-and-road-programme.
86. Stephanie Tang, *HKIAC's New Belt and Road Programme: Does More Need to Be Done?*, Kluwer Arbitration Blog (27 Jun. 2018), http://arbitrationblog.kluwerarbitration.com/2018/06/27/hkiacs-new-belt-road-programme-need-done/.
87. https://beltandroad.hktdc.com/en/hong-kong-advantage.
88. Teresa Cheng, *Belt and Road E-Arbitration and E-Mediation*, Asian Academy of International Law: Belt and Road Summit (11 Sep. 2017), http://www.beltandroadsummit.hk/2017/pdf/programme/DOJ_Ms_Teresa_Cheng.pdf.
89. Sanja Pramod, *Hong Kong*, GAR (22 Oct. 2018), https://globalarbitrationreview.com/insight/the-asia-pacific-arbitration-review-2019/1175881/hong-kong.
90. Zhang Dejiang, *Full Text of Zhang Dejiang's Keynote at Belt and Road Summit*, The Standard (18 May 2016), https://www.thestandard.com.hk/breaking-news/section/3/74885/Full-text-of-Zhang-Dejiang's-keynote-at-belt-and-road-summit.

Administrative Region – officially stated that the city would be able to play a leading role to connect Mainland China and the rest of the world.[91]

Other dispute resolution services, including mediation, continually seek to attract a greater share of cases. Mediation as a form of alternative dispute resolution enjoys a sound reputation in Hong Kong. There are a number of established mediation service providers in Hong Kong, including the Hong Kong Mediation Accreditation Association Limited (HKMAAL), the Hong Kong Mediation Centre and the Hong Kong Mediation Council. Furthermore, several arbitration institutions, including the HKIAC, also provide mediation services.[92]

In addition to internal aspirations for greater market share among various arbitration and mediation service providers in Hong Kong, the arbitration community in Hong Kong as a whole consistently seeks to distinguish itself from other regional arbitral institutions including those found in Singapore that has made considerable efforts in promoting itself as a key arbitration and now mediation venue in Asia.[93] Concurrently, arbitral institutions and trade bodies in Hong Kong continue to explore ways to expand Hong Kong's reputation as a leading arbitration centre.

[C] Judicial Reform: New Initiatives in ICA and ISDS

[1] ICA

The pro-arbitration attitude of the Hong Kong courts has contributed to forming Hong Kong's reputation as a favourable arbitration venue.[94] In order to maintain minimal intervention by the courts, the Court of Final Appeal (CFA) laid down a cautious approach in *Hebei Import & Export Corp v. Polytek Engineering Co Ltd.*,[95] that all courts would closely scrutinise all public policy claims. Yet, at the same time, the CFA placed a high threshold of requiring the alleged infringement to be 'contrary to the fundamental conceptions of morality and justice of Hong Kong'.[96]

Accordingly, in *Gao Haiyan v. Keeneye Holdings Ltd.*,[97] the Court of Appeal stressed and reapplied the usual strict policy of only allowing the refusal of enforcement of arbitral awards in exceptional circumstances. The *Pacific China Holdings Ltd v. Grand Pacific Holdings Ltd.*[98] case reaffirms the court's approach towards maintaining Hong Kong's status as an arbitration-friendly jurisdiction and illustrates the principle that arbitral awards should be set aside in only the rarest of circumstances, where the tribunal's conduct has been egregious. The court held that in order to

91. Hong Kong Economic and Trade Office, *Hong Kong Can Contribute to Belt & Road*, https://www.hketosf.gov.hk/sf/ehk/ehongkong83/beltandroad.htm.
92. www.hkiac.org/en/mediation.
93. *See* e.g., Pasha L. Hsieh, *Liberalizing Trade in Legal Services under Asia-Pacific FTAs: The ASEAN Case*, 18 J. Int'l Econ. L. 153, 168 (2015). Comparing Japan's more recent initiative, *see also* Claxton, Nottage & Teramura, Chapter 10 in this volume.
94. Caldwell, *supra* n. 61, at §4.
95. [1999] 2 HKCFAR 111.
96. Per Sir Anthony Mason at [139].
97. [2012] 1 HKLRD 627.
98. [2012] 4 HKLRD 569.

establish a breach, it must be shown that the tribunal's conduct was of a 'serious' or even 'egregious' nature. In turn, it placed a heavy emphasis on the wide, discretionary case management powers of the arbitral tribunal, which are a cornerstone of international arbitration. This demonstrates that the Hong Kong courts will be slow to interfere with the procedural decisions of arbitral tribunals. The court accepted in *obiter* that it has the discretion not to set aside awards even where a breach is established if it is satisfied that the result could not have been different. The court also held that the burden is on the party wishing to set aside an award to show that it had been, or might have been, prejudiced by the conduct of the tribunal. This shows the strong support of the judiciary for arbitration. Even though the Court of First Instance (CFI) set aside part of an arbitral award on the basis of a serious breach of due process in *China Property Development (Holdings) Ltd v. Mandecly Ltd.*,[99] the CFI maintained a cautious approach and emphasised that the role of the court is to consider the structural integrity of the arbitration proceedings and not to address the substantive merits of the case or the correctness of the award on matters of law or fact.

Important exceptions to the generally pro-arbitration stance in Hong Kong were outlined in the Court of Appeal's consideration of the *China Property Development (Holdings) Ltd v. Mandecly Ltd* [2016] HKCA 207 (CACV 92/2015) case. While the Court of Appeal upheld the CFI's decision, it highlighted that 'some irregularities may be so fundamental and the structural integrity of the arbitration proceeding is so seriously damaged that the court will have no hesitation in setting aside the award'.[100] This may signal that the court will be scrutinising awards more carefully in the future to ensure due process is observed.

[2] ISDS

In January 2018, the Supreme People's Court (SPC) in Beijing announced the establishment of three international courts handling disputes arising from projects under the BRI and issued the 'Supreme People's Court Regulations on Certain Issues in Establishing an International Commercial Court' that came to effect on 1 July 2018.[101] What the SPC meant by 'three international courts' was that three institutions would work together under the umbrella of the China International Commercial Court (CICC): The First International Commercial Court in Shenzhen, Guandong Province; the Second International Commercial Court in Xi'an, Shaanxi Province; and the Fourth Civil Division of the SPC (which is responsible for supervising the two international courts). The aim of the CICC is 'to try [to solving] international commercial cases fairly and timely in accordance with the law, protect the lawful rights and interests of the Chinese and foreign parties equally, create a stable, fair, transparent, and convenient rule of law international business environment'.[102] For now, the jurisdiction of the CICC does not

99. [2015] HKCFI 493 (HCCT 53/2010).
100. *See* para. 8.21 of *China Property Development v. Mandecly.*
101. The text is available at: http://cicc.court.gov.cn/html/1/219/199/201/817.html. *See* further Bath, Chapter 8 in this volume.
102. http://cicc.court.gov.cn/html/1/219/193/195/index.html.

extend to state-investor disputes; it only hears broadly defined international commercial disputes,[103] but the CICC might expand the jurisdiction in the near-future out of necessity. In fact, the CICC's Expert Committee consists of distinguished international arbitration experts who have a strong background in the field of investor-state arbitration.[104]

It is not surprising that China, including Hong Kong, has taken steps to depart somewhat from the traditional ISDS regime, considering the fact that the regime has been under siege in recent years by a few developing countries.[105] However, a major driver of China's inclination to establish its own legal regime to solve BRI-related disputes might be the issue of inconsistent interpretation of ISDS jurisdiction provisions in China's bilateral investment treaties (BITs). Since no comprehensive treaty governing BRI countries is yet to be formulated, the current BRI regime is based on China's existing BITs (BRI treaties). The majority of these BITs came into force during the 1980s and 1990s, reflecting China's status as a host country seeking to attract foreign investment. As China primarily adopted the state-owned economy, the scope of ISDS in those BITs was limited to issue relating to the quantum of compensation for expropriation without a provision for national treatment of investments.[106] These narrow dispute settlement clauses still survive today in China's BITs with developing countries including BRI states and pose difficulty to Chinese investors who are involved in disputes with such countries.

Typically, as in the below text of Article 8(3) of the 1991 PRC-Mongolia BIT, the narrow dispute settlement clauses provides:

> If *a dispute involving the amount of compensation for expropriation* cannot be settled within six months after resorted to negotiations as specified in paragraph 1 of this Article, it may be submitted at the request of either party to an ad hoc arbitral tribunal. ... .[107]

---

103. Matthew S. Erie, *The China International Commercial Court: Prospects for Dispute Resolution for the 'Belt and Road Initiative'*, ASIL Insights (31 Aug. 2018), https://www.asil.org/insights/volume/22/issue/11/china-international-commercial-court-prospects-dispute-resolution-belt.
104. Albert Jan van den Berg, Anna P. Mantakou, Anselmo Reyes, David Unterhalter, Donald Francis Donovan, Emmanuel Gaillard, Fulden Li, Gabrielle Kaufmann-Kohler, Gary Born, George A. Bermann, Hi-Taek Shin, Huang Jin, James Spigelman, Jingzhou Tao, Jingdong Liu, Lu Song, Nayla Comair-Obeid, Neil Kaplan, Peter Malanczuk, Philip Yang. *See* http://cicc.court.gov.cn/html/1/219/235/237/index.html.
105. Leon Trakman, *The ICSID Under Siege*, 45 Cornell Int'l L.J. 603 (2012), pointing out that the siege has been driven by the negative perception of ICSID which has been shared by a few developing countries but has failed to recognise that the institution is the supplicant of its signatories. Unlike those developing countries, China and, especially, Hong Kong may not be willing to abandon the ICSID completely, as evidenced in the recent Australia – Hong Kong Investment Agreement (2019) that allows parties to refer investor-state disputes to any institution, in Article 24.3(b). *See* generally Vivienne Bath & Luke Nottage, *International Investment Agreements in Asia*, in *Handbook of International Investment Law and Policy* (Julien Chaisse, et al. eds., Springer 2020).
106. Vivienne Bath, *'One Belt, One Road' and Chinese Investment*, in *Legal Dimensions of China's Belt and Road Initiative* 165 (Lutz-Christian Wolff, et al. eds., Wolters Kluwer Hong Kong Limited 2016).
107. Article 8 of the 1991 PRC-Mongolia BIT, available at: https://investmentpolicyhubold.unctad.org/Download/TreatyFile/760 (emphasis added).

A concern has been raised over the interpretation of '*a dispute involving the amount of compensation for expropriation*', which had been interpreted broadly by arbitral tribunals until some point.

In *Señor Tza Yap Shum v. The Republic of Peru,*[108] the narrow dispute settlement clause was interpreted for the first time by the ICSID tribunal based on the 1994 PRC-Peru BIT[109] and the ICSID Convention. The tribunal interpreted the clause broadly to conclude that it had subject matter jurisdiction to examine the existence of the alleged expropriation over the Chinese investor's assets. The tribunal stated: first, according to Article 31 of the Vienna Convention on the Law of Treaties (VCLT), the ordinary meaning of 'a dispute involving the amount of compensation for expropriation' was 'a dispute *including* the amount of compensation for expropriation'; second, the objective of the BIT was to promote mutual investments, and thereby the broad interpretation was justified; and third, if the question of the occurrence of an expropriation itself was indeed a matter to be decided exclusively in a Peruvian national court, investor-state arbitration relating to disputes over 'the amount of compensation for expropriation' would absolutely be precluded, because the issue was closely related to the occurrence of an expropriation, and the parties could not resort to arbitration if they had commenced litigation on the matter.[110] Though Peru tried to annul the decision, the ICSID ad hoc annulment committee dismissed the request.[111] The broad interpretation of the narrow dispute resolution clause was later adopted in *Sanum Investments v. Laos.*[112]

However, the United Nations Commission on International Trade Law (UNCITRAL) tribunal in *China Heilongjiang et al. v. Mongolia*[113] rejected such broad interpretation. It construed the narrow arbitration clause of the PRC-Mongolian BIT as follows:

> Arbitration ... would be available in cases where an expropriation has been formally proclaimed and *what is disputed is the amount to be paid by the State to the investor for its expropriated investment*. In other words, *arbitration will be available where the dispute is indeed limited to the amount of compensation* for a proclaimed expropriation, the occurrence of which is not contested. While it may be the case that formally proclaimed expropriations are a less common event than measures having an effect equivalent to nationalisation or expropriation ..., the Tribunal cannot see that an arbitration provision that would nevertheless encompass an entire category of disputes can fairly be said to be lacking *effet utile.*[114]

108. ICSID Case No. ARB/07/6.
109. Article 8 of the PRC-BIT had the same wording as Article 8 of the PRC-Mongolia BIT.
110. Bajar Scharaw, *The (Provisional) End of Debates on Narrow Dispute Settlement Clauses in PRC First-Generation BITs? – China Heilongjiang et al v. Mongolia*, 34 Arb. Int'l 293, 296-7 (2018).
111. ICSID Case No. ARB/07/6 (Annulment Proceeding).
112. (Award on Jurisdiction, 13 Dec. 2013), UNCITRAL, PCA Case No 2013-13.
113. *Beijing Shougang Mining Investment Company Ltd., China Heilongjiang International Economic & Technical Cooperative Corp., and Qinhuangdaoshi Qinlong International Industrial Co. Ltd. v. Mongolia* (PCA Case No. 2010-20), available at: http://res.cloudinary.com/lbresearch/image/upload/v1506936892/s_29117_1035.pdf.
114. *Ibid.*, para. 448 (emphasis added).

The tribunal further stated that 'object and purpose' of the BIT, to promote mutual investments between China and Mongolia, did not permit such broad interpretation as the two countries carefully worded and agreed to the narrow dispute resolution clause in the BIT.[115]

It is interesting that the ICSID tribunal in *Señor Tza Yap Shum v. The Republic of Peru* followed a broad interpretation despite Beijing's current attempt to develop an alternative to the ICSID regime through establishing international courts and expanding the jurisdiction of Chinese arbitration institutions. China's efforts to establish institutions dedicated to solving BRI disputes are understandable given the uncertainty in the approach that had been taken by the ICSID tribunals in interpreting the narrow dispute resolution clauses. Laos and Mongolia are BRI countries, but, in *Sanum Investments v. Laos*, the dispute resolution clause was interpreted broadly whereas, in *China Heilongjiang et al. v. Mongolia*, it was interpreted narrowly. Since certainty is a key to increase foreign investments, it is crucial for Beijing to establish a predictable investment dispute resolution system, to boost investment from Chinese investors into BRI countries.

§6.04 NEW FRONTIERS IN DISPUTE RESOLUTION DEVELOPMENT IN HONG KONG: NEW INITIATIVES IN ICA AND ISDS FOR BRI

[A] Hong Kong: China Interim Measures Arrangement

On 2 April 2019, the Hong Kong Government and the People's Supreme Court of China entered into the Arrangement Concerning Mutual Assistance in Court-ordered Interim Measures in Aid of Arbitral Proceedings by the Courts of the Mainland and of the Hong Kong Special Administrative Region (the Arrangement).[116] Under the Arrangement, parties to arbitral proceedings in Hong Kong conducted by an approved arbitral institution may apply to the Mainland Chinese courts for preservation measures for those proceedings.[117] The Arrangement also sets out the procedures to be followed by

115. *Ibid.*

116. Courtesy English translation is available at, https://gia.info.gov.hk/general/201904/02/P2019040200782_307637_1_1554256987961.pdf. For the background of the Arrangement, *see* generally Wei Sun, *Arrangement Concerning Mutual Assistance in Court-ordered Interim Measures: Interpretations from a Mainland China Perspective – Part I*, Kluwer Arbitration Blog (24 Jul. 2019), http://arbitrationblog.kluwerarbitration.com/2019/07/24/arrangement-concerning-mutual-assistance-in-court-ordered-interim-measures-interpretations-from-a-mainland-china-perspective-part-i/; Wei Sun, *Arrangement Concerning Mutual Assistance in Court-ordered Interim Measures: Interpretations from a Mainland China Perspective – Part II*, Kluwer Arbitration Blog (24 Jul. 2019), http://arbitrationblog.kluwerarbitration.com/2019/07/24/arrangement-concerning-mutual-assistance-in-court-ordered-interim-measures-interpretations-from-a-mainland-china-perspective-part-ii/.

117. Article 3 of the Arrangement. The approved institutions are: HKIAC, CIETAC Hong Kong, ICC, Hong Kong Maritime Arbitration Group, South China International Arbitration Centre and eBRAM International Online Dispute Resolution Centre. *See* https://www.doj.gov.hk/pdf/2019/list_of_institutions_e.pdf.

parties to arbitrations administered by Mainland institutions in order to obtain interim relief from Hong Kong courts.[118]

The Arrangement is the first comprehensive legal instrument through which parties to arbitrations seated offshore 'can seek' interim preservative measures in the Mainland.[119] In other words, the Mainland courts are not obliged by the Arrangement to enforce foreign interim measures. In fact, Article 3 of the Arrangement provides that:

> a party to arbitral proceedings in Hong Kong may, by reference to the provisions of the Civil Procedure Law of the People's Republic of China, the Arbitration Law of the People's Republic of China and relevant judicial interpretations, make an application for interim measure to the Intermediate People's Court of the place of residence of the party against whom the application is made ... or the place where the property or evidence is situated.

However, beyond this Arrangement, there remains no express legal basis in the Mainland for the enforcement of foreign interim orders.[120] While levels of uptake remain to be seen,[121] it is apparent that the new scheme will cement the position of Hong Kong as a BRI dispute resolution hub given formal support for foreign investors to pursue legal rights against investors in Mainland China via arbitration institutions in Hong Kong.[122]

[B] New Players in ISDS

The BRI may pose a challenge to the dominance of ICSID in ISDS. As mentioned above, Beijing has been attempting to create a new dispute regime devoted to international dispute resolution for BRI countries and has, in fact, established new ISDS mechanisms. First, it has expanded the jurisdiction of existing Chinese arbitration institutions, such as Shenzhen Court of International Arbitration (SCIA) and CIETAC, to handle foreign investment disputes. Second, it has established new courts to hear

---

118. Article 6 of the Arrangement.
119. Othmane Benlafkih, *Perspectives: Cross-Border Interim Relief under the Hong Kong–Mainland Bilateral Arrangement*, October-December Corp. Dis. 54 (2019).
120. *Ibid.*, 56. Note that there is an exception of preservative measures for maritime arbitrations seated outside of the Mainland. *See* Jie Huang & Winston Ma, *New Frontiers in International Arbitration for the Asia-Pacific Region (9): Arbitration and Protest in Hong Kong*, Japanese Law and the Asia-Pacific: Japanese Law in Asia-Pacific Socio-Economic Context (1 Nov. 2019), https://japaneselaw.sydney.edu.au/2019/11/new-frontiers-in-international-arbitration-for-the-asia-pacific-region-9-arbitration-and-protest-in-hong-kong/.
121. For the first four months, the HKIAC only had received thirteen applications under the Arrangement. *See* Eric Ng, *The Mainland-HK Arrangement: HKIAC Practice and Experience*, China Bus. L.J. (10 Feb. 2020), https://www.vantageasia.com/mainland-hong-kong-hkiac-experience/.
122. Edern Coënt & Eugene Thong, *One Country, Two Systems: Availability of Interim Measures in China, a New Argument for Hong Kong on the Asia-Pacific Arbitration Stage?*, Kluwer Arbitration Blog (26 Apr. 2019), http://arbitrationblog.kluwerarbitration.com/2019/04/26/one-country-two-systems-availability-of-interim-measures-in-china-a-new-argument-for-hong-kong-on-the-asia-pacific-arbitration-stage/.

international commercial cases.[123] Third, it has built joint arbitration centres to resolve investor-state and commercial disputes with BRI regions, as in the establishment of the China-Africa Joint Arbitration Centre (CAJAC) in 2015.[124] The new comprehensive reforms may 'help to break the monopoly of existing Western-initiated institutions'.[125]

The ISDS reforms by Beijing may offer various dispute resolution options for Hong Kong investors. To solve non-BRI related investor-state disputes, the investors may continue to rely on western institutions such as ICSID, as in *Standard Chartered Bank (Hong Kong) Limited v. Tanzania Electric Supply Company Limited*,[126] and the PCA, as in *Philip Morris Asia Limited (Hong Kong) v. The Commonwealth of Australia*.[127] To solve BRI-related disputes, Hong Kong investors may resort to either the new Chinese dispute resolution institutions or Hong Kong-based institutions.

The multiplicity of ISDS dispute resolution institutions suggests that service providers in the field will continue to distinguish themselves amongst a growing pool of talent. The BRI certainly has introduced new opportunities for Hong Kong-based institutions to increase their caseloads in relation to, but not limited to, investor-state dispute resolution through the use of both arbitration and mediation.

[C] Hong Kong's Contribution to Investor-State Mediation

In recent times, investor-state arbitration has been under siege. This traditional dispute resolution system has been criticised for many reasons including inconsistency in treaty interpretation by ISDS arbitration tribunals; inefficiency in regard to cost and duration (judicialisation); arbitrators' bias; and lack of transparency.[128]

The backlash against ISDS arbitration has resulted in a growing number of commentators,[129] national governments,[130] and international institutions[131] involved in the promotion of investment mediation, in addition to, or instead of, investor-state

123. As mentioned above, those courts are likely to expand their jurisdiction to include foreign investment disputes.
124. Huiping Chen, *China's Innovative ISDS Mechanisms and Their Implications*, 112 AJIL Unbound 207, 208-9 (2018).
125. *Ibid.*, 210. *See also* Bath, Chapter 8 in this volume.
126. ICSID Case No. ARB/10/20.
127. Available at https://pca-cpa.org/en/cases/5/.
128. David Ng, *Discussion Paper for the Session on Investment Mediation*, ISDS Reform Conference: Mapping the Way Forward (13 Feb. 2019), http://isdsreform2019.aail.org/wp-content/uploads/2019/02/ISDS_Discussion_Paper_Investment_Mediation_by_David_Ng-1.pdf. *See also*, for the judicialisation of ICA in general, Nobumichi Teramura, *Ex Aequo et Bono as a Response to the 'Over-Judicialisation' of International Commercial Arbitration* (Wolters Kluwer 2020); Nobumichi Teramura, *Ex Aequo et Bono: An Overlooked and Undervalued Opportunity for International Commercial Arbitration*, Kluwer Arbitration Blog (18 Nov. 2018), http://arbitrationblog.kluwerarbitration.com/2018/11/18/ex-aequo-et-bono-an-overlooked-and-undervalued-opportunity-for-international-commercial-arbitration/.
129. Jack J. Coe. Jr, *Toward a Complementary Use of Conciliation in Investor-State Disputes – A Preliminary Sketch*, 12 U.C. Davis J. Int'l L. & Pol'y 7 (2005); Jack J. Coe. Jr, *Should Mediation of Investment Disputes Be Encouraged, and, If So, By Whom and How?*, 3 Contemporary Issues in International Arbitration and Mediation: The Fordham Papers 339 (2009); Jack J. Coe. Jr, *Settlement of Investor-State Disputes Through Mediation – Preliminary Remarks on Processes, Problems and Prospects*, in *Enforcement of Arbitral Awards Against Sovereigns* 73 (Raymond D. Bishop ed., Juris 2009); Jack J. Coe. Jr, *Concurrent Co-Mediation: Toward a More Collaborative*

arbitration. In particular, in its thirty-sixth session, UNCITRAL Working Group III listed investment mediation as a reform option to address concerns over lengthy and costly ISDS procedures.[132] Investment mediation is also a core dispute resolution procedure outlined in CEPA, as discussed above. Several commentators emphasised the benefits of investment mediation: cost-efficiency; the certainty of settlement; and preserving relationships between parties.[133] Moreover, investment mediation may assist parties to explore creative and innovative solutions outside strict legal remedies, and therefore useful for dealing with polycentric, policy issues involving force majeure claims arising from unforeseen natural disasters,[134] as found in *Vattenfall v. Germany*.[135]

Despite the potential merit and increased efforts directed at the promotion of investor-state mediation, according to UNCITRAL's Working Group III, investment mediation still remains under-utilised in ISDS.[136] The unpopularity of mediation is salient in ICSID,[137] whilst the ICSID Convention provides that '[t]he purpose of the Centre shall be to provide facilities for conciliation and arbitration of investment disputes between Contracting States and nationals of other Contracting States in accordance with the provisions of this Convention'.[138] As of writing, only eleven known conciliation cases (1.6% of total ICSID cases) have been recorded by the ICSID.[139] Some commentators have noted that ICSID conciliation proceedings under

---

Centre of Gravity in Investor–State Dispute Resolution, in *Mediation in International Commercial and Investment Disputes* 61 (Catharine Titi & Katia Fach Gómez eds., Oxford University Press 2019).

130. *See*, e.g., Article 19 of the Investment of Agreement of the CEPA.
131. *See*, e.g., the IBA Rules for Investor-State Mediation that was established to increase resort to mediation for investor-state disputes. *See also* The European Commission, *Consultation Document: Prevention and Amicable Resolution of Disputes Between Investors and Public Authorities within the Single Market* (2017), available at: https://ec.europa.eu/info/sites/info/files/2017-investment-protection-mediation-consultation-document_en_1.pdf.
132. UNCITRAL Working Group III Secretariat, *Annex – Tabular Presentation of Framework for Discussion*, available at: http://www.uncitral.org/pdf/english/workinggroups/wg_3/WGIII-36th-session/149_Annex_Table_-_Framework_for_discussion_070918_v2.pdf.
133. Daniel Weinstein & Mushegh Manukyan, *Making Mediation More Attractive for Investor-State Disputes*, Kluwer Arbitration Blog (26 Mar. 2019), http://arbitrationblog.kluwerarbitration.com/2019/03/26/making-mediation-more-attractive-for-investor-state-disputes/.
134. Shahla Ali & Odysseag G. Repousis, *Investor-State Mediation and the Rise of Transparency in International Investment Law: Opportunity or Threat?*, 45 Denv. J. Intl'l L. & Pol'y 225, 234 (2017).
135. *Vattenfall AB*, ICSID Case No. ARB/12/12. The case arose following the Fukushima nuclear disaster and subsequent decision of German Chancellor Angela Merkel's government to rapidly phase out nuclear power production by 2022. As for the potential applicability of investor-state mediation to the case, *see*: Shahla Ali, *Prospects of Utilizing Investor-State Mediation and UNCITRAL Rules on Transparency for Polycentric Environmental Disaster-Related Disputes: The Case of Vattenfall v. Germany*, in *Trade Development Through Harmonization of Commercial Law* 133, 137 (Muruga Perumal Ramaswamy & João Ribeiro eds., UNCITRAL Regional Centre for Asia and the Pacific 2015). For a more recent potential example in Asia, *see* the Japan-Korea trade and investment tensions as analysed by Claxton, Nottage & Williams Chapter 11 in this volume.
136. UNCITRAL Working Group III Secretariat, *Note by the Secretariat on the Possible Reform of Investor-State Dispute Settlement*, A/CN.9/WG.III/WP. 149, 13 (2018).
137. Ali & Repousis, *supra* n. 134.
138. Article 1(2) of the ICSID Convention.
139. *The ICSID Caseload – Statistics (Issue 2019-1)* 8 (2019).

the ICSID Conciliation Rules and ICSID Additional Facilities Rules often result in a rigid and time-consuming arbitration-like procedural framework.[140]

To increase investment mediation caseload, the ICSID is planning to amend the ICSID Conciliation Rules. It is expected that the protracted nature of ICSID conciliation will be improved,[141] but it will take some time before the amendment is adopted. The ICSID is also preparing to amend ICSID Additional Facilities Rules for making ICSID mediation facilities available in cases where neither respondent nor claimant is the ICSID Contracting State or national of a Contracting State. In addition, the institution is proposing to incorporate a new dispute settlement mechanism, the Mediation Rules, into the Facilities Rules. Some commentators characterise these proposed reforms as small but positive steps.[142]

The challenges identified by the ICSID likewise provide opportunities for dispute resolution institutions in Hong Kong. As of writing, there is no dedicated institution focused on the provision of investor-state mediation, despite its encouraging prospects including already considerable amicable settlement of ISDS disputes across many fields.[143] An increasing number of international investment treaties have included some mention of investment mediation in their corresponding dispute settlement mechanisms. However, very few make it a mandatory step before ISDS arbitration. One rare recent exception is the Hong Kong – United Arab Emirates BIT, signed in 2019.[144]

---

140. Margrete Stevens & Ben Love, *Investor-State Mediation: Observations on the Role of Institutions*, 3 Contemporary Issues in International Arbitration and Mediation: The Fordham Papers 389 (2009).
141. ICSID Secretariat, *Proposals for Amendment of the ICSID Rules 1 Working Paper #2* 1, 356 (2019); ICSID Secretariat, *Proposals for Amendment of the ICSID Rules – Working Paper* Vol. 3 (2018).
142. Ana Ubilava & Luke Nottage, *ICSID's New Mediation Rules: A Small but Positive Step Forward,* Erga Omnes – The SCIL Blog (11 Sep. 2018), http://blogs.usyd.edu.au/erga-omnes/2018/09/icsids_new_mediation_rules.html.
143. Ana Ubilava, *Amicable Settlements in Investor-State Disputes: Empirical Analysis of Patterns and Perceived Problems*, 21 The J. World Inv. & Trade 528 (2020).
144. A second recent example of the host state similarly at least being able to require the foreign investor to go to mediation, before ISDS arbitration, is the Australia-Indonesia FTA signed in 2019, analysed by Ubilava & Nottage Chapter 5 in this volume. By contrast, Australia's new investment agreement with Hong Kong does not provide for compulsory mediation. *See* James Claxton, Luke Nottage & Ana Ubilava, *Pioneering Mandatory Investor-State Conciliation Before Arbitration in Asia-Pacific Treaties: IA-CEPA and HK-UAE BIT*, Kluwer Arbitration Blog (5 Sep. 2020), http://arbitrationblog.kluwerarbitration.com/2020/09/05/pioneering-mandatory-investor-state-conciliation-before-arbitration-in-asia-pacific-treaties-ia-cepa-and-hk-uae-bit/; and Ana Ubilava, *Mandatory Investor-State Conciliation in New International Investment Treaties: Innovation and Interpretation*, Kluwer Mediation Blog (5 Sep. 2020), http://mediationblog.kluwerarbitration.com/2020/09/05/mandatory-investor-state-conciliation-in-new-international-investment-treaties-innovation-and-interpretation/. Compare also various references to conciliation or mediation in e.g., the draft text of the Transatlantic Trade and Investment Partnership, the draft model BIT of Netherlands (2018), the EU – Canada Comprehensive Economic and Trade Agreement (2016), the model BIT of India (2016), the Revised Unified Agreement for the Investment of Arab Capital in the Arab States (2013), Southern African Development Community Model BIT (2012), the ASEAN Comprehensive Investment Agreement, the model BIT of Thailand (2012), and the Investment Agreement for the COMESA Investment Area (2007).

In relation to BRI-related disputes, it is well known that the Central People's Government intends to promote investment mediation instead of investment arbitration.[145] Being at the conjunction point between East and West, and building on the existing CEPA regime, Hong Kong has the potential to be at the forefront of the development of investor-state mediation.

To effectively promote Hong Kong's investment mediation services, relevant institutions must observe fundamental principles of an effective investment mediation mechanism: enshrine the value of the rule of law; and strongly emphasise cost-effectiveness, efficiency, voluntariness, and flexibility.[146] In addition, innovations may be considered, including incorporating transparent multi-party investor-state mediation in some instances.[147] Since many investment cases involve sensitive issues of a confidential nature, confidentiality has been considered an essential element of investment mediation. However, there are mounting concerns that confidentiality infringes the administration of justice. Investment mediation services offered in Hong Kong may overcome such concerns by providing the option of transparent investment mediation.

§6.05 CONCLUSION

Hong Kong's unique position as a gateway to Mainland China and its unique relationship with the Mainland on cross-border enforcement of arbitration agreements and ISDS dispute resolution, make it an ideal location to understand the significant developments in BRI dispute resolution trends. As a Model Law jurisdiction coordinating with China's unique arbitration laws and given the 'flexible structure of the international arbitration system based on a Model Rule framework which allows countries to opt-in or out of particular provisions' we see an example of a dynamic in which 'procedural variation can coexist with a relatively high level of substantive legal uniformity across regions'.[148] Not all elements of the Model Law have been incorporated into the HKAO, and some amendments have been made so as to tailor the law to the unique circumstances of Hong Kong, which have played a positive role in attracting ICA cases on the island.

When comparing the statistics on arbitration cases with other arbitration jurisdictions in Asia, it can be seen that arbitration centres in Korea, Beijing and Singapore have also experienced impressive growth rates. Hong Kong, in the coming years, may succeed in attracting BRI-related investment and commercial cases. Hong Kong's dispute resolution institutions are working hard on this objective. In relation to the BRI, the focus has been not only to attract arbitration cases but ADR cases in general. As such, Hong Kong institutions may benefit from a strategic focus on investor-state

145. Ng, *supra* n. 128, at 13.
146. *Ibid.*, 22-3.
147. Ali & Repousis, *supra* n. 134, at 246.
148. *See* Shahla Ali, *Resolving Disputes in the Asia Pacific Region: International Arbitration and Mediation in East Asia and the West* (Routledge 2011).

mediation which has significant room for development in relation to not only the BRI but also to ISDS cases.

Table 6.1 Number of Arbitration Cases in Leading Asian Arbitral Institutions

Year	*HKIAC*	*The Korean Commercial Arbitration Board*	*Beijing Arbitration Commission*[149]	*Singapore International Arbitration Centre*
2002	320	47	891	38
2012	293	360	1,473	235
2013	260	338	1,627	259
2014	252	382	2,041	222
2015	271	413	2,944	271
2016	262	381	3,012	343
2017	297	385	3,550	452
2018	265	393	4,872	402
2019	308	N/A	N/A	N/A

Source: Data from HKIAC, KCAB, BAC and SIAC.

In Hong Kong, judicial and institutional reforms have played complementary roles in the development of Hong Kong's pro-arbitration approach. Through its line of judicial decisions, Hong Kong courts have articulated and safeguarded the distinct benefits of arbitration, such as the promotion of speed, reduction of costs and party autonomy. Reviews and amendments to the institutional arbitration rules have helped reduce rather than increase the judicialisation of the arbitration process in Hong Kong.

The Hong Kong enforcement model has been praised as there is limited discretion by the courts to refuse enforcement.[150] Some have commented that such strict adherence to upholding arbitral awards or an attitude of minimal judicial intervention, attributable to the desire to support the primacy of arbitration, has been taken too far.[151] The high threshold set by Hong Kong courts (such as in the *Keeneye* case) has acted as a disincentive against frivolous claims on public policy grounds. Nonetheless, scholars have expressed concern that the bar has been set so high that parties subject to irregular awards with genuine issues of public policy are finding it difficult to avail themselves of the public policy exception to enforcement.[152] Reasonable supervision by the courts maintains the integrity of the arbitration process and in turn, enhances

149. BAC statistics include both domestic and international cases.
150. Simon Greenberg, et al., *International Commercial Arbitration: An Asia-Pacific Perspective* para. 9.134 (Cambridge University Press 2011).
151. Choong Yeow Choy & Warren P. Ganesh, *Public Policy Considerations in Arbitral Proceedings in Selected Common Law Jurisdictions*, 44 H.K.L.J. 179 (2014).
152. Weixia Gu & Xianchu Zhang, *The Keeneye Case: Rethinking the Content of Public Policy in Cross-Border Arbitration Between Hong Kong and Mainland China*, 42 H.K.L.J. 1012 (2012).

the confidence of the commercial community.[153] Regarding cross-border award enforcement, some have noted that Hong Kong standards are comparatively more relaxed than international standards.[154]

On the whole, arbitration reform in Hong Kong has been conducted at a macro level with the main objective of aligning regional law with international standards and supporting BRI dispute resolution needs in the region. Such efforts at arbitration reform aim to ensure that Hong Kong is ready to assume its position as a key dispute resolution hub in light of expanding cooperation and ever-increasing levels of investment and trade under the BRI. Figures from the Chinese Ministry of Commerce report that cumulative trade volume between China and economies of BRI jurisdiction has exceeded USD 7.5 trillion by December 2019, with imports and exports of the first eleven months of 2019 with BRI economies reaching USD 1.19 trillion.[155] As of December 2019, China has further concluded 198 cooperation documents with 167 countries and international organisations under the BRI, in addition to establishing working relations with 7 countries on 'unimpeded' trade and 44 countries on bilateral investment cooperation.[156]

While Hong Kong will continue to be a leading arbitration/mediation centre in the Asia-Pacific, BRI policy and relevant legislative/institutional/judicial reform in Hong Kong continue to be largely initiated by the Mainland.[157] At the same time, in line with regional integration policies, Mainland arbitration and mediation centres will continue to coordinate with, learn from, and integrate relevant substantive and procedural aspects of Hong Kong's global dispute resolution architecture in the development of Mainland institutions.

Interparty disputes, whether involving commercial parties or investor states, are expected to arise in line with increased engagement, and expanded trade and investment between China and BRI jurisdictions. Such disputes may be further exacerbated by projected slowdowns in global and regional economies (attributable to a range of factors including but not limited to the COVID-19 Pandemic, the US-China trade war, Brexit and regional unrest). Accordingly, the potential for Hong Kong as a well-established dispute resolution jurisdiction connecting Mainland China to the rest of the world can thus not be overstated.

---

153. James J. Spigelman, *International Commercial Litigation: An Asian Perspective*, 37 H.K.L.J. 859 (2007).
154. Weixia Gu, *15 Years of the Handover: The Rise, Discontent, and Positive Interaction of Cross-Border Arbitration in Hong Kong with Mainland China*, 9 U. Pa. East Asia L. Rev. 44, 51 (2013).
155. Liu Zhihua, *Belt and Road Helps Build Lasting Economic and Trade Relations*, China Daily (12 Dec. 2019), https://global.chinadaily.com.cn/a/201912/12/WS5df18416a310cf3e3557d903.html.
156. *Ibid*.
157. Reyes & Gu identified four stages of arbitration development in the Asia-Pacific region, evaluating Hong Kong (along with Singapore and Korea) as being in Stage 4 or in transition from Stage 3 to 4 (final stage). *See* Anselmo Reyes & Weixia Gu, *Conclusion: An Asia Pacific Model of Arbitration Reform*, in *The Developing World of Arbitration: A Comparative Study of Arbitration Reform in the Asia Pacific* 279, 287 (Anselmo Reyes & Weixia Gu eds., Hart Publishing 2018).

CHAPTER 7

Harmonizing the Public Policy Exception for International Commercial Arbitration along the Belt and Road

Weixia Gu[*]

In the context of a rising volume of cross-border transactions generated by the Belt and Road Initiative (BRI), this chapter argues that a robust legal framework for dispute resolution is required to forge investor confidence and enable BRI's integral goal of economic integration. In light of the substantial levels of harmonization among arbitration laws, arbitration arguably constitutes the primary vehicle for international commercial dispute resolution in an economically integrated Asia under the BRI. Against this backdrop, this chapter argues that the BRI provides a unique opportunity to contemplate the possibility of regional harmonization, as within the Asian economies along the BRI, of the 'public policy' exception to arbitral award enforcement. Such an arbitration initiative in Asia, in which China is anticipated to take a proactive role, holds much potential to project renewed momentum on China as an engine of not only economic power but also 'soft power' transformation in pioneering international legal norms.

§7.01 INTRODUCTION

Officially referred to by the Chinese Government as the BRI (一带一路, yidai yilu), the 'Belt and Road' presently spans and traverses sixty-five countries in Asia, Europe and the Middle East. On 27 March 2015, China's National Development and Reform

* The original version of the chapter was published as Weixia Gu, *China's Belt and Road Development and A New International Commercial Arbitration Initiative in Asia*, 51 Vander. J. Transnat'l L. 1305 (2018). I thank Vanderbilt Journal for allowing re-publication of an updated version of part of the chapter to be included in the book. I also thank the support by the Hong Kong Government Research Grants Council General Research Fund (HKU 17602218; 17609419) and University of Hong Kong's Outstanding Young Researcher Award Scheme.

Commission particularized mechanisms and initiatives for regional cooperation under the BRI.[1] Such activities include establishing unified mechanisms for infrastructure building; standardizing and ensuring compatibility of transport rules; establishing free trade areas; multilateral information exchange and inspection in trade cooperation; bolstering financial regulation cooperation; and promoting cultural exchange and friendship among the Belt and Road nations and their peoples.[2] The BRI seeks not only to stimulate development but also to open up markets and expand trade volume and foreign direct investment (FDI) within the economies under its reach. Crucially, the BRI aims to promote and facilitate wider economic integration amongst the nations of the anecdotal Belt and Road roadmap.

The formation of a de facto economic bloc, including the establishment and operation of cooperation zones, designated funds for infrastructural project financing and investment, as well as a gradual dismantling of trade barriers among the Belt and Road nations, has already yielded substantial increases in regional trade volume. In 2015, China's trade within the Belt and Road region reportedly surpassed USD 1 trillion, accounting for approximately a quarter of China's trade value that year.[3] The resulting potential for expanding cross-border commercial collaboration, trade and investment thus generates a common economic interest – to capitalize on the multiple opportunities produced and stimulated by China's BRI. The strengthening of systems for regional economic cooperation among Belt and Road states and their investors promises collateral benefits for people and markets across all of the Belt and Road economies.

Within this context of a steadily increasing volume of cross-border transactions and joint commercial enterprises, a robust legal framework is required to support and facilitate regional economic integration. A well-functioning dispute resolution system further yields the secondary benefit of increasing transactional efficiency and reducing transactional costs for private investors and state parties to BRI infrastructure projects.

Considering the traditional distrust and reluctance of investors to resolve business disputes through foreign courts, with which they may not be familiar, as well as its potential for offering commercially flexible solutions and particular suitability for mitigating conflicts among different legal systems, international commercial arbitration (ICA) will under market forces form a preferred, indeed optimal, primary vehicle for commercial dispute resolution under the BRI.[4] The prominent level of pre-existing

1. National Development and Reform Commission (NDRC) People's Republic of China, *Visions and Actions on Jointly Building Silk Road Economic Belt and 21st-Century Maritime Silk Road* (28 Mar. 2015), http://en.ndrc.gov.cn/newsrelease/201503/t20150330_669367.html.
2. *Ibid.*
3. Tian Shaohui, *China's Trade with Belt and Road Countries Surpasses 1 Trillion USD in 2015*, Xinhua News (22 Jun. 2016), http://news.xinhuanet.com/english/2016-06/22/c_135458107.htm.
4. Hong Kong's former Secretary for Justice Rimsky Yuen envisioned that opportunities for outward expansion of the local legal and arbitration sectors lay in providing services to alleviating the 'legal uncertainties' along 'One Belt, One Road' countries. *See* Department of Justice (Hong Kong), *Secretary for Justice Promotes Hong Kong's Legal and Dispute Resolution Service in Beijing (with Photos)* (18 Aug. 2015), http://www.doj.gov.hk/mobile/eng/public/pr/20150818_pr.html.

harmonization among the ICA laws of many BRI countries helps make arbitration the ideal dispute resolution mechanism. In addition, as part of a harmonized legal framework, ICA is needed to fulfil the collateral dispute resolution needs of increased commercial trade and investment collaboration and to further the goal of economic integration. Against this backdrop, this chapter contends that the BRI provides a unique opportunity to contemplate the real possibility of a 'geo-legal' harmonization of the public policy exception to arbitral enforcement within Belt and Road nations.

The public policy exception, which expresses fundamental policy considerations for non-enforcement of awards within and by national courts, creates a problem for the generally harmonized system of arbitration laws. Due to the indeterminacy of its ambit, this exception to enforcing ICA awards yields corresponding negative implications for commercial certainty, business efficacy, and investor confidence in light of the BRI. This shortcoming might be regarded as being addressed, in fact, by most jurisdictions' contemporary pro-enforcement approach adopted by courts, encompassing a narrow interpretation and application of the public policy exception. Yet, the approach is not uniform and the high-stake commercial and investment concerns related to the BRI, particularly within China itself, are expected to demand greater delineation and definition of concerns created by this exception to award enforcement and, therefore, the functionality of ICA more generally.

Apart from the public policy exception, there are two recurring themes under the BRI. First, the role of BRI in China's rule-making for resolving investment disputes should not be overlooked. In this respect, rule-making can be further subcategorized into: (i) 'soft-law' – namely harmonization and capacity-building; and (ii) 'hard-law' – which includes treaties, especially when backed by the option of Investor-State Dispute Settlement (ISDS). For soft-law harmonization of arbitral regimes across the BRI region, this chapter argues that the main challenge lies in the public policy exception. Further, China has the potential for rule-making along the BRI region given that the current public policy exception remains uncertain and such uncertainty calls for a 'transnational' standard. Turning to the hard-law perspective, China is also exploring diversification of its dispute resolution dynamics by establishing the China International Commercial Court (CICC) in Shenzhen and Xi'an in 2018.[5] As things currently stand, China's ambition in engaging with rule-making in the adjudication market is evident, but it is not yet achieving the status of a major rule-maker in these fields.

Second, China is a keen player in the ICA market. Several arbitral institutions, including the China International Economic and Trade Arbitration Commission (CIETAC), Beijing Arbitration Commission (BAC) and Shenzhen Court of International Arbitration (SCIA), have attained visibility in the regional and international markets.[6]

---

5. *See* generally Vivienne Bath & Luke Nottage, *International Investment Agreements and Investor-State Arbitration in Asia*, 20/08 The University of Sydney Law School Legal Studies Research Paper 1, 24 (2020), http://ssrn.com/abstract=3544458; Weixia Gu, *The Dynamics of International Dispute Resolution Business in the Belt and Road*, 113 ASIL Procs. 370 (2019); and Bath, Chapter 8 in this volume.
6. Anselmo Reyes & Weixia Gu, *Conclusion: An Asia Pacific Model of Arbitration Reform*, in *The Developing World of Arbitration: A Comparative Study of Arbitration Reform in the Asia Pacific* 279-300, 280 (Anselmo Reyes & Weixia Gu eds., Hart Publishing 2018).

The 2006 Interpretation Concerning the Implementation of the Arbitration Law by the Supreme People's Court in China can be regarded as a symbol of an attempt by the top-level judiciary in China to bring about substantial reform to liberalize the arbitral framework.[7] For instance, drafting defects due to references to ambiguous or multiple arbitration commissions are no longer fatal for establishing the validity of arbitration agreements.[8] Looking forward, China has the potential to become an even more central player in the Asian ICA market. However, lack of official legislation benchmarked directly against standards of the 2006 UNCITRAL Model Law on ICA remains a concern for China's arbitral regime in the long term.[9]

In the subsequent sections, ICA – and in particular, the public policy exception – is first identified as the initial prime target for harmonization efforts. This chapter then considers the practical mechanics of harmonizing the public policy exception, proposing designation of the Asian Infrastructure Investment Bank (AIIB) as a coordinating authority for the drawing up of common standards and normative regulations. The chapter considers possible substantive content of the public policy exception, utilizing a 'negative list' approach, compared to similar harmonization efforts of the European Union (EU) and the Organization for the Harmonization of African Business Law (OHADA). The far-reaching implications of China's BRI amidst a steadily evolving global landscape will also be considered.

§7.02 CHINA'S BRI AND AN ECONOMICALLY INTEGRATED ASIA

The BRI, aided by the AIIB and the Silk Road Fund, is envisaged to play an indispensable role in connecting markets and addressing infrastructural needs across Central Asia and Southeast Asia, in light of existing infrastructural deficits and untapped development potential across the region.[10] Infrastructural development has been confirmed by the literature to hold positive causal relationships with economic growth and poverty reduction.[11] The Asian Development Bank has recently estimated that developing Asia will require investments of USD 26 trillion from 2016 to 2030, or USD 1.7 trillion per annum in order to eradicate poverty, continue growth momentum, and counter the effects of climate change.[12] In this regard, infrastructure investment holds the potential to bolster sustainable, long-term regional economic growth and

7. Weixia Gu, *China's Arbitration Modernisation under Judicial Efforts and Marketisation Waves, in the Developing World of Arbitration: A Comparative Study of Arbitration Reform in the Asia Pacific* 17-38, 25 (Anselmo Reyes & Weixia Gu eds., Hart Publishing 2018).
8. *Ibid.*
9. *Ibid.*, 38.
10. Gilberto M. Llanto et al., *Infrastructure Financing, Public-Private Partnerships and Development in the Asia-Pacific Region*, 22 Asia-Pacific Dev. J. 27 (2015).
11. *Ibid.* For an in-depth discussion of the causal link between infrastructure development and economic output growth in the context of China, *see* Pravakar Sahoo et al., *Infrastructure Development and Economic Growth in China (IDE Discussion Paper No. 261)*, Institute of Developing Economies (October 2010), www.ide.go.jp/English/Publish/Download/Dp/pdf/261.pdf.
12. Asian Development Bank, *Meeting Asia's Infrastructure Needs*, xi (2017), https://www.adb.org/publications/asia-infrastructure-needs.

productivity, and it also increases regional competitiveness by generating commercial activities and creating employment opportunities, which would, in turn, eradicate poverty in the communities.[13]

The infrastructure projects stemming from BRI development are expected to widen commercial collaboration among states and their investors. Market liberalization and reduction of trade barriers under the BRI is further expected to stimulate an abundance of commercial and trade opportunities within a region of increasing economic integration. Economic integration itself yields, broadly, a multitude of benefits, including boosting cross-border trade, affordable transportation of goods and services, homogenization of national trade and fiscal policies, and creation of employment opportunities. In the political economy literature, differing forms and degrees of economic integration are frequently categorized by reference to a spectrum in order of increasing integration.[14] Such forms range from free trade areas, customs unions, common markets, economic unions, through to complete economic integration.[15]

The degree of economic integration to be facilitated by China's BRI development will naturally hinge upon the economic cooperation and national policies of governments in the Asian region. In any event, such integration is anticipated to mature and develop over time as the BRI becomes a cornerstone of regional economic relations and cross-border commercial transactions. The potential development of a de facto zone of economic integration under the BRI, similar to the common market created by what became the EU, will further allow participant countries to access a substantial market, to build export capacities and to strengthen national economic institutions by creating much-needed trade opportunities within and beyond the Belt and Road nations in Asia. In addition, regional economic harmonization reduces transaction and commercial costs, yielding benefits for all parties involved.

The proper and efficient functioning of such a system, regardless of the level of economic integration envisaged, requires a similar level of legal harmonization. As an analogy, one may consider the Uniform Commercial Code published in the United States in 1952, aiming to harmonize the law governing commercial transactions and sales among all American states and territories. Similar to the BRI, the Uniform Commercial Code was conceived in the light of increasingly large volumes of inter-state commercial transactions and a need to harmonize and modernize contract laws. While the end of forging consistency between legal and regulatory norms among China and the Belt and Road nations is to harmonize rather than create uniformity, from a general perspective it still also bolsters the efficiency of trade and commercial transactions, in addition to providing a region-compatible framework for effective dispute resolution.

13. Sahoo et al., *supra* n. 11.
14. Bela Balassa, *The Theory of Economic Integration: An Introduction*, in *The European Union: Readings on the Theory and Practice of European Integration* 126, 127 (Brent F. Nelson & Alexander C.G. Stubb eds., Lynne Rienner Publishers 1998).
15. *Ibid.*

Such benefits can be regarded as a 'cost-savings' motivation for the harmonization of standards through legal transplants.[16] This corresponds to one of the four 'types' of international legal norm transplants identified by Jonathan M. Miller, which can be summarized as follows: as being (a) externally dictated transplants, i.e., those brought about by external forces; (b) cost-saving transplants, i.e., those geared at promoting economic efficiency; (c) entrepreneurial transplants, i.e., those transplants motivated by the expectation of advantage (material or political) to those who propose them; and (d) legitimacy-generating transplants, i.e., those geared at reaping the perceived prestige of adopting foreign norms. While Miller discusses transplantation of norms rather than harmonization, Kozuka and Nottage contend compelling that similar motivations can be applied to harmonization initiatives, as arguably now required under the BRI.

§7.03 ARBITRATION AS A PRIMARY VEHICLE FOR INTERNATIONAL DISPUTE RESOLUTION

Regardless of the public/private nature of the Belt and Road investment, the determinative considerations underlying the selection of dispute resolution mechanisms are applicable to each class of disputes when those arise. Investors, whether in the capacity of private corporations or state governments, tend to distrust dispute resolution mechanisms offered by unfamiliar legal institutions. This is indeed logical from an investor's perspective. Lack of experience or familiarity with the logistics of a foreign judicial system may place a party at a strategic disadvantage, whether real or perceived, vis-à-vis the other local party to the dispute. Such concerns may be exacerbated by an investor's lack of confidence in the judicial independence of certain foreign jurisdictions or their belief in the systems that would 'favour' a local party.

Unlike court litigation, ICA is, therefore, envisioned to act as a primary vehicle for cross-border dispute resolution in disputes arising out of Belt and Road transactions. Increased trade, investment, and commercial opportunities arising from the BRI are expected to generate proportional increases in commercial disputes among states and investors. Due to the transnational nature of commercial dealings promoted under the Belt and Road, such disputes among states and investors may be further classified into two classes. These are, respectively, disputes arising (i) within China; and (ii) outside China, which may be further subcategorized depending on the involvement or otherwise of Chinese parties. ICA should become a favoured means of dispute resolution for both scenarios.

16. Souichirou Kozuka & Luke Nottage, *Independent Directors in Asia: Theoretical Lessons and Practical Implications*, in *Independent Directors in Asia* 468-84 (Dan Puchniak, et al. eds., Cambridge University Press 2017).

§7.04 REGIONAL HARMONIZATION OF THE PUBLIC POLICY EXCEPTION IN ASIA FOR ARBITRAL ENFORCEMENT UNDER THE BRI

[A] The Case for Harmonizing Arbitration Laws in the Asia Region

Harmonization of arbitration laws yields the greatest benefits in terms of commercial certainty, especially in the light of cross-border economic activity in an increasingly globalized world. This section, therefore, seeks to make the case that harmonization of arbitration laws in the Asian region has largely been realized, such that a case may be made for pursuing the next step of harmonizing the public policy exception to arbitral enforcement under Article V(2)(b) of the New York Convention (NYC).

The author pre-emptively recognizes that BRI nations are not limited to, but extend beyond Asian nations, which include approximately sixty-five economies, including Europe and the Middle East. In light of the vast differences in geo-economics, legal systems, cultural values and traditions across these three regions, the contemplation of geo-legal harmonization of international arbitral enforcement and the public policy exception will be limited in the present article to the Asian region. Specifically, the noted geo-legal harmonization efforts are being undertaken by China, Russia,[17] Southeast Asia, South Asia and Central and Western Asia, but geographically excluding economies in Central Europe, Eastern Europe and the Middle East.[18] Table 7.1 illustrates the Belt and Road nations by region.

17. While Russia is categorized as being in Central and Eastern Europe rather than in Asia, Russia is included in this analysis as being an 'Asian' Belt and Road nation due to its geographical spread over both European and Asian continents.
18. Hong Kong Trade and Development Council, *Country Profile,* (2020), http://beltandroad.hktdc.com/en/country-profiles/country-profiles.aspx.

Table 7.1 Belt and Road Nations Categorized by Region

Region	*Belt and Road Nations*	*Number*
China	China	1
Southeast Asia	Brunei, Cambodia, Indonesia, Laos, Malaysia, Myanmar, Philippines, Singapore, Thailand, Timor-Leste, Vietnam	11
South Asia	Bangladesh, Bhutan, India, Maldives, Nepal, Pakistan, Sri Lanka	7
Central and Western Asia	Afghanistan, Armenia, Azerbaijan, Georgia, Iran, Kazakhstan, Kyrgyzstan, Mongolia, Tajikistan, Turkmenistan, Uzbekistan	11
Total the Belt and Road nations in Asia:		*30*
Middle East and Africa	Bahrain, Egypt, Iraq, Israel, Jordan, Kuwait, Lebanon, Oman, Palestine, Qatar, Saudi Arabia, Syrian Arab Republic, Turkey, United Arab Emirates, Yemen	15
Central and Eastern Europe	Albania, Belarus, Bosnia & Herzegovina, Bulgaria, Croatia, Czech Republic, Estonia, Hungary, Latvia, Lithuania, Macedonia, Moldova, Montenegro, Poland, Romania, Russia, Serbia, Slovakia, Slovenia, Ukraine	20
Total the Belt and Road nations outside of Asia:		*35*
Total:		***65***

As noted previously, arbitration laws within the Asian region have largely achieved harmonization due to the adoption of the NYC and the Model Law by most Asian nations along the Belt and Road. In April 2018, 159 and 109 jurisdictions worldwide have acceded to the NYC and the Model Law respectively.[19]

Tables 7.2 and 7.3 below set out the Belt and Road nations in Asia that have acceded to the NYC and the Model Law, respectively. Table 7.2 shows that twenty-eight out of thirty Belt and Road nations in Asia are the NYC Member States. Table 7.3 shows that twenty out of thirty Belt and Road nations in Asia have adopted the Model Law.

The widespread adoption of common ICA norms represents a positive starting point for further harmonization efforts of arbitral enforcement norms among Belt and Road countries. In particular, the ratification of both the NYC and the Model Law by the Russian Federation makes it conceivable that Central Asian economies, particularly those previously of the Soviet Union, will readily follow any further harmonization efforts.[20] As such, a foundation already exists upon which harmonization of the public policy exception to arbitral enforcement under Article V2(b) of the NYC may be contemplated.

---

19. Member jurisdictions of the NYC and Model Law are available at, respectively, http://www.newyorkconvention.org/countries and http://www.uncitral.org/uncitral/en/uncitral_texts/arbitration/1985Model_arbitration_status.html.
20. These 'post-Soviet' Belt and Road nations located in Asia, in addition to the Russian Federation, may include Armenia, Azerbaijan, Georgia, Kazakhstan, Kyrgyzstan, Tajikistan, Turkmenistan and Uzbekistan.

Table 7.2 Adoption of the New York Convention by Belt and Road Nations

Region	*Belt and Road Nations Adopting NYC*	*Number*
China/Russia	China, Russia	2
Southeast Asia	Brunei, Cambodia, Indonesia, Laos, Malaysia, Myanmar, Philippines, Singapore, Thailand, Vietnam	10
South Asia	Bangladesh, Bhutan, India, Nepal, Pakistan, Sri Lanka	6
Central and Western Asia	Afghanistan, Armenia, Azerbaijan, Georgia, Iran, Kazakhstan, Kyrgyzstan, Mongolia, Tajikistan, Uzbekistan	10
Total Belt and Road Nations:		*28*

Table 7.3 Adoption of the Model Law by Belt and Road Nations

Region	*Belt and Road Nations Adopting the Model Law*	*Number*
China/Russia	Russia	1
Southeast Asia	Brunei, Cambodia, Malaysia, Myanmar, Philippines, Singapore, Thailand, Timor-Leste.	8
South Asia	Bangladesh, Bhutan, India, Maldives, Sri Lanka	5
Central and Western Asia	Armenia, Azerbaijan, Georgia, Iran, Mongolia, Turkmenistan.	6
Total Belt and Road Nations:		*20*

[B] The Public Policy Exception under Article V2(b) of the NYC

Under Article V2(b) of the NYC, recognition or enforcement of a foreign arbitral award may be declined, where such recognition or enforcement is considered by a court of the Member State to the Convention to contravene public policy.[21] As the peripheries of 'public policy' are neither restricted nor defined under the Convention, Member States are essentially free to determine the substantive contents and limits of their nation-specific, albeit 'international' rather than 'domestic' conception of public policy.[22] In this regard, Fry contends that such a notion of public policy ought not to be obligatorily 'supranational' or 'truly international' in the sense that it refers to those values considered 'quasi-universal' amongst states rather than those particular to the states themselves. Rather, he maintains that those values can be determined by the state

21. NYC, Article V2(b).
22. While national courts do not always draw a clear distinction between 'domestic' and 'international' concepts of public policy, a wider-ranging 'international' public policy was endorsed by the International Law Association (ILA) in 2003. *See* Pierre Mayer & Audley Sheppard, *Final ILA Report on Public Policy as a Bar to Enforcement of International Arbitral Awards,* 19 Arb. Int'l 249, 251 (2003).

itself, which may legitimately reflect regional or international norms and concerns at its own discretion.[23]

The controversy of the 'free-for-all' public policy exception in the private international law jurisprudence is rooted in the fact that it bestows upon national judicial systems' ultimate control over recognition and enforcement of perhaps otherwise valid foreign arbitral awards, with all the potentials of unpredictability and irregularity in its application. It has been noted that the power of refusal to recognize or enforce arbitral awards goes 'to the heart' of the Convention.[24] The significance lies in that the primary objective of the NYC was to advance collective legislative standards for the enhanced recognition and enforcement of cross-border arbitral awards. Therefore, a broad interpretation of the public policy exception would frustrate the functioning and effectiveness of the Convention, and by extension, efficient operation of the international arbitration system.[25] Even within national boundaries, the vagueness of Article V2(b)'s exception is encapsulated in the general dearth of statutory definitions for public policy.[26] On the other hand, in this regard, Fry astutely argues that a uniform approach of enforcing arbitral awards may compromise the strength of the system such as the attractiveness of ease of enforcement, which also conversely entails negative implications, (for instance, where refusal was based on a procedural defect applicable not only to one but suddenly all states) and the ability of states to regulate events and transactions within their jurisdiction (as a marker of their sovereignty).[27]

Upon endorsing a survey of country reports on the public policy exception, in 2015, the International Bar Association (IBA)[28] observed that while diverse jurisdictions differ in their formulations of international public policy, three subcategories of norms are generally included.[29] These are first, fundamental principles relating to justice and morality; second, rules serving fundamental political, social and economic interests of the nation; and third, international obligations of nations towards other nations or international organizations.[30] As such, the 'minimum' content of a state party's public policy would lie in the fundamental principles or values underscoring its legal order and social fabric – whatever these normative standards and values are determined to be. It is thus clear that judicial systems do not generally allow the 'public

23. James D. Fry, *Desordre Public International under the New York Convention: Wither Truly International Public Policy*, 8 Chinese J. Int'l L. 81, 82 (2009).
24. Richard A. Cole, *The Public Policy Exception to the New York Convention on the Recognition and Enforcement of Arbitral Awards*, 1 Ohio St. J. on Disp. Resol. 367, 372 (1985).
25. NYC, Article 1.
26. A report of the IBA Subcommittee on Recognition and Enforcement of Arbitration found that of over forty jurisdictions surveyed, just two jurisdictions (Australia and the United Arab Emirates) had developed explicit statutory definitions for the concept of 'public policy'. *See* IBA Subcommittee on Recognition and Enforcement of Arbitral Awards, *Report on the Public Policy Exception in the New York Convention* 2 (2015).
27. Fry, *supra* n. 23, at 124.
28. Not to be confused with the ILA, references to which reports will be made in subsequent paragraphs. As both reports of the IBA and ILA engage in comparative research as to the application of the public policy exception among different jurisdiction, the merits of the conclusions of both will be used as appropriate in this article.
29. Mayer & Sheppard, *supra* n. 22, at 255.
30. *Ibid.*

policy' exception to be trotted out as a mere excuse, where all the other lines of attack fail – as suggested cynically in *Richardson v. Mellish*, in which it was commented that '[public policy] is never argued at all but when other points fail' but whose issue must at least reach a minimum standard of fundamentality.[31]

However, in this respect, Gill and Baker, in referring to the IBA, report to identify common themes belying public policy decisions in national courts; note that even beyond an unspoken consensus that public policy issues must be sufficiently fundamental to a nation's normative values, there exist such divergences among different legal systems and cultures as in the expressions of the degree of violation of 'public policy' required to mandate intervention.[32] For instance, whereas civil law systems couch public policy considerations in terms of 'the basic principles or basic ideas of the *legal system* of our country' going to 'the very fundamentals of *public and economic life*' (with emphasis), common law systems tend to refer to specific core values such as considerations going to the 'fundamental norms of *justice and fairness*' (with emphasis).[33] While Gill and Baker categorize such aforementioned definitions of public policy as simply creating the 'overall impression that the values concerned have to be "fundamental" to the particular State',[34] it is worth noting the discrepancies between the formulations of common law and civil law jurisdictions – with possibilities for further alternative formulations under different legal systems themselves pose a source of indeterminacy as to the definition of 'public policy'.

[C] Grounds for Successful Invocation of the Public Policy Exception

The IBA recommends that indeterminacy of the definition of 'public policy' can be mitigated by dividing it into two dimensions: the procedural, and the substantive. 'Procedural' public policy is concerned with upholding formal justice between two arbitrating parties – for instance, relating to the right of due process, or refusing the enforcement of awards obtained by fraud or falsification.[35] In this regard, Gill and Baker note that the content of procedural violations engaging the public policy exception to arbitral enforcement may variously range from virtually universally accepted grounds (such as fraud or falsification of documents) to grounds adopted by the 'majority' of jurisdictions (such as contravention of the res judicata norm), to grounds accepted only by a 'minority' of states (such as contravention of the common law lis pendens doctrine).[36] In any event, it is noted by the IBA report that 'procedural' public policy grounds are more likely to succeed as compared to 'substantive grounds'.

31. Judith Gill & David Baker, *The Public Policy Exception under Article V.2(b) of the New York Convention: Lessons from Around the World*, 8 Asian Disp. Rev. 74, 75 (2006).
32. *Ibid.*
33. *Ibid.* In addition, Gill and Baker further identify a third combined approach enunciated by the Supreme Court of India, which stipulated that enforcement of a foreign arbitral award may be refused on public policy grounds where it was inconsistent with the 'fundamental policy' of Indian law, Indian national interests (civil law concept) or 'justice or morality' (a common law concept).
34. *Ibid.*, 76.
35. IBA Subcommittee, *supra* n. 26, at 15.
36. Gill and Baker, *supra* n. 31, at 78.

In contrast, 'substantive' public policy involves value-laden norms, which inform the interests of public policy.[37] In this regard, the IBA report separates substantive public policy into five main categories: (a) antitrust and competition law; (b) *pacta sunt servanda*; (c) equality of creditors in insolvency situations; (d) state immunity, prohibition of punitive damages; and (e) prohibition of excessive interest.[38] Gill and Baker further note that in relation to the 'substantive' categories, however, they be defined, public policy may be judicially influenced by constitutional and political issues, as well as by legal system.[39] It may be observed that there is a greater divergence among states as to the agreed grounds of 'substantive' public policy.

It is noted by some authors that the 'public policy' under Article V2(b) would, in practice, not necessarily encapsulate all procedural public policy concerns, most already specifically accounted for in Article V1.[40] It is, however, noted that the stipulated bars to arbitral enforcement in Article V1 cover far from all possible procedural defects in the arbitral procedure, such that Article V2(b) may be considered a 'catch-all' for other procedural considerations, in addition to substantive norms.[41]

In any event, as will be discussed later, 'procedural' public policy based on securing fair procedure is often viewed as less contentious as compared to 'substantive' public policy, which is concerned with certain norms based on state-specific priorities or other value judgments.

[D] Harmonizing the 'Public Policy Exception' under Article V2(b) of the NYC

It is noted in the IBA's report that fears over 'indeterminacy' of the public policy exception under Article V2(b) may be more academic than factual. Due to the narrow construction given to the public policy exception by the courts of most Member States, coupled with a pro-enforcement approach of many jurisdictions, even where the exception is raised, it is far more often rejected than not.[42] This trend of practice is in line with the International Law Association's (ILA) 2003 general recommendation that 'international commercial arbitration should be respected save in exceptional circumstances',[43] contained in what is increasingly considered as guidelines of best international practice – that is, the ILA's Interim and Final Reports on Public Policy as a Bar to Enforcement of International Arbitral Awards.[44] It is also noted that Bermann's survey of the interpretation and application of the NYC by the courts of forty-four jurisdictions in 2017 likewise identifies the trend of violations of public policy being construed

37. IBA Subcommittee, *supra* n. 26, at 17.
38. Gill and Baker, *supra* n. 31, at 78.
39. *Ibid.*, 79. In particular, Gill QC and Baker note that the principles of Muslim Sharia Law impact such jurisdictions' view of public policy.
40. Fry, *supra* n. 23, at 92-3.
41. *Ibid.*
42. IBA Subcommittee, *supra* n. 26, at 12.
43. Mayer & Sheppard, *supra* n. 22.
44. International Council for Commercial Arbitration ('ICCA'), *Chapter III – Request for the Recognition and Enforcement of an Arbitral Award*, in *ICCA's Guide to the Interpretation of the 1958 New York Convention: A Handbook for Judges* 107 (ICCA, 2011).

narrowly, much being limited to the violations of the 'most fundamental notions of morality and justice'.[45]

Despite that, potential enforcement arising from the uncertainties in the public policy cases is sufficient to compromise commercial certainty and investor confidence, with adverse effects on the commission of commercial transactions and business in foreign jurisdictions. It is noted that a pro-enforcement approach to arbitral enforcement, as aforementioned, appears to be the judicial practice in China. Between 2000 to 2012, of twelve cases which concerned or included public policy issues, only one succeeded on the basis of the contravention of public policy under Article V2(b) of the NYC.[46] With China being the anticipated primary economic force driving BRI development, her approach towards facilitating commercial endeavours (other than in cases involving elements significantly affecting fundamental national concerns) is expected to set the tone for any harmonization of the public policy exception.

In this regard, it is interesting to note Friedman's conclusions in relation to the public policy defence in the context of American contract law. He analysed a sample of public policy defence cases and found that the public policy cases invoking a specific statute or regulation (48% of the cases sampled) have a 59% success rate. This is in contrast to the public policy cases that either: (i) refer to case law (15%); or (ii) make a 'broad, general appeal' to public policy as a defence (33%) – which succeed just 31% of the time.[47] The takeaway from this appears to be that the specificity of public policy concerns, i.e., those that are clearly defined or based in the precedents, have a higher rate of success in public policy defence than those that refer to a vaguer notion of public policy. This would be illustrative of an appropriate balance of judicial oversight over arbitral enforcement in the context of public policy – to be applied where clearly defined to give reassurance to legislative and commercial certainty.

In light of the utilization of ICA as the primary mode of commercial dispute resolution for Belt and Road transactions together with the Belt and Road Asian nations' high level of harmonization of international arbitration norms and the commercial cost-reducing interest in overcoming any real or imagined uncertainties relating to the public policy exception – the conditions are ripe for taming the 'unruly horse' of public policy.

45. George A. Bermann ed., *Recognition and Enforcement of Foreign Arbitral Awards – the Interpretation and Application of the New York Convention by National Courts* 60 (Springer, 2017).
46. This evidences a 'pro-enforcement' approach generally taken by the Chinese judiciary. *See* He Qisheng., *Public Policy in Enforcement of Foreign Arbitral Awards in the Supreme People's Court of China*, 43 H.K.L.J. 1037 (2013).
47. David Adam Friedman, *Bringing Order to Contracts Against Public Policy*, 39 Fla. St. U. L. Rev. 563, 567 (2012).

§7.05 DETAILS FOR HARMONIZING THE PUBLIC POLICY EXCEPTION UNDER THE BRI

[A] Drawing from the Experiences of the EU and OHADA

It is noted that while countries under the BRI are not yet economically integrated, they cherish the good wishes of being connected. Thus, for these purposes, the EU and OHADA are not perfect comparators. This is because the EU, despite its useful enunciation of a 'regional public policy', exists not solely for the purpose of trade, but acts further as a political bloc dealing with matters as diverse as human rights and regional security - unlike OHADA and the Belt and Road region. However, it is considered that the EU's lengthy experience in matters of economic integration is unparalleled by any other strategic international alliance in the world. In the same vein, where the approach of OHADA of absolute uniformity of business laws - and by extension, public policy - as opposed to harmonization across a host of countries with different national laws and economic considerations is not identical to the Belt and Road region, their single focus on economic integration - as under the BRI - makes them an eligible comparator.

[1] 'EU Public Policy' for EU Member States

A key implication of sovereignty accounted for under Article V2(b) of the Convention is that the EU Member States are judicially free to determine the substantive considerations constituting their jurisdiction's '[international] public policy'.[48] However, due to the supranational nature of EU laws and directives vis-à-vis the EU Member States, individual Member States are further required to take EU law into consideration when determining the substantive content of the public policy.[49] Notably, in *Eco Swiss China Time Ltd v. Benetton International NV* [1999] ECRI 3055, the Court of Justice of the European Union (CJEU) specifically ruled that where an EU Member State's refusal to recognize and/or enforce an arbitral award occurs on public policy grounds, violation of 'EU public policy' must also be treated as a valid ground for annulment.[50] The European Parliament itself affirms the existence of 'EU public policy' as considered in a number of cases by the CJEU.[51]

The EU's experience indicates that the adoption and inclusion of 'regional' public policy considerations by the Member States is compatible with the free determination of sovereign states of the contents of their jurisdiction-specific conception of public policy. It is thus conceivable that 'Asian public policy' similarly encapsulating core Asian interests may be agreed and adopted as part of the national conception of public

48. George A. Bermann, *Reconciling European Union Law Demands with the Demands of International Arbitration*, 34 Fordham Int'l L.J. 1193, 1201 (2011).
49. *Ibid.*
50. Case C-126/97 *Eco Swiss China Time Ltd v. Benetton International NV* [1999] ECR I-3055, 37.
51. Tony Cole et al., *Legal Instruments and Practice of Arbitration in the EU* (2014), http://www.europarl.europa.eu/RegData/etudes/STUD/2015/509988/IPOL_STU%282015%29509988_EN.pdf.

policy by individual nations within the Belt and Road network. Conceivably, a distinction may be made on the basis that the relationship of Member States to the EU is akin to a politically integrated federal union.[52] In contrast, there is no political affiliation among the Belt and Road nations, notwithstanding their geographical proximity and shared economic goals. Nonetheless, political integration ought not to constitute a prerequisite for inclusion of a regional public policy; the presence of common goals or interests should be sufficient.

The substantive contents of 'EU public policy' remain indeterminate. While the CJEU has indicated that individual EU laws and regulations may constitute 'EU public policy' in the specific case, it has yet to enunciate exactly which provisions, or which classes of provisions, are likely to form part of regional public policy.[53] It is noted that while the EU promotes the incorporation of an 'EU public policy' into 'national' public policy, a regionally 'harmonized' public policy is not advanced. The rationale behind the approach of the CJEU is to ensure that civil claims based upon EU laws in the individual Member States would be treated no less favourably as compared to claims based upon domestic laws.[54] As such, there is no implication that the substantive contents of public policy considerations of individual EU nations must be consistent among the common market.

As discussed above, the enunciation of a 'harmonized' public policy exception within the Asia region serves a different purpose in light of the BRI. Mitigating the indeterminacy of jurisdiction-specific public policies through harmonization of their substantive contents promotes the certainty needed to allow the BRI to flourish.

[2] A 'Uniform' Public Policy Under OHADA

The experience of OHADA is considered next. OHADA has taken a different approach from the EU in instituting a 'uniform' public policy as part of its regional implementation of uniform business laws. It should be noted at the outset that the application of uniform public policy under OHADA regime is unrelated to Article V2(b) of the Convention.[55]

Formed under the 1993 OHADA Treaty, OHADA is an alliance of seventeen West and Central African countries, which aims to implement a modernized cross-border regime of uniform business laws and institutions across the participating countries.[56] As the vast majority of OHADA nations are connected as historical French colonies, the OHADA laws, similarly, are derived from the French law.[57] Akin to the infrastructural and economic development motives belying the BRI, the purpose of the unified OHADA laws is to bolster much-needed economic development through the greater

52. Sergio Fabbrini, *Which European Union?* 187 (Cambridge University Press, 2015).
53. Cole et al., *supra* n. 51.
54. Bermann, *supra* n. 48.
55. Article V2(b) will only apply to those OHADA Member States that have ratified the NYC.
56. Claire Moore Dickerson, *Harmonizing Business Laws in Africa: OHADA Calls the Tune,* 44 Colum. J. Transnat'l L. 17, 19 (2005).
57. *Ibid.*, 21.

attraction of foreign investment in the sub-Saharan African region.[58] Supported by OHADA's supranational court, the unification of regional commercial laws[59] not only strengthens the regional rule of law – but also, it is geared at increasing investor confidence by cultivating certainty and bolstering easy accessibility to OHADA's shared business environment.

OHADA's 1999 Uniform Act on Arbitration (Uniform Act) provided an updated, unified set of arbitration laws for the seventeen OHADA nations.[60] Articles 26 and 31 deal respectively with 'international public policy' as one of the six grounds for invalidity of, and the sole ground for refusal to recognize and/or enforce an arbitral award.[61] As 'public policy' refers to OHADA's 'collective' public policy of the Member States as a unit, and the Uniform Act applies to all OHADA jurisdictions, the substantive contents of public policy are not simply harmonized, but actually identical in the seventeen OHADA nations.[62] The significance of Articles 26 and 31 of the Uniform Act is that as long as an award rendered in an OHADA seat jurisdiction is not void due to contravention of OHADA's public policy,[63] it is recognized and enforceable in any other OHADA jurisdiction.[64]

OHADA's uniform regime under the Uniform Act is aimed at maximizing efficiency and commercial certainty for the rendering and enforcement of arbitral awards in the region.[65] However, as with the EU public policy, little legislative guidance is provided as to the substantive content of OHADA public policy and is decided on a case-by-case basis. To further the ends of uniformity, enforcement courts will generally have to accept the conclusions on validity and the subsequent order for recognition in the seat jurisdiction, with appeals to OHADA's supranational court, the Common Court of Justice and Arbitration.[66]

It must be emphasized that OHADA's uniform 'international public policy' implies identical considerations amongst all OHADA Member States. A 'uniform' public policy is more stringent than a 'harmonized' public policy, in that while the former demands complete uniformity in substantive content, the latter only requires them to be mutually consistent. A 'harmonized' public policy provides leeway for individual nations to tailor their public policy according to the particular jurisdictional circumstances, provided that its application does not conflict with the nation-specific public policy of other jurisdictions. Aside from a common interest in regional economic

58. *Ibid.*, 19-20.
59. The OHADA laws are judicially enforced and interpreted by the supranational *Cour Commune de Justice et d'Arbitrage* (CCJA).
60. Francis Ulrigh Ndinga, *The Features of the Arbitration Proceedings under the OHADA Uniform Act on Arbitration Law,* 1 Glob. Scholars J. L. & Confl. Resol. 1, 1-2 (2014).
61. Uniform Act on Arbitration (Uniform Act), Articles 26 and 31, available at https://www.droit-afrique.com/uploads/OHADA-Uniform-Act-1999-arbitration.pdf.
62. Emilia Onyema, *Enforcement of Arbitral Awards in Sub-Sahara Africa,* 26 Arb. Int'l 115, 121 (2010).
63. Uniform Act, *supra* n. 61, at Article 26.
64. *Ibid.*, Article 31. Indeed, an order of recognition and enforcement granted by the court of an OHADA Member State only has to be registered with the courts of the second OHADA Member State in which enforcement is sought. *See* Onyema, *supra* n. 62.
65. *Ibid*, 121.
66. *Ibid.*

development, OHADA's uniform 'public policy' regime is facilitated, by their shared historical experience and French law-based legal systems of many OHADA nations.[67] However, a lack of similar homogeneity among the Belt and Road nations would create virtually insurmountable difficulties in establishing a unified conception of public policy. As such, a 'harmonized' rather than a 'uniform' approach in Asian public policy may be more appropriate as a starting point.

[B] Substantive Contents of a Harmonized Public Policy

As noted in the IBA report, there are certain violations of public policy that appear common to most nations, regardless of variation in legal culture, political framework and level of economic development.[68] For instance, procedural irregularities in the arbitral process amounting to the violation of the right of a party to be heard or to present the case are virtually universally considered contrary to agreed standards of fairness, and thus, public policy.[69] Some substantive matters, such as corruption and fraud, are similarly regarded by most nations as a contravention of public policy.[70] By way of illustration, the discussion below sets out common examples of procedural and substantive matters suggested by the ILA that contravene public policy, where they may be incorporated into a shared Asian public policy framework in international arbitration.

[1] Procedural Contraventions of Public Policy

Procedural public policy contraventions involve defects in the arbitral procedure, which adversely impact on the availability of due process. Non-contentious matters constituting such contravention may include:

- evidence of fraud or corruption in the arbitral process;[71] and
- violations, generally, of due process.[72]

Subject to the agreement amongst the Belt and Road nations, other grounds of procedural contravention of public policy may include, for example, specific procedural issues such as:

- evidence of arbitrator partiality;[73]
- irrational dissonance between the facts and award;[74] or

67. Dickerson, *supra* n. 56, at 15.
68. IBA Subcommittee, *supra* n. 26, at 14-7.
69. *Ibid.*, 15.
70. *Ibid.*, 16.
71. Audley Sheppard, *Interim ILA Report on Public Policy as a Bar to Enforcement of International Arbitral Awards* 19 Arb. Int'l 217, 238 (2003).
72. *Ibid.*, 239.
73. *Ibid.*, 240.
74. *Ibid.*

- decisions made in the absence of reasons.[75]

It was previously noted that Article V(1) of the NYC deals with the refusal of recognition and enforcement of arbitral awards on a number of due process and procedural grounds; *inter alia*, notice of arbitral proceedings and compliance of arbitral process with pre-existing arbitral agreement or laws of the seat jurisdiction. In the same vein as public policy harmonization, with the significant overlap in the categories of procedural irregularities considered under the individual judicial systems as public policy contraventions, it should be possible to develop standards of due process and consistency in the way procedural issues are approached in Belt and Road jurisdictions.[76]

[2] Substantive Contraventions of Public Policy

Substantive public policy contraventions concern the subject matter of the arbitration and the protection of which may be considered contrary to public policy. Such 'proscribed' matters frequently differ amongst different jurisdictions without common ground, due to the variations in policy concerns underlying societal values.[77] The general exception concerns awards which allow the commission of activities universally considered to be illegal or morally objectionable,[78] such as those relating to drug trafficking, corruption or fraud.[79]

However, as discussed in the context of 'EU public policy', while substantive prohibitions may vary depending on the governance policies of individual states, it is submitted that fundamental norms, values and interests shared over an alliance of nations may form part of an individual jurisdiction's public policy. For instance, Article 81 of the Treaty Establishing the European Community, which prohibits practices restricting competition between the Member States, was ruled by the CJEU contrary to regional 'EU public policy'.[80] As fair competition laws are integral to the facilitation of trade and the proper functioning of the free markets, their protection is considered a matter of EU public policy.[81] Such a consideration protects both the economic interests of individual EU Member States, as well the European Community as a regional entity.

It is suggested that similar norms and considerations may be applied to the Asian region regarding the promotion of the economic goals of the BRI. The fundamental interest of the BRI, aside from the development of regional infrastructure, are bolstering cross-border commercial and trade cooperation amongst the Belt and Road nations. Regional prosperity, envisaged as an interest of all jurisdictions in the Belt and Road Asian region, may be facilitated through the application of harmonized public policy. Such substantive norms in the harmonized public policy may include, for example,

75. *Ibid.*
76. IBA Subcommittee, *supra* n. 26, at 14.
77. *Ibid.*, 16.
78. *Ibid.*
79. *Ibid.*
80. Mayer & Sheppard, *supra* n. 22, at 233.
81. *Ibid.*

relatively non-contentious rules such as those against anti-competition agreements, the formation of de facto regional monopolies, and corruption. Other substantive norms, relating to the protection of diplomatic relations amongst nations, may similarly be part of an Asian public policy, considering the objectives of the BRI to increase transnational cooperation. The general approach taken for a first step, from a practical perspective, could be to draft a negative list of factors in which awards are likely to be rejected, including some of the matters highlighted above – such as anti-competition provisions or procedural impropriety.

Harmonization of the public policy exception requires not absolute uniformity, but consistency among the Belt and Road nations. This would imply that while this geo-legal public policy forms just one part of the nation-specific public policy under Article V2(b) of the NYC, remaining nation-specific public policy must be congruent with 'Asian public policy'. It is noted, as above, that judicial custom emphasizes the narrow construction of Article V2(b) of the NYC.[82] This pro-enforcement approach works in tandem with harmonization efforts to tame the 'unruly horse' of public policy.

While there is no existing institution dealing with the coordination of cross-border arbitral enforcement rules per se, it is suggested that in the interim, the AIIB (whose primary function is to provide loans for the BRI development projects) could take a proactive role in coordinating the harmonization of national laws. It could be in the specific context of public policy harmonization or more broadly with regard to trade- and investment-related regulations – forming an integral part of the broad goal of trade facilitation under the BRI. This is possible due to the semi-governmental constitution of AIIB's corporate governance. It would readily allow the adaptation or creation of a new office or a sub-organization to discuss the harmonization of legal norms and regulations pertinent to all Belt and Road nations for their efficient functioning of trade and commerce. By contrast, in the EU, the public policy exception has largely been defined at the highest level of the CJEU, where CJEU is competent only to make judgments of issues being litigated. Such an approach is not recommended since there is no supranational court under the BRI so far (pretty much because the BRI aims to create an economically, rather than a politically integrated zone). Whereas courts may pronounce what public policy 'is' or 'is not' constituted in a particular case, queries as to its concrete and substantive contents are left unanswered with the lack of defined guidelines. For efficiency purposes and to ensure participation of all the Belt and Road nations in determining certain shared matters under the BRI that are against a 'regional' public policy, it would be more desirable to designate a coordination institution such as the AIIB for this purpose.

82. IBA Subcommittee, *supra* n. 26 at 6.

[C] Challenges and Other Aspects of Public Policy Harmonization

[1] Compatibility of Legal Systems and National Cultures Along the Belt and Road

As the Belt and Road's metaphorical 'silk road' moves the wide geographical spread of East Asia, South Asia, and Central Asian regions, it simultaneously navigates common law, civil law, Islamic law systems; as well as a wealth of nations divided along social, cultural, ethnic and religious lines.

First, the definition and span of the public policy concept itself fall to different interpretations among legal systems. The civil law conception of public policy, or *order public*, is frequently viewed as being wider in the application as compared to the traditionally restrictive interpretations to public policy under common law systems.[83] This is compounded by the interaction of jurisdiction-specific social and cultural features. Such social characteristics belie the integral values and interests of a nation, which goes to the root of national conceptions of public policy. For instance, the Islamic concept of public policy revolves around the spirit of Sharia law and its sources.[84] The wide divergences in culture amongst legal systems and values suggest an inherent difficulty in achieving harmonization of the public policy exception, of which contents are informed by the same challenge. This concern may be met with a reiteration of the extent of Asian harmonization applicable by the BRI. The universal prescription of public policy considerations applicable entirely to the Asian region is not the goal of harmonization. The proposed 'Asian public policy' includes defined categories of matters that contravene public policy. This does not preclude nations from retaining other nation-specific public policy considerations, provided that they do not come into conflict with the 'regional' policy. Further, given that the proposed substantive grounds of the 'Asian public policy' largely revolve around the facilitation of economic growth and commercial interactions amongst the Belt and Road nations, there is likely to be less room for contradiction.

Second, there are diverging standards of due process amongst legal systems. Common law jurisdictions may hold parties at arbitration to different standards of procedural fairness as compared to civil law systems, and it is largely based on the idea that due process is connected to natural justice.[85] For instance, while the concept of 'fraud' is well-established under the common law, there may be a definitional variation when the same term is applied in non-common law legal systems.[86] This creates issues insofar as even where a substantive ground for invoking the public policy exception is regionally harmonized, enforcement courts may still be applying diverging standards in determining its application. While it may be theoretically possible to apply a

83. Mayer & Sheppard, *supra* n. 22, at 223-4.
84. *Ibid.*, 219.
85. *Ibid.*, 233.
86. Such is the case of fraud as a ground of refusing reciprocal enforcement of judgments between Hong Kong, a common law jurisdiction, and China, whose system is based upon civil law. *See* Jie Huang, *Interregional Recognition and Enforcement of Civil and Commercial Judgments* (Hart Publishing 2014).

'universal' standard with respect to specific public policy grounds, to do so would be problematic in that inconsistencies with respect to judicial standards between international arbitral enforcement and the remainder of the legal system would be rendered. Such a concern is more difficult to resolve. However, it is ventured that as a matter of a judicial preference for upholding enforcement, enforcement would be denied only on the clear grounds of breach of public policy considerations.

[2] Creation of 'Transnational' Public Policy

A conceptual concern of the proposed harmonized 'Asian public policy' is the creation of 'transnational' public policy. 'Transnational' public policy has been defined by the ILA to refer to a 'truly international public policy ... of universal application, comprising fundamental rules of national law, principles of universal justice, *jus cogens* in public international law, and the general principles of morality accepted by what are referred to as "civilized nations".'[87] 'Asian public policy' would appear to fit into the category of transnational public policy in that it contains considerations that straddle borders and apply to a region of states. This is problematic in that the public policy exception under Article V2(b) of the NYC intends public policy considerations to be nation-specific, albeit 'international' rather than 'domestic' in nature.[88] Further, this is the understanding recommended by the ILA, although such an issue has yet to be conclusively litigated by national courts.[89] In other words, drafters of Article V2(b) of the NYC intended that enforcing states apply their own respective notions of public policy. Nonetheless, as reiterated, the notion of 'regional public policy' adopted by a group of nations is not inconsistent with a nation-specific nature of public policy envisioned under Article V2(b) of the NYC. As stated above, the application of 'Asian public policy' operates in such a way that it constitutes just one category of public policy considerations - as explored above, itself a negative list applied by the jurisdictions. The existence of this region-specific public policy impacts national public policy considerations only so far as there are inconsistencies, which would, in any case, need to be resolved to ensure full cooperation between a nation and a region. As such, harmonization does not limit the ability of a country to define its own public policy. Rather, it aims to bring harmony in the application of the public policy exception.

An additional practical concern may arise with respect to the receptiveness of the Belt and Road countries in adopting aspects of 'regional' or 'transnational' public policy as part of their nation-specific public policy. In particular, it revisits the

87. Mayer & Sheppard, *supra* n. 22 at 220.

88. In other words, a national conception of 'international public policy', rather than 'domestic public policy'. The expression 'international public policy' has been defined by the ILA not to refer to a public policy shared by a number of states, but the part of a public policy belonging to a state, the contravention of which would prevent a party from enforcing a foreign award. *See ibid.*, 251.

89. While some jurisdictions, for instance, France and Switzerland, make a distinction between domestic and international conceptions of public policy, the position of most national courts is uncertain: Bermann ed., *supra* n. 45, at 100.

willingness of the Chinese judiciary – and by necessary extension, the Chinese Government – to broaden the existing narrow definition of its nation-specific 'public policy', which is largely limited to fundamental principles such as the safeguarding of China's national sovereignty, public security, and the integrity of the legal system.[90] To include commercial concerns encapsulated and mandated by 'Asian public policy' under the BRI, it is necessary to ensure the success of the endeavour of China as a proposer and leader of the BRI. While there has yet to be any governmental inclination in this proposal, it is contended that the tangible commercial benefits associated with harmonization, and the illustrations of the EU and OHADA experiences, may lessen the scepticism of adopting a wider take on public policy than currently prevails.

§7.06 CONCLUSION

In light of China's continued economic rise, albeit dented by the COVID-19 pandemic and related global slowdown over 2020, the BRI provides a unique opportunity for increased economic cooperation and integration through the cross-border development of infrastructural projects in the Asian region.[91] Against the backdrop, ICA's advantages make it a primary vehicle in international dispute resolution within the Belt and Road across Asia.

Looking forward, this chapter has sought to demonstrate the distinct advantages and benefits of increased harmonization of arbitration regulatory landscape in the Asian region as a means to bolster and further the multitudinous goals of strengthening cross-border relationships both commercially and geo-politically. The fundamental issue is how to harmonize cross-border arbitral enforcement to ensure the legal and commercial certainty necessary to secure investor confidence. A strong and well-established dispute resolution system is integral. This reduces commercial transactional costs and will be critical in evaluating the success of China's Belt and Road development policy and economic diplomacy strategy.

The BRI provides a golden opportunity for China to take the lead in harmonizing the public policy exception in ICA within the Asian Belt and Road nations. There is a bright future in light of the existing status of harmonization efforts of arbitration enforcement norms through the substantial adoption of the NYC and the Model Law by the Asian economies. The remaining uncertainties around the scope of public policy may create issues of incompatibility in arbitral enforcement, which run against the BRI's goal of economic integration and commercial certainty. As this chapter reveals, reconciliation of national public policies within the Asian region of the BRI should yield significant benefits not only for harmonizing international arbitration norms as a significant mode of dispute resolution development but also for strengthening the recognition of common economic interests under the BRI development. Over time, this

90. Qisheng He, *Public Policy in Enforcement of Foreign Arbitral Awards in the Supreme People's Court of China*, 43 H.K.L.J. 1037, 1043 (2013).
91. Bath & Nottage, *supra* n. 5, at 22.

should consolidate and made inroads towards the goal of enhanced economic integration in the Belt and Road Asian region, and gradually extending to all the sixty-five countries involved in the BRI.

With these principles in mind, and drawing upon experiences of the EU and OHADA, this chapter suggests that the public policy exception to arbitral enforcement in the Belt and Road Asian region could be delineated through a 'negative list' approach. It is further advocated that the creation of 'transnational' public policy, as framed around the common economic interests of the BRI and drawn on existing procedural and substantive common grounds among the Belt and Road nations in Asia, may not be compatible with the requirement of 'national' public policy considerations under Article V(2)(b) of the NYC. However, as discussed, the practical implementation of this suggestion depends much on the receptivity of the Chinese Government in widening the current narrow understanding of China's nation-specific public policy. As 'true harmonization' of the ICA system is an ideal for the increasingly interdependent and globalized world, it is exciting that opportunities brought by China's Belt and Road development may help realize this within the Asian context.

CHAPTER 8

Recent Developments in China in Cross-Border Dispute Resolution: Judicial Reforms in the Shadow of Political Conformity

Vivienne Bath

The rapid expansion of China's international trade and investment in the twenty-first century has necessarily brought with it the need for modern and effective cross-border dispute resolution mechanisms. At the international level, China is playing an active role in the review of investor-state dispute settlement (ISDS) in (United Nations Commission on International Trade Law) UNCITRAL Working Group III and participating in dispute resolution developments in the World Trade Organization (WTO). Domestically, the Supreme People's Court (SPC) has been working to set up new institutions (the China International Commercial Court (CICC)), improve mechanisms for the review and enforcement of arbitral awards and encourage mediation, both domestically and internationally. Much of this activity has been generated and spurred on by the Belt and Road Initiative (BRI) and the anticipated associated increase in cross-border disputes arising from the many commercial transactions involved in the BRI. Its execution also reflects the desire to encourage and expand the international use of Chinese law and build up China as a centre for international dispute resolution. At the same time, however, the Chinese Communist Party (CCP) is tightening its ideological and administrative control over the courts and judicial system. This chapter examines and discusses the implications of these recent developments.

§8.01 INTRODUCTION

The rapid expansion of China's international trade and investment in the twenty-first century has necessarily brought with it the need for modern and effective cross-border dispute resolution mechanisms. China's government and institutions have, in the last two to three years, focused on dispute resolution in several different ways, and in a variety of different fora. The overall picture is one of China expanding the options for the settlement of disputes and improving the quality of its courts and other methods of dispute resolution (with an important objective being to attract international disputes to China and Chinese venues), and engaging actively in international fora. At the domestic level, however, the CCP is tightening its ideological and administrative control over the courts and judicial system.

At the international level, China is playing an active role in the review of ISDS before UNCITRAL.[1] It is also one of sixteen parties participating in the Multi-Party Interim Appeal Arbitration Arrangement Pursuant to Article 25 of the DSU (Dispute Settlement Understanding), the agreement among several large and smaller states which attempts to keep the WTO dispute resolution system functioning.[2] China has, from its inception, been engaged in the WTO side-group Discussions in International Investment Facilitation.[3] Chinese arbitral institutions and others have been actively engaged in international outreach through conferences, seminars, participation in international activities, and signing cooperation and collaboration agreements with foreign arbitration institutions.[4]

At the domestic level, the SPC and Chinese arbitral institutions have been focused on increasing Chinese capacity to deal with cross-border disputes, as well as improving the legal and operational regimes supporting transnational dispute settlement. In the absence of legislative initiatives, the SPC has taken the lead regarding consolidation of the rules relating to arbitration and arbitral awards and working on China's private international law rules relevant to cross-border disputes. The CICC, a new specialist court which is part of the SPC, started hearing cases in 2019. Chinese arbitral institutions have been working to make themselves attractive potential venues both for international commercial arbitration and for ISDS. Mediation continues to be encouraged as part of the so-called diversified method of dispute resolution,[5] coordinating mediation, arbitration and litigation.

Much of this activity has been generated and spurred on by the BRI and the anticipated associated increase in cross-border disputes arising from the many commercial transactions involved in the BRI.[6] Its execution reflects, however, an important

1. Working Group III: Investor-State Dispute Settlement Reform, https://uncitral.un.org/en/working_groups/3/investor-state.
2. European Commission, Multi-Party Interim Appeal Arbitration Arrangement Pursuant to Article 25 of the DSU, JOB/DSB/1; JOB/DSB/1Add/12 (27 Apr. 2020), https://trade.ec.europa.eu/doclib/docs/2020/march/tradoc_158685.pdf; Statement by Ministers, Davos Switzerland (24 Jan. 2020), https://trade.ec.europa.eu/doclib/docs/2020/january/tradoc_158596.pdf. *See also generally* Claxton, Nottage & Williams, Chapter 11 in this volume.
3. WTO, *World Trade Organization, Joint Ministerial Statement on Investment Facilitation for Development* (5 Nov. 2019), WT/L/1072.
4. For example, *see* China International Economic and Trade Arbitration Commission (CIETAC), CIETAC 2019 Work Report, http://www.cietac.org/index.php?m=Article&a=show&id=16871&l=en.
5. SPC, *Opinions on Building the One-Stop Diversified Dispute Resolution Mechanism and the One-Stop Litigation Service Centre* (1 Aug. 2019).
6. *See* generally Gu, Chapter 7 in this volume; Lutz-Christian Wolff & Chao Xi eds., *Legal Dimensions of China's One Belt One Road* (Wolters Kluwer Hong Kong 2016).

motivating factor: the desire to encourage and expand the international use of Chinese law and build up China as a centre for international dispute resolution, as a maritime law centre, a commercial dispute centre and potentially a centre for ISDS, while at the same time maintaining the role and reaffirming the dominance of the CCP over the Chinese justice system.

This chapter looks at recent domestic developments and considers the motivation behind them, the issues which they resolve (and fail to resolve) and their potential impact on cross-border dispute resolution in China.

§8.02 THE ROLE OF THE SPC AND JUDICIAL REFORM

The SPC has taken a leading role regarding cross-border dispute resolution and other judicial reforms. It reflects in its activities the wider policies and initiatives of the government and the CCP, including decisions taken at the Fourth Plenum of the 19th Congress of CCP[7] and ongoing judicial and court reform programs[8] in relation both to dispute resolution generally and to the administration of the courts themselves. Recent SPC initiatives with an impact on international dispute resolution aim to guide and improve the approach of the courts to cross-border disputes and clarify rules relating to the operation of the courts (such as the jurisdiction of the hierarchical levels of the courts), consolidate rules relating to judicial review of arbitration and arbitral awards and improve private international law rules.[9] The SPC has also negotiated agreements with the Hong Kong Special Administrative Region on judgments and arbitration, as well as with other jurisdictions, such as Singapore. Although much of this important work is expressed to be done in the context of the BRI,[10] it is, of course, relevant to cross-border disputes generally.

It must be remembered, however, that the Chinese courts, whether in their regulatory or judicial capacity, do not operate independently.[11] In the current political environment, the CCP has taken steps to affirm that it has absolute leadership over the

7. *See* summary in Jack Kamensky & Erin Slawson, *Five Takeaways from the China's Fourth Plenum*, China Bus. Rev. (7 Nov. 2019), https://www.chinabusinessreview.com/five-takeaways-from-chinas-fourth-plenum/.
8. *See* summary, Susan Finder, *Supreme People's Court's New Vision for the Chinese courts*, Supreme People's Monitor (4 May 2020), https://supremepeoplescourtmonitor.com/2020/05/04/supreme-peoples-courts-new-vision-for-the-chinese-courts/.
9. The SPC has also been active regarding legal work and issues in relation to the COVID-19 pandemic: *see*, e.g., *Guiding Opinions on Several Issues concerning Properly Trying the Civil Cases involving COVID-19 Outbreak in Accordance with the Law (I)*, Fa [2020] No. 12 (16 Apr. 2020), which deals with resolution of contract disputes (particularly regarding claims of force majeure), and *Notice on Strengthening and Standardizing the Online Litigation Work during the Period of Prevention and Control of the Outbreak of Novel Coronavirus Pneumonia*, Fa [2020] No. 49 (14 Feb. 2020).
10. *See*, in particular, SPC, *Opinions on the Supply of Judicial Services and Safeguards by the People's Courts for 'Belt and Road' Construction*, Fa [2015] No. 9 (16 Jun. 2015) (First BRI Opinion); SPC, *Opinions on Further Supply of Judicial Services and Safeguards by the People's Courts for the 'Belt and Road' Construction*, Fa [2019] No. 29 (9 Dec. 2019) (Second BRI Opinion).
11. *See* Björn Ahl, *Judicialisation in Authoritarian Regimes: The Expansion of Powers of the Chinese Supreme People's Court*, 17 Int'l J. Con. L. 252 (2019); Ling Li, *Political-Legal Order and the Curious Double Character of China's Courts*, 6(1) Asian J. Law & Soc. 19 (2019).

courts. CCP control is implemented through a combination of ideological responsibility requirements for judges, control over appointments and reporting requirements, and political and judicial inspection.[12] The coexistence of a more prominent and aggressive CCP approach to the judicial and the legal system (combined with efforts to 'oppose mistaken Western thinking') with initiatives to improve the quality of the courts and the content of the law presents ongoing conceptual and practical problems in the context of international disputes and casts a shadow over the attractiveness of Chinese as a dispute resolution destination.[13] It is important to bear this in mind when considering recent developments in China's approach to dispute resolution.

§8.03 ONE-STOP DIVERSIFIED DISPUTE RESOLUTION AND MEDIATION

Recent years have seen a renewed emphasis on 'diversified dispute resolution': the combination of mediation, arbitration and litigation (as well as access to notarization, third party experts, scholars, appraisers and so on) in order to facilitate the rapid and efficient resolution of disputes.[14] Although this policy is not new in itself,[15] the SPC has recently reiterated the importance of the one-stop diversified dispute system, both in relation to litigation generally and to the settlement of disputes in other areas, including the private economy (through cooperation with the (non-independent) chambers of commerce),[16] intellectual property disputes[17] and financial disputes with the involvement of third-party mediators.[18] The emphasis of the one-stop system is on mediation as the first method of resolving disputes. The integrated system has a number of

12. *Ibid. See also* Jerome A. Cohen, *Law's Relation to Political Power in China: A Backward Transition* 86(1) Social Research: An International Quarterly 231 (2019). Also available at SSRN: https://ssrn.com/abstract=3354939. For a summary of the current position regarding the role of the judiciary, *see* Finder, *supra* n. 8. *See also* ChinaLawTranslate, Jeremy Daum & Susan Finder, *Notes on SPC Research Topics,* (14 May 2020), https://www.chinalawtranslate.com/en/notes-on-spc-research-topics/.
13. *See supra* n. 11; Finder, *ibid.*, quoting Article 5 of the SPC, *Opinions on Thoroughly Implementing the Spirit of the Fourth Plenum of the 19th Party Congress to Advance the Modernization of the Judicial System and Judicial Capacity* (4 Apr. 2020). Available at: http://www.court.gov.cn/fabu-xiangqing-224491.html.
14. SPC, *Opinions on Building the One-stop Diversified Dispute Resolution Mechanism and the One-Stop Litigation Service Centre* (1 Aug. 2019) (2019 Opinion); Guodong Du, *The Future of Mediation in China: Synergy Between Litigation and Mediation,* China Justice Observer (18 Sep. 2019), https://www.chinajusticeobserver.com/a/the-future-of-mediation-in-china-synergy-between-litigation-and-mediation.
15. Bin Li, *China's Diversified Dispute Resolution System* (19 Sep. 2017), reposted at https://adrresearch.net/author/proflisatoohey/.
16. SPC & All-China Federation of Industry and Commerce, *Opinions on Bringing into Play the Advantages of Chambers of Commerce in Mediation and Promoting the Construction of Diversified Resolution Mechanism for Disputes in Sector of Private Economy,* Fa [2019] No. 11 (14 Jan. 2019).
17. SPC, *Opinions on Comprehensively Strengthening Judicial Protection of Intellectual Property,* Fa [2020] No. 11 (15 Apr. 2020), Article 21.
18. SPC, the People's Bank of China and the China Banking and Insurance Regulatory Commission, *Opinions on Comprehensively Advancing the Development of a Diversified Financial Dispute Resolution Mechanism,* Fa [2020] No. 27 (19 Nov. 2019).

purposes: reducing expense and the number of cases before the courts, lowering costs and improving efficiency.[19] However, the top-down regulation and structuring of the integrated system, which links it closely to litigation, and the significant role of the courts in supporting the system and setting up the diversified service centres required by the 2019 Opinion, posits a system with a high degree of centralized institutional involvement and influence – if not control – over alternative methods of dispute resolution. This is notwithstanding the potential involvement of third parties in the process. It remains to be seen whether this will be attractive to commercial entities involved in disputes.

At the international level, China has a long-standing interest in mediation, particularly in the context of the BRI, and various Chinese institutions (such as the China Council for the Promotion of International Trade (CCPIT) and Beijing Arbitration Commission/Beijing International Arbitration Commission (BAC/BIAC)) have entered into agreements to promote international mediation and hybrid arbitration/mediation processes.[20] China signed the United Nations Convention on International Settlement Agreements Resulting from Mediation (the Singapore Convention on Mediation) on 7 August 2019.[21] It has not yet ratified the Convention, and it is not clear when it will be in a position to do so.[22] Reasons given for this include the lack of a consistent domestic legislative framework for mediation, the dominance of the courts in Chinese mediation and the traditional reluctance of the commercial sector to utilize mediation prior to litigation or arbitration.[23]

§8.04 ICA DEVELOPMENTS

Commercial arbitration of China-based disputes, both inside and outside China, has traditionally been a popular method of cross-border dispute resolution and this

19. *Supra* n. 15.
20. *See*, e.g., Silk Road Briefing, *Singapore, China Jointly Write Mediation Rules for Belt and Road Arbitration Courts* (22 Feb. 2019), https://www.silkroadbriefing.com/news/2019/02/21/singapore-china-jointly-write-mediation-rules-belt-road-arbitration-courts/ on the Memorandum of Understanding between China Council for the Promotion of International Trade and Singapore's International Mediation Centre to develop BRI Mediation Rules (24 Jan. 2019); Singapore International Mediation Centre, *SIMC Signs MOU with the Beijing Arbitration Commission/Beijing International Arbitration Center (BAC/BIAC)* (15 Oct. 2019), http://simc.com.sg/blog/2019/10/15/simc-signs-mou-with-the-beijing-arbitration-commission-beijing-international-arbitration-center-bac-biac/.
21. UNTS, C.N.155. 2019.TREATIES-XXII.4 of 8 May 2019, status as at: 17 May 2020. *See* generally Strong, Chapter 14 in this volume.
22. *See* comments in Du, *supra* n. 14, on the need to improve the training and professionalism of Chinese mediators; Susan Finder, *Singapore Mediation Convention & China*, Supreme People's Court Monitor (19 Dec. 2019); *Rooting the Singapore Mediation Convention in Chinese Soil* (1 Sep. 2019).
23. Peter Corne & Matthew Erie, *China's Mediation Revolution? Opportunities and Challenges of the Singapore Mediation Convention*, OpinionJuris (28 Aug. 2019), http://opiniojuris.org/2019/08/28/chinas-media-revolution-opportunities-and-challenges-of-the-singapore-mediation-convention/; Susan Finder, *Singapore Mediation Convention & China (2)*, Supreme People's Court Monitor (10 Dec. 2019), https://supremepeoplescourtmonitor.com/?s=mediation+convention; *supra* n. 22.

continues to be the case. The choice of arbitration was historically supported both by the underdevelopment of the court system and by the difficulty of enforcing foreign judgments in China. For foreign-owned enterprises, the Chinese view has been that 'domestic' (as opposed to foreign-related) disputes should be resolved in China.[24] Statistics issued by Chinese arbitral institutions show a continuous increase in both the number of arbitration cases (both domestic and foreign-related) and their value. The China International Economic and Trade Arbitration Commission (CIETAC) 2019 Work Report[25] states that in 2019, CIETAC accepted 2,716 domestic arbitrations (an increase of 11% over 2018) and 617 foreign-related arbitration cases in 2019 (an increase of 18%), of which 66 were between non-Chinese parties. BAC/BAIC saw an increase of 85% in international commercial arbitrations (163, up from 88), of which 18 involved no Chinese parties.[26]

There have been several recent developments regarding improvement of the environment for international commercial arbitration in China and the greater China area. The Arrangement Concerning Mutual Assistance in Court-ordered Interim Measures in Aid of Arbitral Proceedings by the Courts of the Mainland and the Hong Kong Special Administrative Region[27] came into effect on 1 October 2019. This allows parties to arbitration in Hong Kong or China before a qualified arbitral institution[28] to apply to a Chinese (or Hong Kong) court for interim measures (in China, property, evidence and conduct preservation and, in Hong Kong, for preservation orders, injunctions or other interim measures) in support of the Hong Kong or Chinese arbitration. This is the first time that it has been possible for parties to arbitrations outside mainland China to seek preservation measures in Chinese courts, and it has already proven its value. According to the 2019 HKIAC (Hong Kong International Arbitration Centre) statistical report, it has already processed (in 2019) thirteen applications to ten Chinese courts in respect of assets owned by mainland Chinese parties (60%) and by parties from Hong Kong, the Netherlands, British Virgin Islands and Cayman Islands (40%).[29]

24. On the definition of 'foreign-related' matters, *see* SPC, *Interpretation on Certain Issues Concerning the Application of the 'Law of the People's Republic of China on the Application of Laws to Foreign-Related Civil Relations' (I)*, Fa Shi [2012] No. 24 (effective 7 Jan. 2013), Article 1. Note that to be foreign-related, the dispute must involve at least one foreign party or foreign resident (which does not include a Chinese-incorporated subsidiary of a foreign company), or subject-matter or relevant legal facts located outside mainland China. *See*, however, SPC, *Opinion on the Provision of Judicial Safeguards for the Construction of Pilot Free Trade Zones*, Fa [2016] No. 34, Article 9, which allowed wholly foreign owned enterprises registered in the zone to agree to arbitration outside China.
25. *Supra* n. 4.
26. BAC/BIAC, *2019 Annual Report*, http://www.bjac.org.cn/english/news/view?id=3718.
27. HK Department of Justice, https://www.doj.gov.hk/pdf/2019/arbitration_interim_sc.pdf (Chinese version). Implemented in China by SPC, *Arrangements on Mutual Assistance Between the Courts of the Mainland and the Hong Kong Special Administrative Region for Preservation Measures in Arbitration Proceedings*, Fa Shi [2019] No. 14 (effective 1 Oct. 2019). *See also generally* Ali, Chapter 6 in this volume.
28. A list was compiled by the Department of Justice, after applications were made, and lists the Hong Kong International Arbitration Centre, CIETAC Hong Kong Arbitration Centre, ICC Asia Office; Hong Kong Maritime Arbitration Group, South China International Arbitration Centre and eBRAM International Online Dispute Resolution Centre.
29. HKIAC, *2019 Statistics*, https://www.hkiac.org/about-us/statistics.

The SPC has also been active in clarifying other rules relating to commercial arbitration. They include rules dealing with judicial review, the role of the courts, responsibility for review of decisions, the procedure for enforcing awards and grounds for seeking to prevent enforcement of commercial arbitral awards.

The Provisions on Several Issues Concerning the Trial of Cases Involving Judicial Review of Arbitration (Judicial Review Provisions)[30] and the Relevant Provisions on Issues Concerning Report and Verification of Cases Involving Judicial Review of Arbitration (Report and Verification Provisions)[31] deal with applications to a court for enforcement or revocation of an arbitral award. They reaffirm the principle that a decision not to enforce an award involving a foreign country, Macao, Hong Kong or Taiwan, must be ultimately be made by the SPC (Report and Verification Provisions, Article 2). Domestic awards are also subject to the reporting regime, with the relevant People's High Court generally being the responsible court (Article 3). Decisions to enforce an award are generally not subject to judicial review (Article 22, Judicial Review Decisions).

Articles 13 and 14 of the Judicial Review Provisions reiterate the provision of Article 18 of the Law on the Application of Law in Foreign-Related Civil Relations[32] that the law of the arbitration agreement chosen by the parties should govern the arbitration. In the absence of a choice of law, the courts will look to the law of the seat of the arbitration and where the arbitral institution is based, and, where the application of those laws would lead to a different decision on the validity of the arbitration agreements, will apply whichever law renders the arbitration agreement valid.

The Judicial Review Provisions highlight the differences in enforcement regimes between awards issued by foreign tribunals (and thus enforceable under the New York Convention[33] - under Article 16); awards issued by Chinese institutions in foreign-related disputes (section 274 of the Civil Procedure Law[34] - under Article 17) and awards issued by Chinese institutions in non-foreign-related disputes (which may include awards in disputes involving foreign-owned, or partly foreign-owned, Chinese entities) (section 237 of the Civil Procedure Law). The grounds under section 237 are wider than those set out in section 274, which are limited to lack of a written arbitration

30. Fa Shi [2017] No. 22 (26 Dec. 2017; effective 1 Jan. 2018).
31. Fa Shi [2017] No. 21 (26 Dec. 2017; effective 1 Jan. 2018).
32. Standing Committee of the National People's Congress (effective 1 Apr. 2011). *See also* SPC *Interpretation of the Law on the Application of Law in Foreign-Related Civil Relations*, Fa Shi [2012] No. 24 (28 Dec. 2012; effective 7 Jan. 2013).
33. United Nations Convention on the Recognition and Enforcement of Foreign Arbitral Awards (New York, 10 Jun. 1958). A recent decision of the Guangzhou Intermediate People's Court provides some clarity in relation to so-called "mixed" awards (resulting from arbitration in China by a foreign institution) by ordering the enforcement in China of an award rendered by an ICC tribunal in Guangzhou as a foreign—related Chinese award. *Brentwood Industries v Faanlong Complete Engineering* (2020), discussed in Yves Hu and Clarisse von Wunschheim, *Opening of Mainland China Arbitration Market to Foreign Institutions: Is It Happening, Really?* Kluwer Arbitration Blog (24 Sept. 2020), http://arbitrationblog.kluwerarbitration.com/2020/09/24/opening-of-mainland-china-arbitration-market-to-foreign-institutions-is-it-happening-really/.
34. Standing Committee of the National People's Congress, *Civil Procedure Law of the People's Republic of China* (effective 1 Jul. 2017).

agreement; procedural issues related mainly to the composition of the tribunal; the award exceeding the agreed scope and public policy. The grounds in section 237 also include forged evidence, concealment or evidence and embezzlement, bribery or malpractice of the tribunal.

The Provisions on Several Issues concerning the Handling Cases of Arbitration Award Enforcement by People's Courts (Case Handling Provisions)[35] apply to the enforcement of awards and arbitration-mediation award made by arbitration institutions under the (People's Republic of China) PRC Arbitration Law. The SPC has set out the role of the various levels of courts regarding enforcement and clarified the circumstances under which enforcement may be refused. These include lack of clarity of the award (Article 3); the right of a party not involved in the arbitration to challenge enforcement of an award (where, among other things, the parties to the award have 'maliciously applied for arbitration or engaged in fictitious arbitration' – Article 9) and the terms of Article 237(2)(4) and (5) of the Civil Procedure Law, which provide that an award will not be enforceable where the evidence on which it is based is forged or essential evidence has been concealed from the tribunal (Articles 15 and 16).

These three sets of Provisions thus spell out and reaffirm the role of the courts regarding the enforcement and revocation of awards, as well as reiterating the important role of the SPC in relation to foreign awards. They also provide clarification of several issues relating to public policy. A court may consider the social public interest in not enforcing an award even if it is not raised as a ground by the party protesting enforcement (Article 11 Case Handling Provisions). Where there is an application for the *non-enforcement* of an arbitration-mediation award or an arbitral award issued on the basis of a settlement agreement or mediation agreement between the relevant parties the court may not uphold the application unless the award be against the social public interest (Article 17 Case Handling Provisions). Under the Report and Verification Provisions (Article 3), however, even though generally the relevant High People's Court is responsible for examining and verifying a decision by a lower court that an arbitration award is invalid or should not be enforced, in the case of a cross-provincial dispute, *or where the ground for non-enforcement or revocation is the violation of social public interest,* the decision must be referred to the SPC for examination and verification.[36]

§8.05 ONLINE DISPUTE RESOLUTION

Chinese courts and institutions were looking at the provision and improvement of online dispute resolution prior to 2020, but their efforts to advance online dispute resolution services during the COVID-19 epidemic will almost certainly serve as a foundation for the future online handling of disputes. The 2020 Notice of the SPC on

35. Fa Shi [2018] No. 5 (22 Feb. 2018; effective 1 Mar. 2018).
36. On the question of the Chinese approach to the public policy exception, *see* Gu, Chapter 7 in this volume.

Strengthening and Standardizing Online Litigation Work during the Period of Prevention and Control of the Outbreak of Novel Coronavirus Pneumonia[37] urges the expansion of online litigation, while implementing measures to ensure the identification of parties, prompt review of documents and standardization of procedures. Chinese arbitral institutions have also been urged by the Ministry of Justice to strengthen the construction of online arbitration services.[38] Such institutions as CIETAC already have online arbitration rules, but their focus has been on domestic e-commerce and related disputes.[39] Issues relating to cross-border hearings and evidentiary matters are yet to be resolved, but it can be expected that there will be a continued focus on this area from 2020 onwards.[40]

§8.06 NEW OPTIONS FOR DISPUTE RESOLUTION: THE CICC

The CICC was established in 2018 under the Fourth Civil Division of the SPC.[41] It is comprised of the First International Commercial Court (situated in Shenzhen) and the Second International Court (located in Xi-an, Shaanxi Province).[42] Although the stated impetus for the establishment of the court was Belt and Road dispute resolution,[43] the CICC constitutes a permanent court with the purpose of hearing any international commercial disputes. It is comparable with other international commercial courts, such as the Singapore International Commercial Court established in 2015 (SICC) and other international commercial courts which are being established in various formats in Europe, the Middle East and Central Asia.[44]

37. Fa [2020] No. 49 (14 Feb. 2020).
38. Ministry of Justice, *Guidance on Public Service Work on COVID-19 and Enterprises Returning to Work and Production* (3 Mar. 2020), http://www.moj.gov.cn/government_public/content/2020-03/03/tzwj_3243112.html, discussed in Vincent Chow, *China Pushes for Increase in Online Dispute Resolution as It Reboots Economy*, Law.com International Asia-Pacific (19 Mar. 2020), https://www.law.com/international-edition/2020/03/19/china-pushes-for-increase-in-online-dispute-resolution-as-it-reboots-economy/#.
39. *See*, e.g., CIETAC Online Arbitration Rules (current version, 1 Jan. 2015), Article 1, http://www.cietac.org.cn/index.php?m = Article&a = show&id = 2770&l = en.
40. Compare also the Foreword by Hwang, and the concluding chapter by Ali, Reyes & Teramura, Chapter 15 in this volume.
41. SPC, *Regulations on Several Issues Relating to the Establishment of the International Commercial Tribunal*, Fa She [2018] No. 11 (25 Jun. 2018).
42. *See* CICC, http://cicc.court.gov.cn/ (Chinese and English); Susan Finder, *Update on China's International Commercial Court*, Supreme People's Court Monitor (11 Mar. 2018), https://supremepeoplescourtmonitor.com/?s = update + on + China%27s + international; *Comments on China's international commercial courts*, Supreme People's Court Monitor (9 Jul. 2018), https://supremepeoplescourtmonitor.com/?s = comments + on + China%27s + international; China International Commercial Court starts operating (14 Jan. 2019); *Update from #1 China International Commercial Court* (17 Nov. 2019). *See also* Sheng Zhang, *China's International Commercial Court: Background, Obstacles and the Road Ahead*, 11 J. Int'l Disp. Settl. 150 (2020).
43. Li Yang, *China to Set up Belt and Road Commercial Court*, Belt and Road Portal (28 Sep. 2017), https://eng.yidaiyilu.gov.cn/qwyw/rdxw/29380.htm.
44. *See* Warren & Croft Chapter 2 in this volume; Andrew Godwin, Ian Ramsay & Miranda Webster, *International Commercial Courts: The Singapore Experience*, 18 (2) Melb. J. Int'l L. 18 (2017). Also available at SSRN: https://ssrn.com/abstract = 3095059 and generally Marta Requejo, *International Commercial Courts in the Litigation Market*, MPILux Research Paper 2019 (2). Also available at SSRN: https://ssrn.com/abstract = 3327166.

The CICC is intended to be a high-level commercial court with the specialist expertise to handle substantial and complex disputes. It has jurisdiction to hear (1) a first-instance international commercial dispute[45] for an amount exceeding CNY 300 million (USD 42.3 million) where the parties so agree in writing, and there is an actual connection between China and the dispute;[46] (2) a case referred by a High People's Court to the CICC for trial at first instance; (3) first-instance international commercial cases with significant nationwide impact; (4) applications for preservation, cancellation or enforcement of international commercial arbitration awards; and (5) other international commercial cases that the SPC considers should be tried by the CICC. Since the CICC is part of the SPC, there is no appeal from its decisions, other than pursuant to measures on retrials under the 2012 Civil Procedure Law.[47]

The CICC exists within the framework of the Chinese court system, so various features which distinguish such courts as the SICC are not possible in its structure. For example, a feature of the SICC is that it offers a panel of Singaporean and international judges to hear disputes.[48] The CICC panel is comprised exclusively of Chinese judges, although they are highly experienced and senior judges with international backgrounds and language capabilities who serve on the court in addition to their ordinary duties.[49] They are supported by an International Commercial Expert Committee of the SPC, which can advise on foreign law and mediate disputes. The CICC website also offers the unusual additional feature of a 'foreign law ascertainment platform,' which includes links to a range of Chinese centres which offer services for the ascertainment and proof of foreign law.[50] The CICC also allows a party to present evidentiary materials in English without a translation if the other party agrees.[51] (This trend was followed in recent rules issued for the New Lingang Area, which provide that a foreign litigant may intervene in international commercial disputes in English.[52] It is, however, in contrast to the general rule in litigation, recently reaffirmed by the SPC, that evidence in a foreign language must be accompanied by a Chinese translation.)[53]

There have only been a small number of decisions by the court so far, for example, regarding the existence of an arbitration provision in an international

45. Literally 'foreign-related disputes', which are where: one or more parties is a foreigner, foreign company or stateless; one or more parties resides outside China; the subject-matter of the dispute is outside China or the legal facts that produced, altered or eliminated commercial relations occurred outside China (Reg 2).
46. As to the actual connection test in Article 34 of the Civil Procedure Law, *see* Vivienne Bath, *Overlapping Jurisdiction and the Resolution of Disputes Before Chinese and Foreign Courts*, 17 Y.B. Int'l Private L. 111 (2015-2016).
47. Chapter 16, Procedure for Trial Supervision.
48. Godwin, *supra* n. 44.
49. English capability for judges is required by Reg. 4, *supra* n. 41. For further information on the background of the judges, *see* CICC website, *supra* n. 42, 'About the CICC.'
50. CICC website, *Foreign Law Ascertainment Platform*, http://cicc.court.gov.cn/html/1/218/347/.
51. Reg. 9.
52. SPC, *Opinions on Rendering Judicial Services and Guarantee by People's Courts to the Development of the New Lingang Area in China (Shanghai) Pilot Free Trade Zone*, Fa Fa [2019] No. 31, Article II (5) (13 Dec. 2019).
53. SPC, *Provisions of the Supreme People's Court on Evidence in Civil Proceedings*, Fa Shi [2019] No. 19, Article 1 (effective 1 May 2020); Civil Procedure Law, Article 70.

contract and product liability responsibility of an overseas manufacturer.[54] The CICC aims to set an example in terms of transparency through the prompt publication of judgments (in English and Chinese) which can be expected to be highly influential. There is also a range of research and other material relating to Chinese law on its English and Chinese language website.[55]

§8.07 INTERNATIONALIZATION WITH CHINESE CHARACTERISTICS

Recent years have seen a substantial increase in emphasis by Chinese authorities on cross-border disputes. This extends not just to the extension and improvement of current methods of dispute resolution and the creation of new institutions. It also includes an emphasis on international outreach by courts and arbitral institutions, better education of judges and courts in the elements of international and cross-border law attracting cross-border disputes to China, and expanding the use of Chinese law internationally.

Thus, Chinese arbitral institutions have been engaged in a campaign of international engagement and outreach. Both the BAC and CIETAC comment in their annual reports[56] on their participation in UNCITRAL meetings and report in detail on their outreach to different countries and arbitration institutions. CIETAC reports on its engagement in projects, such as research on BRI international arbitration cases and the international arbitration systems of countries along the Belt and Road. Their reports also emphasize the internationalization of their caseload. CIETAC's report states that parties to arbitrations came from 72 countries and regions, with the United Nations Convention on International Contracts for the Sale of Goods (CISG), and the law of Laos, Australia, Cayman Islands, Italy, South Korea and Hong Kong used as the governing law (in addition to Chinese law). The English language (and English and Chinese) was used in 106 of its arbitrations.[57] Notwithstanding this, the participation of foreign arbitrators in CIETAC arbitrations is surprisingly low (75 in 75 different cases), and the number of cases where neither party is Chinese is also relatively small (although increasing).[58] The HKIAC appears to be maintaining its position as the favoured English speaking arbitration institution in greater China, with 80% of its arbitrations conducted in English. Although HKIAC has fewer cases overall (308 new arbitrations in 2019), HKIAC is also the most international of the three institutions, with parties from 56 jurisdictions and 12 different systems of law involved in its

54. (2019) *Zuigao famin* (1), (2) and (3), SPC Civil Rulings; (2019) *Zuigao Fanshang Chu* (1), available at CICC website (in English and Chinese), *Judgments*, http://cicc.court.gov.cn/html/1/219/211/376/index.html.
55. Liu Tingmei, *The China International Commercial Court (CICC) in 2018*, CICC Website (updated 22 Jul. 2019), http://cicc.court.gov.cn/html/1/219/208/209/1316.html.
56. *CIETAC 2019 Work Report*, *supra* n. 4; *BAC/BIAC 2019 Annual Report*, *supra* n. 26.
57. BAC had cases involving twenty-three countries and regions and five cases applying foreign laws or international conventions (Hong Kong, New York, Kyrgyzstan and CISG) but only point to one foreign law case, under Korean law.
58. In CIETAC's case, there were 75 foreign arbitrators involved in 617 foreign-related cases. BAC did not provide a comparable statistic. There were 66 cases involving non-Chinese parties, up 83% from the previous year (36 cases).

arbitrations. In addition, 81% of HKIAC cases involved only one Hong Kong party, and 35% were completely international.[59]

[A] Internationalization of the Chinese Legal System and Chinese Law

Due to the dominance of Chinese construction companies in BRI projects, many cross-border disputes along the Belt and Road are likely to involve a Chinese party. Current developments internationally as a result of the COVID-19 virus may also see an increase in disputes relating to BRI loan contracts.[60] This raises the question not only of the type and location of dispute resolution mechanisms but also the issue of the law governing the contract and the dispute. The 2010 Law on Application of Laws to Foreign-Related Civil Relations makes clear that the parties to a contract generally have the right to choose the law which governs their contracts (subject to a number of exceptions).[61] The Second BRI Opinion supports the use of foreign laws in domestic free trade zones and encourages a better understanding of foreign law by Chinese courts (Article 3(19)). It emphasizes the importance of better education for the Chinese courts in dealing with cases with international or cross-border features, including a better understanding of international treaties and foreign law, and judicial cooperation across borders (Article 3(16)).

It also reiterates existing Chinese policy regarding the expansion of the use of Chinese law in overseas economic and trade zones.[62] A 2017 Opinion jointly issued by the Ministry of Justice and other government departments called not only for active engagement in the provision of legal services regarding transportation, energy and infrastructure projects but also for the use of external legal publicity campaigns to promote understanding of awareness of China's legal system to relevant countries and

59. HKIAC, *supra* n. 29. Laws applied in HKIAC arbitrations included the law of Hong Kong, England, China, New York, Mongolia, Korea, the Philippines, Switzerland, Macau, Russia, Laos and the CISG. *See also generally* Ali, Chapter 6 in this volume. Note also the recently announced establishment of the International Commercial Dispute Prevention and Settlement Organization under the auspices of the CCPIT and CIETAC, to provide arbitration, mediation, investment arbitration and dispute prevention services internationally. Jian Zhang, *International Commercial Dispute Prevention and Settlement Organization: A Quick Overview*, China Justice Observer (15 Oct. 2020), https://www.chinajusticeobserver.com/a/thing-about-international-commercial-dispute-prevention-and-settlement-organization.
60. James Kynge & Sun Yu, *China Faces Wave of Calls for Debt Relief on 'Belt and Road' Projects*, Financial Times (30 Apr. 2020), https://www.ft.com/content/5a3192be-27c6-4fe7-87e7-78d4158bd39b.
61. Article 10 of the SPC Interpretation on the Law on Application of Laws to Foreign-Related Civil Relations (*supra* n. 32) makes clear that certain mandatory provisions of Chinese law will apply regardless of the agreement of the parties: certain laws on labour, food or public safety, environmental safety, financial safety (foreign exchange administration), anti-monopoly or anti-dumping and others recognized as mandatory laws. The Law contains a general exception to the application of foreign laws which would undermine the 'social and public interests' of China (Article 5).
62. Susan Finder, *Supreme People's Court Updates Its Belt & Road Policies*, Supreme People's Court Monitor (28 Jan. 2020), https://supremepeoplescourtmonitor.com/?s=china+updates+its+Belt, citing the 2019 Decision of the Fourth Plenum of the 19th Party Central Committee; Second BRI Opinion, Articles 3(20) and 4(21).

regions, particularly regarding investment, trade, finance and environmental law.[63] The Second BRI Opinion similarly provides that '[I]t is imperative to expand the influence of Chinese laws and release the typical cases adjudicated by Chinese courts in multiple languages to provide a basis for foreign courts and arbitration institutions to correctly understand and apply Chinese laws and increase the understanding and trust that international commercial subjects have in the Chinese laws' (Article 3(20)). The increased use of Chinese law in international loan and infrastructure contracts, particularly when combined with the establishment of the CICC, is also presumably aimed at increasing the use of Chinese courts and institutions regarding cross-border dispute settlement. This would follow the pattern of the internationalization of, for example, English law and English courts over the twentieth century.

[B] The Domestication of ISDS

China has been an active participant in international investment law and ISDS, both at a multilateral level through its participation in UNCITRAL Working Group III, and at a bilateral and plurilateral level through its many bilateral investment treaties (BITs) and, more recently, free trade agreements.[64] In its submission to Working Group III,[65] the Chinese Government identified a number of major issues with the current system of ISDS which it considered should be studied: arbitral awards lack an appropriate error-correcting mechanism; awards lack stability and predictability due mainly to the use of ad hoc tribunals; there are questions relating to professionalism and independence of arbitrators; third-party funding affects the balance of parties' rights; time frames are too long, and costs are too high. The Chinese submission recommended the study of a permanent appellate mechanism; supported the parties' right to choose arbitrators while improving processes for dealing with arbitrator qualifications and conflicts of interest; and favoured examination of a more effective investment conciliation mechanism and pre-arbitration consultation measures (as a compulsory measure); as well as transparency for third-party funding.[66]

63. Ministry of Justice, the Ministry of Foreign Affairs, the Ministry of Commerce & the Legislative Affairs Office of the State Council, *Opinions on Developing the Foreign-related Legal Service Industry* (9 Jan. 2017) (Article 3(4)).
64. Vivienne Bath, *The South and Alternative Models of Trade and Investment Regulation – Chinese Outbound Investment and Approaches to International Investment Agreements*, in *Reconceptualizing International Investment Law from the Global South* (Morosini & Ratton Sanchez Badin eds., Cambridge University Press 2018). *See* UNCTAD, Investment Policy Hub, *International Investments Agreement Navigator, China*, https://investmentpolicy.unctad.org/international-investment-agreements/countries/42/china.
65. UNCTAD, *Possible Reform of Investor-State Dispute Settlement (ISDS): Submission from the Government of China* (19 Jul. 2019), A/CN.9/WG.III/WP.177, https://undocs.org/en/A/CN.9/WG.III/WP.177.
66. On the innovative mediation step that can be required by the host state before the foreign investor can pursue arbitration, under the Indonesia-Australia free trade agreement signed in 2019, and transparency statistics regarding ISDS awards generally, *see* Ubilava & Nottage, Chapter 5 in this volume. (China has not yet signed the Mauritius Transparency Convention.)

From 2017, following a worldwide trend,[67] Chinese arbitration institutions have also taken an interest in ISDS and issued rules which would allow them to hear or conduct ISDS cases (either under a treaty or pursuant to a contractual agreement). The second BRI Opinion (Article 5(32)) also urges support for 'relevant departments' in improving mechanisms and institutions for international investment dispute resolution and the resolution of international investment disputes in a fair and efficient manner. There have also been some calls for the CICC to have the power to hear ISDS cases.[68]

Arbitral institutions providing specifically for investor-State arbitration include the Shenzhen Court of International Arbitration,[69] with rules which provide for arbitration of ISDS disputes under the UNCITRAL Arbitration Rules; CIETAC and, most recently, BAC/BIAC, both of which have issued tailored ISDS Rules.[70] The institutions have attempted to draft ISDS rules of international quality, consistent with international expectations.[71] The CIETAC international arbitration panel also includes a number of well-known international arbitrators.[72] The BAC/BIAC Rules, issued in 2019, respond to a number of the Chinese suggestions to Working Group III, although they also allow parties to choose the UNCITRAL Arbitration Rules for ISDS. In particular, the BAC/BIAC Rules provide for an 'opt-in' appeal process to an appeal tribunal selected from the panel of arbitrators (on the basis of an error of law, manifest error of fact or lack of jurisdiction);[73] party nomination of arbitrators (from within or outside the BAC/BIAC Panel) (Article 9); compliance by arbitrators with 'codes of ethics for arbitrators that are internationally recognized' (Article 8); mediation at any time before the award is made (Article 37) and provision for disclosure of information relating to third-party funding arrangements (Article 39). Perhaps unsurprisingly, given that so few underlying investment treaties require mediation before arbitration, the Rules do not attempt to incorporate pre-arbitration conciliation procedures or requirements.

It does not appear that any of the Chinese arbitral institutions have received any ISDS cases (in contrast with the HKIAC, which has had two).[74] There are several important issues regarding ISDS in China. First, it is not clear whether the Chinese Government itself would (or could) waive immunity to have an ISDS dispute decided

---

67. Joe Zhang, *China's Largest Arbitration Institution Adopts Its First Investment Arbitration Rules* (28 Sep. 2017), IISD, https://www.iisd.org/blog/china-s-largest-arbitration-institution-adopts-its-first-investment-arbitration-rules.
68. Sheng Gang, *supra* n. 42.
69. SCIA Arbitration Rules (2019) (replacing the 2016 Rules which were in the same form), Article 2(2). http://120.25.66.138/files/fckFile/file/SCIA%20Arbitration%20Rules%20(effective%20from%20Feb_%2021,%202019).pdf.
70. CIETAC International Investment Arbitration Rules (for trial implementation) (effective 1 Oct. 2017), http://www.cietac.org/index.php?m=Page&a=index&id=390&l=en; BIAC Rules for International Investment Arbitration (effective 1 Oct. 2019), http://www.bjac.org.cn/.
71. *See*, however, criticisms of the CIETAC Rules in Sheng Zhang, *supra* n. 42.
72. CIETAC, *International investment Panel of Arbitrators* (1 Sep. 2018), http://cietac.org.cn/Uploads/201809/5ba34355a410e.pdf.
73. *Ibid.*, Article 46 and Appendix E, Rules of Appeal Proceedings for International Investment Arbitration.
74. HKIAC, *2018 Statistics*, https://www.hkiac.org/about-us/statistics. Administered under the UNCITRAL Arbitration Rules, with one seated in Hong Kong and the other seated outside Hong Kong. *See also* Ali, Chapter 6 in this volume.

before a Chinese arbitral institution, and, secondly, it is far from clear whether and how an ISDS award can be enforced against (or in) China in any event, given its stated views on sovereign immunity and the fact that China has entered an exception to the New York Convention on the Recognition and Enforcement of Arbitral Awards limiting enforcement to commercial awards.[75] (The Shenzhen Court of International Arbitration (SCIA) and CIETAC have both attempted to deal with this, to some extent, by nominating Hong Kong as the default seat.)[76]

The Chinese domestic discussion in relation to attracting ISDS disputes to Chinese venues attempts to strike a balance between establishing China as an internationally competitive venue for ISDS and promoting the protection of Chinese interests. For example, the explanatory notes to the ISDS rules provided by CIETAC and the BAC include statements to the effect that being able to have investor-state disputes heard under the auspices of a Chinese arbitration institution would provide protection for Chinese investors (particularly in countries along the Belt and Road where legal risks are high),[77] as well as providing a venue with a better understanding of Chinese law. It is not completely clear, given the attempt to draft internationally acceptable ISDS Rules, why an arbitration under the auspices of CIETAC or BAC/BAIC would result in a better understanding of Chinese law or better protection of Chinese investors than a tribunal appointed under the ISDS Rules. In contrast to the (International Centre for Settlement of Investment Disputes) ICSID Rules, both sets of rules do, however, appear to allow the appointment of one arbitrator of the nationality of each party (which would allow for the appointment of a Chinese arbitrator), even though the chair and/or majority of arbitrators must be of a nationality other than that of either party.[78]

An important question is whether a hearing in China or under the auspices of a Chinese arbitral commission would be attractive to a foreign sovereign state, particularly if the aggrieved investor was a Chinese state-owned enterprise – even if the law governing the dispute was Chinese. As noted above, the aim here appears to be to attract international disputes to China and to stake China's claim to be a major player or 'lawmaker' in international investment law.[79]

75. Meng Chen, *Embracing Non-ICSID Investment Arbitration? The Chinese Perspective*, 39 Nw. J. Int'l L. & Bus.249 (2019), https://scholarlycommons.law.northwestern.edu/njilb/vol39/iss3/1,268, 279 et seq.
76. *Ibid*; *Shenzhen Court of International Arbitration Guidelines for the Administration of Arbitration under the UNCITRAL Arbitration Rules*, Article 3; CIETAC Investment Arbitration Rules, Article 28.
77. *See* CIETAC, *Explanatory Note for CIETAC Arbitration Rules (for Trial Implementation)* (in Chinese), http://cietac.org.cn/index.php?m=Article&a=show&id=14469, Article 1(1).
78. The ICSID Arbitration Rules (Article I, 1(3)) provide that in the case of a three party panel, a party cannot appoint an arbitrator of the same nationality without the consent of the other party, http://icsidfiles.worldbank.org/icsid/icsid/staticfiles/basicdoc/partf-chap01.htm; CIETAC Rules Article 11(3); BAC/BIAC Rules Article 9(3).
79. *Supra* n. 77. Compare generally also Vivienne Bath & Luke Nottage, *International Investment Agreements and Investor-State Arbitration in Asia*, Sydney Law School Research Paper No. 20/08 (26 Feb. 2020), available at SSRN: https://ssrn.com/abstract=3544458.

[C] Unresolved Issues Affecting Cross-Border Dispute Resolution: Chinese Private International Law

An important issue in the process of expanding options and mechanisms for cross-border dispute resolution is the liberalization of Chinese rules of private international law – dealing with the jurisdiction of courts, conflicts of law and enforcement of judgments. There have been some significant recent changes in approach at the judicial level, but in the absence of legislative initiatives, China's private international law regime continues to present several major roadblocks to its program of internationalizing dispute resolution.

Chinese private international law rules are located in a number of different laws. Choice of law rules are generally found in the Law on the Application of Law in Foreign-Related Civil Relations;[80] while laws on such matters as choice of courts, recognition and enforcement of judgments and the jurisdiction of courts are found in the Law on Civil Procedure and the Interpretation of the SPC on the Law of Civil Procedure[81] and other interpretations and opinions of the SPC. There have been significant governmental policy decisions in this area, particularly China's signature of the 2005 Hague Convention on Choice of Court Agreements[82] and the 2018 Singapore Convention on Mediation. Yet the shaping of private international law rules in China to accommodate policies regarding cross-border dispute resolution has been very much left to the SPC, which must work within – and is limited by – the existing legislative framework.

There are several outstanding issues which continue to present issues for cross-border dispute resolution. The first of these is the question of recognition and enforcement of foreign judgments. The basic principle in Chinese law has for a considerable period been that foreign judgments will be enforced only if there is a bilateral judicial assistance agreement or there is reciprocity in terms of enforcement (which has been interpreted to mean that a party seeking to enforce a foreign court judgment in China must show that a foreign court from the relevant jurisdiction has recognized and enforced an equivalent Chinese jurisdiction).[83] The long-standing difficulty of enforcing a foreign judgment in China when compared to China's regime for enforcement of arbitral awards under the New York Convention is an important factor supporting a choice of arbitration rather than litigation in cross border disputes involving Chinese companies.[84] It has also enabled Chinese parties to use as a tactical

80. *Supra* n. 32.
81. SPC, *Interpretations on the Application of the Civil Procedure Law of the People's Republic of China*, Fa Shi [2015] No. 5 (effective 4 Feb. 2015).
82. Convention of 30 June 2005 on Choice of Court Agreements (entered into force 30 Jun. 2005), https://www.hcch.net/en/instruments/conventions/full-text/?cid = 98.
83. Law of Civil Procedure, Articles 281 and 282. Chinese courts do not currently accept as a basis for reciprocal treatment evidence that under the law governing a particular court system, it will recognize foreign judgments. *See* Tu Guangjian, *Private International Law in China* 170-4 (Springer 2016).
84. *See* Guodong Du & Meng Yu, *List of China's Cases on Recognition of Foreign Judgments* (16 Jul. 2019), https://www.chinajusticeobserver.com/a/list-of-chinas-cases-on-recognition-of-foreign-judgments, in which the authors have attempted to collect all cases in which judgments have

defence in a foreign court the anticipated unenforceability of the court's judgment in China.[85]

The increase in Chinese outbound investment and migration of Chinese nationals, along with their China-related disputes, has contributed to the increasing number of cases in which Chinese judgments are presented for enforcement in foreign courts.[86] Conversely, the increased activity of Chinese companies and Chinese expatriates outside China will undoubtedly lead to an increase in foreign judgments brought to Chinese courts for recognition and enforcement. In the context of the BRI and the expected increase in cases involving Chinese companies, both aspects of enforcement are potentially significant. A system where Chinese judgments can be enforced outside China, but foreign judgments cannot be enforced inside China has always been difficult to justify and is now becoming more difficult to sustain. As a result, the establishment of a consistent and effective system for the enforcement of foreign judgments in China is becoming increasingly urgent.

This issue was not addressed in the 2012 (or 2017) revision of the Law on Civil Procedure, Articles 281 and 282 of which provide for recognition and enforcement either on the basis of an international treaty or in accordance with the principle of reciprocity. There has, however, been a good deal of discussion at all levels on the need for an improvement in Chinese rules regarding foreign judgments. There are several ways in which this can be done. As noted above, Chinese courts currently recognize judgments on the basis that an equivalent foreign court has recognized a Chinese judgment, thus requiring the enforcing party to produce such a judgment. Considerable publicity has been given to a small number of judgments of Chinese courts which recognized judgments from Germany, Singapore and the United States.[87] Alternatively, Chinese courts (and others) could adopt the concept of 'anticipatory' reciprocity, whereby the Chinese courts would assume that the relevant foreign court would enforce a Chinese judgment without asking for evidence that it has already done so. The Nanning Statement of the 2nd China-ASEAN Justice Forum[88] supported the adoption of this approach, albeit in a very cautious fashion. This was followed in 2018 by a non-binding and descriptive Memorandum of Guidance between the SPC and the Supreme Court of Singapore on the recognition and enforcement of money judgments

---

been enforced in China (and vice versa) and conclude that only a very small number of foreign judgments have been presented to the Chinese courts for enforcement, with a very low enforcement rate.

85. *See* e.g., argument in *Impala Warehousing and Logistics (Shanghai) Co Ltd v. Wanxiang Resources (Singapore) Pte Ltd* [2015] EWHC 811 (Comm).

86. *Supra* n. 84. In Australia, there have been four recent cases relating to the recognition and enforcement of judgment: *Xu v. Wang* [2019] VSC 269 (refused – abuse of process); *Bao v. Qu; Tian (No 2)* [2020] NSWSC 588 (judgment enforced); *Suzhou Haishun Investment Management Co Ltd v. Zhao & Ors* [2019] VSC 110 (judgment enforced); *Liu v. Ma* [2017] VSC 810 (judgment enforced).

87. *See* Du, *supra* n. 84.

88. Reproduced at China Justice Observer, *Nanning Statement of the 2nd China-ASEAN Justice Forum* 第二届中国-东盟大法官论坛南宁声明 (signed 8 Jun. 2017), https://www.chinajusticeobserver.com/p/nanning-statement-of-the-2nd-china-asean-justice-forum. The forum was hosted by the SPC and attended by high level court officials of ASEAN countries. Note that judges in these countries do not necessarily enjoy the effective legislative power of the SPC.

in commercial cases, which set out the process for enforcement without reference to a requirement for reciprocity to be shown.[89] (Since this follows a number of cases in which Singaporean and Chinese courts have mutually enforced judgments, it can also be argued that reciprocity has already been demonstrated.)[90]

The SPC also addressed the issue of enforcement in both the First BRI Opinion and the Second BRI Opinion. In particular, Article 19 of the Second BRI Opinion mentions in general terms, the adoption of measures to facilitate enforcement and recognition of foreign judgments, while Article 24 adopts the presumption of reciprocity in relation to the enforcement and recognition of judgments of international commercial courts. The long-awaited Interpretation by the SPC on this issue does not, however, appear in the Judicial Interpretation Program for 2020/2021.[91] In the absence of an interpretation - or, better still, a legislative initiative - progress on this issue continues to be slow.[92]

Steps have, however, been taken to facilitate enforcement between Hong Kong and China. The Arrangement on Reciprocal Recognition and Enforcement of Judgments in Civil and Commercial Matters by the Courts of the Mainland and of the Hong Kong Special Administrative Region[93] was signed in January 2019. It expands on - and will, when it comes into force, replace[94] - the existing arrangement for the enforcement of judgments where jurisdiction was taken in accordance with an exclusive choice of court agreement.[95] The new arrangement will apply only to civil and commercial judgments (Article 3) (which do not include preservation measures, anti-suit injunctions or orders for interim relief (Article 4)). There is a range of exceptions, such as cases on the confirmation or validity of arbitral awards and cases on the recognition and enforcement of judgments or arbitral awards of other countries or regions (Article

89. Available at Singapore Supreme Court website, https://www.supremecourt.gov.sg/docs/default-source/default-document-library/spc-mog-english-version---signed.pdf.
90. Toh Kian Sing, Yu Zheng & Anssen Yang, *A Significant Step for Enforcement of Money Judgments in Commercial Cases Between Singapore and China*, SICC News No. 14 (October 2018), https://www.sicc.gov.sg/docs/default-source/modules-document/media-resources/sicc-news-no-14_1c3a840f-6102-4606-8b5d-c22c52edddbf.pdf.
91. Susan Finder, *Supreme People's Court's 2020 Judicial Interpretation Agenda*, Supreme People's Court Monitor (2 Apr. 2020), https://supremepeoplescourtmonitor.com/category/judicial-interpretations/.
92. For a more optimistic analysis, *see* Jie (Jeanne) Huang, *Reciprocal Recognition and Enforcement of Foreign Judgments in China: Promising Developments, Prospective Challenges and Proposed Solutions*, 88 Nordic J. Int'l L. 250 (2019), also available at SSRN: https://ssrn.com/abstract=3359349.
93. Department of Justice (Hong Kong), https://www.doj.gov.hk/eng/public/pdf/2019/Doc3_477379e.pdf (not in force).
94. *Ibid.*, Article 30.
95. Arrangement on Reciprocal Recognition and Enforcement of Judgments in Civil and Commercial Matters by the Courts of the Mainland and of the Hong Kong Special Administrative Region Pursuant to Choice of Court Agreements between Parties Concerned, 2006, amended 2008; Hong Kong Department of Justice, https://www.doj.gov.hk/eng/mainland/pdf/mainlandrej20060719e.pdf. Effective pursuant to Mainland Judgments (Reciprocal Enforcement) Ordinance (Cap. 597) and SPC, *Interpretation on the Arrangement on Reciprocal Recognition and Enforcement of Judgments in Civil and Commercial Matters by the Courts of the Mainland and of the Hong Kong Special Administrative Region Pursuant to Choice of Court Agreements Between Parties Concerned*, issued 12 Jun. 2006, [2008] No. 9.

3). The purpose of this is to exclude the possibility that foreign litigants may seek to obtain recognition and enforcement in China of awards or judgments obtained outside Hong Kong. Article 11 of the Memorandum sets out a number of criteria in relation to recognition: there must be a connection between the requesting court (if it does not have exclusive jurisdiction over the case) and the defendant (such as a residence or an office or branch in the requesting place) or the dispute (place of performance of the contract in the requesting place or infringing act in the requesting place in the case of a tort), or submission in the form of a written jurisdiction agreement or by appearance. However, if all the parties to the dispute reside in the requested state, there must be a connection between the subject matter of the dispute and the requesting court. This would prevent Chinese parties from litigating purely Chinese disputes in Hong Kong and then enforcing the judgment in China (and vice versa).

At the international level, the Hague Convention on Recognition and Enforcement of Foreign Judgments, which aims to create a uniform set of basic rules on the recognition and enforcement of civil or commercial judgments, was concluded on 2 July 2019.[96] China was an active participant in the negotiations on this Convention but has not signed it. As of 3 July 2020, only Uruguay and Ukraine had signed the Convention, and it has not entered into force. The view has been expressed that the Convention reflects China's wish to establish efficient dispute resolution mechanisms for the Belt and Road.[97] However, it is not clear at this early stage whether the Convention will succeed, or when (and whether) China will accede to it.

Other unresolved issues in this area are the Chinese approach to jurisdiction and proceedings running in parallel with similar or identical proceedings in foreign courts. This arises in a number of contexts for several reasons. First, under the Law of Civil Procedure, a court must have a 'substantial connection' with a case or its parties before its jurisdiction can be recognized.[98] This limitation is both unusual and restrictive in the context of international multi-party commercial disputes. In view of the current objective of attracting cases to Chinese institutions, it also potentially operates to the disadvantage of Chinese courts, most of which are subject to the same jurisdictional limitation and cannot hear cases unless the significant connection test is satisfied. If China proposes to be the forum for BRI cross-border disputes of all kinds, not just those which involve Chinese parties, there will have to be changes to this policy.

As mentioned, China has signed the Convention on Hague Choice of Court Agreements, under which Chinese courts would be obliged to recognize the choice of court agreements and recognize and enforce any resulting judgment. Implementation will require a change to the current rules to require recognition of the parties' choice of a neutral forum if this is in a state which is party to the Convention. China has not yet

96. Hague Conference on Private International Law (HCCH), https://www.hcch.net/en/instruments/conventions/full-text/?cid = 137. *See also generally* Ali, Reyes & Teramura, Chapter 15 in this volume.
97. Guodong Du & Meng Yu, *China and HCCH Judgments Convention in 2019* (27 Jul. 2019), https://www.chinajusticeobserver.com/a/china-and-hcch-judgments-convention-in-2019.
98. Bath, *supra* n. 46.

ratified this Convention, although it does already have a similar arrangement with Hong Kong.[99]

A related issue is the question of parallel proceedings. China is a civil law jurisdiction, and a Chinese court with jurisdiction over a dispute under its own rules will therefore accept a case even if there is a concurrent foreign proceeding, or even a foreign judgment unless the foreign judgment has been recognized in a Chinese court.[100] In recent years, Chinese courts have developed a concept of forum non conveniens, pursuant to which they may refuse to hear a case.[101] In practice, the doctrine is very restricted, and cases where it has been applied to reject a case in favour of a foreign (or Hong Kong) court are few.[102] There does not seem to be a move towards resolving this particular issue, although the Hong Kong Memorandum provides that a requested court must refuse to enforce a judgment if the underlying case was brought in the requesting court after a court in the requesting state had accepted an action on the same dispute or a court of the requested place had rendered a judgment or recognized a foreign judgment on the same dispute.

In summary, China's system of private international law continues to be relatively inward-looking regarding jurisdiction and enforcement. Notwithstanding developments in relation to judicial cooperation, Chinese courts are still more inclined to call on concepts of judicial sovereignty than ideas of international judicial comity.[103]

§8.08 CONCLUSION

Recent years have seen several significant new developments in China in relation to cross-border dispute resolution. There has been a high level of activity regarding judicial reform, and a large number of judicial interpretations and regulations issued by the SPC directed at modifying and improving the operation of the courts, improving the process of judicial review and enforcement of arbitral awards and the creation of the CICC. Changes are designed primarily to reinforce and to improve the existing system while positioning dispute resolution within the context of larger policy objectives, such as the BRI. When these are combined with an increased emphasis on international judicial cooperation through the Second Belt and Road Opinion, international outreach by Chinese arbitral institutions and courts and the increased participation of Chinese negotiators in international discussions in UNCITRAL and the WTO, an image is presented of an outgoing, internationally responsive and responsible Chinese judicial and arbitration system.

These initiatives, however, have both positive and negative aspects. The positive aspects - such as the establishment of the CICC, the clarification of procedures regarding the review and enforcement of arbitration decisions, as well as initiatives to

99. *Supra*, n. 95.
100. SPC Interpretation on the Application of the Civil Procedure Law, Article 531.
101. *Ibid.*, Article 532.
102. King Fung Tsang, *China's Rule of Law from a Private International Law Perspective*, 47 Ga. J. Int'l & Comp. L. 93 (2018).
103. Bath, *supra* n. 46.

improve judicial cooperation with Hong Kong courts and arbitral institutions – represent welcome improvements for litigants and others engaged in China-related disputes. Similarly, the emphasis on the integration of litigation, arbitration and mediation into a system of diversified dispute resolution potentially offers more flexible ways to resolve international business disputes, with prospects for stronger and faster enforcement.

The negative aspects are, first, the determinedly China-focused approach to dispute resolution represented by these changes; second, the potential institutionalization of the integrated dispute resolution mechanism; and third, the relationship between the courts, dispute resolution institutions or mechanisms and the CCP.

The Chinese view of cross-border dispute resolution (regarding Belt and Road and other international disputes) increasingly contemplates an increased international role for Chinese law and attracting disputes to China, for which purpose the establishment of credible courts, improvement of existing institutions and better rules on enforcement are essential. Thus, while looking to the outside world, the focus of recent developments is not just to build up the expertise, organization and capability of Chinese organizations, but strongly to encourage the use of Chinese law, Chinese courts, Chinese arbitral institutions and Chinese mediation. While there have been developments which should materially assist with enforcement of foreign arbitral awards, reforms to facilitate reciprocal treatment of foreign court judgments in China, recognition of the parties' choice of foreign fora and limitation of parallel proceedings before foreign and Chinese courts – all of which would require Chinese courts to focus more on judicial comity than judicial sovereignty – are slow in coming. While there is nothing unusual in China's desire to build up its ability to deal with disputes and make itself internationally attractive as a dispute settlement centre, the next step in building up a truly internationalized system should be to build a mutually supportive relationship with foreign courts and legal systems.

Secondly, while the integrated dispute mechanism system offers efficiency and a number of other benefits, it potentially involves the integration of institutions as well as dispute resolution methods, with both the courts and arbitral institutions moving into the mediation area and leaving the role of independent third-party mediators unclear and undefined.

Thirdly, changes to the judicial and dispute resolution system, are, as one would expect, largely driven by domestic considerations and under the shadow of ever tighter political control over the courts and the judicial system within China itself. The emphasis on internationalization, rule of law safeguards, judicial professionalism, expansion and development of dispute resolution methods, protection of rights and application of international rules co-exist with – and must be read in the context of – ever-increasing pressure on the courts and judges to be ideologically committed, subject to the leadership of the Party and its political and judicial inspection mechanisms – to implement CCP policy at both a macro and micro level. This stress between judicial expertise and political conformity is unlikely to change and raises serious ongoing questions about the separation of commercial dispute resolution and Chinese political objectives.[104]

104. Jiangyu Wang, *The [Chinese Communist] Party in China's Legislature and Judiciary*, in *The Chinese Communist Party in Action: Consolidating Party Rule* 181-98 (Lance L.P. Gore & Zheng Yongnian eds., Routledge 2020). Also available at SSRN: https://ssrn.com/abstract=3600636. *See also supra* n. 11.

CHAPTER 9

Malaysia's Involvement in International Business Dispute Resolution

A. Vijayalakshmi Venugopal

Malaysia has had some early but comparatively limited involvement in formally resolving trade disputes, but more engagement in investor-state dispute resolution – including as a home state for investors bringing claims, not just as a host state respondent. Some companies in Malaysia and its main international arbitration centre have also been involved in domain name dispute resolution. That centre and some other organisations have long promoted various types of Alternative Dispute Resolution (ADR), with renewed efforts in recent years to develop new procedures and attract more international commercial arbitrations. Malaysia has also been quite active in negotiating free trade agreements (FTAs). This creates a solid platform to continuing becoming more of a rule-maker in international investment law as well as a significant regional hub for international business dispute resolution services, although Malaysia still has a way to go in both respects compared to larger Asia-Pacific economies and/or more established hubs.

§9.01 INTRODUCTION

This chapter presents an overview of international business dispute resolution cases involving Malaysia. Malaysia's commitments to international organisations and agreements have resulted in Malaysia being subject to actual and potential international business dispute resolution cases, as well as the nation or its investors initiating some others. Malaysia has also been renewing efforts to become a popular regional seat for international commercial arbitration, not only involving Malaysian parties. This is not a definitive discussion of the broad range of such cases but illustrates some of the issues and contexts arising from Malaysia's involvement in international business dispute resolution.

Overall, Malaysia has had some early but comparatively limited involvement in formally resolving trade disputes, but more engagement in investor-state dispute resolution – including as a home state for investors bringing claims, not just as a host state respondent. Some companies in Malaysia and its main international arbitration centre have also been involved in domain name dispute resolution. That centre and some other organisations have also long promoted various types of ADR, with renewed efforts in recent years to develop new procedures and attract more international commercial arbitrations. Malaysia has also been quite active in negotiating FTAs. This creates a solid platform to continuing becoming more of a rule-maker in international investment law as well as a significant regional hub for international business dispute resolution services, although Malaysia still has a way to go in both respects compared to larger Asia-Pacific economies and/or more established hubs.

§9.02 MALAYSIA'S ACTUAL INVOLVEMENT IN INTERNATIONAL BUSINESS DISPUTE RESOLUTION

Malaysia's actual involvement in international business dispute resolution is approached from two perspectives. One involves actual international business dispute resolution cases that Malaysia has been a party to. The second focuses on significant organisations and enforcement provisions in Malaysia, promoting this country as a venue for international business dispute resolution cases.

[A] Malaysia as a Party in International Business Dispute Resolution Cases

Malaysia has been a party in reported international business dispute resolution cases under the World Trade Organization (WTO), in Investor-State Dispute Settlement (ISDS) cases, and under the World Intellectual Property Organization (WIPO). There are not many such cases, but these cases relate to various WTO agreements as a complainant, respondent or third party; investment rights and obligations; and domain name dispute cases as a complainant and respondent.

[1] The World Trade Organization

Malaysia has been a member of the WTO since it came into operation from 1 January 1995, and a member of the General Agreement on Tariffs and Trade (GATT) since 24 October 1957.[1] Since being a member, Malaysia has appeared as:

- a complainant in one WTO case (DS58);
- a respondent in one WTO case (DS1); and
- a third party in twenty-four WTO cases.

1. World Trade Organization, *Malaysia and the WTO*, https://www.wto.org/english/thewto_e/countries_e/malaysia_e.htm.MITI.

As the complainant, Malaysia was one of the earliest Member States to initiate proceedings in the WTO. It joined India, Pakistan and Thailand (with multiple third parties)[2] in the well-known WTO case of *United States – Import Prohibition of Certain Shrimp and Shrimp Products* (DS58). The complainants challenged the United States' ban on importing shrimp and shrimp products from them. This ban applied unless the United States State Department certified that the exporting country minimised the adverse effect of commercial fishing tools on sea turtles.[3]

The Appellate Body decided that this ban was related to the conservation of exhaustible natural resources under Article XX(g), but could not be justified under this Article as it constituted 'arbitrary and unjustifiable' discrimination under the main part of Article XX. It had a 'coercive' effect on WTO members, and its application was rigid and not transparent. Malaysia was not satisfied with the United States amended the law to comply with this decision. The original panel in Article 21.5 (US-Shrimp (Article 21.5 – Malaysia) (DS58)) determined that the United States made serious efforts in good faith to negotiate an international agreement and permit other WTO members to have 'comparably effective' fishing techniques with the United States. The Appellate Body and Dispute Settlement Body (DSB) endorsed the panel's findings.

As a respondent, Malaysia also engaged early on in WTO dispute settlement by contesting a complaint brought by Singapore: *Malaysia – Prohibition of Imports of Polyethylene and Polypropylene* (DS1). Singapore alleged that Malaysia's ban on importing polyethylene and polypropylene under the Malaysian Customs (Prohibition of Imports) (Amendments) (No. 5) Order 1994 violated various provisions under GATT 1994. No other member appeared as a third party in this case. Malaysia amended its import licensing measures for polypropylene and polyethylene products. The WTO was notified that the parties reached a mutually agreed solution, and Singapore withdrew its complaint.

It is unclear why Malaysia has been involved in so few WTO dispute cases. For example, Malaysia has been involved more than Singapore (one WTO case as complainant and none as respondent),[4] but less than Thailand (fourteen WTO cases as complainant and four as the respondent).[5] Abbott has remarked that it was unclear why developing countries generally did not make more complaints to the WTO. Although there is no rule requiring developed and developing countries to be equally involved in WTO disputes, any country's involvement in such disputes can depend on the '... the perceived importance of the problem, the motivation and the circumstances'.[6]

---

2. Australia, Canada, Colombia, Costa Rica, European Communities, Ecuador, El Salvador, Guatemala, Hong Kong, China, Japan, Mexico, Nigeria, Philippines, Senegal, Singapore, Sri Lanka, Venezuela, Bolivia, Pakistan and Thailand.
3. Sea Turtles and Section 609, https://www.state.gov/wp-content/uploads/2019/04/Section-609-One-Pager.pdf.
4. WTO, *Singapore and the WTO*, https://www.wto.org/english/thewto_e/countries_e/singapore_e.htm.
5. WTO, *Thailand and the WTO*, https://www.wto.org/english/thewto_e/countries_e/thailand_e.htm.
6. Roderick Abbott, *Are Developing Countries Deterred from Using the WTO Dispute Settlement System? Participation of Developing Countries in the DSM in the Years 1995-2005*, ECIPE Working

Malaysia has also appeared as a third party, reserving its third-party rights, in twenty-four WTO cases. Of these cases:

- six appear to be independent cases - DS38, DS442, DS456, DS473, DS526 and DS536;
- two cases involve the United States' safeguard measures on the imports of crystalline silicon photovoltaic products - DS545 and DS562;
- five cases involve Australia's measures concerning trademarks and other plain packaging requirements applicable to tobacco products and packaging - DS434, DS435, DS441, DS458 and DS467 (which also generated ISDS proceedings, rejected on jurisdiction grounds in 2015, as mentioned in Chapter 1 of this volume);
- nine cases involve the United States' measures on steel and aluminium products - DS544, DS547, DS548, DS550, DS51, DS552, DS554, DS556 and DS564; and
- two cases involve the United States challenging the Russian Federation's additional duties on certain products from the United States - DS566 and DS585.

Of the six seemingly independent cases, the principal parties were mostly different. None of the complainants was common, nor were the complainants common with the respondents. The respondents were also different between the cases except for two cases involving the United States as the common respondent (DS38 and DS536). Of the latter two cases with the common respondent, though, the subject matter was different, as was the WTO agreements alleged to be violated, except for GATT.[7] Further, the subject matter of the case (measure in issue) and WTO agreements alleged to be violated were different in three of these six cases:

- DS38 involved restrictions on goods and visas for people of Cuban origin under the United States' trade sanctions against Cuba alleged to violate GATT and GATS;
- DS456 involved domestic content requirements on solar cells & modules alleged to violate GATT and TRIMs (the Agreement on Trade-Related Investment Measures); and
- DS526 involved measures involving trade in goods and services, as well as related intellectual property rights, alleged to violate GATS, GATS and (Trade-Related Aspects of Intellectual Property Rights) TRIPS.

Paper No. 01/2007, 1, 14 (2007), https://ecipe.org/wp-content/uploads/2014/12/are-developing-countries-deterred-from-using-the-wto-dispute-settlement-system.pdf.

7. DS38 involved restrictions on goods and visas for people of Cuban origin under US' trade sanctions against Cuba, that were alleged to violate GATT and GATS. However, DS536 involved anti-dumping measures on the imports of fish fillets and other legal instruments, alleged to violate GATT, the Anti-Dumping Agreement (ADA), the Dispute Settlement Understanding (DSU), the WTO Agreement and Vietnam's Protocol of Accession.

The other three cases all involved anti-dumping measures alleged to violate GATT and ADA (Anti-Dumping Agreement) - although:

- DS442 related to imports of certain fatty alcohols;
- DS473 related to imports of biodiesel, with the additional alleged violation of the WTO Agreement; and
- DS536 related to the imports of fish fillets and other legal instruments, with additional alleged violations of the WTO Agreement, Vietnam's Protocol of Accession and the DSU.

However, the common issue of anti-dumping measures in these cases hardly seems typical of cases where Malaysia appeared as a third party for two reasons. First, these are the only cases among the twenty-four cases where Malaysia appeared as a third party involving anti-dumping measures and the ADA. Second, these three cases represent a very small percentage of the total WTO dispute cases involving the ADA (133 cases).[8]

In relation to the two WTO cases involving the United States' safeguard measures on the imports of crystalline silicon photovoltaic products, the respondent in both cases was the United States, but the complainant in the cases was different. The Republic of Korea was the complainant in DS545, while China was the complainant in DS562. However, each case did not refer to the other in the summary of the case report, as in the related cases discussed below, these were the only two cases involving crystalline silicon photovoltaic products.[9] However, the only other cases among the twenty-four cases involving safeguard measures were the nine cases involving the United States' measures on steel and aluminium products discussed below, and sixty-two cases cited the Agreement on Safeguards as being violated.[10] Therefore, it would appear that the crystalline silicon photovoltaic products were more relevant to Malaysia's interest rather than the Agreement on Safeguards (Safeguards).

Five of the cases related to various Member States challenging Australia's *Tobacco Plain Packaging Act 2011* and related laws requiring tobacco products to be sold in uniform plain packages contrary to rights of trademark owners. This was alleged to violate various Articles in the WTO's GATT, Agreement on Technical Barriers to Trade (TBT) and TRIPS. In these cases, Ukraine, as the complainant, requested the panel to suspend its work to work out a mutually agreeable solution and did not request the panel to resume its work before the panel's jurisdiction lapsed (DS434). In the other four cases, the complainants were Honduras (DS435), the Dominican Republic (DS441), Cuba (DS458) and Indonesia (DS467). The panel gave a joint report for these cases.[11] The reports for Indonesia and Cuba were adopted by the

8. WTO, *Disputes by Agreement (as Cited in Request for Consultations)*, https://www.wto.org/english/tratop_e/dispu_e/dispu_agreements_index_e.htm.
9. WTO, *Index of Disputes Issues*, https://www.wto.org/english/tratop_e/dispu_e/dispu_subjects_index_e.htm?id=G233.
10. WTO, *Disputes by Agreement (as Cited in Request for Consultations)*, https://www.wto.org/english/tratop_e/dispu_e/dispu_agreements_index_e.htm.
11. WTO, *Australia - Tobacco Plain Packaging (DS435, 441, 458, 467)*, https://www.wto.org/english/tratop_e/dispu_e/cases_e/1pagesum_e/ds435sum_e.pdf.

DSB, but appealed for Honduras and the Dominican Republic on 23 August 2018, with those appeals still pending as of May 2020 due to the collapse of the WTO Appellate Body (discussed in Chapter 11 of this volume). The panel found that the complainants generally failed to adequately prove the violations alleged.[12]

Of the nine cases involving the United States' measures on steel and aluminium products, all these cases involved alleged violations of GATT and Safeguards. All these cases also included alleged violations of the WTO Agreement except for DS544, DS547 and DS554. Canada and Mexico reached a mutually agreeable solution with the United States in DS550 and DS551, respectively. However, China, India, the European Union, Norway, the Russian Federation, Switzerland and Turkey are still awaiting the panel's report in DS544, DS547, DS548, DS552, DS554, DS556 and DS564.

Of the two cases involving the United States challenging the Russian Federation's additional duties on certain products from the United States (DS566 and DS585), the panel's report is not yet published. Of the expressly related cases discussed above, this is the only series of cases where Malaysia was not a third party in all the cases in the series. In the two cases involving the United States' safeguard measures on the imports of crystalline silicon photovoltaic products, as stated above, although these cases were not cross-referred to each other in the summaries on the WTO website, these were the only two cases involving these products. The five cases involving Australia's measures concerning trademarks and other plain packaging requirements applicable to tobacco products and packaging were cross-referred to each other in the summaries, as were the nine cases involving the United States' measures on steel and aluminium products.

The two cases involving the United States challenging the Russian Federation's additional duties on certain products from the United States were part of a series of cases that were cross-referenced to each other in the summaries. The United States challenged additional duties on certain products from the United States imposed by Canada in DS557, China in DS558, the European Union in DS559, Mexico in DS560 and Turkey in DS561. However, Malaysia did not appear as a third party in these other five cases. Since the summaries state the products involved in these cases as 'certain products', presumably, only the products involved in the first two cases affected Malaysia's interest.

Despite Malaysia being a member of the WTO since 1 January 1995,[13] Malaysia seems to only have been involved in WTO member disputes as a third party once in 1996,[14] six times in 2012,[15] twice in 2013,[16] once in 2017,[17] and fourteen times in

12. *See generally* e.g., Tania Voon, *Third Strike: The WTO Panel Reports Upholding Australia's Tobacco Plain Packaging Scheme*, 20 J. World Inv. & Trade 146 (2019), also available at https://ssrn.com/abstract=3275074.
13. WTO, *Members and Observers*, https://www.wto.org/english/thewto_e/whatis_e/tif_e/org6_e.htm.
14. DS38.
15. DS442 and in the five cases involving Australia's plain packaging issue (DS434, DS435, DS441, DS458 and DS467).
16. DS456 and DS473.
17. DS526.

2018.[18] As a third party, it would then seem that Malaysia is far more active in recent years, which unfortunately is also related to thirteen of the twenty-four cases having a panel constituted, but the panels' reports not being published yet.[19] In the other eleven cases:

- the parties in two cases requested the panel to suspend its work and did not ask the panel to resume its work before the panel's authority lapsed;[20]
- the parties reached a mutually agreeable solution in two cases;[21]
- the panel found that the complainant failed to prove the violations alleged in four cases;[22]
- the respondent was found to have committed some of the breaches alleged in two cases, and the respondent informed the DSB that it intended to fully comply with the findings,[23] or the appellant was satisfied with the respondent's amended Regulations to comply with the panel's findings in one of these cases;[24] and
- the respondent was found guilty of the breaches alleged in one case and the complainant applied for authorisation to retaliate as the respondent failed to comply with the findings (this matter being referred to the original panel).[25]

The WTO agreements alleged to have been violated in these twenty-four cases were:

- GATT – in all twenty-four cases;[26]
- Safeguards – in eleven cases;[27]
- WTO Agreement (Agreement Establishing the World Trade Organization) – in eight cases;[28]
- TRIPS – in six cases;[29]
- TBT – in five cases;[30]

18. DS536, DS545, DS562, in the nine cases involving the United States' measures on steel and aluminium products (DS544, DS547, DS548, DS550, DS551, DS552, DS554, DS556 and DS564), and the two cases involving the United States challenging the Russian Federation's additional duties on certain products from the United States (DS566 and DS585).
19. DS526, DS536, DS545, DS562, seven of the nine cases involving the United States' measures on steel and aluminium products (except for DS550, DS551) and the two cases involving the United States challenging the Russian Federation's additional duties (DS566 and DS585).
20. DS38 and DS434 (1 of the series of five cases involving Australia's plain packaging laws).
21. DS550 and DS51 (2 in the series of nine cases involving the United States' measures on steel and aluminium products).
22. The remaining four cases involving Australia's plain packaging laws – DS435, DS441, DS458 and DS467.
23. DS442.
24. DS473.
25. DS456.
26. DS38, DS434, DS435, DS441, DS442, DS456, DS458, DS467, DS473, DS526, DS536, DS544, DS545, DS547, DS548, DS550, DS551, DS552, DS554, DS556, DS562, DS564, DS566 and DS585.
27. DS545, DS562, DS544, DS547, DS548, DS550, DS51, DS552, DS554, DS556 and DS564.
28. DS473,
29. DS526, DS434, DS435, DS441, DS458 and DS467.
30. DS434, DS435, DS441, DS458 and DS467.

- ADA - in three cases;[31]
- GATS - in two cases;[32]
- TRIMs - in one case;[33]
- DSU - in one case;[34] and
- Vietnam's Protocol of Accession - in one case.[35]

These may appear to be a broad range of Agreements, but they are still limited in comparison to a total of sixty WTO agreements.[36] Overwhelmingly, though, as a major exporter, Malaysia's interest as a third party has been affected by the members' trade in goods (GATT). The number of cases involving some of the other Agreements may be misleading as it is affected by the same agreements being relevant to series of cases rather than separate cases, such as Safeguards being involved in the series of nine cases related to the United States' measures on steel and aluminium products and only two of the other cases.

[2] *Investor-State Dispute Settlement*

Malaysia has been involved in four ISDS cases as a claimant and three cases as a respondent.[37] The earliest case involving Malaysia as a home state of the investor was in 2001 in *MTD Equity Sdn. Bhd. and MTD Chile S.A. v. Chile.*[38] This case involved a bilateral investment treaty (BIT) between Chile and Malaysia signed in 1992. The claimant wanted to construct a residential and commercial complex in Chile. It challenged the Chilean Government's denying a zoning modification necessary for the claimant to construct the residential component of the project. The claimant alleged that Chile breached various provisions of this IIA, including:

- indirect expropriation;
- fair and equitable treatment in terms of the minimum standard of treatment, including denial of justice; and
- arbitrary, unreasonable and/or discriminatory measures.

The parties took their dispute to arbitration conducted by the International Centre for Settlement of Investment Disputes (ICSID). The claimant claimed USD 20 million. The arbitration panel decided in the investor's favour on the second breach alleged above and awarded USD 5.8 million in 2004. This decision was upheld in 2007 in ICSID annulment proceedings.

31. DS442, DS473, DS536,
32. DS38 and DS526.
33. DS456, DS536, DS548, DS550, DS51, DS552, DS556 and DS564.
34. DS536.
35. DS536.
36. WTO, *WTO Legal Texts*, https://www.wto.org/english/docs_e/legal_e/legal_e.htm.
37. UNCTAD, *Investment Dispute Settlement Navigator*, https://investmentpolicy.unctad.org/investment-dispute-settlement.
38. ICSID Case No. ARB/01/7.

The next case involved Malaysia as the home state of an investor, which is noteworthy because Asian investors have been relatively few and late in initiating ISDS cases (as mentioned in Chapter 1 of this volume). The case was brought was in 2003: *Telekom Malaysia Berhad v. The Republic of Ghana.*[39] This dispute involved the Ghana-Malaysia BIT signed in 1996. The investor challenged the government's decision to invite a tender for the management of Ghana's national telecommunication company rather than renewing the investor's telecommunications management contract of this company. The Permanent Court of Arbitration was meant to hear the dispute using the United Nations Commission on International Trade Law (UNCITRAL) arbitration rules. However, this became unnecessary as the dispute was settled between the parties for an undisclosed sum. The case is also noteworthy because it involved government-linked companies on both sides but was run under the ISDS provisions rather than the inter-state arbitration provision also found in the BIT. The governments' interests in the case nonetheless may have facilitated the settlement.[40]

The third case involving an investor from Malaysia came in 2011: *Ekran Berhad v. People's Republic of China.*[41] It related to two BITs, namely, between China and Malaysia in 1988 and between China and Israel in 1995. The investor challenged the government's revocation of the investor's local subsidiary company's rights to a seventy-year leasehold over 900 hectares of land in Hainan province. The government's revocation was allegedly based on the investor's local subsidiary company failing to develop the land as required under local legislation. The ICSID was meant to hear this dispute, but again, the case was settled for an undisclosed sum - this time, even before a panel was constituted. As per ICSID's Arbitration Rule 43(1), the Secretary General issued an order noting the proceeding's discontinuance on 16 May 2013. This claim also drew considerable attention as one of the first and still few ISDS claims brought against China.[42]

The final case involving an investor from Malaysia so far was commenced in 2018: *KLS Energy Lanka Sdn. Bhd. v. Democratic Socialist Republic of Sri Lanka,*[43] under the Malaysia-Sri Lanka BIT of 1982. The investor invested in a wind and solar hybrid power plant renewable energy project and challenged the government's cancellation of this project. The dispute is still pending before the ICSID.

Malaysia was also a respondent in three ISDS cases. The earlier two cases involved the same parties and the same BIT, but different subject matter. The first was in 1994 - *Philippe Gruslin v. Malaysia (I),*[44] under the BLEU (Belgium-Luxembourg

39. PCA Case No. 2003-03.
40. On patterns in settlements following commencement of ISDS arbitrations, compare generally Ana Ubilava, *Amicable Settlements in Investor-State Disputes: Empirical Analysis of Patterns and Perceived Problems*, J. World Inv. & Trade (2020), also available at: https://ssrn.com/abstract=3352181.
41. ICSID Case No. ARB/11/15.
42. *See* generally Bath, Chapter 8 in this volume; and Vivienne Bath & Luke Nottage, *International Investment Agreements in Asia*, in *Handbook of International Investment Law and Policy* (Julien Chaisse, et al. eds., Springer 2020), also available at: https://ssrn.com/abstract=3544458.
43. ICSID Case No. ARB/18/39, UNCTAD, *KLS Energy v. Sri Lanka*, https://investmentpolicy.unctad.org/investment-dispute-settlement/cases/922/kls-energy-v-sri-lanka.
44. ICSID Case No. ARB/94/1.

Economic Union)-Malaysia BIT (1979).The dispute related to the construction sector.[45] The dispute was meant to be before the ICSID, but the parties settled the dispute for an undisclosed sum before the ICSID decided on liability. Under the ICSID's Arbitration Rule 43(1), the arbitrator made an order noting discontinuance on 24 April 1996.

The second case arose in 1999 – *Philippe Gruslin v. Malaysia (II)*, under the same BIT.[46] The claimant from Belgium alleged that the Malaysian government breached the treaty by imposing exchange controls, causing losses in the claimant's investment of securities listed on the Kuala Lumpur Stock Exchange. The claimant claimed USD 2.3 million. The ICSID sole arbitrator agreed by the parties (a former Solicitor-General of Australia, Gavan Griffiths QC) decided in 2000 that it lacked the jurisdiction to hear the case regarding portfolio investment, so found in favour of the respondent. ICSID annulment proceedings were discontinued in 2002.

The final case arose in 2005: *Malaysian Historical Salvors Sdn. Bhd. v. Malaysia*,[47] under the Malaysia-United Kingdom (UK) BIT (1981). The claimant from the UK alleged that the claimant was not owed money under a salvage contract with Malaysia relating to a British vessel that sank in Malaysian waters in 1817. The claimant alleged that this debt arose from the sale of items recovered from the cargo of that ship. The claimant claimed damages of USD 3 million. The claimant alleged that the BIT was breached in a number of ways, including indirect expropriation, unfair and inequitable treatment or minimum standards of treatment, and failing to provide full protection and security. The ICSID arbitrator (Michael Hwang SC from Singapore) also found a lack of jurisdiction by finding that the business venture did not have sufficient characteristics of an 'investment'. However, the decision was instead annulled in its entirety in ICSID annulment proceedings in 2009.[48]

The Arbitration Institute of the Stockholm Chamber of Commerce commented that a 'majority of ISDS cases' are governed by the ICSID, with the 'second-largest group of ISDS cases' being governed by UNCITRAL Arbitration Rules.[49] This is reflected by the dispute settlement bodies in the ISDS cases discussed above involving Malaysia, by an even wider margin. Six out of the seven cases were to be heard by the ICSID, and one case was to be heard by the Permanent Court of Arbitration using the UNCITRAL arbitration rules.

45. No further details are provided regarding the issues in the dispute.
46. ICSID Case No. ARB/99/3.
47. ICSID Case No. ARB/05/10.
48. *See* further Govert Coppens, *Treaty Definitions of 'Investment' and the Role of Economic Development: A Critical Analysis of the Malaysian Historical Salvors Cases*, in *Foreign Investment and Dispute Resolution Law and Practice in Asia* 174-91 (Vivienne Bath & Luke Nottage eds., Routledge 2011).
49. Arbitration Institute of the Stockholm Chamber of Commerce, *ISDS Investor-State Dispute Settlement Factsheet, Arbitration Institute of the Stockholm Chamber of Commerce* 2 (2016), https://sccinstitute.com/media/148946/investor-state-dispute-settlement-isds-_a5_ny-framsida.pdf.

As of 31 December 2019, out of the 1,023 known treaty-based ISDS cases, 674 were concluded, 343 were pending, and six were unknown. Out of the 674 concluded cases:[50]

- 246 (36.5%) were decided in the state's favour;
- 198 (29.4%) were decided in the investor's favour;
- 139 (20.6%) were settled by the parties;
- 77 (11.4%) were discontinued; and
- 14 (2.1%) were not decided in favour of either party – was a finding of liability, but no damages were awarded.

For the seven ISDS cases involving Malaysia, three (42.9%) cases were settled,[51] one decision (14.3%) was declined due to a lack of jurisdiction so resulted in the state's favour,[52] one decision (14.3%) on a lack of jurisdiction was annulled,[53] one investor (14.3%) was awarded USD 5.8 million,[54] and one case (14.3%) is still pending.[55] Nearly half of these cases, then, were settled by the parties themselves, but after being registered under a DSB.

Focusing on the four cases involving a Malaysian investor against different countries, two (50%) were settled between the parties,[56] one (25%) is still pending,[57] and one (25%) was decided in the investor's favour.[58] As such, the majority of these cases were settled. Focusing instead on the three cases involving Malaysia as a respondent, two involved the same Belgian investor and one involved a UK investor. Each of these cases had a different result – one (33.3%) was settled,[59] one (33.3%) was declined due to a lack of jurisdiction so resulted in the state's favour,[60] and one decision (33.3%) on a lack of jurisdiction was annulled.[61] Considering whether Malaysia has been found to be upholding its obligations under BITs, not many ISDS disputes have been initiated and out of those that have, the results are varied. The total results (seven cases) and results by the party (four and three respectively) do not quite follow the patterns of the 674 concluded ISDS cases mentioned above, though this may be misleading due to the small number of ISDS cases involving Malaysia.

50. UNCTAD, *Investment Dispute Settlement Navigator*, https://investmentpolicy.unctad.org/investment-dispute-settlement/country/127/malaysia/.tab-respondent.
51. *Telekom Malaysia Berhad v. The Republic of Ghana* (PCA Case No. 2003-03), *Ekran Berhad v. People's Republic of China* (ICSID Case No. ARB/11/15) and *Philippe Gruslin v. Malaysia (I)* (ICSID Case No. ARB/94/1).
52. *Philippe Gruslin v. Malaysia (II)* (ICSID Case No. ARB/99/3).
53. *Malaysian Historical Salvors Sdn. Bhd. v. Malaysia* (ICSID Case No. ARB/05/10).
54. *MTD Equity Sdn. Bhd. and MTD Chile S.A. v. Chile* (ICSID Case No. ARB/01/7).
55. *KLS Energy Lanka Sdn. Bhd. v. Democratic Socialist Republic of Sri Lanka* (ICSID Case No. ARB/18/39).
56. *Telekom Malaysia Berhad v. The Republic of Ghana* (PCA Case No. 2003-03) and *Ekran Berhad v. People's Republic of China* (ICSID Case No. ARB/11/15).
57. *KLS Energy Lanka Sdn. Bhd. v. Democratic Socialist Republic of Sri Lanka* (ICSID Case No. ARB/18/39).
58. *MTD Equity Sdn. Bhd. and MTD Chile S.A. v. Chile* (ICSID Case No. ARB/01/7).
59. *Philippe Gruslin v. Malaysia (I)* (ICSID Case No. ARB/94/1).
60. *Philippe Gruslin v. Malaysia (II)* (ICSID Case No. ARB/99/3).
61. *Malaysian Historical Salvors Sdn. Bhd. v. Malaysia* (ICSID Case No. ARB/05/10).

Nonetheless, Malaysia has been an early and quite active participant in ISDS proceedings, compared to most other Asian states, and the decisions reached have arguably made significant contributions to the development of international investment law. These experiences have also arguably influenced the drafting not only of Malaysia's investment treaties but also those of the Association of Southeast Asian Nations (ASEAN).[62]

[3] The World Intellectual Property Organization

The World Intellectual Property Organization (WIPO) is a global forum for intellectual property (IP) services, policy, information and cooperation, established in 1967 as part of the United Nations by the WIPO Convention.[63] Malaysia joined the WIPO by accession on 1 October 1988 (in effect from 1 January 1989).[64] Malaysia has acceded to many significant WIPO instruments.[65]

The WIPO Arbitration and Mediation Center provides mechanisms to resolve internet domain name disputes, without the need for litigation in courts. The centre has used the WIPO-initiated Uniform Domain Name Dispute Resolution Policy (UDRP) to process over 46,000 cases.[66] A search of WIPO domain dispute cases involving a party from Malaysia[67] as a complainant showed one case (D2019-3139). There were two cases displayed where a party from Malaysia was a respondent (D2014-0344 and D2019-2862). However, in one of these cases, the complainant was also from Malaysia.

In the three cases involving parties from Malaysia, the parties from Malaysia were complainants in two of the cases (D2019-3139 and D2014-0344) and the respondents were also parties from Malaysia in two cases (D2014-0344 and D2019-2862). All these cases were decided by sole panellists. In two of the cases, the panellists were satisfied with the complainant's evidence and ordered the disputed domain name to be transferred to the respondent (D2019-3139 and D2019-2862), and in the remaining case, the complaint was denied (D2014-0344).

The most interesting and relevant case of the three, although the second is also noteworthy for an unsuccessful claim by one of Malaysia's biggest companies,[68] concerns a Malaysian entity complaining successfully against an American individual recently: *Asian International Arbitration Centre (Malaysia) v. Mark Nowak*

62. Sufian Jusoh, et al., *Malaysia and Investor-State Dispute Settlement: Learning from Experience*, in *International Investment Treaties and Arbitration Across Asia* 216-42 (Luke Nottage & Julien Chaisse eds., Brill | Nijhoff 2018).
63. WIPO, *Inside WIPO, What Is WIPO?*, https://www.wipo.int/about-wipo/en/.
64. WIPO, *WIPO-Administered Treaties, Contracting Parties > WIPO Convention (Total Contracting Parties: 193) > Malaysia*, https://www.wipo.int/treaties/en/ShowResults.jsp?treaty_id = 1& country_id = 124C.
65. WIPO, *WIPO-Administered Treaties, Contracting Parties > Malaysia*, https://www.wipo.int/treaties/en/ShowResults.jsp?country_id = 124C.
66. WIPO, *WIPO ADR, Domain Name Dispute Resolution*, https://www.wipo.int/amc/en/domains/.
67. WIPO, *Search WIPO Cases and WIPO Panel Decisions*, https://www.wipo.int/amc/en/domains/search/.
68. *Genting Berhad v. DomainsByProxy.com / Hans Kam, Nature Malaysia*, Case No. D2014-0344.

(D2019-3139).[69] This dispute concerned the domain name of <klrca.org> that was registered with Go Canada Domains Inc. The complainant filed this complaint with the WIPO Arbitration and Mediation Center on 19 December 2019. The WIPO Arbitration and Mediation Center confirmed that the respondent was the registrant of this domain name and notified the respondent of this complaint. These proceedings began on 9 January 2020. The respondent did not respond to the complaint, so a sole panellist was appointed to hear the dispute.

The complainant is an arbitration centre that was established in 1978, formerly named the Kuala Lumpur Regional Centre for Arbitration (KLRCA). The complainant registered the domain name <klrca.org> on 11 June 2013. The complainant changed its name to the Asian International Arbitration Centre (AIAC) on 28 February 2018. Even as at 25 November 2019, <klrca.org> was used for the complainant's home page, a logo consisting of a device and acronym 'klrca', the name 'Kuala Lumpur Regional Centre for Arbitration' and a description of the complainant having over twenty-five years' experience in arbitration.

The panellist was satisfied that the complainant discharged its burden of proving the following on a balance of probabilities under paragraph 4(a) of the UDRP. First, the disputed domain name was identical or confusingly similar to a trademark in which the complainant has rights. Although the complainant's trademark application was still pending at the time of this case, the complainant established common law rights in the term 'klrca' from the extensive use of this acronym as a trading name and logo since 1978. Although the complainant changed its name in 2018 to AIAC, the complainant still retained residual goodwill in its former name from the duration and extent of previous use that still applied at the date of the complaint. The respondent did not file any response to object to the complainant's trademark right. Accordingly, 'klrca' was found to be identical to the complainant's common law rights in the KLRCA trademark and confusingly similar to the corresponding logo.

Second, under the UDRP, the respondent had no rights or legitimate interests in respect of the disputed domain name. The panellist found that if a complainant establishes a prima facie case that the respondent lacks rights or legitimate interests, the respondent then bears the burden of proof to show that he has rights or legitimate interests in the domain name. If not, the complainant is deemed to have satisfied the second element. Here, the complainant did not authorise the respondent to use its trademark. The respondent is found to have used the 'klrca' domain name to intentionally attempt to attract, confuse and profit from internet users seeking the complainant's products and services. It was not a bona fide use of the domain name. The respondent did not provide any evidence of any other legitimate reason to use the domain name. As such, the complainant established a prima facie case of the respondent's lack of legitimate interest in the domain name, which the respondent has not disproved.

Third, the disputed domain name had been registered and was being used in bad faith. It was unclear if the respondent used the domain name to promote actual

69. *Asian International Arbitration Centre (Malaysia) v. Mark Nowak*, Case No. D2019-3139.

arbitration services or for some fraudulent purpose. However, the respondent clearly registered the disputed domain name with the complainant in mind since the respondent used the full version of the complainant's name on its website to obviously impersonate the complainant. Additionally, the respondent had not disputed the complainant's assertions of bad faith or offered any alternative motivation to use the domain name. Accordingly, the respondent was found to have registered and used the domain name in bad faith. The respondent intentionally attempted to attract internet users to its website for commercial gain by creating a likelihood of confusion with the complainant's trademark. Thus, on 24 February 2020, the panellist ordered that the disputed domain name <klrca.org> be transferred to the complainant.

A party from Malaysia was a respondent in two domain name dispute cases in WIPO. The first was *Genting Berhad v. DomainsByProxy.com / Hans Kam, Nature Malaysia* (D2014-0344)[70] relating to <gentinghighlands.info>. The panellist concluded on 26 May 2014 on this 'finely balanced case' that the complaint should be denied. The respondent was using the domain name to provide information on the complainant's services as a travel destination. In the second case, *Trivago N.V. v. tri-vago Malaysia, Myinfo Asia* (D2019-2862)[71] relating to <tri-vago.com>, the panellist ordered the disputed domain name transferred to the complainant on 5 February 2020. The respondent was providing similar services as the complainant using a confusingly similar domain name without the complainant's permission.

The respondent replied to the complaint in the only case among these three cases where the complaint was denied. Unless the complaint lacks a rational and evidential basis, the panellist may not have an alternate version of the arguments to consider if the respondent does not reply to the complaint.

In addition, Malaysia's involvement in this form of dispute resolution comes through the AIAC managing the Asian Domain Name Dispute Resolution Centre (ADNDRC) since October 2009.[72] The ADNDRC is one of four providers of dispute resolution services relating to disputed generic top-level domain names (gTLDs) authorised by ICANN and the only one in Asia. The AIAC has also been appointed by the Malaysian Network Information Centre (MYNIC) to handle '.my' domain name disputes. On 26 February 2015, The Brunei Darussalam Network Information Centre Sdn Bhd (BNNIC) appointed the AIAC 2015 as t\administrator of all disputes involving the registration or use of .bn (the Brunei country-code top-level domain name).[73] Apart from using the UDRP and UDRP Rules to settle domain name disputes like WIPO, the ADNDRC also uses:[74]

70. *Genting Berhad v. DomainsByProxy.com / Hans Kam, Nature Malaysia*, Case No. D2014-0344.
71. *Trivago N.V. v. tri-vago Malaysia, Myinfo Asia*, Case No. D2019-2862.
72. AIAC, *ADNDRC*, https://www.aiac.world/Domain-Name-Complaints-ADNDRC.
73. AIAC, *DNDR*, https://www.aiac.world/Domain-Name-Complaints-DNDR.
74. AIAC, *Domain Name Dispute Resolution*, https://www.aiac.world/Domain-Name-Dispute-Resolution-Domain-Name-Dispute-Resolution.

- the ADNDRC Domain Name Dispute Supplemental Rules;
- the MYNIC's Domain Name Dispute Resolution Policy (MYDRP), the MYDRP Rules and AIAC Supplemental Rules for disputes involving '.my' domain names; and
- my Domain Registry's Sensitive Name Dispute Resolution Policy (SNDRIP), SNDRIP Rules and AIAC Supplemental Rules for disputes involving '.my' sensitive domain names ('.my' domain names containing sensitive words under the SNDRIP).

[B] Malaysia as a Venue for International Business Dispute Resolution

Malaysia has been quite actively promoting itself as a centre for ADR through organisations focusing on ADR and laws facilitating the reciprocal enforcement of arbitral awards generally, and court judgments from various specified countries. Several organisations promote the awareness of and support the use of ADR, especially the AIAC for arbitration. Malaysia has reciprocal arrangements for enforcement with specific countries under domestic law and international agreements, but these arrangements do not extend to every country or every form of ADR.

[1] Malaysian Organisations Focused on ADR

The main organisations focused on ADR in Malaysia discussed here are the AIAC, the Chartered Institute of Arbitrators (CIArb) (Malaysia Branch) and the Malaysian Institute of Arbitrators (MIArb). The AIAC offers more services related to ADR, including the types of ADR, procedures for ADR hearings, institutional rules and support services. CIArb (Malaysia Branch) focuses more on educating and training of its arbitrators but is part of a broader global (originally UK-based) network. The MIArb also focuses on awareness and training, has institutional rules, provides a forum for ADR hearings and is no longer limited to arbitration but promotes other forms of ADR.

There are many organisations available to act as centres for international arbitration. UNCITRAL provides an illustrative list of over fifty such organisations having links to the UNCITRAL Arbitration Rules.[75] One of these centres is AIAC, before 2018 known as the KLRCA. The AIAC has over forty years of experience in dispute resolution. Providing logistical support for ad hoc arbitrations under the UNCITRAL Rules for Arbitration (as revised in 2013), the AIAC also has developed a suite of its own procedural rules:[76]

- the AIAC Arbitration Rules;
- the AIAC Fast Track Arbitration Rules;

---

75. UNCITRAL, *Arbitration Centres*, https://uncitral.un.org/en/texts/arbitration/contractualtexts/arbitration/centres.
76. AIAC, *Towards a New Decade*, Newsletter #01, 1, 2 (April 2020), https://admin.aiac.world/uploads/ckupload/ckupload_20200416030824_94.pdf.

- the AIAC i-Arbitration Rules (discussed further below);
- the AIAC Mediation Rules; and
- the AIAC Supplemental Rules for UDRP.

The Asian-African Legal Consultative Organization (AALCO) established the KLRCA in Malaysia in 1978. In terms of international links:[77]

- the AIAC held over 30 international conferences and 250 events between 2010 to 2018;
- the AIAC is the only official Court of Arbitration for Sports (CAS) alternative hearing centre in Asia;
- the AIAC's Mediation Rules 2018 are based on the (International Bar Association) IBA Rules for Investor-State Mediation;
- the AIAC is an alternative hearing avenue to the WIPO for domain name dispute resolution regionally and globally – additionally, the AIAC is the Kuala Lumpur Office of the ADNDRC and the exclusive dispute resolution service provider for '.my' and '.bn' disputes;
- the AIAC is an alternative hearing venue for ICSID cases; and
- the AIAC's Arbitration Rules are largely based on the UNCITRAL Arbitration Rules.

The AIAC was the first arbitral institution to have Shariah-compliant arbitration rules (the i-Arbitration Rules). These Rules were launched on 20 September 2012 and came into effect on 9 March 2018. The Rules are suitable for the arbitrations of commercial transactions premised on Islamic principles, such as enabling a tribunal to award a late payment charge determined by the Islamic principles of *ta'widhand gharamah*. The Rules also permit the arbitral tribunal to refer to a Shariah Advisory Council or a Shariah expert on a point related to Shariah principles.[78] The KLRCA received the voter-based Global Arbitration Review Award for 'Innovation by An Individual or Organisation in 2012' for these Rules.[79]

The AIAC now has extensive facilities suitable for dispute resolution hearings. It has twenty-one hearing rooms, twelve breakout rooms, a business centre, a library, an auditorium and multiple dining areas. Some of the rooms offer court recording and transcription (CRT) services capable of video capture, Smart Voice-Tracking microphones and automated Audio-to-Text transcription for ease of user interface. The current building covers 16,430 square metres and is a national heritage site.[80]

77. Arbitration Association, *International Arbitrator Prof. Sundra Rajoo, Ex-Director of AIAC (KL-RCA) in Malaysian Kuala Lumpur, Meets Arbitration.ru*, Arb. J. (20 Jun. 2019), https://journal.arbitration.ru/interview/international-arbitrator-prof-sundra-rajoo-ex-director-of-aiac-klrca-in-malaysian-kuala-lumpur-meets/.
78. *Ibid*: AIAC, *Frequently Asked Questions*, https://www.aiac.world/Frequently-Asked-Questions.
79. AIAC, *KLRCA Wins Global Recognition*, https://www.aiac.world/news/16/KLRCA-Wins-Global-Recognition.
80. AIAC, *Bangunan Sulaiman*, https://www.aiac.world/bangunan-sulaiman.

The AIAC received 3,075 ADR cases in arbitration, adjudication, mediation and domain name dispute resolution from 2010 to 2018.[81] The AIAC received 915 ADR cases in 2018 alone. Forty-two decisions were made on domain name disputes involving '.my' between 2003 and 2020.[82] However, in terms of arbitration cases specifically, the KLRCA received:[83]

- twenty-two arbitrations (twenty domestic and two international arbitrations) in 2010;
- fifty-two arbitrations (forty-nine domestic and three international arbitrations) in 2011;
- one hundred and thirty-five arbitrations (one hundred and eighteen domestic and seventeen international arbitrations) in 2012;
- one hundred and fifty-six arbitrations (one hundred and twenty-eight domestic and twenty-eight international arbitrations) in 2013; and
- one hundred and twelve arbitrations (eighty domestic and thirty-two international arbitrations) in 2014.

Lam Wai Loon[84] credited the improved efficiency of the Malaysian judicial system and the creation of the statutory adjudication regime in the Construction Industry Payment & Adjudication Act 2012 for construction payment disputes with the decreasing number of arbitrations submitted to the KLRCA in more recent years. AIAC has administered over 1,400 adjudication cases, with 2017 recording the highest number – of the 932 cases in 2017, 700 disputes related to construction.[85]

The AIAC has been actively growing as an ADR centre. Though currently more involved in domestic arbitrations and adjudications of construction payment disputes, the AIAC is positioning itself as a centre for international commercial arbitration as well. With various institutional rules based on international rules, being an official alternative hearing venue for other international arbitration organisations in general and for specialised fields, having modern facilities catering for dispute resolution hearings, extensive experience in dispute resolution cases and a growing national and international reputation, the AIAC has been well-positioned to make an even more active contribution to international arbitration dispute resolution.

Sundra Rajoo was a previous director of the AIAC from 1 March 2010, credited as being an active proponent of the centre.[86] He is also credited as being a very visible

81. AIAC, *Committed to the Road Ahead*, Annual Report 2018, 2 (2018), https://admin.aiac.world/uploads/ckupload/ckupload_20191023032658_26.pdf.
82. AIAC, *DNDR*, https://www.aiac.world/Domain-Name-Complaints-DNDR.
83. KLRCA, *KLRCA: Acknowledging the Past, Building the Future* 96 (KLRCA ed., KLRCA 2015).
84. Lam Wai Loon, *Arresting the Crisis of Confidence in Arbitration – a Malaysian Perspective* 128 (Vijay K. Bhatia, Maurizio Gotti, Azirah Hashim, Philip Koh, & Sundra Rajoo ed., Taylor & Francis 2017).
85. AIAC, *Adjudication*, https://www.aiac.world/Adjudication-Adjudication; AIAC, *Construction Sector Sees a Higher Number of Dispute Cases*, https://www.aiac.world/news/252/Construction-sector-sees-a-higher-number-of-dispute-cases.
86. Lam Ko Luen refers to him as 'the man responsible for re-branding KLRCA and putting it on the global map ... actively promoting arbitration as a form of alternative dispute resolution with

representative of the centre, even in international circles.[87] However, he resigned as director on 21 November 2018.[88] A familiar figure in arbitration circles, Vinayak P. Pradhan, succeeded him until his untimely demise on 8 March 2020.[89] It becomes the next director's responsibility to continue leading the AIAC towards making a greater impact on international dispute resolution.

CIArb (Malaysia Branch) is part of an international network of CIArb organisations with over 16,000 ADR practitioners in 149 countries.[90] The Branch is a non-profit organisation with a mandate to '... promote alternative dispute resolution (ADR) as a mode to resolve commercial disputes efficiently.' It has 430 members in Malaysia. The services offered include providing education and training on ADR and recommending procedures relating to ADR to promote international and domestic commercial arbitration.[91]

MIArb was established in 1991 mainly to promote arbitration, but (like AIAC) has since expanded its objectives to encourage other forms of ADR, such as mediation and adjudication. Like the CIArb (Malaysia Branch), the MIArbis also a non-profit and non-governmental organisation, educating the public and running training programs for its members.[92] The MIArb has its own Arbitration Rules[93] and Mediation Rules[94] for parties to adopt. It also provides a forum for private settlement of disputes through ADR.[95]

[2] Enforceability of Awards, Settlements and Judgments

There are provisions made for particular international business dispute resolution awards and judgments to be enforced in Malaysia, but not yet for cross-border settlement agreements.

KLRCA as the centre of choice within the region': Lam Ko Luen, *Arbitration Reform in Malaysia: Adopting the Model Law* 123, 125 (Anselmo Reyes & Weixia Gu ed., Hart Publishing 2018).

87. 'It isn't unusual these days to see Datuk Sundra Rajoo shuttling between multiple countries, talking up the achievements of the Kuala Lumpur Regional Centre for Arbitration (KLRCA)': AIAC, *Starbiz – Up Close and Personal with Datuk Sundra Rajoo* (13 Apr. 2013), https://www.aiac.world/news/24/Starbiz-%E2%80%93-Up-Close-and-Personal-with-Datuk-Sundra-Rajoo.
88. For background, *see* Christine Sim, *Corruption, Immunity, Institutional Arbitration, Should Arbitral Institutions Have Diplomatic Immunity?*, (27 Feb. 2019), http://arbitrationblog.kluwerarbitration.com/2019/02/27/should-arbitral-institutions-have-diplomatic-immunity/?doing_wp_cron=1590393021.6981229782104492187500 and *Sundra Rajoo a/l Nadarajah v. Menteri Hal Ehwal Luar Negeri (Minister of Foreign Affairs), Malaysia & Ors* [2020] MLJU 360.
89. AIAC, *In Memoriam of Mr. Vinayak P. Pradhan (1950 – 2020)*, https://www.aiac.world/Director; FMT Reporters, *'Doyen of Arbitration' Vinayak Pradhan Dies*, (9 Mar. 2020), https://www.freemalaysiatoday.com/category/nation/2020/03/09/doyen-of-arbitration-vinayak-pradhan-dies/.
90. CIArb (UK Branch), *Our Network*, https://www.ciarb.org/our-network/.
91. CIArb (Malaysia Branch), *About the CIArb*, http://www.ciarb.org.my/about/.
92. MIArb, *Institute*, http://www.miarb.com/institute.html.
93. MIArb, *The Malaysian Institute of Arbitrators Arbitration Rules 2000 Edition*, http://miarb.com/files/20111219130124.pdf.
94. MIArb, *The Malaysian Institute of Arbitrators Mediation Rules 2003 Edition*, http://miarb.com/files/20111219124653.pdf.
95. MIArb, http://www.miarb.com/.

Malaysia acceded to the Convention on the Recognition and Enforcement of Foreign Arbitral Awards (NYC) on 5 November 1985, and it came into force on 3 February 1986.[96] Malaysia made a declaration on accession that it would apply the New York Arbitration Convention:[97]

- to the recognition and enforcement of awards made by the other Contracting States only on the basis of reciprocity; and
- only to differences in legal relationships under Malaysian commercial law.

In 2006, the Malaysian Court of Appeal in *Sri Lanka Cricket v. World Sport Nimbus Pte Ltd*[98] held that a foreign award may only be enforced under the New York Arbitration Convention if it is stated in the Malaysian Official Gazette that the state making the foreign award is a Contracting State of the Convention. However, the Malaysian Federal Court in 2009 in *Lombard Commodities Limited v. Alami Vegetable Oil Products Sdn. Bhd.*[99] clarified that the Official Gazette has evidentiary value, but other appropriate evidence can also be used to prove that the state making the foreign award is a Contracting State of the New York Arbitration Convention.[100]

If the arbitration award was made in a Member State of the NYC, the award can be enforced by the High Court in Malaysia under the Malaysian Arbitration Act 2005, as long as the specified grounds for refusing to enforce the award do not apply. The Malaysian Arbitration Act 2005 was based on the UNCITRAL[101] to make it more consistent with 'modern international practice'.[102]

The Malaysian courts have followed other leading and emerging Asia-Pacific jurisdictions for international commercial arbitrations by becoming reluctant to set aside awards beyond the grounds stated in the statute. The Court of Appeal in *Ajwa Food Industries Co (MIGOP), Egypt v. Pacific Inter-Link Sdn Bhd & another appeal*[103] explained that the party applying to set aside the arbitral award bears the burden of proving the grounds of setting aside the award under section 37(1) of the Arbitration Act 2005: 'The court's discretion in setting aside arbitral award is now limited to the narrowly defined circumstances in line with the modern international arbitral practice.' This discretion should be confined to 'a case of patent injustice which the law permits in clear terms to intervene'. Parties should be bound by the arbitral award since they have agreed to use arbitration to settle their dispute. The courts' excessive

96. UNCITRAL, *Status: Convention on the Recognition and Enforcement of Foreign Arbitral Awards (New York, 1958) (the 'New York Convention')*, https://uncitral.un.org/en/texts/arbitration/conventions/foreign_arbitral_awards/status2.
97. New York Arbitration Convention, *Contracting States – List of Contracting States*, http://www.newyorkconvention.org/list + of + contracting + states.
98. [2006] 3 MLJ 117.
99. [2010] 2 MLJ 23.
100. UNCITRAL, *UNCITRAL Secretariat Guide on the Convention on the Recognition and Enforcement of Foreign Arbitral Awards (New York, 1958)* 30-1 (2016), https://uncitral.un.org/sites/uncitral.un.org/files/media-documents/uncitral/en/2016_guide_on_the_convention.pdf.
101. Luen, *supra* n. 86.
102. Sundra Rajoo, *Internationalisation through Institutional Arbitration* 123, 124 (Vijay K. Bhatia, Maurizio Gotti, Azirah Hashim, Philip Koh & Sundra Rajoo eds., Taylor & Francis 2017).
103. [2011] MLJU 1537.

interference 'will defeat the spirit of the Arbitration Act 2005 which is for all intent and purpose to promote one-stop adjudication in line with the international practice'.

The High Court in *JHW Reels Sdn Bhd v. Syarikat Borcos Shipping Sdn Bhd*[104] dismissed the plaintiff's application to set aside a partial award, with costs, as the application was six days beyond the statutory period. This strict application was justified, *inter alia*, because of the Model Law's strict time limits. The High Court in *Mewaholeo Industries Sdn Bhd v. Awan Timur Palm Oil Mills Resources (Johor) Sdn Bhd*[105] also more recently affirmed that: 'The degree of finality that parties to an arbitration proceeding can hope to achieve can be gleaned from Section 8 of the Arbitration Act 2005 which provides that 'No court shall intervene in matters governed by this Act, except where so provided in this Act.'.

The United Nations Convention on International Settlement Agreements Resulting from Mediation[106] was adopted in New York on 20 December 2018 and opened for signature on 7 August 2019 in Singapore, thereafter in New York. It enables international settlement agreements resulting from mediation to be enforced in the Member States, to facilitate international trade by promoting mediation as an effective ADR form. There are several parallels to the NYC for enforcing arbitral awards.[107]

States and regional economic integration organisations can become the Member States of this Convention.[108] As discussed further in Chapter 14 of this volume, fifty-two members have signed the Singapore Convention on Mediation, although the Convention is ratified by four of these states so far – Fiji, Qatar, Saudi Arabia and Singapore. The Convention is in force in these states from 12 September 2020. Malaysia signed this Convention on 7 August 2019, but it has not yet come into force.[109] The government is in the process of amending the Malaysian Mediation Act 2012 to comply with the Singapore Convention on Mediation so it can ratify the latter.[110]

As for cross-border litigation, if dispute resolution awards have been recognised by court orders from countries other than Malaysia, these foreign court judgments can be recognised and enforced by Malaysian courts in specified situations under the Malaysian Reciprocal Enforcement of Judgments Act 1958. Section 4(1) permits a judgment creditor to apply to the High Court within six years of the date of the

104. [2012] MLJU 1790.
105. [2018] MLJU 2024.
106. UNCITRAL, *United Nations Convention on International Settlement Agreements Resulting from Mediation*, https://uncitral.un.org/sites/uncitral.un.org/files/media-documents/EN/Texts/UNCITRAL/Arbitration/mediation_convention_v1900316_eng.pdf.
107. UNCITRAL, *Information Brochure Singapore Convention on Mediation* 2 (2019), https://uncitral.un.org/sites/uncitral.un.org/files/media-documents/uncitral/en/accession_kit_october_2019_website.pdf.
108. UNCITRAL, *United Nations Convention on International Settlement Agreements Resulting from Mediation* (New York, 2018) (the 'Singapore Convention on Mediation'), https://uncitral.un.org/en/texts/mediation/conventions/international_settlement_agreements.
109. UNCITRAL, *Status: United Nations Convention on International Settlement Agreements Resulting from Mediation*, https://uncitral.un.org/en/texts/mediation/conventions/international_settlement_agreements/status.
110. Shanti Abraham, *The Potential of the Singapore Convention in Malaysia* (22 Apr. 2019), https://www.simi.org.sg/News/Singapore-Convention-Seminar-Series/Shanti-Abraham-The-Potential-of-the-Singapore-Convention-in-Malaysia.

judgment to register the foreign judgment. Sections 5-7 provide for situations where a foreign judgment may be set aside or not enforced for specified reasons. These sections are in Part II of this Act. Section 3(1) provides that Part II will apply to superior court judgments of reciprocating countries. Section 2 defines 'reciprocating country' as a country or territory specified in the First Schedule (mostly courts in England and some of its former colonies).

The Court of Appeal in *Mann Holdings Pte Ltd & Anor v. Ung Yoke Hong*[111] reversed the Malaysian High Court's decision to set aside the registration of a Singaporean High Court order. The Court explained that: 'The whole basis of the Act starts with the concept or principle of comity and substantial reciprocity between nations.' The Court later continued that the principle of international comity 'is an internationally recognized and accepted concept, especially within the Commonwealth, with the Courts striving to avoid conflicting decisions between civilized and friendly nations'. The Court noted that this Act extended to the countries listed in the First Schedule, which includes Singapore as in this case. Therefore, once a Singaporean High Court's judgment is properly registered by a Malaysian High Court, it will be 'accorded the same treatment as if it was a judgment given by the High Court of Malaya'. This would also work in reverse: a Malaysian High Court judgment registered under the Singaporean Reciprocal Enforcement of Commonwealth Judgments Act (Chapter 264) would similarly be treated as if it were a Singaporean High Court judgment.

§9.03 MALAYSIA'S POTENTIAL INVOLVEMENT IN INTERNATIONAL BUSINESS DISPUTE RESOLUTION

Malaysia has also agreed to be subject to international business dispute resolution clauses in regional and bilateral FTAs that go beyond the WTO in the depth of commitments (e.g., for trade liberalisation) and scope (e.g., for investment). In 2017, Malaysia's total trade value under Malaysia's FTAs were MYR 1,122.73 billion (exports of MYR 590 billion and imports of MYR 532 billion). Around 63% of Malaysia's total exports in 2017 were from Malaysia's FTA partner countries.[112] As well as lower tariffs, the FTAs generally contain relaxations of quantitative import restrictions, easier custom procedures, improved market accessibility for specified services and easier foreign investment procedures.[113]

The closer analysis below of Malaysia's FTA provisions first allows an assessment of prospects for Malaysia being either subject to formal inter-state dispute settlement or invoking this procedure for violation of substantive commitments. There have been no such cases so far, similarly to other states with FTAs (except, e.g., under the North American FTA). Yet they could grow due to the problems with the WTO DSU

111. [2019] MLJU 101.
112. Ministry of International Trade and Industry (MITI), *FTA*, https://www.miti.gov.my/index.php/glossary/term/54.
113. Malaysia External Trade Development Corporation, *Free Trade Agreements*, http://www.matrade.gov.my/en/malaysian-exporters/going-global/understanding-free-trade-agreements.

associated with the lack of an Appellate Body since December 2019 (discussed in Chapter 11 of this volume). As of May 2020, Malaysia had not joined with Australia, China, Hong Kong, Singapore and thirteen other WTO members in creating an interim appeals authority for WTO disputes.[114] In turn, more engagement in dispute resolution under FTAs may enhance Malaysia's capacity and credibility regarding other forms of cross-border dispute resolution.

Second, an analysis of the FTAs may lead to a consideration of whether Malaysia is becoming more of a 'lawmaker' in international economic law (as mentioned generally in Chapter 1 of this volume). One indicator of this is whether the provisions are quite similar across the treaties, although outcomes depend on negotiating counterparties (especially in regional rather than bilateral treaties). In comparison, for example, relative to per capita GDP, Malaysia shows more consistency in provisions contained in its many BITs than the trend line for other ASEAN states.[115]

In 1967, Malaysia was one of the founding Member States for ASEAN, which now comprises ten states.[116] As such, Malaysia is a party to a number of regional FTAs including:

- the ASEAN-China Framework Agreement on Comprehensive Economic Cooperation (ACFACEC);
- the ASEAN-Korea Framework Agreement on Comprehensive Economic Cooperation (AKFACEC);
- the ASEAN-Japan Framework Agreement on Comprehensive Economic Cooperation (AJFACEP);
- the ASEAN-Australia-New Zealand Free Trade Agreement (AANZFTA);
- the ASEAN-India Framework Agreement on Comprehensive Economic Cooperation (AIFACEP); and
- the ASEAN-Hong Kong, China Free Trade Agreement (AHKFTA).

Overall, such differences suggest that ASEAN (with support from the Member States like Malaysia) have been quite flexible in negotiating the timing and contents of their regional treaties, even with smaller counterparties (like Hong Kong or Australia / New Zealand). Nonetheless, the dispute settlement provisions in these Agreements are primarily focused on arbitration as the dispute settlement form to be used, after the parties have tried to solve the disputes by consultations and considered conciliation and mediation. In addition, most include an ISDS option in the FTA or a related agreement, but the ISDS provisions are not yet in force regarding India and are reportedly not included in the 'ASEAN + 6' Regional Comprehensive Partnership Agreement concluded in late 2019 (as mentioned in Chapter 1 of this volume). As such,

114. *See*, e.g., Singapore Ministry of Foreign Affairs, *Multiparty Interim Appeal Arbitration Arrangement*, https://www.mfa.gov.sg/Overseas-Mission/Geneva/Mission-Updates/2020/04/Multiparty-Interim-Appeal-Arbitration-Arrangement.
115. Luke Nottage, et al., *International Investment Treaties and Arbitration Across Asia A Bird's Eye View, in International Investment Treaties and Arbitration Across Asia* 1, 29 (Luke Nottage & Julien Chaisse eds., Brill | Nijhoff 2018).
116. ASEAN, *Overview*, https://asean.org/asean/about-asean/overview/.

it is possible that Malaysia will become involved in inter-state arbitration under these treaties, especially if the WTO Appellate Body remains paralysed.

Malaysia has signed several bilateral FTAs, which provide perhaps a better indicator (through consistency in drafting) of whether it is emerging as a significant lawmaker in international trade and investment law. However, these are not many such bilateral FTAs (compared especially with Singapore, with a very open economy that facilitates negotiations) and they are mostly with states where there are also mutual commitments through regional FTAs. Malaysia's bilateral FTAs include[117] the Malaysia-Japan Economic Partnership Agreement (MJEPA), the Malaysia-Pakistan Closer Economic Partnership Agreement (MPCEPA), the Malaysia-New Zealand Free Trade Agreement (MNZFTA), the Malaysia-India Comprehensive Economic Cooperation Agreement (MICECA), the Malaysia-Chile Free Trade Agreement (MCFTA), the Malaysia-Australia Free Trade Agreement (MAFTA) and the Malaysia-Turkey Free Trade Agreement (MTFTA).

As with the regional FTAs discussed above, these bilateral FTAs have a specific chapter on inter-state dispute settlement procedures to be used for disputes between the contracting parties on the interpretation, implementation and application of the Agreements generally. The contracting parties may often initiate or terminate good offices, conciliation or mediation at any time to resolve their disputes under these Agreements. Most of the articles in these chapters provide details on such disputes being settled by arbitration. However, there are differences between these provisions relating to dispute resolution between the regional FTAs and between the bilateral FTAs.

Some regional FTAs[118] and bilateral FTAs[119] have an overall express objective for the dispute resolution procedure which can be used to influence the progress and/or outcome of such proceedings while other regional FTAs and bilateral FTAs do not. A second difference in the dispute resolution procedures in the FTAs discussed involves the complaining party's right to establish an arbitral body. This right applies in different specified situations[120] under the Agreements and include different time periods[121] for this right to arise.

The chapter on dispute resolution is expressly excluded from applying to certain other chapters in the regional[122] and bilateral[123] FTAs, though which chapters are excluded is not consistent. Alternative specific forums for dispute resolution are also

---

117. MITI, *FTA*, https://www.miti.gov.my/index.php/glossary/term/54.
118. Such as in Article 1 of Chapter 17 in the AANZFTA, which is absent in Chapter 9 of the AJFACEP.
119. Such as in Article 16.2 of the MNZFTA, which is absent in Chapter 13 of the MJEPA.
120. Such as Article 64 of the AJFACEP compared to Article 6 of the Agreement on Dispute Settlement Mechanism of the Framework Agreement on Comprehensive Economic Cooperation between the Association of Southeast Asian Nations and the People's Republic of China for regional FTAs; and Article 148 of the MJEPA compared to Article 117 of the MPCEPA for the bilateral FTAs.
121. Such as Article 64 of the AJFACEP compared to Article 8 of Chapter 17 of the AANZFTA for the regional FTAs and Article 148 of the MJEPA compared to Article 12.6 of the MTFTA for the bilateral FTAs.
122. Such as in the AANZFTA compared to the AJFACEP.
123. For example, the MJEPA compared to the MPCEPA.

provided for these excluded chapters in some regional and bilateral FTAs[124] but not others. This results in the dedicated dispute resolution chapters applying to different issues in the Agreements; and, even when these chapters are excluded, there are issues without other specific dispute resolution forums being provided, leading to uncertainty.

Some anomalies in the dispute resolution procedures in the regional FTAs include:

- the other party being required to give due consideration to and adequate opportunities the complaining party's requests for consultations involving disputes on any matters covered by the Agreements[125] or specific issues only;[126] and
- the parties right to initiate or terminate good offices at any time being available for some Agreements and not others[127] (though the parties have the right to conciliation and mediation in all these regional FTAs).

Some bilateral FTAs give additional rights that are not found in other bilateral FTAs in relation to dispute resolution. For example:

- the complaining party having the right to select the dispute resolution forum, not being limited to the dispute resolutions forums in the relevant FTA if the dispute arises under the particular FTA and another agreement by which the contracting parties are also bound;[128]
- either party having the right to notify the other of any actual or proposed measure that is likely to materially affect trade in goods between the parties, request information and have technical discussions on any actual or proposed measure;[129]
- the parties being required[130] to enter into consultations or having the option[131] to do so; and
- the dispute being required[132] to be referred to a specified Committee in particular situations or having the option[133] to make this reference.

124. For example, in the AANZFTA and MJEPA, specific dispute resolution procedures provided for investments (which was not specifically excluded), but not for the other chapters that were excluded.
125. Such as Article 6.1 of the AANZFTA and Article 4(1) of the Agreement on Dispute Settlement Mechanism under the Framework Agreement on Comprehensive Economic Cooperation between the Association of Southeast Asian Nations and the Republic of India.
126. Such as Article 4(1) of the Agreement on Dispute Settlement Mechanism of the Framework Agreement on Comprehensive Economic Co-operation between the Association of Southeast Asian Nations and the People's Republic of China.
127. Such as Article 7(1) of the AHKFTA compared to Article 5(1) of the Agreement on Dispute Settlement Mechanism of the Framework Agreement on Comprehensive Economic Cooperation between the Association of Southeast Asian Nations and the People's Republic of China.
128. Article 16.4 of the MNZFTA and Article 12.2 of the MCFTA.
129. Article 2.9 of the MNZFTA.
130. Such as in Article 12.4 of the MTFTA.
131. Such as in Article 115 of the MPCEPA.
132. Such as in Chapter 8 of the MTFTA.
133. Such as in Chapter 7 of the MNZFTA.

The illustrations discussed above indicate that although there are common features provided in dispute resolution procedures specified in FTAs involving Malaysia, there are also significant differences. These extend to different dispute resolution forums being applicable to different situations and different rights being available to the contracting parties. Such variations can have significant effects on the potential dispute resolution procedures available under these regional and bilateral FTAs.

§9.04 CONCLUSION

Malaysia's commitment to international trade has led to Malaysia being bound by various international agreements. Many of these agreements include international dispute resolution clauses, some of which have been enforced by and against Malaysia, although Malaysia has been more involved in ISDS than WTO cases. Malaysia also has relatively few FTAs, especially bilaterally, and (like almost all states) no experience yet in applying the dispute settlement provisions. Those provisions also display quite significant differences, compared to more consistency in Malaysia's drafting of its BITs, so overall it has not yet fulfilled the potential to become a major 'lawmaker' in international economic law. In addition, Malaysia continues to be actively promoted as an international business dispute resolution venue, especially in recent years, including adopting laws and rules based on international standards and training experts connected to international dispute resolution networks. Malaysia, therefore, is a viable contender in the Asia-Pacific region for international dispute resolution.

CHAPTER 10

Disruption as a Catalyst for International Dispute Services in Japan: No Longer Business as Usual?

James Claxton, Luke Nottage & Nobumichi Teramura[*]

The Japanese Government, supported by various stakeholders, has recently been attempting to develop Japan as another regional hub for international business dispute resolution services. Tracking this development is important for both theoretical and practical reasons. How it unfolds should reveal which of various theories for explaining Japanese law-related behaviour have more traction nowadays, especially not only for international commercial arbitration (ICA) but also for investor-state arbitration (ISA). Assessing the new initiatives is also important for legal practitioners and others interested in the practical question of where to arbitrate or mediate cross-border business disputes, particularly in the Asia-Pacific region. This chapter, therefore, focuses mainly on current attempts to promote existing and new international arbitration centres in Japan as well as the recent establishment of the Japan International Mediation Center – Kyoto (JIMC-Kyoto). It locates such developments in the context of intensifying not only competition from other regional venues for dispute resolution services but also the challenges and potential opportunities created by the COVID-19 pandemic since 2020.

* This publication is part of a project funded over 2019 by the University of Hong Kong and University of Sydney researching 'New Frontiers in International Arbitration for the Asia-Pacific Region', https://japaneselaw.sydney.edu.au/2019/02/new-frontiers-in-international-arbitration-for-the-asia-pacific-region-1-hku-usyd-research-project/. It is an updated and expanded version of James Claxton, et al., *Developing Japan as a Regional Hub for International Dispute Resolution: Dream Come True or Daydream?*, 47 J.J.L. (2019).

§10.01 INTRODUCTION: REVISITING 'RELUCTANT CLAIMANTS' IN JAPAN

As of early 2020, amid the COVID-19 pandemic and public concerns around the Tokyo Olympics that had been scheduled to be held in July that year, Japan remained in a transition period that might result in the country moving to the next stage in developing arbitration, albeit belatedly. In a multi-jurisdictional comparative analysis published in 2018, Reyes & Gu identified four stages of arbitration development in the Asia-Pacific region, evaluating Japan (along with Taiwan) as being in transition from Stage 2 to 3. This implies that the country was still required to make efforts in:

- amending legislation along the lines of the 2006 revisions to the Model Law;
- establishing a regional or even an incipient international reputation for its judiciary being supportive of arbitration; and
- putting forward more innovative services in its arbitration institution(s), not just featuring rules and practices modelled on those of rival institutions.[1]

In recent years, Japan has certainly moved forward in such directions through announcing new dispute resolution services[2] and demonstrating a growing interest in playing a more proactive role in investment treaty negotiations and/or investor-state dispute settlement (ISDS) reforms.[3] However, it is rather surprising that the country has not taken such actions until very recently, despite its long-standing reputation as a major exporter (especially since the 1980s) and outbound investor (especially since the 1990s).[4]

The comparatively belated initiatives raise the question of whether Japanese 'non-litigiousness' may have been or still remains a significant impediment to developing international dispute resolution services. Japan's comparatively low per capita civil litigation rate has been a persistent source of fascination among observers, particularly from abroad.[5] They have long argued over whether the main reason for few court filings lies mainly in:

- traditional (non-confrontational) culture;
- institutional barriers (to adversarial court procedures);

1. Anselmo Reyes & Weixia Gu, *Conclusion: An Asia Pacific Model of Arbitration Reform*, in *The Developing World of Arbitration: A Comparative Study of Arbitration Reform in the Asia Pacific* 279, 286-7 (Anselmo Reyes & Weixia Gu eds., Hart Publishing 2018).
2. *See* generally §10.02 and §10.03 of this chapter. *See also* Yoshimi Ohara, *The Asia-Pacific Arbitration Review 2020: Japan*, GAR (24 May 2019), https://globalarbitrationreview.com/benchmarking/the-asia-pacific-arbitration-review-2020/1193378/japan.
3. *See* Nottage & Jetin, Chapter 1in this volume. *See also* generally Vivienne Bath & Luke Nottage, *International Investment Agreements and Investor-State Arbitration in Asia*, 20/08 Sydney Law School Research Paper 1, 26-8 (2020), available at SSRN: https://ssrn.com/abstract=3544458.
4. *Ibid.*
5. Eric A. Feldman, *Law, Culture, and Conflict Dispute Resolution in Postwar Japan*, in *Law in Japan: A Turning Point* 50 (Daniel H. Foote ed., University of Washington Press 2007). Also available at SSRN: https://ssrn.com/abstract=980326.

- elite management (maintaining those barriers, but sometimes by diverting threatening cases into mediation schemes – where complainants may get some partial redress but socio-economic order is largely preserved);
- relative predictability of court outcomes (certainty in law and/or fact determinations);[6] or
- various combinations of these elements depending on the area of law or period in legal history.[7]

Similar diverse arguments have been developed to explain the limited known filings of arbitration by Japanese firms.[8] Commentators have begun by noting the persistent pattern of 'reluctant claimants', first, for arbitration of domestic business-to-business disputes, arguably due to strong 'competition' from reliable courts and court-annexed or other mediation schemes.

Second, a pattern of few filings also seems evident for ICA by Japanese firms, especially for Japan-seated proceedings. This is more surprising because ICA is usually the preferred mechanism for international commercial dispute resolution.[9] The worldwide popularity of ICA arises because it is often difficult to agree on one side's local courts as the forum (due to fear of conceding a 'home court advantage') or even courts of a neutral third country (due to greater difficulties in enforcing judgments worldwide, compared to the enforcement of arbitral awards under the 1958 New York Convention on the Recognition and Enforcement of Foreign Arbitral Awards).

Third, Japanese firms appear to remain 'reluctant claimants' in the burgeoning field of treaty-based ISDS arbitration. Few claims have been formally filed by Japanese investors under international investment treaties,[10] against host states for expropriating or otherwise illegally interfering with their investments. The main venue selected for ISA is the International Centre for the Settlement of Investment Disputes (ICSID), which has attracted 715 claims as of 31 December 2019.[11] Yet its public database lists only three ICSID arbitration cases filed by Japanese investors, all commenced since 2015 under the Energy Charter Treaty and against Spain.[12] However, at least one other

6. For a critical review of the recent restatement of this thesis in J. Mark Ramseyer, *Second-Best Justice: The Virtues of Japanese Private Law* (University of Chicago Press 2015), *see* Marc Dernauer, *Rezensionen / Reviews*, 42 J.J.L. 283 (2016).
7. Luke Nottage, *Translating Tanase: Challenging Paradigms of Japanese Law and Society*, 39 Victoria U.W.L.R. 755 (2006). Also available at SSRN: https://ssrn.com/abstract=921932.
8. Various views are discussed in Tetsuya Nakamura & Luke Nottage, *Japan*, *in International Commercial Arbitration in Asia* 223 (Tom Ginsburg & Shahla Ali eds., Juris 3rd ed. 2012). Also available at SSRN: https://ssrn.com/abstract=2070447.
9. School of International Arbitration, Queen Mary University of London, *2018 International Arbitration Survey: The Evolution of International Arbitration* (2018 Queen Mary Survey).
10. *See* generally Luke Nottage & J. Romesh Weeramantry, *Investment Arbitration in Asia: Five Perspectives on Law and Practice*, in *Investment Law and Dispute Resolution Law and Practice in Asia* 25 (Vivienne Bath & Luke Nottage eds., Routledge 2011). Also available at SSRN: https://ssrn.com/abstract=2041686.
11. *The ICSID Caseload – Statistics (Issue 2020-1)*, https://icsid.worldbank.org/en/Documents/resources/The%20ICSID%20Caseload%20Statistics%202020-1%20Edition-ENG.pdf.
12. *JGC Corporation v. Kingdom of Spain* (ICSID Case No. ARB/15/27); *Eurus Energy Holdings Corporation v. Kingdom of Spain* (ICSID Case No. ARB/16/4); and *Itochu Corporation v. Kingdom of Spain* (ICSID Case No. ARB/18/25). These no doubt related to Spain's abrupt policy

case (based on a one-off investment contract rather than a treaty) has been settled after the Japanese investors threatened to commence arbitration administered by ICSID.[13] There have probably been other such settlements 'in the shadow' of ISA. Japanese investors have also initiated treaty-based ISA claims through their subsidiaries in third countries (such as an ICSID claim by a Nomura subsidiary in the United Kingdom (UK) against the Czech Republic, and recently Bridgestone in the United States of America (USA) against Panama).[14] Furthermore, there have been claims formally filed by Japanese investors under the United Nations Commission on International Trade Law (UNCITRAL) or other non-ICSID Arbitration Rules, notably against India.[15] Those have traditionally involved less transparency, although more and more proceedings tend to become public nowadays,[16] especially under Japan's newer treaties.[17]

---

shift on renewable energy, which have generated extensive treaty-based arbitration claims: *see* generally Yulia S. Selivanova, *Changes in Renewables Support Policy and Investment Protection under the Energy Charter Treaty: Analysis of Jurisprudence and Outlook for the Current Arbitration Cases*, 33 ICSID Rev. 433 (2018).

13. *See*, e.g., Mark Smith & Louise Browning, *Indonesia and Nippon Asahan Aluminium Consortium Reach Settlement*, Dispute Resolution Newsflash (https://www.ashurst.com/en/news-and-insights/legal-updates/indonesia-and-nippon-asahan-aluminium-consortium-reach-settlement/.
14. *Saluka Investments BV (The Netherlands) v. The Czech Republic*, UNCITRAL, Partial Award (17 Mar. 2006); *Bridgestone Licensing Services, Inc. and Bridgestone Americas, Inc. v. Republic of Panama* (ICSID Case No. ARB/16/34). *See also* Damien Charlotin, *Updated With Full Analysis: Many of Panama's Expedited Objections Are Dismissed in Bridgestone Trademark Case, but Arbitrators Won't Let Claimants Claim for Losses Incurred Outside of Panama*, IA Reporter (8 Jan. 2018), https://www.iareporter.com/articles/many-of-panamas-expedited-objections-are-dismissed-in-bridgestone-trademark-case-but-arbitrators-wont-let-claimants-claim-for-losses-incurred-outside-of-panama/.
15. *See*, e.g., *Nissan Motor v. India* (2017), http://investmentpolicyhub.unctad.org/ISDS/Details/828. *See also* Jarrod Hepburn, *An Update on Investment Treaty Disputes Involving the Government of India*, IA Reporter (23 Aug. 2018), https://www.iareporter.com/articles/an-update-on-investment-treaty-disputes-involving-the-government-of-india/, where it was reported that:

    > under a proposed settlement deal, Nissan would receive a payout of around USD 292 million in unpaid incentives offered by the Tamil Nadu state government to locate a manufacturing plant in the state. ... Tamil Nadu Industries Minister MC Sampath was quoted by Reuters news service as saying that a final decision on the settlement would be taken soon, and that the parties were working in a 'conducive environment'. ... Similar to the Vodafone [ISDS] cases, Tamil Nadu had sought an order from the Madras High Court seeking to restrain Nissan's case from proceeding to arbitration.

    In May 2020, the claim was reportedly settled for between USD 185-USD 238 million: Aditi Shah and Sudarshan Varadhan, *Exclusive: Nissan Settles Dispute with Indian State over Unpaid Dues*, Reuters (29 May 2020), https://www.reuters.com/article/us-nissan-india-arbitration-exclusive/exclusive-nissan-settles-dispute-with-indian-state-over-unpaid-dues-sources-idUSKBN2342AR.
16. *See* generally Luke Nottage & Ana Ubilava, *Costs, Outcomes and Transparency in ISDS Arbitrations: Evidence for an Investment Treaty Parliamentary Inquiry*, 21 Int'l Arb. L. Rev. 111 (2018). Also available at SSRN: https://ssrn.com/abstract=3227401.
17. Tomoko Ishikawa, *A Japanese Perspective on International Investment Agreements: Recent Developments*, *in International Investment Treaties and Arbitration Across Asia* 513 (Luke Nottage & Julien Chaisse eds., Brill | Nijhoff 2018).

Nonetheless, the relative paucity of formal ISDS filings by Japanese investors[18] probably helps to explain why Japan has traditionally adopted a somewhat belated and flexible approach towards pressing for and securing ISDS-backed protections in Japan's investment treaties.[19] More recently, however, Japan has been 'catching up' with Korea by concluding more bilateral investment treaties (BITs).[20] Notably, under the Abe Government, Japan has also been playing an active role in pressing for the conclusion of free trade agreements (FTAs) incorporating investment chapters to liberalise and protect cross-border investments. These include the Trans-Pacific Partnership (TPP),[21] and its reincarnation at the 'Comprehensive Agreement for TPP' (CPTPP), re-signed in 2017 (after the Trump Administration withdrew signature by the USA) with minimal changes to the investment chapter.[22] Japan has also expressed somewhat surprisingly strong support for more conventional ISDS procedures in current UNCITRAL deliberations into possible reforms of ISA, thus arguably becoming a more prominent 'rule-maker' in international investment law.[23]

These developments suggest difficulties for a predominantly 'cultural' explanation for relatively few formal filings or corporate interest in ISA on the part of firms from Japan. Diminishing 'institutional barriers' appear more important,[24] although Korean investors seem to be taking advantage of those more aggressively.[25] Similarly, general or even legal 'culture' is hard to posit as the main explanation for comparatively few

18. Compare generally Luke Nottage, *Are US Investors Exceptionally Litigious with ISDS Claims?*, Kluwer Arbitration Blog (14 Nov. 2016), http://arbitrationblog.kluwerarbitration.com/2016/11/14/are-us-investors-exceptionally-litigious-with-isds-claims/. However, *see Macro Trading Co., Ltd. v. People's Republic of China* (ICSID Case No. ARB/20/22). This is arguably the first ISDS case to be based on the 1988 China-Japan BIT: Damien Charlotin, *Japanese Investor Lodges ICSID Arbitration against China*, IA Reporter (30 Jun. 2020), https://www.iareporter.com/articles/japanese-investor-lodges-icsid-arbitration-against-china/.
19. *See* generally, e.g., Shotaro Hamamoto & Luke Nottage, *Foreign Investment In and Out of Japan: Economic Backdrop, Domestic Law, and International Treaty-Based Investor-State Dispute Resolution*, TDM 5 (2011), also available at SSRN: https://ssrn.com/abstract=1724999; and Mapping BITs, *Japan*, http://mappinginvestmenttreaties.com/country?iso=JPN.
20. Compare, http://investmentpolicyhub.unctad.org/IIA/CountryBits/105#iiaInnerMenu; http://investmentpolicyhub.unctad.org/IIA/CountryBits/111#iiaInnerMenu; and recently http://www.meti.go.jp/english/policy/external_economy/trade/FTA_EPA/index.html.
21. Luke Nottage, *The TPP Investment Chapter and Investor-State Arbitration in Asia and Oceania: Assessing Prospects for Ratification*, 17 Melb. J. Int'l L. 313 (2016). Also available at SSRN: https://ssrn.com/abstract=2767996.
22. *See* generally Amokura Kawharu & Luke Nottage, *Renouncing Investor-State Dispute Settlement in Australia, Then New Zealand: Déjà Vu*, 18/03 Sydney Law School Research Paper 1 (2018), available at SSRN: https://ssrn.com/abstract=3116526. After Australia became the sixth of eleven states (with Japan) to complete ratification, the revamped agreement will come into force among the (so far six) Member States from 1 Jan. 2019, *see* https://www.beehive.govt.nz/release/cptpp-underway-%E2%80%93-tariff-cuts-our-exporters-december-30.
23. *See* generally, on UNCITRAL deliberations, Anthea Roberts, *Incremental, Systemic, and Paradigmatic Reform of Investor-State Arbitration*, 112 Am. J. Int'l L. 410 (2018). On 'rule-makers' versus 'rule takers' in international investment law, comparing recently Japan, Korea and others, *see* Bath and Nottage *supra* n. 3.
24. Nottage & Weeramantry, *supra* n. 10.
25. Joongi Kim, *Korea's International Investment Agreements: Policy at the Contours*, in *International Investment Treaties and Arbitration Across Asia* 486 (Luke Nottage & Julien Chaisse eds., Brill | Nijhoff 2018).

ICA filings by Japanese companies.[26] After all, they have had a (long-standing) willingness to pursue arbitrations abroad, originally in core Western venues, like the UK and the US. Japanese firms also now engage increasingly in ICA in major regional hubs, like Singapore and Hong Kong, which have benefitted from the overall expansion in economic activity and arbitration work in the region,[27] particularly over the last decade.[28]

Admittedly, even allowing for the tendency to pursue ICA abroad and the greater confidentiality obligations compared to ISDS proceedings, numbers still seem quite low, compared, for example, to filings by Korean firms.[29] Yet that very difference suggests we should be cautious about attributing few filings to broad notions of traditionally non-confrontational 'Asian culture'. Rather, Japanese behaviour may be partly due to more specific psychological or organisational factors impacting on cost-benefit assessments. One may be a tendency to consider formal dispute resolution as 'throwing good money after bad' since the costs are immediate whereas a win is uncertain. This could reflect a 'costs on-screen, benefits off-screen' problem, noted in other national settings.[30] It might be exacerbated by possibly greater risk averseness among the Japanese, although that is difficult to pinpoint empirically and to apply in contemporary settings.[31] Such risk averseness, combined with a broader 'status quo

26. *Cf.*, e.g., Tony Cole, *Commercial Arbitration in Japan: Contributions to the Debate on Japanese 'Non-Litigiousness'*, 40 N.Y.U. J. Int'l L. & Pol. 29 (2007). Also available at SSRN: https://ssrn.com/abstract=1083371.
27. Luke Nottage, *In/formalization and Glocalization of International Commercial Arbitration and Investment Treaty Arbitration in Asia*, in *Formalisation and Flexibilisation of Dispute Resolution* 211 (Joachim Zekoll, et al. eds., Martinus Nijhoff / Brill 2014). Also available at SSRN: https://ssrn.com/abstract=2987674.
28. SIAC recorded 452 new arbitration cases in 2017; *see* SIAC, *Annual Report 2017*, 11, http://siac.org.sg/images/stories/articles/annual_report/SIAC_Annual_Report_2017.pdf. There were 262 new arbitration cases for HKIAC in 2016, *see* HKIAC, *Annual Report, 2016 Reflections*, 10, http://www.hkiac.org/sites/default/files/annual_report/annual%20report%202016%20%28low%20resolution%29%20v2.pdf; and 79 new cases seated in South and East Asia for ICC in 2017, *see 2017 ICC Dispute Resolution Statistics*, http://library.iccwbo.org/content/dr/STATISTICAL_REPORTS/SR_0040.htm?l1=Statistical+Reports&AUTH=USR_1179&Timeframe=gJn0Fh/C3SJ9wkVUctx9XPHg8IEaixBS9IQv6cwryitUewGAqCJpuw==&AGENT=ICC_HQ.
29. In 2017, fifty-nine South Korean parties were involved in ICC arbitration, in contrast to twenty-nine parties from Japan. *See 2017 ICC Dispute Resolution Statistics*, *supra* n. 28.
30. *See* generally Cass Sunstein, *Cognition and Cost-Benefit Analysis*, 85 John M. Olin Law & Economics Working Paper 1 (1999), available at SSRN: https://ssrn.com/abstract=186669.
31. For example, on one widely known scale, individuals in Japan have a higher score (92) for 'uncertainty avoidance' compared to those in Korea (85), let alone, e.g., Australia (51), https://www.hofstede-insights.com/product/compare-countries/. Some have argued that higher uncertainty avoidance impacts significantly on comparative corporate behaviour (such as CEOs requiring higher takeover premiums and undertaking fewer cross-industry and cross-country takeovers), *see*, e.g., Bart Frijns, et al., *Uncertainty Avoidance, Risk Tolerance and Corporate Takeover Decisions*, 37 J. Banking & Fin. 2457 (2013). However, significant differences over time have been found in other comparative research assuming – admittedly quite ambitiously – that factors found to influence individuals' risk averseness (such as income/wealth and age) map onto nationwide differences in a composite index of propensity towards risk-taking. Specifically, for example, although the US still displays the lowest level of risk averseness among developed countries, this has been growing somewhat over 1995-2009, while diminishing more dramatically from a higher level in Japan over the same period. *See* Alexandrina Scorbureanu & Arne Holzhausen, *The Composite Index of Propensity to Risk – CIPR*,

bias', may also drive a persistent preference for Japanese companies to choose arbitral venues abroad that have a critical mass of annual filings and therefore proven track records.

Commentators have also pointed to various specific institutional barriers that may also continue to make Japan relatively less attractive as the seat for ICA filings. As well as some geographical inconvenience, impediments include access to:

- up-to-date commentaries and especially case law,[32] in English (the lingua franca of ICA),[33] on Japan's legislative regime (although at least since 2003 that is based around the now-familiar 1985 UNCITRAL Model Law on ICA);
- other potential indicia of a pro-arbitration attitude by judges (as its European-style career judiciary does not encourage judges to give extra-judicial speeches to the same degree as in the common law tradition);
- multilingual and expert international arbitrators and counsel; and
- suitable venues for hearings.[34]

In 2017, however, politicians in the ruling Liberal Democratic Party (LDP) began pushing bureaucrats and others to develop measures for Japan to become a more attractive regional hub for (potentially lucrative) ICA and international dispute resolution services more generally.[35] In 2018, a working group comprising fourteen academics, lawyers and in-house counsel identified seven proposals to improve international arbitration services in Japan.[36] They include:

- strengthening the Japan Commercial Arbitration Association (JCAA), the leading national centre for international arbitration;
- encouraging increased presence of outside dispute resolution institutions in Japan;

Allianz Economic Research & Corporate Development Working Paper 147, 13-18 (12 Apr. 2011), https://www.allianz.com/content/dam/onemarketing/azcom/Allianz_com/migration/media/current/en/economic_research/images_englisch/pdf_downloads/working_papers/cipre.pdf.

32. For example, a recent UNCITRAL-supported public resource on the New York Convention lacks a jurisdictional report or any case law related to Japan, *see*, http://newyorkconvention1958.org/.
33. According to *2017 ICC Dispute Resolution Statistics (Language of Awards)*, 'Awards approved in 2017 were drafted in a total of thirteen languages. English remains the predominant language (for 77% of the awards)', in 2 ICC Disp. Res. Bull. 51 (2018).
34. *See* generally Nobumichi Teramura & Luke Nottage, *Arbitration Reform in Japan: Reluctant Legislature and Institutional Challenges*, in *Arbitration Reform in Asia* 83-108 (Weixia Gu & Anselmo Reyes eds., Hart Publishing 2018). Also available at SSRN: https://ssrn.com/abstract=3252270.
35. *See* Luke Nottage & James Claxton, *'Japan Is Back' – for International Dispute Resolution Services?*, Kluwer Arbitration Blog (29 Jan. 2018), http://arbitrationblog.kluwerarbitration.com/2018/01/29/japan-back-international-dispute-resolution-services/.
36. Nihon Keizai Shinbun Writer, *Nihon De Kokusai Chusai 2-Wari-Jaku [Less than 20% of Japanese Companies Seat Their International Arbitrations in Japan]*, Nihon Keizai Shinbun (23 Jul. 2018), https://www.nikkei.com/article/DGKKZO33205960Q8A720C1TCJ000/ (citing the work of the group chaired by University of Tokyo Emeritus Professor Noboru Kashiwagi).

- holding seminars and training for Japanese businesses (perhaps in cooperation with the Japan International Cooperation Agency and the Japan External Trade Organization);
- emphasising marketing abroad;
- attracting international arbitration counsel and arbitrators to Japan (perhaps through tax incentives and greater ease in obtaining visas); and
- the possible establishment of an umbrella organisation to manage international arbitration initiatives.

A final proposal made by this new working group was to bring Japanese facilities and laws bearing on international arbitration in line with standards common in arbitration-friendly jurisdictions. Cost-effective venues have recently become available in Osaka, housed in Ministry of Justice facilities and are on the way in Tokyo.[37]

As for the legislative framework, it was observed in 2018 that doubts remain – in text, if not in practice – about the legality of those who are not registered lawyers in Japan acting as arbitrators and counsel in certain international arbitrations, although views could differ.[38] On 20 May 2020, the House of Representatives amended the *Act on Special Measures concerning the Handling of Legal Services by Foreign Lawyers* (Law No. 66 of 1986). This amendment clearly allows foreign lawyers (engaged abroad, or registered as 'foreign law solicitors' or *gaikokuho jimu bengoshi*) to serve as counsel in Japan-seated arbitrations not only involving Japanese and non-Japanese parties but also among Japanese parties if certain international aspects exist.[39]

There have been other initiatives outside the direct line of vision for the working group that seek to contribute to promoting international dispute resolution in Japan. In November 2020, for instance, the Japan Institute for International Arbitration Research and Training was launched with the support of the Institute of Comparative Law in Japan and Chuo University. The initiative seeks to build capacity by supporting the next generation of Japanese arbitrators, mediators, and dispute lawyers with training and resources. Among other projects, the organization assists students and junior Japanese lawyers to build their professional profiles through participation as speakers in international trainings and conferences.

Tracking how such initiatives unfold will be useful for both theoretical and practical reasons. For scholars, the analysis can offer new insights into what really drives law-related behaviour in contemporary Japan, impacting on this volume's questions as to the trajectory in developing ICA and becoming more influential in ISDS especially compared to other parts of Asia. For practitioners, it can identify and assess

37. The Japan International Dispute Resolution Center, http://idrc.jp/en.
38. Compare Nakamura & Nottage, *supra* n. 8, with Yoshimasa Furuta, et al., *Thoughts on Necessary Change in Japan*, GAR (22 May 2018), https://globalarbitrationreview.com/article/1169880/thoughts-on-necessary-change-in-japan.
39. With effect from 29 Aug. 2020, the amendment allows foreign lawyers to act even in arbitrations among Japanese parties if the substantive governing law is not Japanese law if one of the companies is more than 50% owned by a foreign company, or if the seat of arbitration is outside Japan. The amendment also allows for the minimum three years' experience for registration as a foreign law solicitor to include up to two years' provision of service in Japan plus one year (rather than at least two years) of post-qualification overseas work experience.

Japan as a possibly attractive new option for parties considering forums to resolve commercial disputes outside regular court proceedings, particularly in the economically vibrant Asian region. Accordingly, the rest of this article first assesses attempts to promote ICA, including through existing advertising material from the JCAA.[40] §10.03 then provides an up-to-date report on the establishment of a new JIMC-Kyoto.[41] That might become an attractive complement to ICA in Japan, given the common practice of parties including multi-tiered dispute resolution clauses in cross-border contracts (requiring mediation attempts before arbitration).[42] The challenge in both respects is renewed regional competition from other jurisdictions, including some new contenders, such as Australia.[43]

§10.02 ASSESSING JAPAN'S (IN)CAPACITY IN INTERNATIONAL ARBITRATION

Japan has a long recorded history of seeking to avoid open confrontation and to resolve disputes amicably, but this has not yet translated into resolving many disputes out of court through binding decisions of arbitrators. In the early seventh century, Japan codified Confucian and Buddhist approaches to governing in Prince Shotoku's Constitution, whose first article provides that '[h]armony should be valued, and quarrels should be avoided'.[44] From the seventeenth century, after lengthy political machinations and some bloody conflicts[45] to restore and maintain more centralised control over

40. §10.02 mostly elaborates Nobumichi Teramura & Luke Nottage, *Japan's (In)Capacity in International Commercial Arbitration*, Kluwer Arbitration Blog (17 Nov. 2018), http://arbitrationblog.kluwerarbitration.com/2018/11/17/japans-incapacity-international-commercial-arbitration/.
41. §10.03 elaborates James Claxton & Luke Nottage, *Getting Into Gear: The Japan International Mediation Centre – Kyoto*, Kluwer Mediation Blog (17 Sep. 2018), http://mediationblog.kluwerarbitration.com/2018/09/17/getting-gear-japan-international-mediation-centre-kyoto/. For further background to JIMC-Kyoto, *see* James Claxton & Luke Nottage, *Wa and the Japan International Mediation Centre – Kyoto*, Kluwer Mediation Blog (1 Feb. 2018), http://mediationblog.kluwerarbitration.com/2018/02/01/wa-and-the-japanese-international-mediation-centre/.
42. *See*, e.g., 2018 Queen Mary Survey, *supra* n. 9, finding that the preference for combining alternative dispute resolution with international arbitration had increased from 34% to 50% since 2015 (at 5), and Global Data Trends and Regional Differences, Global Pound Conference Series (2017), reporting that 51% of those surveyed identified preventative pre-dispute or pre-escalation processes as central to the future of commercial dispute resolution (at 13).
43. For a critical assessment of a comparable attempt recently to promote Australia as another regional hub for international arbitration, *see* Luke Nottage & Nobumichi Teramura, *Australia's (In)Capacity in International Commercial Arbitration*, Kluwer Arbitration Blog (20 Sep. 2018), http://arbitrationblog.kluwerarbitration.com/2018/09/20/australias-incapacity-international-commercialarbitration/.
44. H. Gene Blocker & Christopher Starling, *Japanese Philosophy* 37 (State University of New York Press 2001).
45. *See*, e.g., John Dougill, *In Search of Japan's Hidden Christians: A Story of Suppression, Secrecy and Survival* (Tuttle 2012).

the country, the Tokugawa Shogunate implemented a 'didactic' style of mediation that aimed to (re)educate all involved through agreed settlements.[46]

After modern Japan re-opened to the world in the mid-nineteenth century, mediation schemes were introduced to resolve socio-economic and potentially politically controversial issues, such as farm tenancy claims that started to generate growing numbers of court filings from the early twentieth century.[47] After World War II, government-supported mediation schemes were also introduced in the wake of litigation over environmental pollution and other major social issues.[48] Court-annexed mediation also endured for civil disputes more broadly,[49] following a more 'evaluative' style as well, but with perhaps greater reference to legal norms by the mediators (including *bengoshi* lawyers or other legally trained third-party neutrals, with career judges). An even more legalistic style of mediation, despite government funding, similarly characterises the scheme set up to mediate mass claims against the Tokyo Electric Power Company after the 2011 tsunami and consequent nuclear plant meltdown.[50]

These types of schemes, along with the growing efficiency of Japan's civil litigation system anyway, have hampered efforts to develop privately supplied dispute resolution services. In particular, Japanese firms have not regarded international arbitration as an indispensable conflict resolution mechanism.[51] Their understanding of dispute resolution may be summarised as: first, negotiation; second, mediation (but court-annexed); third, litigation; and, fourth, arbitration (if the firms in question know it exists, but many business people and even some Japanese legal practitioners do not realise that arbitration is a viable choice).[52] In short, the use of ICA is still not salient in Japanese business and legal practice.

However, it is too hasty to conclude that the Japanese government has not promoted 'Japanese' ICA in and out of the country. The Ministry of Economy, Trade and Industry (METI) has played a key role over many decades in trying to develop the Japanese arbitration industry.[53] The METI has long supported the JCAA, the dominant

46. Dan Henderson, *Conciliation and Japanese Law: Tokugawa and Modern* (University of Washington Press 1965).
47. Dimitri Vanoverbeke, *Community and State in the Japanese Farm Village, Farm Tenancy Conciliation (1924-1938)* (Cornell University Press 2004).
48. Frank Upham, *Law and Social Change in Postwar Japan* (Harvard University Press 1989).
49. Shusuke Kakiuchi, *Regulation of Dispute Resolution in Japan: Alternative Dispute Resolution and Its Background*, in *Regulating Dispute Resolution: ADR and Access to Justice at the Crossroads* 269 (Felix Steffek & Hannes Unberath eds., Hart Publishing 2013).
50. Joel Rheuben & Luke Nottage, *Now that the (Radioactive) Dust Has Settled: Resolution of Claims from the Fukushima Nuclear Disaster*, 15 Asian Disp. Rev. 126 (2013).
51. Yoshihisa Hayakawa, *Nihon ni okeru Chusai no Rekishiteki Iso [Historical Aspects of Arbitration in Japan]*, 87 Horitsu Jiho 19 (2015).
52. Shigeo Kisa, et al., *Tekisuto-Bukku Gendai Shiho [Japanese Judicial System]* 40 (Nipponhyoronsha 6th ed. 2015).
53. Its jurisdiction ranges from sectors where Japanese firms have long become globally competitive (such as the automotive and electronics industries) to sectors dominated by small- and medium-sized enterprises (SMEs). *See METI Agencies*, http://www.meti.go.jp/english/aboutmeti/agencies/index.html.

and leading arbitration institution in the country, notably by providing former senior officials to serve as JCAA Presidents.[54]

Unfortunately, the JCAA has largely missed out on the boom in ICA across the wider Asian region, particularly over the last ten to fifteen years.[55] Despite modern arbitration rules (updated in 2015, but more dramatically in 2019), fee structures and personnel, the JCAA has attracted only twelve to twenty-seven new case filings annually over 2007-2018.[56] This caseload is very low compared to its counterparts in China, Hong Kong, Singapore[57] and even recently, Malaysia (AIAC)[58] and Korea (KCAB).[59] The JCAA's limited visibility in the global arbitration market is attributable to its (so far largely) fruitless struggle to shake off a reputation abroad as being Japan-focused that partly derives from the fact that almost all its cases involve at least one Japanese party[60] and also the nature of the appointment of its Presidents.[61] Another cause of the limited visibility is the fact that the JCAA lacks credibility for Japanese small- and medium-sized enterprises (SMEs) and even large Japanese companies seeking to include it in cross-border contracts as the arbitral venue.[62] To put it bluntly, the 'Japanese' ICA business has failed to gain not only international but also domestic users.

Given such circumstances, it is understandable that the Japanese government embarked on a new program to shore up the flagging Japanese arbitration scene. In June 2017, the Cabinet of Japan approved the 'Basic Policy on Economic and Fiscal Management and Reform 2017'.[63] This has led to the establishment of the Japan International Dispute Resolution Center Osaka (JIDRC-Osaka)[64] on 1 May 2018, and

54. Yasuhei Taniguchi, *Interview: Shinsetsu Sareta Shingaporu Kokusai Shoji Saibansho Hanji ni Erabareta Sono Haikei [Interview: Appointment as a Judge of the Newly Established Singapore International Commercial Court]*, March 2015 The Lawyers 22 (2015).
55. Takashi Yokoyama, *Arbitration in Japan: Next Chapter*, 2 I.L.Q. 18 (2018); Hiroyuki Tezuka & Youko Maeda, *Ajia Chusai No Tenkai To Nihon [Development of Arbitration in Asia and Japan]*, 87 Horitsu Jiho 13 (2015).
56. Based on statistics provided by the JCAA to the authors. For JCAA's Arbitration Rules, *see* http://www.jcaa.or.jp/e/arbitration/rules.html. The three sets of Rules available since 2019, especially the innovative new 'Interactive Rules' aimed at controlling arbitration costs, appear to be a response to the LDP policy push mentioned in §10.01 and subsequent developments outlined below. *See* generally David Gilmore, et al., *New 2019 JCAA Rules: Is Three a Crowd?*, Kluwer Arbitration Blog (8 Feb. 2019), http://arbitrationblog.kluwerarbitration.com/2019/02/08/new-2019-jcaa-rules-is-three-a-crowd/.
57. 2018 Queen Mary Survey, *supra* n. 9, at 13.
58. AIAC, *CIPAA Conference 2018 – Sharing Solutions* 11-12 (7 May 2018) https://www.aiac.world/wp-content/uploads/2018/CIPAA%20Report%202018.pdf.
59. Sae Youn Kim & Andrew White, *Arbitration Procedures and Practice in South Korea: Overview*, Thomson Reuters Practical Law (1 Sep. 2018), https://uk.practicallaw.thomsonreuters.com/8-381-2907?transitionType=Default&contextData=(sc.Default)&firstPage=true&comp=pluk&bhcp=1.
60. Tezuka & Maeda, *supra* n. 55, at 13.
61. *See* generally Colin Jones, *The Influence of Amakudari on the Japanese Legal System*, 40 J.J.L. 1 (2015).
62. Tatsuya Nakamura, *Nihon No Chusai No Korekara [Future of International Arbitration in Japan]*, in *Kokusai Chusai To Kigyo Senryaku [International Arbitration and Corporate Strategy]* 492 (Koichi Miki, et al. eds., Yuhikaku 2014).
63. https://www.cas.go.jp/jp/seisaku/kokusai_chusai/kanjikai/dai1/gijisidai.pdf.
64. http://www.idrc.jp/index_en.html.

the opening of the International Arbitration Center in Tokyo (IACT)[65] on 1 September 2018. The former does not provide arbitration services but offers reasonably priced and conveniently located specialist facilities for international arbitration hearings and other forms of ADR.[66] The latter is the first Asian international arbitration body specialised in intellectual property disputes.[67]

Those new attempts are part of an inter-ministerial initiative to enhance Japan's status as an international dispute resolution centre. The Justice, Sports, Trade and Transportation ministries in Japan are discussing how they should promote Japan in English as a seat for ICA.[68] Although their main plan is to strategically advertise Japanese ICA to the country and the rest of the world,[69] it is unclear whether they have adequate knowledge about the current position of Japan in the global ICA market. Without sufficient understanding, the government will not be able to promote Japan as an arbitration hub effectively. While their idea is to promote the country as a new attractive venue, can Japan still catch up with other competitors, or are they being too optimistic? A preliminary assessment can be attempted by explaining how the JCAA, as a core part of Japan's arbitration scene, has perceived and projected Japan as a viable seat for ICA. Hence, it is worth evaluating the JCAA's perception of ICA in Japan.

[A] Japan's ICA Capacity

The JCAA earlier published a pamphlet entitled 'Responding to the needs of international business: A guide to international commercial arbitration in Japan' ('JCAA pamphlet').[70] It argues for Japan as a compelling arbitration forum mainly because of a revised Japanese Arbitration Law and a modern Japan that is 'energetic yet refined, fully wired but also enticing: ... where fast-paced international business mixes seamlessly with a cultural yearning to seek consensus amid traditional notions of fair play'.[71]

Regarding arbitration law, the JCAA pamphlet mentions:

- a global standard (the Japanese Arbitration Law was introduced in 2004 based on the 1985 UNCITRAL Model Law);
- party autonomy;

65. https://www.iactokyo.com/.
66. Toshiya Eto, *Japan Plays Catch-up in the International Arbitration Market: Companies Opt for Singapore and Hong Kong to Settle Commercial Disputes*, Nikkei Asian Review (9 Nov. 2018), https://asia.nikkei.com/Business/Business-trends/Japan-plays-catch-up-in-the-international-arbitration-market2?fbclid=IwAR3YedGwTWZeFlSqruIIGionfFNQLk4GTTiMY6iJzG4Sc1AD2OzjNwsF9N0.
67. Nikkei Staff Writers, *Asia's First Patent Arbitration Hub to Open in Tokyo: Quicker Handling of Intellectual Property Battles to Lighten Load on Companies*, Nikkei Asian Review, https://asia.nikkei.com/Business/Business-trends/Asia-s-first-patent-arbitration-hub-to-open-in-Tokyo.
68. Cabinet Secretariat, *Kokusai Chusai No Kasseika Ni Mukete Kangaerareru Sesaku (Chukan Torimatome) [Policy Proposals for Promoting International Commercial Arbitration (Interim Report)]* (2018), https://www.cas.go.jp/jp/seisaku/kokusai_chusai/pdf/honbun.pdf.
69. Cabinet Secretariat, *supra* n. 68, at 5-7.
70. Available at, http://www.jcaa.or.jp/e/arbitration/docs/brochure.pdf.
71. JCAA Pamphlet, *supra* n. 70, at 1.

- court assistance and minimal interference;[72]
- representation by foreign legal counsel (registration is unnecessary to represent clients in ICA cases seated in Japan);
- the New York Convention (Japan was an early signatory, and the Arbitration Law is in line with the treaty).

The first point might surprise some readers as a selling point because Japan was quite late in Asia to adopt the 1985 Model Law, and the Japanese Arbitration Law has still not officially adopted any of the 2006 amendments to the Model Law. However, most Model Law jurisdictions have not adhered to the amendments either,[73] so it could be argued that they do not yet constitute a 'global standard'. Moreover, the Japanese Arbitration Law is partly based on UNCITRAL's deliberations resulting in the 2006 amendments.[74]

As for the attraction of a 'modern' Japan, the JCAA pamphlet claims:

- an advanced nation ('Japan possesses all the facets necessary for reliable and effective resolution of commercial disputes by arbitration';[75])
- good communications and transport connections;
- a business and financial hub (especially around Tokyo); and
- cultural benefits ('equality before the law and fair play are highly valued norms of Japan's democratic society'.[76])

The pamphlet's authors may have been too modest, an enduring trait of Japanese culture, as there are further advantages for choosing Japan as the seat for ICA. Parties can now find Japanese and non-Japanese expert arbitrators based in Tokyo (and even Osaka or Seoul, both not far away), as well as some ICA specialisation among law firms and lawyers (*bengoshi* and *gaikokujimu-bengoshi*).[77] Japanese arbitration institutions also have strong connections with internationally well-known arbitrators from various jurisdictions.[78] In addition, as introduced above, the country has new arbitration centres and support facilities established under the Japanese government's recent pro-arbitration policy. Finally, Japan lies in Asia, although Japan is no longer 'the

72. JCAA Pamphlet, *supra* n. 70, at 2 ('Court intervention in arbitral proceedings is prohibited under the ... Arbitration Law except in specifically defined circumstances. Instead, courts play a supporting role, rendering valuable assistance by appointing arbitrators, serving notice or taking evidence').
73. UNCITRAL, *Status: UNCITRAL Model Law on International Commercial Arbitration (1985), with Amendments as Adopted in 2006*, http://www.uncitral.org/uncitral/en/uncitral_texts/arbitration/1985Model_arbitration_status.html.
74. Koichi Miki & Kazuhiko Yamomoto, *Shin Chusai Hou No Riron To Jitsumu [Theory and Practice of the New Arbitration Act]* 10 (Yuhikaku 2006); Teramura & Nottage, *supra* n. 34, at 90.
75. JCAA Pamphlet, *supra* n. 70, at 8.
76. JCAA Pamphlet, *supra* n. 70, at 9.
77. *See*, e.g., Who's Who Legal, http://whoswholegal.com/search/results/?bSubmitted=true&sFirstName=&sLastName=&sFirmName=&nSearchArea=20&bHasEditions=true&nSubEdition=0&bHasTypes=true&nWebType=0&nSearchCountry=300&ncountrytotal=94&searchsubmit.
78. JCAA, *List of Arbitrators and Mediators (Non-Japanese) Who Have Conducted JCAA Arbitration and/or Mediation Cases Filed Since 1 January 1998*, http://www.jcaa.or.jp/arbitration/0f72fa02e07016f1f51376a89f50cecb8fc406ad.xlsx.

largest economy in the world's most dynamic region'.[79] Japan's political and economic environment has also been stable, particularly in recent years, although it is necessary to monitor the Trump government's unpredictable trade and diplomatic strategies.[80]

[B] Japan's ICA Incapacity

Nonetheless, such advantages need to be weighed against some downsides. The most serious immediate challenge for promoting Japanese ICA is probably still a relative paucity of arbitrators based in Japan who are able to confidently handle arbitration cases in English.[81] Although the Japanese arbitration community has maintained a pool of good-quality arbitrators and attorneys who are fluent in the language, their total numbers remain low.

While the Japanese government and legal profession are aware of this situation and have tried to improve it,[82] their commitment has sometimes come into question. A recent example is the 'Opening Ceremony for JIDRC-Osaka', billed as 'The Future of International Arbitration in Japan' but conducted in Japanese instead of English.[83] To really establish Japan as a new international ADR hub,[84] it seems important to create opportunities to expose local practitioners to legal English and to engage in the lingua franca of contemporary ICA.[85]

Another challenge for seating ICA in Japan is the country's geographical inconvenience. Although certainly not as remote as Australia, for example,[86] Japan is on the outskirts of Asia. Tokyo is one of the world's leading megalopolises. However, the city itself is distant from other major Asian economic centres: seven hours from Singapore; four hours from Hong Kong; three hours from Taipei, Shanghai and Beijing. Tokyo might be an appealing arbitration venue for companies doing business in the city itself or around Japan. Yet other parties, especially Asian corporations with no strong business interests there, will probably continue to favour the very popular regional arbitration venues like Singapore and Hong Kong.[87] It remains unclear whether or not the COVID-19 pandemic from early 2020 will have a long-run impact on ICA practice and especially the popularity of such centres linked in part to their geographical location.

One way to overcome Japan's geographical disadvantage is to develop a niche marketing approach. The establishment of the IACT is a promising experiment,

79. JCAA Pamphlet, *supra* n. 70, at 1.
80. *See* further Nobumichi Teramura, *Australian Perspectives on International Commercial Dispute Resolution for the 21st Century: A Symposium*, June 2018 ACICA Rev. 38 (2018).
81. Taniguchi, *supra* n. 54, at 22.
82. Cabinet Secretariat, *supra* n. 68, at 2-3.
83. http://arbitrators.jp/wp-content/uploads/180426_openingceremony.pdf.
84. Nobumichi Teramura, *Japan – The Next Arbitration Shangri-La?*, Japanese Law and the Asia Pacific (5 Oct. 2017), https://japaneselaw.sydney.edu.au/2017/10/guest-blog-japan-the-next-arbitration-shangri-la/.
85. *2017 ICC Dispute Resolution Statistics (Language of Awards)*, *supra* n. 33.
86. Nottage & Teramura, *supra* n. 43.
87. 2018 Queen Mary Survey, *supra* n. 9, at 9.

although there is a risk of impeding a critical mass in ICA caseload and the development of a consistent 'Japan' brand. (The caseload is already split between the JCAA and TOMAC (Tokyo Maritime Arbitration Commission), and a 'JIDRC-Tokyo' facility was also envisaged on 12 March 2020.[88]) There is also still scope to focus on disputes between parties in the Americas or along the 'Belt and Road' where Chinese investors are involved in multinational consortiums. Moreover, c arbitrations would be helpful to combat geographical inconvenience and regional or global pandemics. So far, few Japanese arbitration institutions (even IACT) seem to be strongly interested in developing online arbitration platforms yet,[89] although this is also true of arbitration institutions worldwide.

A final difficulty relates to some putative 'cultural yearning to seek consensus' in Japan.[90] Given worldwide concerns about the costs, delays and over-formalisation of ICA,[91] can this be niche-marketed for Japan as a positive? This might be done, for example, by emphasising the Arbitration Law's nod to Arb-Med, its practice notably in JCAA arbitrations, and the JCAA's novel 'Interactive Arbitration Rules' added in 2019.[92] Or do the persistence of such concerns show that it is implausible to compete on price, given the information asymmetries in the ICA 'market' (on the demand side) and the growth of large law firms even in Asia (on the supply side)?[93] Is the attraction of consensus even cultural (as opposed to economic), or changing (alongside at least some aspects of Japan's wider legal order)? Or is it something best addressed in separate international mediation proceedings and institutions, as envisaged so far in JIMC-Kyoto?

---

88. http://idrc.jp/en/. However, the opening ceremony of JIDRC-Tokyo was postponed due to the COVID-19 outbreak in the country. *See* JIDRC, *[Postponed] Opening Ceremony of JIDRC-TOKYO (12 March 2020)*, News (28 Feb. 2020), http://idrc.jp/en/news/postponed-opening-ceremony-of-jidrc-tokyo-12-march-2020/.
89. *See also* IACT, *Upcoming Webinar: Managing Coronavirus Impact on Litigation Operations – Mediation & Arbitration* (24 Mar. 2020), https://www.iactokyo.com/events.
90. JCAA Pamphlet, *supra* n. 70, at 1.
91. *See* generally Nobumichi Teramura, *Ex Aequo et Bono as a Response to the 'Over-Judicialisation' of International Commercial Arbitration* (Wolters Kluwer 2020); Nobumichi Teramura, *Ex Aequo et Bono: An Overlooked and Undervalued Opportunity for International Commercial Arbitration*, Kluwer Arbitration Blog (18 Nov. 2018), http://arbitrationblog.kluwerarbitration.com/2018/11/18/ex-aequo-et-bono-an-overlooked-and-undervalued-opportunity-for-international-commercial-arbitration/; Nobumichi Teramura, *The Strengths and Weaknesses of Arguments Pertaining to Ex Aequo et Bono*, 15 Asian Int'l Arb. J. (2019).
92. Articles 48 and 56 of the JCAA's Interactive Rules require the tribunal to summarise key issues and party submissions, and later give its preliminary views before deciding whether to hold hearings to examine witnesses, in writing to all parties, *see* Gilmore, et al., *supra* n. 56. Under the 2018 Prague Rules on the Efficient Conduct of Proceedings in International Arbitration (December 2018), the expression of preliminary reviews is instead discretionary and more limited, seemingly to protect the arbitrators from challenges: *see* Huw Watkins, *Product Differentiation and the JCAA's 2019 Sets of Arbitration Rules* (2019), 21(3) Asian Dispute Rev. 114, 117. On earlier empirical data regarding instead ex parte or caucus-style Arb-Med practice in the JCAA, engaging with statistics analysed by Prof. Tetsuya Nakamura, *see* Luke Nottage, *Arb-Med and New International Commercial Mediation Rules in Japan*, Japanese Law and the Asia Pacific (24 Jul. 2009), https://japaneselaw.sydney.edu.au/2009/07/arb-med-and-new-international-commercial-mediation-rules-in-japan/.
93. Nottage, *supra* n. 27.

§10.03 THE JAPAN INTERNATIONAL MEDIATION CENTRE IN KYOTO

As mentioned at the outset of §10.02 above, the long tradition of court-annexed and government-supported mediation schemes coupled with the general efficiency of Japanese court proceedings has hampered the emergence of privately supported dispute resolution. This is true of mediation as well as arbitration services. Mediation by commercial suppliers has not grown as strongly as in countries like Australia,[94] where developments have often run the other way: the popularity of privately supplied mediation has tended to prompt reforms to court-annexed mediation.[95] Privately supplied mediation services have not expanded much despite, for example, an enactment in 2004 offering advantages for mediation bodies that obtain government certification.[96] Nonetheless, the LDP initiative in mid-2017 created momentum to develop JIMC-Kyoto, which formally commenced operations from November 2018.

Interestingly, the original idea can be traced back to a mediation seminar held in 2015, where discussants had considered the importance of an attractive location and other environmental influences on achieving successful settlements. Participants had agreed that Kyoto would be a particularly attractive place for international mediation. The capital of Japan for more than a millennium, Kyoto, remains known for its traditional architecture and peaceful atmosphere, including religious monuments, teahouses, and gardens. Logistically speaking, as a popular tourist destination, the city also has reliable transportation (lying two hours by bullet train from Tokyo), hotels and other services.

JIMC-Kyoto will also begin operations at a time when international commercial mediation is receiving greater attention and support.[97] This includes reported increases in demand for international mediation[98] and the use of mediation,[99] as well as initiatives to promote mediation to greater effect in certain sectors (such as investor-state mediation).[100]

---

94. *See*, e.g., Laurence Boulle & Rachael Field, *Mediation in Australia: A Comprehensive Treatment of the Theory, Principles and Practice of Mediation* (LexisNexis 2018).
95. *See* generally Shahla Ali, *Court Mediation Reform: Efficiency, Confidence and Perceptions of Justice* (Elgar 2018).
96. Aya Yamada, *ADR in Japan: Does The New Law Liberalize ADR From Historical Shackles or Legalize It?*, 2 Contemp. Asia Arb. J. 1 (2009). Many bodies have registered but few seem to have significant or strongly growing caseloads. The total number of mediation case filings across all certified ADR organisations in Japan has stabilised around 1000 cases each year since 2010, *see* http://www.moj.go.jp/KANBOU/ADR/images/kensu.pdf>. We thank Prof. Moritz Baelz for this reference.
97. *See*, e.g., Eunice Chua, *Feel The Earth Move – Shifts In The International Dispute Resolution Landscape*, Kluwer Mediation Blog (14 Aug. 2018), http://mediationblog.kluwerarbitration.com/2018/08/14/feel-earth-move-shifts-international-dispute-resolution-landscape/ detailing a UNCITRAL conference dedicated, in part, to the rise in mediation.
98. International Mediation Institute (IMI), *International Mediation & ADR Survey, Census of Conflict Management and Stakeholder Trends*, 5 (2016), found that across the globe the interest in international mediation is growing and business advisors, and that potential users understand mediation better.
99. *See*, e.g., Centre for Effective Dispute Resolution (CEDR), the Eighth Mediation Audit (2018), reporting a 20% increase in commercial mediation in the UK since 2016 (at 3).
100. ICSID has proposed draft mediation rules as a new option under its Additional Facility Rules. For a preliminary assessment, *see* Ana Ubilava & Luke Nottage, *ICSID's New Mediation Rules:*

Meanwhile, there is progress towards closing the enforcement gap between international mediation and international arbitration. UNCITRAL has promulgated the 'Singapore Mediation Convention' for the enforcement of international commercial settlement agreements resulting from mediation[101] as well as related amendments to its Model Law on International Commercial Conciliation.[102] The convention, which has fifty-two signatories (but not yet Japan) and was ratified by three states as of March 2020, is set to enter into force from 12 September 2020.[103]

[A] Establishment and Structure of JIMC-Kyoto

The JIMC-Kyoto initiative is closely linked with the Japan Association of Arbitrators (JAA), a non-profit organisation originally established to provide training to arbitrators and to promote alternative dispute resolution. A working group of ten to fifteen JAA members comprising academics, lawyers, in-house counsel, and businesses leaders began meeting in 2017 to iron out the details. The majority of the participants are Japanese, but a few foreigners have been involved in the initiative. The committee has plans for the Centre to offer various support services to international commercial mediations including proposing and appointing mediators, providing mediation facilities, and administering mediations under JIMC-Kyoto mediation rules. Important strides toward this end have already been made.

First, a secretariat comprising a small number of lawyers and assistants employed part-time has been established. Daily operations are managed by a Secretary General who is assisted by a committee subdivided into smaller working groups that have responsibility for different spheres of operations, including panel membership, marketing, and events.

JIMC-Kyoto's operations are based at the peaceful main campus of Doshisha University in central Kyoto. Its postgraduate Law School, established in 2004 as another aspect of justice system reforms in Japan,[104] provides facilities including mediation rooms that are equipped with interpretation booths and private rooms for

---

A Small but Positive Step Forward, Erga Omnes – The SCIL Blog (11 Sep. 2018), http://blogs.usyd.edu.au/erga-omnes/2018/09/icsids_new_mediation_rules.html. ICSID, together with CEDR, the IMI and the International Energy Charter secretariat, has also been offering investor-state mediation training sessions globally.

101. Timothy Schnabel, *The Singapore Convention on Mediation: A Framework for the Cross-Border Recognition and Enforcement of Mediated Settlements*, 19 Pepp. Disp. Resol. L.J. 1 (2019). Also available at SSRN: https://ssrn.com/abstract=3239527.
102. Settlement of commercial disputes, International commercial mediation: draft model law on international commercial mediation and international settlement agreements resulting from mediation, Note by the Secretariat UN Doc A/CN.9/943, 9-13 (2 Mar. 2018), http://undocs.org/A/CN.9/943.
103. *United Nations Treaty Collection, United Nations Convention on International Settlement Agreements resulting from Mediation,* https://treaties.un.org/Pages/ViewDetails.aspx?src=TREATY&mtdsg_no=XXII-4&chapter=22&clang=_en.
104. *See* generally, e.g., Luke Nottage, *Build Postgraduate Law Schools in Kyoto, and Will They Come – Sooner and Later?*, 7 Australian J. Asian L. 241 (2005). Also available at SSRN: https://ssrn.com/abstract=986529.

parties. The fees for the use of these facilities are included in a lodging fee paid to the centre by parties to mediations.

Second, JIMC-Kyoto published rules for administered mediation proceedings in November 2018.[105] The rules comprise modern features and are similar to the mediation rules of other dispute resolution institutions. They provide, for example, that mediation can be instituted either with or without prior party agreement[106] and that the centre will appoint mediators for parties on request.[107]

The rules also clarify how mediation will relate to parallel and subsequent dispute proceedings. They notably prohibit mediators from acting as arbitrators of the same dispute unless the parties agree otherwise.[108] While the rules stop short of providing for hybrid procedures,[109] the centre has published a model escalation clause for mediation-arbitration proceedings.[110] The rules do not prescribe any default style of mediation, which marks a departure from the evaluative style of mediation that is pervasive in most mediations in Japan.

Third, JIMC-Kyoto has published a panel of mediators with input from the Singapore International Mediation Centre (SIMC) and the Hong Kong Mediation Centre. The panel comprises experienced mediators of various nationalities, backgrounds, and areas of specialisation divided into subpanels of mediators residing in Japan, mostly Japanese nationals, and international mediators residing outside of Japan.[111]

[B] Prospects for JIMC-Kyoto

There are several elements that should work in favour of these initiatives in Kyoto. Japan is well placed geographically for disputes between parties from the Americas and Asia, or between some parties within Asia (such as Korean and Chinese firms). There are few dedicated mediation centres in the Asia Pacific, and Japan may be perceived as a neutral place to mediate with reliable services and a pleasant, distinctive environment.

---

105. Japan International Mediation Center in Kyoto, *The Institutional Mediation Rules*, https://www.jimc-kyoto.jp/rules.
106. *Ibid.*, Articles 3.1-3.3.
107. *Ibid.*, Articles 4.4-4.5.
108. *Ibid.*, Article 9. As mentioned in Nottage, *supra* n. 92, the 'arb-med' procedure remains quite common in Japan and a few other Asian jurisdictions. *See further* JCAA Commercial Arbitration Rules (2015) Rule 55, JCAA Commercial Arbitration Rules (2019) Rule 59 and JCAA International Commercial Mediation Rules (2009) Rule 8. The 2018 UNCITRAL Model Law on International Commercial Mediation and International Settlement Agreements Resulting from Mediation (Model Law) (Article 13) likewise allows parties to agree to the mediator acting as an arbitrator in the same dispute.
109. *See*, e.g., the protocol between the Singapore International Mediation Centre Rules and the Singapore International Arbitration Centre (SIAC) entitled 'SIAC-SIMC Arb-Med-Arb Protocol', http://simc.com.sg/siac-simc-arb-med-arb-protocol.
110. Japan International Mediation Center, *Model Clause*, https://www.jimc-kyoto.jp/20190517102057.
111. Panels of resident and non-resident mediators, https://www.jimc-kyoto.jp/mediators#ttl-Resident.

There are also growing opportunities for mediation services in the region. These include, for example, disputes arising out of the Tokyo Olympic Games (deferred from mid-2020) and China's Belt and Road Initiative.[112] Several outside intuitions have already begun to embrace the potential for growth in international mediation services. SIMC notably signed memoranda of understanding with the China International Economic and Trade Arbitration Commission and the Korean Commercial Arbitration Board in August 2019, aimed at jointly promoting mediation services and training mediators.[113]

The coronavirus pandemic in 2020 may also offer new possibilities for mediation services owing to its extensive impact on international business and global supply chains.[114] Disruptions to business, delays, and cancellations strain commercial relations and have already led to a multitude of disputes.[115] In these circumstances, mediation can help cash-strapped commercial firms manage the growing backlog of claims.

JIMC-Kyoto may benefit as businesses come alive to the advantages of mediation in these circumstances. The mediation process is comparatively inexpensive and more likely to preserve relations than adversarial processes like arbitration. It may also be easier to mediate than to arbitrate, during the coronavirus pandemic and even in its aftermath, for practical reasons. Mediations tend to require few participants while arbitrations commonly engage teams of lawyers, supporting staff, experts, and fact witnesses. This amounts to both a commercial advantage of mediation as well as a practical advantage for as long as travel complications and restrictions persist.

Likewise, it may be easier to administer mediations than arbitrations online because mediations tend to be less procedurally complex than many arbitrations. Witness examination and extensive documentary evidence that regularly feature in arbitration are uncommon in mediation. Managing documents and witness online can

---

112. The SIMC, for its part, has already announced that it will collaborate with the Mediation Center of the China Council for the Promotion of International Trade / China Chamber of International Commerce to facilitate the mediation of disputes that arise out of Belt and Road transactions. *See, e.g.*, SIMC, *SIMC and CCPIT Mediation Center Establish International Mediator Panel to Resolve BRI-Related Disputes*, News (25 Jan. 2019), http://simc.com.sg/blog/2019/01/25/simc-and-ccpit-mediation-center-establish-international-mediator-panel-to-resolve-bri-related-disputes/.
113. SIMC, *International Mediation Forum Commemorates a New Era in Dispute Resolution, Highlights Work Needed to Take the Singapore Convention on Mediation Forward*, News (6 Aug. 2019), http://simc.com.sg/blog/2019/08/06/international-mediation-forum-commemorates-a-new-era-in-dispute-resolution-highlights-work-needed-to-take-the-singapore-convention-on-mediation-forward.
114. Constantin-Adi Gavrila, *Reflections in the Age of Coronavirus (COVID-19)*, Kluwer Mediation Blog (14 Mar. 2020), http://mediationblog.kluwerarbitration.com/2020/03/14/reflections-in-the-age-of-coronavirus-covid-19/; Jed Melnick & Simone Lelchuk, *Video Conferencing and Mediating Complex Disputes in the New Normal: Settlements Don't Need to Wait*, N.Y.L.J. (17 Mar. 2020), https://www.law.com/newyorklawjournal/2020/03/17/video-conferencing-and-mediating-complex-disputes-in-the-new-normal-settlements-dont-need-to-wait/?slreturn=20200223061453.
115. Gary L. Benton, *How Will the Coronavirus Impact International Arbitration?*, Kluwer Arbitration Blog (13 Mar. 2020), http://arbitrationblog.kluwerarbitration.com/2020/03/13/how-will-the-coronavirus-impact-international-arbitration/.

be complicated, particularly where interpretation is needed, and witnesses are remote from other hearing participants.

Until 2020, however, JIMC-Kyoto mainly emphasised location and atmosphere as advantages over alternatives. According to the Centre, the peaceful environment of Kyoto and distance from business centres can reduce outside distractions and may more meaningfully engage parties in the mediation process, which can normally be completed in only a day or two. Disputing parties who commit to mediate in Kyoto, rather than in one of their home cities, may demonstrate a level of seriousness and investment in the process that could improve prospects for successful settlements.

JIMC-Kyoto is also considering how to make the centre's services distinctive and reflective of its Japanese roots. Kodai-ji, a temple that is a short distance from the central Kyoto train station, is now available as a venue for JIMC-Kyoto mediations. JIMC-Kyoto is working to secure similar arrangements with other area shrines and temples.

Nonetheless, can JIMC-Kyoto actually emerge as a leading centre for international mediation services? While the JCAA is accredited to offer international commercial mediation services and revised its own mediation rules in February 2020, it has historically struggled to attract mediation (as well as arbitration) cases despite Japan's large economy.[116] As it looks ahead, the JIMC-Kyoto committee has in mind the experience of the JCAA and initiatives that have led other institutions in the region to flourish. Discussions have considered the following issues.

A first topic is international 'in-reach'. Arbitration institutions in Asia that have risen to global prominence include leading international arbitration figures as executives, in management, and as consultants on advisory boards. Working with experts from abroad benefits an institution at the level of operations while reassuring the international community of the capacity and international orientation of the institution.[117]

Second, the committee is alive to the importance of expanded 'international outreach.' Dispute resolution institutions with international aspirations take marketing seriously. This includes less frontal measures like underwriting events and training, supporting student competitions, hosting foreign interns, and maintaining an up-to-date and informative website in English.

Third, transparency has become a trend among dispute resolution institutions. This has made it easier to find information about the leaders, governance structure, case statistics, and lists of arbitrators and mediators of institutions – all normally available online. This is likely to continue, and for institutions entering the market

116. Yoshimi Ohara, *The Asia-Pacific Arbitration Review 2019: Japan*, GAR (29 May 2018), https://globalarbitrationreview-com.wwwproxy1.library.unsw.edu.au/insight/the-asia-pacific-arbitration-review-2019/1170043/japan.

117. The SIAC Board of Directors, Court of Arbitration, and Secretariat each comprise members of various nationalities. They include American, Australian, Belgian, Canadian, Chinese, Dutch, German, French, Indian, Indonesian, Japanese, Korean, Malaysian, Russian, Singaporean and Swedish members.

without established reputations (like JIMC-Kyoto), it is especially important not to leave potential users in doubt about such matters.[118]

A fourth topic concerns cooperation and synergies. The success of dispute resolution institutions in Asia has been propelled by coordination among stakeholders, perhaps most visibly in the case of Singapore. Its government, courts, dispute resolution institutions and legal community collaborate and present a unified front to the public. This has contributed to Singapore's reputation as a hub for international dispute resolution in Asia[119] and beyond.[120]

§10.04 CONCLUSIONS

Can Japan proceed to the next stage of arbitration development, belatedly catching up with the front-runners in the Asia Pacific region? Will this be underpinned by the growing engagement in ISDS and international investment treaty-making, albeit off a low base? The possible expansion of Japan as another regional hub for international dispute resolution has both practical and theoretical resonance. From the standpoint of legal and commercial practice, Japan has long remained well behind Hong Kong and Singapore, now part of the global arbitration lexicon, but also Seoul and Kuala Lumpur, which have a decade-long head start on promotion and development that is now generating growing ICA caseloads.[121] Japan is meanwhile not the only jurisdiction in the Pacific region with hopes to emerge from the shadows, such as Australia, for example, renews its promotional activities and other initiatives.[122] To gain traction in these conditions will require a coordinated and ambitious effort as well as perseverance.[123] Even if Japan and its institutions do earn the trust of potential users, the seeds sown in dispute resolution clauses may not bear significant fruit for a decade or more.

Faced with this reality, Japan would do well to go beyond a general provision of services, to enhance specialisation or targeted marketing. Japan's location at the margin of Northeast Asia might make it a convenient seat for parties distant from Hong

118. Teresa Garcia-Reyes & Michael McIlwrath, *Arbitration Institutions: Five Things Your Website Must Do to Attract Cases* (17 Jan. 2018), http://arbitrationblog.kluwerarbitration.com/2018/01/17/mike/.
119. 2018 Queen Mary Survey, *supra* n. 9, at 10, identifying Singapore as the second most-preferred seat for arbitration (after London) among respondents in the Asia Pacific.
120. 2018 Queen Mary Survey, *supra* n. 9, at 10, identifying Singapore as the third most-preferred seat for arbitration globally as well as fourth among respondents in Europe, fourth among respondents in North America, fourth among respondents in Africa, and third among respondents in the Middle East.
121. *See* generally Ali, Chapter 6 in this volume (on Hong Kong) and Venugopal, Chapter 9 in this volume (on Malaysia). For recent developments in Singapore, *see* Julien Chaisse & Arjun Solanki, Singapore's Amendment to Its International Arbitration Act Pledges Its Leadership in the Asia-Pacific Region (18 Oct. 2020), http://arbitrationblog.kluwerarbitration.com/2020/10/18/singapores-amendment-to-its-international-arbitration-act-pledges-its-leadership-in-the-asia-pacific-region/.
122. *See* especially Monichino & Teramura, Chapter 3 in this volume; and generally Luke Nottage, *International Commercial and Investor-State Arbitration – Australia and Japan in Regional and Global Contexts* (Edward Elgar 2021).
123. This might include the appointment of native English speakers as institutional leaders or the creation of an independent umbrella organisation, *see* Nottage & Claxton, *supra* n. 35.

Kong and Singapore, such as Korean companies that fail to secure Korea as the place of arbitration.[124] Likewise, Japan's historical ties with the US might make it an attractive and geographically convenient seat for American companies with contracting partners in Asia and the Pacific Rim. Belt and Road disputes may present another opportunity, again for reasons of geography, for parties to contract with a Chinese element that want to avoid resolving disputes in Hong Kong. The coronavirus pandemic may prompt legal advisors to diversify the venues they suggest and draft into contracts for ICA and other international dispute resolution,[125] making Japan's recent efforts more visible and impactful.

The emergence of JIMC-Kyoto strikes a new posture for Japan out in front of a potential market for international mediation services rather than running from behind to catch up, as with arbitration. The capacity of the centre could be amplified by integration into the broader international dispute resolution ecosystem in Japan and by synergies with arbitration services through multi-tiered dispute resolution clauses. Prospects might also be buoyed if Japan signs and then ratifies the Singapore Mediation Convention, along with more states regionally and worldwide.

From a theoretical standpoint, the recent and ongoing attempts to establish Japan as a centre for international disputes raise the perennial issue of 'reluctant claimants' and Japanese attitudes towards dispute resolution. In the case of JIMC-Kyoto, cultural drivers, such as affinity for mediation and a tradition of mediation, would not seem enough to sustain the centre even if, as is likely, most early cases will include Japanese parties. Those involved with the project seem to appreciate this constraint and are determined to define the centre by international rather than Japanese standards. This is demonstrated by the emphasis on international outreach in marketing and international 'in-reach' into management. The internationalist approach is also evident through mediator training sessions running in parallel with the establishment of the centre, which has focused on facilitative techniques despite the prevalence of evaluative mediation in domestic proceedings.

The JIMC initiative did not originate with the government or business elite, but rather with key individuals who are now looking to leverage from subsequent government initiatives. The project was largely conceived and implemented by Japanese lawyers whose experience with mediation convinced them of the potential benefit of a dedicated mediation facility in Japan, and the government came on board only after the project was in motion. This offers an alternative narrative to the view shared by some that Japanese dispute resolution culture is top-down and shaped by institutional barriers and/or case management by governmental and big business elites.

Whether Japanese companies will become more willing to favour Japan and Japanese institutions will be an indicator of how much the pull of (corporate) culture remains in play. The present initiatives offer the renewed possibility of persuading Japanese companies to press their contracting counterparties to seat arbitrations in Japan rather than abroad, as South Korea has been able to do effectively to its

124. John Kang, *A Case for Tokyo*, Asian Legal Bus. (3 Jan. 2018), https://www.legalbusinessonline.com/features/case-tokyo/75228.
125. *See* generally Teramura, Ali & Reyes, Chapter 15 in this volume.

benefit.[126] If reluctant Japanese claimants and respondents can at least agree on this point, it will mark an important step towards turning the Japanese dream into a reality.

126. Nottage & Claxton, *supra* n. 35.

CHAPTER 11

Litigating, Arbitrating and Mediating Japan-Korea Trade and Investment Tensions

James Claxton, Luke Nottage & Brett Williams[*]

In July 2019, Japan introduced measures tightening export restrictions to South Korea on three chemicals critical to the manufacture of consumer electronics. The restrictions prompted an animated response by the Korean government, including World Trade Organization (WTO) consultations and threats to terminate an intelligence-sharing agreement. The controversy also filtered down to the public with boycotts of Japanese products in Korea. Tension between the states has been unusually high since 2018 when the Korean Supreme Court affirmed a judgment against Japanese companies accused of forcing Korean nationals to labour in factories during Japan's colonial rule. Japan argued that these claims were precluded by a 1965 treaty normalising post-war relations. While Japan claims that its trade restrictions were not motivated by the judgment, the disputes have contributed to the worst breakdown in cross-border relations in five decades. This chapter evaluates Korea's trade claims against Japan, means of resolving them, and challenges faced in the WTO dispute settlement system. Alternatives or additions to WTO dispute settlement procedures are considered, including claims before the International Court of Justice (ICJ), interstate arbitration, and investor-state dispute settlement (ISDS). Mediation offers an effective means to facilitate negotiations and centralise the trade and treaty disputes in a single forum.

§11.01 INTRODUCTION: COMPLEX MULTI-FACETED TENSIONS

A media and geopolitical storm erupted from mid-2019 after Japan introduced measures affecting exports to the Republic of Korea (Korea). Thunder sounded with

* We thank Ashley Taylor Kelaita, LLM candidate and CAPLUS intern (2019), for superlative research and editorial assistance.

Japan's imposition of certification requirements on three chemicals needed by South Korean companies to make semiconductors, memory chips and displays for consumer electronics (the 4 July Measure). This was followed by lightning and rain when Japan removed Korea from its 'white list' of trusted trading partners (the 2 August Measure), with Seoul retaliating by threatening to reduce military-intelligence cooperation,[1] removing Japan from its 'white list',[2] and threatening to impose countermeasures on trade. The growing geopolitical tempest has brought about the worst breakdown in cross-border bilateral relations in five decades,[3] generating both regional and global ramifications.[4]

Differing rationales for the geopolitical storm have been given. The Japanese government[5] and media[6] tend to emphasise security concerns, namely on shipments of chemicals with potential military applications to North Korea, violating multilateral sanctions. The South Korean government[7] and media,[8] as well as some international news outlets,[9] have often placed more emphasis on the possibility of Japan 'retaliating' for an October 2018 judgment of the Supreme Court of Korea. That decision upheld lower court judgments from 2014 finding major Japanese companies, such as Nippon Steel, liable to compensate claimants alleging that they were forced labourers for the

1. Alastair Gale & Andrew Jeong, *South Korea Stays in Intelligence-Sharing Pact with Japan, for Now*, The Wall St. J. (22 Nov. 2019), https://www.wsj.com/articles/south-korea-stays-in-intelligence-sharing-pact-with-japan-for-now-11574412237 (accessed 10 Mar. 2020).
2. *South Korea Removes Japan from Trade Whitelist as Feud Deepens*, Japan Times (18 Sep. 2019), https://www.japantimes.co.jp/news/2019/09/18/business/south-korea-removes-japan-fast-track-trade-white-list/#.XZRBg-czav4 (accessed 2 Oct. 2019).
3. Lauren Richardson, *Japan's Deepening Diplomatic Crisis with South Korea*, 11(3) EAF Q. 7 (September 2019); Editorial Board, *Abe's Remarkable Political Record Leaves Japan Still Searching for a New Way*, East Asia Forum (2 Sep. 2019), https://www.eastasiaforum.org/2019/09/02/abes-remarkable-political-record-leaves-japan-still-searching-for-a-new-way/ (accessed 2 Oct. 2019); Lee Min-hyung, *Gov't Augments Budget for Diplomacy with Japan*, Korea Times (29 Aug. 2019), https://www.koreatimes.co.kr/www/nation/2019/09/356_274795.html (accessed 2 Oct. 2019).
4. Erin Handley, *What Does Japan and South Korea's Tech Trade Dispute Mean for the Cost of Your Smartphone?*, ABC News (28 Jul. 2019), https://www.abc.net.au/news/2019-07-28/what-does-japan-south-korea-trade-war-mean-for-smartphone-costs/11341254?pfmredir=sm (accessed 25 Sep. 2019); Shim Kyu-Seok, *Seoul Kicks off Dokdo Exercises*, Korea Joongang Daily (26 Aug. 2019), http://koreajoongangdaily.joins.com/news/article/article.aspx?aid=3067170 (accessed 2 Oct. 2019).
5. *METI Chief Seko Defends Tighter Japanese Export Controls Imposed on South Korea*, Japan Times (16 Jul. 2019), https://www.japantimes.co.jp/news/2019/07/16/business/meti-chief-seko-defends-tighter-japanese-export-controls-imposed-south-korea/#.XUilplAlGUZ (accessed 25 Sep. 2019).
6. *Japan to Decide to Remove South Korea from 'Whitelist' on Aug 2*, Nikkei Asian Review (26 Jul. 2019), https://asia.nikkei.com/Spotlight/Japan-South-Korea-rift/Japan-to-decide-to-remove-South-Korea-from-whitelist-on-Aug-2 (accessed 25 Sep. 2019).
7. *Opening Remarks by Deputy National Security Advisor Hyun Chong Kim at Press Briefing* (19 Jul. 2019), http://english1.president.go.kr/BriefingSpeeches/Briefings/444 (accessed 25 Sep. 2019).
8. Do Je-hae, *Korea Strongly Warns against 'Whitelist' Action*, Korea Times (30 Jul. 2019), https://www.koreatimes.co.kr/www/nation/2019/08/356_273101.html (accessed 25 Sep. 2019).
9. Isabel Reynolds & Sam Kim, *Japan Removes South Korea From Trusted Export List*, Bloomberg (2 Aug. 2019), https://www.bloomberg.com/news/articles/2019-08-01/japan-may-decide-on-controlling-exports-to-south-korea (accessed 25 Sep. 2019).

Japanese companies during World War II. The companies, and the Japanese government, have argued that such claims were precluded by a bilateral treaty signed in 1965 to restore diplomatic relations.[10] (Interestingly, similar claims and defences under different bilateral instruments have been raised before Japanese courts by Chinese war-time labourers, generating a settlement with Nishimatsu group companies.[11]) A few media reports also speculated that Japan introduced export restrictions affecting Korea to bolster the appeal of the Abe Administration in upper House of Councillor elections,[12] but it secured another solid victory anyway.[13] Some media sources also suggested that populist Korean President Moon Jae-in may be 'playing to the base' in domestic politics.[14]

On 11 September 2019, Korea formally requested consultations with Japan under Article 4 of the WTO Dispute Settlement Understanding (DSU) in respect of the 4 July Measure only as elaborated in §11.02 below.[15] This is the first stage in the WTO dispute settlement system before a panel is established by the Dispute Settlement Body (DSB).[16] Korea's request might bring to mind the claim successfully brought by the Obama Administration against China over 2012–2014, resulting in China removing export duties and quotas imposed on rare earths, for which it similarly controlled almost all world trade.[17] However, the general exceptions China failed to establish in

10. S. Nathan Park & William Sposato, *Japan and South Korea Don't Have to Love Each Other to Be Allies*, Foreign Policy (2 Jul. 2019), https://foreignpolicy.com/2019/07/02/japan-and-south-korea-dont-have-to-love-each-other-to-be-allies/ (accessed 2 Oct. 2019).
11. *See* book review by Luke Nottage outlining a chapter by Aiko Utsumi that 'begins with a summary of the lawsuits brought in 1998 by Chinese forced labourers against the Nishimatsu Group. The Hiroshima High Court ordered compensation, but the Supreme Court reversed in 2007 based on the 1972 China-Japan Joint Communique in conjunction with the 1952 San Francisco Peace Treaty. Nonetheless, in 2009 the Supreme Court noted that Nishimatsu had acknowledged its historical responsibility, agreed to payments, and would erect a memorial. Utsumi then looks at how different scholars and courts, including recently in Korea, have interpreted such inter-state agreements on Japan's wartime responsibility, insofar as they may preclude private rights to claim compensation': Luke Nottage, *Civil Society and Postwar Pacific Basin Reconciliation: Wounds, Scars and Healing* (Yasuko Claremont, ed, Routledge 2018) – Book Launch, Japanese Law and the Asia-Pacific Blog (8 Jul. 2018), http://blogs.usyd.edu.au/japaneselaw/2018/07/civil_society_and_postwar_paci.html (accessed 25 Sep. 2019).
12. Linda Sieg, *Japan Export Curbs on South Korea May Widen Rift over Wartime Labor Compensation*, Reuters (12 Jul. 2019), https://www.reuters.com/article/us-japan-southkorea-laborers-feud-analys/japan-export-curbs-on-south-korea-may-widen-rift-over-wartime-labor-compensation-idUSKCN1U7101 (accessed 25 Sep. 2019).
13. Purnendra Jain, *Abe and the LDP Remain Dominant after Japan's Upper House Elections*, East Asia Forum (25 Jul. 2019), https://www.eastasiaforum.org/2019/07/25/abe-and-the-ldp-remain-dominant-after-japans-upper-house-elections/ (accessed 25 Sep. 2019).
14. Sieg, *supra* n. 12.
15. Request for Consultations by the Republic of Korea, *Japan – Measures Related to the Exportation of Products and Technology to Korea*, WT/DS590/1. As of 30 Sep. 2019, the EU and Chinese Taipei had requested to join consultations.
16. World Trade Organization, *The Process – Stages in a Typical WTO Dispute Settlement Case*, Dispute Settlement System Training Module: Chapter 6, https://www.wto.org/english/tratop_e/dispu_e/disp_settlement_cbt_e/c6s1p1_e.htm#targetText=There%20are%20three%20main%20stages,party%20to%20implement%20the%20ruling (accessed 9 Oct. 2019).
17. For a discussion of these proceedings and rare earths more generally, *see* David Uren, *Rare Earths: Is There a Case for Government Intervention?*, USSC Analysis (9 Oct. 2019), https://www.ussc.edu.au/analysis/rare-earths-is-there-a-case-for-government-intervention (accessed 9 Oct. 2019).

that case, under Article XX of the General Agreement on Tariffs and Trade (GATT), dealt with health and conservation of natural resources.[18] By contrast, Japan could be expected to raise national security exceptions under Article XXI in the proceedings with Korea. There are even greater differences from a procedural perspective, which we focus on below. However, if the dispute is not resolved by formal consultations and an ad hoc panel rules against Japan, this would only come by 2021 at the earliest. Yet since December 2019, the Appellate Body has not had sufficient Members (full-time 'judges') to hear appeals due to the Trump Administration blocking new appointments until its concerns about dispute resolution and other aspects of the WTO system are adequately addressed.[19] Accordingly, an appeal could stall the resolution of the dispute indefinitely and leave the rights and obligations of the parties unsettled. The US even raised the prospect of blocking the passage of the WTO budget, further clouding prospects for resolution under the auspices of that forum.[20]

The situation becomes even messier when we consider below, in §11.03, other potential interstate dispute resolution processes. Japan could seek arbitration under the 1965 treaty, but that effectively requires the counterparty to provide further consent, which Korea does not seem to want to do. Japan might also consider litigating the treaty before the ICJ. Another option is to invoke interstate arbitration under the Japan-Korea bilateral investment treaty (BIT) in force since 2003, and/or a trilateral investment treaty in force from 2014.[21] However, it may be difficult to prove that the Korean court judgments involved a procedural defect or discrimination towards the Japanese companies creating a denial of justice in violation of the relevant treaties.

A further possibility, mentioned in a very few media reports and considered in §11.04, is that the companies directly initiate ISDS claims, as provided by both investment treaties in lieu of interstate arbitration. This could theoretically include an application to the ad hoc arbitration tribunal to issue interim measures preventing enforcement of the Korean Supreme Court ruling pending determination of claims such as denial of justice.

A major problem for the Japanese companies is that they would have to fork out tribunal, lawyer and expert witness fees – often hefty, even if the claim ultimately

18. Appellate Body Report, *China – Measures Related to the Exportation of Rare Earths, Tungsten and Molybdenum*, WT/DS431/AB/R, WT/DS432/AB/R, WT/DS433/AB/R, adopted 20 May 2015.

19. *See*, e.g., Andrew Stoler, *Crisis in the WTO Appellate Body and the Need for Wider WTO Reform Negotiations*, Institute for International Trade, University of Adelaide (1 Mar. 2019), https://iit.adelaide.edu.au/news/list/2019/04/08/crisis-in-the-wto-appellate-body-and-the-need-for-wider-wto-reform (accessed 25 Sep. 2019).

20. Bryce Baschuk, *U.S. Raises Prospect of Blocking Passage of WTO Budget*, Bloomberg (13 Nov. 2019), https://www.bloomberg.com/news/articles/2019-11-12/u-s-is-said-to-raise-prospect-of-blocking-passage-of-wto-budget (accessed 16 Nov. 2019).

21. *See generally* Saadia Pekkanen, *Investment Regionalism in Asia: New Directions in Law and Policy?* 11(01) World Trade Rev. 119 (2012). *See also Macro Trading Co., Ltd. v. People's Republic of China* (ICSID Case No. ARB/20/22). This is arguably the first ISDS case to be based on the 1988 China-Japan BIT: Damien Charlotin, *Japanese Investor Lodges ICSID Arbitration Against China*, IA Reporter (30 Jun. 2020), https://www.iareporter.com/articles/japanese-investor-lodges-icsid-arbitration-against-china/.

succeeds.[22] A major problem for the Japanese government, in turn, is that ISDS claims brought by the companies would likely further incense not only the current Korean government but also some groups within Korean society (including an association of judges).[23] They and the then opposition party became critical of ISDS especially as it was negotiated into the Korea-U.S. Free Trade Agreement (KORUS), brought into effect from March 2012, and as the first ever treaty-based claim was brought against Korea from late 2012 by a Belgian subsidiary of US-linked Lone Star.[24] One Australian Non-governmental Organisation (NGO) even interprets a Korean newspaper report of current Prime Minister Lee Nak-Yeon as suggesting that Korea may 'abolish' ISDS.[25] More likely he was signalling the need for further rethinking of Korea's investment treaty policy and practice, which has anyway been evolving (e.g., regarding ISDS transparency).[26] Yet an ISDS claim by Japanese companies and/or an award favouring Lone Star would further inflame simmering political tensions, especially as another US investor (Gale) filed a notice to initiate ISDS in 2019 regarding a development in Incheon.[27] Further complicating the attitude towards ISDS from some groups within Korea, Chinese and now Malaysian investors have filed notices of dispute regarding projects on Jeju Island.[28]

As we conclude, in §11.05, given this complex set of potential claims across multiple forums, the best way forward seems to be a negotiated overall settlement, perhaps facilitated by formal mediation.

22. Luke Nottage & Ana Ubilava, *Costs, Outcomes and Transparency in ISDS Arbitrations: Evidence for an Investment Treaty Parliamentary Inquiry* (2018) 21(4) Int. Arb. L. Rev 111, also available at https://papers.ssrn.com/sol3/papers.cfm?abstract_id=3227401.
23. Younsik Kim, *Investor-State Arbitration in South Korean International Trade Policies: An Uncertain Future, Trapped by the Past*, Centre for International Governance Innovation (14 Nov. 2016), https://www.cigionline.org/publications/investor-state-arbitration-south-korean-international-trade-policies-uncertain-future (accessed 25 Sep. 2019).
24. Remarkably, still pending, despite expectations it would be resolved by March 2019: *LSF-KEB Holdings SCA and Others v. Republic of Korea*, ICSID Case No. ARB/12/37; Chae Jong-won & Kim Hyo-jin, *Lone Star's ISDS Suit vs Korea to Be Concluded by March*, Pulse News (5 Nov. 2018), https://pulsenews.co.kr/view.php?year=2018&no=691385 (accessed 2 Oct. 2019).
25. *South Korean Prime Minister Considers Abolishing ISDS*, Australian Fair Trade & Investment Network (16 Jul. 2019), http://aftinet.org.au/cms/node/1757 (accessed 2 Oct. 2019); reproduced at https://bilaterals.org/?south-korean-prime-minister#forum7787 (accessed 2 Oct. 2019).
26. Joongi Kim, *Korea's International Investment Agreements: Policy at the Contours*, in *International Investment Treaties and Arbitration Across Asia* 486-512 (Julien Chaisse & Luke Nottage eds., Brill 2018).
27. Damien Charlotin, *US Investor to Start $2 Billion ICSID Proceedings Against South Korea*, IA Reporter (11 Jun. 2019), www.iareporter.com/articles/us-investor-to-start-2-billion-icsid-proceedings-against-south-korea/ (accessed 2 Oct. 2019).
28. Damien Charlotin, *Malaysian Investor Warns of Arbitration against South Korea over Thwarted Development Project on Jeju Island*, IA Reporter (26 Jul. 2019), www.iareporter.com/articles/malaysian-investor-warns-of-arbitration-against-south-korea-over-thwarted-development-project-on-jeju-island/ (accessed 2 Oct. 2019).

§11.02 KOREA VERSUS JAPAN IN THE WTO

Korea formally requested consultations with Japan under Article 4 of the WTO DSU in respect of the 4 July Measure.[29] This process has officially commenced, with the first consultation between Japan and Korea held on 11 October 2019.[30] At this stage, Korea has not filed any complaint in response to Japan's 2 August Measure to remove Korea from its 'white list'. Whether a WTO Panel would find Japan to have violated substantive commitments under WTO Agreements is not a simple issue, in particular because Japan would most likely claim that its measures can be justified under the security exception in Article XXI of the GATT.

Concerning the Japanese measures, on 1 July 2019, Ministry of Economy, Trade and Industry (Japan) (METI) announced an 'Update of METI's licensing policies and procedures on exports of controlled items to the Republic of Korea', making two changes.[31]

(i) First, with effect from 4 July 2019, Japan ceased to apply certain bulk licences to some exports to Korea (the 4 July Measure). This change had the effect that individual exporters of three chemicals (fluorinated polymide, resist, and hydrogen fluoride) from Japan to Korea would be required to apply for Individual Export Licences. As we understand it, this measure will delay some exports by the period that it takes for an exporter to apply for and receive an export licence. Further investigation would be required to determine whether the measure has any restrictive effect on exports from Korea beyond the time delay inherent in the licensing process.

(ii) Second, on 1 July 2019, Japan initiated a public comment process for a proposed Cabinet Order to remove Korea from a list of countries in appended Table III of the Export Trade Control Order (ETCO). This list is commonly called the 'white list countries' or the 'Preferred Trade Partner List Countries'. Then, on 2 August 2019 (the 2 August Measure), METI announced that the Cabinet had approved the Order to remove Korea from the appended Table III of the ETCO (Cabinet Order No. 378 of 1940).[32]

29. In this request, Korea argued that Japan's 4 July Measure was inconsistent with Japan's obligations under: Articles I, VIII, X, XI:1, XIII:1 and XIII:5 of the GATT; Articles 2, 6, 7, 8, and 10 of the TFA; Article 2 of the TRIMs Agreement; Articles 3.1, 4 and 28.2 of the TRIPS Agreement; Articles VI:1 and VI:5 of GATS; and Article XVI:4 of the Marrakesh Agreement Establishing the World Trade Organization: Request for Consultations, *Japan – Measures Related to the Exportation of Products and Technology to Korea*, *supra* n. 15, [11].
30. Ministry of Economy, Trade and Industry (METI), *Japan Held Consultations with the Government of the Republic of Korea under the WTO Agreement Regarding Japan's Update of Licensing Policies and Procedures on Exports to the ROK* (12 Oct. 2019), https://www.meti.go.jp/english/press/2019/1012_001.html (accessed 6 Nov. 2019).
31. Ministry of Economy, Trade and Industry (METI), *Update of METI's Licensing Policies and Procedures on Exports of Controlled Items to the Republic of Korea* (1 Jul. 2019), https://www.meti.go.jp/english/press/2019/0701_001.html (accessed 2 Oct. 2019).
32. METI, *The Cabinet Approved Partial Amendment to the Export Control Order* (2 Aug. 2019), https://www.meti.go.jp/english/press/2019/0802_001.html (accessed 2 Oct. 2019).

Some further background is necessary.[33] All United Nations (UN) Members are bound by UNS Security Council Resolution 1540 of 2004 obliging Members to impose national controls on export, transit and transhipment of material related to nuclear weapons. Japan is also a party to treaties on non-proliferation of nuclear, biological and chemical weapons, and, in addition, is a party to the international control regimes (which are not strictly treaty regimes). This includes the Nuclear Suppliers Group (NSG) which includes relating to controls on exports of nuclear materials,[34] the Australia Group (AG) relating to controls on exports of material that could contribute to the development of chemical weapons and biological weapons,[35] the Missile Technology Control Regime (MSTCR) relating to controls over exports of missiles and related material that could be used for delivery of weapons of mass destruction (WMD),[36] and the Wassenaar Arrangement (WA) relating to controls on exports of conventional arms and also dual-use goods and technologies.[37] Korea is a participant in the NSG,[38] the AG,[39] a Member of the MSTCR,[40] and of the Wassenaar Arrangement.[41]

National regulation in Japan is implemented under the *Foreign Exchange and Foreign Trade Act* (referred to in Japanese as 'Gaitame-ho'). The key provisions are Article 48-(1), which requires persons exporting certain goods to specified regions set out in a Cabinet Order to obtain permission from METI, and Article 25-1-(1), which requires persons transferring specific technologies relating to specific goods set forth in a Cabinet Order to a foreign person or to a foreign country to obtain permission from METI.

The most important subordinate laws are two cabinet orders. The ETCO specifies the goods that are subject to the requirement under section 48 to obtain permission for exports. Attachment List No. 1 to the ETCO contains a list of the categories of controlled goods.[42] The Foreign Exchange Order (FEO) specifies the technology, including software that is subject to the requirement under section 25 to obtain permission for

---

33. The following bare description of international and Japanese regimes is certainly not comprehensive. The information is mostly drawn from: Center for Information on Security Trade Control (CISTEC), *Overview of Japan's Export Controls* (3rd ed. 2012), available at http://www.aiplanning.net/export_controls.pdf (accessed 2 Oct. 2019).
34. Nuclear Suppliers Group, *Adherence*, http://www.nuclearsuppliersgroup.org/en/adherence (accessed 2 Oct. 2019).
35. The Australia Group, https://australiagroup.net/en/ (accessed 2 Oct. 2019).
36. Arms Control Association, *The Missile Technology Control Regime at a Glance* (July 2017), https://www.armscontrol.org/factsheets/mtcr (accessed 2 Oct. 2019).
37. The Wassenaar Arrangement on Export Controls for Conventional Arms and Dual-Use Goods and Technologies, https://www.wassenaar.org/ (accessed 2 Oct. 2019).
38. Korea became a participant in 1995; *see* Nuclear Suppliers Group, *Participants*, http://www.nuclearsuppliersgroup.org/en/about-nsg/participants1 (accessed 2 Oct. 2019).
39. Korea became a participant in 1996; *see* The Australia Group, *Australia Group Participants*, https://australiagroup.net/en/participants.html (accessed 2 Oct. 2019).
40. Korea became a Member in 2001; *see* Arms Control Association, *supra* n. 36.
41. The Wassenaar Arrangement on Export Controls for Conventional Arms and Dual-Use Goods and Technologies, *About Us*, https://www.wassenaar.org/about-us/ (accessed 2 Oct. 2019).
42. *See Export Trade Control Order (Cabinet Order No. 378 of 1949)* (Japan), available at http://www.japaneselawtranslation.go.jp/law/detail/?vm=04&re=01&id=1925 (accessed 9 Oct. 2019).

exports. Attachment 1 to the FEO contains a list of the categories of controlled technology and software.[43]

Both lists contain Categories 1-15, which are called controlled items. Although Japan has its own classification numbers, the 'controlled items on both lists are basically identical to those of the four international export control regimes'.[44] Both lists also contain Category 16, which contains 'Items other than those under Categories 1 - 15' which is the subject of what is usually called 'catch-all' regulation.

Whereas the List Control required exporters to obtain a licence to export listed goods or technologies, the catch-all control requires exporters to obtain a licence in two situations. One is where METI informs (or orders) the export to obtain a licence for a specific transaction (usually called the 'informed' condition). The second is where exporters are aware that the item will be used for the development, manufacture, use, or storage of WMD or are aware that the end user has been engaging, or used to engage, in the development, manufacture, use or storage of WMD (usually called the 'objective' condition).[45]

In addition, METI maintains an End User List and any exporter seeking to export to an end user on that list must apply to METI for a licence.[46] There are three categories of licences: (i) Individual Export Licences; (ii) Bulk Export Licences; and (iii) Four Types of Special Bulk Licences.

Exporters must apply for Individual Export Licences to export: (a) any controlled item (covered by categories 1-15 under Attachment List No. 1 to the ETCO or Attachment 1 to the Foreign Exchange Order (FEO) unless the export is eligible for a Bulk Export Licence; or (b) any items for which a licence is required under the catch-all provisions.[47] The exporter must lodge information about the transaction and the parties to the transaction and, in particular information about the end user and an End-Use Certificate from the end user. METI will assess the risk of the items contributing to WMD or of items being re-exported to countries or entities of concern.[48]

Second, exporters who are granted a Bulk Export Licence can make multiple exports of controlled items without having to obtain an Individual Export Licence each time. For exports to countries on a list of twenty-seven countries 'that are implementing robust controls as a member of the international export control regimes', it is possible to obtain a General Bulk Licence.[49]

Third, regarding Special Bulk Licences, exporters who obtain Special Bulk Licences can similarly make multiple exports of controlled items without having to

---

43. *Foreign Exchange Order (Cabinet Order No. 26 of October 11. 1980) (Japan)*, available at http://www.japaneselawtranslation.go.jp/law/detail/?ft = 1&re = 2&dn = 1&ia = 03&x = 12&y = 14&co = 01&ky = foreign + exchange + order + cabinet + no. + 260 + of + october + 11&page = 1 (accessed 9 Oct. 2019).
44. CISTEC, *supra* n. 33, at 14.
45. METI, *Overview of the 'List Control' and 'Catch-All Control'*, https://www.meti.go.jp/policy/external_economy/export_control_korea/pdf/gaiyo_en.pdf (accessed 9 Oct. 2019).
46. METI, *End User List* (26 Apr. 2019), https://www.meti.go.jp/press/2019/04/20190426002/20190426002-1.pdf (accessed 9 Oct. 2019).
47. CISTEC, *supra* n. 33, at [5-2-2] 23.
48. *Ibid.*
49. CISTEC, *supra* n. 33, at [5-2-3] 24-5.

apply for a separate Individual Export Licence for each export transaction. Special Bulk Licences are available to exporters not on the list of twenty-seven countries that can establish they meet criteria for eligibility. The main criteria are that the exporter has established an Internal Control Procedure (ICP) that must be submitted to METI and must implement controls in compliance with the ICP. They are also required to report on their compliance annually, to undergo on-site inspection by METI and participate in METI seminars on export control.[50]

It appears that the 4 July Measure does not restrict exports of the three chemicals so it would not breach GATT Article XI:1 (which applies to any restrictions on import or export other than duties or taxes). As Korea has now claimed that the 4 July Measure is inconsistent with Article XI:1,[51] Korea would have to establish that the grant of licences is not automatic. However, the 4 July Measure would likely violate the Most-Favoured-Nation Rule in GATT Article I. This is because exports to other WTO Members of the three chemicals receive an advantage in the form of the expedited export facilitated by the bulk licences not extended to exports into Korea.

The 2 August Measure, as mentioned above, removes Korea from the whitelist of countries which receive less onerous treatment from Japan in relation to controls over exports of a broad range of goods, including both: (i) goods used in the manufacture of any weapons and also (ii) goods that are generally not used in the manufacture of weapons but which could be used in the manufacture of goods. (The second group comprises so-called dual-use goods, and export controls over dual-use goods are frequently referred to as catch-all controls.) Interestingly, Korea has not requested formal consultations to resolve its initial concerns about the 2 August Measure. This may be because Korea has responded by removing Japan from its own 'white list'.

Crucially, Japan would likely claim justification regarding the 4 July Measure (and, if necessary, the 2 August Measure) under GATT Article XXI, and indeed Japan may advance arguments under more than one of the paragraphs of Article XXI. First, to the extent that Japan is obliged under UN Security Resolutions to implement controls over exports of materials, Japan's measures could be justified under the exception in Article XXI(c). Paragraph (c) of Article XXI provides an exemption:

> XXI Nothing in this Agreement shall be construed:
>
> ...
>
> (c) to prevent any Member from taking any action in pursuance of its obligations under the United Nations Charter for the maintenance of international peace and security.

There were no pre-WTO GATT panel reports and there has never been a WTO panel report on Article XX(c).

Under Article 25 of the UN Charter, UN Members are required to carry out decisions of the Security Council. The obligations on UN Members under Security Council Resolution 1540 include a general obligation to prevent the proliferation of

50. CISTEC, *supra* n. 33, at 25.
51. Request for Consultations, *Japan – Measures Related to the Exportation of Products and Technology to Korea, supra* n. 15, [11].

nuclear, chemical or biological weapons and their means of delivery in particular to maintain effective border controls and law enforcement efforts to prevent illicit trafficking in such items, and to maintain effective national export and trans-shipment controls over such items.[52]

Japan may be able to establish that in order to comply with its obligations under Resolution 1540, it is necessary for Japan to apply stricter regulation of exports to Korea involving individual applications for exports. A panel would analyse this objectively, so Japan would need to demonstrate that regulation of exports to Korea should be stricter than exports to countries that are eligible for bulk licences, or are eligible for inclusion on the whitelist.

Second, for any controls not required under a Security Council Resolution, Japan might argue that the restrictions are justified under Article XXI(b) of the GATT. Paragraph (b) of Article XXI provides that:

> Nothing in this Agreement shall be construed
>
> ...
>
> (b) to prevent any Member from taking any action which it considers necessary to the protection of its essential security interests
>   (i) relating to fissionable materials or the materials from which they are derived;
>   (ii) relating to the traffic in arms, ammunition and implements of war and to such traffic in other goods and materials as is carried on directly or indirectly for the purpose of supplying a military establishment;
>   (iii) taken in time of war or other emergency in international relations ... .

There has been just one WTO panel report on Article XXI that included findings under Article XXI(b)(ii): the non-appealed 2019 panel report in *Russia – Traffic in Transit* (with similar reasoning followed recently in *Saudi Arabia – Intellectual Property Rights*).[53] In the pre-WTO period, there were seven complaints involving Article XXI(b), two involving paragraph (b)(ii)[54] and six involving paragraph (b)(iii),[55]

52. Security Council Resolution 1540, UN Doc S/RES/1540 (28 Apr. 2004), at para. 3, and sub-paras 3(c) and 3(d).

53. Panel Report, *Russia – Measures Concerning Traffic in Transit*, WT/DS512/R, adopted 29 Apr. 2019. The same reasoning was subsequently followed (paras 7.241-43) when interpreting the identically worded 73(b)(iii) of the Agreement on Trade-Related Aspects of Intellectual Property Rights, although that security exception was only made out for one of two of the measures impugned by Qatar, in the Panel Report, *Saudi Arabia – Measures Concerning the Protection of Intellectual Property Rights*, WT/DS567/R, issued 16 Jun. 2020.

54. Contracting Parties Decision, *US – Issue of Export Licenses*, GATT/CP.3/SR.22-II/28; Communication from the European Communities, *EEC – Trade Measures Taken by the EC Against the Socialist Federal Republic of Yugoslavia*, GATT/L/6948.

55. Contracting Parties Session, *US – Suspension of Obligations Between the US and Czechoslovakia;* Peruvian Import Restrictions Modification, *Peru – Prohibition of Czechoslovakian Imports*, GATT/L/2844; Draft Decision, *EC, Australia, Canada – Trade Restrictions Affecting Argentina Applied for Non-economic Reasons*, GATT/C/W/402; GATT Panel Report, *United States – Imports of Sugar from Nicaragua*, GATT/L/5607, adopted 12 Mar. 1984, GATT BISD 31S/67; GATT Panel Report (unadopted), *US – Trade Measures Affecting Nicaragua*, GATT/L/6053; *EEC – Trade Measures Taken by the EC Against the Socialist Federal Republic of Yugoslavia*, *supra* n. 54.

but only one case was adopted by GATT contracting parties.[56] In addition, none of those earlier panel reports offer any analysis of what is required to satisfy Article XXI(b)(ii) or (iii).[57]

In the 2019 WTO report in *Russia – Traffic in Transit*, the Panel found that this involves a combination of elements, some of which would involve assessment of what the relevant WTO Member considered to be the case, and some of which involve objective assessments of the particular element of the particular paragraph of Article XXI(b)(i), (ii) or (iii).[58] The Panel did not accept the Respondent's argument that Article XXI(b), by including the phrase 'which it considers necessary', conferred on Russia sole discretion to determine the necessity of any measures taken pursuant to Article XXI(b).[59] Integral to this is that the Panel must not simply accept the Respondent's assertion that it considers the action necessary for the purpose set out in one of the paragraphs (i), (ii) or (iii).[60] The Respondent must establish that there is an essential security interest related to a matter falling within the meaning of paragraphs (i), (ii) or (iii).[61] Japan may have a reasonable prospect of establishing that the situation with exporting to Korea or with at least some exports to Korea falls within each of paragraphs (i), (ii) and (iii).

Falling within the scope of export transactions that would be covered by the regulations applicable to Korea would be any exports of fissionable materials. Japan would argue that control of fissionable material is an essential security interest of Japan. A panel would likely accept that every country has an essential security interest in non-proliferation of nuclear weapons, so some aspects of Japan's measures would likely be justifiable under Article XXI(b)(i). The scope of paragraph Article XXI(b)(ii) is broader. Japan would likely be able to establish that there is a security interest involved that is related to 'the traffic in arms, ammunition and implements of war'. Pursuant to Article XXI(b)(iii), Japan might further argue that the recent history of North Korea's behaviour in conducting missile tests is sufficient to constitute an emergency in international relations, and that its actions regarding exports to South Korea are taken in a time of that emergency in international relations.

Establishing an essential security interest of one of the three types is not enough. Korea would also have to establish that the actions taken are 'actions which [Korea] considers necessary to the protection of the [objectively established] essential security interest'. This enquiry is limited because the text is concerned with whether the Respondent considered the action necessary for protection of the essential security interest, not whether it can be objectively established that the action is necessary for the protection of the essential security interest.

56. *United States – Imports of Sugar from Nicaragua*, *supra* n. 55.
57. For a discussion of these pre-WTO cases, *see* Ji Yeong Yoo & Dukgeun Ahn, *Security Exceptions in the WTO System: Bridge or Bottle-Neck for Trade and Security?*, 19 J. Int. Econ. Law 417, 430-1 (2016).
58. *Ibid.*, paras 7.66, 7.82, 7.100-7.101.
59. *Ibid.*, paras 7.28, 7.57.
60. *Ibid.*, paras 7.27-7.30.
61. *Ibid.*, paras 7.101, 7.132.

However, the Panel in *Russia – Traffic in Transit* stated that the text leaves to every Member to define what it considers to be its essential security interests. Nonetheless the Panel continued:

> [7.132] [T]his does not mean that a Member is free to elevate any concern to that of an 'essential security interest'. Rather the discretion of a Member to designate particular concerns as 'essential security interest' is limited by its obligations to interpret and apply Article XXI(b)(iii) of the GATT 1994 in good faith ...
> [7.133] The obligation of good faith requires that Members not use the exceptions in Article XXI as a means to circumvent their obligations under the GATT 1994. A glaring example of this would be where a Member sought to release itself from the structure of 'reciprocal and mutually advantageous arrangements' that constitutes the multilateral trading system simply by re-labelling trade interests that it had agreed to protect and promote within the system, as 'essential security interests', falling outside the reach of that system.
> [7.134] It is therefore incumbent on the invoking Member to articulate the essential security interests said to arise from the emergency in international relations sufficiently enough to demonstrate their veracity.

The argument that a Member has a discretion to decide issues under Article XXI(b) has a second aspect, the question of necessity, concerning whether the actions taken are necessary for the protection of the Member's essential security interest. The Panel addressed this issue as follows:

> [7.138] The obligation of good faith ... applies not only to the Member's definition of the essential security interests said to arise from the particular emergency in international relations, but also, and most importantly, to their connection with the measures at issue. Thus, as concerns the application of Article XX(b)(iii), this obligation is crystallized in demanding that the measures at issue meet a minimum requirement of plausibility in relation to the proffered essential security interests, i.e. that they are not implausible as measures protective of these interests.
> [7.139] The Panel must therefore review whether the measures are so remote from, or unrelated to, the 2014 emergency that it is implausible that Russia implemented the measures for the protection of its essential security interests arising out of the emergency.

The effect of Japan's actions is to deny exporters the opportunity to apply for General Bulk Licences for export to Korea such that the exporters must apply for Individual Export Licences. According to South Korea, individual applications for export licences 'are placed under increased scrutiny, causing unnecessary delay' for exporters to South Korea.[62]

The Panel would consider the reasons stated by Japan. The announcements by METI give some indication of why Japan considered the actions to be necessary to protect its essential security interests but they do not give a lot of detail. The 1 July announcement of the 'Update of METI's licensing policies and procedures on exports of controlled items to the Republic of Korea' gives two reasons for Japan's actions. The

62. Request for Consultations, *Japan – Measures Related to the Exportation of Products and Technology to Korea, supra* n. 15.

announcement says that METI 'has recently found that certain sensitive items have been exported to the Korea with inadequate management by companies'. A panel would probably not be prepared to rely on this statement on its own without some further elaboration of what inadequate management METI had discovered. The announcement puts more emphasis on another reason:

> Through careful consideration among the relevant ministries in Japan, the Government of Japan cannot help but state that the Japan-ROK relationship of trust including in the field of export control and regulation has been significantly undermined.[63]

However, the METI announcement of 1 July does not give a plausible explanation of how Japan has reached the conclusion that the relationship of trust had been undermined.

The announcement of 2 August adds some further explanation. METI stated that its 2 August Measure 'reemphasise[d] [Japan's] willingness to take strict measures against circumventions and other illicit exports' as well as the 'importance for exporters to exercise self-discipline in undertaking internal export control measures'.[64] Furthermore, METI's more recent press release of 28 August noted that Japan's review of its export control operations was 'designed to ensure proper management of trade in goods and technologies which could potentially be put to military use' and was introduced 'in response to circumstances such as limitations of the Korea's export control system and the operation thereof'.[65] These statements are still likely to be considered as insufficient proof of an 'essential security interest' under Article XXI(b).

By formally pursuing this dispute with Japan, Korea has an opportunity to render a service to the WTO system. Korea can request that Japan provide explicit explanations for why it believes that allowing Korea to remain in the whitelist and remain eligible for bulk licences without exporters having to make individual applications for licences poses a threat to an essential security interest of Japan. Korea could request Japan to make available all evidence showing that actions were necessary to protect its essential security interest.

Korea could attempt to make discussions between Japan and Korea as transparent and open as possible. By engaging in such a process, Korea and Japan would set an example of how Members should behave when justifying measures under GATT Article XXI. Such an approach to Article XXI would help to make it very difficult for a Member to make non-bona fide use of Article XXI as a means to avoid obligations that had been established in reciprocal and mutually beneficial negotiations. Given the way that the recent invocations of GATT Article XXI by the United States (US) have

63. METI, *Update of METI's Licensing Policies and Procedures on Exports of Controlled Items to the Republic of Korea*, *supra* n. 31.
64. METI, *The Cabinet Approved Partial Amendment to the Export Control Order*, *supra* n. 32.
65. METI, *Regarding Today's Announcement by the ROK Government* (28 Aug. 2019), https://www.meti.go.jp/english/press/2019/0828_001.html (accessed 9 Oct. 2019). Japan also issued a statement following consultations with Korea pursuant to Article 4 *DSU* raising similar points (*see* METI, *Japan Held Consultations with the Government of the Republic of Korea*, *supra* n. 30).

challenged the system, demonstrating a best-practice approach would be influential in restoring the boundaries around the appropriate invocation of Article XXI.

Yet there are real procedural problems. Even if a WTO Panel is established following formal consultations and Korea prevails on the merits, this is unlikely to occur before late 2020. This is because, under the DSU, Korea first needs to seek formal bilateral consultations with Japan and then call for formation of an ad hoc panel before the detailed hearings, submissions and panel rulings characteristic of WTO proceedings. On 10 December 2019, however, two of the three remaining Members (or 'judges') of the Appellate Body (AB) stepped down after reaching mandatory retirement. If the USA keeps objecting to any new appointments because of various objections to the DSU procedures and the wider WTO system,[66] the AB will lack a quorum to decide any appeals, including by Japan if the ad hoc panel ruled in favour of Korea. In other words, Korea will have achieved only a pyrrhic victory.

Various WTO Members have proposed reforms aimed at resolving the impasse over the DSU. The European Union (EU) (with support of Australia, China, Korea, Singapore and several others) proposed amendments in late 2018,[67] but the USA was not persuaded.[68] Australia and Japan proposed reforms in April 2019, but so far unsuccessfully, with one trade envoy reportedly stating that the EU, 'China, and Mexico among others severely chastised the joint proposal by Japan and Australia, offering concessions on a platter to the U.S. without securing any commitment from Washington that as a quid pro quo it would agree to the selection process for filling the AB vacancies'.[69] China's recent abandoning of panel proceedings against the EU, contesting methodology for calculating anti-dumping duties, leaves commentators wondering whether China is trying to shore up the WTO's legitimacy or instead set up a competing multilateral system for resolving trade disputes.[70] (On 13 May 2019, China had reiterated its earlier shared proposals for amending the DSU, as part of wider WTO reforms.[71]) No compromise was announced at or around the recent G-20 Summit hosted by Japan in late June.[72]

66. Andrew Stoler, *supra* n. 19.
67. European Commission, *WTO Reform: EU Proposes Way Forward on the Functioning of the Appellate Body* (26 Nov. 2018), https://europa.eu/rapid/press-release_IP-18-6529_en.htm (accessed 2 Oct. 2019).
68. Christopher Hyner, *The United States Rejects the European Union's Proposal to Reform the WTO Dispute Settlement Process*, Lexology (9 Jan. 2019), https://www.lexology.com/library/detail.aspx?g=002f617d-5a3e-41b9-83e6-77ea44a3be91 (accessed 2 Oct. 2019).
69. Ravi Kanth, *Japan, Australia Proposal on AB Reform Comes under Criticism*, Third World Network (24 Apr. 2019), https://www.twn.my/title2/wto.info/2019/ti190421.htm (accessed 2 Oct. 2019).
70. Henry Gao & Weihuan Zhou, *The End of the WTO and the Last Case?*, East Asia Forum (10 Jul. 2019), https://www.eastasiaforum.org/2019/07/10/the-end-of-the-wto-and-the-last-case/ (accessed 2 Oct. 2019).
71. *China's Proposal on WTO Reform* (13 May 2019), https://docs.wto.org/dol2fe/Pages/FE_Search/FE_S_S009-DP.aspx?language=E&CatalogueIdList=254127&CurrentCatalogueIdIndex=0&FullTextHash=371857150&HasEnglishRecord=True&HasFrenchRecord=False&HasSpanishRecord=False (accessed 2 Oct. 2019).
72. Shiro Armstrong, *The Rules Based Economic Disorder after Osaka G20*, East Asia Forum (30 Jun. 2019), https://www.eastasiaforum.org/2019/06/30/the-rules-based-economic-disorder-after-osaka-g20/ (accessed 2 Oct. 2019).

There are also ways to work around the disabled system. One would be that Member States agree not to appeal or to substitute the Panel/AB process for interstate arbitration under DSU Article 25, rarely used since 1995.[73] But this would involve states opting in to a new dispute settlement regime.[74] A more feasible alternative that hems more closely to the present system would be the provision of an alternative body to decide appeals. Indeed, the ministers of sixteen states and the EU released a statement of their intention to create a 'multi-party interim appeal arrangement' on 24 January 2020 at the initiative of Canada and the EU. The appeal arrangement was to be structured like the AB to hear appeals on a provisional basis until the AB becomes operational again.[75] Korea was party to the statement, but Japan was not, so such an interim body would not have jurisdiction over Korea's claims against Japan (unless Japan agreed otherwise). On 27 March 2020, the EU and fifteen other WTO Members (including China but not the US) announced an arrangement to enable appeals outside of the AB for participating states, but neither Korea nor Japan was party to that announcement.[76]

§11.03 JAPAN VERSUS KOREA UNDER THE 1965 TREATY OR TWO INVESTMENT AGREEMENTS

Apart from the trade dispute, Japan might claim against Korea. The 1965 Japan and Korea Treaty on Basic Relations[77] settles and forecloses claims over the treatment of Korean nationals during the period of Japanese colonial rule for a payment by Japan to Korea of USD 2.5 billion (in today's terms) and an offer of favourable loans to Korea. Japan and Korea disagree about whether the treaty was meant to settle only state-level claims or to also extend to private claims by Korean labourers against Japanese businesses.[78]

---

73. Hunter Nottage & Jan Bohanes, *Arbitration as an Alternative to Litigation in the WTO: Observations in the Light of the 2005 Banana Tariff Arbitrations*, in *The WTO in the Twenty-First Century* 212-47 (Yasuhei Taniguchi, Alan Yanovich & Jan Bohanes eds., Cambridge University Press 2007).
74. Jens Hillebrand Pohl, *Seven Months until Appellate Body Apocalypse: Time to Prepare for the Worst Case*, Maastricht University Blog (3 May 2019), https://www.maastrichtuniversity.nl/blog/2019/05/seven-months-until-appellate-body-apocalypse-time-prepare-worst-case (accessed 2 Oct. 2019).
75. Statement by Ministers, Davos, Switzerland, 24 January 2020, https://trade.ec.europa.eu/doclib/docs/2020/january/tradoc_158596.pdf (accessed 10 Mar. 2020); *see also* Dunniela Kaufman, *The Canada-EU Interim Appeal Arbitration Agreement: A Hail Mary Pass, or the Panacea?*, Kluwer Arbitration Blog (21 Sep. 2019), http://arbitrationblog.kluwerarbitration.com/2019/09/21/the-canada-eu-interim-appeal-arbitration-agreement-a-hail-mary-pass-or-the-panacea (accessed 10 Mar. 2020).
76. European Commission, *EU and 15 World Trade Organization Members Establish Contingency Appeal Arrangement for Trade Disputes* (27 Mar. 2020), https://trade.ec.europa.eu/doclib/press/index.cfm?id=2106 (accessed 28 Mar. 2020).
77. *Treaty on Basic Relations, Japan-Republic of Korea, Signed 22 June 1965*, 583 UNTS 33 (entry into force 18 Dec. 1965) ('*Treaty on Basic Relations*').
78. Article II(1) of the *Treaty on Basic Relations* provides that '[t]he Contracting Parties confirm that [the] problem concerning property, rights and interests of the two Contracting Parties and their nationals (including juridical persons) and concerning claims between the Contracting Parties

Article III provides that disputes over treaty interpretation can be settled in interstate arbitration should diplomatic consultations fail. Although Japan invoked this provision on 20 May 2019, after consultations following Korean court execution orders issued in January, Korea has not consented to arbitrate or selected an arbitrator under the treaty. This closes the door on the possibility as there is no authority named in the treaty for default appointments of party arbitrators.[79] While Korea's non-compliance with the arbitration provision may raise the issue of good faith under general international law in principle, the practical consequence for now is that arbitration is stalled, although Japan still seems to hold out hope that the Korean government will change its course.

Japan has also said it is considering bringing the dispute to the ICJ. Like arbitration, this option would require Korea's consent because, unlike Japan, Korea has not made a declaration that the jurisdiction of the ICJ is compulsory or elsewhere consented to give the Court authority over the dispute. While proceedings before the ICJ raise a different set of procedural considerations – including relative efficiency, confidentiality, and access to provisional measures – it is not immediately clear why Korea would be more agreeable to this alternative than arbitration if Japan were to move to institute proceedings.

Japan could instead make collateral claims under the 2002 Japan-Korea BIT or the 2012 trilateral investment agreement among China, Japan and Korea,[80] although the Japanese government does not seem to have raised this possibility publically. Both instruments were in force when the dispute arose, and each provides for mandatory interstate arbitration supported by appointing authorities to act for non-participating parties.

Article 14 of the BIT would allow Japan to commence (United Nations Commission on International Trade Law) UNCITRAL Rules (ad hoc) arbitration against Korea. It usefully adds an expedited procedure for submissions, hearings, and drafting of the arbitral award,[81] but envisages first 'consultations' without specifying any time limit beyond which arbitration can be commenced. Japan may also be disconcerted that there is no express elaboration of a 'loser pays' principle, as has become more common

---

and their nationals, including those provided for in Article IV, para. (a) of the Treaty of Peace with Japan signed at the city of San Francisco on Sept. 8, 1951, is settled completely and finally'.

79. Ministry of Foreign Affairs of Japan, *Failure of the Republic of Korea to Comply with Obligations Regarding Arbitration under the Agreement on the Settlement of Problems Concerning Property and Claims and on Economic Co-operation between Japan and the Republic of Korea* (19 Jul. 2019), https://www.mofa.go.jp/press/release/press4e_002553.html (accessed 2 Oct. 2019).

80. *See* respectively *Agreement between the Government of the Republic of Korea and the Government of Japan for the Liberalisation, Promotion and Protection of Investment*, signed 22 Mar. 2002 (entry into force 1 Jan. 2003) ('*Japan-South Korea BIT*') and *Agreement among the Government of Japan, the Government of the Republic of Korea and the Government of the People's Republic of China for the Promotion, Facilitation and Protection of Investment*, signed 13 May 2012 (entry into force 17 May 2014) ('*Japan-South Korea-China Trilateral Agreement*').

81. *Japan-South Korea BIT*, *supra* n. 80: '4. Unless otherwise agreed by the Contracting Parties, all submissions of documents shall be made and all hearings shall be completed within a period of six months from the date of selection of the third arbitrator, and the arbitral tribunal shall render its decisions within two months from the date of the final submissions of documents or the date of the closing of the hearings, whichever is later.'

(although far from uniform) in international commercial and even investor-state arbitration.[82] The starting point under the BIT is instead that each state bears costs equally, whatever the outcome, subject to tribunal discretion.[83]

Under the trilateral agreement, Article 17 provides that Japan can commence arbitration under the UNCITRAL Arbitration Rules after a mandatory consultation period of six months beginning with a written request for consultations. The scope of the written request, concerning 'any dispute relating to the interpretation or application of [the trilateral agreement]', may not be broad enough to include Japan's request for consultations under the 1965 treaty on 9 January 2019. Assuming notice is not a hurdle, the arbitration procedure mostly mirrors the expedited process and division of costs terms found in the BIT.[84] The most significant difference is that China would be permitted to make submissions and attend hearings as a right.

Apart from these procedural issues, arbitration under an investment treaty may not appeal to Japan as it could narrow the scope of possible claims. Rather than deal directly with the questions of interpretation of the 1965 treaty, the arbitration would concern whether the Korean judiciary breached standards of treatment in the investment treaty by holding Japanese companies liable for forced labour. The standards for resolving this question are expressed differently in the instruments. The BIT promises state treatment that is fair and equitable without qualification while the trilateral agreement links fair and equitable treatment of investors to 'generally accepted rules of international law' and goes on to stipulate that 'a determination that there has been a breach of ... a separate international agreement, does not ipso facto establish that there has been a breach [of the investment treaty]'. Based on the broader treatment standard and indefinite consultation period, the BIT may offer a better option for Japan on balance. That said, the differences in the treatment standards may not be critical because the trilateral agreement contains a most-favoured-nation (MFN) clause. Japan could use this provision to claim that its national investors were owed the broader 'fair and equitable' standard of treatment in the BIT even if claims were brought under the trilateral agreement.

---

82. Catherine Titi, et al., *Excessive Costs & Insufficient Recoverability of Cost Awards*, ISDS Academic Forum, Working Group 1 Concept Paper (14 Mar. 2019), available at https://www.cids.ch/images/Documents/Academic-Forum/1_Costs_-_WG1.pdf (accessed 2 Oct. 2019); Malcolm Langford, Daniel Behn & Laura Letourneau-Tremblay, *Empirical Perspectives on Investment Arbitration: What Do We Know? Does It Matter?*, ISDS Academic Forum, Working Group 7 Concept Paper (15 Mar. 2019), available at https://www.cids.ch/images/Documents/Academic-Forum/7_Empirical_perspectives_-_WG7.pdf (accessed 2 Oct. 2019).
83. *Japan-South Korea BIT, supra* n. 80: '5. Expenses incurred by the chairperson and other arbitrators, and other costs of the proceedings, shall be borne equally by the Contracting Parties. However, the arbitral tribunal may, at its discretion, decide that a higher proportion of the costs be paid by one of the Contracting Parties.'
84. *Japan-South Korea-China Trilateral Agreement, supra* n. 80: '5. Unless otherwise agreed by the disputing Parties, all submissions of documents shall be made and all hearings shall be completed within a period of one hundred and eighty days from the date of selection of the third arbitrator. The arbitral tribunal shall render its award, in accordance with the provisions of this Agreement and the rules of international law applicable to the disputing Parties, within sixty days from the date of the final submissions of documents or the date of the closing of the hearings, whichever is the later.'

To prevail under either investment treaty, Japan would likely have to demonstrate serious procedural irregularities or prove that the Korean Supreme Court's ruling was discriminatory and not merely that the court misinterpreted the terms of the 1965 treaty in reaching its judgment. There are a few public examples of investors successfully challenging court judgments on the basis of protections in investment treaties.[85] Chevron notably convinced an investment tribunal to stay a USD 9.5 billion Ecuadorian court judgment against the company and ultimately recovered damages for denial of justice under the Ecuador-U.S. BIT and violations of customary international law.[86] But the fit with the dispute between Japan and Korea is far from perfect. While the Chevron tribunal found that the court judgment was written by a third party in exchange for payment to the judge, there have been no such allegations of corruption against the Korean courts. More to the point, even if Japan were to convince a tribunal that its nationals were denied justice by the Korean courts, the tribunal would not necessarily need to interpret the 1965 treaty to resolve the claims. Absent a ruling on the meaning of the treaty, the root cause of the dispute would remain unsettled.

§11.04 JAPANESE COMPANIES VERSUS KOREA THROUGH ISDS

As early as 2014, in the wake of the first-instance Korean court judgments against Japanese companies like Nippon Steel, *Investment Arbitration Reporter* commentators had reported that Japanese companies could be preparing ISDS claims against Korea.[87] Apart from questions over the substantive grounds under the relevant treaties, outlined above, how likely are Japanese investors generally to bring ISDS claims?

---

85. Recently, for example, the tribunal in *Manchester Securities v. Poland* ruled in favour of the investor on the basis of a denial of justice as result of a Supreme Court of Poland judgment. The Court, in reviewing and revising the factual findings of lower courts, had denied the investor the chance to rebut these revised factual determinations or submit new evidence. This resulted in a breach of the FET provision under Article II.6 of the US-Poland Business and Economic Relations Treaty: *see* Luke Eric Peterson, *Poland Held Liable for Denial of Justice in Elliot Hedge Fund Arbitration; Unanimous Rigo-Chaired Tribunal Sees 'Egregious' Failing by Supreme Court and Awards $9.5+ Million*, IA Reporter (13 Aug. 2019), https://www.iareporter.com/articles/poland-held-liable-for-denial-of-justice-in-elliott-hedge-fund-arbitration-unanimous-rigo-chaired-tribunal-sees-egregious-failing-by-supreme-court-and-awards-9-5-million/ (accessed 25 Sep. 2019). By contrast, in *Poland v. Uruguay* the majority of the tribunal did not find denial of justice despite Uruguay's Supreme Court and Tribunal de lo Contencioso Administrativo (TCA) making inconsistent interpretations on the validity of the 80/80 Regulation: *Philip Morris Brand Sarl (Switzerland), Philip Morris Products SA (Switzerland) and Abal Hermanos SA (Uruguay) v. Oriental Republic of Uruguay*, ICSID Case No. ARB/10/7, Award (8 Jul. 2016), discussed by Luke Eric Peterson, *The Philip Morris v. Uruguay Award on the Merits: Part One of Our Three Part Analysis Focusing on the Denial of Justice Claims*, IA Reporter (10 Jul. 2019), https://www.iareporter.com/articles/the-philip-morris-v-uruguay-award-on-the-merits-part-one-of-our-three-part-analysis-focusing-on-the-denial-of-justice-claims/ (accessed 25 Sep. 2019).
86. *Chevron Corporation v. Texaco Petroleum Company (Second Partial Award on Track II)*, PCA Case No. 2009-23 (30 Aug. 2018), as discussed in Kyle Dickson-Smith, *An Investment Court that Judges the Judges: A Case of Natural Selection?* 44(2) U.W.A.L. Rev. 71 (2018).
87. Jarrod Hepburn & Luke Eric Peterson, *Analysis: Japanese Companies May Pursue Chevron-Type BIT Arbitration in Response to Korean Court Rulings in Forced Labour Cases*, IA Reporter (10 Jan. 2014), www.iareporter.com/articles/analysis-japanese-companies-may-pursue-chevron-type-bit-arbitration-in-response-to-korean-court-rulings-in-forced-labour-cases/ (accessed 2 Oct. 2019).

Japanese investors were initially very 'reluctant claimants', with an analogy being Japan's 'reluctant litigants' as measured by comparatively few per capita civil suits filed in Japanese courts.[88] In contrast to home countries with much higher ISDS claiming per capita (such as Canada, more so say than the US),[89] there had been only a few indirect treaty-based claims, notably Nomura via its Saluka Investments subsidiary against the Czech Republic (settled in 2007), and Bridgestone via a US subsidiary against Panama (with public hearings over the internet, 29 July–2 August,[90] illustrating incidentally the growing transparency of ISDS proceedings[91]). At least one other threatened ISDS claim was seemingly based on consent to arbitration administered by the International Centre for the Settlement of Investment Disputes (ICSID) contained not in a treaty but in an investment contract, namely between an aluminium smelter consortium and Indonesia. However, this also settled in 2013, so no arbitration was commenced by the Japanese investors.[92]

However, Japanese firms have filed three Energy Charter Treaty claims arbitrations against Spain since 2015.[93] This follows the lead of investors from many other states, also impacted by Spain's abrupt changes in renewable energy policy, so Japanese companies and their legal advisors can reduce costs and other 'institutional barriers' to pursuing formal dispute resolution procedures. Nissan's UNCITRAL Arbitration Rules claim in 2017 under the India-Japan FTA is bolder, as few of the many ISDS claims brought against India (since a 2011 award for Australia's White Industries) have involved investments in manufacturing. This claim may indicate a changing mindset among the leaders of at least larger Japanese companies, towards more active engagement in international arbitration. However, Nissan is quite unusual given its alliance with French shareholder Renault[94] (although that relationship is itself now impacted by securities law prosecutions against CEO Carlos Ghosn).[95]

---

88. *See generally* James M. Claxton, Luke Nottage & Nobumichi Teramura, *Developing Japan as a Regional Hub for International Dispute Resolution: Dream Come True or Daydream?*, 47 J.J.L. 109 (2019), also available at https://papers.ssrn.com/sol3/papers.cfm?abstract_id=3299097 (accessed 2 Oct. 2019).
89. Luke Nottage, *Are US Investors Exceptionally Litigious with ISDS Claims?*, Kluwer Arbitration Blog (14 Nov. 2016), http://arbitrationblog.kluwerarbitration.com/2016/11/14/are-us-investors-exceptionally-litigious-with-isds-claims/ (accessed 2 Oct. 2019).
90. ICSID, *Bridgestone Licensing Services, Inc and Bridgestone Americas, Inc v. Republic of Panama (ICSID Case No. ARB/16/34) – Public Hearing*, News Release (17 Jul. 2019), https://icsid.worldbank.org/en/Pages/News.aspx?CID=333 (accessed 2 Oct. 2019).
91. Luke Nottage & Ana Ubilava, *supra* n. 22.
92. Mark Smith & Louise Browning, *Indonesia and Nippon Asahan Aluminium Consortium Reach Settlement*, Ashurst (1 Feb. 2014), https://www.ashurst.com/en/news-and-insights/legal-updates/indonesia-and-nippon-asahan-aluminium-consortium-reach-settlement/ (accessed 2 Oct. 2019).
93. According to a search on https://icsid.worldbank.org/en/Pages/cases/AdvancedSearch.aspx (accessed 2 Oct. 2019).
94. Peter Campbell, David Keohane & Leo Lewis, *Renault-Nissan Alliance Crumbles with Carlos Ghosn Gone*, Financial Times (18 Jun. 2019), https://www.ft.com/content/6c65eb46-91d9-11e9-b7ea-60e35ef678d2 (accessed 2 Oct. 2019).
95. Jie Ma & Ichiro Suzuki, *Former Nissan Motor Chairman Carlos Ghosn's Release in Doubt as Prosecutors Appeal Bail Decision*, Time (5 Mar. 2019), https://time.com/5543639/carlos-ghosn-nissan-bail/ (accessed 2 Oct. 2019).

Tracing the emergence of claims by Japanese investors generally, the possibility of ISDS claims against Korea now by Nippon Steel and other affected companies cannot be excluded simply on the basis say of some general 'cultural' aversion to formal dispute resolution processes. As for those who still favour instead the 'elite management' theory put forward for such aversion to explain low levels of civil litigation within Japan, whereby government and business elites divert cases away from formal dispute resolution,[96] it is noticeable that peak business associations (especially the Keidanren) have long pressed for ISDS-backed investment treaty protections. And the Abe Administration since 2012 has signed sixteen stand-alone BITs (all with ISDS), albeit still far fewer than Korea, as well as several FTAs. This sends the message that investment treaties are important and to be used, although in highly politicised cases such as this they are probably best used as part of a multilevel negotiation and an overall dispute resolution, as elaborated in §11.05 below.

If Japanese investors were persuaded to pursue Korea under either the BIT or trilateral agreement, claims could be based on the 'fair and equitable treatment' standard in those instruments along the lines previously considered for interstate claims, as discussed in §11.03 above. Procedurally, Article 15 of the BIT envisages the investor seeking 'consultations or negotiation' with the host state for up to three months, then a notice of intent triggering a cooling-off period of at least another three months, before arbitration is possible under the ICSID Convention (as both Japan and Korea are parties), with its more favourable enforcement regime, or any other separately agreed arbitration rules. (Articles 17-18 exclude ISDS for disputes over prudential measures concerning financial services and temporary safeguards for cross-border capital transactions, which are inapplicable here.)

The BIT contains an MFN provision in Article 2 covering 'investment and business activities' that could theoretically be used to commence arbitration more quickly under the dispute resolution provision of the trilateral agreement. This prospect is not especially promising, however, because of the uncertainty about whether a tribunal would extend MFN treatment to dispute settlement and because it is unclear whether the process in the trilateral agreement is actually favourable since it contains a provision for administrative review not present in the BIT. The potential time savings, two months, is almost certainly not worth the risk of litigating these issues.

Article 15 of the trilateral agreement requires more details in the investor's request for consultations so that the dispute can be 'solved amicably', but if no settlement is reached after four months the investor can seek arbitration under the ICSID Convention, UNCITRAL Rules or any other separately agreed arbitration rules. The host state can require the investor to first seek administrative review under any

96. On culture, institutional barriers and elite management theories for low levels of formal filings in Japanese civil courts as well as ISDS disputes involving Asian parties, *see also* Luke Nottage & J. Romesh Weeramantry, *Investment Arbitration for Japan and Asia: Five Perspectives on Law and Practice*, in *Foreign Investment and Dispute Resolution Law and Practice in Asia* 25 (Vivienne Bath & Luke Nottage eds., Routledge 2011), also available at https://papers.ssrn.com/sol3/papers.cfm?abstract_id=2041686 (accessed 2 Oct. 2019).

local requirements, but only for up to four months before arbitration is commenced.[97] (ISDS exclusions regarding certain intellectual property rights or temporary safeguards are again inapplicable here.) While the agreement contains an MFN provision, which might otherwise be used to avoid administrative review, dispute resolution is excluded from the scope of MFN treatment in Article 4(3).

In any case, ISDS filings would mean investors incurring significant arbitration expenses upfront, with empirical studies showing claimants are often unable to recover all lawyer and expert witness expenses even if successful.[98] More importantly, filings by Nippon Steel and others would likely inflame the underlying tension, resulting in boycotts, protests or even strikes around their affiliated companies in Korea. Perhaps for such practical reasons, this point has not been raised by general media, relevant companies or the Keidanren, although the *Investment Arbitration Reporter* has reiterated the possibility of ISDS claims since the Korean Supreme Court judgment late last year.[99]

§11.05 MEDIATION TO ASSIST AN OVERALL NEGOTIATED SETTLEMENT

Given this complex and delicate situation, how could a global settlement be reached? One possibility is for one or more affected Japanese companies to seek direct consultations with Korea, but include a request for mediation to help reach a negotiated outcome. Neither the BIT nor the trilateral agreement mention mediation or conciliation, unlike some investment treaties that refer to it as an option, but mediation can be agreed separately as neither treaty's 'fork-in-the-road' provision preclude this possibility. Recent empirical research highlights the pervasiveness of settlement even after arbitration is filed, contrary to some commentators' scepticism, which underscores the potential for even more settlements through greater use of investor-state mediation.[100]

An advantage of such ad hoc mediation is that skilled mediators could also bring in the host states, and come up with a resolution of the disputes under the 1965 treaty

97. Incidentally, the trilateral agreement is much better for Japanese investors in any disputes against China under the old 1988 BIT. That latter's Article 11(2) provides advance consent by the host state, if the investor seeks arbitration or conciliation 'with reference to' the 1965 ICSID Convention (which both states have acceded to), only for any 'dispute concerning the amount of compensation' for expropriation (which some but not all tribunals interpreting similar wording in other treaties have interpreted also as providing jurisdiction over whether expropriation occurred). Other disputed BIT violations 'may be submitted' to arbitration or conciliation under the respective ICSID Convention rules, but only 'by mutual agreement'.
98. *See* Working Groups 1 and 7 Concept Papers, *supra* n. 82.
99. Jarrod Hepburn, *As Japanese Companies Face Potential Asset Seizure in Korea, Japan Demand Inter-State Arbitration; Potential for Investment Treaty Claims Lurk in Background*, IA Reporter (20 May 2019), www.iareporter.com/articles/as-japanese-companies-face-potential-asset-seizure-in-korea-japan-demand-inter-state-arbitration-potential-for-investment-treaty-claims-lurk-in-background/ (accessed 2 Oct. 2019).
100. Ana Ubilava, *Amicable Settlements in Investor-State Disputes: Empirical Analysis of Patterns and Perceived Problems*, Sydney Law School Research Paper No. 19/17 (2019), also available at https://papers.ssrn.com/sol3/papers.cfm?abstract_id = 3352181 (accessed 2 Oct. 2019).

and before the WTO as well. Mediation has not been so popular in interstate dispute resolution, but successful settlement from mediation of a maritime boundary dispute between Australia and Timor-Leste has highlighted its wider potential for large-scale international disputes nowadays.[101]

There are otherwise few signs that Japan and Korea will be able to work out the dispute on their own at the moment. President Moon has warned of a 'prolonged' conflict and has committed that Korea would 'not be defeated again',[102] while Japan initially resisted engaging in negotiations after Korea refused to arbitrate under the 1965 treaty before proceeding to ratchet up pressure on Korea in the trade dispute. This suggests that the states' positions have hardened as public sentiment on both sides has soured amidst protests, product bans, disruptions to business and tourism, and even self-immolation by Korean nationals in protest against Japan.

While there have been direct negotiations between the states, these have not produced meaningful progress in normalising relations. President Moon and Prime Minister Abe met, for the first time in fifteen months, in late December 2019 before an annual trilateral summit with China. The meeting was followed by vague statements by both leaders about improving relations without any commitments, despite high hopes that the involvement of China and common economic interests in securing regional production chains might catalyse a reconciliation.[103]

More recent events have sent the pendulum swinging back in the directions of escalation. In late 2020, Japan made a second request for WTO consultations with Korea over government support to shipbuilders. Although the underlying dispute predates the dispute over trade restrictions and is factually distinct, the move cannot be isolated from broader relations.[104] Meanwhile, the Supreme Court of Korea is due to liquidate assets seized from Japanese corporations found liable for forced labour by Korean courts. The Abe Administration has said that the corporations should not pay damages voluntarily, leading to speculation about how Tokyo might retaliate if the liquidation occurs.[105]

---

101. Anais Kedgley Laidlaw & Hao Duy Phan, *Inter-State Compulsory Conciliation Procedures and the Maritime Boundary Dispute Between Timor-Leste and Australia*, 10(1) J. Int. Disp. Settlement 126 (2019).
102. Makiko Yamazaki & Ju-min Park, *South Korea Says 'Won't Be Defeated Again' as Japan Trade Row Spirals*, Reuters (2 Aug. 2019), https://www.reuters.com/article/us-southkorea-japan-laborers/south-korea-says-wont-be-defeated-again-as-japan-trade-row-escalates-idUSKCN1US03S (accessed 2 Oct. 2019).
103. Laura Zhou, *China Eager to Help Break Japan-South Korea Stalemate at Summit and Ease Way to Free-Trade Agreement*, South China Morning Post (23 Dec. 2019), https://www.scmp.com/news/china/diplomacy/article/3042990/china-eager-help-break-japan-south-korea-stalemate-summit-and (accessed 10 Mar. 2020).
104. Philip Blenkinsop & Ed Osmond, *Japan Takes Second Complaint to WTO over South Korean Shipbuilding*, Reuters (11 Feb. 2020), https://www.reuters.com/article/japan-southkorea-wto/japan-takes-second-complaint-to-wto-over-south-korean-shipbuilding-idUSL8N2AA4NV (accessed 10 Mar. 2020).
105. Julian Ryall, *As South Korean Courts Chase Japanese Firms for Wartime Claims, Will Abe Retaliate?*, South China Morning Post (12 Jan. 2020), https://www.scmp.com/week-asia/politics/article/3045613/south-korean-courts-chase-japanese-firms-wartime-claims-will-abe (accessed 10 Mar. 2020).

Even responses to the coronavirus outbreak have been cast in political terms. After Tokyo announced a two-week voluntary quarantine of visitors from Korea, Seoul struck back by suspending visas and visa waivers for Japan. This exchange prompted the Director-General of the World Health Organization to encourage the countries to focus on managing the epidemic and not on 'a political spat over travel restrictions'.[106]

High-level officials from the US have tried to extricate the parties from their entrenched positions. An early offer by Donald Trump to mediate did not get traction and even drew an unfavourable comparison to Japan interfering in US relations with Mexico from a former Japanese ambassador to the US.[107] Since then the US has continued to try to play a role in resolving the dispute including calls for a 'standstill agreement' to prevent further escalation of tensions.[108] Yet the US suffers from a credibility problem, as the Trump Administration has itself been using trade policy in a more confrontational way, evidenced by the WTO Appellate Body problem and bilateral trade war with China. Some see that approach as having spread now to Japan's dealings with Korea.[109] Others urge the US to keep exploring ways to 'quietly nudge' both nations to resolve their disputes, but acknowledge the limited scope for informal interventions even for a superpower.[110]

There may be a role to play for current or former officials or politicians from Australia, or from another influential state (such as Singapore), in current negotiations around the WTO DSU, as well as the very significant Regional Comprehensive Economic Partnership (RCEP) concluded on 4 November 2019 but some significant aspects are still left open.[111] Furthermore, Singapore is actively positioning itself as a proponent of international mediation, not least by hosting in August 2019 the diplomatic conference for a new UN Convention on cross-border enforcement of mediated settlement agreements - signing up along with forty-five others (including Korea, China and the USA, but not Australia or Japan) at the event and attracting widespread

106. Jane Chung, *South Korea's Coronavirus Cases Climb above 7,000, Most Cases Traced to Church*, Reuters (7 Mar. 2020), https://www.reuters.com/article/us-health-coronavirus-south-korea/south-koreas-coronavirus-cases-climb-above-7000-most-cases-traced-to-church-idUSKBN20U02M (accessed 10 Mar. 2020). Compare also Kazuhiko Togo, *Can Japan and South Korea Cooperate Against COVID-19?*, East Asia Forum (9 May 2020), https://www.eastasiaforum.org/2020/05/09/can-japan-and-south-korea-cooperate-against-covid-19/ (accessed 8 Jun. 2020).
107. Motoko Rich, Edward Wong & Choe Sang-Hun, *As Japan and South Korea Feud Intensifies, U.S. Seems Unwilling, or Unable, to Help*, New York Times (4 Aug. 2019), https://www.nytimes.com/2019/08/04/world/asia/japan-south-korea-feud.html (accessed 16 Nov. 2019).
108. *Pompeo Calls for 'Standstill Agreement' to Give Feuding Japan and South Korea Time to Cool Off*, Japan Times (31 Jul. 2019), https://www.japantimes.co.jp/news/2019/07/31/national/pompeo-calls-standstill-agreement-give-feuding-japan-south-korea-time-cool-off/ (accessed 2 Oct. 2019).
109. Celeste Arrington, *Japan Claims Its Restricting Exports to South Korea Because of 'National Security'. Here's the Real Reason Why*, Washington Post (18 Jul. 2019), https://www.washingtonpost.com/politics/2019/07/18/japan-claims-its-restricting-exports-south-korea-because-national-security-heres-real-reason-why/?noredirect=on (accessed 2 Oct. 2019).
110. Matthew P. Goodman, *Japan and Korea: Rising Above the Fray*, Center for Strategic & International Studies (6 Aug. 2019), https://www.csis.org/analysis/japan-and-korea-rising-above-fray (accessed 2 Oct. 2019).
111. Peter Drysdale & Mari Pangetsu, *RCEP Is Now Vital in Defending the Global Trading Order*, East Asia Forum (4 Aug. 2019), https://www.eastasiaforum.org/2019/08/04/rcep-vital-to-defend-global-trade-order/ (accessed 2 Oct. 2019).

commentary.[112] Since then, five additional states have signed the convention and two have ratified it.[113] Although the treaty is designed to promote investor-state and commercial mediation, it could heighten interest also in interstate mediation.[114]

Two matters were left open when fifteen negotiating states announced recently that negotiations had been concluded for RCEP. First, although from late 2012 the ten ASEAN states had negotiated with Korea, Japan, Australia, New Zealand, China and India, RCEP was concluded without India – although its later accession is possible, if and when RCEP is signed, ratified and comes into force.[115] Second, the Australian government's formal summary of RCEP outcomes states: 'RCEP does not provide for investor-state dispute settlement. RCEP parties will discuss this question in the future.'[116] Ongoing negotiations about whether and how to add ISDS provisions to RCEP's investment chapter are obviously contentious, even without India and its recent misgivings about ISDS-backed commitments, given the disparate national interests among the remaining fifteen states.[117] Negotiations would be further complicated if there were a collapse in trust and values shared between Korea and Japan over ISDS and investment treaty commitments. Already, some have suggested that the current bilateral tension is behind Korea getting cold feet about seeking to join the regional Comprehensive and Progressive Agreement for Trans-Pacific Partnership (CPTPP), now partly in force (but with ISDS provisions).[118] Japan, with Australia and Singapore, had pushed hard to bring the CPTPP into effect after the Trump Administration withdrew US signature of the earlier Trans-Pacific Partnership FTA.[119]

However, even Australia or Singapore could be seen as having its own interests in the bilateral spat. Better candidates as neutral mediators – especially for a more structured and sustained mediation process[120] – could be senior figures (formerly)

112. Cara Wong, *46 Countries Sign International Mediation Treaty Named after Singapore*, Straits Times (7 Aug. 2019), https://www.straitstimes.com/singapore/key-facts-about-the-singapore-convention-on-mediation (accessed 2 Oct. 2019).
113. UNCITRAL, *Status: United Nations Convention on International Settlement Agreements Resulting from Mediation*, https://uncitral.un.org/en/texts/mediation/conventions/international_settlement_agreements/status (accessed 10 Mar. 2020).
114. Timothy Schnabel, *The Singapore Convention on Mediation: A Framework for the Cross-Border Recognition and Enforcement of Mediated Settlements*, 19 Pepp. Disp. Resol. L.J. 1 (2019).
115. Sourabh Gupta, *India's RCEP Blunder*, East Asia Forum (9 Nov. 2019) https://www.eastasiaforum.org/2019/11/09/indias-rcep-blunder/ (accessed 16 Nov. 2019).
116. Department of Foreign Affairs and Trade, *RCEP Outcomes at a Glance*, available at https://dfat.gov.au/trade/agreements/negotiations/rcep/Pages/regional-comprehensive-economic-partnership.aspx (accessed 16 Nov. 2019).
117. For country reports on all sixteen original negotiating parties to RCEP, *see* Julien Chaisse & Luke Nottage eds., *International Investment Treaties and Arbitration Across Asia* (Brill 2018).
118. Matthew P. Goodman, *supra* n. 110.
119. Luke Nottage, *The TPP Investment Chapter and Investor-State Arbitration in Asia and Oceania: Assessing Prospects for Ratification*, 17(2) M.J.I.L 1 (2016), also available at https://papers.ssrn.com/sol3/papers.cfm?abstract_id=2767996 (accessed 2 Oct. 2019).
120. James M. Claxton, *Compelling Parties to Mediate Investor-State Disputes: No Pressure, No Diamonds?*, Kobe University Social Science Research Paper Series (27 Jan. 2019), available at https://papers.ssrn.com/sol3/papers.cfm?abstract_id=3320087 (accessed 2 Oct. 2019).

within the UN, such as United Nations Conference on Trade and Development (UNCTAD),[121] or another international organisation such as:

(i) the Organisation for Economic Co-operation and Development (OECD),[122] although it is more policy oriented than practice oriented;
(ii) the International Bar Association, which produced investor-state arbitration rules in 2012,[123] although those are hardly used so far and the association's leaders tend now to be full-time practitioners, especially from larger law firms; and
(iii) the International Law Association,[124] instead comprising mostly professors specialising in international law.

The Centre for Effective Dispute Resolution (CEDR), ICSID, the International Mediation Institute (IMI) and the International Energy Charter have been promoting investor-state mediation recently, notably by running courses to train mediators for investment disputes.[125] They too could be consulted for possible mediators, with experience also preferably in WTO law and broader international relations, especially in Asia.

Overall, successful mediation and negotiated settlements tend to arise in two ways. One is where the litigation behind the mediation, including likely costs and delays, has a predictable outcome. (This is one reason sometimes given for low levels of civil litigation in Japan, epitomised by traffic accident data.[126]) But another is where the dispute becomes very complicated, allowing skilled mediators to help parties find novel ways to perceive and develop shared interests. This would not be possible before an adjudicatory forum, like the ICJ or an arbitral tribunal, with a limited mandate to decide claims. An imposed solution, with a perceived winner and loser, might also fail to calm the tide of nationalism, public unrest, and deteriorating relations between the countries. These circumstances offer both a unique opportunity for mediation and a challenge for international dispute resolution.

---

121. UNCTAD, *Investment Policy Hub*, https://investmentpolicy.unctad.org/ (accessed 2 Oct. 2019).
122. OECD, *International Investment Law*, https://www.oecd.org/daf/inv/investment-policy/oecdworkoninternationalinvestmentlaw.htm (accessed 2 Oct. 2019).
123. International Bar Association, *Mission Statement – Mediation Committee*, https://www.ibanet.org/LPD/Dispute_Resolution_Section/Mediation/State_Mediation/Default.aspx (accessed 2 Oct. 2019).
124. International Law Association, *Committees*, http://www.ila-hq.org/index.php/committees (accessed 2 Oct. 2019).
125. International Energy Charter, *Investor-State Mediation Training*, https://energycharter.org/what-we-do/events/investor-state-mediation-training (accessed 2 Oct. 2019).
126. Luke Nottage & J Romesh Weeramantry, *supra* n. 96.

CHAPTER 12

Indian Investment Treaty Practice: Qualitatively and Quantitatively Assessing Recent Developments

Jaivir Singh

This chapter provides a perspective of investment treaty practice from India, which lies at the periphery of what is traditionally associated with the Asia Pacific region. While on the periphery, India has signed investment and trade treaties with many Asia Pacific countries and is also involved in disputes with them. India had in fact endorsed a number of investment treaties with many countries around the world but has recently gone on to denounce all of them and seeks to renegotiate fresh treaties using a template provided by a New Model Treaty that is oriented towards privileging state rights. The chapter begins by a qualitative review of cases that have been instituted against India by investors, followed by a discussion of the many reactions that this has elicited – a New Model Treaty, subsequent denunciation of treaties, signing of new treaties and attempting changes in the domestic law as a device to protect foreign investors. The next half of the chapter assesses these outcomes by looking at econometric evidence pointing to a positive impact of investment treaties signed by India on foreign investment inflows into India, going on to argue that the manner in which state rights have been enhanced in the new treaties – drawing inspiration from trade law – demonstrably curbs investment.

§12.01 INTRODUCTION

Beginning in the 1990s, India signed a number of bilateral investment treaties (BITs) but recently, keeping in line with certain global trends, India has changed its attitude with respect to international investment agreements (IIAs). Most of these treaties have been denounced, and additionally India insists that once the remaining treaties lapse, they have to be renegotiated using a template provided by a New Model Treaty. The new Indian Model Treaty, which was finalised in December 2015 after considerable debate, substantially privileges state rights over investor rights. As recent work by legal scholar Prabash Ranjan contends, the disproportionate tilt towards state rights in the New Model Treaty means that very few countries seeking to protect their outbound investors are willing to agree to the stringent terms required by the Model Treaty.[1] It is hard to predict the future impact of this withdrawal from the world of IIAs on foreign direct investment (FDI) into India. One can only speculate about the effects of this reorientation, with the empirical evidence on the effects becoming visible only with the passage of time. To assess quantitatively the role of recent developments on foreign investment inflows and other dimensions of the economy at the current juncture, one is perforce obliged to extrapolate effects into the future by understanding the nature of the forces that have led us to the current juncture.

It is difficult to precisely hone in on the appropriate set of occurrences that can help assess recent developments, but possibly the best place to begin is by reviewing qualitatively the cases that have been instituted against India by investors. Thus, in §12.02 the key cases against India are described. §12.03 goes on to describe reactions to these cases: the institution of New Model Treaty, the subsequent termination of treaties, the signing of a few new treaties and attempts to change domestic laws. §12.04 consists of the analytical core of the chapter where an attempt is made to assess quantitatively the current developments by first invoking an empirical model that studies the effect of the investment treaties on the inflow of FDI into India before they were denounced. The results of the model show that the erstwhile treaties did play a positive role, allowing us to infer that the absence of strong treaty protection will perhaps indeed dampen future foreign investment into India. To give some substance to this speculation the second part of this section looks at the precise manner in which state rights have been enhanced recently, finding that the shift demonstrably thwarts investment. §12.05 sums up with some concluding comments.

§12.02 THE ISDS ARBITRATION CLAIMS AGAINST INDIA

By 2016, India had one of the largest investment treaty networks in the world: it had signed eighty-three BITs (of which seventy-two had been enforced) and thirteen other IIAs. Almost all made substantive commitments more credible by adding to interstate arbitration and option of investor-state dispute settlement (ISDS) arbitration claims brought directly against host states. When India signed its first treaty (with the United Kingdom (UK) in March 1994, thirty-five years after the first BIT in the world had been signed between Germany and Pakistan), a BIT was widely considered a strategic and appropriate tool for a reform-minded country that was eager to seek foreign capital to help develop its economy. With much of the content behind the provisions of this lean and sparsely worded treaty yet to be decided within the larger ambit of international investment law, the legal implications of such treaties were as yet unclear. As a result, a large proportion of India's BITs (and generally those all over the world) were signed in the 1990s and the early 2000s, as part of a series of liberalising reforms that sought

1. Prabash Ranjan, *India and Bilateral Investment Treaties: Refusal, Acceptance, Backlash* (Oxford University Press, 2019).

to signal that India was an investment-friendly environment, in tune with a trend being followed by many countries all over the world. As can be seen in Figure 12.1 (based on data from the Government of India's Ministry of Finance website), India's trajectory was very much in line with the trend followed by countries all over the world.

Figure 12.1 Number of BITs Signed by India over Time

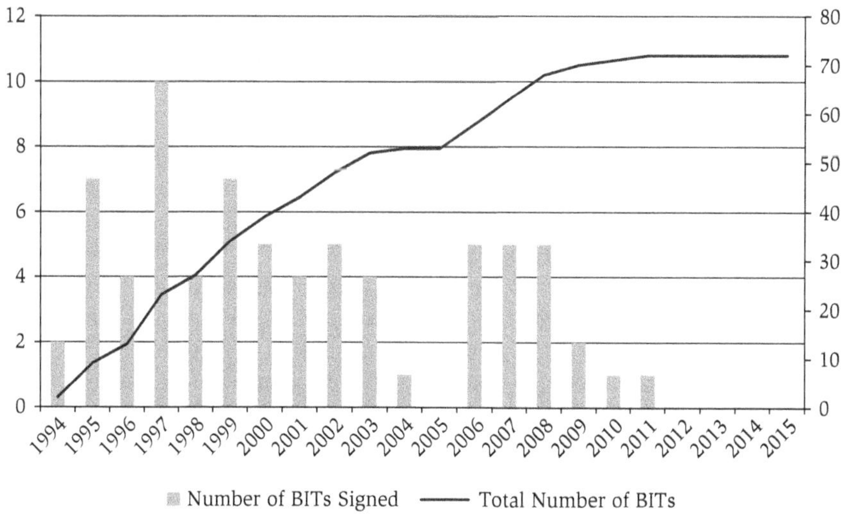

India's first brush with the legal implications of these treaties, however, began at the beginning of the current millennium. Since India had signed many BITs to signal the shift to a more market-friendly policy regime, there was no significant assessment of the binding legal implications that would result from the treaties. Thus, while the investment, substantive standard and arbitration clauses varied across treaties based on the terms brought to the table by the country signing the treaty, from all accounts, at the point that these treaties were being signed India was not strategically vetting the clauses. However, this was also true for a number of other countries, given that the terms contained in such treaties were initially rarely defined and only gained substance and interpretation as a result of treaty practice and arbitral involvement over time.

About a decade or so after India signed its first BIT, the first set of cases (which were settled privately) against the Indian government appeared in 2003. After a hiatus of another eight years, the Indian state had to confront its first full-blown international investment arbitration award in 2011. Soon, over the following years, a considerable number of cases were filed by investors against the Indian state. It is worthwhile outlining the key cases, under three main categories, because the subsequent actions of the Indian state in relation to IIAs appear to react directly to the claims.

[A] The Earliest Case(s)

Foreign investors invoked BITs for the first time in India in relation to the breakdown of the contract with the Dabhol Power Company (owned by a consortium consisting of Enron, GE and Bechtel) to supply electricity to the Maharashtra State Electricity Board. Once the terms of the contract to supply electricity broke down, the matter was moved for international commercial arbitration in London. In addition to this GE and Bechtel filed cases against India through their affiliates in Mauritius, invoking the India-Mauritius BIT, and (US-based) Enron acted similarly by asking affiliates to invoke the India-Netherlands BIT. Apart from this, many of the financial lenders to the project also invoked BITs signed by India with the Netherlands, UK, France, Austria and Switzerland. The multiple cases associated with this contract including those that were initiated as IIA-based arbitrations were settled out of court, with India paying out an undisclosed sum of money to settle the matter. Thus, even though as early as 2003-2004 the BITs signed by India ostensibly came into play, the process did not culminate in arbitral awards through ISDS.[2]

No other case showed up on the horizon until White Industries, an Australian resources company, initiated proceedings against India under the India-Australia BIT in 2010, which culminated in an arbitral award in 2011. Since this is the earliest decision in the Indian experience and plays a role in making one of the central arguments of the chapter, it is worthwhile to lay out the circumstances as well as the contents of this case in some detail. White Industries Australia entered into a contract with Coal India Limited to develop a mine in Piparwar (located in the Indian State of Jharkhand). A dispute arose between the two parties, which ended up being arbitrated by an International Chamber of Commerce (ICC) Tribunal. The tribunal decided to make an award of AUD 4.08 Million in 2002 in favour of White Industries. Soon after the award was granted, Coal India applied to have it set aside in the Calcutta High Court, even though the ICC arbitration had been seated outside India, while at the same time White Industries tried to enforce the award through the Delhi High Court. The Calcutta High Court refused to strike out Coal India's application in 2003 and this decision was again upheld upon appeal in 2004. White Industries appealed the matter in the Indian Supreme Court as a civil case, while in the meantime in 2006 the Delhi High Court stayed the enforcement of proceedings. The Indian Supreme Court started hearing the matter in 2012, which meant that after ten years White Industries had still not received the compensation awarded by the ICC Tribunal in 2002.

Using among other things the 'most favoured nation' (MFN) clause in the Australia-India BIT to draw on provisions in the India-Kuwait BIT, White Industries began IAA-based ISDS proceedings against India in July 2010. Arguing that the ICC arbitration itself was an 'investment' and therefore protected by BITs, White Industries was able to persuade the tribunal that court delays amounted to India's failure to ensure an 'effective means of asserting claims and enforcing rights with respect to investments'. The award in favour of White Industries was worked out as the ICC

2. Preeti Kundra, *Looking Beyond the Dabhol Debacle: Examining Its Causes and Understanding Its Lessons*, 41 Vand. J. Int'l L. 907 (2008).

award plus additional interest calculated from when it was issued in 2002.[3] Apart from expanding the definition of investment to include an arbitral award, this judgment was interesting and quite controversial because it sought compensation from India for the delays caused by the Indian judicial system.

[B] The *2G* Case and Other Claims Related to the Telecommunications Sector

Having faced significant exposure in international arbitration over judicial action in the White Industries award, the Indian judicial system would once again play an important role in sparking BIT-related investor claims. Following a judgment of the Supreme Court of India, companies which had invested in the Indian telecom sector initiated a number of ISDS arbitrations.

At the heart of this was the so-called *2G* case.[4] Relevantly here, the Indian Supreme Court was convinced about corruption in the allocation of the licence-spectrum package to telecom companies and therefore it cancelled all granted licences. This led Sistema (a Russian company), Telenor (a Norwegian company), Axiata, Khaitan Holdings Mauritius Limited and Capital Global and Kaif Investment Limited (all three companies incorporated in Mauritius) to invoke multiple BITs to initiate arbitral proceedings against the Government of India. Some investors - Sistema, Telenor and Axiata - later revised their stance on account of compensatory schemes (offer to participate in spectrum auctions arranged by the government), whereas others - Khaitan Holdings Mauritius Limited and Capital Global and Kaif Investment Limited - moved on to arbitration. The final notice to the Government of India was served by Khaitan Holdings Mauritius Limited, which was also representing Capital Global and Kaif Investment on 30 September 2013. Khaitan Holdings Mauritius Limited filed for USD 140 million in investments made, along with 12% interest from the date of receipt of the investment and claimed that its share of lost shareholder revenue was in excess of USD 1 billion. It has also claimed for the loss of market value of the licences, pegging the amount at USD 300 million. Apparently, investors held various rounds of meetings with government representatives but failed to arrive at a mutually agreeable solution. The firm commenced arbitration under (United Nations Commission on International Trade Law) UNCITRAL Rules,[5] and the case was still to be decided (as of May 2020).

In addition to the cases regarding licensing to provide 2G services, there are two (or more precisely three) prominent cases also associated with telecommunications. In

3. *White Industries Australia Limited v. The Republic of India*, UNCITRAL, http://www.italaw.com/cases/1169#sthash.U7WppHBT.dpuf (accessed 5 May 2020). *See also* Amokura Kawharu & Luke Nottage, '*The Curious Case of ISDS Arbitration Involving Australia and New Zealand*', 44(2) UWA L. Rev. 32 (2008), available via http://www.able.uwa.edu.au/centres/uwalr/issues/2018-volume-44-issue-2 (accessed 5 May 2020).
4. *Centre for Public Interest Litigation v. Union of India and Ors.*, Supreme Court Writ Petition (Civil) No. 423 of 2010, https://main.sci.gov.in/jonew/judis/39041.pdf (accessed 5 May 2020).
5. *Khaitan Holdings Files International Arbitration Against Indian Government*, Moneylife (18 Apr. 2012), http://www.moneylife.in/article/khaitan-holdings-files-international-arbitration-against-indian-govt/34691.html (accessed 5 May 2020).

the first case, the foreign majority stakeholders in ByCell Telecommunications India Private Limited served a notice to the Government of India, alleging violations of the Russia-India and Cyprus-India BITs. ByCell India had about 74% foreign investment by ByCell Holding AG, which was incorporated in Switzerland. The Swiss company was 97% owned by the Cyprus-based Tenoch, which is in turn is owned by two Russian nationals. On account of this jurisdictionally complex structure, the Cyprus and Russia BITs were invoked to initiate the arbitration. The contention for the arbitration was that after granting telecom licences to ByCell, the Department of Telecommunication withdrew the licences after citing security concerns. The contested issues moved through the Indian court system for a number of years and after an adverse ruling,[6] in 2012 ByCell alleged grossly arbitrary and discriminatory treatment against it during the licensing process, thereby frustrating legitimate expectations and denying fair and equitable treatment (FET), by invoking the Russia-India and Cyprus-India BIT.[7] While details are not available, it appears that India has been able to recently win this case.[8]

By contrast, the second case in this category (or rather two related cases arising from the same circumstances) led to arbitral outcomes against India. In 2005 Devas Multimedia, a Mauritius based firm in which two American investment firms *Columbia Capital* and *Telecom Ventures* as well as *Deutsche Telekom* held stakes, signed a contract with Antrix (the commercial arm of Indian Space Research Organisation – ISRO) to provide broadband services in India. After a report from the office of the Comptroller and Audit General (CAG) leaked to the press suggesting corrupt practices associated with the contract, the Indian government led by the United Progressive Alliance (UPA), which was already battling the 2G crisis, pulled out of the contract citing 'force majeure' as well as the argument that the 'essential security interest' of the country required termination of the deal. In response, two cases were filed against India: one by the shareholders of Devas, which included American investors Columbia Capital and Telecom Ventures invoking the India-Mauritius BIT and the second by *Deutsche Telekom* invoking the India-Germany BIT. (In addition to this, Devas Multimedia filed an arbitration case in the ICC, which it won in 2015 and Antrix was ordered to pay USD 672 million to Devas.)

Both of the investment treaty-based proceedings resulted in awards that held against India.[9] In the first case (*CC/Devas (Mauritius) Ltd*), the tribunal held that the

6. *Bycell Telecommunications India Pvt. Ltd. v. Union of India & Ors.*, W.P.(C) No. 8989 of 2009 & CMs 6454, 13362/2009, https://indiankanoon.org/doc/150083441 (accessed 5 May 2020).
7. Shauvik Ghosh, *Now, Bycell Threatens Government with International Arbitration*, Mint (18 Jul. 2012), http://www.livemint.com/Companies/X6OvDi3H699syproZYTBRL/Now-ByCell-threatens-government-with-international-arbitrat.html (accessed 5 May 2020).
8. Press Information Bureau (Government of India), *BIT Claims Against India Dismissed*, Press Release (20 Jan. 2020), https://pib.gov.in/PressReleseDetail.aspx?PRID=1599905 (accessed 2 May 2020). *See also Curtis Defeats $400 Million Investment Treaty Claim Brought Against India*, Curtis (24 Jan. 2020), https://www.curtis.com/our-firm/news/curtis-defeats-400-million-investment-treaty-claim-brought-against-india (accessed 2 May 2020).
9. Analysing inconsistencies in tribunal interpretation, *see* Ridhi Kabra, *Return of the Inconsistent Application of the 'Essential Security Interest' Clause in Investment Treaty Arbitration: CC/Devas v. India and Deutsche Telekom v. India* ICSID Review – Foreign Investment Law Journal (21 Feb. 2020), https://doi.org/10.1093/icsidreview/siz021. On 'essential security interests' in recent trade disputes between Korea and Japan, *see also* Claxton, Nottage & Williams, in this volume.

Indian annulment of the contract violated FET guaranteed by the treaty as well as an expropriation of the claimant's investment, but accepted (by majority) the Indian defence of essential security and adjusted Indian liability accordingly.[10] In the second case (*Deutsche Telekom*), the tribunal also found against India not so much on the grounds of expropriation or violation of FET (in fact these claims were dismissed) but rather it could see no evidence that the annulment was linked to any 'essential security interest'.[11] India challenged the interim award before the Swiss Federal Tribunal, questioning the jurisdiction of the tribunal to hear the case, but the Federal Tribunal dismissed this argument as well as the application for annulment of the award.[12] Payment of the compensation awarded in both cases is awaited, as of May 2020.

[C] Taxation-Related and Other Cases Following from Executive Action

Away from the shadow of judicial decisions aimed at curbing alleged corruption, a rather inexplicable executive action that insists on retrospective taxation has also resulted in a number of investors filing for international arbitration. The narrative of these cases can begin from 2014, when Vodafone International Holdings BV (VIHBV) – a Dutch subsidiary of Vodafone Group Plc (UK) – served a notice of arbitration against the Republic of India under the India-Netherlands BIT, alleging breach of the Netherlands-India BIT for violating FET. The claim centred on legislation authorising the Indian government to tax all sales of Indian assets to overseas buyers over the preceding fifty years. The legislation came into being as a response to a prolonged legal battle between Vodafone and the Indian government concerning Vodafone's acquisition of a majority stake in mobile operator Hutchinson Essar in 2007, which the government insisted gave rise to a tax liability.

This imbroglio culminated in 2012 with the Indian Supreme Court holding that since the acquisition took place overseas, between two foreign companies, Vodafone was not liable to pay tax under Indian law.[13] The Indian Finance Minister subsequently proposed legislative amendments within one month of this ruling to continue legitimising its tax claim, a move that was also approved by the Indian Parliament as a part of the Finance Bill 2012. VIHBV challenged this retrospective amendment to the Indian Income Tax Act in the notice of arbitration it sent to the Government of India. Subsequently, while these arbitration proceedings were still going on, Vodafone Group Plc (the parent company of VIHBV) challenged the same retrospective taxation measures invoking the India-UK BIT. Interestingly India sought an anti-arbitration injunction from the Delhi High Court seeking to restrain Vodafone Group Plc from

10. *CC/Devas (Mauritius) Ltd, Devas Employees Mauritius Private Limited and Telecom Devas Mauritius Limited v. India*, UNCITRAL, PCA Case No. 2013-09, Award on Jurisdiction and Merits (25 Jul. 2016).
11. *Deutsche Telekom AG v. India*, UNCITRAL, PCA Case No. 2014-10, Interim Award (13 Dec. 2017) (DT).
12. *Deutsche Telekom v. India, PCA* Case No. 2014-10, https://www.italaw.com/cases/2275 (accessed 5 May 2020).
13. *Vodafone International Holding B.V. v. Union of India & Anr.*, Civil Appeal No. 733 of 2012, Supreme Court of India, 20 Jan. 2012.

proceeding with the arbitration. The case was dismissed, among other things acknowledging the High Court's limited power to intervene in foreign-seated BIT arbitrations.[14] It has come to pass that in September 2020 the Permanent Court of Arbitration in the Netherlands found that the tax liability imposed by India was in breach of the FET clause of the India-Netherlands BIT and required the Indian government to pay Vodafone INR 850 million.[15]

Cairn Energy, a Scottish energy exploration company, is another foreign company that is facing a USD 1.6 billion tax demand from the Indian government – again following from retrospective taxation legitimatised by the 2012 Finance Bill legislation. Cairn Energy has alleged that India's actions breached several of its obligations under the UK-India BIT, including its obligations to 'create favourable conditions', and ensure FET, as well as 'full protection and security'. It appears that the hearings before the arbitration tribunal are over and that a ruling is expected in the summer of 2020.[16] Related to this is yet another case: Cairn Energy had transferred some of its assets over 2006-2007 to a new company Cairn India and subsequently sold its major shares to Vedanta, another UK-based company. It appears that Vedanta has taken steps to protect its legal position and shareholder interests by initiating a process of treaty arbitration to prevent retrospective tax action by the Indian government.[17]

There are at least three other cases following from executive action. In the first of these cases, the background is that the Government of the Indian State of Tamil Nadu promised several incentives including tax breaks for Nissan to set up a factory in the state in 2008. Nissan had invested in a factory but the promised incentives were not paid out, causing the company to invoke the India-Japan CEPA (Comprehensive Economic Partnership Agreement) and send in a notice to the Indian government in 2016. In the meantime, India has contested jurisdiction arguing that tax matters are not under the purview of the CEPA with Japan, but this was denied by the tribunal.[18] Subsequent press reports seemed to suggest that there may be a settlement between the Indian government and Nissan before an arbitral award is announced.[19] Indeed, the Indian State of Tamil Nadu reached a settlement with Nissan, obliging the company to withdraw its arbitration claim and accepting about one-third of the claimed damages –

14. *Union of India v. Vodafone Group PLC United Kingdom & Anr.*, in the High Court of Delhi CS(OS) 383/2017 & I.A.No.9460/2017.
15. Payaswini Upadyay, *Vodafone Wins Arbitration Against India in Retrospective Tax Case Bloomberg Quint* (25 Sep. 2020), https://www.bloombergquint.com/law-and-policy/vodafone-wins-investment-treaty-case-against-government-of-india (accessed on 20 Oct. 2020).
16. *See* PTI, *Cairn Expects Arbitration Award in Retro Tax Case by This Summer*, Financial Express (10 Mar. 2020), https://www.financialexpress.com/industry/cairn-expects-arbitration-award-in-retro-tax-case-by-this-summer/1894114/ (accessed 5 May 2020).
17. PTI, *Vedanta Slaps Notice of Claims on Government*, The Economic Times (28 Mar. 2015), https://economictimes.indiatimes.com/industry/energy/oil-gas/vedanta-slaps-notice-of-claims-on-government/articleshow/46719147.cms (accessed 5 May 2020).
18. *Arbitration Court Rejects India's Plea in Case against Nissan*, Livemint (29 May 2019), https://www.livemint.com/news/india/arbitration-court-rejects-india-s-plea-in-case-against-nissan-sources-1559130803729.html (accessed 15 Apr. 2020).
19. *Tamil Nadu Close to Settling Nissan Tax Dispute*, The Hindu (29 Feb. 2020), https://www.thehindu.com/news/national/tamil-nadu/tamil-nadu-close-to-settling-nissan-tax-dispute/article30950334.ece (accessed 2 May 2020).

the claim had amounted to USD 660 million.[20] In the second case invoking both the India-South Korea BIT and the bilateral CEPA, Kowepo (Korean Western Power Co.), the South Korean state-owned power utility has sought about USD 400 million in compensation for losses caused by the Indian government allegedly not been able to supply promised fuel for a gas-based power project.[21] In a third case, the Indian government was served notice of arbitration in 2016, invoking the India-United Arab Emirates (UAE) BIT by RAKIA, an investment body of Ras Al-Khaimah, which constitutes one of the seven emirates of the UAE. The Indian government was charged because the Government of the Indian State of Andhra Pradesh government failed to supply bauxite to the investors for their industrial activity as promised. It appears that the refusal by the Andhra Pradesh government was linked to protests from indigenous tribes.[22] The status of the proceedings is not clear and the outcome was pending as of May 2020.

§12.03 REACTIONS TO CASES BY INDIA

One can document three broad responses to such IAA-based arbitration claims against India. One was to finalise a New Model Treaty in late 2015 to replace the one that had been in use since India started signing international investment treaties. The earlier 2003 Model Treaty was based on a 1967 Organisation for Economic Co-operation and Development (OECD) text widely circulated at the time, the *OECD Draft Convention for the Protection of Foreign Property*.[23] The second reaction was to take the position from about the middle of 2016 that all investment treaties would be terminated by March 2017, if possible, and that any country wishing to sign an investment treaty with India must (re)negotiate on the basis of the New Model Treaty. The third response was the move by the Indian state to experiment with alternatives to the standard IIA-led regime of investor protection through joint interpretive statements (JIS), and by subsequently going on to suggesting that special domestic laws will be enacted that will specifically protect foreign investors.

20. Aditi Shah & Sudharshan Varadhan, *Exclusive: Nissan Settles Dispute with Indian State over Unpaid Dues – Sources*, Reuters (28 May 2020), https://www.reuters.com/article/us-nissan-india-arbitration-exclusive/exclusive-nissan-settles-dispute-with-indian-state-over-unpaid-dues-sources-idUSKBN2342AR.
21. Sarita Singh, *Korean Company Starts Arbitration Against India*, The Economic Times (10 Dec. 2019), https://economictimes.indiatimes.com/industry/energy/power/korean-company-starts-arbitration-against-india/articleshow/72449677.cms?from=mdr (accessed 2 May 2020).
22. *RAKIA's Arbitration Notice: Various Issues and India's Response*, GK Today (30 Mar. 2017), https://www.gktoday.in/gk/rakias-arbitration-notice-various-issues-and-indias-response/ (accessed 15 Apr. 2020).
23. Department of Economic Affairs (Government of India), *Transforming the International Investment Agreement Regime: The Indian Experience*, Presentation at the UNCTAD Expert Meeting (25 Feb. 2015).

[A] The New Model Treaty

It is helpful to begin with a brief description of the atmosphere in which the New Model Treaty came to be drafted. Soon after receiving a notice from Vodafone, the government set up an inter-ministerial group (headed by the Revenue Secretary and including secretaries of Department of Economic Affairs, Law and Justice Ministry, Telecom Ministry and Ministry of External Affairs) to look into the issue.[24] The Group was apparently of the opinion that BITs did not cover taxation issues and in particular that this issue was also not covered by the India-Netherlands BIT.[25] Alongside this, the government also decided to review BITs in general and began work on a new model BIT, ostensibly putting on hold the process of signing any more BITs. As this process was taking place, the government started expressing concerns about the nature of BITs emerging here and there also around the world. As an example, the then Finance Minister Chidambaram when addressing the Canada-India Business Council said, while responding to questions around the status of the Foreign Investment Promotion and Protection Agreement, that India could not allow its Supreme Court to be subject to foreign courts or tribunals, and that it seemed unlikely other countries would be willing to do so either.[26]

In addition, the government was also the recipient of demands from a number of civil society groups, whose voice for change became more prominent once more cases against India became noticeable, even under ad hoc UNCITRAL Arbitration Rules that (historically at least) attracted less publicity. One particular instance of note was when the then Prime Minister Manmohan Singh was getting ready to visit the US in 2013, many civil society members wrote a public letter to him making arguments against a potentially damaging India-US BIT, asking that the signing of a treaty should be kept in abeyance till a new model BIT was presented.[27]

In the meantime, the government carried out a review of the 2003 Model BIT, though with little involvement from civil society, domain experts, think tanks, etc. and presented the text of the Draft New Model Treaty (DNMT) to the public. In stark contrast to the earlier Model BIT, the text of the DNMT was consciously and determinedly oriented towards limiting protections offered to investors. The contents of the DNMT are worth noting as in effect almost every provision was a reaction to

24. *Lok Sabha Question by Mr PR Natarajan to the Minister of Commerce and Industry*, Unstarred Question No. 1063, Answered on 12 Aug. 2013.
25. Shauvik Ghosh & Remya Nair, *Vodafone Row outside Ambit of Treaty, Says Govt Panel*, Live Mint (11 May 2012), http://www.livemint.com/Politics/Xa88uGe2Ws1KqrPAjvjYeL/Vodafone-row-outside-ambit-of-treaty-says-govt-panel.html (accessed 5 May 2020).
26. PTI, *Investment Pacts Can't Be Subject to Foreign Jurisdictions – Chidambaram*, Times of India (16 Apr. 2013), http://timesofindia.indiatimes.com/business/international-business/Investment-pacts-cant-be-subject-to-foreign-jurisdictions-Chidambaram/articleshow/19576234.cms (accessed 5 May 2020).
27. G. Manicandan, *We Call upon the Government to Review and Rescind Its Decision to Sign BIT/BIPA with the USA*, Letter to the Prime Minister on behalf of Forum against FTAs (26 Sep. 2013), http://www.bilaterals.org/IMG/pdf/lettter_forum_ag_ftas_us_india_bits_26_sept.pdf (accessed 5 May 2020).

issues that had come up in the cases instituted by investors against India; one could hazard labelling it as a knee-jerk reaction.

[1] The 2014 DNMT:[28] Changes in Definitions, Substantive Standards and Procedure

In the first instance, the DNMT sought to limit the activities of 'Government' that could be questioned in IIA-based arbitration to those performed only by central and state governments, excluding local governments. Thus, while the national treatment clause was retained, it was not to apply to laws or measures taken by regional or local governments. The NDMT was in fact very heavily oriented towards listing a series of issues and items that have to be excluded from the purview of international treaty arbitration. Thus, in addition to the definition of 'investor' barring concerns that do not have real and substantial operations in the home state, the term 'investment' was also confined to expressly exclude interests in government-issued debt, court judgments or arbitral awards (an obvious reaction to the White Industries case and the then ongoing notices generated by the 2G judgment related cases), as well as in holding companies or investment companies. Other articles of the NDMT went on to explicitly exclude umbrella claims by investors as well as non-commercial services provided by the government, presumably referring to the national court system. Perhaps the most prominent exclusion was in relation to 'any taxation measure' – clearly a reaction to the Vodafone case.

The NDMT further removed the bulk of standard substantive standard clauses, so that there is a conspicuous absence of MFN, FET and 'full protection and security' clauses. Instead, these were all replaced by 'Standard of Treatment' that stated that investments could expect to receive limited protection from: (i) 'denial of justice under customary international law', (ii) 'un-remedied and egregious violations of due process', and (iii) 'manifestly abusive treatment involving continuous, unjustified and outrageous coercion or harassment'. There is a long article devoted to expropriation, with a detailed explanation as to what would be construed as expropriation and how a tribunal should assess appropriate compensation and account for mitigating factors in its calculation.

Furthermore, the NDMT set out obligations of investors, which included measures against corruption, disclosures and record-keeping, payment of taxes and compliance with domestic law – requiring demonstrable compliance with these obligations before serving a notice for IIA-based ISDS. As for this procedure, apart from specifying that that arbitration would be carried on under UNCITRAL Rules by a three-person tribunal, the NDMT demanded major changes in the procedure associated with serving notice to the host government. Thus, prior to serving a notice to the government it had to be demonstrated that domestic remedies have been exhausted, the format of the Notice of Arbitration had to identify the precise breach as well as the

28. *See Model Text for the Indian Bilateral Investment Treaty*, https://www.mygov.in/sites/default/files/master_image/Model%20Text%20for%20the%20Indian%20Bilateral%20Investment%20Treaty.pdf (accessed 5 May 2020).

details of compensation demanded, the respondent was to make public the Notice of Arbitration and all pleadings, transcripts, orders and awards (save where specific steps are required to protect confidential information), and the host state could make counterclaims on the basis of investor requirements regarding corruption, disclosure, taxation and non-compliance with domestic law.

[2] The Law Commission Report

The NDMT was released in late 2014. After public consultation, a response came from the respected Law Commission of India (including seconded or past senior judges and other legal experts).[29] The Commission's Report noted that the NDMT was tilted towards privileging the host state against interests of investors. It was generally felt that India should put out a more balanced negotiating text: one that aimed to balance the interests of investors (including importantly the Indian investors increasingly investing abroad) while safeguarding the regulatory powers of the host state. To this end the Report asked for: changes in the Preamble, the incorporation of a more 'asset-based' (albeit closed) definition of investment, taxation not to be excluded from issues covered by the treaty, expropriation definitions to be tempered, the regulatory powers of the government to control money transfers to be moderated, an MFN clause to be reinstituted (albeit a restricted one), measures by state and local governments to be included, and a simplification in the series of procedural innovations (many of them being tried for the first time, borrowed from many jurisdictions and typically part of regional trade agreements).

Of course, the Report of the Law Commission was not entirely antithetical to the NDMT. It appreciated, for example, the call to replace the 'vague fair and equitable' standard with what it thought to be a more clearly phrased standard. That was perceived as bringing the Model Treaty closer to a form that would be compatible with the principles and practice of international law.

[3] The New Model Treaty

The Government of India released the text of its New Model Treaty in December 2015.[30] The final Model Treaty retained the defensive and reactive spirit of the NDMT, although tempered down a bit by following some of the suggestions of the Law Commission. As was the case in the NDMT, there is no explicit reference to the FET standard – the most commonly invoked standard of protection in investment treaty disputes. Instead, the Model Treaty protects against 'measures which constitute a violation of customary international law', invoking a closed list that includes denial of

---

29. Law Commission of India, *Analysis of the 2015 Draft Model Indian BIT*, https://www.latestlaws.com/library/law-commission-of-india-reports/law-commission-report-no-260-analysis-2015-draft-model-indian-bilateral-investment-treaty/.
30. Department of Economic Affairs (Government of India), *Model Text for the Indian Bilateral Investment Treaty*, https://dea.gov.in/sites/default/files/ModelBIT_Annex_0.pdf (accessed 5 May 2020).

justice, fundamental breach of due process, targeted discrimination, and manifestly abusive treatment. There is also no MFN clause at all. Further, as with the NDMT, the emphasis on exhausting local remedies is very prominent in the Model Treaty. An investor may not pursue ISDS arbitration until it has exhausted local remedies, or until five years have passed in pursuit of the exhaustion of local remedies. While investors are protected against measures taken by national, state, and union territory governments, treaty provisions do not apply to local governments.

The New Model Treaty protections are explicitly denied in relation to tax laws or measures taken to enforce tax obligations as well as government procurements, compulsory licences, subsidies, instances of national security, and non-commercial services provided by the government – which could include the national court system. Also excluded from treaty protection are pre-investment activities related to the establishment, acquisition, or expansion of any investment. In addition to these exclusions, the Model Treaty also contains a broad denial of benefits clause, excluding the benefits of the treaty to investments or investors: (1) owned or controlled, directly or indirectly, by persons of that state or a non-party; and (2) that have been established or restructured with the primary purpose of gaining access to the BIT's dispute mechanisms. Among the many exclusions is an interesting set of clauses that list a series of General Exceptions, such as those contained in the General Agreement on Tariffs and Trade (GATT) Article XX, relating to public morals and public order, health, compliance with laws and regulations, the environment, and cultural preservation.

Turning to the clauses of the NDMT that were particularly adverse to FDI and which the Law Commission had spoken up against, there was a removal of the requirement for investors to hold majority-ownership or control to qualify for treaty protection, and of allowances for the host state to bring counterclaims against investors. While a number of types of investment are explicitly excluded from the definition of a qualifying as investment, including portfolio investments, the definition of 'investment' in the Model Treaty is asset based and incorporating a test akin to the *Salini* factors that have been applied by some investment treaty tribunals, though the qualifying investment needs to have certain fundamental characteristics.

[B] Terminations, New Treaties and New Laws

After announcing the New Model Treaty in December 2015, six months later the Indian government decided to make the next set of announcements related to international investment treaties – stating in July 2016 that out of the eighty-three treaties signed, fifty-eight were going to be terminated by 31 March 2017,[31] notably by invoking any applicable unilateral termination clauses provided in the existing treaties. Thereafter countries were expected to renegotiate the terminated treaties based on the New Model BIT and those treaties that were not terminated were to be similarly renegotiated upon

31. PTI, *India to Renegotiate All Bilateral Investment Pacts: Nirmala Sitharaman,* The Economic Times (25 Jul. 2016), https://economictimes.indiatimes.com/news/economy/policy/india-to-renegotiate-all-bilateral-investment-pacts-nirmala-sitharaman/articleshow/53385020.cms?from=mdr (accessed 19 Apr. 2020).

expiry. Nirmala Sitharaman the then Minister of Commerce and Industry (currently the Indian Finance Minister) speaking against the background of the Notice of Arbitration sent to the Indian government by Cairn Energy is reported to have said that the New Model Treaty had been framed precisely to minimise 'Cairn Energy type of dispute'.[32] Stating that the revised Model BIT will form the basis of negotiation for future BITs, Sitharaman is also reported to have said that 'in the new model BIT, taxation matters have been excluded keeping in view of the fact that taxation is an integral function of the state's sovereignty and hence such matters need not be escalated under treaty dispute settlement mechanism'.[33]

Once the termination date came around, and the New Model Treaty came into play, there was a good deal of disquiet among nations seeking to interact with India. For instance, in 2017 there were reports of how India was rejecting an offer from the European Union (EU) to start negotiations for a stand-alone BIT or that the possibilities of going ahead with a Comprehensive Trade and Investment Agreement were not very bright. The individual treaties with many European countries were of course being denounced. Apparently, the Indian government wanted to proceed with negotiations, leaving aside contentious matters (read investment provisions) but the EU was not able to agree to this.[34]

The terms around investment turned out to be the big stumbling block in the case of Canada as well. Canada (an important trading and investment partner of India) was not able to work out a trade or investment agreement because it insisted on an investment agreement as a precursor to or part of a trade agreement. The investment agreement apparently was not successfully brought to fruition because, among other things, Canada was not enthusiastic about the New Model Treaty terms that required all domestic options need to be exhausted before a company can go in for international arbitration, and it also wanted the inclusion of an MFN clause in the agreement.[35] A similar uneasiness can be seen in a press report that was reporting some statements made by the economist Arvind Panagariya (who is otherwise a great supporter of the regime) as to the restrictive nature of the Indian Model Treaty compared to China's approach to IIAs, but also incorporates reference to some of the discontent expressed by the US:

---

32. PTI, *BIT Model to Minimise Cairn Energy Type Dispute: Nirmala Sitharaman,* The Indian Express (8 Aug. 2016), https://indianexpress.com/article/business/economy/nirmala-seetharaman-cairn-energy-dispute-economy-2961422/ (accessed 19 Apr. 2020).
33. *Ibid.*
34. Asit Ranjan Mishra, *India on Collision Course with EU over Trade Treaty,* Livemint (21 Feb. 2017), https://www.livemint.com/Politics/UKLWUwDn33uBuwRrmBRE5M/India-on-collision-course-with-EU-over-trade-treaty.html (accessed 19 Apr. 2020).
35. Amiti Sen Surabhi, *India Refuses Canada's Proposal of Signing Investment Deal Before Free Trade Pact,* The Hindu Business Line (14 Mar. 2017), https://www.thehindubusinessline.com/economy/policy/india-refuses-canadas-proposal-of-signing-investment-deal-before-free-trade-pact/article9583882.ece (accessed 19 Apr. 2020). *See also* Amiti Sen Surabhi, *FinMin to Look into Changes Sought by Canada in Draft Bilateral Treaty,* The Hindu Business Line (26 Apr. 2017), https://www.thehindubusinessline.com/economy/policy/finmin-to-look-into-changes-sought-by-canada-in-draft-bilateral-treaty/article9665816.ece (accessed 19 Apr. 2020).

> Last month, the US Deputy Assistant to the US President and Deputy National Security Advisor for International Economics Adewale (Wally) Adeyemo had blamed India for not being ambitious enough to conclude a BIT ... 'To be frank, we are far apart on number of issues with regard to trade and investment with India. We feel our colleagues in India have not been as ambitious (on concluding BIT) as we want them to be but we remain open,' Adeyemo had said here at a session on India-US Economic Relations.[36]

While this type of disquiet has therefore emerged from major countries from where foreign investment may have been forthcoming, over the past few years, India has ended up signing a small number of treaties and agreements. In 2018 two BITs were signed with Taiwan and Belarus, in 2019 one treaty with the Kyrgyz Republic, and in 2020 an Investment and Facilitation Treaty with Brazil. In addition to this, there are Joint Interpretative Statements over provisions in old remaining treaties, reached with Bangladesh and Columbia. If one were to look at the current website of the Ministry of Finance one will of course find the list of terminated treaties, including, for example, that with Australia. But there is also a long list titled 'BITs (BITs)/Agreements/ Joint Interpretative Statements (JISs) signed subsequent to adoption of Model BIT text 2015' and under this column are listed Iran, Switzerland, Morocco, Kuwait, Ukraine, UAE, San Marino, Hong Kong, Israel, Mauritius, Oman as countries whose treaties are said to be 'under discussion'.[37] These new attempts will be looked at more closely later in this chapter, but before doing so, it is also important to acknowledge the ideological content that feeds the response to international investment treaties in India's post-termination world.

If at least some of the push behind the impulse to replace the old Model Treaty with the New Model Treaty came from left-leaning civil society groups, a similar push encouraging the government to be wary of international trade and investment regimes is also evident from right-wing Hindu nationalist groups that currently dominate Indian politics. In various press reports that follow Indian attempts to sign investment or trade agreements, particularly after the latest populist win of elections by the Bharatiya Janata Party (BJP), there is a good chance that voices from the Swadeshi Jagran Manch (SJM), an arm of the RSS (Rashtriya Sevak Sangh – the ideological organisation that guides Hindu nationalism), can be found speaking up against Indian participation in world trade or investment. As an example, when India hosted an informal World Trade Organization (WTO) mini-ministerial meeting in March 2018 to look for the way forward for that multilateral body, the convener of the SJM Ashwini Mahajan was reported as saying 'After acceding to investment facilitation, our national interests would be at stake.'[38] He also reportedly wrote a letter to the government where he referred to the lack of unanimity among various ministries on investment facilitation,

---

36. PTI, *India's Bilateral Investment Pacts Restrictive: Arvind Panagariya*, The Economic Times (9 Aug. 2016), https://economictimes.indiatimes.com/news/economy/policy/indias-bilateral-investment-pacts-restrictive-arvindpanagariya/articleshow/53613608.cms?utm_source=contentofinterest&utm_medium=text&utm_campaign=cppst (accessed 19 Apr. 2020).
37. The texts of the terminated and new treaties and JISs, as well as other details, can be found on the Ministry of Finance Government of India website, https://dea.gov.in/bipa.
38. Kritika Suneja, *Avoid Backing Investment Facilitation at WTO Meet, Swadeshi Jagaran Manch Cautions Government*, The Economic Times (19 Mar. 2018), https://economictimes.indiatimes

saying that there is little or no evidence that binding rules on investment facilitation will help attract foreign investment into India.[39]

Similarly around October 2019, as the Indian government was ostensibly thinking of joining (but ended up not joining) the Regional Comprehensive Economic Partnership (RCEP), which was essentially a proposed free trade agreement (FTA) between the ten-member ASEAN (Association of Southeast Asian Nations) and six of its biggest trading partners (China, India, Japan, South Korea, Australia and New Zealand), the SJM started lobbying against it by arguing broadly that Indian trade deficits would go up.[40] While speaking up against the RCEP, which India ended up not joining at the end of 2019, Mohan Bhagawat (the head of the RSS) reportedly said:

> to minimise the impact of other immediate crises and the ups and downs of the world economy on our financial system, we need to go to the basics and ponder. We have to formulate our own economic vision keeping in mind our requirements, profile and condition of our people and our resources and potential to realise our national aspirations.[41]

It is precisely this type of *national aspiration* that may have caused India also to move on its latest strategy to govern foreign investment. It was reported in January 2020 that the Indian government has proposed appointing mediators and fast-track courts to settle disputes between investors and the government. An official reportedly said that the 'idea is to attract and promote foreign investment, but a major issue for investors is enforcement of contracts and speedy dispute resolution', but also that: 'Foreign investors have highlighted the enforcement of contracts as one of their biggest concerns, said the second official, adding that improving on this front would also reduce litigation for the government.'[42] The press report goes on to observe: 'The government's thinking is that India may not need to sign investment treaties with other nations if the new law, which is modelled on a BIT, can give confidence to investors, said the first source. A domestic law, however, cannot be a substitute for a BIT as its scope cannot allow investors to take their case to international arbitration, the sources said.' This is of course an attempt to render domestic law as a substitute for international law but that is in complete contradiction of the role of international law – domestic laws may be constitutionally valid but end up breaching obligations under international law. As Prabash Ranjan points out in an op-ed commenting on the issue:

.com/news/economy/policy/avoid-backing-investment-facilitation-at-wto-meet-swadeshi-jagran-manch-cautions-government/articleshow/63358101.cms (accessed 20 Apr. 2020).

39. *Ibid.*
40. R. Jagannathan, *Swadeshi Jagran Manch Is Right. The RCEP Is Not for India, at Least Not as Yet*, Swarajya Magazine (9 Oct. 2019), https://swarajyamag.com/economy/swadeshi-jagran-manch-is-right-the-rcep-is-not-for-india-at-least-not-as-yet (accessed 18 Apr. 2020).
41. Vibha Sharma, *Sangh Affiliate SJM Announces Nationwide Protest Against RCEP*, The Tribune India (11 Oct. 2019), https://www.tribuneindia.com/news/archive/nation/sangh-affiliate-sjm-announces-nationwide-protest-against-rcep-845699 (accessed 9 Apr. 2020).
42. Aditi Shah & Aftab Ahmed, *Exclusive: India Plans New Law to Protect Foreign Investment – Sources*, Reuters (15 Jan. 2020), https://uk.reuters.com/article/us-india-investment-law-exclusive-idUKKBN1ZE151 (accessed 10 Apr. 2020).

> India is a dualist nation when it comes to international law i.e. treaties are not binding domestically (on courts, state governments etc) till the treaty is incorporated into domestic law usually through enabling legislation. If the proposed law aims to incorporate India's BIT obligations under domestic law, it would be a welcome development. However, if the proposed law intends to replace protection to foreign investors under BITs and ISDS, it would be a regressive step.[43]

While this domestic law aimed at foreign investors may or may not come into being, it needs to be also noted as a part of the Budget proceedings 2020 a new Bill was announced, namely the Vivad se Vishwas Bill 2020 – meaning from 'dispute' to 'confidence'.[44] This law has been introduced as an amnesty scheme for direct taxpayers. Section 4(4), 4(5) and 4(7) of the Bill allows for waivers from income tax claims made by the Indian government on foreign investors provided that they pay a one-time specified percentage amount of what they owe to the government and withdraw their arbitration claims from international tribunals.

[C] Summing Up India's Reactions

Overall, the reaction to the investment treaty led cases has caused India to craft a New Model Treaty, which among other things was authored to exclude precisely the types of cases that had come to be brought against India. This has been followed up with the termination or denouncement of erstwhile investment treaties combined with the stated intent of renegotiating future treaties on the basis of the New Model Treaty. One might wish it, but one cannot easily shake off the past,[45] so new cases have continued to pile up under sunset clauses even in terminated treaties. In addition, the weight of pro-state rights in the New Model Treaty has hindered India from being a part of a series of bilateral or multilateral investment agreements, such as RCEP. This, peppered with the nationalist ideology of the currently ruling party, has led India to think it can remedy the current situation by tweaking domestic law – by fashioning a new law to reassure foreign investors and fashioning a tax law to contain the potential effects of adverse rulings by international tribunals.

§12.04 ASSESSING THE DEVELOPMENTS: EMPIRICAL AND THEORETICAL PERSPECTIVES

One way to assess the developments relating to international investment treaties is to go down a familiar refrain from some civil society groups and others, that since the investment treaty system causes substantial financial costs on host countries and

43. Prabash Ranjan, *A Domestic Law May Not Protect Foreign Investments in India*, Hindustan Times (4 Feb. 2020), https://www.hindustantimes.com/analysis/a-domestic-law-may-not-protect-foreign-investments-in-india/story-x4QNAT1o2jBtFhJ1Hq4C2M.html (accessed 20 Apr. 2020).
44. The Direct Tax Vivad Se Vishwas Bill 2020 (Bill No. 29-C of 2020), http://164.100.47.4/BillsTexts/LSBillTexts/PassedLoksabha/29C_2020_LS_EN.pdf (accessed 2 May 2020).
45. *See* Federico M. Lavopa, Lucas E. Barreiros & Victoria Bruno, *How to Kill a BIT and Not Die Trying: Legal and Political Challenges of Denouncing or Renegotiating BITs*, 16(4) J. Int'l Econ. L. 869-91 (2013), available at https://doi.org/10.1093/jiel/jgt025.

constrains the regulatory space, the rebuttal by India and other countries by either exiting the system or attempting to change the terms on which it functions is a correct move in the fight against global capital. This ground is not covered here – in the Indian context, recent work by Prabash Ranjan provides a sufficient critique of the Third World Approach to International Law (TWAIL) analysis along those lines.[46] The core of Ranjan's own work understands recent Indian reaction as an excessive backlash. He sees the reluctance to participate in the rule of law engendered by international law as being inimical for India; rather, he would see India part of an 'embedded liberalism'. In many senses one could not agree more.

In addition, it is important to both elaborate and understand the implications of this backlash. While we do know the empirical effects of having an international investment treaty system impacting on flows of FDI, it is too early to discern the precise effects of dismantling the system on FDI flows. At the best we can infer from the past what India (and potentially others) may be losing in the future by dialling back IIAs. I attempt to do this next by invoking an empirical exercise and then attempt to add further substance by attempting to understand the precise nature of the rights that India wishes nowadays to entrench for the host state.

[A] Empirical Analysis of IIA Impact on FDI into India

There is now a large literature on the effects of the international investment treaty regime across the world.[47] Yet there is little work that looks at the empirical effects of the international investment treaty system specifically on Indian FDI inflows. Here I summarise a recent study on that topic, although it has not yet seen much circulation.[48] It is important to reproduce the contents of the work to make a series of substantial evaluative points.[49] Some of the material may appear technical for those not trained in economics, but the key insights are not difficult to follow.

---

46. Ranjan, *supra* n. 1.
47. For instance, *see* Eric Neumayer & Laura Spess, *Do BITs Increase FDI to Developing Countries?*, 33(10) World Dev. 1567-85 (2005); Peter Egger & Valeria Merlo. *The Impact of BITs on FDI Dynamics*, 30(10) The World Economy 1536-49 (2007); Peter Egger & Valeria Merlo, *BITs Bite: An Anatomy of the Impact of BITs on Multinational Firms*, 114(4) Scandinavian J. of Econ. 1240-66 (2007); Matthias Busse, Jens Königer & Peter Nunnenkamp, *FDI Promotion Through BITs: More Than a BIT?* 146(1) Rev. of World Econ. 147-77 (2010); Axel Berger et al., *Do Trade and Investment Agreements Lead to More FDI? Accounting for Key Provisions Inside the Black Box*, 10 Int'l Eco. and Econ. Policy 247-75 (2013); Shiro Patrick Armstrong & Luke R. Nottage, *The Impact of Investment Treaties and ISDS Provisions on Foreign Direct Investment: A Baseline Econometric Analysis* (2016). Sydney Law School Research Paper No. 16/74, available at https://ssrn.com/abstract=2824090 (with a version forthcoming in Langford Behn et al., *The Legitimacy of Investment Tribunals: Empirical Perspectives* (Cambridge University Press, 2020).
48. A mention has been made, while the work was in progress, in Luke Nottage & Jaivir Singh, *Does ISDS Promote FDI? Pacific Insights from and for Australia and India* Blog of the International Law Association (Australian Branch) (December 2016), http://ilareporter.org.au/2016/12/does-isds-promote-fdi-asia-pacific-insights-from-and-for-australia-and-india-luke-nottage-jaivir-singh/ (accessed 5 May 2020).
49. Jaivir Singh, Vatsala Shreeti & Parnil Urdhwareshe, *The Impact of BITs on FDI Inflows into India: Some Empirical Results* ICRIER Working Paper No. 391 June 2020 via http://icrier.org/pdf/Working_Paper_391.pdf. The study used FDI data published by the Indian Government's

The study exploits one of the key findings suggested in the FDI-Gravity Model literature, namely that the empirical evidence suggests that FDI and trade tend to be complementary rather than substitutes.[50] Thus, in the empirical model specified below, since FDI inflows follow trade, the trade variable is placed on the right-hand side of the equation (as a dependent variable). The volume of trade itself is presumably a product of the forces that make up the Gravity Model, but additionally indicates the tenor of the unilateral policy regime, marking the degree of openness, exchange rate policy and capital control regimes. If the trade variable captures dynamic interactions between India and other nations alongside signalling aspects of the unilateral policy regime, a bilateral policy variable in the form of BITs and FTAs can be thought of as signifying the certainty with which investors can expect a protection of their rights. Using this broad sense, three empirical models were specified to test the impact of BITs on FDI, as well as more broadly the impact of a system governed by international investment treaties on FDI. The model specifications are as follows.

Model I

$$Y_{it} = \alpha + \beta_1 Y_{it-1} + \beta_2 X_{it} + \beta_3 B_{it} + \beta_4 CC_{it} + \varepsilon_{it}$$

Model II

$$Y_{it} = \alpha + \beta_1 Y_{it-1} + \beta_2 X_{it} + \beta_3 B_{it} + \beta_4 CBI_{it} + \beta_5 CC_{it} + \varepsilon_{it}$$

Model III

$$Y_{it} = \alpha + \beta_1 Y_{it-1} + \beta_2 X_{it} + \beta_3 B_{it} + \beta_4 CBP_{it} + \beta_5 CC_{it} + \varepsilon_{it}$$

where:

(i) Y_{it} is the inflow of FDI into India from country i in year t.

(ii) Y_{it-1} is the inflow of FDI into India from country i in year t-1.

(iii) X_{it} is the bilateral trade (total exports and imports) from country i in year t.

(iv) B_{it} is a dummy variable taking the value 1 if a BIT was signed with country i in year t and all years thereafter, or takes the value 0 otherwise.

(v) CC_{it} is a dummy variable which takes the value 1 if a Comprehensive Economic Cooperation Agreement (CECA)/Comprehensive Economic Partnership Agreement (CEPA) was signed with country i in year t and all years thereafter, or takes the value 0 otherwise.

(vi) CBI_{it} is the cumulative number of BITs signed by India in year t.

(vii) CBP_{it} is the cumulative number of BITs signed by partner country in year t.

Department of Industrial Policy & Promotion – data from 2006 till December 2016 can be accessed at https://dipp.gov.in/publications/fdi-statistics/archives, and data before 2006 can be found in the Department's SIA Newsletter archives, which is accessible at https://dipp.gov.in/publications/si-news-letters/archives?field_year_sia_tid = All&field_month_tid = All&page = 13. It was thought best to use the Indian data source because the FDI data sets in the UNCTAD or OECD collections are compiled using data provided by respective governments. The bilateral trade data (total exports and imports from country i in year t) was taken from the World Integrated Trade Solutions (WITS) World Bank database. The data was for 139 countries over 1996-2014. The data on treaties signed by India was gathered from the website of India's Ministry of Finance.

50. *See* Valeriano Martínez, Marta Bengoa & Blanca Sánchez-Robles '*FDI and Trade: Complements or Substitutes? Empirical Evidence for the European Union*' 3(2) Tech. & Inv. 105-12 (2012).

(viii) ε_{it} is the error term (which includes country-specific fixed effects) for country i in year t.

The three model specifications differ from each other in that while *Model 1* incorporates the presence of a BIT as a binary variable, *Model 2* includes the total number of BITs signed by India in year t as an additional cumulative variable and *Model 3* contains the total number of BITs signed by partner country in year t as the additional cumulative variable. Thus, each Model incorporates the BIT variable differently. The other variables reflect relationships that follow from the discussion above – following the observation that FDI follows trade in a complementary manner, the volume of bilateral trade is placed as an explanatory variable. Capturing yet another dimension of the institutional elements in this relationship, the models also include a binary variable as to whether a trade agreement in the form of a CECA or CEPA had been signed with a trading partner or not. Such trade agreements of the CECA/CEPA variety have a chapter dedicated to investment that is more or less along the lines of a BIT.

The estimates of parameters across all three specifications can be seen in the accompanying Table 12.1.[51] The first point to note is that the bilateral trade variable is significant in all the models, albeit with varying degrees of significance. The coefficients associated with the variable as to whether a CECA or CEPA was signed with the partner country are also significant and additionally show the largest marginal effects in all the models. The lagged FDI variable is significant but only in Model 1 and Model 3. However, visible across all three models is the finding that the variable capturing as to whether India signed a BIT with a partner country or not is insignificant – effectively saying that the *individual* signing of BITs did not influence Direct Foreign Investment inflow.

However, the remarkable result of the study can be observed in Model 2 and Model 3. In Model 2 the presence of an additional variable – the *cumulative* BITs signed by India – captures the effects of international investment treaties differently from the individual signing of such treaties. As can be seen the estimated coefficient of this variable is very significant. This tells us that while the individual signing of a BIT with a partner country did not individually have an effect on FDI inflows, the collective consequence of signing a series of investment treaties by India did have a beneficial effect on the inflow of FDI. In Model 3 the presence of investment treaties is captured otherwise from Model 2 – here as the cumulative bilateral treaties signed by the partner country. The estimated coefficient is again very significant. This could be understood as capturing the attitude of the partner country towards investment – thus the greater the number of BITs signed by the partner country, the more conducive it is for investors to invest abroad, and consequently the greater is the volume of FDI inflow into India. Of course, as can be seen in Table 12.1 the estimated marginal effects are quite small, but the high statistical significance of the coefficients definitely demands our attention.

51. The diagnostic details associated with the estimation are not presented here, but the Generalized Methods of Moments (GMM) was used to estimate the model, which corrected for any serial correlation and country-specific fixed effects.

Table 12.1 Parameters Estimated Using Generalised Method of Moments

S. No.	*Variable*	*Model 1*	*Model 2*	*Model 3*
1.	FDI lagged ($\mathbf{Y_{it-1}}$)	0.122** (0.053)	0.078 (0.051)	0.096*** (0.051)
2.	Bilateral trade ($\mathbf{X_{it}}$)	0.508* (0.14)	0.206*** (0.122)	0.272** (0.11)
3.	BIT signed ($\mathbf{B_{it}}$)	0.271 (0.33)	−0.56 (0.432)	−0.589 (0.441)
4.	Cumulative BITs signed by India ($\mathbf{CBI_{it}}$)		0.034* (0.007)	
5.	Cumulative BITs signed by Partner Country ($\mathbf{CBP_{it}}$)			0.068* (0.01)
6.	CECA/CEPA signed ($\mathbf{CC_{it}}$)	1.88* (0.67)	1.16*** (0.616)	1.56** (2.40)
7.	Constant	−1.81*** (−0.98)	−0.96 (0.72)	−2.95* (0.95)

Reprinted from Jaivir Singh, Vatsala Shreeti & Parnil Urdhwareshe, *The Impact of BITs on FDI Inflows into India: Some Empirical Results* ICRIER Working Paper No. 391 June 2020.

* Significant at 1% level of significance.

** Significant at 5% level of significance.

*** Significant at 10% level of significance. (The values in brackets are the robust standard errors.)

These results support the view that institutional support - in particular the system of international investment treaty-based governance - is important for investment flows. To repeat, Model 2 tells us that while signing a particular BIT with a partner country does not necessarily translate into a foreign investment inflow, the cumulative effect of signing a series of treaties has influenced the inflow of foreign investment into India. The cumulative effect is a positive externality or a spillover effect of a series of individual acts of signing BITs - a reputation effect is generated, suggesting that the country must be serious about investor protection since many investment treaties have been signed. Thus, once a whole set of international treaties come into place, they act as a collective signal that international investment arbitration would protect investors in the face of exigencies arising from the actions of host states. Furthermore, having a large number of investment treaties on hand gives investors the opportunity to make use of the most favourable treaties using MFN clauses - as was indeed the case with White Industries. The results of Model 3 reinforce this - the cumulative effect of international investment treaties signed by the partner country seems to assure and encourage investors to invest abroad. In other words, investors in countries attuned towards an orientation to signing IIAs are influenced to invest in a country like India.

In broad terms, these findings point to the fact that the overall governance regime that oversees investment is an important determinant of cross-country investment flows. Of course, intermediate forces such as the volume of trade are important factors in these flows – it was reported in the detailed underlying study that due to issues of multicollinearity the precise impact of foreign trade agreements could not be discerned using this model. However, the variable that captures whether India had signed a CECA/CEPA, which has both a trade dimension and a chapter that is akin to a BIT and thus combining both the forces of trade flows and the governance of investment, is both statistically significant across all models and shows the highest marginal coefficients (i.e., impact).

Overall, the findings of this econometric exercise seem to point to the importance of international instruments governing investment flows. While the presence or absence of a grievance redressal mechanism for foreign investors – that is whether a BIT was signed between the partner countries – does not seem to matter to investors in individual bilateral contexts, the collective institution of having a regime in which investments are protected by the presence of IIAs did help investment flows into India. This in itself does act to counterbalance the much-decried financial and regulatory costs of the investment treaty regime since it cannot be denied that the presence of the regime (at least as per the results of the empirical model) did influence foreign investment in India positively. It follows from this that the dismemberment of this regime will probably act to inhibit some of the foreign investment flow that may have come in if the regime had not been disturbed.

However, a counterargument might be that the regime produced by the New Model Treaty could put its own set of institutions in place, and over time we can have a configuration that protects investors as well as leaving host states less vulnerable to attack. If a straightforward redistribution has been brought into effect without affecting incentives to investors, then this argument could be persuasive, but if we reflect on the manner in which state rights have been strengthened, it will become clear that this is not the case. The New Model Treaty and the handful of new treaties that have been signed subsequently by India carry their structure of rights drawing closely from structure of trade law and practice – a point that was importantly perceived by the Law Commission of India while analysing the NDMT.[52] I turn next to assessing this orientation as a device to govern outcomes relating to foreign investment inflows into India.

[B] Another New Frontier: Shifting Towards Trade-Inspired Rights?

The New Model Treaty is 'new', of course, in a variety of ways. Among other things, it dispenses with many of the traditional substantive standards – as has been noted earlier there is a prominent absence of the MFN, FET and 'full protection and security' clauses, for example, and the expropriation clause being very tightly specified. The abolished substantive clauses have been replaced by the 'Standard of Treatment'.

52. Law Commission of India, *supra* n. 28.

There are also new procedural requirements, among them – asking for domestic remedies to be exhausted before moving to arbitration are new. However, another novelty that needs to be emphasised for analytical purposes here is that a set of explicitly listed government activities are excluded from the ambit of the treaty. Thus, the investment treaty signed with a partner state will not allow any action against the host state in relation to government action regarding tax laws, government procurements, compulsory licences, subsidies, national security, pre-investment activities by investors and non-commercial services provided by the government. Additionally, yet another list is written out in the New Model Treaty – a series of General Exceptions, such as those contained in GATT Article XX, allowing the host state to enact laws and regulations relating to public morals, public order, health, environment, and cultural preservation, which cannot be questioned in any investment treaty-based action against the host state.

In all the three investment treaties signed by India with Belarus, Taiwan and Brazil (that are publicly available), the exclusions or exceptions are just as plentiful as they are in the New Model Treaty.[53] We also do need to take note though that the India-Brazil BIT signed in 2020 varies from the other two treaties with Belarus and Taiwan in that before a dispute goes in for arbitration it has to go through a Joint Committee made up of representatives of the respective governments – a body that administers the treaty. Apart from dealing with disputes, this committee is meant to coordinate and help investors and investments, assisted by an Ombudsman who is expected to deal with 'other party' investors and report back to the Joint Committee. If a dispute is not resolved under the aegis of the Joint Committee, then an ad hoc interstate arbitration can be agreed, but the BIT does not provide advance consent to this procedure (let alone ISDS, allowing direct arbitration claims against the host state). Anyway, the BIT does not allow any interstate arbitration tribunal to award compensation (Article 19(2)). It has been pointed out that this treaty follows more closely the Brazilian rather than Indian Model Treaty, but goes further than both by excluding compensation and thus innovating along the lines of the WTO regime.[54] Under that regime, the Dispute Settlement Body similarly decides if a disputed measure is in conformity with WTO rules and obligations (such as non-discrimination), and then goes on to suggest how to conform to the trade rules (and otherwise allow specified retaliation), but awards no compensation.

53. The texts of the terminated and new treaties and JISs, as well as other details, can be found on the Ministry of Finance (Government of India) website: https://dea.gov.in/bipa. Actually four treaties seem to been signed, but the treaty with Kyrgyz Republic has not been uploaded on the Ministry of Finance website. Over 2017-2018 there were also reports of India signing a BIT with Cambodia that closely followed the New Model Treaty, but that too cannot be found in the public domain: *see generally* Romesh Weeramantry, *International Investment Law and Practice in the Kingdom of Cambodia: An Evolving 'Rule Taker'?* in *International Investment Treaties and Arbitration Across Asia* 303 (Julien Chaisse & Luke Nottage eds., Brill, 2017).
54. Ashutosh Ray, *Dispute Resolution in the India-Brazil BIT: Symbolism or Systemic Reform?*, Kluwer Arbitration Blog (9 Apr. 2020), http://arbitrationblog.kluwerarbitration.com/2020/04/09/dispute- resolution-in-the-india-brazil-bit-symbolism-or- systemic-reform/ (accessed 17 Apr. 2020).

Thus, an important element of the new Indian strategy, as reflected in the India-Brazil BIT, is to impersonate the structure and norms that govern trade in the realm of foreign investment. In addition to mimicking scheduling, the expectation is for diplomatic (read: state-centric) avenues to be primarily used to resolve disputes rather than investor-state arbitration. To assess this strategy a series of questions come before us. Is the governance of foreign trade and foreign investment equivalent? Can the devices used in trade – scheduling, constant diplomatic vigilance keeping in mind the domestic economic interests – sufficiently oversee foreign investment?[55] In answering such questions – it is important to understand the nature of the scheduling in the Indian case – there is no scheduling of sectors of the economy as is the case in most FTAs – rather there is a list specifying all the areas where regulatory control of the state cannot be questioned. Some of this immunity can be interpreted or understood in terms of the global discourse associated with Sustainable Development Goals imposing responsibilities on investors.[56] The General Exceptions relating to public morals, public order, health, environment, and cultural preservation listed in India's recent investment treaties can perhaps be understood along these lines. The positive version of this is the requirement that foreign investors are required to participate in Corporate Social Responsibility activity in all the three treaties signed by India, with this being most extensively articulated in the India-Brazil treaty.

The other category of immunities is different – the tax laws, government procurements, compulsory licences, subsidies, national security, non-commercial services provided by the government presumably such as the judicial system and pre-investment activities by investors. Unlike the case with trade where scheduling is aimed at protecting domestic economic agents or sectors, at least some of these entries are entirely about gathering immunity for sovereign state actions that enable therefore an unbridled exercise of power. The governance of trade in commodities and to a good extent services may be more amenable to scheduling as a country calibrates its trade strategy but the point of governance of investment is to govern a long-term association involving relationship-specific sunk capital. In other words, one would want a legal system that not only is able to handle the needs of long-term contracts but also minimise chances of *ex post* opportunistic behaviour.[57] To the extent a state armed with immunities is conducive to *ex post* opportunistic behaviour, such as indulging in retrospective taxation or invocation of national security to override contracts, this impedes the kind of governance that is needed to encourage investment. The persistent moves by the Indian government to attempt appropriating resources by imposing

55. Expressing caution about simply transposing trade law rules over into international investment law, *see also* generally Jurgen Kurtz, *The WTO and International Investment Law Converging Systems* (Cambridge University Press, 2016).
56. David Gaukrodger, *Business Responsibilities and Investment Treaties Consultation Paper by the OECD Secretariat* (15 Jan. 2020), https://www.oecd.org/daf/inv/investment-policy/Consultation-Paper-on-business-responsibilities-and-investment-treaties.pdf.
57. This invokes a basic reading of the insights offered by new institutional economics/theory of incomplete contracts, the classic sources being Oliver Williamson, *Transaction Cost Economics: The Governance of Contractual Relations* 22(2) J.L. & Econ. 233-61 (1979); and Benjamin Klien, Robert Crawford & Armen Alchain, *Vertical Integration, Appropriable Rents and the Competitive Contracting Process* 21(2) J.L. & Econ. 297-326 (1978).

retrospective taxation is indeed the prominent case in point. As the potential of an adverse ruling in the Cairn case looms, the Indian state is trying to share rents by legislating the Vivad se Vishwas Bill 2020. Such moves, and others like the domestic law aimed at foreign investors, keep power with the host state. Such a governance structure cannot but thwart investment rather than encourage it.

As a contrast it is important to note briefly, before concluding, an instance when the rigours of the international order have improved the governance of long-term contracts. Before India started in earnest on the path of gathering the current levels of immunity, the White Industry case also produced rather important changes in arbitration law in India. Recall that the White Industries case emerged because the ICC Tribunal award kept getting stalled as it passed through the Indian judicial system – so much so that ten years after the award had been granted, the awarded compensation had not reached the investor. Arguing that the ICC arbitration was an 'investment' and therefore protected by BITs, White Industries was able to persuade the ad hoc ISDS tribunal that court delays amounted to India's failure to an 'effective means of asserting claims and enforcing rights with respect to investment'.

Among the many reactions, including the development of the New Model Treaty described above, in August 2014 the Law Commission of India also brought out a report titled *Amendments to the Arbitration and Conciliation Act 1996*.[58] The primary concern of the Report was to suggest amendments that would counter endemic delays that had come to characterise arbitration in India. The Report makes an explicit reference to investment treaties and the White Industries case as one of the justifications for the suggested changes.[59] Consequent to this Report, changes were brought to the Indian Arbitration Act 1996 seeking to prevent future instances of the 'inordinate delay' that had been interpreted by the ad hoc tribunal as denial of 'effective means' to assert claims and enforce rights. The amendment set a time limit of twelve months within which any decision to set aside an arbitral award must be made. It also removed a provision that allowed an automatic stay on the enforcement of an award while a challenge was pending – in effect, this allows awards to be enforced during the pendency of a challenge, unless a stay is specifically sought and granted by the court. The changes in the law also allowed foreign arbitral awards to be enforced by High Courts or higher courts and removed the 'patent illegality' ground added to the 'public policy' exception to enforcing awards,[60] thus preventing courts from reviewing the merits of an arbitral claim during the proceedings for enforcement.

---

58. Law Commission of India, *Amendments to the Arbitration and Conciliation Act 1996* (Report No. 246), http://webcache.googleusercontent.com/search?q=cache:http://lawcommissionofindia.nic.in/reports/Report246.pdf.
59. *Ibid.*, 17-18, noting that: 'The award of the Arbitral Tribunal in White Industries Australia Ltd v the Republic of India, UNCITRAL, Final Award (November 30, 2011), serves as a reminder to the Government to urgently implement reforms to the judicial system in order to avoid substantial potential liabilities that might accrue from the delays presently inherent in the system.'
60. For various pro-arbitration statutory (and case law) developments, *see further*, e.g., Harisankar K. Sathyapalan, *Indian Judiciary and International Arbitration: A BIT of a Control?*, 33 Arb. Int'l 503 (2017). Arguing for the need to harmonise regionally the public policy exception to award enforcement, *see also* Gu in this volume.

§12.05 CONCLUSION

This chapter has described how India has reacted to being taken to task by a series of foreign investors, who have sought remedies from international arbitral tribunals when confronted with long delays characterising the Indian judicial system, imposition of retrospective taxation and instances when the state has not honoured its contractual obligations in long-term investment projects. When confronted with this, except perhaps for the reforms initiated in the *Arbitration and Conciliation Act* partly in reaction to the White Industries case, India has chosen to distance itself from any correction offered by the international investment law order. Rather, it has sought to strategise by restructuring its Model Treaty and to seek immunity against almost every liability that investors have invoked against the Indian state. In this process the manner in which rights have been constructed in favour of the state is inspired by trade rather than investment law – in fact the template is increasingly appropriated from trade. This, it has been argued, has created a space for opportunistic behaviour by the state to appropriate unscrupulously from investors. More recently, realising that it cannot entirely get away with either appropriating via taxation (retrospective) or reneging on long-term contracts, India is trying to offer domestic remedies by attempting some legislation that purports to support foreign investors rather than subjecting itself to an international rule of law.

The exigencies of hypernationalism have caused India to take extremely antithetical statements to any possibility of an international rule of law governing foreign investment. This may be best illustrated by quoting the current Finance Minister reacting to European moves to establish a permanent multilateral investment court.[61] She is quoted as saying: 'We have said no to any investment agreement in which companies can challenge governments ... They want to make this (referring to permanent multilateral investment court) a global template for resolving investor-state dispute ... We rejected it completely. We are opposed to multilateral approach to investment.'[62]

If we are to take the metric of FDI inflows, as shown by the empirical model in this chapter, the overall presence of a notional multilateral protection offered by all the treaties that were signed by India starting in 1994 over a twenty-year period did positively influence the flow of inbound investment. Of course, in the future, a series of other multiple factors that influence foreign investment may keep up the inflow but it would be a loss for the principle that governments cannot act arbitrarily without facing liability under international law. The rules of international law protect against opportunistic behaviour, and in this it is not just an issue about individual investor protection but more broadly about engendering overall growth and development.

61. *See generally* Nottage & Jetin, in this volume; and Amokura Kawharu & Luke R. Nottage, *Models for Investment Treaties in the Asian Region: An Underview*, 34(3) Ariz. J. Int'l & Comp. L., 462-528 (2017), also available at https://ssrn.com/abstract=2845088.

62. *Won't Allow Investors to Challenge Government: Nirmala Sitharaman*, The Economic Times (24 Jan. 2017), https://economictimes.indiatimes.com/news/economy/policy/wont-allow-investors-to-challenge-government-nirmala-sitharaman/articleshow/56744128.cms (accessed 5 May 2020).

CHAPTER 13

FTA Dispute Resolution to Protect Health and the Maritime Environment

Jie (Jeanne) Huang & Jiaxiang Hu[*]

Preventing or managing a global pandemic such as the coronavirus disease of 2019 (COVID-19) requires states to strictly comply with the International Health Regulations 2005 (IHR). However, the IHR lacks a strong enforcement mechanism, like many multilateral environmental protection agreements. Over the past fifteen years, several such conventions have been incorporated into free trade agreements (FTAs) to enhance state compliance and therefore promote environmental protection. A typical example is the International Convention for the Prevention of Pollution from Ships and its Protocols (MARPOL 73/78). Vessels, like viruses, are globally mobile. Vessel-sourced pollution also mirrors human-carried viral infection because the locations of potential harm are unpredictable and widespread. This chapter examines first whether FTAs (especially mega-regional FTAs) can effectively encourage states to comply with MARPOL 73/78. Through this analysis, it generates implications regarding whether the IHR regime could also rely on new or renegotiated FTAs, or be reformed directly, to enhance state compliance with public health initiatives.

§13.01 INTRODUCTION

Whether FTAs can be used to promote trade-related environmental concerns has been quite widely debated.[1] Since the North American Free Trade Agreement (NAFTA)

* This chapter is a considerably updated and expanded version of Jie (Jeanne) Huang & Jiaxiang Hu, *Can Free Trade Agreement Enhance MARPOL 73/78 Compliance?* 43 Tul. Mar. L.J. 59, 59-91 (2018).

1. *See*, e.g., Matthew Rimmer, *Greenwashing the Trans-Pacific Partnership: Fossil Fuels, the Environment, and Climate Change*, 14 Santa Clara J. Int'l L. 488 (2016); Andrew Jensen Kerr, *The Trans-Pacific Partnership and the Construction of a Syncretic Animal Welfare Norm*, 27 Duke Envtl. L. & Pol'y F. 155 (2016); Manjiao Chi, *The 'Greenization' of Chinese BITs: An Empirical Study of the Environmental Provisions in Chinese BITs and Its Implications for China's Future*

signed in 1993, the United States (US) has strongly pushed its trading partners to sustainable trade liberalization without scarifying the environment.[2] Vessel-sourced pollution is a serious threat for the global marine environment. The major international conventions to regulate vessel-sourced pollution are the International Convention for the Prevention of Pollution from Ships and its Protocols (collectively MARPOL 73/78)[3] and the United Nations Convention on the Law of the Sea (UNCLOS).[4] Starting from 2006, the US has incorporated references to MARPOL 73/78 into four of its bilateral FTAs and thereby used trade law to help combat vessel-sourced marine pollution.[5] Most recently the US–Mexico–Canada Agreement (replacing NAFTA) also incorporates MARPOL 73/78.[6] Signed in 2018 by eleven Asia-Pacific states, but not for now the US under the Trump Administration, the Comprehensive and Progressive Agreement for Trans-Pacific Partnership (CPTPP) became the first mega-regional FTA to incorporate MARPOL 73/78. This incorporation was presumably based on a proposal from the US, given its recent treaty practice in this respect, as well as the general influence from the US on the topics and provisions typically found in many Asia-Pacific trade and investment treaties.[7] All these US FTAs and the CPTPP require its members to 'adopt, maintain, and implement laws, regulations, and all other measures to fulfil their obligations' under MARPOL 73/78.[8] However, whether an FTA can effectively encourage states to comply with MARPOL 73/78 has not been well researched. This chapter

Bit-Making, 18 J. Int'l Econ. L. 511 (2015); Kevin Kolben, *A Development Approach to Trade and Labor Regimes*, 45 Wake Forest L. Rev. 355 (2010); Duncan French, *The Changing Nature of 'Environmental Protection': Recent Developments Regarding Trade and the Environment in the European Union and the World Trade Organization*, 47 Neth. Int'l L. Rev. 1 (2000); Ambler H. Moss Jr., *Global Trade as a Way to Integrate Environmental Protection and Sustainable Development*, 23 Envtl. L. 711 (1993); Thomas J. Schoenbaum, *Free International Trade and Protection of the Environment: Irreconcilable Conflict?*, 86 Am. J. Int'l L. 700 (1992).

2. Chris Wold, *Taking Stock: Trade's Environmental Scorecard after Twenty Years of 'Trade and Environment'*, 45 Wake Forest L. Rev. 319, 319-20 (2010).
3. International Convention for the Prevention of Pollution from Ships, 1340 U.N.T.S. 184 (2 Nov. 1973), amended by Protocol of 1978 Relating to the International Convention for the Prevention of Pollution from Ships, 1340 U.N.T.S. 61 (17 Feb. 1978).
4. United Nations Convention on the Law of the Sea, 1833 U.N.T.S. 397 (10 Dec. 1982).
5. The four FTAs are the United States–Peru Trade Promotion Agreement (PTPA), the United States–Columbia Trade Promotion Agreement (Columbia TPA), the United States–Panama Trade Promotion Agreement (Panama TPA), and the US–Korea FTA (KORUS FTA). *See* Office of the United States Trade Representative, *Free Trade Agreements*, https://ustr.gov/trade-agreements/free-trade-agreements/ (accessed 2 Nov. 2018).
6. Articles 24.8 and 24.10 of the US–Mexico–Canada Agreement, https://ustr.gov/trade-agreements/free-trade-agreements/united-states-mexico-canada-agreement/agreement-between (accessed 10 Apr. 2020).
7. Comprehensive and Progressive Agreement for Trans-Pacific Partnership, Ch. 20, Article 20.6 (8 Mar. 2018), https://www.mfat.govt.nz/en/trade/free-trade-agreements/free-trade-agreements-concluded-but-not-in-force/cptpp/comprehensive-and-progressive-agreement-for-trans-pacific-partnership-text/ (last visited 2 Nov. 2018). For comments on CPTPP, *see* Luke Nottage & Vivienne Bath, *International Investment Agreements and Investor-State Arbitration in Asia*, 20/08 Sydney Law School Research Paper 1, 6-8 (2020), https://papers.ssrn.com/sol3/papers.cfm?abstract_id=3544458.
8. United States–Peru Trade Promotion Agreement (PTPA), Article 18.2 (12 Apr. 2006), https://ustr.gov/sites/default/files/uploads/agreements/fta/peru/asset_upload_file953_9541.pdf; United

attempts to fill in that gap. Moreover, the literature on big oil tanker pollution incidents often focuses on civil dispute resolution and compensatory liability between the parties.[9] This chapter explores vessel-sourced pollution from a different perspective: how to prevent such disasters from happening in future, by strengthening national compliance with international law.

The following lays out a hypothetical scenario largely mirroring the recent *Sanchi* incident.[10] Suppose, the *M/V Oceanside*, a Panama-registered oil tanker, collided with a Hong Kong-registered bulk freighter. The tanker was sailing from Iran to South Korea to deliver tonnes of condensate, an ultralight crude oil which is highly volatile when exposed to air and water. The bulk freighter was carrying grain from the US to China. The *Oceanside* caught fire as soon as she hit the freighter. Further suppose that the collision site is within the Zhoushan Fishing Ground, which is one of the biggest in the East China Sea, particularly for mackerel and Atlantic croaker. After collision, the *Oceanside* slowly drifts into Japan's exclusive economic zone, where she ultimately explodes and sinks.

The condensate carried by the *Oceanside* is an ultralight, highly toxic, colourless and odourless version of crude oil, which is difficult to detect and even more combustible than regular crude oil. In our scenario, the explosion would likely have

---

States–Columbia Trade Promotion Agreement (Columbia TPA), Article 18.2 (22 Nov. 2006), https://ustr.gov/sites/default/files/uploads/agreements/fta/colombia/asset_upload_file644_10 192.pdf.

9. *See*, e.g., James D. Fry & Inna Amesheva, *Oil Pollution and the Dynamic Relationship Between International Environmental Law and the Law of the Sea*, 47 Geo. J. Int'l L. 1001 (2016); John D. Kimball, *The Central Role of P&I Insurance in Maritime Law*, 87 Tul. L. Rev. 1147 (2013); Hongjun Shan, *International Recent Developments: China-Vessel-Source Oil Pollution Compensation*, 36 Tul. Mar. L. J. 563 (2012); Muhammad Masum Billah, *The Role of Insurance in Providing Adequate Compensation and in Reducing Pollution Incidents: The Case of the International Oil Pollution Liability Regime*, 29 Pace Envtl. L. Rev. 42 (2011); Natalie Klien & Nikolas Hughes, *National Litigation and International Law: Repercussions for Australia's Protection of Marine Resources*, 33 Melb. U. L. Rev. 163 (2009); Ling Zhu, *Can the Bunkers Convention Ensure Adequate Compensation for Pollution Victims?*, 40 J. Mar. L. & Com. 203 (2009); Yunfu Yang & Cuizhu Lin, *Scope of Losses of Compensation for Damages Due to Oil Pollution of Ships in Chinese Waters*, 2 US-China L. Rev. 55 (2005); Måns Jacobsson, *Oil Pollution Liability and Compensation: An International Regime*, 1 Unif. L. Rev. 260 (1996); Lance D. Wood, *An Integrated International and Domestic Approach to Civil Liability for Vessel-Source Oil Pollution*, 7 J. Mar. L. & Com. 1 (1975).
10. According to the International Maritime Organization (IMO), the Sanchi's registered owner is Hong Kong-based Bright Shipping Ltd., which is on behalf of the National Iranian Tanker Co. The National Iranian Tanker Co. is a publicly traded company based in Tehran and describes itself as operating the largest tanker fleet in the Middle East. The Sanchi had been rented to Hanwha Total Co., which is a 50-50 partnership between the Seoul-based Hanwha Group and the French oil giant, Total. Iranian oil tanker burning off China's coast at risk of exploding, with thirty-two crew members still missing, ABC News (8 Jan. 2018), http://www.abc.net.au/news /2018-01-08/32-missing-oil-tanker-on-fire-after-collision-off-china/9310276; Amanda Erickson, *Four Days on, the Sanchi Oil Tanker is Still on Fire the East China Sea*, The Washington Post (10 Jan. 2018), https://www.washingtonpost.com/news/worldviews/wp/2018/01/08/a-giant-oil-tanker-is-on-fire-and-could-explode-in-the-south-china-sea/?utm_term=.6413da7975b9; *A Costly Message from the Sanchi*, The Japan Times (22 Jan. 2018), https://www.japantimes.co.jp/opinion/2018/01/22/editorials/costly-message-sanchi/#. ('[T]he leakage has split into four separate slicks that cover about 101 square kilometres in total, and could affect an area of up to 200 nautical miles long.')

expelled the *Oceanside's* bunker fuel or the heavy fuel engine oil. While bunker fuel is not as explosive as condensate, it is the dirtiest kind of oil and extremely toxic. Similarly, although bunker fuel is relatively easy to contain and extract from water, even small volumes can damage marine life. If this type of large-scale spill indeed occurs, it would be devastating to the marine life and fishery economy in the East China Sea.

Suppose that after examining the *Oceanside* shipwreck, the investigators concluded that had the *Oceanside* fully complied with the technical requirement for shipbuilding under MARPOL 73/78 the collision would not have led to such a large-scale oil spill. This failure would be largely due to the flag states' failure to effectively require the *Oceanside* to comply with MARPOL 73/78. The *Oceanside* hypothetical should be alarming to coastal states as vessel-sourced pollution creates a serious threat to the surrounding marine environment and species. But the question is: can China or Japan have a remedy under international law?

In addition, the pollution in the *Oceanside* hypothetical also resembles the spread of the coronavirus disease of 2019 (COVID-19) pandemic in 2020. On 31 December 2019, China informed the World Health Organization (WHO) China Country Office about cases of pneumonia with unknown aetiology detected in Wuhan City, Hubei Province of China.[11] From 31 December 2019 through 3 January 2020, China reported a total of forty-four cases to the WHO. On 11 and 12 January 2020, China provided further detailed information to WHO that the outbreak was associated with exposures in one seafood market in Wuhan City. China isolated a new type of coronavirus on 7 January 2020 and shared the genetic sequence of the virus for countries to use in developing specific diagnostic kits on 12 January 2020. As of 8 April 2020, this new virus (COVID-19) had infected a total of 1,353,361 people and caused 79,235 deaths worldwide.[12] As the sanction that the Chinese police imposed on Dr Li Wenliang shows,[13] China is accused of failing to provide a timely report on the virus to the WHO.[14] China disputes whether COVID-19 originated from its territory, although its media had widely reported that the virus first came from people illegally selling, handling, or eating wild animals in January and February 2020.[15] It is not the intention of this chapter to discuss the origin of COVID-19 or who should be liable. Instead, it

11. *Coronavirus Disease of 2019 (COVID-19) Situation Report-1*, https://www.who.int/emergencies/diseases/novel-coronavirus-2019/situation-reports/ (accessed 8 Apr. 2020).
12. *Coronavirus Disease of 2019 (COVID-19) Situation Report-79*, https://www.who.int/emergencies/diseases/novel-coronavirus-2019/situation-reports/ (accessed 8 Apr. 2020).
13. Andrew Green, *Li Wenliang*, 395 The Lancet 682 (2020).
14. Peter Tzeng, *Taking China to the International Court of Justice Over COVID-19*, EJIL: Talk! (2020), https://www.ejiltalk.org/taking-china-to-the-international-court-of-justice-over-covid-19/ (accessed 12 Apr. 2020).
15. *Evidence Is Confirmed That Virus Is Found at Huanan Fish Market*, People's Daily (23 Jan. 2020), http://finance.sina.com.cn/7x24/2020-01-23/doc-iihnzahk6049908.shtml; *Lancet Published Chinese Scholar's Comment: The Relationship Between Novel Coronavirus and Consumption Wild Animals* [Liu Ye Dao Kan fa Zhongguo Xuezhe Pinglun: Xinguan Bingdu Feiyan yu Yewei Xiaofei de Guanxi], China News (12 Feb. 2020), https://m.chinanews.com/wap/detail/zw/sh/2020/02-12/9087971.shtml (accessed 2 Apr. 2020).

focuses on whether the WHO's IHR of 2005[16] contains a mechanism for Member States to efficiently and effectively resolve their disputes, and whether incorporating this international instrument into FTAs may enhance state compliance and therefore better protect public health.

Vessels are like viruses because they are globally mobile. Vessel-sourced pollution also mirrors human-carried viral infection because the locations of potential harm are unpredictable and widespread. In three aspects, the *Oceanside* hypothetical is similar to the spread of COVID-19. First, both incidents are arguably caused by one state who may not comply with an international instrument. For *Oceanside,* the relevant treaty is MARPOL 73/78, while the IHR is involved for COVID-19.[17] Second, both incidents generate harm to other states. In the *Oceanside* hypothetical, fishery industries in China and Japan suffered damage from environmental pollution. Similarly, COVID-19 has caused tremendous losses to people and states regionally and worldwide. Third, neither MARPOL 73/78 nor IHR contain a strong enforcement mechanism to ensure state compliance.

This chapter aims to explore whether FTAs can enhance state compliance to MARPOL 73/78 and then what implications may follow for the IHR. This chapter is divided into four parts. Section §13.02 analyses the role of MARPOL 73/78 in marine environmental protection. It also explains why the US decided to use FTAs to enhance MARPOL 73/78 compliance. Section §13.03 compares MARPOL 73/78 with the CPTPP. It uses the *Oceanside* hypothetical to demonstrate the CPTPP's achievements and deficiencies in enhancing MARPOL 73/78 compliance from four aspects: flags of convenience, the vague role of coastal states, effects on trade or investment, and dispute resolution. Section §13.04 discusses the implications for IHR in the contexts of COVID-19 pandemic. Section §13.05 concludes with proposals to address the deficiencies.

§13.02 THE ROLE OF MARPOL 73/78

Oil tankers first appeared in the late nineteenth century and became very much larger after World War II.[18] In order to address the environmental issues associated with large oil tankers, the United Kingdom organized an international conference in 1954 where the International Convention for the Prevention of Pollution of the Sea by Oil (OILPOL)

16. IHR is an agreement concluded by 196 countries including all WHO Member States. For its texts, *see* https://www.who.int/ihr/publications/9789241580496/en/. For its Member States, *see* https://www.who.int/ihr/legal_issues/states_parties/en/.
17. *See* IHR.
18. According to MARPOL 73/78, '"oil tanker" means a ship constructed or adapted primarily to carry oil in bulk in its cargo spaces and includes combination carriers and any "chemical tanker" as defined in Annex II of [MARPOL 73/78] when it is carrying a cargo or part cargo of oil in bulk': MARPOL 73/78, Annex I, Ch. 1, Reg. 1(4).

was adopted.[19] The OILPOL represents a commitment by participating states to explore solutions to oil tanker pollution.[20]

In 1973, the International Maritime Organization (IMO) held a conference, attended by seventy-one countries, where they adopted the International Convention for the Prevention of Pollution from Ships (MARPOL 73).[21] MARPOL 73 incorporated OILPOL and its various amendments into Annex I to become the primary treaty for eliminating vessel pollution.[22] MARPOL 73 contains two Protocols: Provisions concerning Reports on Incidents involving Harmful Substances (Protocol I), and Arbitration (Protocol II).[23] MARPOL 73 was subsequently amended by the Protocols of 1978, becoming MARPOL 78, at the International Conference on Tanker Safety and Pollution Prevention which was convened by the IMO in February of 1978.[24] MARPOL 78 absorbed MARPOL 73 to form MARPOL 73/78, which entered into force on 2 October 1983.[25] MARPOL 73/78 has five Annexes, corresponding to five different sources of vessel-sourced pollution.[26] MARPOL 73/78 was amended by the Protocol of 1997, whereby a sixth Annex was added.[27] MARPOL states must accept Annexes I and II.[28] Whereas compliance with Annexes III-VI is voluntary, but once accepted, compliance becomes mandatory.[29] As of June 2017, MARPOL 73/78 and Annexes I and II have been accepted by 157 states, representing 99.15% of the world's merchant tonnage,[30] and have contributed to a noticeable decrease in pollution from international shipping.[31]

MARPOL 73/78 and FTAs used to be two parallel lines. They became crossed ever since the US's bipartisan agreement on trade policy relating to FTAs was announced in May 2007.[32] The bipartisan agreement creates a new trade policy template that incorporates a specific list of multilateral environmental agreements

19. Jeff B. Curtis, *Comment, Vessel-Source Oil Pollution and MARPOL 73/78: An International Success Story?*, 15 Envtl. L. 679, 684 (1985); International Convention for the Prevention of Pollution of the Sea by Oil, 1954, 327 U.N.T.S. 3.
20. Curtis, *supra* n. 19, at 684-5.
21. 1340 U.N.T.S. 184 (2 Nov. 1973).
22. IMO, *MARPOL-25 Years* 5 (October 1998), http://www.imo.org/en/KnowledgeCentre/ReferencesAndArchives/FocusOnIMO(Archives)/Documents/Focus%20on%20IMO%20-%20MARPOL%20-%2025%20years%20(October%201998).pdf.
23. MARPOL 73, Protocol I & II.
24. Protocol of 1978 Relating to the International Convention for the Prevention of Pollution from Ships, 1973, 1340 U.N.T.S. 61 (17 Feb. 1978).
25. *Ibid.*
26. MARPOL 73/78, Annexes I & V.
27. IMO, *The Protocol of 1997 (MARPOL Annex VI)*, http://www.imo.org/en/OurWork/environment/pollutionprevention/airpollution/pages/the-protocol-of-1997-(marpol-annex-vi).aspx.
28. MARPOL 73/78, Article 14.
29. *Ibid.*
30. IMO, *Status of Treaties*, http://www.imo.org/en/About/Conventions/StatusOfConventions/Documents/StatusOfTreaties.pdf.
31. The global trend of oil spills shows that after MARPOL became effective, statistics for spills greater than seven tonnes from tankers show a marked downward trend. *See* ITOPF, *Oil Tanker Spill Statistics 2017*, http://www.itopf.com/knowledge-resources/data-statistics/statistics/ (accessed 2 Nov. 2018).
32. *See* Office of the United States Trade Representative, *Bipartisan Trade Deal*, https://ustr.gov/sites/default/files/uploads/factsheets/2007/asset_upload_file127_11319.pdf.

(MEAs) into FTAs, which includes MARPOL 73/78.[33] The bipartisan agreement explains that MARPOL 73/78 is included because the US is a party to the treaty and takes seriously the commitments thereunder.[34] The current Administration and Congress consider that the US has 'nothing to fear from taking on FTA commitments for [MARPOL 73/78] as well and subjecting those commitments to the FTA dispute settlement process where trade or investment are affected'.[35]

The PTPA, the Columbia TPA, the Panama TPA, and the KORUS FTA all incorporate MARPOL 73/78.[36] The US also brought MARPOL 73/78 to the Trans-Pacific Partnership Agreement (TPP), the predecessor of CPTPP.[37] Nevertheless, the TPP does not require its members to ratify all five Annexes of MARPOL 73/78.[38] Its members can maintain existing obligations and make future reservations, exemptions, and exceptions applicable to it under MARPOL 73/78.[39] Therefore, for the first time, MARPOL 73/78 is incorporated into a mega-regional FTA.

MARPOL 73/78 aims to reduce deliberate, negligent, or accidental release of oil and other harmful substances from ships and protect the marine environment.[40] FTAs, such as the CPTPP, affirm the signatories' commitment to 'promote high levels of environmental protection and effective enforcement of environmental laws' and enforce MEA environmental obligations on the same basis as the FTA commercial provisions.[41] However, MARPOL 73/78 and the CPTPP are not perfect agreements. Even the IMO acknowledged that 'a greater effort to impose [the MARPOL 73/78] compliance must be carried out'.[42] One of the key deficiencies of MARPOL 73/78 is its predominant reliance on flag states to ensure MARPOL compliance while neglecting the role of coastal states.[43] A large number of vessels are registered in flag of convenience (FOC) states, which are not incentivized to fully comply with MARPOL 73/78.[44] Though coastal states are often the biggest victims of vessel-sourced oil spills, MARPOL 73/78 provides vague jurisdiction for them to require foreign vessels to meet MARPOL 73/78 standards.[45] As for FTAs, at the core they are not agreements with a

33. *Ibid.*, 2. The list also includes 'the Convention on International Trade in Endangered Species (CITES), Montreal Protocol on Ozone Depleting Substances ... Inter-American Tropical Tuna Convention (IATTC), Ramsar Convention on Wetlands, International Whaling Convention (IWC), and Convention on Conservation of Antarctic Marine Living Resources (CCAMLR)'.
34. *Ibid.*
35. *Ibid.*
36. *See* Office of the United States Trade Representative, *supra* n. 5.
37. The original twelve TPP countries are Australia, Brunei, Canada, Chile, Japan, Malaysia, Mexico, New Zealand, Peru, Singapore, the US, and Vietnam. *See TPP: What Is it and Why Does It Matter?*, BBC (23 Jan. 2017), https://www.bbc.com/news/business-32498715.
38. CPTPP, Ch. 20, Article 20.6.
39. *Ibid.*
40. MARPOL 73/78, Preamble.
41. CPTPP, Ch. 20, Article 20.2.
42. IMO, *MARPOL Annex I- Prevention of Pollution by Oil*, http://www.imo.org/en/OurWork/Environment/PollutionPrevention/OilPollution/Pages/Default.aspx (accessed 4 Nov. 2018).
43. *See* MARPOL 73/78, Articles 3-8. A flag state is the state of the flag a vessel flies. It is also where the vessel is registered.
44. Jim Shaw, *Flag of Convenience – or Flag of Necessity?*, Pacific Maritime Magazine (1 Sep. 2016), https://www.pacmar.com/story/2016/09/01/features/flag-of-convenience-or-flag-of-necessity/455.html.
45. *See* MARPOL 73/78, Articles 3-10.

primary focus on the environment. For example, the CPTPP has been widely accused as weak and unlikely to address environmental concerns.[46] In these contexts, can FTAs enhance the compliance of MARPOL 73/78? This Article tries to provide a tentative answer from four aspects: FOC; the vague role of coastal states; affecting trade or investment between the parties; and dispute resolution.

§13.03 CHALLENGES FOR FTAS TO ADDRESS VESSEL-SOURCED POLLUTION AND PROPOSED SOLUTIONS

[A] FOC

Because of the traditional primacy of flag state jurisdiction, MARPOL 73/78 relies on the flag states to enforce shipping standards,[47] despite FOC states having limited resources or no incentives to fully comply with MARPOL 73/78.[48] Flag states have a primary obligation to inspect or 'survey' vessels when they are put into service or when they apply for a five-year International Oil Pollution Prevention Certificate (IOPP).[49] MARPOL 73/78 also requires flag states to conduct mandatory initial, annual, intermediate, and periodical surveys for '[e]very oil tanker of 150 tons gross tonnage and above, and every other ship of 400 tons gross tonnage and above'.[50] Furthermore, the flag state must ensure that a vessel meets the MARPOL standards with respect to the design, construction, equipment, or manning of vessels before they go into operation.[51] The flag state must immediately investigate MARPOL violations irrespective of where the violation or pollution caused by the violation has occurred.[52]

If a vessel has a valid IOPP, she is regarded for all purposes to be covered by MARPOL 73/78 to the extent of the validity of the certificate, and port states shall accept it.[53] Only when clear grounds exist for believing that the condition of the vessel or her equipment 'does not correspond substantially with the particulars of that certificate' can port states conduct a complete survey of the vessel.[54] Additionally, a

46. Chris Wold, *Empty Promises and Missed Opportunities: An Assessment of the Environmental Chapter of the Trans-Pacific Partnership* 1, 2 (4 Jan. 2016), https://law.lclark.edu/live/files/20857-assessing-the-tpp-environmental-chapter; *see* Matthew Rimmer, *The Trans-Pacific Partnership: Intellectual Property, Public Health, and Access to Essential Medicines*, 29 I.P. J. 277, 280, 292-5 (2017).
47. For example, according to UNCLOS, flag states shall ensure that vessels flying their flag comply 'with applicable international rules and standards': UNCLOS, Article 217(1). They shall enact domestic laws according to applicable international laws to control pollution from ships flying their flag. *See ibid.*, Article 211.
48. Robert Beckman & Zhen Sun, *The Relationship Between UNCLOS and IMO Instruments*, 2 Asia Pac. J. Ocean L. & Pol'y 201, 227 (2017).
49. MARPOL 73/78, Annex I, Ch. 1, Reg. 5.
50. *Ibid.*, Annex I Ch.1, Reg. 4(1).
51. UNCLOS, Article 217(2).
52. *Ibid.*, Article 217(4).
53. MARPOL 73/78, Annex I, Ch. 1, Article 5(1); UNCLOS, Article 217(3). If a vessel has no valid IOPP, the port state 'shall take such steps as will ensure that the [vessel] shall not sail until it can proceed to sea without presenting an unreasonable threat of harm to the marine environment'. MARPOL 73/78, Article 5(2).
54. *Ibid.*

port state may inspect a vessel to verify whether the vessel has discharged any harmful substances violating MARPOL 73/78.[55] If an inspection indicates a MARPOL 73/78 violation, the port state cannot conduct a prosecution and must forward a report with the evidence to the flag state for them to take appropriate action.[56] Upon receiving such evidence, the flag state must investigate the violation and may request further or better evidence from the port state.[57] If the flag state is satisfied with the evidence, it must bring proceedings against the vessel in accordance with its domestic laws as soon as possible.[58] It shall also promptly inform the reporting port state, as well as the IMO, of the actions taken.[59] Therefore, compared with flag states, port states have limited jurisdiction and capacity concerned with MARPOL 73/78 violations.

Since the MARPOL 73/78 enforcement mechanism relies primarily on the flag states,[60] a vessel may evade MARPOL 73/78 standards if a flag state cannot or is not willing to enhance its MARPOL compliance.[61] Over 60% of vessels around the world use FOCs in 2016.[62] A FOC vessel flies the flag of a country other than the country of ownership. A genuine link between the owner of the vessel and the flag state is not required.[63] As vessel registration brings fiscal revenue, states are incentivized to open their registries to foreign vessels. Some FOC states, like Mongolia, do not even have a coastal port but still open their registry to foreign vessels. FOC states have been widely criticized for their ineffectiveness in enforcing MARPOL 73/78 due to a lack of administrative machinery, power, or their simple refusal to investigate or prosecute violations.[64] Enforcing environmental regulations less strictly further incentivizes shipowners to register in those countries.[65] In other words, FOC states waive or weaken their obligations under MARPOL 73/78 in order to attract trade or investment (i.e., registration of foreign vessels). The International Transport Worker's Federation has

55. *Ibid.*, Article 6(2)-(3).
56. *Ibid.*
57. *Ibid.*, Article 6(4).
58. *Ibid.*
59. *Ibid.*
60. Secretariat of the IMO, *Implications of the United Nations Convention of the Law of the Sea for the International Maritime Organization*, 12, IMO Doc. LEG/MISC.8 (30 Jan. 2014) (Implications of the UN Convention), http://www.imo.org/en/OurWork/Legal/Documents/LEG%20MISC%20 8.pdf.
61. Andrew Rakestraw, *Open Oceans and Marine Debris: Solutions for the Ineffective Enforcement of MARPOL Annex V*, 35 Hastings Int'l & Comp. L. Rev. 383, 392 (2012).
62. Craig Moran, *Flags of Convenience: Panama Papers on the High Seas*, World Policy (20 Jul. 2016), https://worldpolicy.org/2016/07/20/flags-of-convenience-panama-papers-on-the-high-seas/. ('[P]erhaps unsurprisingly, Panama is one of the most sought out destinations for ship registrations, followed by Liberia and the Marshall Islands. Together, these "registration havens" account for more than 60 percent of shippers, up from a measly 4 percent in the 1950s.') The figure was around 30% in the 1990s. Mark L. Boos, *The Oil Pollution Act of 1990: Striking the Flags of Convenience?*, 2 Colo. J. Int'l Envtl. L. & Pol'y 407, 412 (1991) (footnote omitted).
63. Boos, *supra* n. 62, at 410 & fn. 22.
64. G.P. Pamborides, *International Shipping Law: Legislation and Enforcement* 10 (1999) (quoting an omitted source); Curtis, *supra* n. 19, at 708 (quoting D. Abecassis, *The Law and Practice Relating to Oil Pollution from Ships* 4, 77 (1978)); Gini Mattson, *MARPOL 73/79 and Annex I: An Assessment of Its Effectiveness*, 9 J. Int'l Wildlife L. & Pol'y 175, 191 (2006).
65. Rebecca Becker, *MARPOL 73/78: An Overview in International Environmental Enforcement*, 10 Geo. Int'l Envtl. L. Rev. 625, 632 (1998) (citing Curtis, *supra* n. 19, at 708).

identified thirty-two FOC states.[66] Eleven other countries on the list of FOC states may have a 'high' or 'very high' risk of inspection violations according to the 2009 annual report by the Paris Memorandum of Understanding (Paris MoU) on their 'black list.'[67] FOC vessels are more likely to cause accidents and pollution, be in poor physical condition, have communication problems, or have inadequately trained and certified crews.[68] Environmental compliance cannot be realized if FOC states are not effectively enforcing MARPOL 73/78.[69]

Moreover, all FOC countries are the least developed countries or countries still developing.[70] These countries often lack resources and/or political will to achieve MARPOL 73/78 compliance. There are two main reasons for this. First, the development of MARPOL 73/78 was closely associated with major marine environmental casualties in developed countries, 'like *Torrey Canyon*, *Amoco Cadiz*, *Argo Merchant*, *Exxon Valdez*, *Erika*, and *Prestige*'; therefore, MARPOL 73/78 is considered as mainly endorsing the environmental concerns of developed countries.[71] The MARPOL 73/78 drafting process did not attract the attention or fully reflect the needs of developing countries. Second, MARPOL 73/78 fails to provide sufficient support for developing countries to fully implement it.[72] While MARPOL 73/78 together with UNCLOS require 'developed countries and international organizations [to provide] financial help, technical assistance, and technology transfer to developing countries', these obligations have never been practically implemented.[73]

The four US FTAs that incorporate MARPOL 73/78 all impose procedural obligations on its Member States regarding investigation and sanctioning of MARPOL 73/78 violations, and disclosure of information and public participation.[74] The CPTPP not only contains these two obligations but also allows subcentral governments, third state,[75] and non-governmental organizations to play an active role in enforcing MARPOL 73/78 compliance. Therefore, this Article uses the CPTPP as our example for its discussion.

66. This includes Panama where *Oceanside*, our hypothetical vessel, is registered. *See* International Transport Workers' Federation, *Flags of Convenience*, http://www.itfglobal.org/en/transport-sectors/seafarers/in-focus/flags-of-convenience-campaign/ (accessed 3 Nov. 2018).
67. *Paris Memorandum of Understanding on Port State Control* 29 (2009), https://parismou.org/sites/default/files/gecorrigeerd%20jaarverslag%202009_0.pdf. The Paris Memorandum of Understanding on Port State Control is an organization consisting of twenty-seven participating maritime administrations in North America and Europe. It aims to eliminate the operation of substandard ships through a harmonized system of port state control. *See ibid.*, 4.
68. Becker, *supra* n. 65, at 634.
69. Rakestraw, *supra* n. 61, at 394; Becker, *supra* n. 65, at 633.
70. Andrew Griffin, *MARPOL 73/78 and Vessel Pollution: A Glass Half Full or Half Empty?*, 1 Ind. J. Global Legal Stud. 489, 507 (1994).
71. Saiful Karim, *Implementation of the MARPOL Convention in Developing Countries*, 79 Nordic J. Int'l L. 303, 331 (2010).
72. *See ibid.*, 336-7.
73. *Ibid.*
74. *See*, e.g., Panama TPA, Ch. 17, Articles 17.3-17.4, 17.7-17.8 (28 Jun. 2007), https://ustr.gov/sites/default/files/uploads/agreements/fta/panama/asset_upload_file314_10400.pdf.
75. A 'third state' refers to a state other than the requesting or the responding state in a vessel-sourced pollution dispute.

The CPTPP imposes on its members new procedural obligations to investigate and sanction MARPOL violations. MARPOL 73/78 avoids interference with its members' domestic law and allows its members to fulfil their investigations and sanctions according to their domestic law. It requires that the sanction for violations specified under domestic law 'shall be adequate in severity to discourage violations ... and shall be equally severe irrespective of where the violations occur'.[76] The CPTPP imposes two new obligations on its Member States. The first is a permissive obligation that sanctions or remedies for MARPOL violations may include a right for victim(s) to seek damages or injunctive relief directly against the violator, or a right to seek governmental action.[77] The second is a compulsory obligation. A CPTPP Member State must provide judicial, quasi-judicial, or administrative methods of enforcement for environmental laws, and importantly, to ensure 'that those proceedings are fair, equitable, transparent and comply with due process of law'.[78] The CPTPP does not explicitly indicate how to interpret the fairness, equity, transparency, and due process of law.[79] This leaves the possibility that these concepts may be interpreted according to international law and held to the international due process standard rather than the domestic law of the relevant Member States. In contrast, MARPOL 73/78 explicitly provides that domestic law shall be applied to investigate and sanction violations.[80]

MARPOL 73/78 only adjusts rights and obligations between states. Disputes involving an interested person residing or established in the territory of MARPOL 73/78 members usually fall into that country's domestic jurisdiction.[81] However, the CPTPP clearly goes beyond state-to-state relationships to explicitly require that a Member State should ensure an interested person has the right to request that state authorities investigate alleged MARPOL 73/78 violations according to the Member State's law.[82] This not only represents a breakthrough with the MARPOL 73/78 regulations but also may pose a significant challenge to the administrative system and judicial order of the CPTPP Member States.[83]

[B] The Vague Role of Coastal States

Coastal states are different from port states and flag states.[84] In our hypothetical, China would be neither a port state nor a flag state for the *Oceanside*, because the *Oceanside* is registered in Panama and it did not plan on entering any port in China. However, on the *Oceanside's* voyage from Iran to South Korea, she would pass China's exclusive

76. MARPOL 73/78, Article 4(4).
77. CPTPP, Ch. 20, Article 20.7(5).
78. *Ibid.*, Ch. 20, Article 20.7(3).
79. *Ibid.*
80. MARPOL 73/78, Article 4.
81. *Ibid.*
82. CPTPP, Ch. 20, Article 20.7(2).
83. *See* Patricia Ranald, *The Trans-Pacific Partnership Agreement: Reaching Behind the Border, Challenging Democracy*, 26 Econ. Lab. Rel. Rev. 241, 245-6 (2015).
84. *See* Food and Agriculture Organization of the United Nations, *Port State Measures* (2002), http://www.fao.org/3/y3536e09.htm#bm9; Food and Agriculture Organization of the United Nations, *Flag State Responsibilities* (2002), www.fao.org/3/y3536e07.htm.

economic zone. China is a coastal state but not a port state. Compared with port states and flag states, the jurisdiction of coastal states is trickier considering the traditional supremacy of freedom of navigation. When MARPOL 73/78 was negotiated, states were contemplating on whether to negotiate UNCLOS. Therefore, MARPOL 73/78 deliberately contains vague provision for the jurisdiction of coastal states.[85] Under Article 4 of MARPOL 73/78, the coastal state can prohibit MARPOL violations 'within the jurisdiction' of the state, but the exact meaning of 'jurisdiction' is not clear.[86] In cases where coastal states discover a MARPOL violation within their jurisdiction, they shall either initiate proceedings in accordance with their own laws or transmit information and evidence to the vessel's flag state for further action.[87]

The degree to which coastal states may regulate foreign ships to prevent vessel-sourced pollution during innocent passage within their territorial waters or navigating their exclusive economic zone is provided by UNCLOS.[88] UNCLOS limits coastal state jurisdiction to two areas: territorial sea, and the exclusive economic zone or the continental shelf.[89] Within their territorial sea, coastal states can exercise sovereignty and adopt laws to control marine pollution from foreign vessels, to the extent that those laws do not hamper innocent passage of foreign vessels.[90] In respect of exclusive economic zones, coastal states may enact laws according to generally accepted international rules and standards to control marine pollution from foreign vessels.[91] UNCLOS also permits coastal states to clearly define a particular area of their respective exclusive economic zones and apply special mandatory measures to control marine pollution from vessels in this area, if the international rules and standards

85. *See* MARPOL 73/78, Article 4; UNCLOS, Article 217(6)-(7); Alan Khee-Jin Tan, *Vessel-Source Marine Pollution: The Law and Politics of International Regulation* 192 (2006) (indicating 'jurisdictional questions remained side-stepped [in MARPOL 73/78] given that the UNCLOS negotiations were by then underway').
86. MARPOL 73/78, Article 4(2).
87. *Ibid.*, Articles 6(2)-(3), 8(3).
88. Implications of the UN Convention, *supra* n. 60, at 12-13. Prior to UNCLOS, the right of the coastal state to intervene on the high seas in case of oil spill was solely regulated by the Convention Relating to Intervention on the High Seas in Cases of Oil Pollution Casualties and the Protocol Relating to Intervention on the High Seas in Cases of Pollution by Substances Other Than Oil. *Ibid.*, Article 221(1) of UNCLOS codifies the basic principles in these instruments. UNCLOS, Article 221(1).
89. UNCLOS, Article 210(5).
90. *Ibid.*, Article 211(4); Anna Miheva-Natova, *The Relationship Between United Nations Convention on the Law of the Sea and the IMO Conventions* 20 (2005), http://www.un.org/depts/los/nippon/unnff_programme_home/fellows_pages/fellows_papers/natova_0506_bulgaria.pdf. This jurisdiction is subject to two conditions. First, if the coastal state has clear grounds to believe a foreign vessel is conducting 'any act of wilful and serious pollution' in its territorial sea, it may physically inspect the vessel and institute proceedings, including detention of the vessel according to the state's laws. UNCLOS, Articles 19(2)(h) & 220(2). The coastal states may not take any preventative measures against a foreign vessel that does not meet the MARPOL requirement for marine pollution while passing its territorial water. Second, the coastal state's jurisdiction should not harm the right of innocent passage of foreign vessels. *Ibid.*, Article 211(4). Therefore, coastal states cannot actively inspect foreign vessels for compliance with the MARPOL 73/78 standards as flag states and port states can.
91. UNCLOS, Article 211(5); Tan, *supra* n. 85, at 196.

cannot meet their special circumstances.[92] If a coastal state has clear grounds to believe that a vessel has violated applicable international rules and standards for marine pollution in its exclusive economic zone, that state may require the vessel to provide information to establish whether a violation has occurred.[93]

Can a coastal state bring a case against a flag or port state for a MARPOL 73/78 violation under an FTA? What remedies are available under FTAs to a coastal state involved in an incident of vessel-sourced pollution? Notably, it is UNCLOS, not MARPOL 73/78, which provides for coastal state jurisdiction of vessel-sourced pollution. The US is not a signatory to UNCLOS. So, the question is, by only incorporating MARPOL 73/78 and not UNCLOS as well, does the US's FTAs create rights and remedies for coastal states in vessel-sourced marine pollution?[94] The application of successive treaties relating to the same subject matter is regulated by Article 30 of the Vienna Convention on Law of Treaties (VCLT) which the US has signed, but not ratified.[95] The UNCLOS should not be considered incompatible with MARPOL 73/78, because it contains several provisions, 'which require States to "take account of", "conform to", "give effect to" or "implement" the relevant international rules and standards developed by or through the "competent international organization"'.[96] These provisions are considered to include MARPOL 73/78.[97] Moreover, Article 311(2) of UNCLOS provides that UNCLOS 'shall not alter the rights and obligations of States Parties which arise from other agreements compatible with this Convention and which do not affect the enjoyment by other States Parties of their rights or the performance of their obligations under this Convention'.[98] Article 311(2) conflicts with Article 311(1), which clearly provides for the priority of UNCLOS.[99] Therefore, according to Article 30(2) of the VCLT, the provisions of MARPOL 73/78 should prevail.[100] Additionally, Article 30(4) further provides that '[w]hen the parties to the later treaty [i.e., UNCLOS]

92. UNCLOS, Article 211(6). The special circumstances are strictly defined and should be concerned with oceanographical and ecological conditions, utilization, the protection of resources, and the particular character of the traffic in the particular area. *Ibid.*
93. *Ibid.*, Article 220(3). The information is limited to the vessel's identity, port of registry, its last and its next port of call, etc.
94. Panama, Columbia, and South Korea are Member States of UNCLOS. *See* United Nations Division for Ocean Affairs and the Law of the Sea, *Chronological Lists of Ratifications of, Accessions and Successions to the Convention and the Related Agreements* (3 Apr. 2018), http://www.un.org/depts/los/reference_files/chronological_lists_of_ratifications.htm.
95. 1155 U.N.T.S. 332, 339-40 (27 Jan. 1980). While the US has not ratified the VCLT, it 'considers many of the provisions of the [VCLT] to constitute customary international law on the law of treaties': US Department of State, *Vienna Convention on the Law of Treaties*, https://www.state.gov/s/l/treaty/faqs/70139.htm (accessed 3 Nov. 2018).
96. Implications of the UN Convention, *supra* n. 60, at 8; Oliver Dörr & Kristen Schmalenbach, *Vienna Convention on the Law of Treaties: A Commentary* 545 (2018). ('[T]reaties are incompatible with each other if their obligations cannot be complied with simultaneously.')
97. Implications of the UN Convention, *supra* n. 60, at 8-10.
98. UNCLOS, Article 311(2).
99. Article 311(1) of the UNCLOS provides that '[t]his Convention shall prevail, as between States Parties, over the Geneva Conventions on the Law of the Sea of 29 April 1958'.
100. Article 30(2) of the VCLT provides that when a treaty 'specifies that the treaty is subject to, or that it is not to be considered as incompatible with, an earlier or later treaty. ... [T]he provisions of that other treaty prevail'. Mark E. Villiger, *Commentary on the 1969 Vienna Convention on the Law of Treaties* 405 (2009) (quoting VCLT, Article 30(2)).

do not include all the parties to the earlier one [i.e., MARPOL 73/78] … [a]s between a State party to both treaties and a State party to only one of the treaties, the treaty to which both States are parties governs their mutual rights and obligations'.[101] Accordingly, MARPOL 73/78 rather than UNCLOS should regulate the legal rights and obligations between the US and its FTA partners.

Nevertheless, if relevant UNCLOS provisions for coastal states jurisdiction on marine environmental protection can be considered a 'international custom' as defined in the United Nations Charter, these provisions can be applied to the US.[102] UNCLOS provides that '[s]pecific obligations assumed by States under special conventions, with respect to the protection and preservation of the marine environment, should be carried out in a manner consistent with the general principles and objectives of this Convention'.[103] The general practice in the application of MARPOL 73/78 and UNCLOS in the international communities also demonstrate states' consensus that MARPOL 73/78 and UNCLOS should be combined so as to provide a complete picture of international law for vessel-sourced marine pollution. Therefore, an argument could be made that the US is bound by the relevant UNCLOS provisions for coastal states jurisdiction on marine environmental protection although it is not a party to the UNCLOS.

Notably, Peru is also not a UNCLOS member, but the PTPA incorporates MARPOL 73/78. However, it is unclear whether UNCLOS provisions for coastal states jurisdiction on marine environmental protection should be applied to both the US and Peru in the context of their FTA. If these provisions have become international custom (as in the authors' opinion they are), they should be applied to the US and Peru.

In footnote 6 of Article 20.6 of the CPTPP, it explicitly indicates that this provision pertains to pollution regulated by MARPOL 73/78.[104] Nothing about UNCLOS is mentioned in the CPTPP. However, the CPTPP is different from the US's FTAs that incorporate MARPOL 73/78, because the CPTPP members are all parties to UNCLOS. Therefore, a stronger argument can be made among the CPTPP members that coastal states can rely on Article 20.6 of the CPTPP, because MARPOL 73/78 needs to be implemented in a manner consistent with the general principles and objectives of UNCLOS, and UNCLOS is considered to be international custom.[105]

[C] Affecting Trade or Investment Between the Parties

Besides MARPOL 73/78, the CPTPP and the US's FTAs that incorporate MARPOL 73/78 all expressly refer to two other MEAs: the Convention on International Trade in

101. VCLT, Article 30(4); Dörr & Schmalenbach, *supra* n. 96.
102. U.N. Charter, Article 38(1)(b).
103. UNCLOS, Article 237(2).
104. CPTPP, Ch. 20, Article 20.6(1), fn. 6.
105. Implications of the UN Convention, *supra* n. 60, at 56-7.

Endangered Species of Wild Fauna and Flora (CITES) and the Montreal Protocol on Substances that Deplete the Ozone Layer (Montreal Protocol).[106]

Regarding environmental protection, all the US bilateral FTAs require that in order to establish a violation of the FTA, '[a] Party must demonstrate that the other Party has failed to adopt, maintain, or implement laws, regulations, or other measures to fulfil an obligation under a covered [MEA] in a manner *affecting trade or investment* between Parties'.[107] Therefore, a violation of an MEA, including MARPOL 73/78, that does not affect trade or investment between parties is not covered by the dispute resolution mechanisms under the FTAs.

Article 20.4 of the CPTPP clearly confirms the original commitments of the CPTPP members to prior MEAs.[108] However, the circumstances in which a member may invoke the CPTPP dispute resolution mechanism for violation of these MEAs vary among the agreements. Although members are encouraged to address any related disputes through CITES, a member's failure to adopt, maintain, and implement its laws and regulations incorporating CITES obligations allows other CPTPP members to bring a claim by utilizing the CPTPP's dispute resolution mechanism.[109] Nevertheless, for MARPOL 73/78 and the Montreal Protocol, a member's failure to maintain its laws and regulations implementing the two conventions does not allow other CPTPP members to bring a claim by utilizing the same dispute resolution mechanism. The claimant needs to prove that the non-implementation affected trade or investment between the parties.[110] Along this vein, commencing the CPTPP dispute settlement mechanism requires more than a violation of MARPOL 73/78; the violation must be (1) sustained and recurring, and (2) affecting trade or investment between the parties.[111] Therefore, a MARPOL 73/78 violation is not a violation of the CPTPP unless it affects trade or investment between the parties.

In the World Trade Organization (WTO) report, *Thailand – Customs and Fiscal Measures on Cigarettes from the Philippines*, the Appellate Body of the WTO laid down a test to determine whether a domestic measure affects trade between the parties:

> The analysis ... requires a careful examination 'grounded in close scrutiny of the "fundamental thrust and effect of the measure itself"', including of the implications of the measure for the conditions of competition between imported and like domestic products. This analysis need not be based on empirical evidence as to the actual effects of the measure at issue in the internal market of the Member

106. *See* Montreal Protocol on Substances that Deplete the Ozone Layer, 1522 U.N.T.S. 29 (1 Jan. 1989); Convention on International Trade in Endangered Species of Wild Fauna and Flora 993 U.N.T.S. 244 (1 Jul. 1975). The Bipartisan Agreement on Trade Policy published in 2007 by Congress and Office of the US Trade Representative identified seven MEAs for inclusion in FTAs, but only three of them are included in the CPTPP. This is possibly because the three are the only MEAs that all CPTPP parties have ratified: International Centre for Trade & Sustainable Development (ICTSD), *Environment in the Trans-Pacific Partnership: A Legal Analysis* 4 (December 2016), https://www.greengrowthknowledge.org/sites/default/files/downloads/resource/ICTSD_environment_trans-pacific_partnership_legal_analysis.pdf.
107. Panama TPA, *supra* n. 74, Ch. 17, Article 17.2, fn. 1 (emphasis added).
108. *See* CPTPP, Ch. 20, Article 20.4.
109. *Ibid.*, Ch. 20, Article 20.17(2), fns. 22-24.
110. *Ibid.*, Ch. 20, Article 20.5.1, 20.6(1), fns. 5 & 8.
111. *See ibid.*, Ch. 20, Article 20.3(4); ICTSD, *supra* n. 106, at 6.

concerned. Of course, nothing precludes a panel from taking such evidence of actual effects into account.[112]

In other words, when imported and like domestic products are subject to a single regulatory regime, only the imported products must comply with additional requirements. This would imply that imported products are treated less favourably, so the measure affects trade between the parties. Without requiring empirical evidence on negative trade effects, this test is favourable for environmental-related trade disputes.

CPTPP requires each Member State to list measure(s) implementing its obligations under MARPOL 73/78, or adopts any subsequent measure(s) that provide an equivalent or higher level of environmental protection as the measure(s) listed. The US-Mexico-Canada Agreement further provides that if a Member State has maintained the measure(s) listed, a violation of MARPOL 73/78 must be in a manner affecting trade or investment between the parties. This means '(i) a person or industry that produces a good or supplies a service traded between the Parties or has an investment in the territory of the Party that has failed to comply with this obligation; or (ii) a person or industry that produces a good or supplies a service that competes in the territory of a Party with a good or a service of another Party'.[113] Consequently, a state may violate MARPOL 73/78 if a person or industry in its territory fails to comply with MARPOL 73/78. Furthermore, according to the US-Mexico-Canada Agreement, when resolving disputes, a panel shall presume that a failure is in a manner affecting trade or investment between the parties, unless the responding party demonstrates otherwise.[114] This allocation of onus of proof favours the Member States who suffer from vessel-sourced marine pollution. This allocation of onus of proof does not exist in MARPOL 73/78, so the US-Mexico-Canada Agreement in this aspect may enhance the protection of marine environment.

[D] Dispute Resolution

MARPOL 73/78 requires parties to negotiate disputes before initiating arbitration.[115] However, it does not provide a clear procedure or timeline for the negotiation, which may prolong the process and delay the establishment of an arbitration tribunal. In contrast, the CPTPP provides a three-step consultation procedure with strict timelines.[116] The three steps are referred to as environment consultations, senior representative consultations, and ministerial consultations. Combined, they should not extend beyond sixty days after the date of receipt of a request under Article 20.20 of the CPTPP, except where the parties agree otherwise.[117] If the dispute is not resolved, the

112. *Appellate Body Report, Thailand-Customs and Fiscal Measures on Cigarettes from the Philippines*, [129], WTO Doc. WT/DS371/AB/R (adopted 17 Jun. 2011) (footnote omitted).
113. The US-Mexico-Canada Agreement, Ch. 24, fn. 15.
114. *Ibid.*, fn. 16.
115. MARPOL 73/78, Article 10.
116. CPTPP, Ch. 20, Article 20.23.
117. *Ibid.*, Ch. 20, Article 20.20-20.23.

requesting party may request consultations under the CPTPP Dispute Resolution Chapter (i.e., Chapter 28),[118] or request the establishment of a panel.[119]

Therefore, compared with MARPOL 73/78 negotiations, the CPTPP consultation procedures are more fully fledged out and detailed. The CPTPP procedures better facilitate dispute resolution because, after a dispute occurs, it is usually difficult for parties to agree upon the consultation procures. Differently from MARPOL 73/78, which provides no procedure for consultation, the tight timeline and clear steps of the CPTPP consultation procedure may be more effective in encouraging parties to focus on negotiations and, if that fails, on establishing the panel.

The most fundamental difference between MARPOL 73/78 and the CPTPP dispute resolution mechanism is that the former adopts an ad hoc 'arbitration' model, whereas the latter resorts to a 'panel' procedure similar to interstate arbitration but inspired also by WTO dispute settlement. They are significantly different in two respects.

The first difference concerns the rules of procedure. MARPOL 73/78 does not provide arbitration procedural rules, but rather allows the arbitration tribunal to decide its own rules.[120] In contrast, the CPTPP provides detailed procedural rules for panels.[121] At the end of the arbitration, MARPOL arbitration tribunals will issue an arbitration award, which is final and cannot be appealed.[122] However, the CPTPP panel will first issue an initial report, which is not immediately final and binding.[123] The disputing parties are then allowed to submit written comments on the initial report to the panel.[124] After considering the comments, the panel may modify its report and make any further examinations it considers appropriate.[125] Then, it will issue a final and binding report.[126] The former type of arbitration procedure is a more traditional way to resolve interstate disputes, whereas the CPTPP's 'initial report + final report' panel system is more innovative. The latter mechanism has been borrowed from the WTO, and is sometimes found in other Asia-Pacific FTAs (such as the investor-state dispute settlement procedure in the Australia-Indonesia FTA signed in 2019, as noted in Chapter 5 of this book). Arguably, the panel procedure is more concerned with ensuring an accurate representation of the parties' arguments and that all matters have been taken into account, rather than providing an opportunity to reargue points of law or fact. This mechanism may help the panel fully deliberate the parties' positions. Ultimately, as the disputing parties' feedback has been taken into account, the final report will more likely be accepted and enforced successfully.

The second difference is in the enforcement mechanism. Unlike trade law, international environmental law traditionally makes use of soft measures such as

---

118. *Ibid.*, Ch. 28, Article 28.5.
119. *Ibid.*, Ch. 28, Article 28.7.
120. MARPOL 73/78, Protocol II, Article VIII.
121. CPTPP, Ch. 28, Article 28.13.
122. MARPOL 73/78, Protocol II, Article X(1).
123. CPTPP, Ch. 28, Article 28.17.
124. *Ibid.*, Ch. 28, Article 28.17(7).
125. *Ibid.*, Ch. 28, Article 28.17(8).
126. *Ibid.*, Ch. 28 Article 28.18.

persuasion, public opinion, international environmental reputation, technical assistance, and financial support to guarantee its implementation, rather than imposing real sanctions. MARPOL 73/78 requires states to immediately comply with any arbitration awards.[127] However, it does not provide a mechanism for enforcement in cases of non-compliance. Therefore, it is not surprising that one commentator has described the MARPOL 73/78 system as 'depend[ing] entirely on voluntary compliance. ... [T]he Member Governments themselves determine whether or not they are in compliance with [MARPOL] regulations a majority of the time'.[128] The IMO does not have the funding and institutional mechanisms to establish a MARPOL enforcement authority.

In contrast, the CPTPP has a stronger enforcement mechanism. Also seemingly inspired by WTO dispute settlement, it allows the complaining state to retaliate by suspending benefits of equivalent effect if the responding state fails to comply with the panel's final report within a reasonable period of time.[129] In considering what benefits to suspend, the complaining state 'should first seek to suspend benefits in the same subject matter as that in which the panel has determined non-conformity'.[130] However, if the complaining state considers that to be impracticable or ineffective, and that the circumstances are serious enough, 'it may suspend benefits in a different subject matter'.[131] Compensation, suspension of benefits, and the payment of a monetary assessment must be temporary and cannot replace full implementation of the panel report.[132] Thus, the CPTPP enforces its environmental obligations with the threat of real trade sanctions. Linking trade retaliation in FTAs with obligations to environmental protection represents a striking progression or cross-fertilization from international trade law.

So far, the MARPOL 73/78 state-to-state arbitration has never been invoked, and there may be two reasons for this. The first has an institutional dimension. The IMO, like many other United Nation (UN) special agencies,[133] considers itself as 'primarily a technical organisation seeking to avoid all political controversy and dispute[s]'.[134] Therefore, most of the marine pollution treaties concluded under the auspices of the IMO contain no or very limited dispute settlement mechanisms. The arbitration mechanism under MARPOL is already comparatively strong, despite the ad hoc nature of the procedure.[135] States hesitate to submit their disputes on the interpretation or implementation of MARPOL 73/78 to arbitration because they hope that disputes will

127. MARPOL 73/78, Protocol II, Article X(1).
128. Becker, *supra* n. 65, at 638.
129. CPTPP, Ch. 28, Article 28.20(1)-(2).
130. *Ibid.*, Ch. 28, Article 28.20(4)(a).
131. *Ibid.*, Ch. 28, Article 28.20(4)(b).
132. *Ibid.*, Ch. 28, Article 28.20(15).
133. For example, the World Intellectual Property Organization defines its objectives as '(i) to promote the protection of intellectual property throughout the world through cooperation among States and, where appropriate, in collaboration with any other international organization, (ii) to ensure administrative cooperation among the Unions': Article 3(i)-(ii) of Convention Establishing the World Intellectual Property Organization Signed at Stockholm on 14 Jul. 1967, 828 U.N.T.S. 5, 11.
134. Robin Churchill, *International Law and Dispute Settlement: New Problems and Techniques* 164 (2010).
135. *Ibid.*

be dealt within the institutional machinery of MARPOL 73/78 (by commission, meeting of the parties, or the Marine Environment Protection Committee of the IMO) rather than by a decision rendered by an arbitration tribunal.[136]

Second, the low number of disputes regarding non-compliance may be due to the fact that states are generally not directly affected by another state's non-compliance, or cannot prove the causalities between the oil spill, the environmental damage suffered, and the defects in the implementation of MARPOL 73/78 by a flag state.[137] The direct maker of an oil spill is the vessel, not the state that fails to fulfil MARPOL 73/78 requirements. In addition, the possibility that the victim coastal states are not complying with MARPOL 73/78 themselves may also contribute to the low number of disputes.[138]

Although all four of the US bilateral FTAs previously mentioned have incorporated MARPOL 73/78, the dispute resolution mechanism under these FTAs has so far never been invoked for vessel-sourced marine pollution. The traditional practice of consensual dispute settlement may reflect the fact that states still believe that the problem of marine pollution is better approached through cooperation rather than unilaterally initiated litigation.[139] The question is whether the strong and compulsory trade dispute resolution system under the CPTPP is compatible with or will change this tradition. Notably, coastal states impacted by vessel-sourced pollution can seek compensation according to the 1969 International Convention on Civil Liability for Oil Pollution Damage (1969 CLC), the 1971 International Convention on the Establishment of an International Fund for Compensation for Oil Pollution Damage (1971 Fund Convention), and the protocols to these conventions.[140] Therefore, states may not have incentives to go through the three-stage consultation, the structured arbitration mechanism under the panel procedure, and ultimately the retaliation mechanism provided by the CPTPP. However, the availability of the CPTPP's compulsory dispute resolution mechanism is an undeniable important symbolic success to encourage MARPOL 73/78 compliance. The shadow it casts may promote diplomatic cooperation in settling issues such as with FOCs.

§13.04 IMPLICATIONS FOR IHR IN THE CONTEXT OF THE COVID-19 PANDEMIC

The IHR require each state party to:

> notify WHO, by the most efficient means of communication available ... within 24 hours of assessment of public health information, of all events which may constitute a public health emergency of international concern within its territory in

136. *Ibid.*, 165-6.
137. *Ibid.*, 166.
138. *Ibid.*
139. *Ibid.*, 165.
140. *See* International Convention on the Establishment of an International Fund for Compensation for Oil Pollution Damage (supplementary to the International Convention on Civil Liability for Oil Pollution Damage, 1969), 1110 U.N.T.S. 58 (18 Dec. 1971); International Convention on Civil Liability for Oil Pollution Damage, 973 U.N.T.S. 4 (29 Nov. 1969).

> accordance with the decision instrument [in Annex 2 of the IHR], as well as any health measure implemented in response to those events.[141]

For events that do not constitute a public health emergency of international concern but are considered an unexpected or unusual public health concern, a state party shall also notify WHO within twenty-four hours of assessment of public health information according to the decision instrument in Annex 2.[142] If there is insufficient information available for a state to complete the decision instrument in Annex 2 of IHR, a state may nevertheless keep WHO advised and consult with WHO on appropriate health measures.[143]

Article 56 of the IHR provides a dispute resolution mechanism in the event of a dispute between parties concerning the above obligations. State parties should first try to resolve their disputes through negotiation, good offices, medication, conciliation, or any other peaceful means of their own choice.[144] If parties fail to reach an agreement, they can refer the dispute to the WHO Director General, who shall make every effort to settle it.[145] If all of disputing Member States accept arbitration as compulsory, states can submit their disputes to interstate arbitration. The arbitration then shall be conducted in accordance with the Permanent Court of Arbitration Optional Rules for Arbitrating Disputes Between Two States. The arbitral awards shall be binding and final to states who accept arbitration.[146]

In four aspects, Article 56 may not effectively and efficiently resolve disputes between Member States, which may explain why the mechanism has not been invoked so far.[147] Addressing the following issues would help Member States to use Article 56 to resolve disputes effectively and therefore enhance IHR compliance and public health outcomes.[148] First, there is no time limit for negotiation, good offices, medication, and conciliation. If one party delays the procedure, it is unclear whether the other party can move to other dispute resolution methods. Second, the legal nature of referring the dispute to the Director General is unclear. Does this mean that the Director General can control the dispute resolution and has authority to issue a binding decision (rather than acting as a settlement facilitator or sort of mediator) even if one party decides to default after referring a dispute for consideration? What is the procedure and time limit for the Director General to resolve the dispute after being referred? If intended to operate as a sort of mediator, what standards of independence or impartiality and natural justice

141. IHR, Article 6.1.
142. *Ibid.*, Article 7.
143. *Ibid.*, Article 8.
144. *Ibid.*, Article 56.1.
145. *Ibid.*, Article 56.2.
146. *Ibid.*, Article 56.3.
147. Gian Luca Burci, *The Outbreak of COVID-19 Coronavirus: Are the International Health Regulations Fit for Purpose?*, https://www.ejiltalk.org/the-outbreak-of-covid-19-coronavirus-are-the-international-health-regulations-fit-for-purpose/ (accessed 11 Apr. 2020).
148. Lawrence Gostin, Mary DeBartolo & Eric Friedman, *The International Health Regulations 10 Years On: The Governing Framework for Global Health Security*, 386 The Lancet 2222, 2225 (2015) (arguing that States Parties should consider pursuing dispute resolution through the Director General or compulsory arbitration, and '[s]uccessful cases by States Parties harmed by travel or trade restrictions or human rights violations would be a powerful precedent to enhance compliance').

should s/he be bound by? The second paragraph of Article 56 merely provides generally that the Director General should 'make every effort to settle [the dispute]'.

A third issue of uncertainty is the relationship between referring a dispute to the Director General under the second paragraph of Article 56 and to arbitration according to its third paragraph. Article 56 does not indicate that referring a dispute to the Director General is a precondition to an arbitration. Arguably, therefore, states can initiate an arbitration without referring the dispute to the Director General. (This possibility therefore would contrast, e.g., with the host state being able to require a foreign investor to attempt mediation, before commencing arbitration, under the 2019 Australia-Indonesia FTA as discussed in Chapter 5 of this book.) However, there still remains a question as to whether any IHR arbitration step could involve the Director General as the arbitrator. Perhaps this issue could be agreed separately by the disputing parties if and when agreeing to arbitration. That raises however a fourth and key issue: the IHR, unlike MARPOL or the CPTPP, do not provide advance consent of the states to arbitration.

The IHR enforcement mechanism of IHR resembles MARPOL 73/78 in two respects. First, if a state fails to provide a timely notification to the WHO regarding a public health emergency of international concern or unexpected or unusual public health event, WHO and other Member States cannot compel this state to carry out its obligation. The IHR also does not provide WHO and other Member States a channel to verify whether a state genuinely has insufficient information available to complete the decision instrument in Annex 2 of IHR. This is like the role of coastal states in MARPOL 73/78. Although they may be severely impacted by vessel-sourced pollution, they have very limited means to compel the flag state to carry out MARPOL 73/78 obligations.

Second, both MARPOL 73/78 and especially IHR have a weak dispute resolution mechanism. Neither convention provides a clear procedure or a timeline for negotiation, good offices, medication and conciliation. Further, unlike MARPOL 73/78 where all Member States have advance consent to compulsory arbitration, the IHR allows its members to declare in writing at any time whether it accepts arbitration as compulsory with regard to all disputes concerning IHR or with regard to a specific dispute in relation to any other Member State accepting the same obligation. Yet no Member State has made such a declaration so far, thus providing advance consent to arbitration (as under MARPOL 73/78).

In addition, compared with the panel system and the retaliation provisions in the CPTPP discussed above in section §13.03, the IHR has limited deterrent effect to force non-conforming members to perform their obligations. As one commentator argues: '[c]ritics have even questioned the binding legal nature of the IHR 2005 given the lack of enforcement or even compliance monitoring mechanisms and the apparent disregard of states parties for WHO's recommendations'.[149] The lack of a strong dispute resolution mechanism in IHR is not surprising because the WHO, like the IMO, has been 'a technical organization based on evidence and science'.[150] The ethos of the

149. Burci, *supra* n. 147.
150. *Ibid.*

WHO is to foster good faith performance of obligations among Member States.[151] Similar to the IMO, the WHO mainly sets technical standards and provides scientific guidance for its Member States. The IMO and WHO are science-based organizations rather than rule-based legal regimes, such as the CPTPP. Therefore, differently from the CPTPP, neither IHR nor MARPOL 73/78 uses sanctions and retaliation options to encourage compliance. However, MARPOL 73/78 started to change this approach by requiring advance consent to arbitration of disputes. The US and several others have further started to change its nature by adding, through FTAs, extra timelines and sanctions for non-compliance with arbitration awards.

§13.05 CONCLUSION AND PROPOSALS

Recent US bilateral FTAs and the CPTPP make a creative contribution to enhance MARPOL 73/78 compliance by imposing new procedural obligations on MARPOL Member States to investigate and sanction violations, and expanding obligations for information disclosure and public participation. Moreover, the CPTPP has included subcentral governments, third state, and non-governmental organizations in its implementation mechanism. Its three-step consultation system may promote negotiation between parties, and its retaliation system may help deter MARPOL 73/78 violations. All these efforts could help to enhance MARPOL 73/78 compliance. However, there are no reports that the FTAs, such as the Panama TPA, have significantly improved compliance with MARPOL 73/78.

Besides the FOC issue, in practice, the FTAs might not significantly enhance MARPOL 73/78 compliance. Theoretically, the CPTPP could encourage non-MARPOL Member States that want to join the CPTPP to sign MARPOL 73/78. However, the majority of states in the world have already ratified MARPOL 73/78 and its two compulsory Annexes, and the CPTPP does not require its members to accept the other four optional Annexes. Accordingly, it is unlikely that the CPTPP can significantly increase MARPOL 73/78 membership. The same argument applies to countries that want to conclude an FTA with the US. While FTAs have a strong dispute resolution mechanism, they are still subject to the threshold of '[a]ffecting trade or investment between the Parties'.[152] As the *Oceanside* hypothetical demonstrates, it is difficult to prove causation between an oil spill and its negative effects on trade or investment. Moreover, because of the different approaches towards dispute resolution in the law of the sea and international trade law, and because of the existence of the 1969 CLC and the 1971 Fund Convention, states may not be incentivized to establish a panel and utilize the retaliation mechanism. The ambiguous status of UNCLOS in US FTAs may

151. Gian Luca Burci & Jakob Quirin, *Implementation of the International Health Regulations (2005): Recent Developments at the World Health Organization*, 22 ASIL Insights (25 Sep. 2018), https://www.asil.org/insights/volume/22/issue/13/implementation-international-health-regulations-2005-recent-developments (indicating that the IHR rely 'largely on a horizontal compliance mechanism, in which states parties can review each other's level of compliance on the basis of reports provided annually to the Health Assembly (Article 54.1)').
152. Panama TPA, Ch. 17, Article 17.3, fn. 1.

limit coastal states' jurisdiction and remedies under the FTAs. All these factors may largely inhibit the capacity of the FTAs to control vessel-sourced pollution.

This leaves two remaining questions. First, are FTAs an effective tool to enhance MARPOL 73/78 compliance? Second, if states do incorporate MARPOL 73/78 into FTAs, can they do better? Regarding the first question, vessel and marine transport are indispensable to international trade, but MARPOL 73/78 is hardly related to trade compared with other MEAs, such as CITES.[153] FTAs may be a sort of 'paper tiger' to control vessel-sourced pollution if their membership is either not large enough or does not include major FOC states. As for the second question, if states are strongly committed to using FTAs to enhance MARPOL 73/78 compliance, they should consider deleting or broadly interpreting the requirement of '[a]ffecting trade or investment between the Parties' when determining whether parties are allowed to invoke FTAs to punish a MARPOL 73/78 violation.[154] FTA dispute resolution tribunals may invoke UNCLOS by treaty interpretation in MARPOL cases. In addition, FTAs may require its members to ratify all MAPROL Annexes rather than allow them to simply accept the compulsory Annexes I and II only.

The same observations apply to the IHR as well. Preventing and combating diseases like COVID-19 requires multilateral joint efforts. However, FTAs are generally bilateral. CPTPP is one of the largest mega-regional FTAs including eleven signatory states, with the possibility of the US one day reinstating its signature and then ratifying along with some further Asia-Pacific states. However, even such membership may not be large enough to controlling global infectious diseases such as COVID-19. Enhance IHR compliance should therefore proceed by direct reform of IHR Article 56. First, the WHO should consider adding time limits to dispute resolution by negotiation, good offices, mediation or conciliation. Second, the legal nature of referring the dispute to the WHO Director General should be clarified. Third, the WHO should consider making arbitration compulsory. Members could be required to consent in advance to submitting their disputes to the Permanent Court of Arbitration at the Hague or purely ad hoc state-to-state arbitration. The world needs a stronger dispute resolution mechanism to safeguard global health under the IHR. If direct reforms are not feasible, then as with MARPOL 73/78 through the CPTPP, incorporating the IHR into FTAs is worth exploring to prevent or manage the next pandemic.[155]

153. The WTO compiled a matrix on measures related to trade to select MEAs, but MARPOL 73/78 was not included. *See*, e.g., WTO, *WTO Matrix on Trade-Related Measures Pursuant to Selected Multilateral Environmental Agreements (MEAs)*, https://www.wto.org/english/tratop_e/envir_e/envir_matrix_e.htm (last accessed 4. Nov. 2018).
154. *See*, e.g., Panama TPA, Ch. 17, Article 17.3, fn. 1.
155. *See* Lawrence O. Gostin & Rebecca Katz, *The International Health Regulations: The Governing Framework for Global Health Security*, 94 Milbank Q. 264, 305, 306 (2016).

CHAPTER 14

Promoting International Mediation Through the Singapore Convention on Mediation

S.I. Strong[*]

This chapter seeks to determine whether and to what extent the recent promulgation of the 2018 United Nations Convention on International Settlement Agreements Resulting from Mediation will promote the use of mediation within the international legal and business communities. The discussion analyses the issue from a unique interdisciplinary perspective, applying concepts from dispute system design (DSD), default theory, psychology, and law and economics to both identify and resolve potential problems with the convention. The chapter also includes data from a recent empirical study conducted by the author on the use of mediation in international commercial disputes. Through this discussion, the chapter hopes to identify how individuals and institutions can complement the effect of the convention to support the development of international commercial mediation in the coming years.

§14.01 INTRODUCTION

For decades, arbitration has been considered the preferred method of resolving cross-border commercial disputes.[1] While that predilection long appeared virtually unassailable, the 2010s saw rising concerns about increased costs, delays and procedural formality in international commercial arbitration, both in the Asia Pacific and

* Although the author was involved with the process of proposing and negotiating the Singapore Convention on Mediation as both a private individual and non-governmental organisation (NGO) representative, the views reflected herein are the author's own and not those of any particular organization.

1. Gary B. Born, *International Commercial Arbitration* 73-93 (2d ed. Wolters Kluwer 2014).

elsewhere. The concerns triggered an intensive debate about potential alternatives to arbitration.[2]

One possibility involved litigation. Advocates of this approach sought to make judicial mechanisms more palatable for multinational actors through two techniques. The first involved the development of international commercial courts that reflect many of the attributes of international commercial arbitration (such as the use of English as the language of choice and/or by the use of foreign judges in addition to national judges).[3] The second involved the adoption of international instruments that increase the international enforceability of forum selection agreements and foreign judgments,[4] thereby mimicking the enforcement regime created in arbitration by the 1958 United Nations Convention on the Recognition and Enforcement of Foreign Arbitral Awards (NYC).[5]

The other solution focused on the expansion of consensus-based mechanisms, such as mediation and conciliation.[6] The latter movement culminated with the United Nations Convention on International Settlement Agreements Resulting from Mediation (Singapore Convention on Mediation), which was adopted on 20 December 2018.[7] On 7 August 2019, an unprecedented forty-six nations signed the instrument at a gala

2. S.I. Strong, *Realizing Rationality: An Empirical Assessment of International Commercial Mediation*, 73 Wash. & Lee L. Rev. 1973, 1982-3 (2016) (hereinafter 'Strong, *Empirical*'); Luke Nottage, *In/Formalisation and Glocalisation of International Commercial Arbitration and Investment Treaty Arbitration in Asia*, in *Formalization and Flexibilisation of Dispute Resolution* 211 (Joachim Zekoll, Moritz Baelz & Iwo Amelung eds., Brill Nijhoff 2014); Nobumichi Teramura, Ex Aequo et Bono *as a Response to the 'Over-judicialisation' of International Commercial Arbitration* (Wolters Kluwer 2020).
3. *International Business Courts – A European and Global Perspective* (Xandra Kramer & John Sorabji eds., Eleven International Publishing 2019); Maya Steinitz, *The Case for an International Court of Civil Justice* (Cambridge University Press 2018); *see also* Bath, Chapter 8 in this volume; Warren & Croft, Chapter 2 in this volume.
4. Convention on Choice of Court Agreements, 30 Jun. 2005, 44 I.L.M. 1294; Convention of 2 July 2019 on the Recognition and Enforcement of Foreign Judgments in Civil or Commercial Matters (Hague Judgments Convention), https://www.hcch.net/en/instruments/conventions/full-text/?cid=137?. At this point, only one country has signed the Hague Judgments Convention. Thirty-two countries (including the Member States of the European Union, which signed on as a regional and international organization) have signed the Convention on Choice of Court Agreements since it opened for signature in 2005.
5. United Nations Convention on the Recognition and Enforcement of Foreign Arbitral Awards, 10 Jun. 1958, 21 U.S.T. 2517, 330 U.N.T.S. 3 (hereinafter 'NYC'). *See* further generally Warren and Croft, *supra* n. 4 at 41.
6. Consensus-based forms of dispute resolution rely on the parties to identify and agree to the terms of the final settlement agreement, either with the assistance of a neutral third-party facilitator (as in mediation and conciliation) or without such an individual (as in negotiation). Although some commentators distinguish between mediation and conciliation, most people have concluded the two terms are basically synonymous. That is the approach that was adopted by UNCITRAL in the Singapore Convention on Mediation and that will be adopted herein: UN Comm. on Int'l Trade Law, Report of the UN Comm. on Int'l Trade Law, Fifty-first Session, UN Doc. A/73/17 (2018) at Annex I, Article 2(3) (hereinafter 'Singapore Convention').
7. *Ibid.*

opening day ceremony in Singapore.[8] Just over one year later, on 12 September 2020, the treaty went into force following ratifications by Singapore, Fiji and Qatar.[9]

Although the Singapore Convention on Mediation was met with a great deal of initial fanfare, it is unclear what effect the instrument will actually have on the use of mediation in the cross-border commercial context. This chapter, therefore, considers whether and to what extent international mediation will be promoted through the Singapore Convention on Mediation, focusing on several issues that have seldom been addressed in the legal literature. In so doing, the discussion does not parse through the individual provisions of the convention itself, since other commentators have already provided those types of analyses.[10]

The chapter begins with a brief outline of the goals of the Singapore Convention on Mediation (section 14.02), followed by a DSD analysis to determine the future efficacy of the convention (section 14.03). The chapter then describes certain structural issues that could create problems going forward (section 14.04) before identifying potential solutions to those concerns (section 14.05). The final substantive section focuses on the effect that various non-legal forces might have on the development of international commercial mediation (section 14.06). The chapter concludes with several forward-looking observations (section 14.07).

§14.02 MEASURING 'SUCCESS': GOALS OF THE SINGAPORE CONVENTION ON MEDIATION

There are a variety of ways to evaluate the success of a legal instrument like the Singapore Convention on Mediation. For example, success could be associated with an increase in the number of mediation agreements signed by international commercial actors or an increase in the number of mediations actually conducted in international commercial settings. Alternatively, success could be associated with a reduction in the amount of time or money it takes to enforce settlement agreements in the cross-border context. These and other measures can and should be studied in the coming years. However, such analyses require not only an empirical baseline to be established but also the passage of a sufficient amount of time in which to measure change. As a result, this chapter ties the success of the Singapore Convention on Mediation to the goals

8. Timothy Schnabel, *The Singapore Convention on Mediation: A Framework for the Cross-Border Recognition and Enforcement of Mediated Settlements*, 19 Pepp. Disp. Resol. L.J. 1, 8 (2019) (hereinafter 'Schnabel, *Convention*').
9. *Status, Singapore Convention on Mediation*, https://treaties.un.org/pages/ViewDetails.aspx?src=TREATY&mtdsg_no=XXII-4&chapter=22&clang=_en (listing 52 signatories as of 2 May 2020).
10. For example, Nadja Alexander & Shouyu Chong, *The Singapore Convention on Mediation: A Commentary* (Wolters Kluwer 2019); Eunice Chua, *The Singapore Convention on Mediation: A Brighter Future for Asian Dispute Resolution*, 9 Asian J. Disp. Resol. 195, 209 (2019); Schnabel, *Convention*, *supra* n. 8, at 14-59; Edna Sussman, *The Singapore Convention: Promoting the Enforcement and Recognition of International Mediated Settlement Agreements*, 42 ICC Bull. (2018).

enunciated in the initial proposal for this treaty.[11] According to that document, 'a multilateral convention on the enforceability of international commercial settlement agreements reached through conciliation' was needed in order to 'encourag[e] conciliation in the same way that the NYC facilitated the growth of arbitration'.[12] Thus, this analysis focuses on comparisons between the Singapore Convention on Mediation and the NYC.

Empirical studies conducted prior to the adoption of the Singapore Convention on Mediation indicated that, at that time, mediation was used relatively infrequently in cross-border business disputes, as compared to other mechanisms.[13] While these findings provide a useful baseline from which to measure future progress in the area of international commercial mediation, they do not provide any information about causation.[14] Indeed, while the empirical findings might seem to suggest that international commercial mediation was a relatively new or underdeveloped phenomenon prior to the signing of the Singapore Convention on Mediation, mediation and conciliation were, in fact, the preferred means of resolving international commercial conflicts in the first half of the twentieth century.[15] It was only after World War II that arbitration became the predominant mode of addressing cross-border business disputes.[16] While the shift may have been due to a number of contributing factors, one major reason was the doubtless the ability of the 1958 NYC to provide easy enforcement of arbitration agreements and arbitral awards in cross-border commercial matters.[17]

When considered from a law and economics perspective, it is clear that the NYC's ability to facilitate easy and predictable enforcement of arbitral awards acted as a 'nudge' in favour of arbitration since neither litigation nor mediation offered an equally efficient enforcement regime.[18] Indeed, the proposal for the Singapore Convention on Mediation explicitly noted that '[o]ne obstacle to greater use of conciliation ... is that

11. Proposal by the Government of the United States: Future Work for Working Group II, UN Doc. A/CN.9/822, at 3 (2 Jun. 2014) (hereinafter 'US Proposal').
12. *Ibid.*
13. Chua, *supra* n. 10, at 204; Kim M. Rooney, *Conciliation and Mediation of International Commercial Disputes in Asia and UNCITRAL'S Working Group on the International Enforcement of Settlement Agreements*, 18 Asian Disp. Rev. 195, 197-8 (2016); Strong, *Empirical, supra* n. 2, at 2023.
14. Empirical researchers must be careful not to extrapolate beyond the boundaries of the data. Lee Epstein & Gary King, *The Rules of Inference*, 51 U. Chi. L. Rev. 1, 9-10 (2002).
15. Eric A. Schwartz, *International Conciliation and the ICC*, 10 ICSID Rev.-Foreign Investment L.J. 98, 99 (1995).
16. Linda C. Reif, *Conciliation as a Mechanism for the Resolution of International Economic and Business Disputes*, 14 Fordham Int'l L.J. 578, 614-5 (1991); Schwartz, *supra* n. 15, at 107.
17. Lucy Reed, *Ultima Thule: Prospects for International Commercial Mediation* 21 (18 Jan. 2019), NUS Centre for International Law Research Paper No. 19/03, https://ssrn.com/abstract=3339788 or http://dx.doi.org/10.2139/ssrn.3339788; S.I. Strong, *Beyond International Commercial Arbitration? The Promise of International Commercial Mediation*, 45 Wash. U. J. L. & Pol'y 11, 38 (2014) (hereinafter 'Strong, *Promise*').
18. Richard H. Thaler & Cass R. Sunstein, *Nudge: Improving Decisions About Health, Wealth, and Happiness* 6 (Yale University Press 2008). In 2019, this phenomenon changed for both mediation and litigation. *See supra* n. 4. 'Nudges' can be defined as 'interventions that maintain freedom of choice, that do not impose mandates or bans, but that nonetheless incline people's choices in a particular direction'. Cass R. Sunstein, *Deciding by Default*, 162 U. Pa. L. Rev. 1, 5 (2013).

settlement agreements reached through conciliation may be more difficult to enforce than arbitral awards, if a party that agrees to a settlement later fails to comply'.[19] The Singapore Convention on Mediation was, therefore, intended to level the playing field as between arbitration and mediation by providing an equally quick and inexpensive means of enforcing settlement agreements arising out of international commercial mediation.[20]

In so doing, the drafters of the Singapore Convention on Mediation did not seek to give preferential treatment to mediation but instead merely intended to eliminate one of the primary discrepancies between international commercial mediation and international commercial arbitration.[21] The question, therefore, is whether a change in the enforceability of mediated settlement agreements will have the desired effect on the use of mediation in international commercial settings. The answer may be discovered through a DSD analysis.

§14.03 DSD AND THE SINGAPORE CONVENTION

DSD 'is not a dispute resolution methodology itself' but instead reflects 'the intentional and systematic creation of an effective, efficient, and fair dispute resolution process based upon the unique needs of a particular system'.[22] DSD has been used to understand the historical evolution of particular dispute systems; to evaluate the operation of existing disputes systems; and to design or redesign dispute systems.[23] A full DSD analysis includes four stages: '(1) taking design initiative, (2) assessing or diagnosing the current situation, (3) creating systems and processes, and (4) implementing the design, including evaluation and process or system modification'.[24] Notably, this final step - implementation - is iterative in nature, requiring periodic revaluation of the system to determine whether and to what extent it is meeting the goals identified by the designers.[25]

DSD has been a fundamental part of the Singapore Convention on Mediation from its inception.[26] Indeed, the United States (US) Government's proposal for a new convention in the area of international commercial mediation was triggered by a 2014 law review article that consciously undertook a DSD analysis to understand why

19. US Proposal, *supra* n. 11, at 2.
20. Alexander & Chong, *supra* n. 10, at 7-11.
21. Strong, *Promise, supra* n. 17, at 28.
22. Susan D. Franck, *Integrating Investment Treaty Conflict and Dispute Systems Design*, 92 Minn. L. Rev. 161, 177-8 (2007); *see also* Nancy H. Rogers et al., *Designing Systems and Processes for Managing Disputes* 4-5 (2d ed. Wolters Kluwer 2018).
23. Stephanie Smith & Janet Martinez, *An Analytic Framework for Dispute System Design*, 14 Harv. Negot. L. Rev. 123, 124 (2009).
24. Rogers et al., *supra* n. 22, at 16. Other commentators suggest a seven-step process, although the basic elements are relatively similar. Hallie Falder, *Designing the Forum to Fit the Fuss: Dispute System Design for the State Trial Courts*, 13 Harv. Negot. L. Rev. 481, 486-7 (2008).
25. Rogers et al., *supra* n. 22, at 16.
26. S.I. Strong, *Applying the Lessons of International Commercial Arbitration to International Commercial Mediation: A Dispute System Design Analysis*, in *Mediation in International Commercial and Investment Disputes* 39, 39-60 (Catharine Titi & Katia Fach Gómez eds., Oxford University Press 2019).

multinational businesses preferred arbitration over mediation, despite the various benefits associated with mediation.[27] That article not only provided a historical overview of the development and legal status of international commercial mediation in the twentieth and early twenty-first centuries but also compared the legal environment surrounding international commercial mediation to that of international commercial arbitration and international commercial litigation.[28] The text ultimately concluded that systemic reform of the legal framework surrounding international commercial mediation was necessary to eliminate invisible 'nudges' in favour of arbitration[29] and provided specific guidance on what a new international convention in the area of international commercial mediation should look like.[30] While the Singapore Convention on Mediation ultimately diverged from the suggestions contained in the article, the article nevertheless described how filling a gap in the legal environment surrounding international commercial mediation could effectively promote the use of mediation in the cross-border business context.[31] This rationale was subsequently reflected in the US proposal to the United Nations.[32]

The first three steps of the DSD process – taking the design initiative, assessing the current legal environment and creating a new system or feature – have now been completed for the Singapore Convention on Mediation.[33] The fourth stage of the process – implementation – is currently underway, as states work to ratify the convention and adopt national legislation intended to give domestic effect to that instrument.[34] However, the concept of implementation, from a DSD perspective, also involves an evaluation of the effectiveness of the new system or feature.[35] While this latter process is in some ways premature, given that the convention has only recently gone into effect, it may be useful to keep a watchful eye on certain structural issues in order to determine whether additional modifications to the design of the system will eventually need to be made.[36] This analysis is found in the following section.

27. Strong, *Promise*, *supra* n. 17, at 11. The article was presented to and discussed at a public meeting of the US State Department's Advisory Committee on Private International Law (ACPIL) in February 2014. Hal Abramson, *The New Singapore Mediation Convention: The Process and Key Choices*, 20 Cardozo J. of Conflict Resol. 1037, 1040 (2019); Schnabel, *Convention*, *supra* n. 8, at 4, n. 17.
28. Strong, *Promise*, *supra* n. 17, at 19-28.
29. *Ibid.*, 12-13, 31-2.
30. *Ibid.*, 16-32.
31. *Ibid.*, 29-38.
32. US Proposal, *supra* n. 11, at 2.
33. Rogers et al., *supra* n. 22, at 16; S.I. Strong, *The Role of Empirical Evidence and Dispute System Design in Proposing and Developing International Treaties: A Case Study of the Singapore Convention on Mediation*, 20 Cardozo J. on Conflict Resol. 1103 (2019) (hereinafter 'Strong, *Case Study*').
34. This is a lengthy and important task. For example, Timothy Schnabel, *Implementation of the Singapore Convention: Federalism, Self-Execution, and Private Law Treaties*, 30 Am. Rev. Int'l Arb. 265, 273-88 (2019) (hereinafter 'Schnabel, *Implementation*').
35. Rogers et al., *supra* n. 22, at 16.
36. It would also be useful to conduct a variety of empirical studies on international commercial mediation now to help establish a baseline that can be used to measure future progress on a variety of issues. These might include issues like the number of international commercial contracts that currently include mediation provisions or the length of time it currently takes for a settlement agreement arising out of international commercial mediation to be enforced.

§14.04 STRUCTURAL CONCERNS

As noted previously, this chapter does not undertake a detailed analysis of the individual provisions of the Singapore Convention on Mediation since other scholars have already conducted such studies.[37] Instead, it is sufficient for current purposes to note that the Singapore Convention on Mediation was intentionally modelled on the NYC, both in terms of its intended impact and as a matter of structure.[38] For example, both instruments include only a limited number of grounds upon which an objection to the enforcement of the final outcome of a proceeding can be based.[39] However, the Singapore Convention on Mediation diverges from the NYC in at least one important regard, namely with respect to the way the Singapore Convention on Mediation focuses exclusively on the back end of the mediation process (i.e., the settlement agreement) while the NYC addresses both the back end (i.e., the award) as well as the front end (i.e., the arbitration agreement) of the arbitral process.

This strategy is, in many ways, contrary to what might have been expected. At a conceptual and practical level, international commercial arbitration appears to have benefitted as much from provisions in the NYC relating to the easy enforcement of arbitration agreements as it has from provisions relating to the easy enforcement of arbitral awards, although the drafters of the NYC did not decide to add a provision facilitating enforcement of arbitration agreements until relatively late in the deliberation process.[40] Given the success of the dual-purpose model, the initial DSD analysis that triggered the US proposal for the Singapore Convention on Mediation strongly suggested the development of a mediation convention that, like the NYC, addressed both the front end of the mediation process (i.e., the initial agreement to mediate) as well as the back end of the process (i.e., the final settlement agreement).[41]

These suggestions were subsequently supported by empirical research presented to Working Group II of the United Nations Commission on International Trade Law (UNCITRAL), the body responsible for drafting the Singapore Convention on Mediation, early in the deliberation process.[42] The research in question involved a large-scale

However, but there are many other matters that could usefully be measured now, before the Convention comes into force on a widespread basis.

37. Alexander & Chong, *supra* n. 10; Chua, *supra* n. 10, at 209; Schnabel, *Convention, supra* n. 8, at 14-59; Sussman, *supra* n. 10, at 42.
38. Schnabel, *Convention, supra* n. 8, at 1.
39. NYC, *supra* n. 5, Article 5; Singapore Convention, *supra* n. 6, Article 5. Article 5 of the Singapore Convention on Mediation sets out three main categories of objections: one involving the disputing parties, another involving the settlement agreement and a third involving the mediation procedure itself. *Ibid.* The convention also allows courts to refuse to grant relief *sua sponte* on the grounds of public policy grounds or the fact that the subject matter of the dispute cannot be settled by mediation. *Ibid.*
40. NYC, *supra* n. 5, Articles II(1), V; Warren & Croft, *supra* n. 3.
41. Strong, *Promise, supra* n. 17, at 32.
42. S.I. Strong, *Use and Perception of International Commercial Mediation and Conciliation: A Preliminary Report of Issues Relating to the Proposed UNCITRAL Convention on International Commercial Mediation and Conciliation*, http://papers.ssrn.com/sol3/papers.cfm?abstract_id =2526302. The study was cited by the Secretariat and various governments in their submissions to Working Group II and discussed orally during the Working Group II meeting in February 2015. UN Secretariat, Settlement of Commercial Disputes: Enforceability of Settlement Agreements

international survey[43] that investigated behaviours and attitudes relating to international commercial mediation as well as various normative issues relevant to a possible convention involving international commercial mediation.[44] According to the data, enforcement of settlement agreements that had some type of international element was, or was perceived to be, significantly more difficult than enforcement of settlement agreements that were entirely domestic.[45] This data was useful from a DSD perspective because it justified a back-end convention like the Singapore Convention on Mediation. However, the data also showed that enforcement of mediation agreements that had some type of international element was, or was perceived to be, significantly more difficult than enforcement of mediation agreements that were entirely domestic.[46] This information suggested an equal need for international action addressing the front end of the mediation process.[47]

Respondents were also asked to indicate whether they thought an international instrument on international commercial mediation would encourage the use of mediation in cross-border business disputes, and if so, what type of instrument. According to the study, 68% of the respondents believed that a convention addressing mediation agreements would encourage mediation within their home jurisdictions, with an additional 20% indicating that such an instrument might be useful.[48] A slightly higher percentage of respondents – 74% – believed that an international instrument dealing with the back end of the mediation process would encourage mediation in their jurisdiction, with an additional 18% indicating that such an instrument might be useful.[49] While these results may initially appear to justify UNCITRAL's decision to focus on the back end of the process, no statistical studies were run on the data, so it is unknown whether the difference in percentages (68% versus 74%) is significant.

The respondents were then asked whether they thought international action in this field should proceed on a single-subject basis (i.e., either relating only to mediation

Resulting From International Commercial Conciliation/Mediation – Revision of UNCITRAL Notes on Organizing Arbitral Proceedings, Comments Received from States, Note by the Secretariat, UN Doc. A/CN.9/WG.II/WP.188 at 6 n. 7 (23 Dec. 2014); Note by UNCITRAL Secretariat, Settlement of Commercial Disputes: Enforceability of Settlement Agreements Resulting From International Commercial Conciliation/Mediation, UN Doc. A/CN.9/WG.II/WP. 187, at 6 n. 16 (27 Nov. 2014); UNCITRAL, Working Group II, Sound Recordings of Meetings, http://www.uncitral.org/uncitral/en/commission/working_groups/2Arbitration.html; Schnabel, *Convention, supra* n. 8, at 4, n. 17. The final version of the study was subsequently published in the *Washington and Lee Law Review*. Strong, Empirical, *supra* n. 2, at 1973.

43. Strong, *Empirical, supra* n. 2, at 2017, 2019-20. The study generated responses from 221 participants in 51 countries and included private practitioners and neutrals (arbitrators, mediators, conciliators and judges) as well as those who worked as in-house counsel or in governmental or institutional settings, such as arbitral institutions. *Ibid.* (noting 15% of respondents came from the Asia-Pacific region).
44. *Ibid.*, 1998.
45. *Ibid.*, 2053-5.
46. *Ibid.*, 2050-1.
47. This conclusion was reinforced by data indicating that the vast majority of cross-border commercial mediations arise as a matter of contract rather than through other means. *Ibid.*, 2026.
48. *Ibid.*, 2051-2.
49. *Ibid.*, 2055-6. The open comments section of the survey also demonstrated the intensity of support for a convention in this area of law. *Ibid.*, 2061-3.

agreements or only to settlement agreements) or on a dual-subject basis (i.e., relating to both mediation agreements and settlement agreements), as is the case in arbitration.[50] Survey participants were overwhelmingly (75%) in favour of a dual-subject convention that addressed both the beginning and end of the mediation process.[51] However, of the respondents who preferred a single-subject convention, more supported an instrument focusing on settlement agreements (19%) rather than on mediation agreements (6%).[52]

Respondents were asked to describe, in their own words, why they favoured the approach they did. One principle that was repeated numerous times reflected the idea that:

> addressing both the beginning and the end of the mediation process would 'ensure effectiveness', 'give [international commercial mediation] more legitimacy', and 'encourage more general acceptance'. Thus, one respondent stated that if the proposed convention 'does not address both issues, its practical effectivity is doubtful'. This result would likely occur because, in the words of another participant, '[t]he enforceability of one without the other will fall short of providing the level of confidence needed for parties to embark in mediation or conciliation'.[53]

Given the amount of support for a dual-subject convention, it may seem odd that UNCITRAL nevertheless chose to focus exclusively on the back end of the mediation process. According to those involved in the deliberation process, the US only included settlement agreements in its initial proposal because of a desire to simplify the deliberation process.[54] The idea was that it was better to obtain agreement on a more limited instrument rather than fail to reach agreement on a more ambitious project. That strategy appeared wise, given that the proposal almost stalled in the first days of deliberation,[55] but the question nevertheless arises whether adopting a single-subject instrument will achieve the goals identified by proponents of the convention.

Looking forward, two outcomes appear possible. On the one hand, the absence of a front-end enforcement mechanism in the Singapore Convention on Mediation may preclude the type of full flourishing of mediation that proponents of the instrument hoped for. This is the result anticipated by commentators who believe that the absence of provisions allowing the easy enforcement of mediation agreements could lead to diminished use as well as diminished usefulness of the instrument because parties would not have sufficient confidence in the mediation process overall.[56] On the other hand, the convention may lead to an increase in the use of mediation in the

50. *Ibid.*, 2056-7.
51. *Ibid.*, 2057.
52. *Ibid.*, 2057.
53. *Ibid.*, 2058.
54. US Proposal, *supra* n. 11, at 3; Alexander & Chong, *supra* n. 10, at 17-18.
55. Schnabel, *Convention, supra* n. 8, at 5.
56. Alexander & Chong, *supra* n. 10, at 17-18; Maryam Salehijam, *The Role of the New York Convention in Remedying the Pitfalls of Multi-Tiered Dispute Resolution Clauses*, in *60 Years of the New York Convention: Key Issues and Future Challenges* 35, 40, 51-2 (Katia Fach Gómez & Ana M. Lopez-Rodriguez eds., Wolters Kluwer 2019); *see also* Lars Kirchoff, *Constructive Interventions: Paradigms, Process and Practice of International Mediation* 285 (Wolters Kluwer

international commercial arena despite the absence of a provision on mediation agreements,[57] partially as a result of the convention and partially as a result of other 'nudges', such as those promoting mediation as a matter of domestic law[58] and as a matter of international investment law.[59] However, the expanded use of mediation would likely generate increased litigation about potential breaches of mediation agreements[60] since the vast majority of mediations in the international commercial realm arise as a matter of contract rather than through other means.[61]

Interestingly, both scenarios would appear to benefit from a parallel instrument that addresses mediation agreements. While such an initiative would be welcomed by many individuals and institutions, little if anything is known or written about how national and international actors decide to develop and pursue particular proposals for new international instruments.[62] Indeed, the initial process of determining which ideas to develop is almost entirely hidden from public view, even though the decisions are critical to international law and policy, 'since whoever controls the agenda has control over the scope of the governance system and its ability to change over time'.[63] As a result, it is useful to discuss how DSD might help generate useful solutions going forward. Those matters are addressed in the next section.

2008); Carrie Menkel-Meadow, *The Future of Mediation Worldwide: Legal and Cultural Variations in the Uptake of or Resistance to Mediation*, in *Essays on Mediation: Dealing With Disputes in the 21st Century* 21, 30, 36 (Ian Macduff ed., Wolters Kluwer 2016).

57. The concept of 'increased use' might be reflected in more actual mediations and/or more mediation agreements, either on their own or as part of multi-tiered dispute resolution provisions (step clauses).
58. Somewhat unusually, UNCITRAL revised the 2002 Model Law on International Commercial Conciliation (now referred to as the 2018 Model Law on International Commercial Mediation and Settlement Agreements Resulting From Mediation) at the same time it drafted the drafting of the Singapore Convention on Mediation. Schnabel, *Convention, supra* n. 8, at 7; *see also* UNICTRAL Model Law on International Commercial Mediation and Settlement Agreements Resulting From Mediation, https://uncitral.un.org/en/texts/mediation/modellaw/commercial_conciliation. A number of countries in the Asia-Pacific region have adopted some form of the 2002 model law, including Malaysia in 2011 and Bhutan in 2015. Shahla Ali, *Forming Transnational Dispute Settlement Norms: Soft Law and The Role of UNCITRAL's Regional Centre for Asia and the Pacific* (Edward Elgar 2021). Other regions within Asia have been influenced by the rules, including Hong Kong, Singapore, Japan and to some extent mainland China. *Ibid.*, 77.
59. At least one investment treaty has recently required foreign investors to mediate if requested by the host state prior to proceeding to arbitration. Indonesia-Australia Comprehensive Economic Partnership Agreement (2019) (hereinafter 'IA-CEPA'), https://www.dfat.gov.au/trade/agreements/not-yet-in-force/iacepa/iacepa-text/Pages/default; *see also* Ubilava & Nottage, Chapter 5 in this volume. The Singapore Convention on Mediation might be extended to address at least some investment disputes, such as those involving construction or natural resource extraction. Schnabel, *Convention, supra* n. 8, at 22-3 (offering the view of one of the primary drafters of the Singapore Convention on Mediation). However, the primary focus of the Convention is on commercial disputes. *Ibid.*
60. Strong, *Promise, supra* n. 17, at 32-4.
61. Strong, *Empirical, supra* n. 2, at 2026.
62. Ian Brownlie, *Principles of Public International Law* 609-11 (7th ed. Oxford University Press 2008).
63. Eric B. Bluemel, *Overcoming NGO Accountability Concerns in International Governance*, 31 Brook. J. Int'l L. 139, 162 (2005) (noting that '[s]elf-interest may dominate such agenda-setting formulations, as actors with an interest in the status quo may reject change through the formulation of the agenda').

§14.05 POTENTIAL SOLUTIONS TO STRUCTURAL CONCERNS

The best, if not the only, real solution to structural concerns involving the Singapore Convention on Mediation involves the creation of a parallel instrument facilitating the enforcement of mediation agreements.[64] However, development and adoption of an international convention is not a simple endeavour since proponents of such an endeavour must not only comply with best practices in DSD but must also cultivate connections with individuals and institutions with the skills, knowledge and desire to take and sustain a design initiative.[65] Because international lawmaking is, for the most part, a state-centric process,[66] prospective reformers are, therefore, advised to find a way to connect with representatives in their national governments who can and will champion the idea both within the relevant organization and with external audiences.[67]

The experience of the Singapore Convention on Mediation demonstrates how such access can be gained. First, prospective dispute system designers can offer their assistance directly to their national governments, as occurred when the author of the 2014 law review article that ultimately led to the Singapore Convention on Mediation presented the idea for a new instrument at a meeting of the US State Department's Advisory Committee on Private International Law (ACPIL).[68] Individuals who are based in the US are fortunate in that Federal Advisory Committee Act requires the State Department to establish Advisory Committees in a number of different fields, thereby providing interested individuals with the means of connecting with first-level decision makers.[69] However, there is no guarantee that the State Department will adopt any particular proposal. Indeed, some ideas languish for years without any forward

64. Strong, *Promise, supra* n. 17, at 32-4 (providing suggestions on the shape of such an instrument).
65. Rogers et al., *supra* n. 22, at 60-1.
66. Cedric Ryngaert, *Non-State Actors: Carving Out a Space in a State-Centered International Legal System*, 63 Neth. Int'l L. Rev. 183, §§1, 6 (2016).
67. S.I. Strong, *Clash of Cultures: Epistemic Communities, Negotiation Theory, and International Lawmaking*, 50 Akron L. Rev. 495, 508-9 (2017) (hereinafter 'Strong, *Epistemic Communities*') (discussing internal and external audiences in the international lawmaking process). It can be useful to find support within the hierarchical line of authority in a decision-making institution, as shown by the experience with the Singapore Convention on mediation. Schnabel, *Implementation, supra* n. 34, at 265 n. * (noting the role that John Kim, then Assistant Legal Adviser for Private International Law, played in the proposal process).
68. Abramson, *supra* n. 27, at 1040; Schnabel, *Convention, supra* n. 8, at 4; Strong, *Case Study, supra* n. 33, at 1107, 1115.
69. FACA Database, https://www.facadatabase.gov/FACA/FACAPublicPage (last visited 20 Dec. 2019). ACPIL and other State Department Advisory Committees not only allow the State Department to gauge stakeholder support for various international initiatives but also to obtain ideas from the public about areas where law reform is necessary or useful. Notice of public meetings of these groups is provided through the US Federal Register. For example, 82 Fed. Reg. 43068-01 (13 Sep. 2017) (giving notice of a meeting to discuss upcoming work at UNCITRAL involving arbitration and mediation); 81 Fed. Reg. 72639-01 (20 Oct. 2016) (giving notice of a meeting to discuss ongoing projects involving private international law); 81 Fed. Reg. 50591-01 (1 Aug. 2016) (giving notice of a meeting to discuss the work of UNCITRAL on international settlement agreements); 80 Fed. Reg. 51864-01 (26 Aug. 2015) (giving notice of a meeting to discuss ongoing projects involving private international law, including those involving mediation and conciliation); 79 Fed. Reg. 60229-01 (6 Oct. 2014) (providing notice of a meeting to discuss ongoing projects at UNCITRAL); 79 Fed. Reg. 38642-01 (8 Jul. 2014) (providing notice of

movement, thereby underscoring the need to conduct proper research and analysis (optimally a full DSD analysis) before presenting a proposal to the relevant decision makers.[70]

The US is not the only country with a public consultation process. Other nations, including those in the Asia-Pacific region, have adopted similar mechanisms to allow interested individuals and organizations to provide input on proposed actions. For example, Australia engages in public consultations in a number of fields, including matters governed by the Department of Foreign Affairs and Trade.[71]

While a number of countries have adopted public consultation processes, not all of the procedures are the same. For example, although ACPIL appears open to receiving new ideas for international initiatives from members of the public, other advisory committees in both the US and elsewhere limit the type of assistance that is sought.[72] Canada's Department of Justice is an example of the latter approach, noting in its Policy Statement and Guidelines for Public Participation that:

> [r]ather than a broad commitment to public participation on every issue, the Policy Statement supports participation activities only where the issues and timelines are such that public input will make a contribution to the policy development process. ... Determining the policy areas that will include a public participation component is the responsibility of the appropriate departmental authority.[73]

While these types of restrictions undoubtedly appear reasonable from the perspective of a government agency seeking to streamline its operations and focus on its own policy priorities, mechanisms that limit the ability of individuals and groups to propose new projects involving international law can pose problems as a matter of both practice and principle. Indeed, one commentator has argued that recent initiatives regarding transparency and public consultations in international law have done little to increase the diversity of voices in the realm of international lawmaking.[74] Fortunately, individuals seeking to take the design initiative have other ways of conveying their ideas and research to the appropriate authorities.

---

a meeting to discuss the US proposal to UNCITRAL prior to the UNCITRAL Working Group II meeting); Strong, *Case Study*, *supra* n. 33, at 1115.

70. Strong, *Case Study*, *supra* n. 33, at 1115.
71. Business Consultation, Australian Government, https://consultation.business.gov.au/Consultation/Common/Search/ConsultationAdvancedSearch.aspx. In recent years, in addition to issue-specific public and private consultations, the Department's Trade and Investment Law Branch has invited experts from various groups (including non-governmental organizations) to participate in twice-yearly 'outreach event' workshops aimed at providing an update on the government's current activities and thinking as well as hearing suggestions for future work. International law experts from the federal Attorney General's Department are involved in these events as well.
72. Strong, *Case Study*, *supra* n. 33, at 1116.
73. Policy Statement and Guidelines for Public Participation – Department of Justice, Government of Canada, https://www.justice.gc.ca/eng/cons/pol.html.
74. Diane Desierto, *Are 'Transparency' Procedures and Local Community 'Consultations' Enough? A Human Rights 'Feedback Loop' to International Economic Law Reforms of 2018*, EJIL: Talk! (12 Dec. 2018), https://www.ejiltalk.org/are-transparency-procedures-and-local-community-consultations-enough-a-human-rights-postscript-to-2018-reforms-in-international-economic-law/.

One way that individuals interested in helping the international lawmaking process can become engaged is through direct communications with supranational organizations responsible for promulgating international law. Perhaps the most forward-looking body in this regard is the European Union, which has created the European Citizens' Initiative (ECI) to provide 'a unique and innovative way for citizens to shape Europe by calling on the European Commission to make a legislative proposal'.[75] Although this initiative has a number of problems, most notably with respect to the level of discretion exercised by the Commission in deciding whether to pursue a citizen proposal, the ECI at least provides people with no formal connection to government agencies with an opportunity to shape international law.[76]

The European Union has also created the Civil Society Dialogue, which operates as part of the European Commission Directorate General (DG) for Trade.[77] This initiative is slightly more bureaucratic in that it involves representatives from various stakeholder groups engaging in discussions with DG Trade officials rather than individual citizens participating directly with the officials, but it still facilitates the transmission of ideas about new international instruments to the relevant decision makers.[78]

Another model is seen at UNCITRAL, which occasionally issues open calls for interested individuals and organizations to engage in discussions about possible future works.[79] However, this type of direct communication is relatively infrequent.[80] Instead, UNCITRAL, like many other UN and international bodies, typically obtains the views of non-state-affiliated individuals and groups through recognized NGOs.[81] While this process is meant to foster transparency and public participation in the international lawmaking process, there can be significant discrepancies in how and when NGOs can

75. Official Register, The European Citizens' Initiative, http://ec.europa.eu/citizens-initiative/public/welcome (noting that the process is initiated through a petition with one million signatures).
76. Nikos Vogiatzis, *Between Discretion and Control: Reflections on the Institutional Position of the Commission Within the European Citizens' Initiative Process*, 23 Eur. L.J. 250, 250-1 (2017).
77. European Commission, Objectives, Civil Society Dialogue, https://trade.ec.europa.eu/civilsoc/csd_proc.cfm.
78. *Ibid.* In 2020, the European Commission initiated a study to determine how well the Civil Society Dialogue was operating, which complies with best practices in DSD. Consultations, European Commission, https://trade.ec.europa.eu/doclib/press/index.cfm?id=2134.
79. For example, Events, UNCITRAL, https://uncitral.un.org/en/events/25-26.03.2019 (advertising an open public meeting for 'experts from governments, private sector, academic and the non-profit sector' to assist UNCITRAL Working Group I on Micro, Small and Medium-sized Enterprises (MSMEs) regarding possible work involving multiparty contracts).
80. FAQ – Methods of Work, UNCITRAL, http://www.uncitral.org/uncitral/en/about/methods_faq.html (discussing whether individuals can take part in UNCITRAL and Working Group sessions). However, such interactions may be on the rise. UN Comm. on Int'l Trade Law, Report of the UN Comm. on Int'l Trade Law, Forty-third session, UN Doc. A/65/17 (2010) at Annex III, paras 11, 15 (hereinafter 'UNCITRAL Working Procedures') (encouraging increased contact between the Secretariat and outside experts, including through the convening of colloquia).
81. *A Guide to UNCITRAL: Basic Facts About the United Nations International Trade Commission* 8 (2013) (hereinafter 'UNCITRAL Guide'), http://www.uncitral.org/pdf/english/texts/general/12-57491-Guide-to-UNCITRAL-e.pdf; Strong, *Epistemic Communities*, *supra* n. 67, at 507.

participate in international discourse.[82] For example, NGOs may be allowed to observe proceedings freely but may be limited with respect to the extent to which they can contribute to floor debate, provide materials for the consideration of delegates and/or propose new initiatives.[83] This latter feature is particularly important since, as previously noted, the ability to control the agenda of a particular group or meeting has a significant impact on the lawmaking process.[84]

While some differences in the treatment of NGOs and other groups can be found in the rules of procedure governing the relevant body, other protocols are less transparent since they may rely on unwritten discretionary norms, such as the personal preferences of the chair of the group in question.[85] Although UNCITRAL has tried to minimize these types of differences by instituting a standardized work process for chairs to follow, discretion is, of course, necessary when managing complex multilateral deliberations.[86] However, the lack of transparency can be problematic, particularly for those who are new to the system. Indeed, the effectiveness of new and diverse voices in international lawmaking can be severely hindered in a variety of ways. The first involves well-known disparities regarding funding, sophistication and institutional knowledge.[87] The second involves a more subtle but equally pervasive phenomenon known as the status quo bias, which is discussed in the following section.

---

82. Alexander Gillespie, *Transparency in International Environmental Law: A Case Study of the International Whaling Commission*, 14 Geo. Int'l Environ. L. Rev. 333, 337 (2001). Some of the most detailed guidance on NGO participation at the UN is found in a 1996 document adopted by the Economic and Social Council (ECOSOC), which gives effect to Article 71 of the United Nations Charter regarding NGO participation in international lawmaking at the United Nations. ECOSOC Res. 996/31, Consultative Relationship Between The United Nations And Non-Governmental Organizations, 49th plen. mtg. (25 Jul. 1996); *see also* UN Charter, Article 71 (giving NGOs status in ECOSOC); Note by the Secretariat, UNCITRAL Rules of Procedure and Methods of Work, UN Doc. A/CN.9/638/Add.5 (2007) at 12 (hereinafter 'UNCITRAL Methods of Work') (discussing the rights of observers).
83. UNCITRAL Guide, *supra* n. 81, at 1, 8, 11-12; UNCITRAL Working Procedures, *supra* n. 80, at Annex III (outlining the working methods of UNCITRAL); UNCITRAL Methods of Work, *supra* n. 82, at 11-18; Gillespie, *supra* n. 82, at 337, 339-40. At UNCITRAL and particularly Working Group II, the norm has been to allow NGOs to contribute in the debate concurrently with state delegates. However, there is no way to know how the chair prioritizes interventions that are pending since he or she has broad discretion to decide how to control the course of discussion. Note by the Secretariat, UNCITRAL Rules of Procedure and Methods of Work, UN Doc. A/CN.9/638/Add.3 (2007) at 2-3 (hereinafter 'UNCITRAL Presiding Officer'). Furthermore, NGOs at UNCITRAL do not appear able to independently propose new work projects. UNCITRAL Working Procedures, *supra* n. 80, at Annex III, paras 5, 7.
84. Bluemel, *supra* n. 63, at 162.
85. Potentially significant variations arise across different fields of substantive expertise. For example, Karsten Nowrot, *Legal Consequences of Globalization: The Status of Non-Governmental Organizations Under International Law*, 6 Ind. J. Global Legal Stud. 579, 591-2 (1999); Strong, *Case Study*, *supra* n. 33, at 1118.
86. UNCITRAL Presiding Officer, *supra* n. 83, at 3-6 (discussing the duties of the presiding officer).
87. Melissa J. Durkee, *The Business of Treaties*, 63 UCLA L. Rev. 264, 267-8 (2016) (noting that businesses can experience a marked advantage over other groups in terms of access to and influence over the international lawmaking process); Genevieve Tung, *International Trade Law and Information Policy*, 42 Int'l J. Legal Info. 241, 251-2 (2014) (noting the US Trade Act of 1974 gave corporate NGOs a preferential role in advising on international treaties). The persuasiveness of a particular NGO can also vary depending on the field of endeavour (since some issues may be considered more suitable for NGO participation than others) or on the reputation of the

§14.06 EFFECT OF NON-LEGAL FORCES ON THE DEVELOPMENT OF INTERNATIONAL COMMERCIAL MEDIATION

Lawyers are often most comfortable analysing legal phenomena, such as those relating to structural defects in international instruments or problems associated with the development of new conventions. However, the biggest challenge to the development of mediation in the cross-border commercial context may arise not as a matter of law and policy but instead as a result of certain non-legal forces, most notably a psychological phenomenon known as the status quo bias.

Empirical researchers have defined the status quo bias as an emotional preference for the established legal or social norm, regardless of the rationality of that preference.[88] In most cases, litigation is considered the status quo in dispute resolution, but the 'nudge' created by the NYC may have created a new status quo – arbitration – in the international commercial setting.[89] In either event, mediation is viewed as the newcomer to the field and, therefore, may be viewed more critically than would be appropriate under a purely rational analysis.

Because the status quo bias is largely unconscious, it can be very difficult to overcome. The first step is for people to recognize that they may be operating under this type of cognitive distortion. A heuristic known as the 'Reversal Test' can help individuals appreciate whether and to what extent their thinking is affected by the status quo bias.[90]

Psychologists have suggested that there is little that can be done to offset the pull of the status quo beyond calling on decision makers to be even-handed in weighing up the available options.[91] However, law and policymakers may be able to neutralize some or all of the weight of the status quo bias through the strategic use of nudges.[92]

Perhaps the strongest type of nudge involves the creation of a legal default.[93] Long before the concept of nudges became popular, law and economics scholars recognized that legal defaults affect rational decision-making by increasing the attractiveness of the established norm at both a psychological and economic level.[94] At this

---

NGO itself, in that those organizations that have relevant technical expertise and that demonstrate unbiased analysis will likely be more influential than those that appear largely or entirely self-interested. UNCITRAL Guide, *supra* n. 81, at 11; Strong, *Epistemic Communities*, *supra* n. 67, at 507.

88. Nick Bostrom & Toby Ord, *The Reversal Test: Eliminating Status Quo Bias in Applied Ethics*, 116 Ethics 656, 660 (July 2006); Robert A. Prentice & Jonathan J. Koehler, *A Normality Bias in Decision Making*, 88 Cornell L. Rev. 583, 597 (2003).
89. S.I. Strong, *Truth in a Post-Truth Society: How Sticky Defaults, Status Quo Bias and the Sovereign Prerogative Influence the Perceived Legitimacy of International Arbitration*, 2018 U. Ill. L. Rev. 533, 564 (hereinafter 'Strong, *Status Quo Bias*').
90. *Ibid.*, 576-8.
91. William Samuelson & Richard Zeckhauser, *Status Quo Bias in Decision Making*, 1 J. Risk & Uncertainty 7, 9 (1988).
92. Sunstein, *supra* n. 18, at 5 (defining nudges); Thaler & Sunstein, *supra* n. 18, at 6 (same).
93. Sunstein, *supra* n. 18, at 5 (2013) (noting that 'default rules, even or perhaps especially if they appear to be invisible, count as prime "nudges"').
94. Russell Korobkin, *The Status Quo Bias and Contract Default Rules*, 83 Cornell L. Rev. 608, 612 (1998). Parties are often unwilling to incur the transaction costs associated with contracting around legal defaults.

point, the default mechanism for dispute resolution is clearly litigation.[95] However, the pull of the default in the cross-border commercial context is offset to a large degree by the NYC, which imposes a significant 'nudge' in favour of arbitration by offering certain benefits (such as a fast, predictable and relatively inexpensive means of enforcing arbitration agreements and arbitral awards) to actors in that particular market.[96]

Notably, the Singapore Convention on Mediation - like the NYC - does not seek to change the dispute resolution default norm in international commercial matters. However, the process of offering an additional benefit to parties in international commercial mediations (i.e., easy enforceability of settlement agreements) may help the Singapore Convention on Mediation offset the pull of the litigation default.[97]

As useful as this technique may be, it may not be enough. However, countries that are inclined to increase the use of mediation in cross-border business disputes can adopt other types of nudges that can visibly or invisibly move popular beliefs and behaviours regarding this particular mechanism. For example, some countries have 'nudged' their residents toward mediation in the domestic realm by requiring parties to pursue mediation either prior to filing a claim or prior to trial.[98] Additional nudges could arise at the international level, either by explicitly requiring mediation as a precondition to investment arbitration[99] or by increasing the use of mediation in interstate disputes.[100] While these techniques would not change litigation's status as the legal default or affect the structural defects of the Singapore Convention on Mediation, they might perhaps minimize the influence of the status quo bias by normalizing mediation as part of the dispute resolution process.[101]

§14.07 CONCLUSION

The unprecedented number of initial signatories to the Singapore Convention on Mediation would seem to suggest similarly unqualified success for mediation now that

95. Strong, *Promise*, *supra* n. 17, at 28; Strong, *Status Quo Bias*, *supra* n. 89, at 564-6.
96. *Strong, Promise, supra n. 17, at 28; Strong, Status Quo Bias, supra n. 89, at 564-66.*
97. While states have promulgated various international instruments that are meant to minimize the differences between litigation and other dispute resolution mechanisms (such as arbitration and mediation) in the international commercial realm, those initiatives have not been very successful to date. *See supra* n. 4.
98. Civil Procedure Act 2005 s. 26 (Australia); Civil Procedure Rules (England and Wales), Practice Direction - Pre-Action Conduct and Protocols, para. 8 (suggesting use of alternative dispute resolution prior to filing of an action in England and Wales); Sarah Konnerth, Note, *Pro Se, No Say?: The Impact of Presumptive Mediation in the New York State Court System on Self-Represented Litigants*, 88 Fordham L. Rev. 1365, 1382 (2019) (discussing a 2019 requirement in New York that all matters filed in state court will presumptively be sent to mediation); S.I. Strong, *Defining the Litigation Default*, 37 Civ. J. Q. 463, 467-8 (2018) (hereinafter 'Strong, *Default*') (discussing mediation in England and Wales).
99. IA-CEPA, *supra* n. 59; *see also* Ubilava & Nottage, *supra* n. 59.
100. Claxton, Nottage & Williams, Chapter 11 in this volume (proposing a solution to the trade and investment tensions between Japan and Korea that escalated in 2019).
101. Strong, *Default*, *supra* n. 98, at 467-8.

the instrument has come into force.[102] However, there is no guarantee that the convention will indeed promote mediation in the way that the drafters intended. As a result, proponents of international commercial mediation can and should do more to ensure the wide flourishing of mediation in this field.

First and foremost, individuals and institutions should seek to broaden the reach of the convention by encouraging states that have not yet signed and ratified the instrument to do so as soon as possible.[103] The Singapore Convention on Mediation can only achieve its goal of promoting and expanding the use of mediation 'in the same way that the NYC facilitated the growth of arbitration' if the instrument is in force in a significant number of countries.[104]

Next, proponents of international commercial mediation can try to offset the pull of the status quo bias by educating individuals about the existence and nature of these types of cognitive distortions and by seeking to normalize mediation within their legal systems. State actors can assist in this process by increasing the role that mediation plays in domestic forms of dispute resolution. While it is impossible to change litigation's status as the legal default, some of the distorted thinking that arises in this area of law and practice might be minimized or neutralized by various nudges. One type of nudge that has been discussed herein involves requirements to attempt mediation prior to initiating an action in court or prior to trial. While the private nature of arbitration precludes would make it difficult for governments to impose similar types of requirements in the arbitral process, arbitral institutions might amend their rule sets to reflect similar requirements in the future. Alternatively, arbitrators can encourage parties to engage in mediation in the early stages of a dispute, even in the absence of a formal requirement to do so.

Finally, the international community can consider the possibility of adopting a parallel convention addressing the enforceability of mediation agreements in the international commercial sphere. This type of initiative may be some years away, but steps can be taken now to assist in that process. For example, it would be useful for scholars to conduct empirical research on a variety of issues to provide a baseline for future comparisons and DSD analyses. Particular attention can and should be made to issues relating to the enforceability of mediation agreements since those appear to be an area of weakness in the existing legal regime.

As important as the Singapore Convention on Mediation may be in encouraging the use of mediation in cross-border business disputes, it is only a single instrument. If international commercial mediation is to flourish, individuals and institutions around the world must continue their efforts to educate, inform and implement change. Only then will the goals of drafters be met.

102. *See supra* nn. 7-8.
103. Schnabel, *Implementation*, *supra* n. 34, at 265.
104. US Proposal, *supra* n. 11, at 3.

CHAPTER 15

Expanding Asia-Pacific Frontiers for International Dispute Resolution: Conclusions and Recommendations

Nobumichi Teramura, Shahla Ali & Anselmo Reyes

Asia's emergence as a global economic powerhouse has corresponded with a prolonged upward trend in international commercial arbitration (ICA) cases involving Asian parties, as well as a belated expansion of investor-state dispute settlement (ISDS) arbitrations involving Asian states or investors. Further accelerating the eastward shift in international dispute resolution, various initiatives to improve support for ICA and ISDS have been taken, and alternatives (such as international commercial courts and international commercial mediation) have been promoted. This book aimed to examine significant 'new frontiers' for Asia-Pacific cross-border business dispute resolution, focusing on major economies in East and South Asia and countries (such as Australia) that are closely linked economically and geographically. The foregoing chapters have discussed this broad theme, focusing on developments in Australia, Japan, Hong Kong, China, India and Malaysia, while paying attention to broader regional initiatives (such as China's Belt and Road Initiative (BRI)) and recent international instruments (such as the Singapore Convention on Mediation (entering in force from 12 September 2020[1])). This concluding chapter highlights key findings in the individual chapters and identifies some challenges for the post-COVID-19 era.

§15.01 INTRODUCTION

Over the last fifty years, the Asia-Pacific region has experienced strong economic growth. As of 1970, the nominal gross domestic product (GDP) of the region was around USD 493 billion, about two-thirds of Europe's GDP (around USD 726 billion)

1. United Nations Convention on International Settlement Agreements Resulting from Mediation (New York, 2018).

and less than half of North America's GDP (around USD 1.7 trillion).[2] By 2018, the GDP of the Asia Pacific had reached USD 29.4 trillion, while that of Europe was around 16 trillion, in contrast to North America's GDP of USD 22.3 trillion.[3] The implication is that the Asia-Pacific region has surpassed Europe and North America on the economic scale. It is expected that this growth will continue, although possibly at a slower rate as a result of the COVID-19 pandemic.[4]

The economic expansion of the Asia Pacific is linked to its increasing share of global trade and investment. In Chapter 1, Nottage and Jetin demonstrated that such an increase has been underpinned by the regional development of global value chains (GVCs) and an increase of foreign direct investment (FDI). The increasing participation of 'Factory Asia' in GVC trade and the consequent FDI inflows have been among the main engines of the region's economic growth.[5] Although China has played a central role in the development of Asian GVCs, two recent shocks – the COVID-19 pandemic and trade tensions between China and the US – are likely to have lasting impacts on China's role among GVCs, as Chinese, American and Japanese multinational enterprises (MNEs) relocate plants from China to Vietnam and other Southeast Asian nations.[6] Accordingly, in the long term, the surge in Asian GVC trade is unlikely to abate overall, relocations largely taking place within Asia itself.

Asia's emergence as a global economic powerhouse has corresponded with a prolonged upward trend in ICA cases involving Asian parties, as well as a belated expansion of ISDS arbitrations involving Asian states or investors. Further accelerating

2. *See* https://data.worldbank.org/indicator/NY.GDP.MKTP.CD?locations=Z4-8S-Z7. The Asia-Pacific region consists of East Asia, South Asia and the Pacific.
3. *Ibid.*
4. Valentina Romei & John Reed, *The Asian Century Is Set to Begin: The Region Was the Envy of Europe in 17th Century and the World Is about to Turn Full Circle,* Financial Times (26 Mar. 2019), https://www.ft.com/content/520cb6f6-2958-11e9-a5ab-ff8ef2b976c7; Jonathan Woetzel & Jeongmin Seong, *We've Entered the Asian Century and There Is No Turning Back,* World Economic Forum (11 Oct. 2019), https://www.weforum.org/agenda/2019/10/has-world-entered-asian-century-what-does-it-mean/; Scott Foster, *COVID-19 Tilts the Future Toward Asia: Asia Returns to Work while America Struggles to Regain Its Footing in What Looks Like a Historical Tipping Point,* Asia Times (14 May 2020), https://asiatimes.com/2020/05/covid-19-tilts-the-future-toward-asia/.
5. Nottage & Jetin, Chapter 1 in this volume.
6. *Ibid*; Finbarr Bermingham, *China's Manufacturing Exodus Set to Continue in 2020, Despite Prospect of Trade War Deal,* South China Morning Post (9 Jan. 2020), https://www.scmp.com/economy/china-economy/article/3045141/chinas-manufacturing-exodus-set-continue-2020-despite; Bernama, *Chinese Firms Relocating to Malaysia Amid Trade War, Says Economist,* New Straits Times (5 Aug. 2019), https://www.nst.com.my/news/nation/2019/08/510255/chinese-firms-relocating-malaysia-amid-trade-war-says-economist; Kenneth Rapoza, *New Data Shows U.S. Companies Are Definitely Leaving China,* Forbes (7 Apr. 2020), https://www.forbes.com/sites/kenrapoza/2020/04/07/new-data-shows-us-companies-are-definitely-leaving-china/#207a988b40fe; Kenneth Rapoza, *Coronavirus Could Be The End Of China As A Global Manufacturing Hub,* Forbes (1 Mar. 2020), https://www.forbes.com/sites/kenrapoza/2020/03/01/coronavirus-could-be-the-end-of-china-as-global-manufacturing-hub/#56aac89a5298; Junko Horiuchi, *Japanese Firms Moving Production Sites to Southeast Asia as Coronavirus Outbreak Disrupts Supply Chains* (11 Feb. 2020), https://www.japantimes.co.jp/news/2020/02/11/business/japanese-firms-moving-production-southeast-asia-coronavirus-supply-chains/#.XstfIGgzZnI; Keita Nakamura, *Japan to Help Shift Manufacturing to ASEAN from China after Virus Disrupts Supply Chains,* The Japan Times (5 May 2020), https://www.japantimes.co.jp/news/2020/05/05/business/japan-manufacturing-asean-china-coronavirus-supply-chains/#.Xsthj2gzZnI.

the eastward shift in international dispute resolution, various initiatives to improve support for ICA and ISDS have been taken, and alternatives (such as international commercial courts and international commercial mediation) have been promoted. Asia has thus been generating enhanced opportunities for dispute resolution services.

This book aimed to examine significant 'new frontiers' for Asia-Pacific cross-border business dispute resolution, focusing on major economies in East and South Asia and countries (such as Australia) that are closely linked economically and geographically. The principal questions posed were: (1) whether existing and new venues for ICA could improve their attractiveness through law reform, case law development, and other measures, despite worries about cost and delay; (2) whether emerging concerns about ISDS-backed investment treaty commitments would prompt Asian states to become rule-makers in international investment law, rather than be mere rule-takers; and (3) whether innovations in existing or new fields might assist the Asia-Pacific region in developing international dispute settlement further. The forego-ing fourteen chapters have discussed these broad themes, focusing on developments in Australia, Japan, Hong Kong, China, India and Malaysia. These chapters also note broader regional initiatives, including some developments in well-established jurisdic-tions such as Singapore[7] as well as China's BRI) and recent international instruments (such as the Singapore Convention on Mediation (entering in force from 12 September 2020[8]). This concluding chapter highlights key findings in the individual chapters and identifies some challenges for the post-COVID-19 era.

§15.02 FROM RULE-TAKER TO RULE-MAKER

The lessons from this book's chapters are clear: the Asia Pacific is in the process of transforming itself from rule-taker to rule-maker in international dispute resolution. The efforts remain a work in progress, but the region is steadily moving in that direction, balancing different levels of economic development among the region's disparate states and territories.[9] A corollary is the diminishing influence of the US on investment treaties and ISDS within the region and an increase in regional innovation in ICA.

7. Hannah Kim, *Paris Arbitration Week Recap: Recent Developments and Key Arbitration Trends in Asia*, Kluwer Arbitration Blog (15 Jul. 2020), http://arbitrationblog.kluwerarbitration.com/2020/07/15/paris-arbitration-week-recap-recent-developments-and-key-arbitration-trends-in-asia/ (referring to proposed International Arbitration Act (IAA) reforms in Singapore, including an 'opt-in' appeal mechanism to the High Court on a question of law arising from an arbitral award and an option for parties to waive or limit the grounds to set aside an arbitral award, provided that the agreement is reached after the award is rendered).
8. United Nations Convention on International Settlement Agreements Resulting from Mediation (New York, 2018).
9. On this point, a comprehensive study focusing on ICA developments in the Asia Pacific can be found in Anselmo Reyes & Weixia Gu, *Conclusion: An Asia Pacific Model of Arbitration Reform, in The Developing World of Arbitration: A Comparative Study of Arbitration Reform in the Asia Pacific* 279-300 (Anselmo Reyes & Weixia Gu eds., Hart Publishing 2018).

Australia is rarely perceived as a leader in the development of ICA and ISDS,[10] due in part to its geographical remoteness.[11] As Monichino and Teramura point out, the judiciary and arbitration institutions in Australia have been making concerted efforts to push the country to the next level by means of the International Arbitration Act (IAA), amended notably in 2010 based on the 2006 UNCITRAL Model Law on International Commercial Arbitration (UNCITRAL Model Law).[12] Australian courts have applied this legislation in an increasingly internationalist (and therefore pro-arbitration) spirit. However, Australian case law, institutional development and legislative reform (even in relation to confidentiality, as noted by Nottage[13]) have not been markedly novel. They have typically adopted what was already prominent in ICA practice abroad. Ubilava and Nottage observe a similar phenomenon in Australia's recent engagement in international investment treaty lawmaking, which largely reflects a US-style approach to treaty drafting, notwithstanding an interesting investor-state mediation provision in a 2019 treaty with Indonesia.

On the assumption that innovations are not necessary for Australia to become successful in the competitive market of international dispute settlement, will the country remain a rule-taker even if it decides to establish a new Australian International Commercial Court as recommended by Warren and Croft?[14] The answer is likely to be 'yes' because establishing an international commercial court is no longer novel, having been adopted in other Asia-Pacific jurisdictions, such as Singapore and China.[15] Distinguishing the prospective Australian International Commercial Court from its competitors in other jurisdictions will be a challenging but meaningful task for the Australian judiciary. Currently, judges with specialist international commercial, investment and financial dispute experience are dispersed among Australia's federal and state jurisdictions. As Monichino and Teramura propose, consolidating that expertise into one intermediate Court of Appeal through an amendment of the IAA may be a way of meeting that challenge head-on.

Japan is yet to become a rule-maker for ICA and ISDS. Claxton, Nottage and Teramura discuss recent initiatives by the Japanese government to boost ICA caseloads in the country. Those initiatives include the establishment of the Japan International

10. Nobumichi Teramura, et al., *Judicial Control of Arbitral Awards in Australia*, in *The Cambridge Handbook of Judicial Control of Arbitral Awards* forthcoming (Larry A. DiMatteo, et al. eds., Cambridge University Press 2020); Luke Nottage & Nobumichi Teramura, *Australia's (In)Capacity in International Commercial Arbitration*, Kluwer Arbitration Blog (20 Sep. 2018), http://arbitrationblog.kluwerarbitration.com/2018/09/20/australias-incapacity-international-commercialarbitration/.
11. Given that the travel and quarantine restrictions that have been imposed worldwide as a result of the COVID-19 pandemic have led to a surge in the use of videoconferencing for the conduct of transnational litigation and arbitration (including the taking of evidence for trials), it is doubtful that Australia's geographical position should be regarded as any serious impediment to its development as an international dispute resolution centre in the future.
12. Monichino & Teramura, Chapter 3 in this volume.]
13. Nottage, Chapter 4 in this volume.
14. Warren & Croft, Chapter 2 in this volume.
15. Marta Requejo, *International Commercial Courts in the Litigation Market*, Max Planck Institute Luxembourg for Procedural Law Research Paper Series (22 Feb. 2019), https://papers.ssrn.com/sol3/papers.cfm?abstract_id=3327166##.

Dispute Resolution Center (JIDRC) in Tokyo and Osaka as well as the International Arbitration Center in Tokyo (IACT). The JIDRC has been envisaged as the Japanese equivalent of Maxwell Chambers in Singapore, the revamped premises of the Hong Kong International Arbitration Center (HKIAC) and the Asian International Arbitration Centre (AIAC) in Kuala Lumpur, and the Seoul International Dispute Resolution Centre. The IACT has promoted itself as the first Asian international arbitration hub specialising in intellectual property (IP) disputes. However, it is an open question of how successful these modest steps will be.[16] In addition, although the Japanese Government has shown interest in taking a more proactive role in investment treaty negotiations and ISDS reform, it remains to be seen whether its pragmatic and cautious approach will strengthen Japan's status in international investment treaty lawmaking. Japan may have had a better chance of influencing treaty negotiations and drafting during the 1980s when its economy was sometimes dubbed as 'Number One' by commentators,[17] but that was before the bubble burst, and the Japanese economy stagnated during the 1990s.[18]

In the present economic environment, significantly more 'trial and error' will arguably be needed before Japan becomes a rule-maker in international dispute settlement. The establishment of the Japan International Mediation Center – Kyoto (JIMC – Kyoto) is one such experiment. Claxton, Nottage and Williams further suggest that Japan should encourage the use of mediation to resolve its ongoing trade and investment tensions with South Korea. This would demonstrate the utility of international mediation as a means of resolving complex multi-stakeholder disputes in a single forum,[19] and show a new way forward for resolving other increasingly complex regional cross-border disputes in a post-COVID-19 world.

As a financial hub connecting China and the West, Hong Kong has long been a major arbitration centre for the Asia Pacific and the world. The cosmopolitan city has contributed enormously to the development of international business dispute resolution by offering balanced procedural and substantive reforms and innovations over many years.[20] Ali shows how Hong Kong is now focusing on updating its frameworks for dispute resolution settlement to attract more ICA and ISDS cases relating to the BRI. Among recent reforms in this vein have been the Investment Agreement of the Mainland and Hong Kong Closer Economic Partnership Arrangement (2017), BRI-specific initiatives from the HKIAC and the China International Economic and Trade

16. For past modest reforms of ICA in Japan, *see* generally Nobumichi Teramura & Luke Nottage, *Arbitration Reform in Japan: Reluctant Legislature and Institutional Challenges, in Arbitration Reform in Asia* 83-108 (Weixia Gu & Anselmo Reyes eds., Hart Publishing 2018).
17. Ezra F. Vogel, *Japan as Number One: Lessons for America* (Harvard University Press 1979).
18. Gary Saxonhouse & Robert Stern eds., *Japan's Lost Decade: Origins, Consequences and Prospects for Recovery* (Wiley-Blackwell 2004); Luke Nottage & Leon Wolff, *Corporate Governance and Law Reform in Japan: From the Lost Decade to the End of History?*, in *Japanese Management: In Search of a New Balance Between Continuity and Change* 133-66 (Rene Haak & Markus Pudelko eds., Palgrave Macmillan 2005).
19. Claxton, Nottage & Williams, Chapter 11 in this volume.
20. Shahla Ali, *Balancing Procedural and Substantive Arbitration Reforms: Advancing International Arbitration Practice in Hong Kong, in The Developing World of Arbitration: A Comparative Study of Arbitration Reform in the Asia Pacific* 39-66 (Anselmo Reyes & Weixia Gu eds., Hart Publishing 2018).

Arbitration Commission Hong Kong Arbitration Centre (CIETAC Hong Kong), and the Arrangement Concerning Mutual Assistance in Court-ordered Interim Measures in Aid of Arbitral Proceedings by the Courts of the Mainland and of the Hong Kong Special Administrative Region (2019). These should help Hong Kong to continue as a leading dispute resolution centre in the Asia-Pacific region.

No doubt, recent events in Hong Kong have raised questions about its future role as a preferred seat of international arbitration.[21] In moving toward greater integration with Mainland China while retaining a distinct common law system, the thrust of BRI-related rulemaking will be driven by Mainland institutions. Ali notes that:

> BRI policy and relevant legislative/institutional/judicial reform in Hong Kong continue to be largely initiated by the Mainland. At the same time, in line with regional integration policies, Mainland arbitration and mediation centres will continue to coordinate with, learn from, and integrate relevant procedural and substantive aspects of Hong Kong's global dispute resolution architecture in the development of Mainland institutions.[22]

This circumstance suggests that Hong Kong is unlikely to become a rule-maker for a growing BRI caseload. It will instead offer insights from which future reforms elsewhere (especially in Mainland China) will be developed. It is likely that Hong Kong will continue to offer unique rulemaking and institutional contributions to the area of investor-state mediation, IP, general commercial and financial dispute resolution; however, as Ubilava and Nottage point out that, in contrast to Australia's 2019 treaty with Indonesia, Hong Kong's new treaty with Australia does not contain a provision allowing a host state to require mediation before arbitration.

China is already a rule-maker for BRI dispute settlements, having commenced the ambitious project to increase its connectivity with the rest of the world and thereby enhance its geopolitical influence. Anticipating a growth in BRI-related disputes, the country established the China International Commercial Court (CICC), which presently comprises the First International Commercial Court in Shenzhen, Guangdong Province, the Second International Commercial Court in Xi'an, Shaanxi Province; and the Fourth Civil Division of the Supreme People's Court (SPC). Ali envisages that, through the BRI, the CICC will enable China to become a rule-maker in international commercial and investor-state dispute resolution.[23]

Focusing on ICA and the substantial levels of harmonisation that exists among arbitration laws in the Asia Pacific, Gu argues that the BRI will allow China to promote regional harmonisation further, in particular among Asian economies along the Belt and Road, albeit with the safeguard of the public policy exceptions to the enforcement of foreign arbitral awards.[24] Reflecting on China's extensive experience in negotiating investment treaties and on certain emerging ISDS cases, Bath surmises that China

21. Sourabh Gupta, *Hong Kong's High Degree of Autonomy in the Balance,* East Asia Forum (26 Jun. 2020), https://www.eastasiaforum.org/2020/06/26/hong-kongs-high-degree-of-autonomy-in-the-balance/.
22. Ali, Chapter 6 in this volume.
23. *Ibid.*
24. Gu, Chapter 7 in this volume.

intends to play a more active role in any multilateral review of ISDS procedures. For example, in its submission to UNCITRAL Working Group III, China has proposed a number of reforms which, if implemented, could attract more ISDS cases into the country. Outlining other developments impacting on ICA and cross-border litigation, Bath contends that, at the same time as it has been tightening political control internally, China has been contemplating an enhanced role for Chinese law and Chinese institutions in the resolution of BRI and other international disputes.

In recent years, India has emerged as a more credible market for ICA[25] and attracted attention for its attempts to elevate its position in investment treaty lawmaking. Although it had a large network of international investment agreements (IIAs) with regional and other partners, India unilaterally opted to denounce IIAs when permitted to do under those instruments (as with Australia in 2017) and to let other IIAs lapse. This policy was in reaction to a wave of inbound ISDS claims (beginning with one from an Australian mining company decided in 2011). Singh explains how India aimed to replace existing IIAs with a new 2016 Model Treaty that significantly favours host states over investors.[26] Summarising his econometric analysis of the positive cumulative impact of the IIAs signed by India up to 2015, Singh warns that, if systematically adopted, the new template could significantly curb the influx of foreign investment. Despite this, it appears that India has had little hesitation in sacrificing economic development in order to turn itself from a rule-taker to a rule-maker in international investment law. Singh links this attitude to growing nationalism, noting that in late 2019 India declined to join the Regional Comprehensive Economic Partnership (RCEP) free trade agreement (FTA) involving the ten states of the Association of Southeast Asian Nations (ASEAN), Australia, New Zealand, China, Japan and Korea.

Malaysia has recently appeared on the international dispute settlement map. Venugopal observes that, over the last decade, Malaysia has been successfully promoting itself as a regional centre for Alternative Dispute Resolution (ADR), thanks to competitive arbitration institutions, an increasingly pro-arbitration judiciary, and legislation based on the UNCITRAL Model Law (enacted in 2005, and amended in 2018 in light of the 2006 Model Law revisions). Venugopal suggests that the contribution by the AIAC – formerly known as the Kuala Lumpur Regional Centre for Arbitration (KLRCA) – should not be underestimated. A major achievement was for AIAC to become the first institution to have shariah-compliant arbitration rules (the i-Arbitration Rules), for which it received the voter-based Global Arbitration Review (GAR) Award for 'Innovation by an Individual or Organisation in 2012'. This has led to AIAC (and hence Malaysia) becoming a regional leader for Islamic commercial arbitration. This may presage further growth thanks to the development of Islamic banking and finance worldwide.[27]

---

25. *See* generally Hiro Naraindas Aragaki, *Arbitration Reform in India: Challenges and Opportunities, in The Developing World of Arbitration: A Comparative Study of Arbitration Reform in the Asia Pacific* 221-49 (Anselmo Reyes & Gu Weixia eds., Hart Publishing 2018).
26. Singh, Chapter 12 in this volume.
27. Thomas Panighetti, *I-Arbitration: Not the Newest Apple(R) Product, but Sharia Law in International Commercial Arbitration*, 5 Y.B. Arb. & Med. 287 (2013); Maria Bhatti, *Islamic Law and International Commercial Arbitration* (Routledge 2018).

However, despite Malaysia's significant involvement in inbound and outbound ISDS cases and some influence on ASEAN treaty practice, Venugopal suggests that Malaysia has yet fully to become a rule-maker in international investment treaty-making. For example, Malaysia has disparate ISDS provisions in its FTAs. It also has divergent inter-state dispute resolution provisions, which have never been applied. Although it has been a third party in twenty-four World Trade Organization (WTO) disputes, it has been a complainant (against the US) in one WTO case and a respondent in another (brought by Singapore). Venugopal is concerned that, despite the risk of 'different dispute resolution forums being applicable to different situations and different rights being available to the contracting parties', Malaysia lacks the experience to handle such diversity.

Overall, the six jurisdictions surveyed have been moving towards becoming rule-makers for international dispute resolution at varying rates and with differing degrees of success. Malaysia and China may be seen as taking the lead, having become rule-makers for specific areas of international dispute resolution: respectively, Islamic law-related arbitration and BRI dispute settlement. Hong Kong would not be far behind. The city might well weather recent events and maintain its present large volume of cases. But even then, its pursuit of rulemaking in ICA and ISDS may be given lower priority in light of the present a shift by some institutions to concentrate on BRI-related dispute resolution. While this decision makes economic sense, as pointed out by Ali and Gu, Hong Kong will likely follow Mainland China's lead as a rule-maker on BRI disputes, the BRI being a project of the Central People's Government.

The other three jurisdictions – Australia, Japan and India – remain engaged in the process of trial and error and, therefore, have yet to establish a clear roadmap to becoming rule-makers for ICA and ISDS. This is notwithstanding sustained efforts by their leading arbitration lawyers, judges, academics and institutions. India's experiment with its Model Treaty template for IIA negotiations may be a bold initiative, but it is doubtful whether many other countries will accept ostensibly protectionist provisions. The worst scenario for India would be to find itself excluded from a discussion over the future of ISDS evolution as a result of a collective rejection of the new template by its key economic partners.

All six jurisdictions may climb further up the ladder to becoming rule-makers by participating in recent innovations within the Asia-Pacific region. One innovation relates to the International Convention for the Prevention of Pollution from Ships and its Protocols (MARPOL 73/78), whose reach has been expanded through FTAs and specifically their dispute settlement provisions. Another innovation is the Singapore Convention on Mediation.

Huang and Hu explore the opportunities that are likely to be brought about by MARPOL 73/78. Their analysis considers how future FTAs might similarly incorporate other international instruments, such as those of the World Health Organisation (WHO), dealing with pandemics like COVID-19.[28] By 2018 MARPOL 7378 had been accepted by 157 states, representing 99% of world merchant tonnage, thereby leading

28. Hu & Huang, Chapter 13 in this volume.

to a perceptible decrease in pollution from international shipping. But its dispute resolution mechanism is weak in that Contracting States must have an open-ended negotiation before referring a dispute to ad hoc arbitration. Huang and Hu explain that the situation has improved for the Asia Pacific, thanks to the incorporation of MARPOL 73/78 into the Comprehensive and Progressive Agreement for Trans-Pacific Partnership (CPTPP) (in force from 2019). That provides for MARPOL 73/78-related disputes to follow a compulsory procedure with strict timelines. If consultation is unsuccessful, a complainant may request that a panel similar to an inter-state arbitration tribunal being set up in accordance with detailed procedural rules. The CPTPP also reinforces environmental obligations under MARPOL 73/78 with the threat of trade sanctions. Huang and Hu argue that the sophisticated dispute resolution procedure may not boost the number of MARPOL 73/78 state-to-state arbitrations. On the other hand, if the CPTPP were to be revised in modest ways, the Asia-Pacific region could become even more of a rule-maker in a significant area of international dispute settlement, thereby enhancing ocean protection. Drawing an analogy between the global mobility of vessels and viruses, Huang and Hu suggest that states may similarly safeguard global health by beefing up the WHO's International Health Regulations of 2005 (IHR) with a strong dispute resolution mechanism and incorporating the IHR into CPTPP and other FTAs.

The Singapore Convention on Mediation holds out the potential for the Asia-Pacific region to become a rule-maker in international commercial mediation. This is not only because it is the first United Nations (UN) treaty named after Singapore.[29] It is also because many Asian countries have expressed interest in updating their legal infrastructures to incorporate mediation, having had a strong tradition of using mediation informally as a means of resolving disputes. This is often said to be due to an emphasis on harmony within the community prevalent in Asian cultures and politics.[30] A renewed focus on mediation consequent upon the coming into force of the Singapore Convention on Mediation would provide an arena in which Asian states can innovate.

Accordingly, Strong advances useful proposals on how the Asia-Pacific region should go about contributing to the development of international mediation.[31] Recognising that the Convention alone will not ensure success in the promotion of mediation, she recommends that proponents of international commercial mediation should encourage non-Member States to accede to the Convention as soon as possible. They should at the same time inform potential stakeholders of the disadvantages in terms of time and cost of international litigation and ICA; highlight the utility of mediation in

29. Nadja Alexander, *It's Done: The Singapore Convention on Mediation*, Kluwer Arbitration Blog (9 Aug. 2019), http://mediationblog.kluwerarbitration.com/2019/08/09/its-done-thesingapore-convention-on-mediation/.
30. Eunice Chua, *The Singapore Convention on Mediation – A Brighter Future for Asian Dispute Resolution*, 9 Asian J. Int'l L. 195, 203-5 (2019); Eunice Chua, *Why Asian States Should Sign Up to the Singapore Convention on Mediation*, Khmer Times (11 Jul. 2019), https://www.khmertimeskh.com/622749/why-asian-states-should-sign-up-to-the-singapore-convention-on-mediation/.
31. Strong, Chapter 14 in this volume.

international commercial settings; and consider adopting a parallel convention to fill a gap in the Singapore Convention on Mediation – the enforcement of agreements to mediate cross-border disputes.

To summarise, this book has demonstrated various regional 'rulemaking' initiatives in international commercial and investment treaty arbitration, as well as other forms of transnational business dispute resolution. The jurisdictions in or closely connected with Asia, as introduced in this book, have been moving towards becoming a collective rule-maker for cross-border dispute settlement. Even before the COVID-19 pandemic, the Asia-Pacific region was the new frontier in international business dispute settlement. Will it continue to be so after COVID-19?

§15.03 THE ASIA-PACIFIC REGION IN THE AGE OF COVID-19

The COVID-19 pandemic has fundamentally and irrevocably affected our lives. As of 1 July 2020, the number of confirmed cases of COVID-19 across the world has surpassed 10 million, and the number of deaths has exceeded half a million.[32] It is impossible to predict with certainty how the pandemic will affect the world, including the trajectory for Asia-Pacific dispute resolution.[33] In these unprecedented times, will it still be possible for the Asia-Pacific region to further cross-border dispute settlement? We conclude by identifying five challenges for Asia-Pacific institutions in the brave new world of the COVID-19 era.

First, there is the challenge of technology. This means adapting to the use of remote conferencing, which has become the new normal of dispute resolution under COVID-19.[34] Virtual hearings ceased to be science fiction long ago.[35] Since then, many have advocated a more intensive use of the internet for the conduct of litigation, arbitration and mediation.[36] But it has only been recently that reliable technology for

32. https://covid19.who.int/.
33. Luke Nottage & Tom van Laer, *COVID-19 in Asia and Beyond: We Are Story Characters Living in a New Story World*, Japanese Law and the Asia-Pacific: Japanese Law in Asia-Pacific Socio-Economic Context (6 May 2020), https://japaneselaw.sydney.edu.au/2020/05/covid-19-in-asia-and-beyond-we-are-story-characters-living-in-a-new-story-world/.
34. Maxi Scherer, *Remote Hearings in International Arbitration: An Analytical Framework*, 37 J. Int'l Arb. (2020).
35. Jasna Arsic, *International Commercial Arbitration on the Internet – Has the Future Come Too Early?*, 14 J. Int'l Arb. 209 (1997).
36. Mohamed S. Abdel Wahab, *The Global Information Society and Online Dispute Resolution: A New Dawn for Dispute Resolution*, 21 J. Int'l Arb. 143 (2004); Gabrielle Kaufmann-Kohler & Thomas Schultz, *The Use of Information Technology in Arbitration*, Jusletter (5 Dec. 2005), http://lk-k.com/wp-content/uploads/The-Use-of-Information-Technology-in-Arbitration.pdf; Teramura, et al., *supra* n. 10 (recommending Australia to promote ODR to overcome its geographical remoteness). In addition, China International Economic and Trade Arbitration Commission (CIETAC) adopted CIETAC Online Arbitration Rules in 2009: https://arbitrationlaw.com/sites/default/files/free_pdfs/CIETAC%20Online%20Arbitration%20Rules.pdf. Note that their focus has been domestic e-commerce and related disputes, as pointed out by Bath, Chapter 8 in this volume.

remote hearings has become available at an affordable price.[37] Despite this, as well as some early initiatives within the Asia-Pacific region,[38] utilisation of the available technology in domestic and cross-border dispute resolution had been slow due to a deeply entrenched preference for physical hearings among judges, arbitrators, mediators, and lawyers.[39] Now, thanks to the lockdowns, social-distancing and travel restrictions that have been imposed to curb COVID-19, virtual hearings have overnight become standard.[40] A few applications (e.g., Zoom CISCO Webex, Microsoft Teams and Blue Jeans), some being innovations of Asian entrepreneurs,[41] have become indispensable for the conduct of dispute resolution domestically and internationally.[42] Capitalising on the availability and affordability of these applications (especially of Zoom), Asia-Pacific institutions have been hosting regular online seminars – webinars – on a range of COVID-19- related topics, as a means of enhancing their visibility, not just within the Asia Pacific, but to the world at large.[43] Additionally, in a bid to bolster their credentials as rule-makers, Asia-Pacific institutions have been issuing guidelines on best practices for the conduct of remote hearings.[44] Much more can be done to exploit the full potential of currently available technology. It will be imperative if they are to survive through the COVID-19 era for Asia-Pacific institutions to grapple with the

37. Jordan Novet, *Why Zoom Has Become the Darling of Remote Workers During the COVID-19 Crisis*, CNBC (21 Mar. 2020), https://www.cnbc.com/2020/03/21/why-zoom-has-become-darling-of-remote-workers-amid-covid-19-outbreak.html.
38. *Seoul Protocol on Video Conference in International Arbitration* (18 Mar. 2020), https://globalarbitrationreview.com/digital_assets/9eb818a3-7fff-4faa-aad3-3e4799a39291/Seoul-Protocol-on-Video-Conference-in-International-Arbitration-(1).pdf.
39. Kaufmann-Kohler & Schultz, *supra* n. 36, at 5.
40. Janet Walker, *Virtual Hearings – the New Normal*, GAR (27 Mar. 2020), https://globalarbitrationreview.com/article/1222421/virtual-hearings-%E2%80%93-the-new-normal; Gary L. Benton, *How Will the Coronavirus Impact International Arbitration?*, Kluwer Arbitration Blog (13 Mar. 2020), http://arbitrationblog.kluwerarbitration.com/2020/03/13/how-will-the-coronavirus-impact-international-arbitration/?doing_wp_cron=1591689286.1524488925933837890625; Mirèze Philippe, *Offline or Online? Virtual Hearings or ODR?*, Kluwer Arbitration Blog (26 Apr. 2020), http://arbitrationblog.kluwerarbitration.com/2020/04/26/offline-or-online-virtual-hearings-or-odr/?doing_wp_cron=1591690339.1163289546966552734375. For precise definition of 'remote hearings', 'virtual hearings' and 'ODR', *see* Scherer, *supra* n. 34.
41. Zoom was founded by Eric Yuan from China, and CISCO Webex was co-founded by Subrah Iyar from India and Min Zhu from China.
42. Chahat Chawla, *International Arbitration During COVID-19: A Case Counsel's Perspective*, Kluwer Arbitration Blog (4 Jun. 2020), http://arbitrationblog.kluwerarbitration.com/2020/06/04/international-arbitration-during-covid-19-a-case-counsels-perspective/?doing_wp_cron=1591756099.5273880958557128906250.
43. For example, *HKIAC Webinar Series* (https://www.hkiac.org/content/hkiac-webinar-series); *SIAC International Arbitration Webinar Series 2020* (https://www.siac.org.sg/2013-09-18-01-57-20/2013-09-22-01-20-47/siac-international-arbitration-webinar-series-2020); *ADR Online – An AIAC Webinar Series* (https://www.aiac.world/events); *ACICA Webinars* (https://acica.org.au/acica-webinars/). *See also* Luke Nottage, *Will the COVID-19 Pandemic Be a Long-Term Game Changer for International Arbitration?*, Kluwer Arbitration Blog (16 Jul. 2020), http://arbitrationblog.kluwerarbitration.com/2020/07/16/will-the-covid-19-pandemic-be-a-long-term-game-changer-for-international-arbitration/?doing_wp_cron=1594949609.2157111167907714843750.
44. *HKIAC Guidelines for Virtual Hearings* (14 May 2020), https://www.hkiac.org/sites/default/files/ck_filebrowser/HKIAC%20Guidelines%20for%20Virtual%20Hearings_2.pdf; *ACICA Online Arbitration Guidance Note* (May 2020), https://acica.org.au/wp-content/uploads/2020/05/ACICA-Online-Arbitration-Guidance-Note.pdf.

implications of the paradigm shift in the delivery of dispute resolution services and re-invent themselves accordingly.

Second, there is an economic challenge. It is anticipated that there will be a spike in commercial disputes as a result of COVID-19.[45] It is easy to see why. The world has entered into what looks to be a profound financial recession.[46] Unemployment is rising globally.[47] Many established businesses, whether small, medium or large, have failed or are finding themselves on the brink.[48] In these trying times, debtors will be terminating or breaching contracts, while creditors will be insisting on performance in whole or part. Cashflow will be a worry. Few will have the financial resources to undertake protracted and expensive litigation or arbitration to settle their disputes. There will be a premium on being able to achieve speedy settlements. In such an environment, mediation comes into its own as a mode of dispute resolution. Thus, in order to maintain caseloads at anywhere near pre-COVID-19 levels, Asia-Pacific institutions will need to come up with creative protocols and techniques (involving, in particular, the use of remote hearing technology) for cost-effective and time-efficient mediations.

Third, as a corollary to economic woes, there is the challenge of protectionism. Long before the pandemic, globalism was under attack, and the free flow of goods and services was under threat. For example, mention has been made of tensions between the US and China, as well as trade restrictions between Japan and South Korea.[49] We are currently seeing squabbles among China, the US, the EU, the UK and Canada on the extent to which technology should be made available to or shared with China,[50] with other Asian countries being forced to take sides.[51] The pandemic has exacerbated the predicament, with the closure of borders and wholesale restriction on travel among Asian countries and between the Asia Pacific and the rest of the world.[52] The upshot

45. For example, *see* London Court of International Arbitration (LCIA), *2019 Annual Casework Report* 3 (LCIA 2020) (noting that '[i]n the first quarter of 2020, the LCIA has seen a spike in new cases, and in the medium-term the COVID-19 crisis will undoubtedly lead to additional cases'). *See also* generally Jörg Risse & Antje Baumann, *Thinking Ahmad: Dispute Resolution after the Corona Crisis*, 4 SciedsVZ 165 (2020).
46. World Bank Group, *Global Economic Prospects*, A World Bank Group Fragship Report 3ff (June 2020), https://openknowledge.worldbank.org/bitstream/handle/10986/33748/978146481553 9.pdf.
47. International Labour Organisation (ILO), *COVID-19 and the World of Work. Fourth Edition: Updated Estimates and Analysis*, ILO Monitor (27 May 2020), https://www.ilo.org/wcmsp5/groups/public/@dgreports/@dcomm/documents/briefingnote/wcms_745963.pdf.
48. World Bank Group, *supra* n. 46, at 42.
49. Claxton, Nottage, & Williams, Chapter 11 in this volume.
50. Wei Sheng, *'Five Eyes' Look in Different Directions on Huawei: National Security Experts Describe Diverging Approaches*, technode (17 Jun. 2020), https://technode.com/2020/06/17/five-eyes-look-in-different-directions-on-huawei/; Scott Bade, *How Huawei is Dividing Western Nations*, TechCrunch (28 Mar. 2020), https://techcrunch.com/2020/03/28/how-huawei-is-dividing-western-nations/.
51. Amalina Anuar, *ASEAN, 5G and the Great Tech Game*, East Asia Forum (29 Apr. 2020), https://www.eastasiaforum.org/2020/04/29/asean-5g-and-the-great-tech-game/.
52. Daniel Wagner, *Coronavirus Pandemic Is Hastening the Death of the Globalised Order and the Rise of a 'Me First' World*, South China Morning Post (23 May 2020), https://www.scmp.com/comment/opinion/article/3085389/coronavirus-pandemic-hastening-death-globalised-order-and-rise-me.

has been an unprecedented drop in the demand for goods and services worldwide.[53] Countries have taken (or are likely to take) steps to prop up their local businesses, at least temporarily, and to keep them from being wound up.[54] The situation is unlikely to improve in the short to medium term. Commentators are sceptical of V-shaped economic recovery and have instead predicted a U- or even L-shaped recovery as the more likely scenario.[55] Creditors could find in consequence that, in Asian countries with weak adherence to the rule of law, it will become more difficult to enforce foreign judgments or arbitral awards against local businesses. The public policy ground, highlighted already by Gu in this volume, will likely be more frequently invoked by the courts in those countries as a reason for refusing recognition and enforcement.[56] The challenge for Asia-Pacific jurisdictions will be to resist chauvinist pressures and instead apply their laws in an even-handed and transparent manner, even though that may lead to financial difficulties for numerous domestic businesses.[57]

Fourth, internal social and political challenges persist in many Asian jurisdictions. Malaysia, for example, seems to have a never-ending problem with corruption and related political unrest.[58] These problems, if left unresolved, will inevitably colour the way in which the relevant Asian jurisdictions are viewed by foreign investors and traders. The popularity of such jurisdictions as international, regional or quasi-regional dispute resolution centres will suffer in consequence. Hong Kong is also now a special case in point. Given anxiety over the durability of the 'one country, two systems' model,[59] with Hong Kong becoming like another city in Mainland China,[60] some have expressed concerns about the impartiality of the HKIAC and arbitrations administered

53. *Ibid.*
54. For example, *see* Ian Roberts, et al., *COVID-19 Singapore: Guide to (Temporary Measures) Act 2020,* Clyde&Co: Insight & Knowledge (8 Apr. 2020), https://www.clydeco.com/insight/article/covid-19-singapore-guide-to-temporary-measures-act-2020; Squire Patton Boggs, *Impact of COVID-19 on Insolvency Laws: How Countries Are Revamping Their Insolvency and Restructuring Laws to Combat COVID-19* (8 Apr. 2020), https://www.restructuring-globalview.com/wp-content/uploads/sites/21/2020/04/Impact-of-Global-Insolvency-Laws_.pdf; Mario Draghi, *Draghi: We Face a War against Coronavirus and Must Mobilise Accordingly,* Financial Times (26 Mar. 2020), https://www.ft.com/content/c6d2de3a-6ec5-11ea-89df-41bea055720b; International Monetary Fund (IMF), *Policy Tracker,* Policy Response to COVID-19 (2020), https://www.imf.org/en/Topics/imf-and-covid19/Policy-Responses-to-COVID-19.
55. David Rodeck, *Alphabet Soup: Understanding the Shape of a COVID-19 Recession,* Forbes (8 Jun. 2020), https://www.forbes.com/advisor/investing/covid-19-coronavirus-recession-shape/.
56. *See,* for example in Italy, Matthias Weller, *Italian Self-Proclaimed Overriding Mandatory Provisions to Fight Coronavirus,* Conflict of Laws.net (19 Mar. 2020), http://conflictoflaws.net/2020/italian-self-proclaimed-overriding-mandatory-provisions-to-fight-coronavirus/.
57. For example, *see* Mimi Zou, *The Supreme People's Court of China Just Released it Guiding Opinion on COVID-19 Related Civil Disputes,* Linkedin (20 Apr. 2020), https://www.linkedin.com/pulse/supreme-peoples-court-china-just-released-guiding-opinion-mimi-zou.
58. Bridget Welsh, *'Old Malaysia' Triumphs for Now,* East Asia Forum (7 Mar. 2020), https://www.eastasiaforum.org/2020/03/07/the-persistence-of-old-malaysia/.
59. ABC/Wires, *What's in Hong Kong's New National Security Law Imposed by China, and Why Is It So Controversial?,* ABC News (1 Jul. 2020), https://www.abc.net.au/news/2020-07-01/what-is-in-hong-kongs-new-china-imposed-national-security-law/12409024.
60. Jeppe Mulich, *The End of Hong Kong Autonomy,* East Asia Forum (31 May 2020), https://www.eastasiaforum.org/2020/05/31/the-end-of-hong-kong-autonomy/.

by it.[61] Doubts have even been expressed as to the Special Administrative Region's commitment to maintaining an independent judiciary and upholding the rule of law.[62] Those perceptions, however unwarranted, will have to be addressed. At heart is Hong Kong's reputation as an international dispute resolution centre. If that is compromised, Hong Kong will cease to be a leading international dispute resolution centre. The challenge will be to persuade the world that, notwithstanding the complexity and challenges of recent events, Hong Kong remains a trusted venue for dispute resolution where the rule of law is paramount. The HKIAC has been making significant efforts in this regard. In a recent letter issued in June 2020, it outlined its ongoing commitment to neutrality through oversight by its Council and Appointments Committee comprised of international and local experts; a track record of enforcing arbitral awards against entities of all nationalities, including those based in Hong Kong and Mainland China; and its processing of twenty-four applications under the PRC-HK Interim Measures Arrangement 2019 and issuance of preservation orders in respect of at least CNY 4.9 billion (USD 705 million) worth of assets located on the Mainland.[63]

Finally, there are what might be called 'legacy' challenges, that is, the host of general issues – by no means unique to the Asia Pacific – that were around long before COVID-19. Examples of such issues are: (1) ensuring diversity in the appointment of judges and arbitrators; (2) ensuring transparency in the dispute resolution process; (3) reducing the carbon footprint of those engaged in the provision of dispute resolution services; (4) reducing the cost, duration and technicality of litigation and arbitration; and (5) ensuring access to commercial dispute resolution services for all who might need them, so that resort to such services will not be perceived as the preserve of the wealthy.[64] These problems have not gone away just because of COVID-19. They remain pressing. The challenge will be for Asian jurisdictions to face them with urgency, not just to wait and see how other countries deal with them.

---

61. Sarah Grimmer, *Distinction and Connection: Hong Kong and Mainland China, a View from the HKIAC*, GAR (24 May 2019), https://globalarbitrationreview.com/insight/the-asia-pacific-arbitration-review-2020/1193369/distinction-and-connection-hong-kong-and-mainland-china-a-view-from-the-hkiac.
62. Greg Torode & James Pomfret, *Hong Kong Judges Battle Beijing over Rule of Law as Pandemic Chills Protests*, Reuters (14 Apr. 2020), https://www.reuters.com/investigates/special-report/hongkong-politics-judiciary/.
63. HKIAC, *Hong Kong Remains a Neutral and Effective Seat of Arbitration*, News Articles (29 Jun. 2020), https://www.hkiac.org/news/hong-kong-remains-neutral-and-effective-seat.
64. *See* generally Luke Nottage, *In/formalization and Glocalization of International Commercial Arbitration and Investment Treaty Arbitration in Asia, in Formalisation and Flexibilisation of Dispute Resolution* 211-49 (Joachim Zekoll, et al. eds., Martinus Nijhoff / Brill 2014); Daniel Bethlehem, *The Greening of International Dispute Settlement?: Stepping Back a Little?*, Eighth Annual Charles N. Brower Lecture on International Dispute Resolution (26 Jun. 2020), https://twentyessex.com/wp-content/uploads/2020/06/The-Greening-of-International-Dispute-Settlement-Sir-Daniel-Bethlehem-ASIL-June-26-2020.pdf.

Index

G

H

I

R

S

T

U

1. Moshe Hirsch, *The Arbitration Mechanism of the International Center for the Settlement of Investment Disputes,* 1993 (ISBN 07-923-1993-1).
2. Aida B. Avanessian, *Iran-United States Claims Tribunal in Action,* 1993 (ISBN 18 533-3902-4).
3. Isaak I. Dore, *The UNCITRAL Framework for Arbitration in Contemporary Perspective,* 1993 (ISBN 18-533-3573-8).
4. Vesna Lazić, *Insolvency Proceedings and Commercial Arbitration,* 1998 (ISBN 90-411-1115-8).
5. Joachim Frick, *Arbitration in Complex International Contracts,* 2001 (ISBN 90-411-1662-1).
6. Katherine Lynch, *The Forces of Economic Globalization: Challenges to the Regime of International Commercial Arbitration,* 2003 (ISBN 90-411-1994-9).
7. Christoph Liebscher, *The Healthy Award: Challenge in International Commercial Arbitration,* 2003 (ISBN 90-411-2011-4).
8. Hamid G. Gharavi, *The International Effectiveness of the Annulment of an Arbitral Award,* 2003 (ISBN 90-411-1717-2).
9. Abdulhay Sayed, *Corruption in International Trade and Commercial Arbitration,* 2004 (ISBN 90-411-2236-2).
10. Gabrielle Kaufmann-Kohler & Thomas Schultz, *Online Dispute Resolution: Challenges for Contemporary Justice,* 2004 (ISBN 90-411-2318-0).
11. Christopher R. Drahozal & Richard W. Naimark (eds), *Towards a Science of International Arbitration: Collected Empirical Research,* 2005 (ISBN 90-411-2322-9).
12. Ali Yeşilirmak, *Provisional Measures in International Commercial Arbitration,* 2005 (ISBN 90-411-2353-9).
13. Christian Bühring-Uhle, *Arbitration and Mediation in International Business,* second revised edition, 2006 (ISBN 978-9-041-12256-8).
14. Bernard Hanotiau, *Complex Arbitrations: Multi-party, Multi-contract and Multi-issue – A Comparative Study*, Second Edition, 2020 (ISBN 978-94-035-1261-7).
15. Loukas A. Mistelis & Julian D.M. Lew (eds), *Pervasive Problems in International Arbitration,* 2006 (ISBN 978-9-041-12450-0).
16. Julian D.M. Lew & Loukas A. Mistelis (eds), *Arbitration Insights – Twenty Years of the Annual Lecture of the School of International Arbitration, Sponsored by Freshfields Bruckhaus Deringer,* 2006 (ISBN 978-9-041-12606-1).
17. Mark Kantor, *Valuation for Arbitration: Compensation Standards, Valuation Methods and Expert Evidence,* 2008 (ISBN 978-9-041-12735 8).
18. Christoph Brunner, *Force Majeure and Hardship under General Contract Principles: Exemption for Non-Performance in International Arbitration,* 2009 (ISBN 978-90-411-2792-1).

19. Loukas A. Mistelis & Stavros L. Brekoulakis (eds), *Arbitrability: International & Comparative Perspectives*, 2009 (ISBN 978-90-411-2730-3).
20. Sam Luttrell, *Bias Challenges in International Commercial Arbitration: The Need for a 'Real Danger' Test*, 2009 (ISBN 978-90-411-3191-1).
21. Monique Sasson, *Substantive Law in Investment Treaty Arbitration: The Unsettled Relationship Between International Law and Municipal Law*, Second Edition, 2017 (ISBN 978-90-411-6103-1).
22. Ileana M. Smeureanu, *Confidentiality in International Commercial Arbitration*, 2011 (ISBN 978-90-411-3226-0).
23. Won Kidane, *China-Africa Dispute Settlement: The Law, Economics and Culture of Arbitration*, 2011 (ISBN 978-90-411-3674-9).
24. Karel Daele, *Challenge and Disqualification of Arbitrators in International Arbitration*, 2012 (ISBN 978-90-411-3799-9).
25. Crina Baltag, *The Energy Charter Treaty: The Notion of Investor*, 2012 (ISBN 978-90-411-3428-8).
26. Alexandra Diehl, *The Core Standard of International Investment Protection: Fair and Equitable Treatment*, 2012 (ISBN 978-90-411-3869-9).
27. Manuel Indlekofer, *International Arbitration and the Permanent Court of Arbitration*, 2013 (ISBN 978-90-411-4766-0).
28. Günther J. Horvath & Stephan Wilske (eds), *Guerrilla Tactics in International Arbitration*, 2013 (ISBN 978-90-411-4002-9).
29. Albert Badia, *Piercing the Veil of State Enterprises in International Arbitration*, 2014 (ISBN 978-90-411-5162-9).
30. Nadja Erk, *Parallel Proceedings in International Arbitration: A Comparative European Perspective*, 2014 (ISBN 978-90-411-5264-0).
31. Simon Vorburger, *International Arbitration and Cross-Border Insolvency: Comparative Perspectives*, 2014 (ISBN 978-90-411-5419-4).
32. Ahmad Ali Ghouri, *Interaction and Conflict of Treaties in Investment Arbitration*, 2015 (ISBN 978-90-411-5417-0).
33. Reto Marghitola, *Document Production in International Arbitration*, 2015 (ISBN 978-90-411-5159-9).
34. Alfonso Gómez-Acebo, *Party-Appointed Arbitrators in International Commercial Arbitration*, 2016 (ISBN 978-90-411-6671-5).
35. Jonas von Goeler, *Third-Party Funding in International Arbitration and Its Impact on Procedure*, 2016 (ISBN 978-90-411-5015-8).
36. Dean Lewis, *The Interpretation and Uniformity of the UNCITRAL Model Law on International Commercial Arbitration: Focusing on Australia, Hong Kong and Singapore*, 2016 (ISBN 978-90-411-6700-2).
37. Stavros Brekoulakis, Julian D.M. Lew & Loukas Mistelis (eds), *The Evolution and Future of International Arbitration*, 2016 (ISBN 978-90-411-7004-0).
38. Rémy Gerbay, *The Functions of Arbitral Institutions*, 2016 (ISBN 978-90-411-6217-5).

39. Maximilian Clasmeier, *Arbitral Awards as Investments: Treaty Interpretation and the Dynamics of International Investment Law*, 2017 (ISBN 978-90-411-8357-6).
40. Tony Cole (ed.), *The Roles of Psychology in International Arbitration*, 2017 (ISBN 978-90-411-5921-2).
41. Pietro Ferrario, *The Adaptation of Long-Term Gas Sale Agreements by Arbitrators*, 2017 (ISBN 978-90-411-8232-6).
42. Jacob B. van de Velden, *Finality in Litigation: The Law and Practice of Preclusion – Res Judicata (Merger and Estoppel), Abuse of Process and Recognition of Foreign Judgments*, 2017 (ISBN 978-90-411-8342-2).
43. Dolores Bentolila, *Arbitrators as Lawmakers*, 2017 (ISBN 978-90-411-8354-5).
44. Giacomo Marchisio, *The Notion of Award in International Commercial Arbitration: A Comparative Analysis of French Law, English Law, and the UNCITRAL Model Law*, 2017 (ISBN 978-90-411-8391-0).
45. Csaba Kovács, *Attribution in International Investment Law*, 2018 (ISBN 978-90-411-9675-0).
46. Mary Mitsi, *The Decision-Making Process of Investor-State Arbitration Tribunals*, 2019 (ISBN 978-90-411-9600-2).
47. Ahmet Cemil Yıldırım, *Interpretation of Contracts in Comparative and Uniform Law*, 2019 (ISBN 978-94-035-1130-6).
48. Beata Gessel-Kalinowska vel Kalisz, *The Legal, Real and Converged Interest in Declaratory Relief*, 2019 (ISBN 978-94-035-1244-0).
49. Maximilian Pika, *Third-Party Effects of Arbitral Awards: Res Judicata Against Privies, Non-mutual Preclusion and Factual Effects*, 2019 (ISBN 978-94-035-1273-0).
50. Yulia Levashova, *The Right of States to Regulate in International Investment Law: The Search for Balance Between Public Interest and Fair and Equitable Treatment*, 2019 (ISBN 978-94-035-0931-0).
51. Flavia Marisi, *Environmental Interests in Investment Arbitration: Challenges and Directions*, 2020 (ISBN 978-94-035-1723-0).
52. Martina Magnarelli, *Privity of Contract in International Investment Arbitration: Original Sin or Useful Tool?*, 2020 (ISBN 978-94-035-2020-9).
53. Xu Qian, *Water Services Disputes in International Arbitration: Reconsidering the Nexus of Investment Protection, Environment, and Human Rights*, 2020 (ISBN 978-94-035-2203-6).
54. Nobumichi Teramura, Ex Aequo et Bono *as a Response to the 'Over-Judicialisation' of International Commercial Arbitration*, 2020 (ISBN 978-94-035-2073-5).
55. Bruno Guandalini, *Economic Analysis of the Arbitrator's Function*, 2020 (ISBN 978-94-035-2265-4).
56. Zena Prodromou, *The Public Order Exception in International Trade, Investment, Human Rights and Commercial Disputes*, 2020 (ISBN 978-94-035-2031-5).
57. Jürg Künzle, *Multiple Contracts and Coordination in International Construction Projects: A Swiss Law Analysis*, 2020 (ISBN 978-94-035-2024-7).

58. Cornel Marian, *The State's Power to Tax in the Investment Arbitration of Energy Disputes: Outer Limits and the Energy Charter Treaty*, 2020 (ISBN 978-94-035-1752-0).
59. Luke Nottage, Shahla Ali, Bruno Jetin & Nobumichi Teramura (eds.), *New Frontiers in Asia-Pacific International Arbitration and Dispute Resolution*, 2021 (ISBN 978-94-035-2855-7).

www.ingramcontent.com/pod-product-compliance
Lightning Source LLC
LaVergne TN
LVHW020645300926
849161LV00004B/825